University Textbook Series

Especially Designed for Collateral Reading

HARRY W. JONES
Directing Editor
Professor of Law, Columbia University

ADMIRALTY
Grant Gilmore, Professor of Law, Yale University.
Charles L. Black, Jr., Professor of Law, Yale University.

AGENCY, PRINCIPLES OF
The late Merton L. Ferson, Dean Emeritus, University of Cincinnati College of Law.

COMMERCIAL TRANSACTIONS—Selected Statutes
Robert Braucher, Professor of Law, Harvard University.
Arthur E. Sutherland, Jr., Professor of Law, Harvard University.

CONFLICT OF LAWS, Third Edition
The late George W. Stumberg, Professor of Law, University of Texas.

CORPORATIONS
Norman D. Lattin, Professor of Law, University of California, Hastings College of the Law.

CRIMINAL LAW
Rollin M. Perkins, Professor of Law, University of California, Hastings College of the Law.

ESTATES IN LAND & FUTURE INTERESTS, PREFACE TO
Thomas F. Bergin, Professor of Law, University of Virginia.
Paul G. Haskell, Professor of Law, Georgetown University.

EVIDENCE: COMMON SENSE AND COMMON LAW
John M. Maguire, Professor of Law, Harvard University.

EVIDENCE, STUDENTS' TEXT ON THE LAW OF
John Henry Wigmore.

JURISPRUDENCE: MEN AND IDEAS OF THE LAW
The late Edwin W. Patterson, Cardozo Professor of Jurisprudence, Columbia University.

LEGAL RESEARCH, FUNDAMENTALS OF, with 1964 Assignments Pamphlet
Ervin H. Pollack, Professor of Law, The Ohio State University.

PROPERTY
John E. Cribbet, Professor of Law, University of Illinois.

THE STUDY OF LAW, INTRODUCTION TO
Bernard C. Gavit, Late Professor of Law, Indiana University.

TORTS
Clarence Morris, Professor of Law, University of Pennsylvania.

TRUSTS, Second Edition
Ralph A. Newman, Professor of Law, University of California, Hastings College of the Law.

THE LAW OF
CORPORATIONS

By

NORMAN D. LATTIN

Professor of Law, The Ohio State University
College of Law

Brooklyn
THE FOUNDATION PRESS, INC.
1959

Lattin Corporations F.P.Inc.
5–1967

"Legal doctrines are not self-generated abstract categories. They do not fall from the sky; nor are they pulled out of it. They have a specific juridical origin and etiology. They derive meaning and content from the circumstances that gave rise to them and from the purposes they were designed to serve. To these they are bound as is a live tree to its roots."—Mr. Justice Frankfurter, concurring in the result of Reid v. Covert, 354 U.S. 1, at 50, 77 S.Ct. 1222, at 1248, 1 L.Ed.2d 1148, at 1182 (1957).

PREFACE

Modern business corporation law in America is barely a half-century old, though its roots were well started by the middle of the nineteenth century. And, were one to define "modern" as the period during which the really great advances were made through legislation and the common law, I should be inclined to place the period as starting at approximately the second quarter of the present century.

Adequate statutes were few prior to 1925, but shortly after that date the Ohio, Michigan and California corporation statutes were thoroughly overhauled with the result that practically new statutes, drafted by committees of lawyers and legal scholars who practiced or taught in the business associations area and who were competent to do the job, were enacted. True, Delaware in 1899 had adopted a new corporation law which purported to be "a safe, well-guarded and comprehensive law under which this important franchise may be obtained and by which the rights and interests of the individuals and the public will be protected and preserved." [1] The Delaware act was intended to compete with that of New Jersey and those of other states having "liberal" statutes and there was much criticism at the time of projecting a statute with provisions sufficiently broad to attract incorporators from other states to use this rather than their own less "liberal" statutes. There is still controversy as to just how safe certain portions of the Delaware statute, in the latest revision of 1953, are. But the fact remains that, during this period of unusual legislative activity in the field of corporations, it has become less necessary in many states for incorporators to use the laws of other states to obtain the features desired for smooth corporate functioning.

The modern statutes have attempted to permit a business using the corporate form to carry on conveniently and effectively as previous business experience has proved necessary if the machine age is to accomplish its mission. Doubts have been raised, however, as to whether these statutes and the case-law of the period have kept abreast of the needs for higher ethical standards in the world of business. The tremendous power which a board of directors wields in carrying on a corporate enterprise has ramifications which extend to the farthest removed customer, the ultimate consumer, the lowliest employee, a host of creditors and of shareholders, and to the corporation's competitors. The oppor-

---

1. Journal of Del. senate, 1898, page 10.

tunity for profitable dealing in the company's shares and other securities, and of the use of inside information for other lucrative ventures places a premium on the integrity demanded of fiduciaries in the position of directors and officers. Furthermore, Professor Adolf A. Berle, Jr., has pointed out that there are 135 corporations owning 45% of the industrial assets of the United States which means, in terms of world production, "nearly one-fourth of the manufacturing volume of the entire world." [2] One has to be naïve, indeed, not to suspect that there is behind such enormous aggregations of capital a significant influence not only on the economic side of the economy but on the political side as well. Morality of a high sort is demanded when power plays so important a part. There is no need of laboring the point.

While modern corporation statutes have, for the most part, provided well for the large, publicly held corporation, they have, almost without exception, failed to recognize the need of adequate provisions for the closely held corporation, sometimes called the incorporated partnership, and for the "one-man" corporation. Such corporations have existed for a long time, the first significant case involving important corporate principles being, perhaps, Salomon v. A. Salomon & Co., Ltd.,[3] actually a one-man corporation with qualifying shares in the hands of his family. Since there is no policy in any state prohibiting contracts limiting liability to a certain fund or group of assets there should be no objection to a statute permitting one man to incorporate (there are a few such statutes), permitting informal action by the shareholders should they decide that they do not desire a board of directors, or action by the sole shareholder, if such he be. It should be said that the North Carolina Business Corporation Act which became effective on July 1, 1957, does have some interesting provisions for this type of corporation. Until such time as statutes fill this gap, the tortuous route via the common law, over which battles are fought each year, will have to be pursued. The draftsman has a difficult job, though not an impossible one, of reaching most of the desired objectives under present corporation statutes but the day will come, I feel sure, when his job will be made easier because of statutory aid.

The present volume was written with the purpose of clarifying, where possible, the "law" of corporations and to present in as simple language as accuracy would permit the major principles which have been in the making since the early days of the Amer-

2. The 20th Century Capitalist Revolution, page 25 (1954). The figures are those of Professor M. A. Adelman of the Massachusetts Institute of Technology, states Professor Berle.

3. [1897] App.Cas. 22 (House of Lords).

ican corporation. Where decision or statutory law has seemed out of line with reason, it has been criticised, as justly it should be. The notes contain statutory examples of what is happening in practically all of the important areas of the subject. I have attempted, too, to stress the drafting problems, for many cases that have arrived in courts might well not have, had the draftsman known thoroughly the legal difficulty involved or had he used more circumspect language in his instrument. The matter of control in the closely held as well as in the publicly held corporation has been emphasized by showing what the law demands in the way of fiduciary obligation when control is exercised by directors or by shareholders. The emphasis has been upon present-day problems, and the bulk of the book is devoted to them. Where I have thought that some mention should be made of the federal taxing statutes so as to put one on guard as to the possibility of tax savings, I have discussed the problem and cited materials where a more adequate treatment may be found. In a work of this sort, more cannot be expected, for the law of corporations is much too large a subject to have interjected an extended discussion of the law applicable to the taxation of corporations or of other business associations. I have devoted a little more space to the discussion of the partnership, limited partnership, joint stock company, partnership association and the Massachusetts or business trust than is usually found in one-volume treatises. My chief reason for doing this is to give the lawyer a means of comparison which will enable him to give his client a view of other business associations that may fit his needs better, perhaps, in some business ventures, than the private corporation.

My footnotes indicate the writers preceding me who have helped me substantially in the writing of this text. It was impossible, however, to include all of the useful materials. The several recent casebooks on corporations, including one in which I am a co-compiler and co-author, have been of immeasurable help in pointing out valuable raw materials and at times in giving the authors' judgment on the direction the ever-changing law of corporations is taking. I am especially indebted to Dean Frank R. Strong of the College of Law, The Ohio State University, and to the University administration for a generous fellowship leave for the purpose of finishing this book, and for an almost unlimited amount of secretarial assistance provided by the College, and to Dean John D. Lyons of the University of Arizona College of Law who so courteously permitted me to use the Law College's library during six months while engaged in writing a portion of this volume. To them go my gratitude and thanks; and likewise to those whose articles, notes, casebooks and texts have been of aid as my footnotes will show. To my students who over the years have been astute critics of the materials used in my courses in Corporations and Corporation Finance should go a lion's share of praise and thanks for the probable influence they have had on the manner of approaching this now completed task.

NORMAN D. LATTIN

Columbus, Ohio
January, 1959

SUMMARY OF CONTENTS

•

TABLE OF CONTENTS

xiv

TABLE OF CONTENTS

Chapter 4. Evolution and Formation of Corporations; Legal Effects When Defectively Formed— Continued

Chapter 6. Postincorporation Management: Directors; Officers; Agents—Continued

TABLE OF CONTENTS

xix

Chapter 9. The Use of Shares to Acquire Corporate Assets—Continued

xxi

†

CORPORATIONS

Chapter 1

THE ROLE OF THE LAWYER IN DETERMINING WHAT FORM OF BUSINESS ASSOCIATION IS BEST SUITED TO HIS CLIENT'S NEEDS

§ 1. The Lawyer's Function

The function of the lawyer extends not only to legal matters in drafting the essential contracts and documents which are involved in setting up a business form for his client, and in complying with various statutes and regulations, but reaches out beyond legal matters to areas of convenience and utility of which the client may have the barest knowledge. The client may already be in business as an individual assisted by agents and servants, or may be using the partnership or some other form of business association to accomplish his business purpose. He may be starting a new enterprise or purchasing one now being run by others. Or he may have a unique plan of doing business which he hopes to develop and, in the process, to make a profit for himself with the desire of retaining control over his business unit, or with the simpler anticipation of taking his profit at the earliest moment and permitting others to assume the burden of developing his idea. He may have made contracts in anticipation of his business venture, or taken options or assignments of patent or other rights. His enthusiasm may have led him to purchase, in anticipation of the promotion of his project, lands to be developed or options upon the same. But, whatever his present situation may be, he needs advice as to what business association will best suit his plan and he has come to his lawyer to discuss the matter.

§ 2. Forms of Business Association

At the first conference with his client, the business venture will be ascertained and its ramifications probed. Does the client have others who are interested and who are willing to join him in some business form to develop his plan? Is the project of such a size that the financing of it cannot be assured by those immediately interested in its promotion? Is it a new business or has it been carried on by the client as an individual proprietor or by a partnership of which he is a member, or through some other type of business association? In any case, have obligations been incurred in anticipation of promoting the venture? If business has been carried on in some business association form, what are the liabilities and obligations of the association to outsiders and among the associates? Are there sufficient taxing advantages to be gained by using a particular business form and are these of such importance that another form, more convenient and, perhaps, more protective should not be used? Is the business such as to require licenses or franchises? Is it one which, if incorporated, comes within special statutes designed for the purpose, such as banks, insurance companies, utilities and the like? Is it to function within the borders of a single state, or will it exercise its powers in a number of states? It may be that it is to operate not only within the United States but in foreign countries, and special problems will arise concerning the law of such countries, including the matter of treaties existing between the United States and those countries. Here, too, taxing incidents may be important. If a branch of the business is to be established in a foreign state, what business form will be most effective in that state?

The problems are legion and they will not all arise at the moment of inception of the business form used. The lawyer, however, must anticipate them. As the business progresses, he must be prepared to advise his client on the practical as well as the legal side of the business. If the business started as a partnership, limited partnership or other business association, the time may come when it is advisable to change to the corporate form. Or, if it began as a modest project in corporate form within state borders, doing an intrastate business, but has developed and extended its business to other states, the opportune moment may have arrived when practical and legal advantages may suggest incorporation in several states with a holding company at the top of the pyramid. Practical advantages may outweigh whatever legal ones there are, or the reverse, and the lawyer must weigh them in the light of the client's needs.

§ 3. The Individual Proprietorship—Some Fundamental Considerations

Business may be carried on in a number of forms, the individual proprietorship being the simplest. Here, the individual as such, either with or without the aid of agents or servants, carries on for himself. If he functions without the aid of others his obligations in contract and his liabilities for wrongdoing are remedied primarily by the law of contracts and torts. His standard of conduct may be prescribed by statute in a particular business and, in any case, by the common law. Apart from some contractual limitations upon his unlimited liability, his liability is complete, that is, unlimited. Those who give him credit must rely upon his assets and his credit standing. Otherwise, some guaranty, suretyship or other security arrangement may be required to bolster up what is lacking in assets and credit rating.

If the individual proprietor is to be assisted by agents and servants, the rules and principles of the law of agency and of master and servant come into play. Statutes protecting workmen against health and danger hazards, against unemployment and loss of service due to injury or illness, against the day when the employee will be retired, and other legislative acts which secure him through his union membership the right to bargain collectively and to strike in proper cases, to join or not to join the union, and to be free in making his choice without coercion from his employer, may be applicable. Other statutes may require the employer to deduct from the wages of his employees amounts due under social security and income tax legislation and pay them over to the government. The lawyer of today must be prepared to give his business client the advice which will keep him from unintentional mishaps which may result in controversies with his local and federal governments.

§ 4.   Balancing of Ponderables and Imponderables in the Choice of Business Association

The objective may be the starting of a new business, the continuation of an old one in a new business association form, or the purchase of an existing business through the use of a newly formed business association or, perhaps, through the purchase of the shares or of an interest in an existing business association.

Apart from the ever changing problems of taxation, problems which can be touched upon but incidentally in a work of this kind, there are certain ponderables and imponderables which must be weighed in the choice of a business association. Continuity of existence of the business, centralization of control, legitimate devices to obtain and keep control, limited or unlimited liability of the associates, the possibility of death, bankruptcy, insanity, inadequate performance or poor health and old age of the associates, probability of expansion and the necessity of obtaining capital from outside sources, the ease or difficulty of holding and disposing of property both personal and real, of bringing suit and defending the same, of the use of authority or the abuse of it by the associates, of the amount of "red tape" involved in making reports to governmental agencies, of complying with state and federal securities acts, and of the expense involved in setting up the particular business association, should be analyzed and weighed before determining what business form should be recommended.

As important in making a determination is a body of well settled law which may be relied upon with some confidence that problems as they arise will be solvable upon a reasonably predictable basis so that guesswork may be reduced to a minimum. This last is quite as important to the business client as to his legal adviser, for in the area of business transactions, including those peculiar to the various business associations, it is not only desirable but necessary that the ambit of legal action be ascertainable with reasonable certainty. A bad rule of law may be better than none at all or than one which casts doubts as to its meaning or the extent of its application. Yet there are, and must remain, some areas where principles broad in outline, indefinite in scope, and uncertain in their application to a particular set of facts, exist as guideposts to the lawyer and judge alike in solving their problems.

Statutes which pertain to various business associations will have an important influence and their absence or inadequacy may discourage the use of a particular business association form. For example, the use of the joint stock company, once a vigorously thriving business association, would no doubt be ruled out in many states because of no or little legislation concerning this form of association, although the common law offers solutions to many of the important problems. The "Massachusetts" or business trust, thoroughly understood in some states, though not in others, may have the same fate, for there is little legislation concerning the business trust except in a few states. The local corporation statute may not have kept abreast of modern corporate development and be abandoned in favor of some foreign corporation statute that offers more elasticity in matters of importance in corporate functioning. Likewise, if the partnership is being considered as a solution to the business needs of the client, whether or not the state in which the business is to be carried on has adopted the Uniform Partnership Act or the Uniform Limited Partnership Act, or has effective statutes and a body of common law of its own to pinpoint the significant problems, will be important in the final selection of a business form for the purpose at hand.

Other matters of local or federal significance will also have a bearing on the selection of a business device capable of meeting the needs of the particular client. The progress of the law, whether statutory or decisional, will determine future action.

§ 5. The Arsenal of Business Association Forms

A text on corporations is not the place to discuss, more than briefly, the law of other business associations. It seems desirable, however, to outline their major features for the ultimate purpose of affording a means of comparison with the corporate form. A knowledge of their special characteristics is also necessary for an informed judgment on the choice of association to be made.

There are six forms of business association in use in the United States: (1) the partnership, in which is included the joint venture, (2) the limited partnership, which is a statutory thing, (3) the partnership association or limited partnership association which exists in a few states by statute and approaches the corporation in its statutory qualities, (4) the joint stock company which existed at common law and which has been considerably aided in some states by legislation, (5) the "Massachusetts" or business trust, a common law device aided by statute in a few states, and (6) the corporation. Unincorporated associations not for profit, such as labor unions and clubs, non-profit corporations, and cooperatives are without the scope of this work.

§ 6. The Partnership

While many decisions state that "partnership results from contract, express or implied,"[1] it is important to note that the Uniform Partnership Act[2] omits all reference to contract in defining a partnership as "an association of two or more persons to carry on as co-owners a business for profit."[3] The latter is a more accurate statement, for partnership results when two or more persons operate a business in such a manner that the law imposes partnership liability upon them. They may actually have intended not to be partners and have expressed their intent orally or in formal written articles of partnership. Yet, if they

---

1. For an example, see Martin v. Peyton, 246 N.Y. 213, 158 N.E. 77 (1927). Chancellor Kent's definition, 3 Kent's Commentaries 20 (7th ed. 1851), is somewhat more specific: A partnership is a "contract of two or more competent persons, to place their money, effects, labour and skill, or some, or all of them, in lawful commerce or business, and to divide the profit, and bear the loss, in certain proportions." Original edition (1828) at page 2 of volume 3.

2. This important act had been adopted in 35 states, Alaska (now a state) and Guam, through 1956: Alaska, Arizona, Arkansas, California, Colorado, Delaware, Guam, Idaho, Illinois, Indiana, Kentucky, Maryland, Massachusetts, Michigan, Minnesota, Missouri, Montana, Nebraska, Nevada, New Jersey, New Mexico, New York, North Carolina, Ohio, Oklahoma, Oregon, Pennsylvania, South Carolina, South Dakota, Tennessee, Utah, Vermont, Virginia, Washington, West Virginia, Wisconsin, Wyoming. 7 U.L.A., Supp.1957.

3. UPA § 6(1).

have carried on their business venture by associating together as co-owners for profit, they cannot escape the legal effects of partnership.[4]

Except where partnership liabilities have been imposed by estoppel through appearances set up by the conduct of the apparent partner or partners,[5] "persons who are not partners as to each other are not partners as to third persons."[6] Whether they are partners as to each other, then, will be tested by the definition set forth in the paragraph above, and not upon their actual intent.

The term "co-owner" in the definition needs some clarification, for it may lead the novice to believe that co-ownership means literally what it seems to say, that is, co-ownership of the partnership assets. What is meant is that the associates, that is, the partners, have the power of ultimate control, thus distinguishing the partnership from the relationship existing between principal and agent.[7] The power of ultimate control in the latter relationship rests in the principal; in the partnership, all partners have the power of ultimate control, though they may agree among themselves that one or more of them shall have the sole authority to carry on the business of the partnership. A third party, without knowledge of the agreement among partners, would obtain a valid contract executed by the unauthorized partner for his firm because of this principle.[8] Each partner has the authority of a general agent in carrying on the partnership business. The limitation of authority does not divest him of the power to make the contract but does deny to him the right to make it, and would subject him to liability to his partners. Thus, while co-ownership of partnership assets is present in the great majority of partnerships, it need not be, for a partner may contribute only his services and still have the status of partner with all the incidents of that relationship.[9]

The definition rules out associations not for profit, such as unincorporated unions, lodges, clubs and the like.[10] Such organ-

---

4. Martin v. Peyton et al., supra, note 1.

5. UPA § 16. Even the opinions on this point sometimes fail to express what the Commissioners on Uniform State Laws intended, as in Nelson v. Abraham, 29 Cal.2d 745, 177 P.2d 931, 933 (1947), where it is stated: "A partnership connotes coownership in the partnership property with a sharing in the profits and losses of a continuing business."

6. UPA § 7(1).

7. Commissioners' Note to § 6(1), 7 U.L.A. 11–12 (1949).

8. UPA § 9(1) and (4). § 18 provides that, "subject to any agreement between them" "(e) All partners have equal rights in the management and conduct of the partnership business."

9. McBriety v. Phillips, 180 Md. 569, 26 A.2d 400 (1942).

10. Cahill v. Plumbers, etc., Local 93, 238 Ill.App. 123 (1925); State v. Sunbeam Rebekah Lodge No. 180 of Hermiston, 169 Or. 253, 127

izations are governed by the rules of principal and agent. Whether an association organized to carry on a business as co-owners for the profit of others than the associates, for example for the benefit of an educational or charitable institution, would qualify under the definition of partnership, is a debatable question. Lindley, in his famous English work, says there is a partnership, but Gilmore, speaking for the American scene, thinks not.[11] Gilmore states that "if one conducts a business the profits of which do not belong to him, he cannot be considered as a proprietor of the business, nor held to a principal's liability with respect thereto." [12] Perhaps the inadequacy of this assumption lies in failing to consider the associates as "proprietors" who have the ultimate control of the business though the profits go to others. Had the Commissioners intended to confine the term "profit" to that of the co-owners, the addition of the words "to themselves" would have made their intent clear. But the clause is not there, so the broader interpretation is justified.

Under the early cases, profit sharing alone was frequently held to constitute the associates a partnership.[13] It has been stated that "Every man who has a share of the profits of a trade ought also to bear his share of the loss. And if anyone takes part of the profit, he takes a part of that fund on which the creditor of the trader relies for his payments." [14] But the great case of *Cox v. Hickman* [15] relegated profit sharing to a secondary position and emphasized the mutual agency of the associates as being of more importance. This concept was adopted by the Uniform Partnership Act.[16] Thus, under the Act, profit sharing in a business is but prima facie evidence that one so associated is a partner, but no inference is to be drawn in case of profits

---

P.2d 726 (1942). In the latter case, it was held that where no statute controlled, an unincorporated non-profit association was incapable of taking title to land and that § 79-302, O.C.L.A., which authorizes a partnership to take title in the partnership name, was not applicable. But see, on this point, Byam v. Bickford, 140 Mass. 31, 2 N.E. 687 (1885), where a deed to an unincorporated non-profit association, though not effective as such, was held to create a tenancy in common in the members. The Oregon court refused to follow this doctrine, and since there were no heirs, the realty devised by will escheated to the state.

§ 8(3) UPA states: "Any estate in real property may be acquired in the partnership name. Title so acquired can be conveyed only in the partnership name." See also UPA § 8(4) and § 10.

11. Lindley, A Treatise on the Law of Partnership 10–11 (10th ed. 1935); Gilmore, Partnership 6 (1911).

12. Gilmore, supra, note 11, at 10–11.

13. Grace v. Smith, 2 Wm.Bl. 998 (1775); Waugh v. Carver, 2 H.Bl. 235, 126 Eng.Rep. 525 (1793); Leggett v. Hyde, 58 N.Y. 272, 17 Am. Rep. 244 (1874); Aspinwall v. Williams, 1 Ohio 84 (1823); Wood v. Vallette, 7 Ohio St. 172 (1857).

14. Grace v. Smith, supra, note 13.

15. 8 H.L.Cas. 268 (1860).

16. See particularly UPA §§ 6 and 7.

received in payment of a debt, as wages, as annuities to a widow or representative of a deceased partner, as interest on loans "though the amount of payment vary with the profits of the business," or as consideration for the sale of good will of a business or of other property.[17] Sharing in profits by joint tenants, tenants in common or by the entirety, or because of joint or common property, or part ownership, in itself does not create partnership obligations and liabilities.[18] Likewise, the sharing of gross profits, whether or not the participants have some common interest in the property from which the gross returns are derived, does not in itself create partnership liability.[19]

While the typical partnership will be one in which there is co-ownership of assets, a sharing not only of profits but of losses as well, and a community of control, the sharing of profits and the power to exercise control are the basic essentials which the Act anticipates. Whenever profit sharing through association for business exists, close questions will arise concerning the character of the association where some elements of control, such as supervision or veto powers, may be exercised.[20] Men may be willing to lend their money to others on a profit sharing basis, or be not averse to holding property in common with others where the object is to benefit through the profits made by the use or sale of the property, but be quite unwilling to take the risk of partnership liability. The experienced lawyer will recognize the legal difficulties involved where some control over the business venture is retained by the lender or common owner. And if the client comes to him at the inception of his business venture, a carefully drawn contract avoiding mutual agency and ultimate control, but with modest protective provisions not approaching too closely the periphery of danger, will result. Nevertheless, especially when creditors are seeking to hold the associates as partners, the uncertainties of judicial decision loom large for, "By no human ingenuity would a Partnership Act which does not abolish common law partnership, enable a person who reads it to tell in every supposable case whether there is or is not a partnership." [21] Subtle matters of policy play their part in the determination of whether unlimited liability shall be imposed, and such matters are imponderable.

(a) **Joint ventures.** Where two or more persons combine to profit from a single business enterprise, limited in scope and duration and not intended to have the continuity of the usual

---

17. UPA § 7(4).

18. UPA § 7(2).

19. UPA § 7(3).

20. For an excellent example, see Martin v. Peyton, 246 N.Y. 213, 158 N.E. 77 (1927).

21. William Draper Lewis, The Uniform Partnership Act, 24 Yale L.J. 617 (1915).

general business partnership, the relationship is sometimes described by the term "joint venture" or "joint adventure." [22] There is no precise definition of the term, but most courts have used it to describe the singleness of the enterprise. Its duration may be for a shorter or longer time, even for a period of years.[23] Except in minor details, the law of partnership is applied to joint ventures, and even the minor differences asserted are not such in fact as partnership cases of the regular sort have illustrated.[24] It would be better for courts to discontinue the use of the term except in those rare instances where partnership law is not applicable to the factual pattern. And, even then, since much confusion has already been caused by the use of the term, it would be better to abandon its use in any case.

(b) The principle of delectus personae. While individuals, partnerships, corporations, and other associations may, under the Uniform Partnership Act, be members of partnerships,[25] the common type is composed of individuals. By a principle described in the Latin phrase *delectus personae* or *delectus personarum,* membership in a partnership may not be obtained except with the consent of all the partners.[26] There is the right to select its own membership, and neither the assignment of a partner's interest in the partnership, nor a sale of it on execution, nor a devise of it by will, nor an inheritance, can force the remaining partner or partners to take in as a partner the assignee, purchaser on execution sale, devisee or heir. This right

22. Nelson v. Abraham, 29 Cal.2d 745, 177 P.2d 931 (1947).

23. Walls v. Gribble, 168 Or. 542, 124 P.2d 713, 714 (1942): "A joint adventure differs from a copartnership principally in that, while a copartnership is usually formed for the transaction of a general business of a particular kind, a joint adventure is usually, but not necessarily, limited to a single transaction, although the business of conducting it may continue for a number of years."

24. Preston v. State Industrial Accident Commission, 174 Or. 553, 149 P.2d 957 (1944). See the thorough analysis in Comment: The Joint Venture: Problem Child of Partnership, 38 Calif.L.Rev. 860 (1950), where the writer concludes: "It is unfortunate for the courts to attempt the construction of two systems of law when the administration of justice would be greatly facilitated by the recognition of the joint venture for what it is, a partnership. The most rational view is that the courts should apply it directly, by command of the Uniform Partnership Act where that law is in force, and by principle and convenience where common law governs." See also Comment, The Business Joint Venture in Louisiana, 25 Tulane L.Rev. 382 (1951).

25. UPA § 2 defining "person" and § 6(1) defining "partnership." There is a major difficulty, as will later be seen, in considering a corporation as a member of a partnership, chiefly because a corporation, under the corporation statutes, must be managed by its board of directors. If, as is the case in the partnership, all members have equal rights in the conduct of the partnership business, the two statutes run afoul of each other. The matter of policy in the corporate field has been a hard one to overcome.

26. UPA § 18(g): "No person can become a member of a partnership without the consent of all the partners."

to select its own membership does not ordinarily exist in associations having shares, as in case of corporations, joint stock companies, or "Massachusetts" or business trusts, though contracts providing for reasonable restrictions upon the transfer of shares, if they do not encroach too heavily upon the policy behind the restraint upon alienation principle, will be enforced.[27] The partners may waive this right by agreement as they do in case of the joint stock company where authority to run the business is delegated to a board of directors or trustees. When control is separated from ownership, there is little reason for the principle of *delectus personarum.*

(c) Unlimited liability. A controlling factor in determining whether the general partnership should be used is the unlimited liability of the partners. If, in fact, a partnership exists, partners cannot escape unlimited liability simply by an agreement among themselves that certain of them shall be liable only to the extent of their contributions to the partnership or upon some other proportionate sharing basis. Among themselves, such a contract has validity, but as to third persons dealing with the partnership or those tortiously injured by acts of the partners done within the scope of the partnership business, such persons are protected and all partners are unlimitedly liable. While the sharing of losses is usually anticipated in partnership ventures, an agreement to share losses is not a necessary element in the determination of whether the association is a partnership.[28] Furthermore, where there is no agreement that profits and losses are to be shared unequally among the partners, all partners share equally though their contribution to capital may have been on a different basis.[29] This last statement, however, applies to partners *inter se* and not to their liability to third persons which remains unlimited.

At common law, the liability of partners for torts committed in the prosecution of the partnership business was joint and several[30] while their liability upon contracts was considered joint.[31] To the lawyer, the important distinction between joint, and joint and several liability is that, where jointly liable, all partners must be joined in suit since their obligation is joint, and therefore all must join if suing on a joint obligation. But where there is joint and several liability, one or more partners

27. See page 339, infra.

28. Roy C. Whayne Supply Co. v. McGowan, 213 Ky. 102, 280 S.W. 491 at 492 (1926), where it is stated: "Sharing losses as well as profits was once thought to show partnership, but is no longer reputed infallible, since one may be a partner without it."

29. Greiss v. Platzer, 131 N.J.Eq. 160, 24 A.2d 408 (1942); UPA § 18 (a).

30. Weaver v. Marcus, 165 F.2d 862 (4th Cir. 1948).

31. Kadota Fig Ass'n of Producers v. Case-Swayne Co., 73 Cal.App.2d 796, 167 P.2d 518 (1946).

may be sued for the entire liability, that is, there need be no
joinder of all. Statutes have varied on this matter, some of
them making all partnership liability joint and several, some
making it joint, and case law must be examined for interpretations which at times seem to do violence to the particular statute.[32] The Uniform Partnership Act places joint and several
liability upon partners for torts committed by a partner while
acting in the ordinary course of the partnership business or
with the authority of his co-partners, and in certain breaches of
trust, and joint liability for all other debts and obligations of
the partnership.[33]

(d) Unstable character of partnership. Due to the several
circumstances under which a partnership may be "dissolved,"
this form of business association has an instability which must
be weighed in the light of the greater stability of corporations
and other associations having transferable shares. "Dissolution" has been defined in the Uniform Partnership Act as "the
change in the relation of the partners caused by any partner
ceasing to be associated in the carrying on as distinguished from
the winding up of the business." [34] While lawyers have frequently used the term "dissolution" to include not only the act
of terminating the business but also the acts thereafter following in the process of winding up the business and distributing
its assets, this confusion in the use of the term should no longer
exist.[35] As the Commissioners have stated, "In this act dissolution designates the point in time when the partners cease to
carry on the business together; termination is the point in time
when all the partnership affairs are wound up; winding up, the
process of settling partnership affairs after dissolution." [36] Dissolution, then, is a change in legal relationship caused by a partner's ceasing to be associated in the partnership venture, the
partnership continuing for the purpose of being wound up.[37]

The agreement of the partners may have provided for a
definite time period during which the partnership business is to
be carried on. Or, if no time period has been agreed upon, one
or more partners may elect to discontinue the business and wind
it up. Or, even where a time period has been agreed upon, all
partners may decide to dissolve their firm. Or the agreement
may have provided for the expulsion of a partner upon the happening of stated conditions and, in good faith, the partner has

32. Commissioners' Note to § 15, 7
    U.L.A. at 86 (1949).

33. UPA §§ 13, 14 and 15.

34. UPA § 29.

35. See Commissioners' Note, 7 U.L.
    A. 165–166 (1949).

36. Supra, note 35.

37. UPA § 30. McIver v. Norman,
    187 Or. 516, 205 P.2d 137 (1949);
    McKinley v. Long, 227 Ind. 639, 88
    N.E.2d 382 (1949); Schneider v.
    Newmark, 359 Mo. 955, 224 S.W.2d
    968 (1948).

been expelled. Or some statute or circumstance may have made it unlawful longer to carry on the business or to carry on the particular business in the form of a partnership. Or, it may be, that a partner has died or become bankrupt. Dissolution results under the above circumstances and if some, but not all of the partners desire to carry on the same business under an arrangement with the departing partner or his estate as by purchasing his interest, where the business may legally be carried on, a new partnership results. The retiring partner and the deceased partner's estate [38] will be liable for debts contracted and torts committed to the time of dissolution which made either liable during the time of his existence as a partner. This liability he cannot escape except by contract with the third persons involved where it has been agreed that his liability will be less than that of a partner, a contract which those dealing with the partnership may well hesitate to make.[39] In any case, he will be liable for the torts with which his partnership would be chargeable.

Even if the partnership agreement is for a specified time and the time has not yet passed, a partner may withdraw and thus cause a dissolution though he will be liable for damages caused by virtue of his breach of the agreement.[40] Thus, a partner has the power to bring about a dissolution of the partnership at his will for any reason, good or bad. This, in itself, is a possibility which those investing capital in a business venture may wish to avoid. They cannot avoid it in a general partnership.

Furthermore, a partner may have been declared a lunatic in some judicial proceeding, or may have been shown to be of un-

---

38. UPA § 36(4) provides: "The individual property of a deceased partner shall be liable for all obligations of the partnership while he was a partner but subject to the prior payment of his separate debts."

39. There is a further possibility in UPA § 36(2) which provides: "A partner is discharged from any existing liability upon dissolution of the partnership by an agreement to that effect between himself, the partnership creditor and the person or partnership continuing the business; and such agreement may be inferred from the course of dealing between the creditor having knowledge of the dissolution and the person or partnership continuing the business." See also UPA § 36(3).

40. While the English law is contra to this view (see Crawshay v. Maule, 1 Swanst. 495 (1818)), the weight of American authority supports the statement as does UPA § 31(2). See Commissioners' Note, 7 U.L.A. 170 (1949), for other authority. "There can be no such thing as an indissoluble partnership." Atha v. Atha, 303 Mich. 611, 6 N.W.2d 897, at 899 (1942), quoting from an earlier Michigan case which, in turn, had quoted from Skinner v. Dayton, 19 Johns. 513, 538, 10 Am.Dec. 286, at 294 (N.Y.1822): "Even where partners covenant with each other, that the partnership shall continue seven years, either partner may dissolve it the next day, by proclaiming his determination for that purpose; the only consequence being that he thereby subjects himself for damages for a breach of his covenant."

sound mind, or have become incapable through age, accident or disease of performing his partnership duties, or have so conducted himself as to have affected prejudicially the carrying on of the business, or have breached his partnership agreement wilfully and persistently or otherwise carried on so as to make it impracticable for the other partners to function as partners with him, or, perhaps, the business cannot be carried on except at a loss, or other circumstances may indicate that dissolution is equitable. In such cases, the Uniform Partnership Act provides for dissolution, on the application by or for a partner, by decree of the court.[41] If a partner sells his interest in the partnership, the purchaser may immediately force liquidation if the partnership is one at will, and if for a specified term may force it upon the termination of the period.[42] Also, under the Uniform Partnership Act, where a judgment creditor of a partner has a charging order upon the interest of the partner,[43] provision is made for dissolution by court decree upon application of the judgment creditor under the circumstances set forth in Section 32(2).

These uncertainties are of sufficient importance to warrant careful consideration in any case, and should be presented to a client who desires the assured continuity of his business enterprise, in spite of some advantages, considered hereafter, which the partnership form has over other business associations. Death of a partner, and the consequence of dissolution thereby, can be provided for by the partnership agreement and the testamentary will of the partner so that its effects may be alleviated as by a provision that the deceased's partnership interest shall remain in the partnership for a stated period and/or an agreement that the remaining partners may purchase it at a figure to be determined by book valuations, or in some other manner, at a time therein stated. Some of the other circumstances under which dissolution may occur can likewise be foreseen and contracted for, and should be, for the protection of the remaining partner or partners. Cross-insurance upon the lives of the partners in favor of the surviving partners for the payment or partial payment of the deceased partner's interest is a possible solution to the perhaps present inability of the surviving partners to settle with the deceased's estate without seriously crippling the business itself. Insurance companies have devised plans for such contingencies which may be had for the asking and the lawyer should consult such plans and make his recommendations accordingly. Death is one contingency which is certain and a lawyer would indeed be delinquent in his duty to

41. UPA § 32(1).   **43.** UPA § 28(1).

42. UPA § 32(2) (a) and (b).

his client in drawing up a partnership agreement which failed
to provide for this event.

(e) Partnership property. There was no difficulty at common
law in a partnership's acquiring personal property or choses in
action in the partnership name though the name might be an
artificial one. The partners became the legal owners. The
failure to recognize the partnership as a legal person distinct
from its members and the rules which had developed in conveyancing made the transfer of realty to the partnership a more
difficult matter. If a conveyance was made to a partnership in
a partnership name which included the name of a partner, legal
title to the realty vested in the named partner and he held as
trustee for the partnership. Some courts, however, went a bit
further and held that parol evidence might be used to show who
were the partners and that they obtained a title as tenants in
common.[44] But the fact that legal title vested in the named partner had its dangers, for he could convey to one who had no
knowledge of his position of trust a good legal title, thus divesting the equitable interest of the partnership.

The Uniform Partnership Act removed the uncertainty of
the existing law concerning conveyancing to and from the partnership. Under the Act, real property can be conveyed to the
partnership in the partnership name, though it be a fictitious
one, and when title is so held it may be conveyed, when authorized, by a partner in the partnership name.[45] Even when the
partner has no authority to convey, if the conveyance was made
for apparently carrying on in the usual way the business of the
partnership, the conveyance will be valid unless the grantee had
knowledge of the partner's lack of authority.[46] But even if the
property was conveyed to a grantee with notice, his subsequent
grant for value to one without notice of the partner's lack of
authority is valid as against the partnership.[47] Thus, the Act
recognizes, for this purpose, the legal entity of the partnership
with reasonable provisions for protecting the firm and giving
the necessary security to a bona fide grantee.

Furthermore, if a partner with authority to convey executes
a conveyance in his own name where the property is held in
the partnership name, the grantee obtains an equitable title to
the property.[48] And where title is in one or more of the part-

---

44. Crane, Partnership 190 (2d ed.
     1952). A better and more ac-
     curate term to use is "tenancy in
     partnership," a term used in § 25
     UPA to designate the interest of a
     partner in the partnership stock.
     Note, 17 Mich.L.Rev. 190 (1918).

45. UPA §§ 8(3) and 10(1).

46. UPA § 9(1). See note 50, infra.

47. UPA § 10(1).

48. UPA § 10(2).

ners, but not in the names of all, those in whose names the title is, where the record does not disclose the partnership interest, may convey a valid title to a good faith purchaser for value though the act of those partners in conveying would not otherwise have bound the partnership.[49] "Where the title to real property is in the name of one or more or all the partners, or in a third person in trust for the partnership, a conveyance executed by a partner in the partnership name, or in his own name, passes the equitable interest of the partnership, provided the act is one within the authority of the partner, under the provisions of paragraph (1) of section 9." [50]

Thus, at common law, partnership realty might be held by one, several or all of the partners, or by one not a member of the partnership in trust for the partnership. Under the Act, while such usages are preserved, the simplest and most effective manner of holding realty is in the name of the partnership.

(f) What is firm property? It is at times difficult to ascertain just what property belongs to the partnership and what belongs to the individual members of the firm, for an individual partner's property may be used in the business without any intent to make it partnership property. It may be loaned rather than contributed as a part of a member's capital contribution. The problem is important in the determination of priorities between partnership and individual creditors in equity and in the matter of attachments and executions made by such creditors at law. It is also important in the winding up of a partnership, for if the property is the individual property of a partner it may not be sold and the proceeds proportionally distributed to the other members of the firm. As among themselves, the partners may determine what property shall be partnership stock and what shall remain their individual property. And, generally, the determination of the partners is controlling as to third persons dealing with the partnership, though the appearances thus created by them may be the means of estopping them from asserting their individual rights in the property, at least until the claims of those able to raise an estoppel are satisfied. Whether or not the property is to be considered a part of the firm assets is primarily a question of intention with inferences drawn

---

49. UPA § 10(3).

50. UPA § 10(4). § 9(1) reads as follows: "Every partner is an agent of the partnership for the purpose of its business, and the act of every partner, including the execution in the partnership name of any instrument, for apparently carrying on in the usual way the business of the partnership of which he is a member binds the partnership, unless the partner so acting has in fact no authority to act for the partnership in the particular matter, and the person with whom he is dealing has knowledge of the fact that he has no such authority."

from the manner of acquisition and use of the property where the intention has not otherwise been made manifest.[51]

The Uniform Partnership Act has two simple statements on partnership property: "(1) All property originally brought into the partnership stock or subsequently acquired by purchase or otherwise, on account of the partnership, is partnership property. (2) Unless the contrary intention appears, property acquired with partnership funds is partnership property." [52]

(g) Nature of partner's interest in partnership property. In specific partnership property a partner is co-owner and holds as a tenant in partnership.[53] The common law had developed the tenancy in common and the joint tenancy whose legal incidents are well known and to which the courts naturally proceeded for analogies which might be useful in the determination of problems involving partnership property. While the fact of co-ownership of partnership property by the partners was evident, the legal incidents which followed therefrom, due to the particular nature of a partnership and the conflicting interests of partners, creditors, spouses and legal representatives of the partners, were not clear. The right of survivorship of a joint tenant upon the death of the other, for example, is a workable concept in the field of partnership law if limited to the peculiar needs of the legal situations presented, for it gives the surviving partner or partners, rather than the legal representative of the deceased, the property which is needed in the winding up of the partnership. But the early courts, not satisfied with a useful analogy, applied as well other legal incidents of joint tenancies to the partnership scene. The close application of these principles produced inequities which later courts attempted to rectify, and in their attempt "produced very great confusion." [54] "Practically this confusion has had more unfortunate effect on substantive rights when the separate creditors of a partner attempt to attach and sell specific partnership property than when a partner attempts to assign specific partnership property not for a partnership purpose but for his own purposes." [55] The Uniform Partnership Act proceeds to end this confusion by using the term "tenant in partnership" and by spelling out the incidents of such a tenancy.

Under the Act, a partner, "subject to the provisions of this act and to any agreement between partners," has an equal right

51. See the discussion in Crane, Partnership 173 et seq. (2d ed. 1952).

52. UPA § 8(1) and (2). See Block v. Schmidt, 296 Mich. 610, 296 N. W. 698 (1941).

53. UPA § 25(1).

54. Commissioners' Note, 7 U.L.A. 145 (1949).

55. Supra, note 54.

with his partners, for partnership purposes but for no other purpose without the consent of his partners, to possess specific partnership property. This right is not assignable "except in connection with the assignment of rights of all the partners in the same property," is not subject to attachment or execution except for claims against the partnership, in which case the partners cannot claim any right under the homestead or exemption laws, vests in the surviving partner or partners upon his death, or if he is the last surviving partner and death occurs it vests in his legal representative, but such partners, or the legal representative of the last surviving partner, have no right to possess the partnership property except for a partnership purpose. And "A partner's right in specific property is not subject to dower, curtesy, or allowances to widows, heirs, or next of kin." [56] Thus, in effect, the partnership assumes the habiliments of a legal person, for the limited purposes outlined above. The confusion resulting from joint tenancy concepts thus disappears and in its place is substituted a workable concept for the partnership form of business.

(h) Partner's interest in the partnership. As distinguished from a partner's interest in specific property in the partnership is his interest in the partnership which is his share in the profits and surplus and is considered personal property.[57] This interest, under the Act, is assignable but this does not of itself dissolve the partnership nor, during the continuance of the partnership, does it entitle the assignee to participate in the firm as a partner. It does give the assignee the right to receive the profits to which his assignor was entitled and, in case of dissolution, the assignee is entitled to receive whatever interest would have been received by his assignor had he then been a partner.[58] The common law, however, held that an assignment by a partner of his interest constituted a dissolution without more. The wisdom of the Act's provision is apparent when it is realized that frequently assignments are made by a partner as security for a loan and that, under such circumstances, he has no intent of giving up his relationship as partner. Barring some other cause for dissolution, he continues as a partner with the obligations and rights of a partner.[59] In a sense, the partner's interest is thus treated as if the firm were a legal person, somewhat comparable to the position of a shareholder in a corporation when he sells or pledges his shares.

It has been said that "No question as to partnership property has been more confused by the decisions than that of the

---

56. UPA § 25.

57. UPA § 26.

58. UPA § 27.

59. UPA § 31, Causes of Dissolution, and pp. 11–13, supra.

rights of separate creditors of a partner, seeking to apply the debtor partner's share or interest to the payment of a separate debt by attachment or execution." [60]   The problem as it existed at common law must be left to texts on partnership for it is too involved for discussion here.[61]   But the conflict arose out of the view that a partnership was not a legal person capable as such of holding property in its own right and the equitable concept that partnership assets should first be applied to pay firm debts and the individual assets of the partners to pay their individual debts.   Had the courts generally recognized the partnership as a legal person rather than an aggregate of persons holding title, such problems would have been resolved much as they have been in case of the corporation.   It should not pass unnoticed, however, that when courts of their own volition adopted a concept that, under certain circumstances, the assets of the partnership must first go to the payment of partnership debts and those of the partners to the settlement of their private debts they were, in a real sense, giving a qualified legal personality to the partnership.

(i) **The partnership as a legal entity.**   One of the major advantages of corporations is that the law considers them distinct legal personalities, thus simplifying the holding of property, the bringing of suits, the separation of individual from corporate interests, and giving rather complete dominance of control in a management composed of a board of directors.   The common law, however, was reluctant to build legal personalities from groups whether formed for business purposes or not, as in unions, or in clubs, though they might act in unison and purport to act in a manner comparable to that of a corporation.   It was thought that the legislative process was necessary to create legal personality though the arguments were frequently strong for judicial creation to produce desirable economic and social results.   The civil law, on the contrary, recognized the separate personality of partnerships and a few states so recognized it.[62]

---

60. Crane, Partnership 205 (2d ed. 1952).

61. Crane, supra, note 60, at 205 et seq.

62. See Crane, Partnership 11 (2d ed. 1952); People of Puerto Rico v. Russell & Co., 288 U.S. 476, 53 S.Ct. 447, 77 L.Ed. 903 (1937), discussing the sociedad en comandita under the Puerto Rican law; Rosario v. Sucesores De Sobrino Y Compania, 78 F.Supp. 463 (D.C. Puerto Rico 1948); Brinson v. Monroe Auto. & Supply Co., 180 La. 1064, 158 So. 558, 96 A.L.R.

1206 (1934); Henderson's Estate **v.** Comm'r of Internal Revenue, 155 F.2d 310 (5th Cir. 1946)—Louisiana law; Rubio Savings Bank of Brighton v. Acme Farm Products Co., 240 Iowa 547, 37 N.W.2d 16 (1949).   Scottish law is provided for in § 4(2) of the English Partnership Act of 1890 [53 and 54 Vict. c. 39] as follows: "In Scotland a firm is a legal person distinct from the partners of whom it is composed, but an individual partner may be charged on a decree or diligence directed against the firm, and on payment of the debts is

The common law was able conveniently to fashion from the whole cloth the de facto corporation [63] and, when occasion demanded it, to tailor a subsidiary corporation, albeit a legal person, to that of a parent corporation in such a manner as, for the purpose at hand, to make the parent in effect a combination of the two.[64] But in case of the partnership, the common law staked its belief upon the aggregate theory, failing to recognize the firm as a legal person distinct from the members comprising it. This was the theory finally adopted by the Uniform Partnership Act. As Judge Learned Hand has written: "The Uniform Partnership Act . . . did not . . . make the firm an independent juristic entity. The Commission did indeed start out to do so, and if Dean Ames had lived, considering his partiality for the mercantile conception of a partnership . . . , he might have succeeded in impressing that mould upon the act. But after his death, the Conference in 1911 after a very full discussion chose to retain the pluralistic notion of the firm, as the English chancellors had painfully worked it out from the bare common-law, which recognized only joint owners and joint obligors . . . That was procedurally full of difficulties, and permitted some injustice, both of which it was the purpose of the Act to abate; but the essentials of the old model were preserved." [65]

Although the Uniform Partnership Act failed specifically to give legal personality to the partnership, several portions of it inferentially recognized the concept. It has already been noted that the Act permits conveyances to and from the firm in

entitled to relief *pro rata* from the firm and its other members." 7 U.L.A. 252 (1949).

63. See infra, p. 160 et seq., for a discussion of the de facto corporation.

64. See Berle, The Theory of Enterprise Entity, 47 Col.L.Rev. 343, at 349–350 (1947).

65. Helvering, Comm'r of Internal Revenue v. Smith, 90 F.2d 590 at 591–592 (2d Cir. 1937). But compare the words of the same judge in Comm'r of Internal Revenue v. Lehman, 165 F.2d 383, 7 A.L.R.2d 667 (2d Cir. 1948), cert. denied 334 U.S. 819, 68 S.Ct. 1085, 92 L.Ed. 1749 (1948). See Commissioners' Prefatory Note, 7 U.L.A. 1–2 (1949), on the matter of the adoption of the aggregate theory as opposed to the entity theory of partnership. On the taxation point involved, see page 25, infra.

In Williams v. McGowan, Comm'r of Internal Revenue, 152 F.2d 570, at 572 (2d Cir. 1945), Judge Learned Hand states: "Our law has been sparing in the creation of juristic entities; it has never, for example, taken over the Roman 'universitas facti'; and indeed for many years it fumbled uncertainly with the concept of a corporation. One might have supposed that partnership would have been an especially promising field in which to raise up an entity, particularly since merchants have always kept their accounts upon that basis. Yet there too our law resisted at the price of great and continuing confusion; and, even when it might be thought that a statute admitted, if it did not demand, recognition of the firm as an entity, the old concepts prevailed."

the partnership name whether the name be an artificial one or one which contains the name of a partner,[66] that a partner has no right to possess specific firm property except for partnership purposes and that the right vests, upon his death, in the remaining partner or partners, and that it is not subject to dower, curtesy, or allowances to widows, heirs, or next of kin,[67] and that a partner's interest in the firm is merely his share in the profits and surplus, assignable true, but not effective to dissolve the partnership.[68] These provisions recognize the two interests, that of the partnership and that of the partner, much as if they were distinct legal personalities.

Another instance of virtually recognizing the partnership as an entity is that in which a judgment creditor of an individual partner, under this Act, may obtain a charging order against the debtor partner's interest in the partnership, have a receiver appointed to receive the debtor's share of profits and other moneys due or coming due to him from the partnership, and foreclose the debtor partner's interest subject to its redemption by other partners.[69] Thus, the judgment creditor of the individual partner acquires no greater rights than the individual partner had and, if there is a sale under the foreclosure, the purchase of the partner's interest may be made without causing a dissolution.[70] But, upon application of the purchaser, dissolution may be decreed after the termination of the specified term of the partnership, or if it was a partnership at will when the charging order was issued, dissolution may be decreed immediately.[71] An attachment or writ of execution upon specific partnership property is thus outlawed as far as individual partner's creditors are concerned.[72] The remedy is for an order charging the partner's interest, whatever it may be, in the partnership.

The Act contains other provisions recognizing the division of interests. The application of an insolvent firm's assets to pay firm creditors and of the individual partner's assets to pay his own creditors before either group of creditors may benefit from the other's assets—also recognized as an equitable principle at common law—is best explained by attributing legal personality to the partnership. And "When partnership property and the individual properties of the partners are in possession of a court for distribution, partnership creditors shall have priority on partnership property and separate creditors on individual property, saving the rights of lien or secured creditors

66. Supra, p. 14.
67. Supra, pp. 16–17.
68. Supra, p. 16.
69. UPA § 28.

70. UPA § 28(2).
71. UPA § 32(2).
72. UPA § 25(2) (c).

as heretofore." [73] Furthermore, when a partner is bankrupt or is insolvent, his separate creditors come first, then the partnership creditors.[74]

Under the Act, too, when a new partner is admitted to an existing partnership without liquidation of the firm his contribution to the partnership assets (as well as that of his co-partners) is subject to the obligations created by the partnership before he became a member, though he is not personally liable for such prior obligations.[75] Unless he assumed such prior obligations, the common law did not thus hold his contribution subject to them, as his entry into the partnership created a new partnership whose combined assets became liable for obligations incurred thereafter. It should be said that the common law did look diligently to find an assumption of liability by the new partnership of the debts of the old, and frequently found it, but the Act now makes the matter clear.[76] Thus, in effect, the firm may be considered a legal unit for this purpose.

Statutes in many states authorize suit against the partnership in its artificial or firm name by service upon one or more partners, usually providing that a judgment shall bind the assets of the firm and the individual property of the partners served with process, thus recognizing the firm as if it were a legal person holding its property as such. The Bankruptcy Act has also adopted the view that partnership creditors have a prior claim to partnership assets and individual creditors to individual partners' assets, and the Uniform Fraudulent Conveyance Act treats the partnership as a legal entity in the determination of whether a conveyance is fraudulent as to partnership creditors.[77]

Whether a partnership is a legal entity for the purpose of contracting with a partner of the firm and whether two partnerships of which there is a common member or members may so contract is a problem which has caused some difficulty. It was hard for the common law to conceive that an obligor might at the same time be an obligee, though in a different capacity, and that he might be both plaintiff and defendant in the same suit. But as Justice Story has said, " . . . there never has been any difficulty in proceeding in courts of equity . . . Courts of equity, in all such cases, look behind the form of the transactions to their substances; and treat the different firms, for the purposes of substantial justice, exactly as if they were composed of strangers, or were in fact corporate companies." [78]

73. UPA § 40(h).

74. UPA § 40(i).

75. UPA §§ 17, 41(1).

76. Commissioners' Note, 7 U.L.A. 100 (1949).

77. See Bankruptcy Act § 5 (11 U.S. C.A. § 23) and Uniform Fraudulent Conveyance Act §§ 2(2) and 8 (1951).

78. Story, Equity Jurisprudence § 680 (3d English ed. 1920).

It is indeed surprising that the common law, so elastic and imaginative in some areas, has proceeded with such blind spots in others. The traditions and practices of merchants doing business in the partnership form might well have furnished the necessary perspective for a liberal adoption of entity concepts in this field. Yet, bogged down with concepts of joint ownership for a quite different set of purposes, the common law was indeed shortsighted in failing to meet the business needs by giving legal personality to the partnership.

However, the common law, through a high fiction, considered partnership realty converted into personalty "so that the firm might deal with it as personalty for the purposes of paying debts and selling or settling partnership affairs, to the exclusion of the rights of heirs, widows or creditors of individual partners. As soon as partnership purposes were fully accomplished, however, the remaining realty was regarded as resuming its nature as such. This theory of conversion was employed to describe the subordination of the land to partnership purposes." [79] The Uniform Partnership Act [80] has been rightly interpreted to create an out and out conversion of partnership realty into personalty so that it never reverts to realty for any purpose, thus making the conflict of interests clear from the moment the realty is acquired by the partnership for its uses until it is liquidated and its assets distributed. Again, it may be said that such treatment, whether by the common law or under the Uniform Partnership Act, inferentially recognizes the partnership as a legal entity.

(j) Some advantages of the partnership. The informal manner in which a partnership may be formed and its business conducted, free from the red tape of governmental regulation, is one advantage that should not be ignored. The agreement may be oral or written, though, as a matter of practice, it should be carefully thought out and reduced to writing in the light of matters heretofore discussed and the particular needs of the partners. If the Uniform Partnership Act is in force in the state, a glance at its provisions will show that the rights and duties of partners are thus-and-so unless otherwise agreed upon, thus permitting variations from the statutory norm which a wise draftsman will consider. For example, the matter of propor-

---

79. Ballantine, Lattin and Jennings, Cases and Materials on Corporations 25 (2d ed. 1953).

80. § 26; Lewis, The Uniform Partnership Act, 24 Yale L.J. 617, 637 (1915). Professor Burdick in his article, Partnership Realty, 9 Col. L.Rev. 197, at 216 (1909), had recommended treating the partnership as a legal entity "at least as far as firm title is concerned; and give full effect to the principle that a partner is not a co-owner of firm property, but that his interest in it is only a right to his proportion of the cash assets of the firm after its debts are paid."

tionate sharing of profits and losses, of delegation of management to one or several of the partners, of salaries for services, if some partners are to have salaries—partners are not entitled to remuneration for services unless provided for—, and other important matters may be specifically included in the agreement, and should be. This is quite as true at common law. The various contingencies upon which a partnership may be dissolved make necessary a carefully drawn agreement aimed at a practical solution which will protect the partners who may wish to continue the business without financial embarrassment to those partners. If the partnership is composed of an even number of partners, occasions will arise when action may be impossible because of a tie vote much as similar action may be prevented by a tie vote in a corporate board of directors of similar composition. Provision for the arbitration of such partnership matters by impartial arbitrators with an agreement to abide by their determination may seem desirable; or, perhaps, if the partners have great confidence in a fellow partner, they may give him more than one vote in case there is a tie, or voting power may be arranged on the basis of capital contributions.

Matters such as the name of the partnership, the partners composing it, the date when the partnership agreement is to take effect, the purposes of the partnership, the location of its business, and the life duration of the partnership are ones which are basic and would, no doubt, be thought of by a neophyte in this legal area. Contributions by the named partners to the partnership stock, whether of realty, personalty, cash, choses in action, or services should be specifically set forth, as well as any loans to the firm whether of specific property or cash. How the profits and losses are to be shared, i. e., in what proportion, remuneration for services, if any, management by stated partners if such is the arrangement, voluntary and compulsory retirement, purchase and sale of a retiring or deceased partner's interest with a method to determine its value, cross-insurance of partners for the purpose of having a fund to purchase a deceased partner's interest, the specific duties that partners are to perform, the settlement of disputes through arbitration or otherwise, books of account to be kept, accounting periods when profits and losses are to be determined, banking arrangements including who is to sign checks and notes and upon whose authority loans may be procured, who is to hire and discharge employees of the partnership and to determine their salaries or wages, are all matters which should call for expression in the agreement of partnership. Other provisions may be thought desirable, and the problems of the particular partnership will determine many of them. In drafting partnership articles, the simple, direct and accurate statement which the layman can grasp should be the rule, for laymen have to work within the confines of such agreements and should not have to pursue their attorney for an opinion as to the meaning of what should have been clear in the first instance.

(k) Taxing advantages. Another advantage which to date has prevailed is in the realm of federal income taxation. While the income of a corporation is heavily taxed before profits or surpluses are derived out of which dividends may be paid, the shareholder receiving dividends must also include them as income to himself and also be taxed. Hence, in a real sense, there is double taxation. Partners, on the other hand, are liable for income tax only in their individual capacity, that is, the income of a partnership is not first taxed as if the firm were a legal entity, and the profits taxed again as income when distributed to the partners.[81] However, a return for each taxable year is required to be made by the partnership for information purposes.[82] The distributive share of each partner, whether distributed or not, is taxable to him as an individual.[83] Thus the partnership, whether general or limited, may be used to reduce the tax burdens which fall heavily upon corporations or "associations" under the statute. The policy of the Federal Internal Revenue Code, however, is to tax as corporations, associations having essentially the qualities of corporations, namely, management through some device approaching that of a board of directors in a corporation, as in joint stock companies and Massachusetts or business trusts, and continuity of existence as in these organizations, as by the use of transferable shares or by agreements among themselves which further such continuity without dissolving the association as would a change in membership in a partnership. "The term 'association' is not used in the Internal Revenue Code in any narrow or technical sense. It includes any organization, created for the transaction of designated affairs, or the attainment of some object, which, like a corporation, continues notwithstanding that its members or participants change, and the affairs of which, like corporate affairs, are conducted by a single individual, a committee, a board, or some other group, acting in a representative capacity." [84]

---

81. I.R.C.1954 (26 U.S.C.A.) § 701. After the manuscript for this volume went to press, Congress enacted taxing provisions under which certain small business corporations having not more than 10 shareholders may elect to be taxed in the manner of a partnership, that is, upon the undistributed taxable income of the corporation, the taxpayer to include in his gross income the proportion he would have received had the corporation distributed the fund in dividends. I. R.C. §§ 1371–1377; 6037 (corporation must file an informational return under this section); 27 U. S. Law Week 87–89 (August 26, 1958).

82. I.R.C.1954 (26 U.S.C.A.) § 6031.

83. I.R.C.1954 (26 U.S.C.A.) § 702.

84. Fed. Tax Reg. § 39.3797–2; 26 C.F.R. (Part 1) § 39.3797–2.

Because of the scope of the definition of the term "association" there is a pitfall which should be avoided if the partnership hopes to escape the taxation to which corporations and "associations" are subject. Thus, if control is placed in one or more members, but not all, of a general partnership, or in one or more, but not all, of the general partners in a limited partnership, *and* the partnership is not dissolved by the death of a partner or upon his transfer of interest in the partnership, an association results under the Internal Revenue Code and it is taxed as if it were a corporation. "An unincorporated association, though a partnership under state law, may nevertheless be included within the term 'corporation' within the definition of the revenue law." [85]

There is, however, a new provision in the 1954 Code which permits partnerships which qualify under the provision to be taxed as if they were corporations. Election to be so taxed must be by the unanimous action of the partners and the partnership must not have more than 50 members. Other conditions are attached to this privilege. Circumstances may exist whereby tax savings may be made through such an election.[86]

Prior to the 1954 Internal Revenue Code, there had been considerable controversy over the manner of treatment of a gain or loss in the sale of a partner's interest in the firm. Was his interest to be treated as a *single* capital asset similar to shares in a corporation although composed of fractional interests in the partnership assets some of which could not be properly considered as "capital assets" in an individual's tax return? The Commissioner had contended that there should be an individual partnership-item treatment as in the case of the sole proprietorship. And this view had some support in the courts.[87] But eventually a number of federal courts held that "when a partnership is dissolved, either by the act of the parties, by operation of law, by the death of a surviving party, or by a decree of court after litigation between the partners, the moneys received by the withdrawing partner for his share of the assets, even if payable over a period of years are *not* income, but the

---

85. Poplar Bluff Printing Co. v. Com'r, 149 F.2d 1016, at 1018 (8th Cir. 1945). For interesting cases where management was placed in one or more of the profit sharers with continuity of existence of group anticipated, see Herman v. U. S., 81 F.Supp. 963 (D.Mo.1949); Wabash Oil & Gas Ass'n v. C. I. R., 160 F.2d 658 (1st Cir. 1947), cert. denied 331 U.S. 843, 67 S.Ct. 1533, 91 L.Ed. 1853 (1947).

86. I.R.C. § 1361; 26 U.S.C.A. §§ 701 et seq., Guide to Internal Revenue Code of 1954, pages 95–97, discussing § 1361.

87. See, for example, Helvering v. Smith, 90 F.2d 590, at 591–592 (2d Cir. 1937). But compare the words of the same judge, Learned Hand, in Com'r v. Lehman, 165 F. 2d 383, at 386, 7 A.L.R.2d 667 (2d Cir. 1948), cert. denied 334 U.S. 819, 68 S.Ct. 1085, 92 L.Ed. 1749 (1948).

distributing of capital assets from which a capital gain or loss results." [88]   The Commissioner had reluctantly taken this view after he apparently saw the futility of obtaining much judicial recognition of his own view.[89]

However, this approach opened up certain loopholes of tax escape and resulted in amendments in the 1954 statute.[90]   While the single capital asset rule has been codified by § 741 of the 1954 provisions on the issue of the treatment of a withdrawing partner's interest in the firm, a change in the previously accepted common law rule was made which restricts the single capital asset view considerably.   This change provides that where what the selling partner receives is attributable to his share of unrealized receivables or substantially appreciated inventory, these items are to be treated as ordinary gain or loss, the gain to be taxable as income.   The purchaser of the partner's interest may exclude from his gross income when such is later realized on the receivables or inventory, an amount equal to the income recognized to the seller from such items, providing he elects to so adjust the basis of the partnership assets.[91]   Gains which are outside the area taxable as income are treated as capital gains and losses as capital losses.[92]   Further discussion must be left to treatises on federal income tax problems.[93]

In the paragraphs above referring to the rule of capital gains and losses, the underlying assumption has been that the partner who sold his interest, or the partnership which dissolved and distributed its assets, carried on no longer the partnership affairs.   However, the partners may desire to form a corporation and transfer the partnership assets to the corporation for stock in the latter.   This can be done tax-free if the statute is followed though there is a resulting dissolution of the partnership.[94]   However, there are sometimes circumstances under which it may be wiser to have the incorporation a taxable

88.   Chief Judge Yankwich in Herbert v. Riddell, 103 F.Supp. 369, at 382–383 (D.C.Cal.1952).   See Willis, Handbook of Partnership Taxation 178–179 (1957).

89.   Willis, op. cit. supra note 88, 179.   See Note, Theory of the Tax Treatment of the Sale of a Partnership Interest, 52 Col.L.Rev. 257 (1952).

90.   Note, 52 Col.L.Rev. 257, at 265–266 (1952), which points out the dangers of the single capital asset view.

91.   I.R.C. of 1954 (26 U.S.C.A.) § 751 and Regulation § 1.751–1.

92.   I.R.C. of 1954 (26 U.S.C.A.) § 741 and Regulation § 1.741–1.

93.   See Miller, Capital Gains Taxation of the Fruits of Personal Effort: Before and Under the 1954 Code, 64 Yale L.J. 1, at 33–43 (1954); Jackson (and others), The Internal Revenue Code of 1954: Partnerships, 54 Col.L.Rev. 1183, at 1214 et seq. (1954); C.C.H. Standard Fed.Tax Rep, Par. 3900 et seq. (1957).

94.   I.R.C.1954 (26 U.S.C.A.) § 351.

event. For such refinements treatises on federal income taxation must be consulted.[95]

Family partnerships are likewise used for the purpose of avoiding the heavy surtaxes upon one family member by distributing the income among several members of the family. As far as husband and wife partnerships are concerned, the problem of forming a partnership to reduce income taxation is no longer of practical importance as the Internal Revenue Code now permits husband and wife to make a joint return of their combined incomes, no matter what the source, with payment by each of a separate tax on half of the total.[96] But the problem remains important where other family members are brought into partnership ventures in order to lessen the taxes of the high-income-bracket member. Originally, it was thought that the participating family members must contribute either assets originating with them or substantial services to a partnership so formed in order to gain the advantage of distributing the income and having the benefit of the lower taxing brackets thus made possible by individual tax returns of the several family partners.[97] Later, the Supreme Court attempted to correct this misapprehension and placed the emphasis upon the family members' good-faith intent to be partners, the fact that the family-member partners had been given their partnership interest or the funds with which to purchase it, and that no substantial services in the management of the partnership were anticipated or performed, being matters to consider, with all others, in the determination of whether there was an honest intent to form and carry on the partnership.[98]

The troublesome matter of a gift of a partnership interest by the high-income-bracket member to one or more of the family members has been handled in a more satisfactory manner by a 1951 amendment to the Internal Revenue Code which provides that "A person shall be recognized as a partner [for income tax purposes] if he owns a capital interest in a partnership in which capital is a material income-producing factor, whether or not such interest was derived by purchase or gift from any other person." [99] A new section added the same year provides that the distributive share of the donee shall be includible in his gross income "except to the extent that such share is determined

95. Willis, Handbook of Partnership Taxation 477 (1957).

96. I.R.C.1954 (26 U.S.C.A.) § 2, formerly § 12(d).

97. Com'r v. Tower, 327 U.S. 280, 66 S.Ct. 532, 90 L.Ed. 670 (1946); Lusthaus v. Com'r, 327 U.S. 293, 66 S.Ct. 539, 90 L.Ed. 679 (1946).

98. Com'r. v. Culbertson, 337 U.S. 733, 69 S.Ct. 1210, 93 L.Ed. 1659 (1949).

99. I.R.C.1954 (26 U.S.C.A.) § 704(e) (1). See also Regulation § 1.704–1 (e); C.C.H. (Surrey and Warren), Federal Taxation, Current Law and Practice, pages 6309–6313 (1957).

without allowance of reasonable compensation for services rendered to the partnership by the donor, and except to the extent that the portion of such share attributable to donated capital is proportionately greater than the share of the donor attributable to the donor's capital." [100]   And the section further provides that an interest purchased by a family member from another family member shall be considered as if created by a gift from the seller for income tax purposes, the fair market value of the purchased interest to be considered as donated capital.

Concerning family partnerships, the 1954 Internal Revenue Code and Regulations recognize that income from a partnership is derived from two sources, by the use of capital and of services contributed by the partners.   And the provisions of the family partnership sections must be read in the light of their relationship to § 61 which expresses the general principle that income is to be taxed to the person who earns it whether by his own services or the use of his capital.[1]   Thus, even if the partner received his interest by gift, if he in fact owns a capital interest over which he has control and the partnership "is one in which capital is a material income-producing factor," the donee-partner will be taxed and not the donor except for income produced by him.[2]

Whether the informality of carrying on a business under the general partnership form with little regulation by the state plus the savings in taxation that may be available through the use of this form are of sufficient importance to outweigh what advantages are present in other business association forms must be determined in the particular case.   There will, of course, be other tax considerations, such as the additional outside personal income of the prospective partners when added to the probable profits of the partnership, matters which must be weighed by comparing the taxing results with those of a corporation or "association" where reasonable amounts from profits may be retained as additional working capital or where stock may be issued as a dividend freezing a surplus into capital.   Reasonable salaries of associate-shareholders may be deducted as expenses of a corporation, whereas there is no such possibility of deducting partners' salaries as expense in the partnership.   The Revenue Act still treats favorably corporations earning not more than $25,000.   If the corporate normal-tax net income is not more than that amount, there is a flat rate.   If above $25,000, a heavier rate on the amount of excess is applied.   And if the corporation is subject to the accumulated earnings tax as pro-

---

100. I.R.C.1954 (26 U.S.C.A.) § 704 (e) (2).

1. Regulations, § 1.704–1(e) (1) (i).

2. I.R.C.1954 (26 U.S.C.A.) § 704(e) (1).

vided for in the 1954 Internal Revenue Code, §§ 531 and 535, it will pay in addition a much heavier tax on this excess.[3] As taxing statutes are amended or added to more frequently than other statutes, a vigilant eye must be kept upon them for changes that will affect existing preferences and thus give argument for or against the use of a particular business association.

§ 7. The Limited Partnership

The limited partnership is a purely statutory thing which had its inception in this country in 1822 by virtue of a New York statute patterned after the French Civil Code.[4] Many states thereafter modeled their limited partnership acts after this early New York act. In 1916, the National Conference of Commissioners on Uniform State Laws approved the Uniform Limited Partnership Act to give more liberal protection to limited partners than the preceding state statutes and their holdings under them had given. By 1957 thirty-six states, Alaska and Hawaii had adopted the Act and it seems probable that others will do the same.[5]

The limited partnership is a hybrid type of firm in which limited liability is by statute given to the limited or special partners while unlimited liability remains in the management group of partners. There must be one or more general partners in such firms. Statutory requirements are specific as to the conditions precedent necessary to the formation of the limited partnership and these uniformly require a filing of the articles or certificate of limited partnership in some public office where those who contemplate dealing with such firms may ascertain the facts which the statute requires to be stated. The courts have, in general, required a literal following of the statutory requirements and a failure in this respect to substantially comply has resulted in the imposition of unlimited liability upon the limited partners. Furthermore, the limited partners must take no part in the management of the business as this will make them liable as general partners.

3. For a good discussion on the taxing advantages or disadvantages see Symposium on the Close Corporation, 52 Nw.U.L.Rev. 345, 355 et seq. (1957).

4. On the early history of limited partnerships on the continent, see Moorhead v. Seymour, 77 N.Y.S. 1050 (1901); Ames v. Downing, 1 Bradf. (N.Y.) 321 (1850).

5. Alaska, Arizona, Arkansas, California, Colorado, Florida, Georgia, Hawaii, Idaho, Illinois, Indiana, Iowa, Maryland, Massachusetts, Michigan, Minnesota, Missouri, Montana, Nebraska, Nevada, New Hampshire, New Jersey, New Mexico, New York, North Carolina, Ohio, Oklahoma, Pennsylvania, Rhode Island, South Dakota, Tennessee, Texas, Utah, Vermont, Virginia, Washington, West Virginia, Wisconsin.

An exposition of the New York Act of 1822 and subsequent legislation amending it will be found in 38 McKinney's Con.Laws of N.Y.Ann. title "Partnership Law," page 129 et seq.

It has been noted that one may now lend money to a partnership and contract for a return of a part of the profits in lieu of interest with comparative safety (except in one or two jurisdictions) if he does not retain the power of control over the business affairs.[6] In a leading case where such a loan was made, minor matters of control such as supervision and a veto power over certain transactions were held not to have created partnership liability. The Commissioners on Uniform State Laws thus concluded, partially because of the lending possibility, that this "deprived the existing statutory provisions for limited partners of any practical usefulness."[7] After all, why run the risk of strict statutory interpretation, with its attendant result of creating unlimited liability where limited liability was contemplated, when the same result of sharing profits could be accomplished through a profit-sharing loan to a general partnership? Furthermore, the lender may compete with other creditors of the partnership, whether the partnership be limited or general, whereas the limited partner has no such right as to his capital contribution.

The Uniform Limited Partnership Act proceeds upon the following reasonable assumptions: (1) that no public policy exists which requires one who contributes capital to a firm and shares profits therein, even where some measure of control is reserved, to become unlimitedly liable for debts of the firm *provided* that creditors, when they gave credit, had no reason to believe the capital contributor was so bound; (2) that those who conduct a business in which they are unlimitedly liable should be able to acquire further capital by associating with themselves others who contribute capital and acquire rights of ownership in the venture *provided* such capital contributors do not compete with creditors for the business assets.[8] With this broad philosophic basis it was thought that the rigidity of the existing limited partnership acts which tended to discourage the use of the limited partnership and frequently forced business men into the use of the corporate form "ill suited to many business conditions" might be alleviated or, indeed, be cured by the adoption of the Uniform Limited Partnership Act.[9] Many of the old statutes had provisions in them that if the certificate or affidavit required by statute to be filed was materially false the statutory result was to make all liable as general partners. Such provisions were strictly construed against the limited or special partners. In an important case interpreting the Uniform Limited Part-

6. Supra, page 8; Martin v. Peyton, 246 N.Y. 213, 158 N.E. 77 (2d Cir. 1927).

7. Commissioners' Note, 8 U.L.A. 3 (1922).

8. Supra, note 7, at 4.

9. See supra, note 7, at 3.

nership Act which had been adopted in Illinois to supersede the old act, it was said that "To such extent was this tendency (to interpret strictly against the limited partners) recognized in the mercantile world that it was considered hazardous for one to invest money in a partnership enterprise upon the faith of compliance with limited partnership statutes, which were quite commonly regarded as a trap to catch the unwary rather than a proper means to a desirable end. To relieve from such undue hazard, and make more safe to investors not participating in the business, the employment of their capital in partnership enterprises, as well as to bring about uniformity in such matters, the 'Uniform Limited Partnership Act' was drafted and submitted to the Legislatures of the different states." [10] That so many jurisdictions have adopted the Act bears witness to its greater efficacy to suit the needs of business and satisfy the desire of the inactive investor to secure, with reasonable certainty, limited liability comparable in many ways to that of a shareholder in a corporation.

Under the Act, a limited partnership is one "formed by two or more persons under the provisions of § 2, having as members one or more general partners and one or more limited partners." [11]   The limited partners as such are not bound by the partnership obligations,[12] that is, they are not, as are general partners, individually liable for such obligations.

§ 2 states the formalities necessary to form such a partnership and requires a signed and sworn certificate stating the partnership name, character of business, location of its principal place of business, name and residence address of each partner with designations of who are general, and who special, partners, the term during which the partnership is to exist, the amount of cash and property, the latter to be described and the agreed valuation to be stated, to be contributed by each limited partner; additional contributions, if any, and the times at which or the events upon which such shall be made, by each limited partner; the time, if agreed, when each limited partner is to have returned to him his contribution; "the share of the profits or the other compensation by way of income which each limited partner shall receive by reason of his contribution;" the right of a limited partner (if given) to substitute an assignee-contributor in his place with the terms and conditions of the substitution; the right (if given) of partners to admit additional limited partners; the right (if given) of priority among limited partners as to

---

10. Cir. J. Alschuler in In re Marcuse & Co., 281 F. 928, at 934 (7th Cir. 1922), aff'd sub nom. Giles v. Vette, 263 U.S. 553, 44 S.Ct. 157, 68 L.Ed. 441 (1924).

11. § 1 ULPA.

12. § 1 ULPA.

their contributions or as to compensation by way of income; the right (if given) of continuation of the business after the death, retirement or insanity of a general partner by the remaining general partners; and the right (if given) of a limited partner to demand and receive property other than cash in return for his contribution. The certificate is required to be filed in an office to be inserted by the adopting state,[13] and the further provision is made that "A limited partnership is formed if there has been substantial compliance in good faith with the requirements of paragraph (1)," the substance of which is contained in the above delineation of the information which is required to be set forth in the certificate.[14]

In spite of the Commissioners' philosophic basis that no public policy exists which requires a contributor of capital to a partnership to be unlimitedly liable, even where some measure of control by him is reserved, the Act provides that a limited partner does not become liable as a general partner "unless, in addition to the exercise of his rights and powers as a limited partner, he takes part in the control of the business." [15] "Control" is not defined in the Act, and there lurks within the possible connotations of this term a rather formidable danger to limited partners. "Would one act of control or participation in the management be sufficient to turn a limited partner into a general partner? This liability is not expressly restricted to the period of participation in the management. Specific provisions as to the extent to which a limited partner may give advice or participate in business transactions without becoming liable as a general partner are much needed." [16]

The Act also provides that the limited partner may make his contributions in cash or other property, but not in services.[17] There had been some question under earlier acts whether a requirement for the cash contribution by the limited partner was met by a payment by check [18] and, in one jurisdiction where a check was held valid compliance, it had been held that there must be *payment* of the check prior to the filing of the certificate in order to qualify as payment in cash,[19] otherwise unlimited

---

13. § 2(1) (b) ULPA.

14. § 2(2) ULPA.

15. § 7 ULPA.

16. Ballantine, Lattin & Jennings, Cases and Materials on Corporations 41 (2d ed. 1953).

17. § 4 ULPA.

18. Not "actual cash payment" under earlier New Jersey act, though drawer of check had funds in bank ready for payment. McGinnis v.

Farrelly, 27 F. 33 (C.C.S.D.N.Y. 1886). Check held valid in payment, White v. Eiseman, 134 N.Y. 101, 31 N.E. 276 (1892); Chick v. Robinson, 95 F. 619, 37 C.C.A. 205, 52 L.R.A. 833 (6th Cir. 1899), interpreting an early Michigan statute; Rothchild v. Hoge, 43 F. 97 (C.C.E.D.Va.1890), interpreting former Virginia statute.

19. Durant v. Abendroth, 69 N.Y. 148, 25 Am.Rep. 158 (1877). See also Myers v. Edison General Elec-

liability would result. It seems inconceivable today when checks are the usual means of payment that a court would fail to recognize a check, provided funds were available to satisfy it, as "cash" contributed by a limited partner, especially since the Act provides that, upon "substantial compliance" with § 2, paragraph 1, a limited partnership results. It may be legitimately argued that so long as payment of the check results, the main object of supplying a fund available to creditors has been accomplished; more ought not to be insisted upon. One purpose of limited partnership is to protect the limited partner by subjecting his capital contribution alone to the liabilities of the firm.[20] Liberal interpretation, rather than narrow construction of the Act, should be the rule, not the exception.[21]

The Uniform Limited Partnership Act contains no statement as to when the certificate must be filed. Suppose it has been executed but not filed when the business itself was begun. Debts may have been created prior to the filing or subsequent thereto. Would the limited partners be individually liable for such debts? In a recent case where the debt under consideration had been incurred subsequent to the filing, which filing had been made forty-nine days after execution, it was held that the limited partners were not individually liable for the debt, the court saying: "The prevailing opinion as to the construction of statutes of this character is that they are remedial in nature and are to be construed with a view to effecting the purpose of the statute and at the same time protect the public . . . No time is fixed by the act within which such filing and recording must be done, and it must therefore be held that a reasonable time is allowed. What is a reasonable time must be determined by the circumstances of the particular case." [22] But one may be skep-

---

tric Co., 59 N.J.L. 153, 35 A. 1069 (1896).

Under the former Arkansas Limited Partnership Law (6 Ark.Stat.1947 Ann. § 65–208) which required an affidavit stating "that the sums specified in the certificate to have been contributed by each of the special partners to the common stock have been actually and in good faith paid in cash," it was held that part payment in cash at the time of filing the certificate and affidavit with later payment in cash of the full amount stated did not qualify as compliance with the statute and was a false statement "making all persons interested in such partnership . . . liable for all engagements thereof as general partners." The quoted words are those of the former Arkansas

Lattin Corporations F.P.Inc.—3

statute. Kistler v. Gingles, 171 F. 2d 912 (8th Cir. 1949), noted in 48 Mich.L.Rev. 347 (1950). Arkansas adopted the ULPA in 1953.

20. Lanier v. Bowdoin, 282 N.Y. 32, 24 N.E.2d 732 (1939), reargument denied 282 N.Y. 611, 25 N.E.2d 391 (1940).

21. As a rule of construction § 28(1) ULPA has this provision: "The rule that statutes in derogation of the common law are to be strictly construed shall have no application to this act."

22. Stowe v. Merrilees, 6 Cal.App.2d 217, 44 P.2d 368, at 369 (1935). Accord under earlier New York Limited Partnership Act, Levy v. Lock, 5 Daly (N.Y.) 46, 47 How.Prac. 394 (1874).

tical about the debts created prior to filing, for "The purpose of requiring such filing and recording is to acquaint third parties with the essential features of the partnership arrangement . . ." [23] Such failure to file under some circumstances may well be held fatal to the limited liability of the special partners for debts incurred prior to filing. In such cases, the analogous situation of the failure to file articles or certificates of incorporation before starting the corporate business are instructive.[24] However, § 11 of the ULPA provides that one who has made his contribution to the capital of what he erroneously supposed to be a limited partnership does not become a general partner if, upon discovering the mistake, he "promptly renounces" his interest in the profits, "or other compensation by way of income." As a matter of practice, no lawyer should permit a limited partnership or a corporation to start on its business career prior to the performance of all statutory conditions precedent to its formation and any conditions precedent required for the commencement of business activities.

The Act provides that the surname of a limited partner may not, except in the exceptions stated, appear in the partnership name; otherwise, the limited partner becomes a general partner to creditors whose credit was extended "without actual knowledge that he is not a general partner." [25]

Under earlier statutes, false statements in the certificate, though unknown by the limited partner, had been a source of perplexing difficulty and a danger which the unsuspecting investor could not easily avoid. A false statement in the certificate, under the Uniform Act, does not in itself make the limited partner individually liable unless he knew the statement to be false,[26] and then only to one who suffered loss by reliance upon such a statement. Furthermore, there is a provision that the certificate shall be amended when it contains a false or erroneous statement.[27] To the limited partner, such a provision becomes important when, subsequently to his signing of the certificate, he discovers a false statement, for, if he has a "sufficient time before the statement was relied upon to enable him to cancel or amend the certificate, or to file a petition for its cancellation or amendment" as provided in another section, and has not taken advantage of the cancellation or amendment provisions, he will be individually liable to one who has suffered loss by reliance upon

---

23. Stowe v. Merrilees, supra, note 22, 44 P.2d at 370.

24. See page 163, infra.

25. § 5 ULPA. The exceptions stated in this section are (1) where the surname is also that of one of the general partners, or (2) where,

prior to his becoming a limited partner, the business had been carried on, under a name in which his surname appeared.

26. § 6 ULPA.

27. § 24(g) ULPA.

the false statement.[28]   If his fellow partners refuse to execute an amendment to rectify the false statement, provision is made in the Act for court process to accomplish the desired end.[29]

(a) Defective limited partnerships. A radical departure from the earlier limited partnership acts is that contained in a provision of the Uniform Limited Partnership Act to the effect that a person contributing to the capital of a business conducted by a person or partnership who erroneously believes that he has acquired the status of a limited partner in a limited partnership is not, so long as he confines his activities to those permitted by a limited partner, a general partner of the person or partnership, or bound by the obligations of such a person or partnership, provided that, upon discovering his mistake, he "promptly renounces his interest in the profits of the business, or other compensation by way of income." [30]   Of course, even under the above circumstances, if he takes part in the control of the business, he would be liable as a general partner.[31]   In a case where the certificate of limited partnership was executed while a prior limited partnership act was in force, but was not filed until its repeal and the adoption of the Uniform Act, for a business venture not permissible of operation by a limited partnership under the Act, it was held that the limited partners were protected as such, since they had contributed to the capital erroneously believing that they had become members of a limited partnership.[32]   There had been no attempt to organize under the Uniform Act as adopted in Illinois, yet the provisions of the Act were applied by the court.   The legislative purpose of relieving special partners from the strictness of the earlier statutes and decisions, emphasized the court, called for liberal construction, adding, "Its application should not be restricted to cases where there was an attempt to organize a limited partnership under the act." [33]   And even where a limited partnership had been formed under a previous act but was so defectively formed that, under earlier holdings the limited partners would have been considered general partners, the subsequent adoption of the Uniform Act, though there had been no attempt to comply with its provisions,

28. § 6(b) ULPA. § 25 contains the requirements for amendment and cancellation of certificates.

29. § 25(3) and (4) ULPA.

30. § 11 ULPA. A few states, prior to the Uniform Act, had provisions protecting the good faith special partner. Warren, Corporate Advantages Without Incorporation, 309–310 (1929).

31. § 7 ULPA. That this is the only exception to non-liability un-

der § 11, see Case Notes, 8 U.L.A. 24 (1922).

32. Giles v. Vette, 263 U.S. 553, 44 S.Ct. 157, 68 L.Ed. 441 (1924), aff'g In re Marcuse & Co., 281 F. 928 (7th Cir. 1922). The Illinois version of the ULPA was under construction.

33. Giles v. Vette, supra, note 32, 263 U.S. at 563, 44 S.Ct. at 161.

has been held, by virtue of § 11, to give the limited partners the protection that section affords. Said the court, "We hold . . . that section 11 will apply to relieve all those persons who have erroneously believed that they have become limited partners, either in a partnership organized under the old statutes, or in one organized under the Uniform Act." [34] This liberal holding, if followed elsewhere, gives considerable protection to limited partners in partnerships formed under more rigid statutes with their harsh case-law interpretation, where the limited partnership continues to exercise its powers without complying with the state's later enactment of the Uniform Act.

Upon discovery of his mistaken belief that he has become a limited partner, he must promptly renounce "his interest in the profits of the business, or other compensation by way of income." [35] While the language seems clear that prompt renunciation of his interest in profits or compensation as income to be later paid, and not a return of profits already paid if received under his contract of limited partnership, is the test of non-liability as a general partner, some doubt had been raised in *Giles* v. *Vette* [36] where renunciation had been accompanied by a return of profits antecedently paid. The court had said that "All dividends on the $190,000 were returned. It need not be decided whether such return was necessary." [37] The point was directly involved in a recent Maryland case where the mistaken special partner did not return profits received prior to the liquidation of the partnership at which time there were no profits to be renounced. The court agreed that his renunciation gives protection if it extends to the *interest* he has in profits not yet paid over. This conclusion, said the court, "is fortified from the standpoint of verbiage by the general usage of the word 'renounce' which does not commonly have the meaning of 'return'. It is

---

34. Rathke v. Griffith, 36 Wash.2d 394, 218 P.2d 757, at 763, 18 A.L.R. 2d 1349 (1950), based upon the broad language of Giles v. Vette, supra note 27, and in the face of § 30(2): "A limited partnership formed under any statute of this state prior to the adoption of this act, until or unless it becomes a limited partnership under this act, shall continue to be governed by the provisions of sections 9966 to 9975, inclusive, Remington's Revised Statutes. . . ." Hill, J., dissented, stating at page 765 of 215 P.2d: "The majority writes this subsection out of the statute. I cannot agree that we have the right so to do." See pages 761–762

discussing this section in the light of § 11. And see § 28(3) ULPA: "This act shall not be construed . . . to affect . . . any right accrued before this act takes effect." The Rathke case cites a companion case in the federal district court in accord but unreported and affirmed in Baumer Foods, Inc. v. Griffith, 166 F.2d 433 (9th Cir. 1948), in a "laconic opinion," certiorari being denied in 334 U.S. 828, 68 S.Ct. 1339, 92 L.Ed. 1756 (1948).

35. § 11 ULPA.

36. Supra, note 32.

37. Supra, note 32, 263 U.S. at 563, 44 S.Ct. at 161.

generally used in the sense of giving up a right, or a claim." [38] The debts had been contracted four years after the supposed special partner had received his last profit distribution from the firm. In traditional common-law fashion the court stated that it did not have to decide what would be required of the special partner if profits had been received by him after the debts of the claimant had been contracted. Again, it seems obvious that he should be protected in such a case if he received no more in profits than his contract of limited partnership called for and made renunciation promptly upon later discovery that the limited partnership was defective. Barring some argument of a transfer of partnership assets in fraud of creditors, an argument of a quite different sort, which would seem not ordinarily to exist if profits in a true sense have been distributed, there is no good reason to suppose that "renounce" means "return" under these facts any more than under the facts which the court had before it.

The Uniform Act does not lay down any criteria for determining what constitutes renunciation. From the cases thus far decided, it is apparent that the most informal sort of act indicating that the special partner has given up his claim to the future distribution of profits (or other compensation by way of income) will suffice, as where he executes a bill of sale conveying his interest to the general partners,[39] or returns the profits he has received, though he had no obligation to do so.[40]

While a limited partner may not compete with creditors of the limited partnership for his capital contribution, the Act permits such competition for loans to and contractual obligations with the firm.[41] Such competition is not permitted in the general partnership nor among the general partners and creditors in a limited partnership.[42] But a limited partner may not, as to his competitive claims, receive or hold any partnership property as collateral security, "or receive from a general partner or the partnership any payment, conveyance, or release from liability, if at the time the assets of the partnership are not sufficient to discharge partnership liabilities to persons not claiming as general or limited partners." Any violation of these prohibitions is considered a fraud on the creditors of the partnership.[43]

---

38. Gilman Paint & Varnish Co. v. Legum, 197 Md. 665, 80 A.2d 906, at 910, 29 A.L.R.2d 286 (1951), citing with approval and quoting from a note in 71 U. of Pa.L.Rev. at 150–151 (1923).

39. Rathke v. Griffith, supra, note 34.

40. Giles v. Vette, supra, note 32.

41. § 13 ULPA. See also § 16 concerning the withdrawal or reduction of a limited partner's contribution.

42. § 40 Uniform (General) Partnership Act which states the rules for distribution of partnership assets after dissolution.

43. § 13 ULPA.

Limited partners, under the Act, may contract among themselves for priority over other limited partners as to a return of their contributions, as to their compensation by way of income, or in other matters, this being somewhat analogous to what may be done in the corporation by the creation of classes of preferred shareholders. But such agreements must be made in the certificate and their absence puts all limited partners on an equal footing.[44] Such partners are entitled to the share of profits or other compensation agreed upon in the certificate with a proviso "that after such payment is made, whether from the property of the partnership or that of a general partner, the partnership assets are in excess of all liabilities of the partnership except liabilities to limited partners on account of their contributions and to general partners." [45]

Mention should be made of a provision which permits a person to be a general partner and a limited one in the same partnership at the same time. By this provision, he has all the rights and powers, and is subject to the restrictions, of a general partner, but, with respect to his contribution, as between the other partners, he has the rights of a special partner.[46] Thus, he may have a preferred position as between partners, but be liable as a general partner as to third persons, a qualified security which permits him to share in the control of the firm.

As to judgment creditors of a limited partner, a court may issue a charging order upon his interest to satisfy the debt, may appoint a receiver, make other orders, give directions and make inquiries "which the circumstances of the case may require." There may be redemption of the special partner's interest thus charged out of the separate property of a general partner, but not out of partnership property. And these remedies are not deemed exclusive of others which may be available.[47]

Provisions are also made for the protection of limited partners which give them the rights of general partners in the inspection of partnership books, in requiring full information, upon demand, of partnership affairs, for formal accounting of the firm's "affairs whenever circumstances render it just and reasonable," and for dissolution and winding up by court decree.[48] Further protection is given them by requiring their unanimous consent or ratification when the general partners act in contravention of the certificate, or when they act in such a way as to make it impossible to carry on the ordinary business of the partnership, or confess a judgment against the partnership, or possess or assign their rights to specific partnership property for

44. § 14 ULPA.   47. § 22 ULPA.

45. § 15 ULPA.   48. § 10 ULPA.

46. § 12 ULPA.

other than firm purposes, or admit another as a general partner, or a person as limited partner (unless the certificate so provides), or continue the business with firm property on the death, retirement or insanity of a general partner, unless the certificate gives the right.[49]

In the distribution of assets after dissolution of the partnership, the limited partners, after the payment of creditors of the firm, are given a preference over the general partners first, as to their share of profits and other compensation by way of income on their capital contributions, and second, as to their return of capital contributions, and these preferences come in ahead of any loans that the general partners may have made to the firm,[50] as well as ahead of the general partners' capital contributions. If no priorities among special partners have been set up in the certificate or an amendment thereto, they share in the partnership assets "in respect to their claims for capital, and in respect to their claims for profits or for compensation by way of income on their contributions respectively, in proportion to the respective amounts of such claims." [51]

By the Act, a limited partner may assign his interest and the assignee has the right to become a substituted limited partner if all the members, exclusive of the assignor, consent to it, or if the certificate empowers the assignor to give his assignee the right. Upon amendment of the certificate to accord this change, the assignee becomes a substituted limited partner with all the rights and powers and subject to all restrictions and liabilities of his assignor except liabilities of his assignor of which he had no knowledge and which he could not ascertain from the certificate. However, the assignor is not, by virtue of his assignment, relieved from liability to the partnership for obligations set out in Sections 6 and 17 of the Act. And if the assignee does not become a substituted limited partner his rights, by the assignment, extend only to the rights his assignor would have had in the share of profits or other compensation by way of income and the return of his contribution.[52]

The executor or administrator of a deceased special partner has all the rights of a limited partner in the settlement of his estate and the power, if the deceased had it, to constitute his assignee a substituted limited partner. The estate is, of course, liable for all the deceased's liabilities as a limited partner.[53]

---

49. § 9 ULPA. Compare the protection given general partners in § 9, Uniform (General) Partnership Act.

50. § 23(1) ULPA. § 23 sets up the order of payment in the settlement of accounts upon winding up the partnership affairs.

51. § 23(2) ULPA.

52. § 19 ULPA.

53. § 21 ULPA.

Upon the death, retirement or insanity of a general partner, the partnership is dissolved unless the business is continued by the surviving general partners under a provision of the certificate giving this right, or unless all members of the firm consent to the continuance.[54]

There are also provisions in the Act concerning the withdrawal or reduction of a limited partner's contribution with protective features in favor of creditors of the firm.[55] This is somewhat comparable to the redemption of shares by a corporation where the shareholder's contract provides for such or to the purchase of its own shares by a corporation where creditors will not be injured by such purchase.[56] However, care should be taken in drawing up the certificate to provide specifically for withdrawal or reduction of a limited partner's contribution, for the Act provides that if no time is stated in the certificate for the return of his contribution (or for the dissolution of the partnership), a limited partner may demand its return after he has given a six months' notice in writing to the other members of the firm.[57] And if the limited partner makes his rightful demand and is unsuccessful in procuring it, he is given the right to have the partnership dissolved, an event which a wise draftsman will avoid.

While a special partner who has withdrawn his contribution at a time when there remains partnership property sufficient to pay the then existing creditors seemingly has protection even when, later, the assets have been dissipated or have depreciated in value to the extent that such creditors cannot obtain satisfaction therefrom, an important New York case has indicated that he is still liable to the extent of the contribution withdrawn plus interest upon it from the time of withdrawal.[58] This is harsh doctrine in view of the specific statement in § 16(1) (a). As Chief Judge Cardozo put it, "We think his obligation to creditors to the extent of his limited liability can be discharged by nothing less than payment." [59] It was pointed out that, standing alone, § 16(1) (a) "might seem to justify the contention that the payment might be kept if what was left was then adequate, though inadequate thereafter. The inference is seen to be erroneous when we read the section following. By § 17(4) it is provided that 'when a contributor has rightfully received the return in whole or in part of the capital of his contribution, he is

---

54. § 20 ULPA.

55. § 16 ULPA.

56. See pages 444–445, infra for a discussion of these problems.

57. § 16(2) (c).

58. Kittredge v. Langley, 252 N.Y. 405, 169 N.E. 626, 67 A.L.R. 1087 (1930). The court was faced with

a limited partnership created under the previously existing New York statute of 1897, but also justified its holding under the ULPA. The partnership had been dissolved before the adoption of the ULPA in New York.

59. Ibid. 252 N.Y. at 419, 169 N.E. at 631.

nevertheless liable to the partnership for any sum, not in excess of such return with interest, necessary to discharge its liabilities to all creditors who extended credit or whose claims arose before such return.' " [60] And § 23 which regulates the distribution of assets upon dissolution further substantiates this result, thought the court. The Uniform Act was not in force at the time the litigative facts occurred and not for a considerable period thereafter. But as sagacious a judge as Cardozo thought it desirable to discuss the provisions of the Act which, in his view, would likewise sustain the holding. From the above, it seems apparent that a wise counselor, where possible, would insist upon the payment of all existing partnership debts before he allowed his special partner client to accept the return of his contribution. Furthermore, in view of the danger of future liability, the certificate should be so drafted as to require this.

There are also provisions in the Act concerning the cancellation or amendment of the certificate of limited partnership setting up the events calling for cancellation or amendment and the form by which the amendment or cancellation is brought about,[61] concerning who are proper parties to proceedings by or against a limited partnership,[62] concerning rules of construction in the interpretation of the Act,[63] and concerning the matter of limited partnerships existing under statutes of the adopting state prior to the adoption of the Uniform Act.[64] This last provision contains authority for such partnerships formed under statutes prior to the Act to become limited partnerships under the Act by complying with the conditions there set forth.

(b) Taxing incidents of limited partnerships. Thus far, the limited partnership has been accorded the same taxing advantages under the federal statutes as those which prevail in the case of general partnerships.[65] The same note of caution should be expressed here as there against the creation of a limited partnership with continuity of life through freely transferable partnership interests which purport to make the transferee a partner without dissolving the firm together with the creation of a management group (i. e., centralized management) of less than all the managing partners (i. e., the general partners), due to the broad definition of "association" in the federal statute.[66] The taxing of the partnership as an "association" may result if the

---

60. Ibid. 252 N.Y. at 420, 169 N.E. at 631.

61. § 24, concerning when the certificate shall be cancelled or amended; § 25, concerning the requirements for amendment and for cancellation of certificate.

62. § 26 ULPA.

63. § 28 ULPA. And see § 29 for cases not provided for in the Act.

64. § 30 ULPA.

65. See discussion, page 24 et seq., supra.

66. See discussion, pages 24–25, supra.

draftsman has failed to note the extent of the definition and to keep his limited partnership outside its bounds.

(c) Conclusions. The limited partnership, under the Uniform Limited Partnership Act, offers much more security to the limited partners than did the legislation which preceded it. In states where the Uniform Act has not yet been adopted, a lawyer may well pause before advising a client to use this form of business association, for the dangers to limited partners in some states are great. Where the Uniform Act has been adopted, notice should be taken of local differences which have been incorporated into the particular enactment as some of these differences are material. The wise lawyer will still consider whether the loan to a general partnership, with a profit-sharing return, with provisions for periodic reports, examination of records, etc., of the partnership, but with no ultimate control by the lender, is not a safer transaction than the relationship created through the use of the limited partnership. But in states where profit-sharing still persists as a controlling test of partnership liability, or where profit-sharing is overemphasized, he may be justifiably cynical as to the use of the lending device where a sharing of profits is to be the return for the use of the loan. If the limited partnership seems advisable, he will comply with the local statute and its interpretation by the courts in order to avoid the pitfalls which may make special partners into general ones. His advice to the special partners should always include a specific warning that they must not participate in the management or control of the business; otherwise, they lose the very protection which they sought through the use of this business form. If the investor desires to participate in management and also wishes limited liability, he cannot procure it through the use of the partnership device except through contractual provisions with third parties who deal with the partnership.

§ 8.   Partnership Associations with Limited Liability

In a few states there are statutory provisions for associations with limited liability which are usually designated as partnership associations. They differ from limited partnerships in that all members have limited liability, as in the modern corporation, the members holding transferable shares as in corporations. Usually, the transferee must be elected to membership in such associations and, if not elected, he is entitled to be paid for the interest which he purchased or which devolved upon him by the death of the former owner.[67]   Some statutes provide that the

---

67.   14 Mich.Stat.Ann. (1937), § 20.91; Ohio Rev.Code § 1783.05; 59 Purdon's Pa.Stat.Ann. § 383.

statement filed to create such an association may specifically grant the transferee membership, but, barring this, he must be elected in order to be a member.

Partnership association statutes provide for a "statement" of certain facts, somewhat similar to those required to be stated in articles or certificates of incorporation, to be filed in a designated office or offices and, if not filed, the association will be a general partnership. Such associations are required to have added to their names the word "Limited", and its omission renders all members, at least those who participate in the omission, liable "for any indebtedness, damage or liability arising therefrom." [68] And, generally, all papers, advertisements, contracts, letter-heads, and other instruments must be signed or labelled in such a manner. Provisions are also made for the holding of property in the firm name and for suits by or against such associations to be brought in the firm name, the association being considered an entity for such purposes as in the case of corporations.

Where partnership associations exist, they are managed by a board of managers, comparable to a board of directors in a corporation, but usually the statute provides for a minimum *and* maximum number of managers.[69] The Ohio statute also provides that not less than three nor more than twenty-five persons may form such an association, thus containing a limitation which is not found in modern statutes for the formation of corporations.[70] A limitation as to the life of such associations to twenty years is a common provision, with or without a provision for renewal, thus differing from the usual unlimited life of the modern corporation,[71] though in accord with the earlier statutes limiting corporate life. There are other provisions as to capitalization, payment by the members for their shares, formalities necessary when obligations of more than a stated amount are incurred, annual elections of managers, dissolution, etc.

Except where a particular business or trade may be organized under such statutes but not under the local corporation act, it is doubtful whether such organizations are any longer

---

68. 14 Mich.Stat.Ann. (1937), § 20.-93; 59 Purdon's Pa.Stat.Ann. § 382 (participants in omission are liable); Ohio Rev.Code § 1783.02 (participants in omission are liable); 42 N.J.Stat.Ann. 42:3–3(3) (participants in omission are liable).

69. 14 Mich.Stat.Ann. (1937), 1957 Cum.Supp. § 20.95, not less than 3 nor more than 7; 59 Purdon's Pa. Stat.Ann. §§ 401 and 402, the latter providing for not less than 3 nor more than 9.

70. Ohio Rev.Code § 1783.01.

71. 59 Purdon's Pa.Stat.Ann. § 441 (as amended in 1931), with provision for renewal of life in § 444; 14 Mich.Stat.Ann. (1937), § 20.91, with no provision for renewal; Ohio Rev.Code § 1783.01, with no provision for renewal; 42 N.J.Stat. Ann. 42:3–2, with no provision for renewal.

necessary or desirable.   There are dangers, not so threatening in the corporate field, of failing to comply substantially with the statutory provisions with the result that the members will be un-limitedly liable, and of innocently making material misstatements in the required filed statement or in failure to keep a subscription book, when required, which bring about this same unfortunate result.[72]   Generally, such partnership associations are subject to the "law" of corporations rather than that of partnerships or limited partnerships.[73]   But for purposes of federal jurisdiction based upon diversity of citizenship, such entities created by legislative fiat have not been able to convince the courts that they are citizens.[74]   There is no good reason, apart from the convenience of federal courts in keeping their dockets free from such suits, for the distinction made.

Whether a partnership association, without local statutory aid, may sue or be sued in its partnership name in a jurisdiction other than where formed, as in the case of corporations, is a question primarily depending upon the sympathy or lack of it entertained by the courts of the forum.   There is no inherent difficulty in the concept that such associations are entities for the purpose of suit, of holding property and doing business, just as are corporations.   The essential difference between the two organizations is that in the partnership association there exists the right to select its members (delectus personarum) whereas in the corporation, there is no such right given by law.   Thus, one remnant of general partnership law is retained.   An early Massachusetts case reluctantly held that a Pennsylvania partnership association was not an entity for the purpose of suit in Massachusetts, the opinion stating that "If the question were an open one in this commonwealth, it might well be held that such an association could be considered to have so many of the characteristics of a corporation that it might be treated as one." [75] Precedent in Massachusetts, thought the court, foreclosed a different holding.   But the Massachusetts court had previously held that an English joint stock company formed under a deed of settlement, to which Parliament had given several incidents of

---

72. See, for examples, Eliot v. Himrod, 108 Pa. 569 (1885); Hite Natural Gas Company's Appeal, 118 Pa. 436, 12 A. 267 (1888); Hill v. Stetler, 127 Pa. 145, 13 A. 306, 17 A. 887 (1889).

73. Rouse, Hazard & Co. v. Detroit Cycle Co., 111 Mich. 251, 69 N.W. 511, 38 L.R.A. 794 (1896); Staver & Abbott Mfg. Co. v. Blake, 111 Mich. 282, 69 N.W. 508, 38 L.R.A. 798 (1896); Armstrong v. Stearns, 156 Mich. 597, 121 N.W. 312 (1909).

74. Great Southern Fireproof Hotel Co. v. Jones, 177 U.S. 449, 20 S.Ct. 690, 44 L.Ed. 842 (1900), overruling Andrews Bros. Co. v. Youngstown Coke Co., 86 F. 585 (6th Cir. 1898).

75. Edwards v. Warren Linoline & Gasoline Works, Limited, 168 Mass. 564, 47 N.E. 502, at 503, 38 L.R.A. 791 (1897).   Accord as to New York joint stock association, Taft v. Ward, 106 Mass. 518, at 524 (1871).

corporateness but had legislated specifically that it was not a corporation, was, for purposes of taxation, "associated"—a term used in the taxing statute—under the laws of a foreign state, and hence taxable in a manner different from that available to individuals through treaty provisions then operable.[76] The case went to the Supreme Court of the United States where all except Mr. Justice Bradley held that the association was a corporation taxable as such under the statute which had used the terms "incorporated or associated under the laws of any government or state other than one of the United States," [77] a holding which the Massachusetts court had carefully avoided.[78] Taken from its specific setting, the arguments of the majority justices in the Supreme Court would warrant the conclusion that a partnership association, which in reality is a statutory joint stock association, is suable as an entity outside its state of birth. And if it is a "corporation," it would seem, contrary to what the Supreme Court has held, to be a "citizen" in the sense that diversity of citizenship would entitle it to federal court jurisdiction. Taxing statutes, however, have to be watched, for they frequently tax as corporations organizations having some of the incidents of corporateness, and holdings which classify such organizations as corporations for the purpose of taxation are highly insecure bases for arguing that other corporate incidents should follow. But legislative fiat, such as exists in the case of partnership associations, and which gives personality to the group in much the same manner as do corporation statutes, offers extremely valid arguments for pursuing corporate personality results without other statutory aid, including that of suit by and against such associations in the association name in a foreign jurisdiction.

Pennsylvania has still another statutory business device called a "registered partnership" which gives to all its members limited liability. Electric light and power, banking and trust, gas, water, railroad, street railway and traction businesses are excluded from using this device. Such partnerships are formed by subscribing, acknowledging and recording articles of partnership and publicizing certain information about them. The word "registered" must be added to the partnership name and a list of the partners must be kept posted at the principal place of business with the capital subscribed by each, the amount paid upon the subscriptions of each, with words "Limited Liability" added to the name of each. The shares are transferable and, in the

---

76. Oliver v. Liverpool & London Life & Fire Insurance Co., 100 Mass. 531 (1868).

77. Liverpool Ins. Co. v. Commonwealth of Massachusetts, 10 Wall. (77 U.S.) 566, 19 L.Ed. 1029 (1870).

78. See the discussion of these cases in Warren, Corporate Advantages Without Incorporation, 412–425 (1929).

absence of any regulation providing that transferees thereupon become members, such transferees must be elected to membership and, if not elected, may obtain the "book value" of their interest. Property is held in the name of the partnership and suits are brought by and against it in the firm name. Provision may also be made for management of the firm by less than all the partners.[79]

(a) **Taxing incidents.** The partnership association, having the essential features of a corporation, comes within the definition of the term "association" under the federal income tax provisions and is thus taxable as corporations are taxable.[80] Hence, the advantages which general and limited partnerships have in this area are not available to such organizations. The Pennsylvania registered partnership would seem to come within the term "association," at least when it is managed by a representative or a representative group rather than by all of the partners.

(b) **Conclusions.** Barring local reasons for the use of the partnership association, where these organizations exist, the right to select its own members seems to be the only argument in its favor. Actually, reasonable restrictions may be placed upon the transfer of shares in a corporation to reach much the same result, thus overcoming this seeming advantage. The comparatively small amount of case law on this type of association, as compared with the voluminous amount on corporations, should be thoroughly considered before recommending a partnership association instead of a corporation. The danger of incurring unlimited liability through the failure to comply substantially with the statutory provisions also looms large against their use. Such factors must be weighed well before recommendations are made to use the partnership association.

§ 9. The Joint Stock Company

Unlike corporations, the joint stock company or association has existed, as a common law business association, without appealing to the state for its right to exist. It acquires its existence by articles of association closely approximating those of articles or certificates of incorporation, having by agreement continuity of life, transferable shares whose transfer does not result in the dissolution of the company, and the business of which is managed by a board of trustees or directors in much the same manner as a corporation is managed by its board of directors.

Unlike shareholders in a modern corporation, the shareholders in a joint stock company do not have limited liability.

---

79. 59 Purdon's Pa.Stat.Ann. § 241   80. See discussion on page 25, of
  et seq.   text, supra.

Theirs is the liability of partners in the ordinary business partnership, and this liability cannot be avoided by any provisions in the articles of association, though it may be avoided by contracts with third parties doing business with the joint stock company. Unless aided by statute, these business organizations cannot be sued or sue in the name of the company but are subject to the same rules with reference to suit existing in the law of partnership, that is, all members must be joined where liability is joint though one, several or all may be sued where the liability, as in tort, is joint and several. However, in the joint stock company, only the trustees or directors, or their agents, may make valid contracts for the company, thus differing from the ordinary partnership. Through the use of transferable shares, delectus personarum is surrendered and, through representative control, the inherent right of partners to community of control, is lost. It should be noted that, in partnership associations previously discussed, though in a sense joint stock companies, statutes have given the shareholders limited liability as in the case of the modern corporation. This big advantage, then, is not one given to joint stock companies as that term is usually used in this country, though in England the term has included common law joint stock companies unlimited as to liability as well as those formed or registered under Parliamentary legislation as corporations having limited liability.

It has been said that "The principal feature of the joint stock association is the right of perpetual succession. In this respect it is like a corporation, and enjoys all the advantages flowing from such a privilege." [81] Uninterrupted continuity of life is indeed a characteristic which encouraged the use of this device both from the standpoint of stability and of securing the necessary capital from numerous investors who otherwise would have been reluctant or unwilling to share in such enterprises.

Since joint stock companies were not considered entities distinct from their shareholders for the purpose of holding property, title was usually vested in trustees who might be one or more of the directors, or in shareholders who were not directors. If title to the property were held by the directors or managing trustees who *also* had ultimate control of the business, the result would be a business or "Massachusetts" trust, the incidents of which are discussed in the following section. A careful drafting of the association articles will make the matter clear if a joint stock association is the device desired. The name "joint stock company" or "syndicate" or some other terminology indicating joint action with transferable shares is not controlling.

---

81. Matter of Jones, 172 N.Y. 575,
at 580, 65 N.E. 570, at 571 (1902).

(a) **Statutory joint stock companies.** Where statutes have provided for joint stock associations as, for example, in New York, such associations have sometimes been called statutory joint stock companies. Thus, the New York statute, while not delineating the things that must be set forth in the articles of association, does specify that the articles may provide that the death of a stockholder or a transfer of shares shall not work a dissolution of the association, that the articles may prescribe the number of directors which may not be less than three, and that any other provisions "not inconsistent with law" may be included.[82] Provision is made for the filing of a certificate with the secretary of state and the clerk of the county in which the association's principal place of business is to be carried on setting forth certain facts specifically required and providing that the officers who fail to comply shall be jointly and severally liable to pay a penalty to the state.[83] Real property is held in the name of the president and is conveyed by him, as president, and limitations are placed upon acquisitions of realty by such associations.[84] Provisions are made for changing the company's articles of association which are fairly similar to, but simpler than those concerning the amendment of corporate articles or certificates of incorporation. While its capital stock may be increased or reduced, the amount "shall not be reduced below the amount of its paid-up capital stock, nor shall it be reduced if the liabilities of the association exceed its assets," thus safeguarding, in some measure, its creditors.[85]

While there is no provision stating the minimum number of stockholders required for a joint stock company, a section authorizing injunctions suspending the business of such associations mentions "association(s), consisting of seven or more persons." [86]

The statute also provides that suits may be maintained by or against joint stock companies in the name of the president or treasurer but neither is personally bound to pay the judgment, this in effect being a judgment against the company the satisfaction of which may be from company assets.[87] The statute, however, does not relieve the stockholders of their unlimited liability but provides that, where an action has been brought against an officer, another action for the same cause may not be

82. New York General Associations Law, § 3.

83. Ibid. § 4, Cum.Ann.Pocket Part (1957).

84. Ibid. § 6.

85. Ibid. § 7.

86. Ibid. § 10.

87. Ibid. §§ 12, 13 and 15. Under Ohio Rev.Code § 1745.01, "Any unincorporated association may contract or sue in behalf of those who are members and, in its own behalf, be sued as an entity under the name by which it is commonly known and called."

brought against a stockholder "until after final judgment in the first action, and the return, wholly or partly unsatisfied or unexecuted, of an execution issued thereupon." [88]   However, there is no indication in the statute that the action need be brought *first* against the president or treasurer rather than against the members of the joint stock association.   In fact, except as to the prohibition concerning the bringing of an action against the members until judgment and return of execution unsatisfied where the action was originally started against the president or treasurer, the statute specifically states that it does not prevent an action against all the members *except* as theretofore prescribed.[89]

There are also provisions in the New York statute which regulate the doing of business of similar foreign associations within the state of New York.[90]

Statutory provisions have made it easier for joint stock associations to hold and convey property, sue and be sued, and carry on business generally in somewhat easier fashion than under the common law.   The one important thing that the common law made clear was that such organizations were to be managed by their boards of directors or trustees and that there was no sharing of control by the associates in the sense that their contracts or acts on behalf of the association would bind it, as in case of the partnership.   And there was, of course, common law recognition that, by their agreement, the transfer of a member's shares, whether by the member during his life or by operation of law upon his death, did not dissolve the association.   The right to select its own membership as in the partnership was bargained away by the members in the articles of association.   Unlimited liability, the necessity for all to join or be joined in suit, with the usual exception in case of joint and several liability, the manner of holding property real or personal, and other incidents of partnership remained, barring statutory aid.

§ 10.   The Business or "Massachusetts" Trust

The business trust, frequently called "Massachusetts" trust because of its reputed origin there in this country,[91] is a cross between the joint stock company and the conventional trust with some of the characteristics of each.   It is a common law device invented to give continuity of life and limited liability to the owners of shares in the trust thus providing two of the main advantages of the corporation.   Organized by a deed or declaration

88.   Ibid. § 16.

89.   Ibid. § 17.

90.   Ibid. Article 4.

91.   Professor Warren, in his work, Corporate Advantages Without In- corporation, at 382 (1929), states that "A business trust is often called a Massachusetts Trust because such trusts have probably been used in Massachusetts more than in any other one state."

of trust, the title to the property of the trust is in named trustees and their successors, with ultimate control in the trustees.[92] The agreement provides for continuity of life through the use of freely transferable shares, similar to shares of stock, the successors in interest becoming members of the trust. Such trusts have at times been set up without reference to a time period during which they are to function, at other times with a definite time stated as, for example, "for 75 years unless sooner terminated by the vote of ⅔ the outstanding shares," [93] or for a period equal to that of lives in being or lives in being plus 21 years, some draftsmen apparently fearing that the rule against perpetuities applied to business trusts. That the rule against perpetuities was not intended to apply to the business trust is perhaps sufficiently well established today to allay such fears.[94] If "ultimate control" is given to trustees who run the business, the beneficiaries are not liable to creditors of the trust beyond the amount they agreed to contribute.[95]

There are some states, however, that have refused to recognize the business trust, classifying this device as a partnership or joint stock company.[96] But generally, however, business trusts have been recognized as something different from other business organizations. The arguments for limited liability of the certificate holders are these: Beneficiaries of a trust are not personally liable either for contracts executed by the trustees or

---

92. Where other elements of a valid business trust were present, it has been held that failure to put title of the property in the trustees makes the beneficiaries liable as partners. Brown v. Bedell, 263 N. Y. 177, 188 N.E. 641 (1934).

93. Commissioner of Corporations and Taxation v. City of Springfield, 321 Mass. 31, 71 N.E.2d 593 (1947).

94. That a business trust is not the sort of organization to which the rule against perpetuities was intended to apply, see Hamrick v. Bryan, 21 F.Supp. 392, at 396 (D. Okl.1937), citing in support of the statement: Hart v. Seymour, 147 Ill. 598, 35 N.E. 246 (1893); Howe v. Morse, 174 Mass. 491, 55 N.E. 213 (1899). And see Baker v. Stern, 194 Wis. 233, 216 N.W. 147, 58 A.L.R. 462 (1927); 156 A.L.R. 22, at 76–78 (1945). But statutes may limit the life of the trust as in Liquid Carbonic Co. v. Sullivan, 103 Okl. 78, 229 P. 561 (1924).

95. Goldwater v. Oltman, 210 Cal. 408, 292 P. 624, 71 A.L.R. 871 (1930), a case of first impression in California.

96. Texas has classified them as general partnerships, stating in the same breath "that the association formed by the writing termed a declaration of trust was that species of partnership called a joint-stock company." Thompson v. Schmitt, 115 Tex. 53, 274 S.W. 554, at 558 (1925). Said the court, at 560: The certificate holders attempted "to secure the very exemption from liability for the debts of the mercantile business they were providing the money to conduct which the statutes accord only to special partners in a limited partnership." See also Hildebrand, Liability of Trustees, Property, and Shareholders of a Massachusetts Trust, 2 Tex.L.Rev. 139, at 165 (1924); 4 Tex.L.Rev. 57, at 67 (1925). *Accord:* Willey v. W. J. Hoggson Corp., 90 Fla. 343, 106 So. 408 (1925); Ing v. Liberty Nat. Bank, 216 Ky. 467, 287 S.W. 960 (1926).

for their torts committed in the process of carrying out the trust. The trustees are personally liable and, in the case of contracts made within the authority granted them, they are entitled to reimbursement from the trust estate. If that is not sufficient, they cannot pursue the beneficiaries unless there is an agreement by the beneficiaries to reimburse them.[97] As the trust estate is not considered a legal person at common law, it cannot make contracts, or sue or be sued at law upon the trustees' engagements, but a creditor has a derivative right in equity against the trust estate in cases where the trustees are entitled to reimbursement from the estate. And if, by agreement, the trustees are given the right of reimbursement from the *beneficiaries*, the creditors are entitled to a derivative right against the beneficiaries if the trustees fail to pay and the trust estate is insufficient.[98]

It is customary, however, to provide in the declaration of trust that all contracts shall be the obligations of the trustees, and that the trustees shall insert into every order, contract or obligation made by them a stipulation that neither they nor the beneficiaries shall be held personally liable but that all persons dealing with the trustees shall look only to the property of the trust for payment.[99] While it is much safer for the trustee to sign, "The X Oil Co., by T, trustee, officially, not personally," there is growing authority to the effect that an exculpatory clause of a trust agreement, if known to the third party dealing with the trust, relieves the trustees and shareholders of liability.[1] Preferably, the exculpatory provision should be included in each contract or instrument to avoid the danger of a law suit. But it is arguable that, today, anyone dealing with what he knows to be a business trust should be charged with notice of the almost universal practice of placing in the trust agreement an exculpatory clause and hence should be barred from proceeding against the

97. 2 Scott, Trusts § 278 (1939). But, in England, the law has allowed the trustee reimbursement from the beneficiaries where the trust estate is insufficient.

98. 2 Scott, Trusts § 278 (1939).

99. Goldwater v. Oltman, 210 Cal. 408, at 426, 292 P. 624, at 631–632, 71 A.L.R. 871, at 883–884 (1930), sets out such a provision verbatim. And see declaration of trust provisions in Pennsylvania Co. for Insurances on Lives and Granting Annuities v. Wallace, 346 Pa. 532, 31 A.2d 71, at 74 (1943).

1. See Pennsylvania Co. for Insurances, etc. v. Wallace, supra note 99, 31 A.2d at 77; Schumann-Heink v. Folsom, 328 Ill. 321, 159 N.E. 250, 58 A.L.R. 485 (1927). But see Comment, 27 Calif.L.Rev. 432, at 433 (1939). And, under a provision of the Uniform Negotiable Instruments Law which exempts one, duly authorized, who has signed "for or on behalf of a principal or in a representative capacity," from liability, trustees in a business trust who have so signed such instruments have been held not to be personally liable. Williams v. Schulte, 103 S.W.2d 543 (Mo.App.1937); Charles Nelson Co. v. Morton, 106 Cal.App. 144, 288 P. 845 (1930); Bowen v. Farley, 256 Mass. 19, 152 N.E. 69 (1926); Megowan v. Peterson, 173 N.Y. 1, 65 N.E. 738 (1902).

trustees for more than can be obtained from the trust estate, where the trustees have signed as representatives of the trust. As was said by Chief Justice Maxey of the Supreme Court of Pennsylvania, "The manner of the signing of the mortgage and bond 'Lancaster Apartment Company of Philadelphia, by its Trustees' (naming them) certainly should have put the company on inquiry as to whether or not the trustees were personally liable on the obligation." [2]

A trust formed for the purpose of carrying on a business has been a useful device approaching closely the advantages of a corporation. "Thus the corpus of the trust corresponds to the capital of the incorporated company, the trustees to the board of directors, the beneficiaries to the stockholders, and the declaration of trust to the charter." [3] The holders of certificates of beneficial interest in a business trust have the same right to examine the records of trustees as do shareholders in a corporation.[4] And, where the right to vote is given, such certificate holders may, like their shareholder opposites, vote by proxy.[5] They, like shareholders, receive a distribution of profits in accordance with the declaration of trust provisions and, upon dissolution of the trust, are entitled to their ratable distribution of the corpus of the trust after liabilities payable out of the corpus are satisfied. Certificates of interest with preferences, comparable to preferred stock in a corporation, are legally possible if desired.[6]

Business trusts may be within constitutional or statutory definitions of "corporation" or "association" and, if so, may be required to comply with regulations and statutory provisions if these are within the area of definition. Thus, for purposes of federal income taxation, business trusts are taxed similarly to corporations.[7] And, where a business trust formed in another

---

2. Pennsylvania Co. for Insurances, etc. v. Wallace, supra, note 99, 31 A.2d at 78. But in R. F. C. v. Goldberg, 143 F.2d 752 at 756–757 (7th Cir. 1944), it is pointed out that the Illinois cases have insisted upon an exculpatory provision in the contract with a third party or that he actually have notice of such a provision in the declaration of trust. However, as long ago as 1893, William W. Cook, author of a leading work on private corporations, was able to say, "[T]he trust instrument generally provides that neither the shareholders nor trustees shall be liable [for the debts] but that does not bind a creditor unless he agrees to it in his contract or actually knows about it." Cook, The Mysterious

Massachusetts Trusts, 9 A.B.A.J. 763, at 766 (1893).

3. Schumann-Heink v. Folsom, 328 Ill. 321, at 325, 159 N.E. 250, 58 A.L.R. 485 (1927). See also Morrissey v. Com'r, 296 U.S. 344, at 359, 56 S.Ct. 289, at 296, 80 L.Ed. 263 (1935).

4. Wallace v. Malooly, 4 Ill.2d 86, 122 N.E.2d 275 (1954).

5. Comstock v. Dewey, 323 Mass. 583, 83 N.E.2d 257 (1949).

6. See Hauser v. Catlett, 197 Okl. 668, 173 P.2d 728 (1946), where a business trust was set up with both common and preferred shares.

7. I.R.C.1954 (26 U.S.C.A.) § 7701(a) (3); Fed.Tax Reg. (1955) § 39.-3797-2; Morrissey v. Comm'r, 296

state doing business in Michigan attempted to sue in Michigan on a promissory note given by the defendant, the statutory definition that "The term 'corporation' as used in this Act shall be construed to include all associations, partnership associations and joint stock companies having any of the powers or privileges of corporations, not possessed by individuals or partnerships, under whatever term or designation they may be defined and known in the state where organized," was held to bar suit when the trust had not complied with the foreign corporation provisions of the Michigan statutes.[8] Statutory definitions of similar phrasing have been the means of requiring the trust to comply with the securities statutes in the registration and issue of its shares [9] and, in a recent case which depended upon such a definition, it was held that, in order to sell its shares legally, it must incorporate.[10]

(a) The matter of "ultimate control." Where "ultimate control"—a phrase of undefined limits—is in the shareholders of a business trust and not in the trustees, the relationship created is held to be in the nature of a partnership or joint stock company.[11] If "the certificate holders are associated together by the terms of the 'trust' and are the principals whose instructions are to be obeyed by their agent who for their convenience holds the legal title to their property," there is a partnership.[12] And, as

U.S. 344, 56 S.Ct. 289, 80 L.Ed. 263 (1935).

8. Hemphill v. Orloff, 238 Mich. 508, 213 N.W. 867, 58 A.L.R. 507 (1927), aff'd 277 U.S. 537, 48 S.Ct. 577, 72 L.Ed. 978 (1928). Also see State ex rel. Range v. Hinkle, 126 Wash. 581, 219 P. 41 (1923), where constitutional provision was similar to that in the Michigan constitution and statute, and Weber Engine Co. v. Alter, 120 Kan. 557, 245 P. 143, 46 A.L.R. 158 (1926). See generally Ann., 156 A.L.R. 22, at 180 et seq. (1945).

But see Manufacturer's Finance Trust v. Collins, 227 Mo.App. 1120, 58 S.W.2d 1004 (1933), where, in interpreting similar language, the court found no provision in the trust deed which purported to give those who executed it any powers or privileges not possessed by an individual, and hence there was no necessity to comply with the foreign corporation statute.

9. Wagner v. Kelso, 195 Iowa 959, 193 N.W. 1 (1923); Groby v. State, 109 Ohio St. 543, 143 N.E. 126 (1924); Note, State Regulation of Foreign Business Trusts, 41 Harv. L.Rev. 86 (1927).

10. Rubens v. Costello, 75 Ariz. 5, 251 P.2d 306 (1952), reaffirming its position in Reilly v. Clyne, 27 Ariz. 432, 234 P. 35, 40 A.L.R. 1005 (1925).

11. First Nat. Bank of New Bedford v. Chartier, 305 Mass. 316, 25 N.E. 2d 733 (1940); State Street Trust Co. v. Hall, 311 Mass. 299, 41 N.E. 2d 30, 156 A.L.R. 13 (1942), but it was not intended that the Uniform Partnership Act should apply to such defective business trusts to give a beneficiary (partner) the right to have the defective trust (partnership) dissolved. Since the defective business trust is more in the nature of a joint stock company, it would seem that the Uniform Partnership Act would not apply anyway.

12. Williams v. Inhabitants of Milton, 215 Mass. 1, 102 N.E. 355, at 357 (1913). In this leading case, the only powers the beneficiaries could exercise were to consent to an alteration or amendment of the

Professor Bogert states, "The courts probably use the word 'associated' in this connection to describe the provision for joint activity in the exercise of powers vested in the cestuis, and not merely the provision for meetings." [13]

Whether the court describes the power reserved by the beneficiaries as "ultimate control" or "ultimate authority," or in terms of beneficiaries and trustees being associated together in such a manner as to make the trustees their agents, the problem still remains one of outguessing the judicial mind as to what remnants of authority retained will put the beneficiaries in jeopardy of the unlimited liability of partners. Some rude awakenings have occurred in this area to the dismay of innocent beneficiaries and to the surprise of the attorneys who fashioned the particular business trust. One is led to suspect, quite rightly it would seem, that decisions in this area turn upon policy matters that rarely find expression in the case at hand. Ideas that limited liability could be obtained without statutory or contractual aid and that continuity of business life might be acquired through a combination of common law trust and joint stock company principles were not easily sold to a conservative judiciary.

More than thirty years ago Judge Calvert Magruder [14] who was then a professor of law at Harvard Law School wrote: "Where a business is thus conducted under a declaration of trust, with the management exclusively vested in trustees, neither the power in the shareholders, (1) to fill vacancies among the trustees, nor (2) to elect trustees at stated intervals, nor (3) to remove trustees, nor (4) to alter or amend the declaration of trust, nor (5) to terminate the trust, nor (6) any combination of these powers, should be held to turn the trust into a partnership contrary to the intent of the parties." [15] His main thesis was that, even with such powers retained by the beneficiaries of a business trust, the beneficiaries had not associated together to carry on as co-owners a business for profit, the partnership concept. Usually the cases have involved business trusts which have contained several devices for control by the beneficiaries and when the supposed business trust has been held to be a partnership or joint

---

trust and to terminate it before the time fixed in the declaration of trust, after the trustees had recommended such action. "But they cannot force the trustees to make such alteration, amendment or termination." (102 N.E. at 358.)

13. 2 Bogert, Trusts § 297 (1935).

14. Now Chief Judge of the United States Court of Appeals for the First Circuit.

15. Magruder, The Position of Shareholders in Business Trusts, 23 Col.L.Rev. 423, at 443 (1923). And, as circuit judge, he wrote: ". . . we think this instrument (declaration of trust) should be considered as analogous to a corporate charter and as broadly interpreted." Bomeisler v. M. Jacobson & Sons Trust, 118 F.2d 261, at 265 (1st Cir. 1941).

stock company there has been no pointing out of the specific provision or provisions for control which convinced the court that the trustees were agents of the beneficiaries rather than principals in their own right.

Cogent arguments exist for liberal judicial holdings supporting business trusts with rather basic but indirect powers of control reserved by the beneficiaries. For example, there has been no policy anywhere against obtaining limited liability by contract. And, in the case of the common law trust, limited liability of the beneficiary was the rule *without special contract* with the third party dealing with the trustee. The trustee was liable, and this the third party knew; and the trust estate, if available to the trustee for his obligations under the trust, was in equity available to the third party. The trustee could, by contract, limit his liability and frequently did by an agreement which sent third parties to the trust estate for their only redress. Of course, there was no way of limiting the trustee's tort liability. With this in mind, there seems to be no valid reason why a court which has the problem of determining whether "ultimate control" has been given to the trustees should not examine the local corporation statute to ascertain what it permits the shareholders to do in the way of controlling the action of the directors and, if no more control has been retained by the beneficiaries of the business trust, by analogy, hold that the business trust is valid, carrying with it the usual incidents. If it finds, as it will in many states, that shareholders have the power to remove directors at will, to elect new ones to fill vacancies, to amend the corporate articles, to merge or consolidate with other corporations, to determine whether all or a large part of its assets shall be sold, to dissolve, and to do other things by shareholder vote, this will indicate that there is no policy which places shareholders in the position of principals with the directors as their agents. Is there any more reason why beneficiaries of a business trust who go no farther in the way of indirect control than the corporation statute permits shareholders to go should be held to a partnership liability for failing to give the trustees "ultimate control?"

Liberal authority has permitted beneficiaries to hold annual elections of trustees,[16] to subject trustees to removal by the bene-

16. Home Lumber Co. v. Hopkins, 107 Kan. 153, 190 P. 601 (1920) (The question involved only whether the state charter board must consider and pass upon the merits of the plaintiff's application to sell its stock in Kansas. In a dictum, the court stated that plaintiff was a "corporation" for purpose of doing business in Kansas.); Comm'r of Corporations and Taxation v. City of Springfield, 321 Mass. 31, 71 N.E.2d 593, at 598 (1947).

ficiaries,[17] to alter or terminate the trust agreement,[18] and to have a combination of powers including the power to elect annually the trustees, by vote of three-quarters in value of shares to fill vacancies, remove any or all of the trustees, alter or terminate the trust or to substitute a new trust agreement for the one terminated,[19] without creating the principal-agent relationship which results in unlimited liability to the beneficiaries. However, as a practical matter, in drafting deeds of business trust, one should be conservative in providing for any control over trustees by the beneficiaries unless the jurisdiction has taken a liberal view on the matter of control. This is particularly wise advice in jurisdictions that have had little experience with the business trust or where courts, for some reason, have frowned upon obtaining limited liability except through statutory procedures or direct contractual agreements.

There lurks a danger, apparently not yet discovered by the courts in this country, of unlimited liability in the beneficiaries based upon their implied agreement to indemnify the trustees. As Professor Scott has written: "In some cases it is possible to spell out such an agreement (to indemnify the trustee) even in the absence of express words to that effect, particularly where

---

17. Downey Co. v. Whistler, 284 Mass. 461, 188 N.E. 243 (1934); Rhode Island Hospital Trust Co. v. Copeland, 39 R.I. 193, 98 A. 273 (1916) (could remove and appoint new trustees). See Ann. 156 A.L.R. 22, at 116–117 (1945).

18. Comm'r of Corporations and Taxation v. City of Springfield, 321 Mass. 31, 71 N.E.2d 593 (1947), could terminate by vote of two-thirds of outstanding shares; Rhode Island Hospital Trust Co. v. Copeland, 39 R.I. 193, 98 A. 273 (1916), by two-thirds vote, the trustees consenting, the trust deed could be altered or trust terminated; In re Winters' Estate, 133 N.J.Eq. 245, 31 A.2d 769 (Prerog.Ct. 1943), two-thirds in interest could alter or amend the declaration of trust. See Ann., 156 A.L.R. 22, at 118–119 (1945).

19. Loring v. U. S., 80 F.Supp. 781 (D.Mass.1948). In this case the business trust had been formed in 1899. The specific problem before the court was whether trustees are "employees" within the meaning of the Social Security Act. The retention of the broad powers

stated in the text above by the beneficiaries was not discussed. Judge Ford stated: "There can be no real right to control a trustee who by his own dissent can invalidate any order given to him." (Page 785.) A trustee deals as "principal in all matters of trust business." (Page 786.) It seems clear that Judge Ford was distinguishing between the sort of direct control involved in carrying on the ordinary trust business and that which indirectly results from elections, removals of trustees, terminating the trust, etc. And see also U. S. v. Griswold, 124 F.2d 599 (1st Cir. 1941), and Bomeisler v. M. Jacobson & Sons Trust, 118 F.2d 261 (1st Cir. 1941), where beneficiaries retained the right to call meetings and, by majority vote, elect successor trustees, fix trustees' compensation, authorize the issuance of additional certificates of beneficial interest, and terminate the trust. Some courts fail to understand this difference. See, for example, Goldwater v. Oltman, 210 Cal. 408, 292 P. 624 at 629 (1930), where the court, in a dictum, stated: "If trustees are sub-the settlor is also the beneficiary of the trust," [20] which is often the case in business trusts. Professor Bogert expresses surprise that no American court has considered the possibility of thus reaching the beneficiaries through the trustees. He states that if reimbursement is ever justified in trust cases, this is the clearest instance for its application.[21] However, there is usually a clause in the trust agreement that the beneficiaries are not to be liable for debts of the business trust. If such provisions mean that the trustee has surrendered any right of reimbursement he may have from an implied agreement, there would still be limited liability for the beneficiaries. Professor Warren, however, has felt that such a clause thus interpreted should be held contrary to public policy.[22] However, whether there is any public policy involved in obtaining limited liability in this way would seem to depend upon whether the manner in which the legislature has provided for obtaining limited liability should be considered exclusive of other methods, including that attempted by contract. And even in Texas where business trusts are held to be partnerships it has been pointed out that the courts have accepted evidence of rather dubious value from which an inference has been drawn of an agreement between the creditor and the trustees that only the trust estate shall be liable for the creditor's claim.[23]

(b) Statutes on business trusts. While the common law did not recognize the trust estate as a legal personality capable of suing or being sued, or of contracting as a legal unit, some statutes have given the business trust legal personality for some purposes. In Massachusetts a statute permits the trust estate to sue or be sued at law upon its contracts and for torts committed by its trustees' negligence in carrying on the trust business, and

ject to being removed by shareholders, and are dependent upon them for election, it is apparent that the ultimate control of the organization rests in the shareholders."

For a good example of the reservation of powers over the actual business of the trust, see Bank of America Nat. Trust & Savings Ass'n v. Scully, 92 F.2d 97 (10th Cir. 1937). The reservation of such powers was held to result in partnership liability of the beneficiaries. In First Nat. Bank of New Bedford v. Chartier, 305 Mass. 316, 25 N.E.2d 733 (1940), where the trust deed provided for an annual election of trustees with terms of one year with right of removal for cause, a right to fill vacancies, to change by-laws at any special or annual meeting, a special meeting being callable by as few as five

shareholders, it was held that the shareholders had ultimate control which gave them unlimited liability. More recently, in Kadota Fig Ass'n of Producers v. Case-Swayne Co., 73 Cal.App.2d 796, 67 P.2d 518 (1946), where the shareholders reserved the power of replacement and periodic election of the trustees, the court held that the trust "must be treated as a copartnership business."

20. 2 Scott, Trusts § 278, at page 1547 (1939).

21. 2 Bogert, Trusts § 296, at page 370 (1953).

22. Warren, Corporate Advantages Without Incorporation, at 391 et seq. (1929).

23. 2 Bogert, Trusts § 299, at pages 376–377 (1953).

service upon one of its trustees is sufficient.[24] But it has been held that the business trust is not a legal entity for the purpose of making contracts, the statute merely permitting its assets to be reached in an action at law for debts which the trustees have contracted.[25] Nor does the statutory right to sue the trust estate relieve the trustees from their common law liability when there is no agreement to that effect.[26] However, it has been held that one who deals with a business trust as such and receives from it anything of value will be estopped to deny its existence.[27] This is comparable to the loose estoppel used by some courts to sustain suits by a defectively organized corporation against those who have dealt with it on a corporate basis.[28] The Massachusetts statute also provides for filing of the declaration of trust and carries a criminal penalty for failure to file.[29] And certain reports must be made annually by the trust.[30]

(c) Advantages of business trusts. Where recognized, there is still much to be said for the use of the business trust as a device for carrying on business. Limited liability of the beneficiaries and centralized management in one or more trustees are two very distinct advantages gained without incorporation. The fact that the trustees may apply in equity, as in other trusts, for directions in the execution of the trust also has its merits.[31] Continuity of life through the use of transferable shares, as in a corporation, gives the organization an advantage over organizations where each new member has to be chosen by unanimous agree-

24. Larson v. Sylvester, 282 Mass. 352, 185 N.E. 44 (1933); 6 Ann. Laws of Mass. 1955, Ch. 182, § 6. Similarly, in Wagoner Oil & Gas Co. v. Marlow, 137 Okl. 116, 278 P. 294 (1929); Williams v. Schulte, 103 S.W.2d 543 (Mo.App.1937). And see Oklahoma statute set out in Liquid Carbonic Co. v. Sullivan, 103 Okl. 78, 229 P. 561 (1924).

25. Dolben v. Gleason, 292 Mass. 511, 198 N.E. 762 (1935).

26. Tebaldi Supply Co. v. Macmillan, 292 Mass. 384, 198 N.E. 651 (1935); Larson v. Sylvester, 282 Mass. 352, 185 N.E. 44 (1933).

27. General American Oil Co. v. Wagoner Oil & Gas Co., 118 Okl. 183, 247 P. 99 (1926); id. v. id., 127 Okl. 208, 260 P. 780 (1926).

28. See infra, p. 166.

29. 6 Ann.Laws of Mass. 1955, ch. 182, § 2.

30. 6 Ann.Laws of Mass. 1955, ch. 182, § 12.

31. Business trusts are generally subject to the same principles of law as trusts which are of the older, historically traditional type. Hauser v. Catlett, 197 Okl. 668, 173 P.2d 728, at 735 (1946). But see Magruder, Cir.J., in Bomeisler v. M. Jacobson & Sons Trust, 118 F.2d 261, at 265 (1st Cir. 1941), where he wrote: "It may well be that in such trusts (i. e., the conventional type) the trust instrument should be construed strictly in order to afford maximum protection to the beneficiaries. But these rules evolved to govern the traditional type of trust, cannot be carried over and applied without change in the field of business trusts of the type here presented. . . . It can scarcely run with the hares and hunt with the hounds by disclaiming corporate analogy when this becomes inconvenient."

ment. Also, death or disability of a beneficiary does not terminate the trust. While suit must be brought by trustees and against them—i. e., the trust is not a legal personalty—this is not a large disadvantage. Some statutes have wisely changed this. Since there is little legislation in many states on the business trust, great elasticity is possible through the contract set forth in the declaration of trust.[32] The lack of legislation also explains the absence of red tape which is so prevalent today in case of the corporation. In the taxing statutes of some states, though not in the federal income tax provisions, there may still be some taxing advantages.

(d) **Disadvantages of the business trust.** The fact that some courts do not thoroughly understand this business device and, suspicious of limited liability obtained through the device, apply narrowly the tests of ultimate control, is a distinct disadvantage to the use of the business trust in such jurisdictions. If used, great care must be taken in drawing up the declaration of trust to be sure that no element of control may be sufficiently important to be declared "ultimate control." That the body of law concerning business trusts is still negligible in many jurisdictions and that there are, consequently, many unsettled problems there, may be controlling in the choice of a business association. A resourceful use of analogies found in ordinary trust law, and in partnership and corporation law, should be useful, and particularly so in a court sympathetic to the business trust, not only in solving the usual problems in this area but in extending the bounds of usefulness of the business trust by a liberal interpretation of that weasel phrase "ultimate control."

---

32. For a specimen form of declaration of trust, see Ann. 156 A.L.R. 22, at 65–71 (1945), with a check list at 73–74.

Chapter 2

THE CORPORATION AS A LEGAL UNIT DISTINCT FROM ITS SHAREHOLDERS

§ 1. Meaning of This Concept of Separate Personality

One of the several practical advantages of the corporation is that the law has seen fit to clothe this institution with legal personality. Whether there are many, few, or but one shareholder, the principle that a corporation is a legal unit separate from its shareholders, whose property is its own, whose contracts are personal to itself, whose debts do not charge its shareholders personally but must be collected from the corporation, whose torts committed by its employees within the course of their employment or by its agents within the scope of their authority are chargeable to it, whose suits must be brought in the corporate name, is one of convenience which dictates that corporate rights and liabilities be not confused with those of even its sole shareholder. This is practical and logical and, if it were not so, in case of corporate injury a multiplicity of suits would result, each based upon the indirect injury to the shareholder's shares.[1] And the confusion would be great in the area of conflicting claims of creditors of one or both. Except in the unusual case, the wrongful act which injures the corporation and indirectly causes damage to its outstanding shares is the basis for but one suit by the corporation or by a shareholder exercising his derivative right [2] for the benefit of his corporation, for the shareholders are presumably made whole if the corporation obtains restitution or compensation from the wrongdoer.[3]

In some extreme cases, where injustice would result if the principle were not applied with some elasticity, courts have rightly deviated in order to avoid harsh results and, at times, to eliminate circuity of action.[4] And, particularly in parent-subsidiary cases, courts are rightly on their guard with a close scrutiny of the facts of corporate family life to protect the interests of third parties and shareholders as well as those of the subsidiary corporation.

---

1. In re John Koke Co., 38 F.2d 232 (9th Cir.1930), cert. denied 282 U.S. 840, 51 S.Ct. 21, 75 L.Ed. 746 (1930); Green v. Victor Talking Machine Co., 24 F.2d 378, 59 A.L.R. 1091 (2d Cir.1928), cert. denied 278 U.S. 602, 49 S.Ct. 9, 73 L.Ed. 530 (1928).

2. See infra, pp. 346 et seq.

3. See cases in note 1, supra.

4. State Trust & Savings Bank v. Hermosa Land & Cattle Co., 30 N.

In the colorful language of Mr. Justice Holmes, "A leading purpose of such (corporation) statutes and of those who act under them is to interpose a nonconductor, through which, in matters of contract, it is impossible to see the men behind." [5] And the court there held that the contract of the corporation whose property, including its trademarks, trade rights, and good will had been sold to the plaintiff with an agreement that it would go out of business, be dissolved, and would not engage in a similar business in competition with the plaintiff, did not bind its shareholders who were members of one family and its connections, all of whom had notice of the agreement. The corporation's agreement was personal to it and not binding upon its shareholders. Where the shareholders, or some of them, are of real importance in such a transaction, a contract should be obtained with them as well as with the corporation, not to engage in a similar business as individuals, members of a partnership or any other business association, or as shareholders in a competing corporation, for a reasonable time and within reasonable geographic bounds.

§ 2.   The Dual Cause of Action Area

The concept that the corporation is a legal unit distinct from its shareholders is a deceptively simple one, and close cases arise in which the corporation suffers injury by the wrongful act of a third person or by its directors, and the shareholder is also injured through a depreciation in the value or selling price of his shares where, due either to a relationship between the shareholder and the defendant or to the particular type of act creating liability, both the shareholder and the corporation may have a cause of action. Attempts have been made to delineate the area wherein the corporation and shareholder may each have a cause of action. It has been said that "For a shareholder to obtain a personal right of action there must be relations between him and the tortfeasor independent of those which the shareholder derives through his interest in the corporate assets and business," [6] as, for example, where a shareholder has pledged his stock with the directors and they have wrongly exercised corporate powers with

M. 566, 240 P. 469 (1925)—sole shareholder, in action against his corporation, was permitted to set off a personal claim against plaintiff; United States Gypsum Co. v. Mackey Wall Plaster Co., 60 Mont. 132, 199 P. 249 (1921); Knight v. Burns, 22 Ohio App. 482, 154 N.E. 345 (1926); Lerner v. Stone, 126 Colo. 589, 252 P.2d 533 (1952). *Con-*

tra: Gallagher v. Germania Brewing Co., 53 Minn. 214 (1893).

5. Donnell v. Herring-Hall-Marvin Safe Co., 208 U.S. 267, at 273, 28 S.Ct. 288, at 289, 52 L.Ed. 481 (1908).

6. Green v. Victor Talking Machine Co., 24 F.2d 378, 59 A.L.R. 1091 (2d Cir.1928), cert. denied 278 U.S. 602, 49 S.Ct. 9, 73 L.Ed. 530 (1928).

a resulting impairment of the value of the pledgor's stock.[7] But
this concept is too narrow. Suppose the directors intentionally
carry on the corporate business in such a way that the corporate
stock is depreciated to a price below its market or intrinsic value,
this with the intent of buying up the stock at the lower price.
And suppose further that the stock in the market falls from $10
to $1 a share. Suppose, too, that the corporation has been dam-
aged in its credit standing and cannot longer obtain necessary
bank loans or other financing to carry on its business. The
shareholder tries to sell his shares at their intrinsic value of $10
but finds that he will have to take a loss of $9 per share if he
sells. Does he as well as the corporation have a cause of action?
Should his cause of action depend upon whether he has sold his
shares at $1 per share and later discovered the directors' skull-
duggery; or that he has tried to sell his shares and has found no
takers at their intrinsic value; or that the type of act upon
which he bases his suit is a depletion of assets caused by his directors' wrongful acts; or that his suit is based upon false representations made by his directors concerning the assets and
management of the corporation and that they had wrongfully
procured a "stop order" of the Securities and Exchange Commission by which trading in its stock was impeded and restrained? If he, as well as the corporation, has an action, is it based
upon some relationship other than that of shareholder?

The law is clear that, had he sold his stock in our hypothetical case, and later discovered the intentionally fraudulent action
of the board, his remedy would be in tort against the delinquent
directors.[8] Corporate recovery at this point would not help him.
Should it make a difference, as far as his recovery is concerned,
whether he has sold his shares, if he has tried to and has then
refused to sell because of the inadequacy of the price, or whether
he has not tried at all? Walter, J., in *Coronado Development*

---

7. General Rubber Co. v. Benedict,
215 N.Y. 18, 109 N.E. 96, L.R.A.
1915F, 617 (1915); Cutler v. Fitch,
231 App.Div. 8, 246 N.Y.S. 28
(1930). In Ritchie v. McMullen, 79
F. 522 (6th Cir.1897), the complaint
alleged a conspiracy to depreciate
the value of a pledgor's stock for
defendants' own purposes. Taft,
Cir.J., wrote at page 533: "It is
undoubtedly true, as the circuit
court held, that a stockholder,
merely as such, cannot have an action in his own behalf against one
who has injured the corporation,
however much the wrongful acts
have depreciated the value of his

shares . . . But we are of
opinion that this principle has no
application where the wrongful
acts are not only wrongs against
the corporation, but are also violations by the wrongdoer of a duty
arising from contract or otherwise,
and owing directly by him to the
stockholders."

8. Von Au v. Magenheimer, 126 App.
Div. 257, 110 N.Y.S. 629 (1908), affirmed without opinion 196 N.Y.
510, 89 N.E. 1114 (1909); Backus
v. Kirsch, 264 Mich. 73, 249 N.W.
469 (1933); Walsham v. Stainton, 1
DeG., J. and S. 678, 46 Eng.Rep.
268 (1863).

Corporation v. *Millikin,*[9] thought not and refused to dismiss a complaint on this ground. But the Appellate Division, in a questionable decision, thought otherwise, stating through Glennon, J.: "It is not alleged in the pleading here under attack that plaintiff lost the benefits of a sale which it otherwise would have made; that it could have sold the stock to a prospective purchaser or that it even contemplated its sale. The question arises as to what damages, if any, plaintiff actually has sustained. It is not alleged that the intrinsic value of the stock has been affected in any way by the acts of the so-called conspirators. The charge that 'Bagdad shares have been rendered practically valueless and have become unsalable in the market to the direct damage of plaintiff in the sum of $600,000' is not sufficient. Plaintiff in order to succeed in this action would have to show that it actually suffered special damage."[10]

A considerable body of authority exists to the effect that even though the directors or third person acted with malice toward the shareholder, the depreciation in the value of his stock due to the corporate injury gives him no personal right against the delinquent directors or other person.[11] Recovery by the corporation is supposed to return his depreciated shares to their former value. The *Coronado* case contains a dictum that no recovery should be allowed where the shareholder still holds his shares *and* the tortious act was one in which there was "a wrongful withholding or taking or dissipation" of corporate property.[12] "In general," stated Judge Walter, "I think the test must be whether or not assets of the corporation have been lost or destroyed or depreciated or its business interfered with, for if so there is a direct injury to the corporation and recovery therefor should go to it so that all stockholders may benefit from the recovery in proportion to their stockholdings, and if not no right of the corporation has been invaded and it is not justly entitled to any recovery."[13]

However, in *Sutter* v. *General Petroleum Corporation,*[14] a shareholder-plaintiff alleged that he had been fraudulently induced by the defendants to form a corporation and to invest in it, and that the corporation was fraudulently induced to lease from

---

9. 175 Misc. 1, 22 N.Y.S.2d 670 (Sup. Ct.1940), but complaint was dismissed because of insufficient allegation of damages in 262 App.Div. 504, 30 N.Y.S.2d 548 (1941).

10. 262 App.Div. 504, at 505, 30 N.Y. S.2d 548, at 549 (1941).

11. Green v. Victor Talking Machine Co., 24 F.2d 378, 59 A.L.R. 1091 (2d Cir.1928), cert. denied 278 U.S. 602, 49 S.Ct. 9, 73 L.Ed. 530

(1928); Hidalgo v. McCauley, 50 Ariz. 178, 70 P.2d 443 (1937); Shenberg v. DeGarmo, 61 Cal.App. 326, 143 P.2d 74 (1943).

12. 175 Misc. 1, at 5, 22 N.Y.S.2d 670, at 675 (Sup.Ct.1940).

13. 175 Misc. 1, at 5, 22 N.Y.S.2d 670, at 674 (Sup.Ct.1940).

14. 28 Cal.2d 525, 170 P.2d 898, 167 A.L.R. 271 (1946), noted in 35 Calif. L.Rev. 453 (1947).

the defendants defective oil drilling machinery which collapsed, rendering the corporate business and its shares worthless. The court held that the stockholder, where he is directly and individually injured, may sue as an individual for damages attributable to the tortious act of the defendant, including the depreciation resulting to his stock, and that the corporation has an action for the wrong which resulted in such depreciation of its shares. This may well amount to double recovery. While the court cited the *Coronado* case, it apparently did not accept in full Judge Walter's conception that where corporate property is lost by the wrongful act of the defendant, the corporation is the only party entitled to sue.

Another approach might well be made to this problem. While directors are primarily fiduciaries to their corporation, they are frequently held as fiduciaries to their shareholders. There is reason for making them strictly accountable as fiduciaries to their shareholders when they intentionally run the corporation with the objective of shareholder injury. It would seem that intentional injury would warrant a shareholder's personal action even where he has not parted with his stock and the depreciation in value of his stock came by way of the intentional depletion of assets, even though the corporation might recover, in its own right, the full amount of the depletion from the directors involved. The possibility of double recovery in such a case is no more damaging to the directors (and why should anyone be concerned about it under such circumstances) than in case of other intentional and malicious tortfeasing where punitive damages are possible. The infusion of morals into this area of the law can be justified, if need be, on the fiduciary obligation theory which has been used in other areas of the law to good effect.

§ 3. Informal Corporate Action; Confusion of Shareholder Action with Corporate Action

Modern stock corporation statutes provide that the corporation shall be managed by a stated number of directors, usually three or more, to be chosen by the shareholders having voting rights. A shareholder, as such, whether or not he holds all of the corporation's outstanding shares, has no management rights except as he may be elected to the board of directors or appointed by it with authority to act. As we shall presently see, there are certain formal requirements such as proper notice before a board meeting, the existence of a quorum of the board at the meeting, and action by it as a body where conflicting views may clash before a decision is reached, which are necessary for proper corporate action. But men being human are likely to slip in some or all of the formal requirements and act as if they were the corporation. A sole shareholder, for example, may proceed to deal with the corporate assets as if, in fact, they were his own. Suppose he personally conveys, mortgages or devises by will these assets? If creditors are not injured by his action, should a court hold invalid such a conveyance, mortgage or devise?

It is probable that legislative intent in specifying that a board of directors shall manage the corporation was to protect the shareholders in the operation of the corporate business. At least, every shareholder has the right to insist that corporate action be carried out as prescribed by the statute. It may be that the legislature had a dual purpose in mind and was also aiming its legislation at the protection of those who deal with the corporation. It seems doubtful if the state has any interest beyond this. But some courts, failing to see the probable reasons behind the statutory requirement, have hewed strictly to the line and held void action taken by a sole shareholder or by the unanimous vote of the shareholders.[15] Fortunately, most modern authority has been more realistic and taken a liberal view and, barring injuries to creditors, has supported a rule that contracts, conveyances, mortgages and devises will be judicially recognized if made by a sole shareholder or by unanimous vote of the shareholders, although not authorized by the board.[16] Some courts have reasoned that the corporation is the sole shareholder's alter ego.[17] Others have rationalized that the sole shareholder's authority is

15. See Charlestown Boot & Shoe Co. v. Dunsmore, 60 N.H. 85 (1880). In Gashwiler v. Willis, 33 Cal. 11, 91 Am.Dec. 607 (1867), the shareholders had unanimously authorized the sale of the corporate property and three directors who were also shareholders were authorized by the shareholders to sign the deed, though there had been no board meeting. However, all members of the board were present at the shareholders' meeting. The deed was properly signed. In as ridiculous a holding as one will find, the court held the deed invalid. Said the Court at page 19: "Had the stockholders all executed a deed to the property, they could have conveyed no title, for the reason that it was not in them. . . ." And see Conro v. Port Henry Iron Co., 12 Barb. 27 (Sup. Ct.N.Y.1851), where the court held similarly on a lease of the property, and England v. Dearborn, 141 Mass. 590, 6 N.E. 837 (1886), where a chattel mortgage executed by the president who owned all of the shares except two was held invalid

because not authorized by the board.

16. Salmon v. Fitts, 67 F.2d 681 (5th Cir.1933); In re Michael J. Hughes & Co., 110 F.Supp. 577 (D. N.J.1953); Copeland v. Swiss Cleaners, 255 Ala. 519, 52 So.2d 223 (1951); Burger v. Western Sand & Gravel Co., 237 S.W.2d 725 (Tex.Civ.App.1950); Matter of Bauer, 289 N.Y. 326, 45 N.E.2d 897, 144 A.L.R. 543 (1942); Norma Mining Co. v. Mackay, 241 F. 640 (9th Cir.1917); Warner Fuller, The Incorporated Individual: A Study of the One-Man Company, 51 Harv. L.Rev. 1373, at 1387 (1938). But see other modern authority *contra:* Dos Pueblos Ranch & Improvement Co. v. Ellis, 8 Cal.2d 617, 67 P.2d 340 (1937); Garmise v. McDonough & Co., 197 Ill.App. 527 (1944).

17. Nat. Bank of Commerce v. Pingree Co., 62 Utah 259, 218 P. 552 (1923); Roberts v. Hilton Land Co., 45 Wash. 464, 88 P. 946 (1907); Wenban Estate, Inc. v. Hewlett, 193 Cal. 675, 227 P. 723 (1924).

coextensive with that of the board.[18] The same rationalizing is justified when the shareholders act unanimously. In reality they are the corporation and a governing board is provided for their convenience. They may waive this statutory protection if they do so unanimously. As was stated in a New Jersey case: " . . [W]here the functions normally pertaining to a board of directors are in the particular instance performed by the stockholders themselves, they by common consent dispensing with the election of directors, the agency for the company may result as clearly as if action by a board of directors had intervened; for such directors would themselves be no more than agents for the body of stockholders." [19] Whatever the reasoning, a desirable result is reached. But to keep the record straight, formal corporate action ought, wherever possible, to be required to ratify the transaction entered into by informal corporate action.

Where a sole shareholder has created an ambiguity which has misled one dealing with him to believe that he is contracting with the shareholder personally, the shareholder will be personally liable though he intended only to represent his company.[20] If he has so confused his own dealings with those of his corporation that segregation of the accounts of each is impossible, and particularly when he has depleted the corporate assets which would otherwise have gone to corporate creditors, it is not unjust that he should be personally held for corporate obligations.[21]

§ 4. "Piercing the Corporate Veil"—Semantics Versus Realism

A variety of metaphorical language has been used by the courts when they find it desirable to hold the real owners of the corporation, i. e. the shareholders, when the corporate form has been used for a purpose not permitted by the legislative privilege of carrying on in this form. Much of this language has appeared in parent-subsidiary cases though it is quite as applicable to the natural-person-solely-owned corporation or to one operated by unanimous consent of the shareholders where the corporation has more than one shareholder. Where the corporation has been used as an "instrumentality" or "adjunct" of the parent, or is

18. Hanson Sheep Co. v. Farmers' & Traders' State Bank, 53 Mont. 324, 163 P. 1151 (1917).

19. Murphy v. W. H. & F. W. Cane, Inc., 82 N.J.L. 557, at 563, 82 A. 854, at 856 (1912).

20. Wittman v. Whittingham, 85 Cal.App. 140, 259 P. 63 (1927). "Where the sole shareholder makes an agreement lacking precision of intent, the cases indicate that the courts will not split hairs to relieve him of personal responsibility." Warner Fuller, The Incorporated Individual: A Study of the One-Man Company, 51 Harv.L.Rev. 1373, at 1383 (1938). And see Tynes v. Shore, 117 W.Va. 355, 185 S.E. 845 (1936); Rutz v. Obear, 15 Cal.App. 435, 115 P. 67 (1911).

21. Warner Fuller, supra, note 20, at 1381; R. U. Archawski v. Hanioti, 129 F.Supp. 410 (D.N.Y.1955).

merely an "alias" or "dummy" or "agency" or "alter ego" of the
parent, the "corporate veil" will be "pierced" and the persons behind it exposed to the bright light of liability. They, not the
corporation, were the real actors on a stage already set by themselves. If all this colorful language means is that the corporation
is an agent of the shareholders who are the principals, there can
be no quarrel with it though it does have a tendency to confuse.
The corporation may, like a natural person, be an agent of natural or artificial persons. But the language has not been confined
thus narrowly. It has been used to explain results which have
a legitimate and realistic basis of explanation in the doctrine
which limits the use of the corporate privilege to decent and fair
objectives, and where the privilege is used in a manner not contemplated as a proper use of the corporate device it will be struck
down and its shareholders held because of their misuse of the
privilege.

The classic statement of when a corporation will be looked
upon as an association of persons rather than a legal entity was
made by District Judge Sanborn a half-century ago: "If any
general rule can be laid down, in the present state of authority,
it is that a corporation will be looked upon as a legal entity as a
general rule, and until sufficient reason to the contrary appears;
but when the notion of legal entity is used to defeat public convenience, justify wrong, protect fraud, or defend crime, the law
will regard the corporation as an association of persons." [22]
The principle is too broad to be of practical use in specific cases,
but it does put moral content into the law concerning the use of
the corporate privilege. It might be paraphrased thus: " . . .
[T]he entity will be disregarded when it is necessary to promote
justice or to obviate inequitable results." [23] Again, as a definite
yardstick it has the fault of Judge Sanborn's statement but the
merit of warning users of the corporate form that there are moral limitations attached to the privilege. More useful because it
points out some specific instances where the "corporate veil will
be pierced" is Professor Warner Fuller's statement that where

22. U. S. v. Milwaukee Refrigerat-
or Transit Co., 142 F. 247 at 255
(C.C.Wis.1905).

23. Warner Fuller, The Incorporated Individual: A Study of the One-
Man Company, 51 Harv.L.Rev.
1373, at 1402 (1938). Rippey, J.,
dissenting, in Boro Park Sanitary
Live Poultry Market, Inc. v. Heller,
280 N.Y. 481, 21 N.E.2d 687, at 690
(1939), wrote: "While at law a
corporation is an entity, a 'personality,' separate and distinct from
its shareholders, members or officers, nevertheless, where the interests of justice require and under some circumstances the corporate form may be disregarded.
. . . That rule is not limited
to any specific class of cases or to
any particular subject-matter or
to the relative position of the parties in the litigation. Its foundation is broad enough to warrant
its application wherever the peculiar facts in the particular case under consideration in the interests
of justice demand, even where the
rights and interests of third parties are involved."

"the corporate devise has been used to defraud creditors, to evade existing obligations, to circumvent a statute, to achieve a monopoly, or to protect knavery or crime," courts have held that the corporation may not be used for such ends.[24]

§ 5. Inadequate Capitalization as a Basis for Shareholder Liability

The modern corporation, contrary to its older counterpart, the joint stock company, has as one of its most important characteristics the ability, through the process of incorporation, of giving its shareholders limited liability. If the shareholder gives the consideration which the statute requires in payment of his shares, neither the corporation nor its creditors may, as a general rule, require him to pay more. But modern statutes do not state what aggregate capitalization will be considered sufficient in any case to give the shareholders limited liability. However, many of them do prescribe a minimum amount which must be subscribed and/or paid in before the corporate business may be started and, if this requirement is violated, a remedy is usually given in the form of a cause of action against the board of directors. A common provision permits the corporation to be formed with $500 or $1,000 of stated capital subscribed and/or paid in.[25] While it is not stated in the statute that the corporation must have sufficient capital to meet the normal requirements of the particular business, judicially imposed rules have assumed that since the owners of the business are no longer individually liable they must supply the corporation with a substitute for this privilege of limited liability, and that substitute is capital contributions through the issue of shares sufficient to meet the reasonable requirements of the particular business.[26]

24. Warner Fuller, supra, note 23, at 1401. And Wormser, Piercing the Veil of Corporate Entity, 12 Col.L.Rev. 496, at 517 (1912), a quarter of a century earlier had used almost identical words: "When the conception of corporate entity is employed to defraud creditors, to evade an existing obligation, to circumvent a statute, to achieve or perpetrate a monopoly, or to prevent knavery or crime, the courts will draw aside the web of entity, will regard the corporate company as an association of live, up-and-doing, men and women shareholders, and will do justice between real persons."

25. Ohio Rev.Code § 1701.04(A) (5)—articles must state the amount of stated capital with which the cor-

poration will begin business which shall not be less than $500; Kan. Gen.Stat.1949, § 17–2802G, as amended by L.1953, c. 125, § 4—minimum amount to commence business shall be not less than $1,-000; A. L. I. Model Business Corp. Act § 48(g) (Rev.1953)—$1,000.

26. Arnold v. Phillips, 117 F.2d 497 (5th Cir.1941), cert. denied 313 U. S. 583, 61 S.Ct. 1102, 85 L.Ed. 1539 (1941); Weisser v. Mursam Shoe Corp., 127 F.2d 344 (2d Cir.1942); Del Golfo de California S. A. De C. V. v. Resnick, 47 Cal.2d 792, 306 P.2d 1 (1957); Dixie Coal Mining Co. v. Williams, 221 Ala. 331, 128 So. 799 (1930), where sole shareholder was held when corporation was undercapitalized, though statute permitted corporations to be

Arnold v. *Phillips* [27] illustrates well the principle of adequate capitalization as a condition to limited liability. Arnold obtained a Texas charter for the Southern Brewing Company, the capital being fixed at $50,000. He paid cash and took 498 shares, furnishing the two other directors with one share each as qualifying shares. While the brewery was being built it became evident that $50,000 would not finish it. Arnold advanced $70,000 on demand notes to the corporation. The plant was built at a cost of approximately $115,000. To begin operations, Arnold made further advances and, by the end of the first fiscal year a demand note for the $75,500 advanced to date was given; a little later a note for approximately $80,000 was substituted with interest at 6% and this was secured by a deed of trust on the whole plant. For two years the business prospered and was able to pay Arnold $45,000 as salary, $19,000 as interest on his note, and $27,400 upon the principal amount of the note leaving a balance of approximately $52,000 on the note. After all of these payments had been made, the books showed a surplus of about $97,000. Then business fell off and a few months later Arnold had to make further advances which eventually amounted to about $47,000. During this depressed period Arnold took no salary and was paid no interest on his advances. With his advances totalling approximately $99,000 (which included the balance of $52,000 of initial advances), Arnold foreclosed on the plant and, upon public sale, made the only bid for it, which bid was the amount of his

formed with a minimum of $1,000 stated capital. And in Ohio Edison Co. v. Warner Coal Corp., 79 Ohio App. 437, 72 N.E.2d 487 (1946), as one of the grounds for holding the parent not liable for the subsidiary corporation's debts, the court stated that "It (the subsidiary) operated the business of mining the coal and had a substantial capital reasonably regarded as adequate to enable it to operate its business and pay its debts as they matured. Various unforeseen economic factors intervened to defeat this expectation." See also Luckenbach S. S. Co., Inc. v. W. R. Grace & Co., Inc., 267 F. 676 (4th Cir.1920), cert. denied 254 U.S. 644, 41 S.Ct. 14, 65 L.Ed. 454 (1920), where two affiliated corporations were involved but inadequate capitalization was the basis of holding one affiliate though there was no evidence of direct intervention by it in the business of the other; Wallace v. Tulsa Yellow Cab Taxi & Baggage Co., 178 Okl. 15, 61 P.2d 645 (1936), where an affiliate was grossly undercapitalized in the risky taxi business for which public liability insurance could not be procured except at very high rates, and compare Elenkrieg v. Siebrecht, 238 N.Y. 254, 144 N.E. 519, 34 A.L.R. 592 (1924); Harman v. Mobile Homes Corp., 317 Mich. 233, 26 N.W.2d 757 (1947). But see Moe v. Harris, 142 Minn. 442, 172 N.W. 494 (1919), where the corporation had no shareholders and no capital. Corporate formalities alone were emphasized. It is doubtful whether the court really understood the problem. It spoke in terms of de jure and de facto corporations and held that if a body was one or the other, the incorporators would not be liable. But this does not necessarily follow as the above cases clearly show.

27. Supra, note 26. See also Albert Richards Co., Inc. v. The Mayfair, Inc., 287 Mass. 280, 191 N.E. 430 (1934).

debt. Bankruptcy occurred six months later, the unsecured indebtedness being about $66,000. Upon the trustee's petition, the district court set aside the duly recorded deed of trust against the bankrupt's entire plant, cancelled the foreclosure of it by sale, and adjudged the bankrupt corporation the owner of the property free from the deed of trust. The upper court held the initial advances necessary to complete the plant, equip it and start it on its course were, as the district court found, capital, "a sort of interest-bearing redeemable stock; and that as a matter of law these contributions could not, as against corporate creditors, either precedent or subsequent, be turned into secured debts by afterwards taking and recording a trust deed to secure them. There was no debt to be secured." [28] The later advances made by Arnold, thought the court, were as if they had been made by a bank, and Arnold might compete with corporate creditors, keeping his mortgage security, just as a lending bank might have. With two years of prosperity, the court felt that the original investment of $50,000 plus the initial advances ($75,500) constituted adequate capital ($125,500). The court found no other basis upon which to hold Arnold than that of inadequate capitalization of his company—there was no fraud and no using of the corporation as an agent or as an "instrumentality or 'other pocket' for Arnold's main business of contracting."

There was also another interesting angle to *Arnold* v. *Phillips* which the court discussed. It involved an affiliate of the Brewing Company, the Monte Carlo Distributing Co., formed with a capital of but $1,000, eight shares of which were held by Arnold and two qualifying shares by others. With this insignificant capitalization, the affiliate was expected to buy and resell the output of the Brewing Company and did handle about 80% of its business. At time of bankruptcy, it owed the Brewing Company about $80,000. The court thought that Monte Carlo was but "an agency of Southern Brewing Company," that its assets and liabilities were really those of that company, and that a bankruptcy court could so hold. The inadequate capitalization was the point of emphasis.

While most of the cases holding the shareholders when the corporation has been inadequately capitalized have been parent-subsidiary or affiliated corporation cases, there is no good reason why any distinction should be made between this type of case and the case of the corporation whose shares are held by natural persons. *Arnold* v. *Phillips* is a case in point. But this case involved a one-man corporation with no innocent shareholders. Suppose one innocently subscribed to shares and became a

28. Arnold v. Phillips, supra, note 26, at 501.

shareholder in a corporation which was undercapitalized and was later called upon to disgorge to creditors who now found it impossible to collect from the corporation. Might he argue from an analogy drawn from cases involving "corporations" so inadequately formed that they are neither de jure nor de facto corporations that he should not be individually liable unless he is found to have been an "active" shareholder?[29] If he has purchased shares for investment purposes and has not participated actively in the management of the corporation ought he to be liable any more than in the analogous case? In fact, is not the court ignoring the de jure corporate device in undercapitalization cases just as it refuses to recognize a corporation when it fails to arrive at the de facto organization stage? If there is any reason for distinguishing "active" from "inactive" shareholders in the pursuit of a basis for liability, it would seem that the distinction would be valid in both types of case.

(a) When is a corporation adequately capitalized? It may be that the popcorn man on the corner with little to anticipate in the way of credit for his immediate needs and with small danger of large tort liability would be adequately capitalized at the minimum of $500 or $1,000 set forth in his local statute. Or, if no amount is set forth, for a rather nominal amount. But what of the owner of a fleet of taxis or the flying instructor who has a couple of training planes which he uses in his school of instruction? If they incorporate, what is to be the test of adequate capitalization so that they can be sure that they will not be held individually for the debts or tort claims of their corporations?

The scope and magnitude of the contemplated operations of the corporation is one important item to be reckoned with.[30] The courts sometimes use the phrase "substantial capital," at times connecting it with the very business being operated by the corporation, as "substantial capital reasonably regarded as adequate to enable it to operate its business and pay its debts as they matured."[31] For how long must it be able to operate its business and pay its debts as they mature? In *Arnold* v. *Phillips,* the court held that Arnold's advances to complete the brewery and those he made during the first year of the corporate business were rightly to be considered capital. The corporation

---

29. Baker v. Bates-Street Shirt Co., 6 F.2d 854 (1st Cir.1925); Fay v. Noble, 7 Cush. (61 Mass.) 188 (1851), to the effect that those who acted for the "corporation" were acting without authority since there was no principal and, consequently, were principals themselves.

30. Pepper v. Litton, 308 U.S. 295, 60 S.Ct. 238, 84 L.Ed. 281 (1939). See Latty, Subsidiaries and Affiliated Corporations, 119–128, 133–138 (1936).

31. Ohio Edison Co. v. Warner Coal Corp., 79 Ohio App. 437, 72 N.E.2d 487 (1946).

was for a while successful and later unsuccessful. Arnold also made loans to his corporation during the latter period. These loans, the court held to be debts which Arnold could make claim for to the trustee in bankruptcy of the corporation. The court in that case, as is always true where shareholders are sought to be charged with corporate debts on the basis of inadequate capitalization, was looking backwards at events that had already happened. It could point out the inadequacies of capital at early points of lending by the sole shareholder. But it seems obvious that capitalization reasonably adequate to carry on the particular business must always be tested as of the time of the inception of corporate existence rather than near its economic death. And if there are hazards in the particular type of business, as in case of the taxi company or of the incorporated flying instructor, these must be considered as well as the probable liabilities from other sources and the time it may take for the corporation to put itself on a paying basis.

There are many things that contribute to the financial downfall of a business enterprise, and lack of adequate capital is but one of these. No hard and fast rules have yet been laid down to test the adequacy or inadequacy of the capital of a corporation. Probably no more should be expected of men who start a new enterprise than what reasonably prudent men with a general knowledge of the particular type of business and its hazards would determine was reasonable capitalization in the light of any special circumstances which existed at the time of incorporation of the now defunct enterprise. If the business has previously been carried on in some other business association form, experience should have indicated pretty clearly what capitalization may be reasonably adequate.[32]

§ 6. Effect of Using the Corporate Device to Evade Statutory Prohibitions

The separate personality concept has frequently led to the use of the corporation for the purpose of accomplishing indirectly that which could not have been done directly. Where a parent corporation dominated both a subsidiary railroad and a subsidiary coal company (it owned all the stock of each), the court held that there had been a violation of the Hepburn Act. The railroad was transporting its own coal for purposes other than its own use. Affiliated corporations had been used to accomplish a purpose which the statute did not permit.[33] The holding, by a

32. Latty, supra, note 30. At the designated pages will be found useful material on the subject of what is adequate capitalization. And see Symposium on the Close Cor- poration, 52 N.W.U.L.Rev. 345, at 368–372 (1957) where undercapitalization is discussed.

33. The case involved an application of the Sherman Anti-Trust Act and

holding company formed for that purpose, of controlling stock in two competing railroad corporations was held to be in violation of the Sherman Anti-Trust Act.[34]   The use of a holding company to avoid a statutory double liability provision placed upon shareholders in banking corporations was held not to relieve the shareholders in the holding company from this double liability.[35]   And the use of an affiliated corporation by the controlling shareholders of the Pabst Brewing Company, the affiliate being used to secure payments of rebates from carriers over which the Brewing Company shipped its product, was held to be a violation of the Elkins Act making such rebates illegal.[36]

the Hepburn Act (Commodities Clause of the Act to Regulate Commerce) which prohibited a railroad to transport in interstate commerce any article or commodity produced or mined by it except for its own use. In this case, U. S. v. Reading Co., 253 U.S. 26, at 62, 40 S.Ct. 425, at 434, 64 L.Ed. 760 (1920), Mr. Justice Clarke wrote: "It would be to subordinate reality to legal form to hold that the coal mined by the Coal Company, under the direction of the Holding Company's officials, was not produced by the same 'authority' that operated the Reading Railway lines. The case falls clearly within the scope of the act, and for the violation of this commodity clause, as well as for its violation of the Anti-Trust Act, the combination between the Reading Railway Company and the Reading Coal Company must be dissolved."

But see U. S. v. Elgin, Joliet & Eastern Ry. Co., 298 U.S. 492, 56 S.Ct. 841, 80 L.Ed. 1300 (1935). In the later case of U. S. v. South Buffalo Ry. Co., 333 U.S. 771, 68 S.Ct. 868, 92 I.Ed. 1077 (1948), Mr. Justice Jackson describes the *Elgin* case as standing for the principle "that the prohibition against a railroad company transporting any commodity which it owns or in which it has an interest, except for its own use, does not prevent it from transporting commodities of a corporation whose stock is wholly owned by a holding company which also owns all of the stock of the railway, unless the control of the railway is so exercised as to make it the alter ego of the holding company." A further statement from the same opinion is illuminating: "It is enough to say that if the *Elgin* case

were before us as a case of first impression, its doctrine might not now be approved."

In Keystone Mining Co. v. Gray, 120 F.2d 1 (3d Cir.1941), noted in 55 Harv.L.Rev. 140 (1941), a carrier attempted to do by use of a subsidiary what it could legally have done itself. But Congress had shown pretty clearly that it did not favor subsidiaries for this purpose.

34.   Northern Securities Co. v. U. S., 193 U.S. 197, 24 S.Ct. 436, 48 L.Ed. 679 (1904), "Those who were stockholders of the Great Northern and Northern Pacific and became stockholders in the holding company are now interested in preventing all competition between the two lines, and, as owners of stock or of certificates of stock in the holding company, they will see to it that no competition is tolerated." Mr. Justice Harlan, 193 U.S. at 327, 24 S. Ct. at 452.

35.   Anderson v. Abbott, 321 U.S. 349, 64 S.Ct. 531, 88 L.Ed. 793, 151 A.L.R. 1146 (1944), rehearing denied 321 U.S. 804, 64 S.Ct. 845, 88 L.Ed. 1090 (1944). Justices Jackson, Roberts, Reed and Frankfurter dissented, Jackson writing the dissenting opinion.

36.   U. S. v. Milwaukee Refrigerator Transit Co., 142 F. 247 (C.C. Wis.1905). And see id. v. id., 145 F. 1007 (C.C.Wis.1906), where the charges against the Pabst Brewing Co. were dismissed "for failure of proof," Judge Baker concluding that "the majority of the brewing company stock is owned by persons that have no interest in the refrigerator company." Hence, they were not receiving rebates. The

The corporate device had been used to reach a result not permitted by the statute.

In one area, however, the use of the corporate form to accomplish what the sole shareholder could not have legally done as a natural person and bound himself thereby has, in a few decisions, been held legitimate. The area is that of usurious loans. Statutes frequently provide that corporations are not covered by the statutes limiting the interest that may be charged in case of loans to natural persons. There is, perhaps, good reason for the distinction. But suppose a natural person is told that he cannot get the loan he asks for, though he has property which would justify the loan, but that if he will incorporate and put the same property into the corporate jackpot and mortgage it as security a loan will be granted the corporation at a rate of interest which would have been usurious had the natural person been the borrower. Is not this using the corporate device to evade a definite statutory policy? *Jenkins v. Moyse* [37] held not, though it would seem that it clearly was. Professor Ballantine felt that the decision was sound because there was no proof of borrower-oppression and no inequity resulted from the borrower's voluntary act.[38] On the other hand, Dean Stevens disagrees, and rightly so, for this was a loan for personal needs and the lender demanded incorporation for the sole purpose of exacting usurious interest.[39] However, there is too little case law to justify a bold statement that a solely owned corporation may be used for this purpose.

brewing company was paying the full legal freight rates and the Pabsts, through their sole ownership of Milwaukee Refrigerator Transit Co., were the beneficiaries of the rebates. However, a decree was entered against the Transit Co. and the railroad companies.

37. 254 N.Y. 319, 172 N.E. 521, 74 A.L.R. 205, Ann. at 211 (1930). The rationalization of the court was that the corporation was being used to do just what the law permitted. Accord: Carozza v. Federal Finance & Credit Co., 144 Md. 227, 131 A. 332 (1925). But see Western States Acceptance Corp. v. Tuttle, 210 Cal. 51, at 54, 290 P. 574, at 575 (1930); H. A. S. Loan Service v. McColgan, 21 Cal.App. 551, 133 P.2d 391 (1943) and comment, "Disregarding the Corporate Entity" as a Regulatory Process (H. W. Ballantine), 31 Calif.L.Rev. 426 (1943); In Sodi, Inc. v. Salitan, 68 So.2d 882 (Fla.Sup.Ct.1953), it was held that, because the statute excepting corporations from the usury laws had been repealed and the new statute was broad enough to prohibit the charging of usurious rates to corporations, there was no authority to bind the corporation to usurious rates from the provision in the corporation statute empowering corporations "To borrow money at such rates of interest and upon such terms as it, or its board of directors, may deem necessary or expedient and shall authorize or agree upon; . . . ." The court held that the borrowing authority was "merely a recognition that a corporation must act through its responsible and authorized officers and requires an agreement by them fixing the interest rate to make it a corporate obligation."

38. Ballantine, Corporations 306 (Rev. ed. 1946).

39. Stevens, Corporations 78 (2d ed. 1949).

The use of the corporation to avoid a statutory policy is one of the clearest cases where courts will act to hold the owners accountable in the same manner as if the corporation had not been used.

It was argued in *Jenkins* v. *Moyse* that the corporation should be treated in the same manner as the sole shareholder behind it. A similar argument was used in *Boro Park Sanitary Live Poultry Market, Inc.* v. *Heller* [40] where a family of four brothers and their mother were the sole shareholders, directors and officers of their corporation. The corporation, in the immediate past, had employed members of the defendant union but now desired to carry on without any outside help. The union contract had expired and the sole shareholders proceeded to carry on by themselves. By picketing and other methods the defendant union sought to "induce or compel" the corporation to employ union members and to enter into a new contract with the union. The union had refused to admit the shareholders as members on the ground that they were employers and hence not eligible to membership. The corporation sought to enjoin the union from picketing and from interfering with its business. While statutes were involved, the problem boiled down to "whether in this case of corporate employer and its stockholders who labor for wages in its business [they] stand in the relation of employer and employee." [41] Had the business been carried on as a partnership, the partners would not be held as employees. Should the same be held here? The majority of the court thought not, holding that "The corporate entity is . . . in this case not a fiction. It is the form chosen by the stockholders for the conduct of the business. It hires the stockholders for the conduct of the business. It hires the stockholders to work for it. They are paid by it. They are subject to discharge by it." [42] While the shareholders might not be eligible for union membership because they share in the profits of the business "and their interests may not coincide with the interest of other workers," the controversy of whether union members or the shareholders should be employed to do the work remained a "labor dispute" and the Court of Appeals sustained the Appellate Division in its dismissal of the complaint for failure to state a cause of action. Rippey, J., writing a dissenting opinion, felt that the interests of justice required that the corporate form be "disregarded." "Practically, under the peculiar facts in this particular case, the four brothers and the mother were the corporation and were not servants of the corporation in any sense

40. 280 N.Y. 481, 21 N.E.2d 687 (1939). See notes in 20 B.U.L.Rev. 132 (1940); 9 Brooklyn L.Rev. 94 (1939); 25 Cornell L.Q. 132 (1939).

41. Ibid. 21 N.E.2d at 688.

42. Ibid. 21 N.E.2d at 688.

except by legal fiction . . .. The defendants cannot 'justi-fy wrong' by asserting the contrary." [43] Here, the family had used the corporate form, not to evade the provisions of a statute but legitimately, and found themselves bound by the usual entity principle. In order to evade the statute and the decision of the New York Court of Appeals, the family formed a partnership and obtained the remedy they had previously sought.[44]

§ 7. Use of the Corporate Form to Avoid Contracts or Other Obligations

The attempt to use the corporate form to hinder, delay or defraud creditors has been no more successful than the use of a natural person for the same purpose. From an early time courts have held that the real parties in interest, the owners, cannot avoid 13 Elizabeth, Chapter 5, and the statutes patterned after it by incorporating themselves and conveying their property gratuitously to their dummy.[45] The rules applicable are the same as where no corporation is used.

Fundamentally, the problem is the same when a corporation is used to avoid a contractual liability or duty. In the now famous case of *Pepper* v. *Litton* [46] the facts, while somewhat complicated, involved the use of the one-man corporate device to prevent the recovery of royalties due under a lease. Through a maze of transactions and a series of cases in state and federal courts, the plaintiff eventually got her judgment. The corporate device had been used in a manner and for a purpose the statute did not permit.

---

43. Ibid. 21 N.E.2d at 690. Hubbs, J., concurred; O'Brien, J., took no part in the decision. Having lost their argument, the family group turned itself into a family partnership and, asking for the same relief, received it. Kershnar v. Heller, 14 N.Y.S.2d 595 (Sup.Ct.1939), modified in 258 App.Div. 751, 15 N.Y.S.2d 451 (1939), and permanent injunction granted in 259 App.Div. 850, 20 N.Y.S.2d 406 (1940), rehearing denied 259 App.Div. 1030, 21 N.E.2d 389 (1940), motion to appeal denied 283 N.Y. 775, 28 N.E.2d 980 (1940).

44. See note 43, supra.

45. Booth v. Bunce, 33 N.Y. 139 (1865); Hibernia Ins. Co. v. St. Louis & New Orleans Transp. Co., 13 F. 516 (C.C.Mo.1882) (Shareholders in a corporation organized another transferring all of its property to the second corporation

without paying the debts of the first. Held: To full extent of the assets received, the obligations of the first corporation may be enforced against the second); First Nat. Bank of Chicago v. Trebein, 59 Ohio St. 316 (1898) (A natural person formed a corporation and transferred his assets to it to evade his creditors. Held: Corporation was in substance the sole shareholder and its assets could be pursued).

46. 308 U.S. 295, 60 S.Ct. 238, 84 L. Ed. 281 (1939). Higgins v. California Petroleum & Asphalt Co., 147 Cal. 363, 81 P. 1070 (1905), was similar, a transfer of corporate properties to a second and then a third corporation, each substantially identical, to avoid the payment of royalties. The court held all three jointly liable for the royalties on the lease.

But hard cases sometimes make poor law and so it was in *Berry* v. *Old South Engraving Co.*[47]   The Old South Engraving Co. had an agreement with the plaintiff union regulating the conditions of employment and pay of its employees. The union, it was alleged, had, contrary to the agreement, given better terms to competing engraving companies "who were permitted to pay employee members of the said Union less than the rates established by said agreement." Upon failing to obtain comparable terms for its employees, the shareholders and officers organized a new company, the Old South Photoengraving Corp., which gave 9,000 of its issue of 12,000 shares of no-par value stock to the old company for its assets and business. The shareholders purchased the remaining shares in the new company in proportion to their shareholdings in the old one. The old company then carried on no business, though it had not been dissolved, and the new company hired non-union labor and carried on as before. The union sought to enjoin the violation of its agreement and damages. Although the shareholders of the new company were the same, its assets the same, its officers the same, its name practically the same and it was, for all practical effect, the old company in new clothing, the court held that "The motive of the officers, directors and stockholders of the old corporation as individuals, that is the desire of these incorporators of the new corporation to secure through the instrumentality of a corporation authority to do business exactly like the business done by the old corporation, without the burden of the commercial agreement as to the employment of union labor, cannot be regarded as fraudulent in fact or in law."[48]   The court held the bill properly dismissed against the old company "as it did not break the contract by ceasing to employ either members of the union or anybody else." And, since the new company had never contracted with the union, the bill was properly dismissed against it. Fortunately, the great bulk of authority is opposed to this holding.[49]   Here was a clear case of the use of the corpo-

---

47. 283 Mass. 441, 186 N.E. 601 (1933), noted in 47 Harv.L.Rev. 135 (1933); 32 Mich.L.Rev. 551 (1934); 18 Minn.L.Rev. 597 (1934).

48. Ibid., 186 N.E. at 604.

49. Ballantine, Corporations, at 303–304 (Rev. ed. 1946), calls this a "bare-faced evasion" which most jurisdictions would not stomach. See interesting case of Ducasse v. Am. Yellow Taxi Operators, 224 App.Div. 516, 231 N.Y.S. 51 (1928), where contract of original corporation was enforced against successive corporations into which orig-

inal had merged, but enforcement extended only to numbers of taxi meters actually leased by original corporation.

The Massachusetts court has recently done better. In Packard Clothes, Inc. v. Director of Division of Employment Security, 318 Mass. 329, 61 N.E.2d 528 (1945), an individual transferred his property to a solely owned corporation which did the same business and hired the same employees as before, under the same management. As an individual he had acquired a merit rating which, he argued, should be avail-

rate device by the same persons who, through their first corporation, had made a contract with the plaintiff, with the sole purpose of ridding themselves of a disadvantageous contract. Though no mention was made of it in the decision, could it be that the claimed economic inequality caused by the union's giving better terms to the old company's competitors was the inarticulate premise behind the holding? If there was an actual breach of agreement on the union's part in this respect, a proper solution would have been to require the union to do equity before expecting any from the court, and a return to the agreed terms would have been insisted upon before listening to the arguments for an injunction.

§ 8. The Sole Shareholder in Competition with Other Corporate Creditors

In the famous case of *Salomon v. A. Salomon & Co., Ltd.*,[50] Salomon, a solvent bootmaker, formed a limited company to take over his business, had his wife, self and five children sign the Memorandum of Association which, under the English Law, is comparable to articles of incorporation or the certificate of incorporation under American law, took over £1,000 in cash, £10,000 in debentures which were liens upon the corporate property, and one share over half (20,001 shares of £1 par value) of the authorized capital stock in fully paid shares, six shares being issued to members of his family, one to each, as qualifying

able to his corporation. The defendant had rejected the plaintiff's claim that the new corporation was simply its sole shareholder. The court held that the plaintiff-corporation was the successor employing unit in toto and was entitled to the merit rating under the statute previously acquired by its sole shareholder. "It is competent to pierce the veil of the corporation and to disregard the corporate form, and consider substance rather than form in order to carry out the legislative intent."

In N. L. R. B. v. Hopwood Retinning Co., Inc., 104 F.2d 302 (2d Cir. 1939), Monarch Retinning Co., Inc., was formed to take over the property of Hopwood Retinning Co., Inc., after Hopwood had been ordered to cease and desist from unfair labor practices, to reinstate employees locked out earlier and to pay them for wages lost. Monarch argued that it and its officers were not liable for violating the order against Hopwood. Held: Mon-

arch was formed for the purpose of avoiding the order. It was the alter ego of Hopwood and it, and its officers, are guilty of contempt. The facts also indicate that Monarch was undercapitalized. And see Walling, Adm'r of Wage and Hour Division, etc. v. James V. Reuter, Inc., 321 U.S. 671, at 674, 64 S.Ct. 826, at 828, 88 L.Ed. 1005 (1944). Here, after N. L. R. B. had ordered the corporation to cease violating the Fair Labor Standards Act, the corporation dissolved and the family behind it carried on as an unincorporated group.

Compare N. L. R. B. v. Timken Silent Automatic Co., 114 F.2d 449 (2d Cir.1940) with the *Hopwood* case, *supra*. See particularly Judge Clark's dissent. He cites *Hopwood* and states that *Timken* will be confusing in the light of the first case, as there the successor corporation was held.

50. [1897] App.Cas. 22 (House of Lords).

shares. A little later Salomon's company, having failed, was in liquidation proceedings and Salomon presented his claim for payment of his debentures. If Salomon's claim were allowed the unsecured creditors of the company would obtain nothing on their claims. It seemed clear that the property Salomon turned over to his company was overvalued and that the capital supplied for which shares were taken was inadequate to carry on the venture. The trial court [51] held that the company was Salomon's agent and that company creditors could have sued him personally. The Court of Appeals [52] took the view that the corporation was a kind of trustee created for an illegal purpose, namely, to pervert the corporate form to defraud creditors. With either view prevailing, Salomon would have lost his case. But the House of Lords [53] held that, although it was a one-man company formed to obtain limited liability (a legitimate purpose) and that the stockholders, other than Salomon, were dummies, nevertheless it was a corporation and a different person from its sole shareholder. The legality of the one-man company under the English statute was thus established. Hence, the court allowed Salomon to keep his secured claim for £10,000 just as if he had been an outsider lending this sum to the corporation. This case also established the principle that literal compliance with the corporation statute is all that is required— that dummy incorporators, dummy shareholders with qualifying shares, and dummy directors, all with but a nominal interest in the company, are competent to form it and carry it on.[54]

51. Broderip v. Salomon, L.R. [1895] 2 Ch. 323, 329–332.

52. Broderip v. Salomon, L.R. [1895] 2 Ch. 323.

53. Supra note 48. See Dollar Cleansers & Dyers v. MacGregor, 163 Md. 105, 161 A. 159 (1932), for contrary result.

54. See Kahn-Freund, Some Reflections on Company Law Reform, 7 Mod.L.Rev. 54, at 54–55 (1944), where he calls the decision in Salomon v. A. Salomon & Co., Ltd., "a calamitous decision," and further states that the privilege of limited liability through incorporation ought to be confined to "risky ventures" and that the partnership, either general or limited, "ought to be the usual type of business association."

The American statutes were generally interpreted in the same manner, namely, that dummy incorporators, shareholders and directors fulfilled the statutory requirements. This made it possible for a corporation, through indirect action, to incorporate a subsidiary. Kardo Co. v. Adams, 231 F. 950 (6th Cir. 1916), reversing American Ball Bearing Co. v. Adams, 222 F. 967 (D.Ohio 1915), which had held that, under the Ohio statute, bona fide stockholding was intended, and that these provisions were mandatory. Since one natural person or a corporation could by use of dummies so incorporate, would it not be better to provide by statute that one person, natural or artificial, may alone incorporate? See 28 Iowa Code Ann. §§ 491.1 and 491.2; Ky.Rev.Stat.1953, § 271.025, as amended by L.1954, c. 33; 15 Mich.Stat.Ann. [1957 Cum.Supp.] §§ 21.2 and 21.3, as amended; and Wis.Bus.Corp.Law of 1951, § 180.-44. These statutes permit one individual to incorporate and the Michigan statute also specifically permits partnerships and corpora-

Having provided a corporation with capital sufficient for its ordinary needs is there any reason why a sole or controlling shareholder should not be able to lend money to his corporation, with or without security upon its assets, and compete with the corporation's outside creditors? If, under similar conditions, outsiders had lent money and taken security upon the corporate assets, there would be no question of the outsider's right to do this. Then, should not the sole shareholder, whether natural person or corporation, be able to do the same and compete as any outsider might with other creditors of the corporation? There are many decisions which so hold [55] but, almost without exception, these cases indicate that courts will scrutinize carefully the good faith and fairness of the sole shareholder's deal with his corporation before they will let him compete with other creditors.[56] He has inside knowledge of the condition of his corporation and the temptation is great to protect his own interests in a failing corporation by taking security for past loans or for accrued salary which he has failed to collect, in which case he is not only asking to compete but to be considered a secured creditor. If he is to compete at all under such circumstances it should be as a general creditor with general creditors. And, if he has been careless in failing to keep adequate accounts of his transactions with his company, or has allowed his claims to remain dormant for an unreasonable time, the careful scrutiny of the court is a fair guarantee that he will not even be allowed to compete with other corporate creditors.[57] Undercapitalization in any event will prevent his competing with other creditors even where his claim is honest, his records properly kept, and his pursuit prompt.[58]

tions, the Kentucky statute also permitting corporations, to be incorporators.

55. Wheeler v. Smith, 30 F.2d 59 (9th Cir.1929); Coffman v. Maryland Publishing Co., 167 Md. 275, 173 A. 248 (1934); Arnold v. Phillips, supra, p. 70 of text, allowed the mortgage security of the later loans made by Arnold to come in ahead of the corporation's general creditors. And, of course, Salomon v. A. Salomon & Co., Ltd., [1897] App.Cas. 22 (House of Lords).

56. Dollar Cleansers & Dyers, Inc. v. MacGregor, 163 Md. 105, 161 A. 159 (1932); New York Trust Co. v. Island Oil & Transport Corp., 56 F.2d 580 (2d Cir.1932). And see notes in 46 Harv.L.Rev. 823 (1933);

32 Mich.L.Rev. 121 (1933); 82 U. of Pa.L.Rev. 868 (1934); 45 Yale L. J. 1471 (1936).

57. Warner Fuller, The Incorporated Individual: A Study of the One-Man Company, 51 Harv.L.Rev. 1373, at 1386–1387 (1938) and cases cited. See also, Pepper v. Litton, 308 U.S. 281, 60 S.Ct. 238, 84 L.Ed. 281 (1939). In Vennerbeck & Clase Co. v. Juergens Jewelry Co., 53 R.I. 135, 164 A. 509 (1933), the court allowed the sole shareholder's claim for salary emphasizing the fact that he had kept his accounts accurately and honestly.

58. See again Arnold v. Phillips, supra, p. 70 of text. Compare Albert Richards Co. v. The Mayfair, 287 Mass. 280, at 288, 191 N.E. 430, at 433 (1934).

§ 9. The Solely Owned Corporation in Insolvency Proceedings

In bankruptcy proceedings, it has been stated, "[C]ourts of bankruptcy are essentially courts of equity, and their proceedings inherently proceedings in equity." [59] Such courts are, by the statute, granted powers to allow and disallow claims and to reject them in whole or in part "according to the equities of the case" though they may previously have been allowed.[60] Whether the claimant be a director, officer, or shareholder of his corporation the equitable power is there. Nor does the fact that the claim has been reduced to judgment guarantee that the claimant will be treated in the same manner as outside creditors. The director, officer and dominant or controlling shareholder or group of shareholders occupy a position of trust—each is a fiduciary—whose dealings with the corporation will be subjected to rigorous scrutiny not only to ascertain whether there was good faith but also to find out whether there was fairness to the corporation and those who are interested in it. "The essence of the test is whether or not under all the circumstances the transaction carries the earmarks of an arm's length bargain. If it does not, equity will set it aside. While normally that fiduciary obligation is enforceable directly by the corporation, or through a stockholder's derivative action, it is, in the event of bankruptcy of the corporation, enforceable by the trustee. For that standard of fiduciary obligation is designed for the protection of the entire community of interests in the corporation—creditors as well as stockholders." [61] And, under the reorganization provisions of the bankruptcy statute, the court has the same power and duty to avoid unfairness and injustice.

It frequently happens in bankruptcy proceedings, whether for the purpose of liquidation or reorganization of an insolvent corporation, that creditors or shareholders do not seek to hold the sole or controlling shareholder liable for the insolvent corporation's debts but rather to prevent the exercise of his claim, whether secured or unsecured, against his corporation. What is now known as the "Deep Rock doctrine" arose out of such a case.[62] A parent corporation had undercapitalized its subsidiary and allowed it to become greatly in debt. Mismanagement by the parent was glaring. Insolvency resulted and, in a reorganization proceeding under the statute, the parent corporation pre-

---

59. Local Loan Co. v. Hunt, 292 U.S. 234, 240, 54 S.Ct. 695, 697, 78 L.Ed. 1230, 93 A.L.R. 195 (1934).

60. U. S. Fidelity & Guaranty Co. v. Bray, 225 U.S. 205, 217, 32 S.Ct. 620, 625, 56 L.Ed. 1055 (1911).

61. Mr. Justice Douglas in Pepper v. Litton, 308 U.S. 295, at 306–307,

60 S.Ct. 238, at 245, 84 L.Ed. 281 (1939).

62. Taylor v. Standard Gas & Elect. Co., 306 U.S. 307, 59 S.Ct. 543, 83 L.Ed. 669 (1939). The doctrine gets its name from the subsidiary of Standard Gas & Elect. Co., Deep Rock Oil Corporation.

sented its claim, based upon an open account, in competition with other creditors and security holders. The court subordinated the parent's claim not only to the claims of other creditors of the subsidiary but also to those of its preferred shareholders who are in no real sense creditors of any kind but actually part owners of the business. Subordination of claims in such proceedings is as flexible as the proverbial chancellor's foot is long. The court has discretion to subordinate or not to subordinate, and if it subordinates the sole shareholder's claim or that of the parent in a parent-subsidiary situation it may go the whole way as in *Deep Rock* or simply subordinate the claim to the claims of the unsecured creditors, or stop at some other point.

Such claims will be disallowed if they are "fictitious or a sham" but where they do not fall within this class the cases "involve simply the question of order of payment. At times equity has ordered disallowance or subordination by disregarding the corporate entity. That is to say, it has treated the debtor-corporation simply as a part of the stockholder's own enterprise, consistently with the course of conduct of the stockholder. But in that situation as well as in the others to which we have referred, a sufficient consideration may be simply the violation of rules of fair play and good conscience by the claimant; a breach of the fiduciary standards of conduct which he owes the corporation, its stockholders and creditors. He who is in such a fiduciary position cannot serve himself first and his cestuis second." [63]

§ 10. Problems Where the State is Sole Owner of its Corporation's Shares

For various purposes a sovereign state may use corporations formed under its laws, or in the United States under the

---

63. Mr. Justice Douglas in Pepper v. Litton, 308 U.S. 295, at 310–311, 60 S.Ct. 238, at 247, 84 L.Ed. 281 (1939). In the *Deep Rock* case, Mr. Justice Roberts, speaking of the "instrumentality rule" which the petitioners had argued to preclude the allowance of the parent corporation's claim, continued: "It (the instrumentality rule) is not, properly speaking, a rule, but a convenient way of designating the application in particular circumstances of the broader equitable principle that the doctrine of corporate entity, recognized generally and for most purposes, will not be regarded when so to do would work fraud or injustice. The principle has been applied in appropriate circumstances to give minority stockholders redress against wrongful injury to their interests by a majority stockholder." Taylor v. Standard Gas & Elect. Co., 306 U.S. 307, at 322, 59 S.Ct. 543, at 550, 83 L.Ed. 669 (1939). For notes on this case, see 24 Cornell L.Q. 587; 34 Ill.L.Rev. 94 (1939); 28 Mich.L.Rev. 88 (1939); 16 N.Y. U.L.Q.Rev. 648 (1939); 25 Va.L. Rev. 849 (1939). In Comstock v. Group of Investors, 335 U.S. 211, at 237, 68 S.Ct. 1454, 1467, 92 L.Ed. 1911 (1948), Mr. Justice Murphy (dissenting) explains the Deep Rock Doctrine.

laws of the several states or by act of Congress. Problems arise as to whether the corporation may be sued without the consent of the state, whether its property may be taxed by a state within the United States, and whether its property is to be treated as property of the United States or of the corporation quite apart from its sole owner in other cases.

As might be expected there has been little consistency or logic in these cases. In government-owned corporations the property of the corporation is held to be that of the United States.[64] Thus courts have broken down the corporate entity and glanced into the government's safety deposit box to see who owns the shares. However, when a governmentally owned corporation carries on part of the state's business in this form, recent cases have consistently held that the government may not defend by asserting that it has given no consent to be sued.[65] More frequently than not the Congressional act authorizing the use of a corporation for the particular governmental function states that the corporation may sue or be sued and, apart from this customary practice, when the act fails to state this, the fact that Congress has authorized the use of a corporation would, in itself, warrant the conclusion that the corporation has the powers which the state or District of Columbia statute, whichever is used, gives it. And the power to sue and to be sued is usually specifically stated as a power and, if not, it is implied.

---

64. For a recent case so holding, see Southern Pacific Co. v. Defense Supplies Corp., 64 F.Supp. 605 (D. Cal.1946), aff'd sub nom. Southern Pacific Co. v. R. F. C., 161 F.2d 56 (9th Cir.1947) and Note in 20 So.Calif.L.Rev. 293 (1947); Inland Waterways Corp. v. Young, 309 U.S. 517, 60 S.Ct. 646, 84 L.Ed. 90 (1940). The Chief Justice and Justices Roberts and McReynolds dissented. Mr. Justice Frankfurter wrote the majority opinion which held that a national bank may pledge its assets to secure a deposit of a government-owned corporation, stating at 60 S.Ct. 650: "The funds of these corporations are, for all practical purposes, Government funds; the losses, if losses there be, are the Government's losses."

65. Bank of United States v. Planters' Bank of Georgia, 9 Wheat. (U.S.) 904 (1824); Sloan Shipyards Corp. v. U. S. Shipping Board, 258 U.S. 549, 42 S.Ct. 386, 66 L.Ed. 762 (1922). In Keifer & Keifer v. R. F. C., 306 U.S. 381, at 390–391, 59 S.Ct. 516, at 518–519, 83 L.Ed. 784 (1939), Mr. Justice Frankfurter, after stating that "Congress may . . . endow a governmental corporation with the government's immunity," adds, "But always the question is: has it done so?" He then continues: "Congress has provided no less than forty of such corporations discharging governmental functions, and without exception the authority to-sue-and-be-sued was included. Such a firm practice is partly an indication of the present climate of opinion which has brought governmental immunity from suit into disfavor, partly it reveals a definite attitude on the part of Congress which should be given hospitable scope." The corporation in question had been created by R. F. C. which, in the statute creating it, gave it power to sue and be sued. The court thought that Congress must have intended the same power to sue and be sued should be in the corporation so created by R. F. C.

On the other hand, when states have attempted to tax the government-owned corporation courts have permitted this chameleon-like entity to revert to its original governmental color and to defend on the basis that such a corporation is an agency of the United States and possesses its rights and privileges.[66] But Congress has the power to determine the extent to which its corporate business shall be subject to or exempt from such state taxing legislation. And, since most of the cases where the problem has been presented involved corporations formed to carry out strict governmental functions, such as to aid in the prosecution of a war, rather than to carry on an enterprise which private corporations with public ownership of their shares might have done, it is doubtful whether the principle is as rigid as is sometimes assumed.[67]

When the corporation makes claims in bankruptcy or where the status of its employees is involved, the courts have been quick to hold that the corporation does not obtain the preferences it would be entitled to under the bankruptcy statute had the United States not used the corporate form and that the employees do not have the same status as employees of the government.[68] This Gilbert and Sullivan approach reached a climax in a recent case where a government-owned corporation sued an-

---

66. Clallam County v. U. S., 263 U.S. 341, 44 S.Ct. 121, 68 L.Ed. 328 (1923); King County v. U. S. S. B. Emergency Fleet Corp., 282 F. 950 (9th Cir., 1922); Thurston, Government Proprietary Corporations, 21 Va.L.Rev. 351; ibid. 465, at 485 (1935). In an article by Lilienthal and Marquis, The Conduct of Business Enterprises by the Federal Government, 54 Harv.L.Rev. 545, at 596 (1941), the authors state: "Despite the recent sharp contractions of the doctrine of intergovernmental immunity from taxation, it appears still to be true that Congress has power to determine the extent to which these federal business activities shall be subject to or exempt from state taxation." They continue: "The court is now more apt to require definite evidence of a congressional purpose to exempt the federal enterprise from state taxation." (Page 596.) And see Mr. Justice Stone in Graves v. People of State of New York ex rel. O'Keefe, 306 U.S. 466, at 480, 59 S.Ct. 595, at 598, 83 L.Ed. 927 (1939).

67. See Thurston, Government Proprietary Corporations, 21 Va.L.Rev. 351; id. 465, at 482 (1935); Li-

lienthal and Marquis, The Conduct of Business Enterprises by the Federal Government, 54 Harv.L.Rev. 545, at 596, footnote 134 (1941); note 66, supra.

68. Sloan Shipyards Corp. v. U. S. Shipping Board, 258 U.S. 549, 42 S.Ct. 386, 66 L.Ed. 762 (1922); U. S. v. Wood, 290 F. 109 (2d Cir., 1923); Mellon v. Michigan Trust Co., 271 U.S. 236, 46 S.Ct. 511, 70 L.Ed. 924 (1926); Thurston, supra, note 67 at 487. In fact, salaries of employees of government-owned corporations are taxable by the states, at least where Congress has shown no intent otherwise. Graves v. People of New York ex rel. O'Keefe, 306 U.S. 466, at 479, 59 S.Ct. 595, at 598, 83 L.Ed. 927 (1939). And the income of employees of state-owned corporations, unless the corporation is essential to the preservation of the state government—i. e., if the particular governmental business cannot be carried on by a private enterprise— is taxable by the federal government. Helvering v. Gerhardt, 304 U.S. 405, 58 S.Ct. 969, 82 L.Ed. 1427 (1938).

other government-owned corporation and the United States for damages to wool shipped by the libellant on a vessel owned by the United States. The suit was to establish a claim against an insurance company. Circuit Judge Frank wrote: "It seems clear to us that the complete ownership of the Defense Supplies Corporation by the United States shows this to be nothing more than an action by the United States against the United States. The Act (Suits by Admiralty Act) would appear to contemplate no such action." [69]

§ 11. Determination of Enemy Character of Corporations During War

The two World Wars have raised important problems under trading with the enemy acts where corporations have been the actors. The most famous English case is *Daimler Co., Ltd.* v. *Continental Tyre & Rubber Co., Ltd.,*[70] which arose during World War I. A German corporation owned 23,398 of 25,000 shares issued by a corporation formed under the English statute, three Germans, residents of Hanover, owning 1,600 shares, the two remaining shares being held one each by the secretary, a naturalized German, and the corporation's managing director, a German citizen, both residing in England. The Secretary, however, was the only resident in England at the time he brought suit on behalf of the corporation for a debt owed by the defendant. The House of Lords held that the enemy character of a corporation must be determined by something other than the corporate birth-place. Said Lord Parker of Waddington: "My lords, I think that the analogy is to be found in control . . . . The acts of a company's organs, its directors, managers, secretary, and so forth, functioning within the scope of their authority, are the company's acts and may invest it definitely with enemy character. It seems to me that similarly the character of those who can make or unmake those officers, dictate their conduct mediately or immediately, prescribe their duties and call them to account, may also be material in the question of the enemy character of the company." [71] Since all directors were German and at the time residents of Germany, and since all but one shareholder were Germans in Germany, all being "the King's enemies," no one could be validly appointed to bring suit. Thus the control test, which looked behind the

69. Defense Supplies Corp. v. U. S. Lines Co., 148 F.2d 311, at 312 (2d Cir., 1945), cert. denied 326 U.S. 746, 66 S.Ct. 43, 90 L.Ed. 446 (1945).

70. [1916] 2 A.C. 307 (House of Lords).

71. Ibid. at 340. The "control" test was codified by an English statute in World War II. Trading with the Enemy Act, 1939, 2 and 3 Geo. VI, c. 89, § 2(1) (c); 26 Halsbury's Stat. of Eng. 326 (2d ed. 1951).

corporate entity to see who had the power to control, became the law of England.

In the United States the separate entity theory of corporations has been, until recently, rigidly followed. Thus, if the corporation was incorporated within the United States, it acquired no enemy character through the character of its shareholders, directors or officers even though all of them were citizens and residents of an enemy state.[72] The decisive tests in the classification of corporations as "enemy" were "organization under the laws of an enemy state or a foreign corporation doing business in an enemy state." [73] However, the shares of enemy shareholders in a non-enemy corporation were properly seized as enemy property.[74] These interpretations were made under the 1917 Trading with the Enemy Act.[75]

The TEA of 1917 was amended in 1941 prior to the formal entry of the United States into World War II.[76] Regulations were issued under the amendments and the early regulations accepted the control test.[77] "Thus, a domestic corporation was deemed under the control of a 'national of a foreign country' when a substantial portion of its capital was represented by funds which belonged to blocked nationals." [78] Eventually, the Supreme Court held that interpretations under the 1917 TEA

---

72. Hamburg-American Line Terminal & Navigation Co. v. U. S., 277 U.S. 138, 48 S.Ct. 470, 72 L.Ed. 822 (1928), where a German corporation owned all of outstanding stock of a New Jersey corporation. Held: Its property is nonenemy property. Mr. Justice McReynolds stated that Congress might have taken the view that when all of the stock is held by enemy shareholders, that made the New Jersey corporation an enemy alien. But Congress did not take that view. And see (same result) in Behn, Meyer & Co., Ltd. v. Miller, Alien Property Custodian, 266 U.S. 457, 45 S.Ct. 165, 69 L.Ed. 374 (1925), where majority stock was held by a German in an English (Straits Settlement) corporation, doing business in the Philippines.

73. Fink, That Pierced Veil—Friendly Stockholders and Enemy Corporations, 51 Mich.L.Rev. 651, at 655 (1953).

74. Ibid. at 655.

75. 50 U.S.C.A.Appendix § 2.

76. Trading with the Enemy Act, 50 U.S.C.A.Appendix §§ 2, 5, 9(a), as amended by First War Powers Act of 1941. The term "enemy" is defined in 50 U.S.C.A.Appendix § 2 as follows: "The word 'enemy', as used herein, shall be deemed to mean, for the purposes of such trading and of this Act—

"(a) Any individual, partnership, or other body of individuals, of any nationality, resident within the territory (including that occupied by the military and naval forces) of any nation with which the United States is at war, or resident outside the United States and doing business within such territory, and any corporation incorporated within such territory of any nation with which the United States is at war or incorporated within any country other than the United States and doing business within such territory."

77. § 5(E) (ii) of Executive Order 8389.

78. Fink, That Pierced Veil—Friendly Stockholders and Enemy Corporations, 51 Mich.L.Rev. 651, at 659 (1953).

could not stand in light of the 1941 amendments and held that "enemy taint can be found if there are enemy officers or stockholders; even in the presence of some nonenemy stockholders," [79] and that the presence of nonenemy stockholders did not prevent the seizure of the corporate assets. But the court further held that when assets of a corporation organized under a neutral country's laws were seized because of enemy stockholding or office-holding "the rights of innocent stockholders to an interest in the assets proportionate to their stockholdings must be fully protected." [80] How this can be done without a sale of the corporation's assets, the paying off of legitimate creditors and a distribution of the shareholder's proportionate interest to him is a baffling problem.[81] However, there is an analogy offered by the appraisal statutes which permit dissenting shareholders, when certain fundamental changes are made, to be paid the fair value of their shares. Appraisal procedures might well be used for this purpose.[82]

79. Kaufman v. Societe Internationale Pour Participations Industrielles et Commerciales, S.A., 343 U.S. 156, 72 S.Ct. 611, at 613, 96 L.Ed. 853 (1952). Mr. Justice Reed wrote a dissent which was joined in by the Chief Justice (Vinson) and Mr. Justice Minton, a part of which follows: "The result reached by the Court is brought about by a disregard of the ordinary incidents of the relation of a stockholder to a corporation. A stockholder has no present interest in the physical property of an unliquidated corporation." (72 S.Ct. at 616.) And, further: "Where the corporation subjects its assets to forfeiture by aiding our enemies, the corporation should pay the penalty. The friendly stockholder should not be permitted by strained statutory interpretation to withdraw his contributions to the funds that were used to our injury and so reduce the assets available for war claimants." (72 S.Ct. at 617.)

80. Mr. Justice Black in the Kaufman case, supra, note 79, 72 S.Ct. at 613. The majority justices felt that such suits could be more appropriately resolved by § 9(a) than through a multiplicity of separate actions even though the corporate action was not for the benefit of all shareholders but only the nonenemies.

81. In volume 14, No. 12, pages 9 and 10 of the magazine "The Reporter" for June 14, 1956, in an article "Enemy Assets—The $500,000,000 Question" by William Harlan Hale and Charles Clift, the authors state that Ernest K. Halbach, a Philadelphian of German descent, former president of and majority shareholder in General Dyestuffs, "a creation of the I. G. Farben-I. G. Chemie group," was paid by the United States Government which had seized the corporate stock under the TEA Act, the sum of $557,550 for his majority interest in the corporation. This was (and is) a highly successful corporation and the solution by settlement reached in this case is one possible under the later *Kaufman* decision. The same article, page 10, reports that Halbach has brought suit to have the settlement set aside on the grounds that he had been forced to accept the reward under duress. The article states (page 10) that an Alien Property official estimates the stock may have been worth $5,000,000 at the time suit was brought.

82. See page 515 et seq., infra, for a discussion of appraisal rights.

§ 12. The Corporation as a "Citizen" for Purpose of Federal Jurisdiction Based upon Diversity of Citizenship; as a "Person" Where Constitutional Guarantees are Threatened

The Supreme Court took a tortuous route to arrive at the rule that, for purposes of jurisdiction in the federal courts, a corporation is a citizen of the state in which it was incorporated, this without reference to the citizenship of its shareholders.[83] Chief Justice Marshall, faced with the problem of recognizing or not recognizing a corporation for this purpose, stated flatly that "That individual, intangible, and artificial being, that mere legal entity, a corporation aggregate, is certainly not a citizen; and, consequently, cannot sue or be sued in the courts of the United States, unless the rights of the members, in this respect, can be exercised in their corporate name." [84] Thus, if the shareholders were citizens of a state different from that of the other party to the suit, jurisdiction was obtained. Some years later the court took the position that, for purposes of federal jurisdiction, the shareholders of a corporation are conclusively presumed to be citizens of the state where their corporation was incorporated.[85] But when P, a citizen of New Jersey, owning stock in a New York corporation, brought suit against the corporation and D, both residents and citizens of New York, and it was urged that P was conclusively presumed to be a citizen of New York so that there was no diversity of citizenship, the court promptly held that there was no such presumption and that jurisdiction was obtained.[86] Until quite recently, the rule first stated above, has been recognized for obtaining federal jurisdiction on diversity grounds when the amount involved was over $3,000, exclusive of interest and costs. Recently § 1332 of

83. Northern Securities Co. v. U. S., 193 U.S. 197, 24 S.Ct. 436, 48 L.Ed. 679 (1904); Great Southern Fire Proof Hotel Co. v. Jones, 177 U.S. 449, 20 S.Ct. 690, 44 L.Ed. 842 (1900) (The direct holding was that a Pennsylvania limited partnership association is not a corporation for purposes of federal jurisdiction under the diversity of citizenship clause).

84. Bank of United States v. Deveaux, 5 Cranch (U.S.) 61, at 86, 3 L.Ed. 38 (1809).

85. Marshall v. B. & O. R. Co., 16 How. (U.S.) 314, 14 L.Ed. 953 (1853). But the court also spoke of the corporation as a citizen as did the earlier case of Louisville, Cincinnati & Charleston R. v. Letson, 2 How. (U.S.) 497, 11 L.Ed. 353 (1844). And see Frederick Green, Corporations as Persons, Citizens, and Possessors of Liberty, 94 U. of Pa.L.Rev. 202, at 216–217 (1946), stating: "When the jurisdictional clauses of the Constitution and the Judiciary Act spoke of citizens, they meant to include corporations." The Australian High court construed its Constitutional provision giving the court jurisdiction in cases "between residents of different States" of Australia as applying only to natural persons. See Frankfurter, The Distribution of Judicial Power Between United States and State Courts, 13 Cornell L.Q. 499, at 524 (1928).

86. Doctor v. Harrington, 196 U.S. 579, 25 S.Ct. 355, 49 L.Ed. 606 (1905).

Title 28 U.S.C.A. has been amended, raising the jurisdictional amount to one exceeding $10,000, exclusive of interest and costs. And § 1332(c) provides that "For the purposes of this section. . . . A corporation shall be deemed a citizen of any State by which it has been incorporated and of the State where it has its principal place of business." And subsection (d) defines "States," as used in the section, as including the Territories, the District of Columbia, and the Commonwealth of Puerto Rico. These amendments took effect on the date of their approval, July 25, 1958, applying only in case of actions commenced after the date of enactment. Though other business associations such as the joint stock company, the partnership association or the business trust frequently have many of the characteristics of corporations, and are at times treated like corporations, the diversity of citizenship rule has not been applied to cover them. Citizenship of the individual members or of the trustees if different from that of the other party to the suit is the test.[87]

The question was early raised whether a corporation was a "citizen" within Article 4, Section 2, Clause 1, of the federal constitution, so as to be entitled to "all privileges and immunities of citizens of the several states." In two important early cases [88] the court held that a corporation did not qualify under this provision. Thus a corporation may be compelled to comply with the corporation laws of a foreign state in which it intends to do business, or may be kept out of the state entirely if the state so wills.[89] But a corporation is a "person" entitling it to due process and equal protection of the laws,[90] and "Within the

87. Great Southern Fire Proof Hotel Co. v. Jones, 177 U.S. 449, 20 S.Ct. 690, 44 L.Ed. 842 (1900) (a Pennsylvania limited partnership association, though declared by statute to be a citizen, was held not to be a citizen for diversity purposes); Ex parte Edelstein, 30 F.2d 636 (2d Cir. 1929), cert. denied sub nom. Edelstein v. Goddard, 279 U.S. 851, 49 S.Ct. 347, 73 L.Ed. 994 (1929) (an unincorporated association held not a citizen for diversity purposes). The civil law sociedad en comandita has some interesting features not present in partnerships formed in common law countries. In People of Puerto Rico v. Russell & Co., 288 U.S. 476, 53 S.Ct. 447, 77 L.Ed. 903 (1933), noted in 47 Harv.L.Rev. 136 (1933), the court held personality in such an organization so complete that it saw no adequate reason for treating it differently, for purposes of federal jurisdiction, from corporations organized under state laws.

88. Bank of America v. Earle, 13 Pet. (U.S.) 519, 10 L.Ed. 274 (1839); Paul v. Virginia, 8 Wall. (U.S.) 168, 19 L.Ed. 357 (1868).

89. Paul v. Virginia, supra, note 88.

90. Kentucky Finance Corp. v. Paramount Auto Exchange Corp., 262 U.S. 544, 43 S.Ct. 636, 67 L.Ed. 1112 (1923). A corporation has been held to be a "person" under the Civil Rights Act and, within the meaning of the equal protection and due process clauses, is entitled to freedom of speech and of the press. Grosjean v. American Press Co., Inc., 297 U.S. 233, 56 S.Ct. 444, 80 L.Ed. 660 (1936); Pennekamp v. Florida, 328 U.S. 331, 66 S.Ct. 1029, 90 L.Ed. 1295 (1945); Burstyn, Inc. v. Wilson, 343 U.S. 495, 72 S.Ct. 777, 96 L.Ed. 1098 (1951); N. A. A. C. P. v. Patty, 159 F.Supp. 503, at 518–519 (D.Va.1958) (holding that a nonprofit corporation has the same constitutional right). See Note, 66 Yale

meaning of federal statutes about venue, a corporation is an 'inhabitant' of the district where it has its principal office, keeps its books, and transacts the business relating to its corporate organization, and is a 'resident' of the state by which it was incorporated," and is one of "the people" entitled to the benefit of the Fourth Amendment protecting it against unreasonable searches and seizures.[91] However, a corporation created by act of Congress is not a "citizen" of any state nor is one born under the statutes of the District of Columbia,[92] when it argues diversity of citizenship for the purpose of federal jurisdiction. And it has been held that a corporation is not a "citizen" within the meaning of the Fourteenth Amendment, Section 1, prohibiting the states from making or enforcing any law which shall abridge the privileges or immunities of citizens of the United States.[93]

§ 13. Parent-Subsidiary and Affiliated Corporations

It has been said that "One of the major impediments to an accurate perception of what the corporation is doing, and why, is that most large corporations are in fact a complicated series of top holding companies, subsidiary holding companies, operating companies and various types of developmental, sales, credit, and other service companies. With this intricate and interesting corporate machinery, it becomes ever more difficult to tell who controls the corporation, where the impetus towards corporate action originates, or whose purposes are primarily served."[94] And yet subsidiary and affiliated corporations, when properly employed, have been useful devices during a period of great corporate expansion.

L.J. 545 (1957). But see the concurring opinion of Justice Stone in Hague v. C. I. O., 307 U.S. 496, at 527, 59 S.Ct. 954, 83 L.Ed. 1423 (1939), where he expresses the opinion that the privileges and immunities which § 1 of the 14th Amendment secures are those only of natural persons: that a corporation "cannot be said to be deprived of the civil rights of freedom of speech and of assembly, for the liberty guaranteed by the due process clause is the liberty of natural, not artificial persons." It is pointed out in N. A. A. C. P. v. Patty, supra, that this statement cannot be authoritative as but one other justice concurred in it.

91. Frederick Green, Corporations as Persons, Citizens, and Possessors of

Liberty, 94 U. of Pa.L.Rev. 202, at 203, 209 (1946).

92. Thurston, Government Proprietary Corporations, 21 Va.L.Rev. 351, at 391, 392 (1935); ibid. 465 (1935), and authority cited. But see 28 U.S.C.A. § 1332(c) quoted at page 89, supra.

93. Western Turf Ass'n v. Greenberg, 204 U.S. 359, 363, 27 S.Ct. 384, 386, 51 L.Ed. 520 (1907); Selover, Bates & Co. v. Walsh, 226 U.S. 112, 126, 33 S.Ct. 69, 57 L.Ed. 146 (1912). And see Henderson, The Position of Foreign Corporations in American Constitutional Law (1918).

94. Timberg, Corporate Fictions, Logical, Social and International Implications, 46 Col.L.Rev. 533, at 576 (1946).

In a real sense subsidiary and affiliated corporations are but a variation of the one-man company. They are usually formed by the parent corporation and it holds all but the qualifying shares of stock. Or the relationship may derive from the purchase of all of the shares of, or a controlling interest in, a corporation already doing business. The end result is the same.

While earlier corporations found it difficult legally to hold shares in other corporations, except where such shareholding was incidental to some purpose for which the corporation was formed [95] or where shareholding was for the purpose of temporarily investing funds not immediately needed in the business,[96] statutes or legally permissible purpose clauses giving the corporation authority to hold shares in other corporations made the subsidiary possible. It is perhaps doubtful whether statutory authority, as originally given, was intended to authorize corporations which have, in the first instance, insulated their shareholders against unlimited liability, to insulate themselves against unlimited liability by forming one or more wholly owned corporations to serve as shock absorbers in some risky or other part of the business. And, incidentally, to reinsulate the shareholders of the parent corporation in this process. At times, the same result has been accomplished by one shareholder's holding all the shares in two or more corporations formed to carry on different departments or functions of one business enterprise. Such corporations are called affiliates.

The fact that nearly all modern statutes require three or more incorporators to incorporate and that many of them require a board of directors of three or more who must be shareholders did not, as we have seen, prevent the accomplishment of the parent-subsidiary relationship. Natural persons, who might in fact have no interest in the corporation, were held capable of signing the articles or certificate of incorporation. The parent would supply the directors of the subsidiary (if necessary) with a share apiece to qualify them, the remaining shares being held by the corporation. If there was no requirement that directors be shareholders, the parent would take all of the shares issued. Had the courts taken the position that bona fide substantial shareholding by the incorporators was a requirement, the subsidiary, as we know it, would not have been possible.[97]

95. State ex inf. Atty. Gen. v. Missouri Pacific Ry. Co., 237 Mo. 338, 141 S.W. 643 (1911). But it was generally held that, without statutory authorization, a corporation could not be an original subscriber in a new corporation.

96. Booth v. Robinson, 55 Md. 419 (1880). Probably a minority view

in the United States but was the English rule.

97. The civil law does not permit dummies to form corporations or hold shares. In many civil law countries the law does not recognize a corporation with but one shareholder. The Roman law concept is that a corporation "is and must con-

Once having recognized the validity of subsidiaries and affiliates, the main problem was to keep within proper bounds a doctrine which permitted reinsulation. The courts have no ready or simple answer to solve the numerous problems arising out of parent-subsidiary-affiliate relationship. Professor Latty who has written an illuminating treatise on this subject has concluded that no concept of separate corporate personality will alone suffice to solve an actual problem. Policy factors, he concludes, are much more important than any formula which has yet been prescribed.[98]

All courts agree that sole or majority shareholding alone will not make the parent liable for the subsidiary's contracts or torts.[99] Nor will the fact that the same directors, or some of them, sit upon both corporations' boards. At times courts have seemed to give great weight to the formalities used in keeping the parent and subsidiary appearing as if they were two corporations with different shareholders, directors, and officers. In these cases, emphasis has been placed upon such things as separate board meetings for each, separate bank accounts, payment of employees out of the appropriate bank account, executing contracts in the name of the corporation intended to be bound, non-interference by parent's officers in the business of the subsidiary as by ordering the latter's officers and employees to act as if they were employees of the parent, and generally carrying on as two corporations with no family connections.[1]

Holdings based in main upon findings that the formalities had been kept would indeed be superficial. But as Cardozo, J.,

tinue to be a contract among several individuals." These shareholders must be bona fide ones, that is, real owners of the shares they hold and not mere dummies. The Commercial Law of Mexico, for example, requires at least five shareholders at the time of incorporation and any reduction below this after incorporation results in immediate dissolution. Colombia law is similar. If the shareholders fall below five, there is no way to make up the deficiency, as by issuing more stock to new shareholders. And the directors make themselves liable if they initiate new operations after the number of shareholders falls below five. Furthermore, some countries, by statute, do not permit more than a certain percentage of capital to be owned by foreign shareholders. Spain, for example, does not permit more than 25% to be owned by foreign shareholders

where the corporation engages in a "new industry." Alyea, Subsidiary Corporations Under Civil and Common Law, 66 Harv.L.Rev. 1227, 1229–1235 (1953).

98. Latty, Subsidiaries and Affiliated Corporations 16 and 220 (1936); Latty, The Corporate Entity as a Solvent of Legal Problems, 34 Mich. L.Rev. 597, at 609 (1936). Professor Ballantine had earlier come to practically the same conclusion. See Ballantine, Separate Entity of Parent and Subsidiary Corporations, 14 Calif.L.Rev. 12, at 18–19 (1925).

99. Stone v. Cleveland, C., C. & St. L. R. Co., 202 N.Y. 352, 95 N.E. 816, 35 L.R.A.,N.S., 770 (1911); Berkey v. Third Avenue Ry. Co., 244 N.Y. 84, 155 N.E. 58, 50 A.L.R. 599 (1926), motion for rehearing denied 244 N. Y. 602, 155 N.E. 914 (1927).

1. Berkey v. Third Avenue Ry. Co., supra, note 99.

stated in a leading case involving a parent and its subsidiary, "The whole problem of the relation between parent and subsidiary corporations is one that is still enveloped in the mists of metaphor. Metaphors in law are to be narrowly watched, for starting as devices to liberate thought, they end often by enslaving it." [2] With true realism this great judge followed the quoted statement with a warning that "the essential term to be defined is the act of operation. Dominion may be so complete, interference so obtrusive, that by the general rules of agency the parent will be a principal and the subsidiary an agent. Where control is less than this, we are remitted to the tests of honesty and justice." [3] But the consistent maintenance of separate organization of the subsidiary, which he considered "the mark of separate existence," he thought also important in the determination of a case. However, the formalities indicating separate organization and operation should not be considered of too great weight for "Those familiar with present day methods of corporate control will not be so naïve as to suppose that the complete domination in fact of its subsidiaries by a holding company owning all their stock is in any way inconsistent with scrupulous recognition of their separate corporate entities, or with the maintenance of separate accounts and distinct personnels of officers and directors." [4] Acts of control are the important facts to be ascertained as Cardozo had pointed out in the *Berkey* case.[5]

Some of the factors already considered in previous sections which point to liability of the parent for its subsidiary's contracts and torts are inadequacy of capitalization of the subsidiary, confusion of parent's with those of subsidiary's business transactions—"If the process or activity could have been tagged by the parties but was not, there seems no compelling reason why the courts should do the tagging *ex post facto* for them" [6]

2. Ibid, 244 N.Y. at 94, 155 N.E. 61, at 96 of 244 N.Y., at 62 of 155 N.E., Crane, J., wrote a dissenting opinion in which Pound, J., joined. They felt that in operation, control and dominance the Third Avenue Ry. was the Forty-second Street Ry.

3. Ibid. 244 N.Y. at 95, 155 N.E. at 61. Compare Berkey case with Lehigh Valley R. Co. v. Dupont, 128 F. 840 (2d Cir. 1904) and Lehigh Valley R. Co. v. Delachesa, 145 F. 617 (2d Cir. 1906). Also, Ross v. Pennsylvania Railroad, 106 N.J.L. 536, 148 A. 741 (1930).

4. Mr. Justice Stone, dissenting, with whom Justices Brandeis and Cardozo joined, in United States v. Elgin, Joliet & Eastern Ry. Co., 298

U.S. 492, at 506, 56 S.Ct. 841, at 846, 80 L.Ed. 1300 (1936).

5. Ibid. 298 U.S. at 507, 56 S.Ct. at 846. And, for an excellent analysis of actual control, see Weisser v. Mursam Shoe Corp., 127 F.2d 344, 145 A.L.R. 467 (2d Cir. 1942), opinion by Frank, Cir. J. And see Kingston Dry Dock Co. v. Lake Champlain Transportation Co., 31 F.2d 265, at 267 (2d Cir. 1929), L. Hand, Cir. J., writing the opinion. Compare this with what is said in North v. Higbee Co., 131 Ohio St. 507, 3 N.E.2d 391 (1936).

6. Douglas and Shanks, Insulation From Liability Through Subsidiary Corporations, 39 Yale L.J. 193, at 206 (1929).

—, and the use of a subsidiary to evade statutory prohibitions or to avoid contractual or other obligations. And, of course, the use of an affiliated corporation for similar purposes has been considered quite as obnoxious. The failure to keep strictly the formal matters distinguishing parent from subsidiary may be an example of confusing parent's and subsidiary's transactions. And where there is direct intervention or intermeddling of parent in subsidiary's business, or in a particular transaction, it is not difficult to find that the parent is using its subsidiary as its agent.

Douglas (now Mr. Justice Douglas) and Shanks in a much cited article claimed that the following four standards would keep business units from being treated as assimilated: [7]

(1) A separate financial unit for each, "sufficiently financed so as to carry the normal strains upon it."

(2) The day-to-day business should be kept separate with records similarly kept.

(3) The formal barriers between the two management structures should be maintained. Separate meetings of the board, etc., should be rigidly adhered to.

(4) The two units must not be represented as one.

The application of these standards will not explain all of the cases but they are of aid in explaining a large proportion of them. But more important, probably, is the determination of the primary question, whether the corporate privilege has, in good faith and honesty, been used for legitimate corporate ends.[8] And what are "legitimate corporate ends" is a question whose answer depends upon a rather uncertain word called "policy."

§ 14. Parent-Subsidiary and the Theory of "Enterprise Entity"

Professor Berle has advanced the thesis that when courts have recognized de facto corporations they have constructed a new entity, not intended by the statute under which the incorporators have failed substantially to comply, but justified "from the reality of the underlying enterprise, formed or in formation." [9] Likewise, when a court recognizes two or more corporations as if they were but one, it has raised a new personality which, again, is not spelled out in any statute but is based upon the fact that, actually, there is but one enterprise. "In effect what happens is that the court, for sufficient reason, has deter-

---

7. Ibid. at 196–197.

8. See Ballantine, Separate Entity of Parent and Subsidiary Corporations, 14 Calif.L.Rev. 12, at 18–19 (1925).

9. Berle, The Theory of Enterprise Entity, 47 Col.L.Rev. 343, at 344 (1947). See also Latty, op. cit. supra note 98, at 196.

mined that though there are two or more personalities, there is but one enterprise; and that this enterprise has been so handled that it should respond, as a whole, for the debts of certain component elements of it. . . . The facts which induce courts to do this are precisely the facts which most persuasively demonstrate that, though nominally there were supposed to be two or more enterprises, in fact, there was but one. The economic fact pushes through the paper differentiations embodied in the corporate certificates; and liabilities are dealt with in accord with the business, instead of the legal fact of corporate entity." [10]

The economic fact pushed through in an interesting case decided in the same year as that of Professor Berle's article.[11] California Zinc Company owned zinc mines in a remote part of California. The plaintiff railway company, all of whose shares were owned by the plaintiff Zinc Company, alleged that practically all of its line had been inundated by the back waters caused by the building of the Shasta Dam in California, and sought damages for this injury. The Zinc Company alleged that a large part of its mines had been inundated. It appeared that the Glidden Company owned all of the shares of the Zinc Company which it operated so as to secure an adequate and continuous supply of zinc for its business. Glidden Company, however, was not a party to the suit. Plaintiffs alleged that the operation of the mines and of the railway company was "a single integrated enterprise," arguing that the two should be considered a "single property" for the taking of any part of which they were entitled to recover not only the value of the part taken but also any consequent damage to the remainder. Since the Zinc Company had no means except through its subsidiary to move its zinc out of the mountains, it was argued that the taking of the railway virtually destroyed the value of the part of the mines untouched by the waters. The Government argued that there were two causes of action and that they could not be joined. The court overruled the Government's demurrer and permitted the single cause of action, holding that the plaintiffs were entitled to go to trial and, if they proved "a single integrated enterprise," the Zinc Company "probably would be entitled to recover for any consequential damage to its remaining property as the result of the taking of the railway." [12] Had

---

10. Berle, op. cit. supra note 9, at 350. And see H.A.S. Loan Service v. McColgan, 21 Cal.App. 551, 133 P.2d 391 (1943), where an affiliated corporation was used to evade usury and franchise tax laws. The court seems to have relied upon the single enterprise theory.

11. California Zinc Co. v. U. S., 112 Ct.Cl. 577, 72 F.Supp. 591 (1947).

12. Ibid. 72 F.Supp. at 593. See also U. S. v. Powelson, 118 F.2d 79, at 86 (4th Cir., 1941), rev'd on other grounds, 319 U.S. 266, 63 S.Ct. 1047, 87 L.Ed. 1390 (1943).

Glidden Company joined as a plaintiff and been able to show that other zinc was not obtainable, or, if so, in smaller quantities or at a higher price, might it not also have argued "single integrated enterprise" and asked for consequential damages covering its injury? One wonders at what point a court would call a halt to the single integrated enterprise doctrine when, instead of being sued, the parent and its subsidiaries sue as in the *California Zinc* case. There are problems of legal causation interesting to contemplate. And, even though the court recognizes the plaintiffs as being a single integrated enterprise does this mean that a person injured through the negligence of the railway might validly argue that California Zinc Company and Glidden are liable for the tort committed by the subsidiary?

Like so many other attempts to rationalize results, Professor Berle's explanation of what happens when the court requires a subsidiary's obligation to be assumed by the parent depends upon an unknown and uncertain element, namely, the finding by the court of "sufficient reason." And in the *California Zinc* case the court not only emphasized the single integrated enterprise possibility but stated, "Where it is necessary to do so in order to do justice, the courts have not infrequently disregarded the separate entities and treated the two corporations as one." [13] And courts may well differ as to what is "justice" in a particular case.

13. California Zinc Co. v. U. S., supra, note 11, 72 F.Supp. at 593.

Chapter 3

PREINCORPORATION MANAGEMENT:
PROMOTERS; SUBSCRIPTIONS

---

§ 1. The Meaning of "Preincorporation Management"

The term "preincorporation management," as used in this chapter, envisages activities carried on by the "preincorporators" [1] or promoters not only prior to actual incorporation whereby the business unit acquires its legal personality but beyond into the organization stage to the point where it is able to carry on the business for which it has been formed. The term "preincorporation," strictly interpreted, would have this chapter stop short of the act which constitutes the birth of the corporation. But several of the problems involving preincorporation activity do not come to a head until the corporation has acquired its existence and further events have occurred, results which are traceable to the earlier period.

§ 2. Who are Promoters?

Prior to launching a business association of any kind someone must have been interested in a patent, a mine, a new idea of achieving a business goal, a new business or the possibility of a new competitor in an old business, or perhaps the combining of two or more business associations into a new corporation or the purchase of stock in several corporations for control and economy of operation purposes. Any one of the objectives named above (and many more) must first be discovered by someone; and after discovery someone must have thought out the economic possibilities of the new venture—what market is there for the product; how much financial support outside the persons immediately interested in developing the idea will be needed; what labor will be required and is it available; what raw materials will be needed; where is the best location for the business; what legal problems are involved; what property, patent rights, licenses, options and contracts should be obtained immediately, that is, prior to incorporating. If the project is a sizeable one requiring that a considerable amount of outside

---

1. A term used by the late Professor E. Merrick Dodd of Harvard Law School. "Promoters" is the term used by the courts and, since it has such wide usage, will be adhered to in this book.

funds be procured, there will be joint efforts between those interested in the promotion and investment bankers who have organizations through which shares can be sold to the public and who will underwrite the issue. Thus the work of promotion involves discovery, investigation and analysis, and the assembly of property, personnel and finances, and those who operate in one or more of these areas are called promoters.[2]

§ 3. **Relation of Promoter to Promoter**

Suppose promoter A, through long study, has a plan which has excellent prospects of financial gain provided he can obtain one or more promoters to supply some of the funds necessary to carry out his plan. He goes to B, discloses his plan, tells B that he himself will put up $200,000 if B will join him and contribute a similar amount. B is impressed, tells A so but asks A to submit his plan and papers to B's attorney. B's attorney is likewise impressed, tells B so. B personally thereafter takes advantage of A's plan by using the ideas expressed orally and in writing and makes large profits for himself. A then brings an action for an accounting asking for a decree that he is entitled to a share of the profits so made by B. In a case with approximately these facts the court held that A had no action in equity as equity will not enforce an agreement to make an agreement, if such there was in this case. The plan, or idea, was not property —mere ideas are not capable of legal ownership and protection. A could, of course, recover his manuscript containing his plan.[3] And, had the action been brought on the law side for damages the result would have been the same as ideas, unless they are

2. Old Dominion Copper Mining & Smelting Co. v. Bigelow, 203 Mass. 159, 89 N.E. 193, at 201 (1909) discusses promoters: "In a comprehensive sense promoter includes those who undertake to form a corporation and to procure for it the rights, instrumentalities and capital by which it is to carry out the purposes set forth in its charter, and to establish it as fully able to do its business. Their work may begin long before the organization of the corporation, in seeking the opening for a venture and projecting a plan for its development, and it may continue after the incorporation by attracting the investment of capital in its securities and providing it with the commercial breath of life." See also Henderson v. Plymouth Oil Co., 15 Del. Ch. 40, 131 A. 165, at 170 (1925).

See Guthmann & Dougall, Corporate Financial Policy 180–192 (2d ed. 1948); ibid. 186–211 (3d ed. 1955); excerpt from same in Ballantine, Lattin and Jennings, Cases and Materials on Corporations 161–162 (2d ed. 1952). "A promoter is one who brings together the persons who become interested in the enterprise, aids in procuring subscriptions and sets in motion the machinery which leads to the formation of the corporation itself." See page 146, infra, for a definition of "promoter" under the federal Securities Act of 1933.

3. Haskins v. Ryan, 71 N.J.Eq. 575, 64 A. 436 (1906), aff'd without opinion 75 N.J.Eq. 623, 73 A. 1118 (1909). See Note, Recognition of Legal Rights in Ideas, 47 Harv.L. Rev. 1419, at 1424 (1934).

of the kind that can be copyrighted or patented, may be freely filched.[4]

As long as the ideas are in the realm of probable expectancy, with little certainty that the promoter will receive the anticipated benefits from his plan, the law has hesitated to give legal rights to him when he has exposed his plan to others who have breached the confidence placed in them. When there is a strong or reasonable probability that the promoter will be able to consummate his plan, there is no valid reason (except the difficulty of proof) why the law should not protect him against those who have gained his confidence and wilfully taken advantage of him. The theft of ideas, given in confidence, where there is a strong probability of consummation is arguably analogous to the sort of interference with contractual relations that justifies a remedy. In fact, strong probability of consummation is but one short step from contract. One might describe such interference as an unfair trade practice in the realm of corporate promotions, though there seems to be no such category in the business world. Furthermore, morality in promotion schemes has not been very high and this may, in some measure, account for the judicial skepticism displayed in the failure to protect ideas, especially when they have been exposed to probable participants for the very purpose of realizing their money-making value through promotion.

There is danger, then, in the initial planning of disclosing too much before a contract or some relationship is entered into between promoters. The practical thing for the promoter who has an idea or plan ready to submit in concrete finished form which cannot be protected by copyright or patent is to disclose a minimum and, before disclosing the essential parts of his idea or plan, to contract with his prospective promoter that the latter, for a stated consideration and the further consideration of the first promoter's promise to disclose, in detail, his written idea or plan, will neither disclose any part of the plan to others nor use any part of the plan personally, as a member of any business association including membership through the holding of shares in a corporation except upon further written agreement between the two.[5] The agreement should also provide

---

4. Prosser, Torts 753 (2d ed. 1955): "The copying or imitation of ideas, styles, designs, advertising layouts or schemes, and even the physical appearance of articles in trade, have been held, in the absence of any patent, copyright or deception as to the identity or source, to be privileged, apparently on the theory that the right to compete is the right to imitate, and there can be no monopoly as to such commercial methods."

5. See Bristol v. Equitable Life Assurance Soc., 132 N.Y. 264, at 267, 30 N.E. 506, 507 (1892); Logan, Legal Protection of Ideas, 4 Mo.L. Rev. 239, 253 et seq. (1939). Even where the contract agreeing not to

that, if the prospective promoter elects to aid in the promotion, he shall have the right to upon the terms stated by so indicating in writing.

Frequently a joint adventure or confidential relationship between promoters can be worked out and, in such a case, the law of partnership or of fiduciaries may be invoked. Since partners owe each other the duty of utmost good faith until the partnership is terminated or abandoned, if one partner takes advantage of the plan of promotion and bars the other from its fruits, the second may recover his share of the profits in accordance with the original agreement in an action for an accounting. And, of course, if one joint adventurer refuses to perform according to his contract, he will be liable in damages for any injury proximately attributable to the breach.[6]

§ 4. Preincorporation Contracts of Promoters

It is frequently desirable as a practical matter to obtain options, enter into contracts for the purchase of land, buildings, machinery and materials, and for the performance of services prior to the incorporation of the business unit for whose benefit such transactions are to be consummated. Since there is no principal in existence at the time contracts are entered into, an antiquated agency doctrine prevents the application of agency principles to these transactions.[7] The party dealing with the promoters may, and usually does know that the corporation is nonexistent, and the agreement may read "by and on behalf of the M Corporation, a corporation to be formed," and the promoters may sign in similar manner, yet the end result is usually interpreted to be a contract between the promoters and the other contracting party which, when "adopted" by the corporation after it has been formed makes it the contract of the corporation but does not, of itself, relieve the promoters of contractual liability.[8]

disclose or use has been entered into, courts have further required that the idea be new, novel and valuable. Note, Sales: Property in Ideas, 31 Cornell L.Q. 382, at 390–391 for practical suggestions (1946).

6. Brown v. Leach, 189 App.Div. 158, 178 N.Y.S. 319 (1919).

7. 2 Restatement, Agency § 326 (1933): "An agent purporting to make a contract with another for a principal whom both know to be nonexistent or wholly incompetent does not necessarily become a party to the purported contract; unless otherwise agreed, the agent is a party to such a contract." But "by manifesting consent," the purported principal becomes a party to the original transaction and 1 Restatement, Agency § 104 (1933), Comment b, calls this "adoption." See, for valid criticism of the rule, Note, Outmoded Concept Dominates Law of Promoters' Preincorporation Contracts, Stanford Intramural L.Rev. 119 (June, 1948).

8. The leading English case is Kelner v. Baxter, L.R. 2 C.P. 174 (1866), which required a "new contract" if the corporation was to be bound. And see Newborne v. Sen-

As was stated in a leading case, "When a party is acting for a proposed corporation, he cannot, of course, bind it by anything he does at the time, but he may (1) take on its behalf an offer from the other, which, being accepted after the formation of the company, becomes a contract; (2) make a contract at the time binding himself, with the stipulation or understanding that if a company is formed it will take his place and that then he shall be relieved of responsibility, or (3) bind himself personally without more, and look to the proposed company, when formed, for indemnity." [9] The contract in the case from which the quoted portion was taken was between the plaintiff and "D. J. Geary for a bridge company to be organized and incorporated." It was held to be Geary's personal contract and that he took the chances of the incorporation of the company and of its indemnifying him. The court, however, pointed to one element which, in itself perhaps justified the holding, namely, that "work was certainly to be begun and probably completed (and a large part paid for) before it was possible that this corporation should come into existence." [10]

There are good practical reasons why a corporation should not come into existence charged automatically with the contracts and other obligations incurred by its promoters on its behalf prior to its birth.[11] But when the other contracting party knows that the agreement is for the benefit of a corporation to be formed and the contract so states, and the corporation is later formed and adopts the contract, is there any valid reason why the promoters should also be held to liability after the adoption? From these facts alone it would seem to reasonable business men that a novation was intended by both contracting parties though

solid (Great Britain), Ltd., [1954] 1 Q.B. 45, 1 All E.R. 708 (1953). See also Abbott v. Hapgood, 150 Mass. 248, 22 N.E. 907, 5 L.R.A. 586, 15 Am.St.Rep. 193 (1889). But see King Features Syndicate v. Courrier, 241 Iowa 870, 43 N.W.2d 718, 41 A.L.R.2d 467, Ann. at 477 (1950); O'Rorke v. Geary, 207 Pa. 240, 56 A. 541 (1903); Margady v. Weissman, 74 N.Y.S.2d 280 (Sup.Ct.1947), aff'd without opinion, 272 App.Div. 412, 72 N.Y.S.2d 412 (1947), which require adoption only to bind the corporation, representing the usual rule in the United States.

9. O'Rorke v. Geary, 207 Pa. 240, 56 A. 541, at 542 (1903). Where notes had been signed by promoters in the name of the proposed corporation prior to incorporation and had been later adopted by the corpora-

tion and partial payments made by the corporation to the payee, it was held that, without a novation or release by the payee, the promoters could be held for the remainder of the debt. Wells v. J. A. Fay & Egan Co., 143 Ga. 732, 85 S.E. 873 (1915). See Ann. 41 A.L. R.2d 477 (1955), Personal liability of promoter to third person on or with respect to contract made for corporation or in aid of promotion.

10. O'Rorke v. Geary, supra, note 9, 56 A. at 542.

11. Preston v. Liverpool, Manchester, etc. Ry., [1856] 5 H.L.C. 605, at 618, 10 Eng.Rep. 1037, at 1043; Clifton v. Tomb, 21 F.2d 893, at 900 (4th Cir., 1927); Air Traffic & Service Corp. v. Fay, 196 F.2d 40, at 42 (D.C. Cir., 1952).

nothing was said about it.[12] But not to lawyers or judges. Most
courts have refused to recognize a novation without further indication that the parties intended that the promoter should not
be liable after the company had adopted his contract. Fortunately, some courts have searched for and found seemingly insignificant facts indicating an intent to deal on a novation basis.[13]
It is but a short step to recognizing a novation without additional facts which, under the circumstances, would seem to be
superfluous. And, it seems certain that before long some pro-
gressive court will recognize the possibility of an agency for a
nonexistent principal, under the above circumstances, and will
call the act of "adoption" by the corporation a "ratification"
with all of the incidents that follow from the usual ratification
case in agency.

It should be stated that there is a good deal of loose language in the cases to the effect that what makes the corporation
liable is its "ratification" of the contract made by the promoter
in its behalf. Under present concepts, the accurate term is
"adoption." A true ratification relates back to the time of the
agent's act while an adoption relates to the time when the corporation accepts the contract as its own.[14]

Some courts speak of the promoter's contract as one for the
benefit of a corporation to be formed and that the corporation
may sue as a third party beneficiary.[15] As in an agency-ratifica-
tion theory, the time of entering into the contract and the form
in which it appears (i.e., whether required to be in writing or

12. See 1 Williston & Thompson,
Contracts § 306 (Rev. ed. 1936); 2
Restatement, Agency, § 326, Comment a (1933). See also McEachin
v. Kingman, 64 Ga.App. 104, 12 S.
E.2d 212 (1940), where the result
was reached, but a dissenting
judge stuck to ancient doctrine
that the promoter was an agent
for a nonexistent principal and
hence was liable even though the
corporation adopted the contract.

13. See McEachin v. Kingman, supra, note 12; Strause v. Richmond,
etc., Co., 109 Va. 724, 65 S.E. 659,
132 Am.St.Rep. 937 (1909); Carle
v. Corhan, 127 Va. 223, 103 S.E.
699 (1920); E. H. Warren, The
Progress of the Law; Corporations, 34 Harv.L.Rev. 282, at 289–
291 (1921).

14. McArthur v. Times Printing Co.,
48 Minn. 319, 51 N.W. 216 (1892).
This will make a material differ-

ence when the statute of limitations or of frauds is in issue. The
promoter's written contract was
held to satisfy the statute of frauds
provision concerning contracts not
performable within one year where
the adoption theory was used in
Meyers v. Wells, 252 Wis. 352, 31
N.W.2d 512 (1948). But, in Mansfield v. Lang, 293 Mass. 386, 200
N.E. 110 (1936), which did not recognize the adoption theory, it was
held that the corporation, by properly authorized agent, after incorporation must sign a writing on its
behalf to meet the statute of frauds
provision. A true ratification theory would require no further writing by the corporation as the promoter's writing would suffice.

15. Eden v. Miller, 37 F.2d 8 (2d Cir.,
1930) in a dictum, noted in 44
Harv.L.Rev. 126 (1930); Belle Isle
Corp. v. MacBean, 30 Del.Ch. 373,
61 A.2d 699, at 709 (1948).

not) would relate back to the time when the contract was entered into by the promoter.

While a promoter may obtain an offer for the projected corporation, or may bind himself without an agreement of novation trusting for a corporate adoption which will be followed by complete performance, or may bind himself with a provision that, upon adoption by the corporation, the other contracting party will look solely to the corporation for performance, that is, an agreement of novation, he still has some choices not yet mentioned. He may secure an option for his company, or for himself but transferable to it, and be liable for no more than the price of the option. Or he may promise only that he will form a corporation and see to it that the contract is adopted by it.[16] It is probable that, as a practical matter, the promoter will want a binding contract with the outside contracting party and that the option or the binding contract with a provision for novation will better suit his needs than some of the remaining possibilities.

§ 5. Meaning of "Adoption" of Promoters' Contracts

The formal manner of adoption of promoters' contracts is by express assumption by the board of directors of such contracts. But frequently no formal action is evidenced. The corporation through its properly chosen officials may have accepted the benefits of a preincorporation contract with knowledge of its existence and the terms thereof and be held to have "adopted" it. It must be one, however, which such officials have authority to make.[17] But to be bound by the burdens of such contracts it must also appear that benefits were accepted with full knowledge of the essential facts.[18]

That a distinction should be made in the manner of adoption between contracts with outside parties and those by the promoter for his services in the promotion is arguable, for the promoter's interest in his own contract with brother-promoters is likely to be heavily weighted in his favor. Some cases have taken the view that there is no corporate liability to promoters for services or expenses in obtaining the charter, in securing subscriptions to the capital stock, and in otherwise perfecting the organization of the corporation, where these services have been rendered in expectation that they would be paid for, unless an express promise is made by the corporation after its organi-

---

16. See Elggren v. Snyder, 75 Utah 370, 285 P. 640 (1930).

17. McArthur v. Times Printing Co., 48 Minn. 319, 51 N.W. 216 (1892).

18. Morgan v. Bon Bon Co., 222 N.Y. 22, 118 N.E. 205 (1917); Gardiner v. Equitable Office Bldg. Corp., 273 F. 441 (2d Cir., 1921); Bryan v. Northwest Beverages, Inc., 69 N.D. 274, 285 N.W. 689, 123 A.L.R. 717 (1939).

zation, or unless the general law or a charter provision imposes the obligation.[19]   Other cases, with more reason, have raised an implied promise to pay by the acceptance of the benefits of such services and expenses.

There are certain expenses such as the attorney's fee for legal advice and for drawing up the articles or certificate of incorporation, franchise taxes, filing fees, etc., which are incurred prior to incorporation and which the corporation simply by its birth, ought, perhaps, to be charged with as if it had formally adopted the contracts made for it by the promoters.   Furthermore, by using its corporate powers with knowledge of the debts incurred in obtaining its existence has it not accepted the benefits conferred with notice of the burdens?   A leading case answered this in the negative, saying: "This is not a case in which the corporation can accept or refuse the benefits of a contract.   Under the instant record it had no choice.   Like a child at its birth it must be born in the manner provided.   There is no volition on its part."[20]   While user per se of its charter and by-laws did not constitute an adoption the evidence showed that, at a board meeting, one of the directors instructed the attorney to obtain a permit to sell the corporate shares so that the company might acquire funds with which to pay him, an instruction apparently accepted by all of the board members.   This, held the court, was an adoption and the corporation was bound to pay the plaintiff-attorney.   But was the court right in the first instance in holding that a *user* of corporate powers is not an adoption?   While the corporation is in no position to prevent its birth, its governing body is certainly in a position to say it will or will not use the powers given it; and a voluntary user with knowledge of the burdens attached thereto ought to be sufficient to constitute an adoption.

Some courts permit a quasi-contractual recovery for these necessary expenses.[21]   Professor Berle would hold the corpora-

19. See cases cited pro and con in Gardiner v. Equitable Office Bldg. Corp., supra, note 18 at 445. In Indianapolis Blue Print & Mfg. Co. v. Kennedy, 215 Ind. 409, 19 N.E.2d 554 (1939), it was argued by the corporation that an express promise was necessary to bind it, but the court held otherwise. See Ohio Rev.Code § 1701.29, which specifically authorizes corporations to pay their preincorporation expenses.

20. Kridelbaugh v. Aldrehn Theatres Co., 195 Iowa 147, 191 N.W. 803 (1923). In Weatherford, M. W. & N. W. R. Co. v. Granger, 86 Tex.

350, 24 S.W. 795, 40 Am.St.Rep. 837 (1894), the court distinguished between the contract itself, benefits (bonuses raised by promise that railroad would pass through named points) which the corporation had accepted resulting in the adoption of the contract, and the promise to pay a fee for obtaining the benefits so accepted, saying that the latter was not adopted by accepting the benefits. This is certainly a very dubious distinction which, apparently, has no support elsewhere.

21. Ramsey v. Brooke County Bldg. & Loan Ass'n, 102 W.Va. 119, 135

tion to contracts made for it by its promoters, including attorneys' fees for advice and for drawing up the articles on his "enterprise entity" theory, having regard for the fact that, during this early promotion period, the promoters "owe the highest duty and good faith in determining the amount of such liability since they are virtually dealing with themselves." [22] This makes sense as the promoter-corporation-to-be-formed situation is *sui generis* and needs a different treatment from that found in contract and agency law. At this late date it is probably too much to expect that courts, without the aid of legislation, will proceed on a different tack to obtain sailing on a smoother sea.

§ 6. Legislative Treatment of Preincorporation Contracts

Thus far there has been little legislation on the subject.[23] The Michigan statute reads: "No contract made by the incorporators for or on behalf of any corporation to be formed preliminary to the filing of the articles shall be deemed to be invalid or ineffectual because made prior to such filing, and all property held by such incorporators for the benefit of the proposed corporation shall be deemed to be the property of such corporation." [24] The Michigan court held that the statute abrogated the rule that promoters could not make contracts on behalf of, that is, as agents for a corporation to be formed and that, "upon organization of such corporation, by adoption" the contract became the exclusive one of the corporation and other contracting party. Under the Michigan statute, it would seem that the word "ratification" would be the proper one instead of "adoption" for the statute has changed the rule that an agent cannot represent a nonexistent principal so as to consummate a contract which the principal, now existing, may ratify.[25]

Another approach has been made under a Kansas statute which gives the corporation thirty days after the filing of an affidavit, in compliance with Section 15 which has reference to

S.E. 249, 49 A.L.R. 668 (1926). Ballantine, Corporations 112 (Rev.ed. 1946), says the better opinion is contra. But why so? The corporation is protected for recovery may be had only upon a reasonable value basis. The corporation has received benefits and should be required to pay for them.

22. Berle, The Theory of Enterprise Entity, 47 Col.L.Rev. 343, at 358 (1947).

23. See Isaacs, The Promoter: A Legislative Problem, 38 Harv.L. Rev. 887 (1925); Ehrich and Bunzl,

Promoters' Contracts, 38 Yale L.J. 1011 (1929).

24. Mich.Stat.Ann. § 21.8 (1937).

25. In re Montreuil's Estate, 291 Mich. 582, 289 N.W. 262 (1939). The court makes it clear that the agency rule has been changed, saying, "Plaintiff contends that there can be no agency in behalf of a nonexistent principal. This must be qualified by stating, unless sanctioned by law." See note on this case and on the statute, 38 Mich. L.Rev. 1266 (1940). See also Bil-Gel Co. v. Thoma, 345 Mich. 698, 77 N.W.2d 89 (1956).

corporate accomplishment of the conditions precedent to commencing business, in which to disaffirm or repudiate its preincorporation obligations. The statute actually includes more, for it specifically mentions obligations incurred *before* and *after* the organization of the corporation.[26] Thereafter, the "promoters, subscribers and incorporators" are released from all personal liability on such obligations contracted in the corporate name.

Nothing is said in the Michigan statute as to whether the promoter is liable if the anticipated corporation is not later formed or if the corporation when formed fails to ratify the contract. If pure agency doctrine is applied, the agent, if he has kept within the scope of his authority which, in this situation, would seem to be whether he has made a contract within the anticipated powers of the corporation, would not be liable. If, through his fault, the corporation was not formed or if, through his later influence with the board, it was not ratified, he should be held personally as under the common law prior to the statute. The Kansas statute seems clearly to say that promoter-liability is there, unless contracted away, until the passage of the stated time during which the corporation does not disaffirm. This is statutory novation by inaction.

§ 7. The Drafting Problem — Protecting the Promoter

The discussion in the last few sections indicates pretty clearly the difficulties in the law which the draftsman must overcome. These need not be repeated. Since binding agreements are generally preferable, the promoter's contract for his proposed corporation will bind him in all jurisdictions. But there should always be a provision for novation upon the adoption of the contract by the corporation. And it is desirable to provide for the contingency that, due to no fault of the promoter, the corporation acquires no existence; and the further contingency that, due to no fault of his, the corporation has failed to adopt the contract. Offers and options, if used, should cause no more trouble in their drafting than in other cases except that the draftsman should not forget that the corporation to be formed is the real party in interest.

26. Kan.Gen.Corp.Code § 2807 [Kan. Gen.Stat.Ann. § 17–2807], noted and criticised in 54 Harv.L.Rev. 154 (1940). Compare § 109(4) of the English Companies Act, 1948, reading: "Any contract made by a company before the date at which it is entitled to commence business shall be provisional only, and shall not be binding on the company until that date, and on that date it shall become binding." See Palmer's Company Law 243 (19th ed. 1949) explaining this section.

§ 8.   Preincorporation Subscriptions

To be sure that there will be a body of contributors to the capital of the corporation to be formed, it is often desirable to obtain subscriptions to its stock prior to its incorporation. Frequently, statutes provide that a certain amount of capital stock be subscribed before incorporation and some statutes require that subscriptions be made in the articles which must also be signed by these subscribers. On the other hand, some statutes say nothing about preincorporation subscriptions but provide for the opening of books of subscription by the incorporators after the filing of the articles or by the board of directors after they take office. Where specific methods of subscribing were set up in corporation statutes, early cases were rigid in interpreting them to mean that the statute set out the exclusive method—that another method would not be tolerated. Fortunately, modern authority has been more lenient and informal subscriptions are recognized though a statute may prescribe a formal method.[27]

Extreme informality in the manner of statement of subscription agreements has sent many cases to high courts for determination. If such subscriptions are to be of practical value to the promoters, the subscribers must be bound by them until the corporation has been formed and has had a chance to accept or repudiate them. By mutual promises between and among the several subscribers this desirable result can be obtained.

The usual type of subscription agreement which courts have been called upon to interpret reads something like this: "We, the undersigned, hereby subscribe for the number of shares set opposite our names of the $10 par value common stock in the X Hotel Company, a corporation to be organized under the laws of Y state with authorized capital stock of 100,000 shares of $10 par value common stock for the purpose of building and operating a hotel business in the city of Z, state of Y, and we promise to pay for each share its par value at the call of the Board of Directors."[28] This may be followed by the signatures of many

---

27. See Dodd and Baker's Cases and Materials on Corporations 693–694 (2d ed. 1951); Windsor Hotel Co. v. Schenk, 76 W.Va. 1, 84 S.E. 911 (1915), where the court stated: "Even in those states in which it has been held that a subscription can be made only in the statutory mode, the ground of the decisions is that the statute either expressly or impliedly prohibits a subscription in any other form. This view necessarily implies the validity of the subscription and the right to make such a contract, unless the statute denies it . . ."

28. See subscription agreements in Bryant's Pond Steam-Mill Co. v. Felt, 87 Me. 234, 32 A. 888, 33 L.R.A. 593, 47 Am.St.Rep. 323 (1895); Coleman Hotel Co. v. Crawford, 3 S.W.2d 1109, 61 A.L.R. 1459 (Tex. Com.App.1928); Windsor Hotel Co. v. Schenk, 76 W.Va. 1, 84 S.E. 911 (1915); Capps v. Hastings Prospecting Co., 40 Neb. 470, 58 N.W. 956 (1894).

subscribers who have had an opportunity to examine the names above their own; or, as is frequently the case, individual subscription blanks may be furnished the subscribers and they may or may not know who else has subscribed to the venture. In either case, many courts will interpret the subscription as an offer to subscribe to shares, which offer may be revoked by any subscriber at any time prior to the formation of the company *and* acceptance by it of the offer.[29] A few courts have interpreted an agreement with a double aspect, as where several persons agree to form a corporation and to subscribe to its shares, as a contract among the subscribers themselves *and* a continuing offer to the proposed corporation which, when accepted by the corporation, creates shareholders from subscribers.[30] And a few of these have held that the offer is irrevocable without the consent of all parties to the subscription agreement.[31]

Many subscription agreements are less formal and complete than the illustration in the preceding paragraph. And barring some statutory provision requiring a writing, oral subscription agreements are valid. If the agreement is merely an offer, the statute of frauds is not involved.[32] It is in no sense a contract of purchase or a sale of shares to be issued. "A subscription is different from a contract of purchase and sale, being a contract to issue or create new shares, as contrasted with an agreement for the transfer of title to shares already in existence." [33] However, those jurisdictions taking the view that the particular agreement is a contract between or among subscribers would be concerned with the contracts-not-to-be-performed-within-a-year provision of the statute of frauds. However, such agreements usually contemplate prompt action and it would be un-

---

29. Bryant's Pond Steam-Mill Co. v. Felt, supra, note 28, quoted portion at page 109 of the text, infra. As to the practical basis of the majority rule the court said: "And in view of the fact that such subscriptions are often obtained by overpersuasion, and upon sudden and hasty impulses, we are not prepared to say that the rule of law which allows such a revocation is not founded in wisdom." 32 A. at 890.

But the cases are unsatisfactory on the point of whether the subscriber may withdraw after corporate birth or, at least, after organization.

30. Minneapolis Threshing Co. v. Davis, 40 Minn. 110, 41 N.W. 1026, 3 L.R.A. 796, 12 Am.St.Rep. 701

(1889). And see Coleman Hotel Co. v. Crawford, 3 S.W.2d 1109, 61 A. L.R. 1459 (Tex.Com.App.1928) with notes in 7 Tex.L.Rev. 312 (1929); 27 Mich.L.Rev. 467 (1929).

31. Minneapolis Threshing Co. v. Davis, supra, note 30.

32. The statute of frauds provisions that might apply are those having reference to a sale of things or choses in action and to contracts not to be performed within a year.

33. Ballantine, Corporations 442 (Rev.ed. 1946); 2 Williston and Thompson, Contracts § 521 (Rev. ed. 1936); 12 Fletcher, Cyc. of Corporations § 5576 (Perm. ed. 1932). But a sale of shares comes within the statute of frauds provisions in the Uniform Sales Act § 4.

usual, indeed, to find a subscription agreement which is not to be performed within a year.

§ 9. Preincorporation Subscriptions—Time and Manner of Acceptance

There is a good deal of confusion in the manner of statement of when the subscriber becomes a shareholder and at what point it is too late for him to withdraw. If it is simply a matter of contract law the offer does not become binding as a contract until the corporation has accepted it, and it cannot accept it until it has been born and has officials with authority to accept. But it is more than a contractual problem. Businesswise it is advisable that a body of subscribers be bound to contribute to the corporate capital at the earliest point where such an intention to be bound can be spelled out. From the corporation's standpoint there is not the same reason for action on its part after it has come into existence that there is in the preincorporation contracts made on its behalf by promoters. Those who have subscribed hastily and inadvisedly have the opportunity to withdraw, barring a contract which binds them to their fellow subscribers and creates an irrevocable offer, prior to actual incorporation.

Take the disarming statement in a leading case [34] that "If the subscriber's promise to take and pay for shares remains unrevoked till the organization of the proposed corporation is effected and his promise has been accepted, then we have all the elements of a valid contract; . . ." What is meant by "till the organization . . . is effected?" And, further, does the word "accepted" need explanation? Until recently the Ohio statute provided that after the articles of incorporation had been filed the incorporators might open *books of subscription* for the purpose of acquiring a body of shareholders.[35] Nothing was said about preincorporation subscription agreements, nor is anything stated about these in the 1955 statute. The statute did provide, as does the 1955 one, for a later meeting of shareholders for the purpose of electing directors, drawing up by-laws (code of regulations) etc. Would the corporation have been organized for the purpose of accepting preincorporation subscriptions upon the filing of the articles under such a statute? Who would accept them, the incorporators? That would seem to be a reasonable conclusion. And if the corporation came into exist-

34. Bryant's Pond Steam-Mill Co. v. Felt, 87 Me. 234, 32 A. 888, at 889, 33 L.R.A. 593, 47 Am.St.Rep. 323 (1895). See also Collins v. Morgan Grain Co., 16 F.2d 253 (9th Cir. 1926).

35. Old Ohio Gen.Code §§ 8623–10 and 8623–11. New Ohio Rev. Code § 1701.09, enacted in 1955, provides that, after the filing of the articles, the incorporators shall receive subscriptions for shares.

ence with a board of directors which some statutes provide shall be set up in the articles or certificate of incorporation, would not the corporation be organized the moment it obtained its existence under the statute, whether or not the statute required some conditions precedent to doing business, that is, organized for the purpose of accepting subscriptions? That, too, would seem to make sense.

Then, what more is needed? If there has been a formal acceptance by the incorporators, in the first illustration, or by the directors, in the second, or by officials appointed by them for the purpose of accepting these offers, a formal acceptance would have been made. To create liability no notice of this acceptance need be given the subscriber under American law [36] though the English law is contra; [37] that is, the right to withdraw the offer is lost by acceptance, without notice, under the former law. And placing the names of the subscribers on the corporate books as shareholders, making a call for part payment or payment, or other act indicating corporate acceptance will suffice to foreclose a subscriber from later withdrawing his offer. He has now become a shareholder.

The exact point at which a subscriber becomes a shareholder is not so important, perhaps, as whether the subscriber may withdraw after the corporation has obtained its formal existence, whether "organized" or not. Pennsylvania seems to have handled the problem exceedingly well in light of the practical needs of this business unit. In *Berwick Hotel Co. v. Vaughn* [38] the rule was recognized that "If . . . (the subscriber) desired to withdraw his subscription and separate himself from the intended corporation, he certainly could do so by proper notice to that effect, provided he gave such notice previous to filing the application for charter." This rule gives weight to the business needs of the new corporation and is in no way disadvantageous to the subscribers. Professor Frey has contended that, even under the rule as stated, the rights of the corporation and of the shareholder should not be considered mutual—that is, the subscriber can no longer withdraw but the corporation should have a right to choose what subscribers should become

36. Dictum in Gillespie v. Comacho, 28 Hawaii 32 (1932); Richelieu Hotel Co. v. International Military Encampment Co., 140 Ill. 248, 29 N.E. 1044 (1892). Compare Hawley v. Upton, 102 U.S. 314, at 317, 26 L.Ed. 179, at 180 (1880), which involved a postincorporation subscription agreement.

37. Palmer's Company Law 89 (19th ed. 1949); Buckley, The Companies Acts 62 (12th ed. 1949).

38. 300 Pa. 389, 150 A. 613, 71 A.L.R. 1340 (1930). In Massachusetts, the right to withdraw seems to exist up to the time when the corporation has been formed and organized so that it may function as a legal unit for the purpose of accepting subscriptions. Dodd and Baker's Cases and Materials on Corporations 708 (2d ed. 1951).

shareholders to protect itself from irresponsible subscribers and from the possible overissue of its authorized stock.[39] Both of these matters can be taken care of by the subscription agreement, but, barring such an agreement, the suggestion has merit.

It has been pointed out that under the Pennsylvania rule, which is one of convenience, no corporate acceptance of preincorporation subscriptions is necessary as in other cases of contract involving offers. Though a deviation from usual contract principles, such principles do not serve well the particular function for which they have been employed. And when that is the case the analogies to agency and contract rules should be abandoned and new ones fashioned to fit the subject.[40] Recent statutes have taken over where the common law has failed.

§ 10.　Drafting of Preincorporation Subscription Agreements

The chief difficulty, as we have seen, is to make the preincorporation agreement binding until the corporation has been formed and organized to the point where it can accept or reject it. If the particular jurisdiction takes the view that the agreement is simply an offer which can be withdrawn at any time before corporate organization *or* before corporate organization *and* acceptance, it will be desirable to make the offer irrevocable if possible. English draftsmen have been able to do this by giving the promoter an irrevocable power of attorney by authorizing him to subscribe for shares in the name of the subscriber. Such agreements have been held irrevocable because of the creation of an agency coupled with an interest.[41]

In some states preincorporation subscription agreements have taken the form of a contract with a trustee for the projected corporation, the promises to pay being to the trustee. These, too, have been held to be irrevocable by the subscribers.[42]

39. Frey, Modern Development in the Law of Preincorporation Subscriptions, 79 U. of Pa.L.Rev. 1005, at 1019 (1931). And see Morris, Legal Effect of Preincorporation Stock Subscriptions, 34 W.Va.L.Q. 219 (1928).

40. Lukens, The Withdrawal and Acceptance of Preincorporation Subscriptions to Stock, 76 U. of Pa. L.Rev. 423, 428, 431 (1928); Schwenk, Preincorporation Subscriptions: The Offer Theory and —What is an Offer? 29 Va.L.Rev. 460 (1943).

41. Carmichael's Case, [1896] 2 Ch. 643, 16 Eng.Rul.Cas. 799 (C.A.) (the promoter was to be paid out of

money raised by the issue of shares); Pole's Case, [1920] 2 Ch. 341, aff'g [1920] 1 Ch. 582 (Authority was given by an underwriter to a syndicate of underwriters to apply for shares for him not taken by the public. Held: A power coupled with an interest and irrevocable).

42. West v. Crawford, 80 Cal. 19, 21 P. 1123 (1889) (court called the agent a "trustee of an express trust"—a trustee for the subscribers); San Joaquin Land & Water Co. v. West, 94 Cal. 399, 29 P. 785 (1892) (court used the term "agent" and not "trustee" but held that the money collected by him from the subscribers belonged to the corpo-

Since agencies coupled with an interest have been recognized in other areas of American law, there is no good reason for believing that they would not be accepted in this area.[43]

§ 11. Statutory Provisions Concerning Preincorporation Subscriptions

With the present confusion in this area, it is not surprising that statutes have begun to appear to simplify and make practical what the common law has failed to do. The recent Model Business Corporation Act [44] contains a provision that such subscriptions are irrevocable for six months, unless otherwise provided in the subscription agreement. However, if all subscribers consent to a revocation it is permitted.[45] The older Uniform (later known as "Model") Business Corporation Act of 1928 contains a provision making such subscriptions irrevocable for one year, unless otherwise provided in writing and, after that period it is revocable unless prior to revocation a certificate of incorporation has been issued as provided in another section. The filing of the articles creates shareholders from subscribers without further act.[46] The statutes of several states have similar or somewhat similar provisions, although they vary on matters such as the irrevocability of the subscriptions.[47]

ration); Horseshoe Pier Amusement Co. v. Sible, 157 Cal. 442, 108 P. 308 (1910); Drake Hotel Co. v. Crane, 210 Mo.App. 452, 240 S.W. 859 (1922).

43. Compare Electric Welding Co., Ltd. v. Prince, 195 Mass. 242, 81 N. E. 306 (1907). See Restatement, Agency § 138 (1933), on powers coupled with an interest.

44. Drafted by a committee of the American Bar Association, an early draft being published in 1946. A revision of this was published in 6 The Business Lawyer, 1 to 112 (November 1950) and this was known as the Model Business Corporation Act (Revised). It was revised again and published by the Committee on Continuing Legal Education of the American Law Institute and will be designated in this text as the A.L.I. Model Business Corporation Act (Rev.1953). See Garrett, History, Purpose and Summary of the Model Business Corporation Act, 6 The Business Lawyer 1 to 7, preceding the Act itself (November 1950). Some additional revisions and optional sections were printed in 1955.

45. A.L.I. Model Business Corporation Act § 16 (Rev.1953).

46. § 5, II, § 6, Model (formerly "Uniform") Business Corporation Act of 1928, 9 U.L.A. 64–66 (1951).

47. See 5 Idaho Code § 30–109 (1948); Ill.Smith-Hurd Ann.Stat. § 157.16; Baldwin's Ky.Stats.Ann. §§ 271.065 and 271.075 (1955); West's La.S.A.–Rev.Stat. § 12:6; 15 Mich.Stats.Ann. § 21.5, par. 2, § 21.8 (1937); Minn.Stat.Ann. § 301.17, subd. 2(1) (makes preincorporation subscriptions irrevocable for 60 days after issuance of certificate of incorporation and if not accepted within that period they are void); A recent (1955) Ohio statute is interesting. In Ohio Rev.Code § 1701.01(F), defining "shareholder," one whose name appears on the corporate books as an owner is a shareholder as are those who have subscribed to shares, whether the subscription was received by the incorporators or the directors, unless the articles, regulations or subscription contract provides otherwise.

§ 12. Revocation of Preincorporation Subscriptions—to Whom Made and How

If the subscriber's offer is not irrevocable he may withdraw it at any time prior to that event which either creates the status of shareholder or an event after which he can no longer withdraw. Withdrawals have usually been informally made, frequently by word of mouth and, if made to a proper party and clear in their intent to withdraw, will be valid.[48] In *Collins* v. *Morgan Grain Co., Inc.*,[49] the subscription was by telegram to one of the promoters and the withdrawal was oral and made to the same promoter. Said the court, "There was simply an offer, and it is always competent to prove by parol the revocation of an offer, whether the offer be written or oral."

While the withdrawal may be informal, to whom must it be made? The cases are few on this point and no flat rules have been laid down. What is reasonable under the circumstances is an elastic principle which gives much leeway for interpretation.[50] Notice of withdrawal given to the promoter or other authorized person who took the subscription, as long as he is exercising such authority, would be adequate as held in the *Collins* case. And if at a later point the statute designates incorporators or the board of directors who have been named in the articles as those who are to "organize" the corporation, notice to them prior to acceptance (if withdrawal is possible at this late date) would certainly be adequate.

§ 13. Liability of Subscriber for Subscription Price—Defenses to Liability

After shareholder status has been acquired through any of the methods discussed, the corporation has a cause of action upon the shareholder's contract to pay the price there set out. Shareholder status may be acquired without the issue of a certificate, according to the usual and better view, for the certificate is merely evidence of the ownership of shares. But the shareholder may have several defenses to such a suit. If the corporation is materially different from the one represented in the subscription agreement or there is a material change in its stock structure, the subscriber is not bound to pay for or accept membership in the corporation. It is not the corporation to whose

---

48. See Berwick Hotel Co. v. Vaughn, 300 Pa. 389, 150 A. 613, 71 A.L.R. 1340 (1930), where there may have been an attempted withdrawal but court said the notice thereof must be unequivocal.

49. 16 F.2d 253 (9th Cir.1927).
   Lattin Corporations F.P.Inc.—8

50. See Hudson Real Est. Co. v. Tower, 161 Mass. 10, 36 N.E. 680 (1894); Canyon Creek Elev. & Mill Co. v. Allison, 53 Mont. 604, 165 P. 756 (1917); Berwick Hotel Co. v. Vaughn, supra note 48.

shares he subscribed, but a different one.[51] While the agreement may not be overly specific as to corporate purposes, the provisions in the corporate articles or certificate must tend to accomplish those purposes.[52] Of course, if the provisions in the articles are merely statements of what would be considered as incidental to the purposes stated in the agreement, there is no violation of the agreement as the same provisions would have been read into the articles by a court posed with the problem of determining whether corporate purposes have been exceeded.

In case of preincorporation, but not of postincorporation, subscriptions, the subscriber is entitled to a de jure corporation if he is to be bound. This is considered a condition precedent impliedly imposed.[53] In either case, the life of the de facto corporation can be taken in a quo warranto proceeding, though the risk is negligible. The fact that, after incorporation, the prospective subscriber at least has the opportunity to discover whether his organization is de jure or de facto seems of little importance. Even lawyer-subscribers do not make such a search. But there is a larger chance that a corporation already in existence will have creditors who should be protected, whereas if a call is promptly made for payment of preincorporation subscriptions creditor risk may be slight. However, if the corporation has a de facto existence, the preincorporation subscriber should not have this defense if payment of his subscription is necessary to satisfy creditors.[54]

One important case has raised the question whether preincorporation subscribers have a right to share in the organiza-

51. Dean Stevens objects to this type of statement. He says: "It would be more accurate to say either that there is no contract because the acceptance is not in the terms of the offer, or that, though the offer has been accepted, the change which had been made makes it impossible for the corporation to perform." Stevens, Corporations 403–404 (2d ed. 1949).

52. Harlie R. Norris Co., Ltd. v. Lovett, 123 Cal.App. 640, 12 P.2d 141 (1932); Marysville Elect. Lt. & Pow. Co. v. Johnson, 109 Cal. 192, 41 P. 1016, 50 Am.St.Rep. 34 (1895). But see Coleman Hotel Co. v. Crawford, 3 S.W.2d 1109, 61 A.L.R. 1459 (Tex.Com.App.1928), where subscription agreement stated purposes to be to purchase a site, construct and own a modern fireproof hotel of not less than 50 rooms. Before articles were filed it was

decided to rent the hotel for a stipulated rental which the subscriber-defendant thought much too low. He contended that renting the hotel was a material change from the original plan. It was held that the subscriber was liable. See same case on retrial, Crawford v. Coleman Hotel Co., 16 S.W.2d 307 (Tex.Civ.App.1929) and notes in 7 Tex.L.Rev. 312 (1929); 27 Mich. L.Rev. 467 (1929).

53. Dorris v. Sweeney, 60 N.Y. 463 (1875) (also business included more than he had signed for); Capps v. Hastings Prospecting Co., 40 Neb. 470, 58 N.W. 956 (1894); Tonge v. Item Pub. Co., 244 Pa. 417, 91 A. 229 (1914).

54. Stevens, Corporations 401 (2d ed. 1949); see Frey, Modern Developments in the Law of Preincorporation Subscriptions, 79 U. of Pa.L.Rev. 1005 (1931).

tion of their company, that is, to participate in the election of the first board of directors (where these have not already been set up in the articles or certificate of incorporation), participate in the making of by-laws and share in other initial basic shareholder transactions. There were numerous subscribers but only five persons became incorporators, each having subscribed to one share of preferred stock, their subscriptions being in the articles of incorporation. These five waived the statutory notice to shareholders, met, organized the company, adopted by-laws and elected themselves directors. They then proceeded to adopt some very important resolutions involving the purchase of property for the company, payment for it in stock and bonds, the authorization to issue shares, to contract for the construction of a hotel upon the property purchased and to lease the corporate property to another prospective corporation. They also resolved to issue a large number of shares to themselves and others for services as promoters. When called upon to pay for his shares, the plaintiff refused, setting up, among other reasons, the fact that he had not been given the opportunity to participate in the organization of the company. The court held that the subscription was a conditional one—"that the law contemplates and guarantees participation by the stockholders in the organization of the corporation." Those holding a majority of shares "subscribed for in the certificate (of incorporation)" could accept, "on behalf of the corporation, the subscriptions made before issuance thereof." The shareholders thus created would then be entitled to participate in the organization of their corporation.[55] Here the court implied the condition and held that the subscriber need not pay for his shares. On its facts the case is inherently right for if the new corporation is to be started off by interested promoters holding a nominal amount of stock there is grave danger that they will be benefited at the expense of subscribers who have a substantial interest in the corporation. This is quite as bad as having saddled upon it the preincorporation contracts without acceptance by the corporation after it is organized.

55. Windsor Hotel Co. v. Schenk, 76 W.Va. 1, 84 S.E. 911 (1915), citing Baltimore City Pass. Ry. v. Hambleton, 77 Md. 341, 26 A. 279 (1893), and St. Paul, etc., Railroad Co. v. Robbins, 23 Minn. 439 (1877). Ballantine, Corporations 61 (Rev.ed. 1946), expresses the opinion that a more substantial ground of objection was the fraud of the promoters to the subscribers to whom was owed the fiduciary duty of good faith in the organization of the company. Compare Kenyon v. Holbrook Microfilming Service, Inc., 155 F.2d 913 (2d Cir.1946). Learned Hand, Cir. J., stated: "The context (of the Delaware statute) shows that what is meant is that the incorporators shall have charge of so much as is necessary to start the business going by getting in the money and electing the board." The Ohio statute spells out what the incorporators may do after the articles are filed. Ohio Rev.Code §§ 1701.09 and 1701.10.

Occasionally the problem of whether a preincorporation subscriber may defend a suit by the corporation upon his agreement on the ground that his subscription was obtained by misrepresentations made by the promoters or their agents, has arisen. If the corporation has received notice of the true facts prior to acceptance of the subscription the subscriber should have no difficulty in defending on this basis. But the agency difficulty which has continually confused the courts in this area is again troublesome here. Some courts, seeing that the facts of precorporate life are not so different from those following incorporation, at least with reference to subscriptions, have applied the same rules they have used in postincorporation subscriptions where these have been obtained by misrepresentations of corporate officers or agents.[56] Other courts have not been so realistic and have reached contrary results.[57] Under the former decisions the subscriber may usually rescind his subscription and recover what he has paid upon it. And, of course, the subscriber has a personal cause of action in deceit against the promoter who has made fraudulent misrepresentations or who has fraudulently concealed essential facts to procure the subscription, if he has been damaged thereby.

Another factor which may have a bearing on whether the preincorporation subscriber may rescind his subscription for fraud is the theory of some courts that such subscription agreements constitute irrevocable offers and contracts inter se to subscribe, sometimes spoken of as "trilateral agreements," notably in Pennsylvania.[58] While, under the Pennsylvania decisions, the subscriber's offer does not become irrevocable until the "filing (of) the application for charter," [59] if he remains silent until this deadline has been reached he not only may not withdraw but "he also enters into contractual relations with each other subscriber or shareholder in similar position" [60] this without further move on his part. This, as Professors Dodd and Baker have pointed out, "has been made a convenient means to deny rescission of a subscription for misrepresentation by the corporation or its agents or promoters, and to deny effect to special conditions or agreements affecting particular subscriptions." [61] Admitting the logical difficulties involved in holding otherwise, this seems

56. Rhoades v. Banking, Trust & Mfg. Co., 125 Va. 320, 99 S.E. 673 (1919); Stone v. Walker, 201 Ala. 130, 77 So. 554, L.R.A.1918C, 839 (1917).

57. Rapid Hook & Eye Co. v. De-Ruyter, 117 Mich. 547, 76 N.W. 76 (1898); Oldham v. Mt. Sterling Imp. Co., 103 Ky. 529, 45 S.W. 779 (1898).

58. See Dodd and Baker's Cases and Materials on Corporations 713 (2d ed. 1951).

59. See Berwick Hotel Co. v. Vaughn discussed at page 110, supra.

60. Dodd and Baker, supra, note 58, at 713.

61. Ibid. and cases cited in their footnote 9.

like a highly artificial way of deciding individual rights when fraud or mistake of this sort is involved. The only merit observable in such an approach is that the corporation blossoms forth with a body of shareholders under obligation to pay the subscription price if one undefrauded shareholder can be found who insists upon going ahead with the corporate business, or if all have been defrauded, if one defrauded subscriber can be found who so insists. Should one ignore the fact that subscribers act in reliance upon statements made by those who solicit subscriptions and that each subscriber relies upon the truthfulness of these statements and acts upon them in subscribing? Consequently, may it not be said that each subscriber consents to whatever relationship the court finds exists—whether an offer which may be revoked, one which may not be revoked without unanimous consent, or whether it results in a contract between and among subscribers—only upon the implied condition that no material misstatements have been made, whether innocently or fraudulently, to obtain his subscription? If such be the case, a court should have no logical difficulty, even, in permitting rescission. Whatever conditions have been set up to protect creditors will, of course, also have a bearing on the solution of this problem.

Under most modern corporation statutes there is no requirement that all of the originally authorized capital stock be subscribed and paid in before business may be started. If anything is said about this important matter it is in the form of a requirement that a minimum capital, but not less than $500 or $1,000— usually a rather nominal amount—be stated in the articles as the amount with which the corporation will commence business, with a prohibition against starting business before the amount so stated has been subscribed and paid in. Formerly, it was customary to require that all of the original authorized capital stock, or a certain percentage of it, be subscribed and paid in. And a subscriber had a good defense when sued upon his subscription agreement if the full amount required had not been in good faith subscribed. This was held to be an implied condition to the corporation's right to enforce payment. Since modern corporation statutes do not generally provide for more than a nominal amount of capital to be subscribed and/or paid in before starting business, there is no longer an implied condition that more than the minimum named in the articles or statute need be subscribed.[62] But the subscription agreement itself may provide

---

62. See Norton v. Lamb, 144 Kan. 665, 62 P.2d 1311 (1936). For older cases requiring that all or a stated proportion of capital stock must be subscribed, see Salem Mill Dam Corp. v. Ropes, 6 Pick. (23 Mass.) 23 (1827); Anvil Min. Co. v. Sherman, 74 Wis. 226, 42 N.W. 226, 4 L.R.A. 232 (1889); 4 Fletcher, Cyc. of Corporations §§ 1557 et seq. (Perm. ed. 1931).

as a condition precedent to subscriber liability that a named substantial amount shall be subscribed, otherwise the agreement shall be considered invalid.[63]

Any of the above possible defenses to liability upon his subscription agreement may be waived by the subscriber and, if waived, the corporation may recover the subscription price.

§ 14. Subscriptions upon Special Terms—Conditions Precedent and Subsequent

Conditional subscriptions are of two kinds, one based upon the performance of an act or the accomplishment of a result upon which the subscriber's liability depends; the other, by which he becomes liable as in other cases of absolute subscriptions but with special terms which, if breached, give him a cause of action for damages. The first is correctly called a subscription upon a condition precedent; the second, sometimes designated one upon a condition subsequent, is better described as a subscription upon special terms. The example given at the end of the last section whereby the subscription agreement was to be considered invalid if a designated amount of capital stock should not be subscribed is one of a true condition precedent. While the subscriber may waive such a condition, he may always defend by asserting and proving that the prescribed amount of capital stock has not been subscribed. Or the agreement may anticipate shareholder status immediately but without the right to vote or to receive dividends until full payment has been made for the shares. Payment, then, is a condition precedent to full shareholder status.

On the other hand, suppose one subscribes to shares in a corporation which promises to do something in the future such as building and running its railroad through County A, State B. May the subscriber refuse to pay the subscription price until the corporation actually builds and runs its railroad as promised or is he under a legal obligation to pay, and, if the promises are not kept, sue to enjoin or for damages? Such an agreement anticipates payment upon call (How else can the railroad be built?) and, if the agreement is broken by the corporation, the subscriber's redress is for damages or, if the intended violation is caught in time, an injunction may be proper.[64] Or suppose the agreement was that payment for the shares was to be out of dividends later declared by the corporation and the company at

63. In Coleman Hotel Co. v. Crawford, 3 S.W.2d 1109, 61 A.L.R. 1459 (Tex.Com.App.1928), a subscription agreement had a clause: "This subscription to be valid only upon condition of not less than $50,000 total solvent subscriptions being obtained."

64. McMillan v. Maysville & Lexington R. Co., 15 B.Mon. (54 Ky.) 218, 61 Am.Dec. 181 (1854).

no time has had a fund out of which dividends could be declared. May creditors be defeated by the subscriber's defending on the theory that this is a condition precedent to payment—any payment—for his shares? This, too, is a subscription on special terms and, while a solvent corporation could not enforce payment in any other way, the creditors could in a proper case.[65]

It is sometimes doubtful whether the agreement is one on special terms or upon conditions precedent. The policy of protecting creditors and other subscribers has led to construing such ambiguous agreements as subscriptions on special terms rather than upon conditions precedent.[66]

§ 15.   Special Terms for Special Subscribers

The preceding section has assumed without statement that whatever conditions were present were either available to all subscribers or, if not, were consented to by those to whom they were not available. It sometimes happens that collateral promises are made, either orally or in writing, which are not meant for the ears or eyes of subscribers generally but which purport to give substantial advantages to the "special" subscriber. His agreement may call for payment of his shares out of dividends only while the other subscribers have promised to pay cash. Or, perhaps, his agreement is to take 100 shares but the special promise to him is that if he later elects he may cut his subscription to 50 shares. Or his special agreement may be that if the old oak falls—or upon any other condition—he will not be liable on his subscription. Insofar as other subscribers do not know of the special terms given him, they are in a true sense being misled. They had a right to expect that all subscriptions were on the same footing or, if they were not, that they would be informed prior to subscribing so that they might subscribe with their eyes open. Such agreements are considered fraudulent and void and are not available as a defense when the corporation sues to enforce the subscription nor when creditors are involved, which is an even clearer case.[67]

But suppose, as a part of a subscription agreement, there is a promise that if the subscriber so elects the corporation will repurchase his shares at the same price he paid for them. This type of provision has frequently been recognized as valid if the corporation at time of payment has a fund out of which the purchase may legally be made even when the jurisdiction has adopted the rigid rule that a corporation has no power to re-

---

65. See Norton v. Lamb, 144 Kan. 665, 62 P.2d 1311 (1936).

66. See Ballantine, Corporations 458 (Rev. ed. 1946).

67. Norton v. Lamb, supra, note 65; Upton v. Trebilcock, 91 U.S. 45, 23 L.Ed. 203 (1875).

purchase its own shares.[68]   This is considered an exception.
And today when there is considerable statutory recognition of
the right of a corporation to purchase its own shares out of
surplus or at other times out of capital when creditors will not
be injured, the agreement would be perfectly valid.   Professor
Ballantine has felt that such agreements have "the same unfair
effects as an option to cancel or reduce or release a subscription,"
further stating that their recognition is of "very dubious policy." [69]   But the same danger is not present in this situation that
exists in the other special-terms-for-special-subscribers' agreements.   The subscriber is under obligation to pay for his shares
in the first instance, so the capital is there to be used by the corporation as in case of the contributions by other subscribers
who do not have the benefit of the agreement to repurchase.
Furthermore, unless the corporation is in position to repurchase
from funds set up by the statute or from those which the court
as a common law matter has ruled must be present the contract
is of no practical value to the shareholder who has it.   If there
are funds from which the purchase may legally be made, the
chances are slight that other shareholders will be injured though,
in those states where a repurchase may be made out of capital
provided creditors will not be injured, there is some danger of
injuring other shareholders.[70]   The informed subscriber will
know that this possibility exists and may be on his guard against
it.

§ 16.   Release, by Corporation, of Subscriber's Obligation to Pay for His Shares

Closely allied with the problem last discussed in the preceding section is the attempted release of a subscriber from his obligation to pay for his shares.   Instead of using assets of the company with which to buy in its shares the corporation releases a
subscriber and thus loses an asset which it has not yet acquired,
that is if the subscriber is solvent and able to pay for his shares.
The effect on existing creditors of the company is the same—
fewer assets to pay their debts.   But if the same protective device
is thrown around the release as exists in case of a purchase of its
own shares by a corporation, there would seem to be little objection unless it can be said that the other subscribers have a

---

68. Schulte v. Boulevard Gardens
Land Co., 164 Cal. 464, 129 P. 582,
44 L.R.A.,N.S., 156, Ann.Cas.1914B,
1013 (1913); Williams v. Mary-
land Glass Corp., 134 Md. 320, 106
A. 755 (1919); Grace Securities
Corp. v. Roberts, 158 Va. 792, 164
S.E. 700 (1932); In re Tichenor-
Grand Co., 203 F. 720 (D.N.Y.1913).

69. Ballantine, Corporations   459
(Rev. ed. 1946).

70. Notably Massachusetts and Wisconsin.   Dodd and Baker's Cases
and Materials on Corporations
1233 (2d ed. 1951).

right to the released subscriber's contribution unless they waive it. The same result could be reached circuitously by having the solvent shareholder pay for his shares and immediately having the corporation, by board action, repurchase for the same price. Assuming that the purchase was from a proper fund, the transaction would probably be considered valid.

But, as Professor Ballantine has shown, by a "quirk of the law" contracts of repurchase have not been as strictly limited as releases of subscriptions.[71] The corporate management may, in case the subscriber is unable to pay for his shares [72] or to effect a good faith compromise based upon a valid consideration[73] release the subscriber from his obligation; otherwise, the consent of all the shareholders is necessary and conditions must be such as will not result in fraud upon present or future creditors.[74] In fact, in one important case, it was argued that if no creditors existed at the time of cancellation, and all shareholders agreed to it, there could be no attack later upon its validity. But the court held that subsequent creditors and those who had previously dealt with the company had the right to rely upon the retention of the "working capital" at the amount named in the corporate articles, the publication of which amounted to a continuous "holding out to all the world . . . that the capital is paid or subscribed." [75] It seems like pretty high nonsense to assume that business men in giving credit rely that much upon the amount of capital stock set forth in articles or in balance sheets and, if they did, to conclude that they further assume that the figure will always remain the same until they are notified otherwise. They are much more interested in liquid assets and current liabilities, credit ratings and previous paying experience than in any statement of the company's capital stock. But throughout corporation law there is this assumption which ought to be reexamined wherever it appears. Such statements are usually tied to a pronouncement that unpaid subscriptions are a trust fund for the benefit of creditors, a doctrine which is discussed elsewhere in this book.[76]

71. Ballantine, Corporations 460 (Rev. ed. 1946).

72. Murphy v. Panton, 96 Wash. 637, 165 P. 1074 (1917), a dictum.

73. Ibid.

74. Ibid.

75. Ibid. The court used the term "working capital" as the amount named in its articles and not as the term is usually used today. Union Trust Co. v. Amery, 67 Wash. 1, 120 P. 539 (1912). But see Myers v. C. W. Toles & Co., 287 Mich. 340, 283 N.W. 603 (1939), where the release was by unanimous action and the corporation had a surplus equal to the amount of the released subscription. Creditors existed at the time of the release. The release was held valid. Said the court (283 N.W. at 613): "We fail to see where the cancellation of a subscription differs from a purchase by the corporation of shares of its own stock."

76. See pages 404; 414 et seq., infra, on the doctrine that capital stock constitutes a trust fund for the benefit of creditors.

§ 17. Postincorporation Subscriptions

Subscriptions sought by a corporation after it has been formed may constitute offers from the company to become shareholders [77] or solicitations of offers from subscribers to become shareholders.[78] In the first type the subscriber becomes a shareholder immediately; in the second, upon acceptance of his offer by the corporation. In either case there may be statutory or contractual limitations on full shareholder status prior to payment for his shares and present-day statutes tend to prohibit the issuing of the share certificate until the full price has been paid. But whether the company is making an offer or seeking one depends upon its intent.

Whether the corporation is seeking subscriptions to the originally authorized capital stock or to shares later authorized, there should be no confusion as to what is intended. But the manner in which the subscription agreement is phrased has at times caused courts to find an intent to make a contract of sale which does not become effective in creating shareholder status until title has passed to the subscriber. Whereas, in the case of a subscription which has been accepted, shareholder status arises upon acceptance and the shareholder is liable to pay for his shares upon proper call, the breach of a contract to purchase merely makes the "subscriber" liable for damages caused by the breach. When the corporation is insolvent or in bankruptcy and creditors cannot be satisfied except by enforcing payment of unpaid or partially paid subscriptions the distinction becomes vital. In case of the true subscription, the now shareholder is liable for what remains to be paid on the subscription price. This, in spite of the fact that his shares are perhaps worthless at this point. But if the agreement is interpreted as an executory contract to purchase shares, it has been held that since the corporation is not now in a position to perform its promise by issuing a valid certificate, the consideration has failed and the so-called purchaser is relieved from payment.[79]

The agreement that title to the stock shall not pass until a later time and that stockholder rights shall not commence until that time, which time is usually set as the date upon which full

---

77. Kennebec Housing Co. v. Barton, 123 Me. 293, 122 A. 852 (1923); Greer v. Chartiers Railway Co., 96 Pa. 391, 42 Am.Rep. 548 (1881).

78. L. E. Fosgate Co. v. Boston Market Terminal Co., 275 Mass. 99, 175 N.E. 88 (1931).

79. Stern v. Mayer, 166 Minn. 346, 207 N.W. 737, 46 A.L.R. 1167 (1926); Boroseptic Chem. Co. v.

Nelson, 53 S.D. 546, 221 N.W. 264 (1928), noted in 13 Minn.L.Rev. 257 (1929). The Minnesota Business Corporation Act § 16, XI (Minn. Stat.Ann. § 301.17, subd. 11, as amended in 1955) now provides that contracts for the purchase of shares from a corporation shall for all purposes have the same status as accepted subscriptions.

payment is completed, are the facts courts have emphasized as showing an intent not to create shareholder status presently.[80] What courts so holding have failed to sense is that the analogy to sales is a poor one for this area. Whether the agreement concerns the original issue or one later authorized it is for the purpose of creating a fund to be used in the corporate business in ways that may result in profit to all the contributors to it and which, translated into assets of various kinds including promises to pay for this eventual participation, may be relied upon by those doing business with the corporation and, whether or not relied upon, should go to pay corporate obligations. "As far as liability to or for the benefit of creditors is concerned, it should not make any material difference that one is a 'purchaser' on installments rather than a 'subscriber', or that he will not be entitled to exercise the full privileges of a shareholder until full payment." [81]

Good draftsmanship pointing toward shareholder status at the time the agreement is entered into, with the retention of some shareholder rights until full payment has been made, should make these contract-of-sale holdings impossible. While the holdings have not as a rule emphasized the use of the words "subscribe" or "subscription" or "sale" or "purchase" as being determinative of what the agreement actually is, if it is intended to be a subscription agreement terms of subscription, and not of sale, should be used. If it is intended to be a sale of treasury stock, for example, then let terms of sale and purchase be used with a clear indication of when title passes creating shareholder status. Retention of possession by the corporation of the certificate until full payment has been made should be included as a provision securing the corporation against nonpayment, with provisions for a sale of the shares so represented upon failure to comply with the terms of the agreement and for liability for any deficiency resulting therefrom. In fact, the local statute may contain a provision prohibiting the delivery of a share certificate until the full price has been paid with, perhaps, provisions for the forfeiture and sale of the shares upon breach of the agreement.

§ 18. Underwriting Agreements

At an earlier date the term "underwriting" was defined as "an agreement entered into before the shares are brought before the public, that in the event of the public not taking up

---

80. See cases in note 79, supra.

81. Ballantine, Lattin and Jennings, Cases and Materials on Corporations 189 (2d ed. 1953), and materials cited in footnote 6 of same. See also Reagan v. Midland Packing Co., 298 F. 500 (D.Iowa 1924).

the whole of them, or the number mentioned in the agreement, the underwriter will, for an agreed commission, take an allotment of such part of the shares as the public has not applied for." [82] Or, as a later case stated, "It is an agreement by the subscribers to insure the sale of the bonds at par, and if they are not sold to others then to purchase and pay for them at par. . . ." [83] But here, as well as in subscription agreements, draftsmen have sometimes used a terminology not justified in strict underwriting agreements or underwriting language in, perhaps, a subscription agreement which has led to expensive litigation to determine what was intended. For example, the term "underwriting" appeared in the title and in the body of an agreement which was otherwise a meticulously drafted subscription agreement with an agency to sell the shares subscribed under the conditions set out in the agreement. [84] It is quite as important that when the instrument is one intended to be for underwriting, that the language not be in terms of a subscription to shares, or of a lending. Such an agreement is neither one nor the other but a contract to take and pay for those securities which the public has failed to sign for. [85] Even though all of the underwritten securities are sold the underwriter's commission is earned as in case of analogous insurance contracts where the insured event never comes off.

The term "underwriter" has a much more expanded meaning under the federal Securities Act of 1933, § 2(11) [86] where the underwriter is defined as "any person who has purchased from an issuer with a view to, or offers or sells for an issuer in connection with, the distribution of any security, or participates or has a direct or indirect participation in any such undertaking, or participates or has a participation in the direct or indirect underwriting of any such undertaking; but such term shall not include a person whose interest is limited to a commission from an underwriter or dealer not in excess of the usual and customary distributors' or sellers' commission. . . . [T]he term issuer shall include, in addition to an issuer, any person directly or indirectly controlling or controlled by the issuer, or

82. In re Licensed Victuallers' Mutual Trading Ass'n, L.R. 42 Ch.Div. 1, at 6 (C.A.1889).

83. Busch v. Stromberg-Carlson Telephone Mfg. Co., 217 F. 328 (8th Cir. 1914).

84. Positype Corp. of America v. Flowers, 36 F.2d 617 (7th Cir. 1929), cert. denied 281 U.S. 762, 50 S.Ct. 461, 74 L.Ed. 1170 (1930).

85. In Busch v. Stromberg-Carlson Telephone Mfg. Co., supra note 83,

it was argued that an agreement to underwrite $100,000 principal amount of bonds upon a commission of 5% was, in legal effect, a loan. The court properly decided that it was an underwriting agreement. The underwriter was thus held liable though the company became insolvent and the bonds worthless after the underwriting contract had been entered into.

86. 15 U.S.C.A. § 77b(11), as amended in 1954.

any person under direct or indirect common control with the issuer." The term includes the "strict" underwriter discussed in the above paragraph unless he purchases for investment and not to distribute and the one who purchases an issue outright to sell to the public. It includes "underwriters of the underwriter" who agree to take over all or part of the underwriting risk assumed by the original underwriter.[87] Today the underwriter who purchases from the issuer an issue, taking the risk of distribution, is probably the more common type.

§ 19. Securities Acts ("Blue Sky" Laws), State and Federal, and Their Application to Subscriptions to Shares

Prior to 1911 in the United States there were few statutory regulations concerning the issue and sale of securities. In that year, Kansas enacted a fairly comprehensive statute [88] and it acquired the colorful name of "Blue Sky Law," a law which was aimed at protecting the public in the purchase of securities which had little behind them but the blue sky. The name has persisted. Today, with the exception of Alaska, Nevada and Delaware (since 1953), all states and the District of Columbia have statutes regulating the issue and sale of corporate and other securities.[89] Starting with the Securities Act of 1933, the federal government has enacted a series of statutes aimed at the regulation and sale of securities and of those who carry on the business of underwriting or selling securities, and for other rather closely allied purposes.[90] At this point we are concerned primarily with requirements relating to preincorporation subscriptions and those postincorporation subscriptions of the initial issue of shares, that is, those which are preincorporator or promoter instilled.[91]

The majority of state blue sky statutes today require a registration, either by qualification of specified issues or transactions, or by notification or description of other specified issues

87. Matter of Reiter-Foster Oil Corp., 6 S.E.C. 1028, 1035 (1940). Rule 142(a) [17 Code of Federal Regulations § 230. 142 (1949 ed.)]. General Rules and Regulations Under the Securities Act of 1933 is important in defining "participates" and "participation" as used in § 2(11) set out in the text above. On the topic generally, see Loss, Securities Regulation, 106–120 (1951).

88. Kan.Laws 1911, c. 133. For the historical background of the Blue Sky laws, see Loss and Cowett, Blue Sky Law 1–10 (1958).

89. See Loss, Securities Regulation (1951), Supp.1955, App.B, 407–408, where is listed all of the state "Blue Sky" legislation with citations to the sections in the statutes. This book is the most useful one yet to appear on this subject to the present time. And see Loss and Cowett, op. cit. supra note 88, 432–433.

90. The federal acts important here are the Securities Act of 1933, 15 U.S.C.A. § 77a et seq., and the Securities Exchange Act of 1934, 15 U.S.C.A. § 78a et seq.

91. Blue Sky legislation is exhaustively and critically treated by Loss and Cowett, Blue Sky Law (1958).

or transactions, frequently calling for broker-dealer registration as well.[92]   Unless the subscription is for an issue made exempt by the particular statute or comes within an exempted transaction such as that exempting the initial subscription or sale of voting shares when the total number of shareholders after such subscription or sale is not more than a stated number, these blue sky statutes are usually broad enough to cover publicly solicited preincorporation subscriptions as well as those which are sought after incorporation.   The local statute should be consulted before taking any subscriptions to ascertain whether statutory requirements must be met before taking them.   "About half the states exempt all stock subscriptions whenever no commissions were paid or expenses incurred prior to incorporation," [93] but that exception is likely to be rare.   Usually criminal sanctions and civil remedies are provided in case of violation of the compliance requirements.   If in doubt about the application of the statute or of the regulations promulgated by the securities commission of the state, the best practical advice is to consult the commissioner of securities before taking any subscriptions.

The federal Securities Act of 1933 must be complied with where subscriptions are to be taken before or after incorporation unless the subscriptions are within the area of exempted securities or of exempted transactions.   The exemption of "Any security which is a part of an issue offered and sold only to persons resident within a single State or Territory, where the issuer of such security is a person resident and doing business within or, if a corporation, incorporated by and doing business within, such State or Territory," [94] is important as is the provision which permits the Securities and Exchange Commission, by its rules and regulations, to exempt certain securities "if it finds that the enforcement of this sub-chapter with respect to such securities is not necessary in the public interest and for the protection of investors by reason of the small amount involved or the limited character of the public offering; but no issue of securities shall be exempted under this subsection where the aggregate amount at which such issue is offered to the public exceeds $300,000." [95] Another important exemption pertinent here is that of transactions of an issuer not involving any public offering.[96]

92. Ballantine, Lattin and Jennings, Cases and Materials on Corporations 677–678 (2d ed. 1953), part of "Note on Securities Acts ('Blue Sky Laws') State and Federal," 675–679.

93. Loss, Securities Regulation 43 (1951).

94. § 3(a) (11) of the Securities Act of 1933, 15 U.S.C.A. § 77c(a) 11, as amended in 1954.

95. § 3(b), ibid., 15 U.S.C.A. § 77c(b).

96. § 4(1), ibid., 15 U.S.C.A. § 77d (1) as amended in 1954.   The term "public offering" is explained in an opinion by general counsel in S.E.C. Release 285 (1935), 11 Fed.Reg. 10953 (1946).   The most recent important case on what constitutes a "public offering" is S. E. C. v. Ralston Purina Co., 346 U.S. 119, 73 S.Ct. 981, 97 L.Ed. 1494 (1953).

Where compliance with the federal act is necessary, a registration statement requiring full disclosure of material facts must be filed with the Commission and become effective and, in case of sale or offer of the securities for subscription or sale, a prospectus meeting the requirements of the statute must be prepared and used as required.[97] If the offering is to be made in several states, it will be necessary to comply with the statutes in these several states as well as with the federal act.[98] Some of the state acts have been amended to provide for a simplified registration when the corporation has complied with the federal act by perfecting its registration statement and providing the prospectus there required.

The important practical difference between the federal and most state securities legislation is that, if all the material facts are disclosed in the registration statement under the federal act, the Securities and Exchange Commission has no power to stop the issue; but under state acts the administrative body or official usually has the power to prevent the issue if it appears to be fraudulent or unfair to prospective shareholders. The full disclosure and the offer and sale through the use of a prospectus of like quality is supposed to open the eyes of the prospective subscriber and no paternalistic protection is deemed necessary thereafter. State legislation is paternalistic and offers somewhat more protection, when the administrative body is awake to its job, than does the federal approach. Furthermore, the state acts quite generally permit administrative protective action after the securities have been sold to the public.

§ 20. Promoters' Profits—Promoters' Frauds—the Old Dominion Copper Company Cases

The problems in this section revolve around the original issue of shares or an issue that is contemplated at the preincorporation stage to be made immediately, or almost so, after incorporation. Promoters are often greedy fellows, and if not greedy, overoptimistic as to the value of their contribution to the future world of shareholders supporting their venture. They are entitled to the fair value of their contribution to society based upon honest evaluations of what they contribute. The chief difficulties arose prior to the "invention" of no-par value

Comment on case in 21 U. of Chi. L.Rev. 113 (1953). See Notes in 52 Mich.L.Rev. 298 (1953); 48 Nw. U.L.Rev. 771 (1954); 3 Utah L.Rev. 519 (1953).

97. See §§ 5, 6, 7, 8, 10, Securities Act of 1933, 15 U.S.C.A. §§ 77e–77j as amended.

98. See Rohrlich, Some Current Thoughts on Corporate Capitalization, 1 Vand.L.Rev. 553 (1948); Smith, State "Blue-Sky" Laws and the Federal Securities Acts, 34 Mich.L.Rev. 1135 (1936).

shares when the dollar sign on par value shares meant that "meal or malt" must have been contributed to the extent of par value so that shareholders who paid the full par value would not have their shares diluted.[99] If courts had held—which they did not— that authorization to issue par value shares meant that it was illegal to issue them for less than par even with notice to and the agreement of the remaining body of shareholders, problems all along the line would have been simplified.[1] No statute has been found which directly authorized the issue of par value shares at less than par except under very special conditions set forth in the statute, which conditions justified such action. And such statutes are rare indeed. In fact, the common law looked with a jaundiced eye upon issues at less than par where creditors were concerned and placed definite restrictions upon such issues.[2]

In the *Old Dominion Copper Company cases,* Bigelow and Lewisohn, two reputable promoters, became owners of mining properties with the purpose of organizing a corporation under the laws of New Jersey to develop them. While they and their syndicate were the only persons interested in the corporation they sold to it for 130,000 shares of $25 par value, a total of $3,250,000, properties which had cost them approximately $1,-000,000 and which were perhaps worth in the neighborhood of $2,000,000 in the market.[3] As part of their original plan they intended to sell the additional 20,000 shares, and did sell them, or rather their corporation sold them, to subscribers who had no notice of the profit taken by the promoters and their syndicate, at their par value of $25 or a total of $500,000. An independent

---

99. No-par value shares were first authorized in 1912 by a New York statute. Laws of N.Y., 1912, c. 351.

1. See Scully v. Automobile Finance Co., 12 Del.Ch. 114, 109 A. 49 (1920); Note, 39 Harv.L.Rev. 757 (1926). Handley v. Stutz, 139 U.S. 417, 11 S.Ct. 530, 35 L.Ed. 227 (1891), sustained a sale of par value stock at less than par by "an active corporation . . ., a 'going concern,' finding its original capital impaired by loss or misfortune, . . . for the purpose of recuperating itself and providing new conditions for the successful prosecution of its business . ." "To say that a corporation may not, under the circumstances above indicated, put its stock on the market, and sell it to the highest bidder, is practically to declare that a corporation can never increase its capital by a sale of shares, if the original stock has fallen below

par." And see Harman v. Himes, 64 App.D.C. 252, 77 F.2d 375 (D.C Cir. 1935), where an unsuccessful attempt was made to come within the limitations of Handley v. Stutz. The English practice does not permit shares to be sold for less than par. Buckley on the Companies Acts 141–142 (12th ed. 1949); Gower, Modern Company Law 104 (1954). Permission may be obtained from the court under § 57 of the Companies Act of 1948, but this is so difficult and cumbersome that the section is rarely used.

2. See Handley v. Stutz and Harman v. Himes, supra note 1. See later discussion of this problem at page 412 et seq., infra.

3. A market value "largely due to the skilful manipulation" of Bigelow and Lewisohn. Old Dominion Copper Mining & Smelting Co. v. Bigelow, 203 Mass. 159, 89 N.E. 193, 40 L.R.A.,N.S., 314 (1909).

board of directors had not passed upon the initial transaction of these promoters. The balance sheet in practically all of promoters' profit cases would show the properties at their inflated value. But if such properties are honestly reported on the corporate balance sheet at cost ($1,000,000) or at their instrinsic value ($1,000,000 or approximately that) it is evident that there was an immediate dilution of the innocent shareholders' shares of $15 per share so that the actual value of each share would be $10. If the market value ($2,000,000) were set up as an asset, the dilution per share would be $8.33 and its value would be $16.67. In both cases the innocent shareholder is making a gift of considerable size to the promoters and the corporation is being deprived of the capital to which it is entitled to develop its properties for the benefit of the whole shareholder group. However, at the time the profit was taken and the additional shares issued to innocent shareholders the stock on the market was at par or better and remained so for a long time thereafter.

Several years later the evil day arrived. The corporation was insolvent and it was discovered then that the promoters had taken a large profit and somewhere along the way had unloaded their stock on the public. Bigelow was still in Massachusetts where the local courts could get service upon him. But Lewisohn was then dead, having died while a citizen of New York, and his estate was in New York. The *Bigelow* case went to the Massachusetts courts and the *Lewisohn* one to the federal court on diversity of citizenship grounds. The corporation appeared as party-plaintiff in both suits and originally similar remedies seem to have been sought—rescission of the sale of the mining property and a return of the shares given in purchase thereof (which was impossible for neither held shares at this time) or, in the alternative, to recover the secret profits made by the promoters.[4]

In the *Bigelow* case the Massachusetts court held that promoters owe a fiduciary duty to the corporation promoted not to take a secret profit from it and, if they do, they must disgorge at the suit of their corporation. This fiduciary duty extended not

---

4. Old Dominion Copper Mining & Smelting Co. v. Bigelow, 188 Mass. 315, 74 N.E. 653, 108 Am.St.Rep. 479 (1905). Defendant had demurred to the petition which seems to have been in the alternative for rescission or for an accounting of the shares disposed of. The court found no necessity to say what remedies were available. The demurrer was overruled. In the trial of the case, the remedy sought was to recover secret profits made by Bigelow and Lewisohn in a sale of properties to their corporation. Id. v. Id., 203 Mass. 159, 89 N.E. 193, 40 L.R.A.,N.S., 314 (1909). In the United States Supreme Court, the action was stated as one in equity to rescind the sale of mining rights and property, or in the alternative, to recover "damages" for the sale, that is, breach of trust. Old Dominion Copper Mining & Smelting Co. v. Lewisohn, 210 U.S. 206, 28 S.Ct. 634, 52 L.Ed. 1025 (1908).

only to the shell of their creation but continued "until the promoter has completely established according to his plan the being which he has undertaken to create," [5] which in this case meant that the innocent subscribers to the 20,000 shares constituted a part of the company to which the promoters owed this fiduciary duty. Recovery of the total secret profits made by the two promoters—joint trustees had breached their trust—was allowed though a large part of the recovery would benefit the holders of guilty shares as well as those holding innocent shares. As an important *dictum* the court stated that if at the time a company is brought out the promoters intend to remain its sole owners and not seek contributions from innocent shareholders in the future, but later company exigencies require that additional stock be issued, the promoters may not be liable, though they make no disclosure of their profits previously taken.[6] Presumably by this time the water in the stock has been absorbed by earnings or its market price has reflected its actual value. In either case, the new shareholder may deal with his eyes open. But there is danger in this situation, as in the one in *Bigelow,* and courts should scrutinize carefully each case for indications that, perhaps, would warrant the carrying of the fiduciary obligation thus far in an appropriate case.

"Fundamentally," stated Rugg, J., in *Bigelow,* "the action is to recover profits obtained by a breach of trust." If the promoter is a fiduciary in the strict sense he should be required to disgorge the difference between the total par value (or market value if established) he took in stock and the *cost* of the property given as consideration for the stock. But, in the *Bigelow* case, the market value of $2,000,000 was allowed to be set off against the market value of shares taken by the promoters. Judge Rugg speaks of "the wholly unwarranted profit of $1,250,000 kept secret from other initial shareholders." If the $1,000,000 purchase price had been used the profit would have been $2,250,000, which is quite a difference.[7]

Some courts have distinguished between the purchase by one who, at the time of purchase, has no intent of promoting a corpo-

---

5. Old Dominion Copper Mining & Smelting Co. v. Bigelow, 203 Mass. 159, 89 N.E. 193, at 206, 40 L.R.A., N.S., 314 (1909).

6. In re British Seamless Paper Box Co., 17 Ch.Div. 467 (C.A.1881) so held. And see Jeffs v. Utah Power & Light Co., 136 Me. 454, 12 A.2d 592 (1940).

7. The actual recovery is set forth in Hyams v. Old Dominion Mining & Smelting Co., 82 N.J.Eq. 507,

at 509, 89 A. 37, at 38 (1913). See Note, Measure of Recovery Against a Promoter Who Sells Property to a Corporation in Breach of Fiduciary Duty, 7 U. of Chi.L.Rev. 534, at 538 and 544 (1940); Weston, Promoters' Liability: Old Dominion v. Bigelow, 30 Harv.L.Rev. 39, at 41 (1916). As to the liability of strict trustees, see 3 Bogert, Trusts and Trustees § 489 (1935).

ration and selling the property to it and the purchase by a promoter with the intent of organizing a corporation and selling the property to it at a profit. In the first situation, it is held that there is no duty to disclose the purchase price but only that the now promoter is the seller; he was not in a fiduciary relation to any corporation at the time of his purchase.[8] If he fails to disclose, recovery will be based upon the fair value of the property rather than its purchase price. And if par value shares have been taken the recovery will be the difference between the total par value (or market value if established) of the shares taken by him and the fair value of the property. In the second situation, the promoter is held to be a fiduciary from the start and, according to some cases, he must disclose the purchase price; otherwise, he may be required to disgorge the difference between the total par value (or market value if established) of shares taken and the cost to him of the property transferred for the shares.[9]

The Massachusetts court suggested four ways by which a promoter could take a profit and not be held accountable for it at a later time:

(a) By providing an independent board not directly or indirectly under the promoter's control and making a full disclosure to them;

(b) By making a full disclosure of all material facts to all of the original subscribers in the corporation;

(c) By procuring a ratification of his contract after disclosing its circumstances by obtaining the vote

8. Densmore Oil Co. v. Densmore, 64 Pa.St. 43 (1870); Henderson v. Plymouth Oil Co., 15 Del.Ch. 231, 136 A. 140 (1926), aff'd 16 Del.Ch. 347, 141 A. 197 (1928); same case 15 Del.Ch. 40, 131 A. 165 (1925); same case, 19 F.2d 97 (3d Cir. 1927). And see Old Dominion Copper Mining & Smelting Co. v. Bigelow, supra, note 5, 89 N.E. at 212.

9. Gluckstein v. Barnes, [1900] App. Cas. 240 (H.L.) (there was also misrepresentation involved); Pietsch v. Milbrath, 123 Wis. 647, 101 N.W. 388, 102 N.W. 342, 68 L.R.A. 945, 107 Am.St.Rep. 1017 (1905). In an interesting note in 7 U. of Chi.L. Rev. 534, at 538 (1940), it is stated that "The traditional treatment of this question by the courts in terms of whether the property was acquired by the promoter before or after he became a fiduciary of the company has been found inadequate. Certainly, there would seem to be no reason for so distinguishing the amount of disclosure which the promoter must make in resale. If the policy for requiring disclosure is to be realized, the remedy which the company is given should be sufficiently rigorous to compel the desired disclosure. A prophylactic rule would require the promoter to disgorge all secret benefits arising from the transaction. Should courts hesitate to apply so complete a sanction, then the right of the promoter to retain any secret profit from property sold to the corporation should depend upon whether he has borne sufficient risks in the ownership of the property to entitle him to compensation therefor, such compensation to be made in terms of any increase in its value during his ownership."

of the shareholders of the completely established corporation; or

(d) By subscribing personally to all of the shares
of stock contemplated as a part of the promotion
scheme.[10]

We shall want to discuss at some length the fourth method suggested by the court but before doing so we should examine the
Lewisohn holding.

The *Lewisohn* case was handled in a quite different manner
by Mr. Justice Holmes who wrote the opinion. Where those who
presently hold all of the outstanding stock have consented to the
profit with full knowledge of the facts, neither they nor their
corporation may object later. The fact that new shareholders are
to be brought in under the plan and are brought in later without
notice cannot matter. " . . . [T]he plaintiff cannot recover
without departing from the fundamental conception embodied in
the law that created it,—the conception that a corporation remains unchanged and unaffected in its identity by changes in its
members." The legislature may make this change but not the
judges. Furthermore, wrote Holmes, if we looked through fiction
to facts, substantial justice would not be accomplished "if the
corporation were allowed to disregard its previous assent in order to charge a single member with the whole results to which
$13/15$ of its stock were parties, for the benefit of the guilty, if
there was guilt in anyone, and the innocent alike." [11] The court
specifically refused to discuss whether the $2/15$ of innocent shareholders, or their assigns, had any personal claim against the promoters.

It should be mentioned that the New Jersey statute under
which *Old Dominion* got its life provided that stock issued for
property should be issued only "to the amount of the value" of
the property so purchased.[12] In the face of such a statute, it is
surprising that courts would permit a watering of corporate
stock even if all agreed to it and creditors were not injured. The
statute would have justified a holding that the legislature has determined as a matter of policy that, if the corporate privilege is

---

10. Old Dominion Copper Mining &
Smelting Co. v. Bigelow, 203 Mass.
159, 89 N.E. 193, at 202, 40 L.R.A.,
N.S., 314 (1909).

11. Old Dominion Copper Mining &
Smelting Co. v. Lewisohn, 210 U.S.
206, at 216, 28 S.Ct. 634, at 637, 52
L.Ed. 1025, at 1031 (1909).

12. N.J.Pub.Laws 1889, p. 414, § 4;
ibid. 1893, p. 444, § 2, cited in Old
Dominion, etc., Co. v. Bigelow, 203
Mass. 159, 89 N.E. 193, at 198, 40

L.R.A.,N.S., 314 (1909). At time
corporation promised to pay promoter $30,000 in shares for his se-
cret process, it was thought to be
good; the process turned out to be
valueless. In a suit to compel the
issue, it was held that a worthless
process was not "property" and
corporation was not bound to issue.
Trotta v. Metalmold Corp., 139
Conn. 668, 96 A.2d 798, 37 A.L.R.2d
906 (1953).

used, its terms must be complied with; and that no agreement among the owners could defeat this legislative policy. But both courts assumed that if the promoters went through the proper ritual watered stock could be floated, at least insofar as the corporation's owners were concerned. And this was the normal conception, one which has bred some pretty unsatisfactory law, so unsatisfactory that one author has concluded that "For generations judicial remedies for promoters' frauds and the recovery of secret profits have stood as a monument to judicial ineptitude." [13]

We have seen that the watered stock taken by the promoters is increased in value by the cash contribution of the par value made by each innocent subscriber and that his share is immediately diluted. Then, why is not the cause of action his rather than the corporation's? How has the corporation been injured so that it may, under the *Bigelow* holding, sue for its own benefit? Is it because the contemplated capital contribution of par from each shareholder, unless the corporation unshackled agrees to less, has not been received and that the corporation has been crippled by its shortage of capital? Or is it because each original shareholder, unless otherwise notified before he subscribes, has the right to insist that par value be paid in cash, property or services, these last at their actual or reasonable value? If it is the shareholder's cause of action, he should be bringing the suit and if he collects the difference between the actual value of his diluted share and the par value thereof (or market value if it has one), are not his damages taken care of? [14] Guilty shares would not be entitled to anything and Justice Holmes' practical difficulty would be solved. When the corporation sues to recover secret profits is it perhaps upon the theory that, upon recovery, the corporation will then be the one in which the innocent shareholders had intended to subscribe and the one which, with the additional capital gives the corporation a reasonable chance to succeed? There is no doubt that the innocent subscribers had a right to expect that there would be in assets $3,750,000 worth, less the expense of organizing, this capital to be devoted to the business. Actually, they found themselves in a corporation which had either $1,500,000 or $2,500,000 worth of assets with par value stock outstanding in the amount of $3,750,000. The promoters, by milking their corporation, had not given it a chance to sell its shares to the best advantage and, if the chance had been given,

13. Reuschlein, Federalization—Design for Corporate Reform in a National Economy, 91 U. of Pa.L. Rev. 91, at 108 (1942).

14. The proper measure of shares of stock taken by a promoter is the market value at the time of taking, and not the par value. Ballantine, Corporations 829 (Rev. ed. 1946).

the avid enthusiasm of the public in this case would no doubt have encouraged the purchase of the same shares at par.

The cases, for the most part, have assumed that the cause of action belongs to the corporation basing their reasoning upon the fiduciary obligation owed by the promoter to the corporation, rather than to the individual shareholder, and the "corporation," under the *Bigelow* holding which represents the better and majority view is "the completely established corporation," that is, "completely established according to his (the promoter's) plan the beginning of which he has undertaken to create." There is no disagreement between the Supreme Court's and Massachusetts' concept that the promoter owes a fiduciary obligation to the corporation but only as to what constitutes the corporation to which the duty is owing.[15]

Thus far we have spoken of secret profits taken in par value shares of the company's stock. The issues are the same when profits in cash or property are secretly taken by the promoter under circumstances similar to those already discussed. If this were not so all the promoter would have to do would be to obtain subscriptions and payment thereon while the corporation was still in his control, take his secret profit and then turn the company over to its legitimate owners. His fiduciary obligations are obviously as clear here as in the *Bigelow* situation. But the fourth method by which he may take a profit, and a secret one at that, with all the earmarks of a fraudulent deal is that suggested by the Massachusetts court and agreed to by the Supreme Court of the United States, namely, by taking all the stock himself and selling it to the public.

§ 21. Promoters' Profits—Where Promoter takes all Shares Contemplated as a Part of the Promotion Scheme

Both the United States Supreme Court in *Lewisohn* and the Massachusetts Supreme Judicial Court in *Bigelow* recognized this method as being a safe one as far as corporate attack was concerned. The promoter takes all of the shares to be issued and

---

15. In Davis v. Las Ovas Company, Inc., 227 U.S. 80, 33 S.Ct. 197, 57 L.Ed. 426 (1912), not all of the promoters knew of the profit being taken by other promoters. The corporation was allowed to recover the secret profits. "The standing of the corporation results from the fact that there were innocent and deceived members of the corporation when the property was taken over by it." 33 S.Ct. at 199. That a recovery would enure to the guilty as well as to the innocent shareholders did not disturb the court. English authority is in accord. New Sombrero Phosphate Co. v. Erlanger, 5 Ch.Div. 73 (C.A. 1877), aff'd 3 App.Cas. 1218 (House of Lords 1878). An Arizona decision held that a single innocent shareholder, although he may in the meantime have sold his shares, satisfies the requirements of a corporate cause of action. Hughes v. Cadena DeCobre Mining Co., 13 Ariz. 52, 108 P. 231 (1910).

himself sells them to the public. The same inflated value due to the overvaluation of property or services is there but the promoter, as between himself and his corporation, may take as many shares as he likes and is free from corporate attack even on behalf of his transferees whose stock is as thoroughly depreciated by this method as in the Bigelow state of facts. As in the case where the original plan calls for additional shares to be issued by the corporation to the public, this plan of the promoter anticipates the unloading of his shares on uninformed purchasers from him and the innocent purchaser should have a remedy similar to the one in *Bigelow*. The difference between the two factual situations and the legal results were later explained by the Massachusetts court in what is perhaps the leading case on the point, as follows: [16]

"When one as an original subscriber buys stock directly from a corporation in conformity to the plan for its promotion, the parties to the transaction are the subscriber and the corporation. The subscriber has the right to assume that the corporation has been honestly organized. There is something akin to an implied representation on the part of the corporation that there has been no breach of duty toward it on the part of its promoters. The invitation to the public to become original subscribers to stock as a part of the scheme of promotion imports a representation by promoters that the corporation has been honestly organized without violation of their fiduciary duty to it. The scheme of promotion contemplates an assumption of this nature by original subscribers because there is a general presumption in favor of honesty . . .   Therefore, when there has been a breach of that duty, equity affords to such original subscriber a right to enforce a remedy for the wrong done to the corporation resulting in harm to him by reason of his relation to it as an original subscriber. Where one is not an original subscriber to stock but purchases shares from a broker or other vendor of stock, the corporation is not a party to the transaction. If any wrong is committed on the buyer, it is by the seller, not by the corporation. The buyer, under those circumstances, is not in a position to enforce rights of the corporation. Such a case bears some analogy to the rule that, where the act of an intelligent and responsible human being intervenes between an original cause and a result-

16. Hays v. The Georgian, Inc., 280 Mass. 10, 181 N.E. 765, at 770, 85 A.L.R. 1251, Ann. at 1262 (1932), noted in 47 Harv.L.Rev. 1031 (1934); 19 Va.L.Rev. 274 (1933); Ball v. Breed, Elliott & Harrison, 294 F. 227 (2d Cir. 1923), cert. denied 264 U.S. 584, 44 S.Ct. 333, 68 L.Ed. 861 (1924). "The law unquestionably is that the corpora-tion cannot for the benefit of its shareholders recover promoters' secret profits if all of the capital stock passed through the hands of the promoters to the public." Thaxter, J., in Jeffs v. Utah Power & Light Co., 136 Me. 454, 12 A.2d 592 (1940), noted in 54 Harv.L.Rev. 139 (1940); 19 Texas L.Rev. 198 (1941).

ing damage, the law will not look beyond the cause most recently operative."

The question immediately arises as to whether the promoter when he himself sells or sells through a broker is under any duty to disclose to his purchaser that these shares are part of an issue which he took in payment for property or services at an inflated value. And there seems to be no answer except in noncommittal dicta in case law.

Why should the court in the analysis above have any doubt that a wrong exists as to both the corporation and the buyer? The corporation has lost its opportunity to sell to best advantage its shares [17] and the buyer from the promoter has received a share which he had a right to assume had brought into the corporate treasury its par value for whatever consideration the statute permits shares to be issued. And has not the buyer the right also to assume that if the promoter or his agent disposes of his shares as part of the promotion plan that a disclosure of any profit unknown to the buyer will be made to him before purchase? This is no ordinary sale where the seller is under no obligation to tell his buyer what he paid for the thing sold. Would not a court be justified in holding that the promoter (or his agent for sale) impliedly represents that there has been no breach of fiduciary duty on his part toward his corporation or toward those to be brought in by a sale of his own shares under the promotion plan? What the Massachusetts court failed to see was that the facts which were the basis for its dictum (and its later case) were right in line with those of its direct holding, namely, that the full blown corporation planned by the promoters was not that in which the promoters were sole shareholders but the later one in which some or all of the shareholders were uninformed ones. It was the same trap that Mr. Justice Holmes fell into in *Lewisohn* by placing more emphasis upon the corporate form than convenience demands. As Professor Ballantine has stated so well the promoter "has had the aid of ingenious lawyers who have been more than a match for the lawyers on the bench whose duty it was to regulate him." [18]

Promoters have at times used a variation of the above by taking all of the stock in their corporation and returning a portion by gift to be sold to the public by the corporation for its own benefit, or to be sold to the public by the corporation as representative of the promoters, the proceeds to go to the promoters. Shares returned by gift are considered "treasury shares" and a common law rule permits such shares to be sold at less than par

17. See Ballantine, Corporations 842 (Rev. ed. 1946): "This is analogous to the well established doctrine of liability of directors for misappropriating corporate opportunities."

18. Ibid. 826.

value.   Fortunately, the majority holdings consider the sale of treasury shares under the above circumstances as if they were subscriptions by innocent incoming shareholders and allow a corporate cause of action to recover secret profits.[19]   Other courts have held such sales to have the same legal significance as if the promoters themselves had made them.[20]   But "if the transaction was a mere trick or species of jugglery to relieve the promoters from any liability" it has been suggested that even the minority position would change.[21]   How unsuspecting can one in judicial robes be?   Is this device ever used by promoters who plan immediately or almost immediately to unload their stock on the public except as "a mere trick or species of jugglery," and when they find it necessary to make a gift of their own stock to the corporation so that it may obtain the finances with which to carry on for the moment the corporate business, is anything more needed to open the judicial eye?[22]   It would seem that when promoters turn back to their corporation stock they have taken for overvalued property or services so that it may be sold for them, there should be but one answer—estoppel for misleading subscribers into believing that they are dealing with the corporation and not with the promoters.   And the corporate cause of action would seem to be the more practical one.

§ 22.   The Use of a Combination of Preferred and Common Shares in the Promotion Process

Suppose the promoters use preferred shares having a preference as to earnings and as to assets upon dissolution and common shares, the latter being taken in toto for overvalued property and services.   The plan envisages the sale of the preferred to the public with no notice of the transaction involving the common, and the preferred is so sold.   The promoters individually sell their shares so that, as far as the transferees are concerned,

19.   California-Calaveras Mining Co. v. Walls, 170 Cal. 285, 149 P. 595 (1915) ;   Torrey v. Toledo Portland Cement Co., 158 Mich. 348, 122 N. W. 614 (1909).   See Mason v. Carrothers, 105 Me. 392, 74 A. 1030 (1909), where several shareholders holding preferred and common shares brought the action.   The promoters had taken all of the common shares and had returned $200,000 worth of them to the corporation to "sweeten" the sale of $100,000 worth of preferred shares to be sold without disclosure of the promoters' profits.   As explained in Jeffs v. Utah Power & Light Co., 136 Me. 454, 12 A.2d 592, at 599 (1940), "The theory of Mason v. Carrothers . . . is that the plaintiffs, having paid value for common stock, were injured by reason of the fact that other similar stock had been issued to others without consideration."   The plaintiffs had paid "on the basis of $100 for one share of preferred stock and two shares of common."

20.   Henderson v. Plymouth Oil Co., 16 Del.Ch. 347, 141 A. 197 (1928).

21.   Ibid. 141 A. at 207.

22.   The best explanation the author has found of the legitimacy of such a gift by promoter to corporation is contained in Re Pipe Line Oil Co., 289 F. 693, at 701–702 (6th Cir. 1923).

they are in no position to bring a derivative action to recover for the corporation's benefit the secret profit made, at least under the theory of *Hays* v. *The Georgian, Inc.,* [23] representing the traditional view. May the innocent preferred shareholders bring a derivative action in such a case? If the initial organizational expenses have been paid by the promoters there is no immediate dilution of the preferred shares as there was of the common shares in *Bigelow* and *Lewisohn.* But the cushion of protection behind their investment is not what it was represented to be. In *Jeffs* v. *Utah Power & Light Company* [24] the court had that problem complicated by too many other factors to make a really good case on the point. Thaxter, J., after plaintiffs had argued "that they had a right to assume that the 300,000 shares of common stock and the 78,370 of second preferred represented $37,837,000.00 of assets," stated: "Assuming it all to be true they nowhere allege that their stock is worth any less than they paid for it. But beyond this counsel cite no case holding that a preferred stockholder has any absolute right to compel common stockholders to pay in full for the common stock issued to them, nor is any such case not based on a statute likely to be found." [25]

If it were simply a question of whether the stock was worth less than was paid for it, a choice would have to be made between the stock's actual value and its market value at the time the promoters took their profit. In the *Bigelow* and *Lewisohn* cases the market value was par or above for a considerable period after these promoters and their syndicate took their profit. The actual value of the stock in these two cases, that is the asset value behind the innocent shares, was much less than par. But does the problem end there? Was not counsel right in the *Jeffs* case in arguing that the preferred shares were entitled to the additional cushion which payment of par for the common shares would have given them? And we return again to a factor present in all secret profits cases, namely, that the corporation is injured in losing the opportunity to sell its shares at the most advantageous price to it, a thing that seems to have been lost sight of in these cases. That no case could be found supporting the absolute right of which Judge Thaxter speaks is just another instance where, as in every other case where new problems arise, new law must be made (or "found," if the court prefers the term) to fill the gap.[26]

---

23. 280 Mass. 10, 181 N.E. 765, 85 A.L.R. 1251 (1932), noted in 47 Harv.L.Rev. 1031 (1934); 19 Va.L. Rev. 274 (1933).

24. 136 Me. 454, 12 A.2d 592 (1940), noted in 54 Harv.L.Rev. 139 (1940); 19 Texas L.Rev. 198 (1941).

25. Ibid. 12 A.2d at 601.

26. The court distinguished Mason v. Carrothers, 105 Me. 392, 74 A. 1030 (1909). See note 19, supra. In the *Jeffs* case the shareholders bringing suit owned only preferred shares. There were other difficulties also. There was no definite allegation as to the actual value of the property turned over by the

§ 23. The Use of No-par Value Shares in the Promotion Process

No-par value shares have the advantage of carrying no dollar sign upon them. If 50,000 no-par shares are issued to promoters as consideration for the transfer of Blackacre which cost them $5,000 and is reasonably worth no more than this can subscribers of the same class of no-par shares who are brought in as part of the promotion scheme but who pay $10 a share complain that they were not notified of the previous deal? If 50,000 additional shares are issued at $10 a share it is obvious that there is an immediate dilution of the second 50,000 shares and an inflation of the first shares issued. The promoters, if allowed to keep this inflationary value, will compete in dividends, preemptive and other rights, and in distribution of assets upon dissolution, for each share is equal to every other share except as its contract gives it greater or lesser rights. Because of this possibility of unjust preference, a rule has developed which calls for equal contribution from those shareholders issued no-par shares at approximately the same time unless some good business reason can be assigned for the difference in price. As stated by one court: "While an arbitrary sale of the same issue of stock at different prices to different persons would not be sanctioned, such differential sales will be sustained, if based on business and commercial facts which, in the exercise of fair business judgment, lead directors to follow such a course." [27] "Business and commercial facts" may warrant the issuing of no-par shares to promoters at a price different from that of subscribers coming into the corporation as part of the promotion scheme. But fair value for services, property, ideas and risk should be strictly "fair value."

Another difficulty which confronts the issuer of no-par shares is that statutes frequently require the incorporators, if they are given authority to accept subscriptions to such stock, or the directors to put a price upon it at the time of issue or, in some cases, within a short time thereafter if issued for property. This must be capitalized or, if the statute permits, part of it capitalized and the remainder thrown into paid-in or capital surplus. For all practical purposes this puts no-par value stock issued to promoters in the par value category, and if they accept it with the dollar sign thus placed upon it for property or services at an inflated

---

promoters. It was also not clear whether plaintiffs' shares had, in the hands of previous owners, consented to the transactions of which plaintiffs complained. The plaintiffs had, to boot, bought their stock several years after the promoters had taken their profit, if profit there was. And it did not appear that any of plaintiffs bought their stock from the company, nor during the promotional stage. To top matters, there was actually a cushion represented by junior securities of about $5½ millions.

27. Atlantic Refining Co. v. Hodgman, 13 F.2d 781, at 788 (3d Cir. 1926); Bodell v. General Gas & Electric Corp., 15 Del.Ch. 420, 140 A. 264 (1927).

value their position is no better than if the dollar sign had appeared on the certificate itself. No-par, as well as par value stock may be watered.[28] Of course, the devices suggested by the Massachusetts court in *Bigelow* may be used to secure the promoters' profit as in the case where par value shares are used.

An interesting successful attempt was made in *Piggly Wiggly Delaware, Inc.* v. *Bartlett*[29] to combine the use of par value preferred shares with no-par value common shares, the promoters taking 15,000 of the latter in exchange for a system of vending merchandise for which they had paid $1,000. The preferred shares were sold to the public without a disclosure of this transaction. The promoters' no-par shares were sold through company officials for approximately $100,000 and, after deducting certain promotion expenses, the promoters divided the remainder among themselves. The corporation sued to recover the secret profits. The bill was dismissed, the court saying: "There was a full bona fide consideration for the sale by the company to Bartlett and his associates of fifteen thousand shares of the capital stock of no-par value. Had this stock had a par value, and had stock of par or face value exceeding the value of the rights purchased been issued, a different question would arise."[30] This is another illustration of the abuse by promoters through their control of the corporation, at the promotion stage, of their fiduciary duty to their corporation whereby they have deprived it of its opportunity to float its securities at the best price available. Furthermore, the appearances set up by the promoters in having the company officials dispose of their no-par shares with no disclosure that it was promoters' stock that was being sold, should have been the basis of an estoppel justifying, under the better rule, a recovery of the profit from the promoters. Beyond this, the cushion which the preferred shareholders had a right to expect was behind their shares was nonexistent.

A safe way of assuring promoters compensation for services or payment for property would be by disclosure to an impartial board or to the incoming preferred shareholders of the services rendered and of the property transferred, with the claimed value in one case and the cost to the promoters in the other, with an agreement to accept 15,000 no-par value shares for these services and this property. If the preferred shares carry preferences as to dividends and to assets upon dissolution to the extent of the shareholders' initial contribution, they will lose

28. Livingston v. Adams, 226 Mo. App. 824, 43 S.W.2d 836 (1931), cert. denied by Supreme Court, 1932. But see G. Loewus & Co., Inc. v. Highland Queen Packing Co., 125 N.J.Eq. 534, 6 A.2d 545 (1939).

29. 97 N.J.Eq. 469, 129 A. 413, 65 A.L.R. 1353 (1935).

30. Ibid. 129 A. at 418. Ballantine, Corporations 842 (Rev. ed. 1946), considers the case badly decided.

only the cushion that otherwise would have been expected in a stock set-up of this kind. The promoters would be paid on the basis of profits with little expectation, perhaps, of obtaining any of the corporate assets if later the corporation were dissolved.[31] This may well prove acceptable to those who are financing the venture through their subscriptions to preferred stock. If the promotion is successful the promoters will reap their benefit chiefly through earnings and if earnings are exceptional the value of the common shares will be increased.

Consideration should also be given to the use of low par value shares of one cent, five cents, ten cents, etc., for use in a promotion plan. With a conservative valuation of the consideration given for these shares, there should be no difficulty with problems involving overvaluation or of secret profits. If the promotion plan is substantially sound, another class of shares, with sufficient preferences to make them attractive, could be used to finance the plan. If the venture proved successful, both classes of shares would benefit and the promoters would obtain an adequate return for their promotion. That is, if the share-contracts are carefully drawn.

§ 24. Where Bond and/or Note Holders are Part of the Promotion Scheme—McCandless v. Furlaud

In the most famous case since the *Old Dominion Copper Company cases,* the promotion scheme was carried out by the use of several subsidiary corporations but the plan itself contemplated that mortgage bonds as well as mortgage notes be used to finance the promotion and these with all of the stock passed through the promoters' hands and were sold by them and their agents to the public. The bonds were taken at a discount of $10 per $100 and the notes at a discount of $12 per $100 while about ⅚ of the stock issued was taken as a bonus, the remaining ⅙ at 50¢ a share. The property transferred for bonds, notes and stock was greatly overvalued so that an honest balance sheet drawn up after the initial transactions were consummated and promoters' profits taken would show assets of a value of approximately $3,000,000 and liabilities (bonds and notes) of $5,000,000. It should be said that the promoters took their profit out of cash derived from a sale of the bonds and notes and from a sale of stock at $10 per share. Thus it was apparent that, from the beginning, the corporation was insolvent.

Action was brought by the receiver of the corporation against the promoters for an accounting. The District Court

---

31. See Berle, Compensation of Bankers and Promoters Through Stock Profits, 42 Harv.L.Rev. 748, at 752 (1929). The English use "founders" or "deferred" shares for this purpose. Palmer's Company Law 69 (19th ed. 1949).

held that by force of the false statements in the circulars as to the purpose of the issue of bonds and notes, the promoters were trustees for the benefit of their corporation and of the holders of its mortgage debt to the extent of the difference between the proceeds received by the promoters and the amount they turned over to the corporation. Judgment was denied against any of the promoters for the proceeds of the shares of stock. The Court of Appeals reversed the District Court on the doctrine of *Lewisohn* that the corporation had knowledge through its promoter-shareholders and that if there was any cause of action it was available to the defrauded creditors but not to the corporation or its receiver. The United States Supreme Court held that *Lewisohn* did not control. Here, the corporation was insolvent from the outset with liens beyond the value of its assets. And no consent of its shareholders could make such conduct lawful as far as creditors were concerned, or when challenged by the receiver as the representative of creditors. "There is no occasion," wrote Mr. Justice Cardozo, "to consider whether the corporation itself at the instance of new shareholders would be permitted to disaffirm the fraud and maintain a suit in equity for appropriate relief. We put that question by. Enough that the receiver has the requisite capacity." [32] And even though the company were not actually insolvent, thought the court, "there would be a wrong to bondholders and noteholders if assets were depleted to the very brink of insolvency after fraudulent misrepresentations to the effect that there was an ample margin of security." But the court thought that this was something more than deceit to be redressed in damages at the suit of defrauded creditors. "What is here is a tort growing out of the fraudulent depletion of the assets by men chargeable as trustees if they have failed to act with honor." [33] The promoters were trustees as to the bonds and notes and as to the shares which they took, "the transaction being a unit, infected with a common vice. Everything of profit arising out of the abused relation must now be yielded up," including the $850,000 derived from the sale of bonus shares at $10 per share.

Four justices dissented, Mr. Justice Roberts writing the dissenting opinion. It was the minority's opinion that *Lewisohn* covered this case and that *Lewisohn* was being overruled; that the decree of the Circuit Court of Appeals should be affirmed. The corporation, thought the minority, had no cause of action and the receiver could have no greater right. "The so-called fiduciary relation of promoters," wrote Mr. Justice Roberts, "may

32. McCandless v. Furlaud, 296 U.S. 140, at 160, 56 S.Ct. 41, at 47, 80 L.Ed. 121 (1935). Accord: Bovay v. H. M. Byllesby & Co., 27 Del.Ch. 381, 38 A.2d 808 (1944), noted in

34 Calif.L.Rev. 435 (1946); 43 Mich. L.Rev. 978 (1945).

33. McCandless v. Furlaud, supra, note 32, 296 U.S. at 164, 56 S.Ct. at 49.

be availed of by the corporation only in virtue of the equity of innocent stockholders defrauded by the promoters' scheme." [34]   If creditors have been defrauded, which may have been this case, they must bring the action and not the corporation or its receiver.

McCandless v. *Furlaud* extends the fiduciary obligation of promoters to creditor security holders whose securities comprise a part of the initial promotion scheme along with the shares to be issued initially so that the corporate cause of action is proper when the promoters have taken profits resulting in corporate insolvency or near insolvency.   While the opinion itself does not mention expressly the corporate right to a fair capitalization which will give some assurance of corporate success, and the promoters' fiduciary duty not to impair the company's chances by depriving it of necessary capital, this is perhaps a fair inference from the holding, at least where creditor security holders have been created.   The judgment requiring the promoters to disgorge the receipts from the sale of the bonus stock was directly in the face of the *Lewisohn* case.   The court's explanation that the transaction was a "unit" infected with a common vice is not convincing for all such promoters' transactions are such whether or not creditor security holders are involved.

A better explanation would be that the cushion, which was reasonably represented by the $850,000 for which the promoters' bonus shares were sold, had been removed without notice to and consent of the other security holders.   But the net result of the holding was good and it may be that the doctrine of *Lewisohn* is on the way out, if it is not already there as Mr. Justice Roberts felt.

§ 25.   Other Remedies—by Rescission—Suits by or in Favor of Individual Security Holders

In the preceding sections the discussion has centered around the corporate cause of action to recover secret profits taken by promoters.   Because of the fraudulent concealment of the profit and the issue of shares for grossly overvalued services or property, rescission by the corporation is a proper remedy, at least

---

34.   Ibid. 296 U.S. at 173, 56 S.Ct. at 53.   The minority disagreed in material respect with the finding of fact of the majority.   The *McCandless* case was noted in many law reviews some of which follow: 24 Calif.L.Rev. 465 (1936); 3 U. of Chi.L.Rev. 484 (1936); 36 Col. L.Rev. 488 (1936); 49 Harv.L.Rev. 785 (1936); 34 Mich.L.Rev. 1189 (1936); 45 Yale L.J. 511 (1936). In accord with Mr. Justice Roberts' statement that *Lewisohn* applied only to shareholders, see Allenhurst Park Estates, Inc. v. Smith, 101 N.J.Eq. 581, 138 A. 709 (1927), holding that bondholders were not entitled to notice of promoters' profits.   The corporation in this case was solvent and bondholders were not actually injured.   But, as part of the original promotion scheme, should they not be entitled to notice of what promoters have taken before they subscribe to bonds?

where corporate creditors or other security holders will not be injured by a cancellation and return of the shares, rather than a recovery in cash to the extent of the water in them.[35]   When promoters have taken their profit in cash or property a rescission does not present the same difficulties for a return of such assets gives both creditors and security holders further security.

It has already been suggested [36] that if the real injury is to the shareholder who comes into the promotional scheme uninformed and pays cash to the extent of the par value of his shares and finds his shares diluted by promoters' shares taken for services or property at inflated values, the cause of action in a real sense is his.   On the other hand, in the analogous situation where directors or officers intentionally or negligently misuse their powers so that corporate losses result and the shareholders' shares are depreciated in value because of this, the usual and only remedy is by the corporation or by an action brought derivatively by a shareholder for the benefit of his corporation.[37]   The resulting judgment, if satisfied, is supposed to take up the slack in the depreciated shares.

The courts have not been consistent in the promoters' profit cases as to whose cause of action it is.   If individual frauds have been perpetrated against subscribers through fraudulent representations made in connection with the subscription and sale of the shares, the shareholder has his remedy for damages and, in a proper case, for rescission.   This follows from basic tort law. The failure of promoters to perform their fiduciary duty of disclosing the profits or other advantages taken by them is clearly analogous.   Concealment, when there is a duty to disclose, amounts to fraud.   In *Downey* v. *Byrd,* a class action by shareholders, on behalf of themselves and others similarly situated, against promoters without joining the company, was permitted in a factual situation similar to that in *Lewisohn* and *Bigelow.* Said the court: "We have undertaken to show that promoters occupy a fiduciary relation towards the subscribers to the stock

---

35.   The problems centering on creditors' rights generally in watered stock cases are discussed at page 403 et seq., infra.

Erlanger v. The New Sombrero Phosphate Co., 3 App.Cas. 1218 (H.L. 1878);   Diamond State Brewery, Inc. v. de la Rigaudiere, 25 Del. Ch. 257, 17 A.2d 313 (1941)—"If the issuance of stock was void, cancellation is the proper remedy; if merely voidable 'then that form of relief is to be adopted which would seem to be most in accord with all the equities of the case.' "

And where rescission and cancellation of shares were requested in Scully v. Automobile Finance Co., 12 Del.Ch. 174, 109 A. 49 (1920), the court took upon itself the authority to decree that the water be taken up by payment in dollars as "the most equitable form of relief." The corporation was solvent.

36.   See page 133, supra.

37.   See Chapter 8, infra, where shareholders' derivative actions are discussed.

of a corporation which they are promoting; and when such promoters promote a bubble, an equitable action will lie against them for injuries sustained by subscribers, on account of the fiduciary relation which they sustain towards the subscribers . . ." [38] And in *Hyde Park Terrace Co.* v. *Jackson Brothers Realty Co.*,[39] it was held proper for the corporation to bring the action on behalf of the injured shareholders, any recovery to be held in trust for them. In an analogous situation where officers had taken excessive salaries and some shareholders had acquiesced in this, the corporation was held a proper party to sue as trustee of its nonacquiescing shareholder-beneficiaries.[40] The innocent shareholders, in a similar case, were allowed to bring the action for their own benefit.[41] And, of course, if any redress is proper under the doctrine of the *Lewisohn* case it would have to be upon the theory of individual injury, the cause of action being that of the innocent shareholder or his transferee.

While traditionally the action for cancellation of shares taken by promoters for inflated values in services or property is held to be a corporate one, several courts have permitted non-assenting shareholders whose shares have been diluted to bring the action either individually or by a class suit.[42] The reasoning behind these cases is that the real injury is to the shareholder, not the corporation, and the action is not in the interest of the corporation but for the protection of individual rights. And it has been held in the same jurisdiction that either the shareholders individually or by class suit or the corporation by itself or through a derivative suit brought by one or more shareholders may bring such an action.[43] In any suit for the cancellation of watered stock there is always the danger that creditors may be injured by

---

38. Downey v. Byrd, 171 Ga. 532, 156 S.E. 259 (1930). *Contra:* Barrett v. Shambeau, 187 Minn. 430, 245 N.W. 830 (1932).

In the analogous case of Harris v. Rogers, 190 App.Div. 208, 179 N.Y. S. 799 (1919), noted in 33 Harv.L. Rev. 979 (1920), all but 25% of the shareholders had released or waived their claims against negligent directors. A class action by innocent shareholders was held proper.

39. 161 App.Div. 699, 146 N.Y.S. 1037 (1914).

40. Matthews v. Headley Chocolate Co., 130 Md. 523, 100 A. 645 (1917).

41. Brown v. DeYoung, 167 Ill. 549, 47 N.E. 863 (1897). Compare Voorhees v. Mason, 245 Ill. 256, 91 N.E. 1056 (1910); Keenan v. Eshleman,

23 Del.Ch. 234, 2 A.2d 904, 120 A.L. R. 227 (1938).

42. See Shaw v. Staight, 107 Minn. 152, 119 N.W. 951, 20 L.R.A.,N.S., 1077 (1909); Mason v. Carrothers, 105 Me. 392, 74 A. 1030 (1909).

43. Mason v. Carrothers, supra note 42, an action brought by 11 shareholders; Scully v. Automobile Finance Co., 12 Del.Ch. 174, 109 A. 49 (1920), action by 4 shareholders to have promoters' shares cancelled but court, of its own accord, changed remedy to assessment to take up the water, this in a solvent company; Jeffs v. Utah Power & Light Co., 136 Me. 454, 12 A.2d 592 (1940), a derivative action; Diamond State Brewery, Inc. r. de la Rigaudiere, 25 Del.Ch. 257, 17 A.2d 313 (1941), corporation brought action to cancel.

such cancellation. This is clearly the case when the corporation is insolvent or nearly so. In cases where creditors may be injured unless the water is taken up by payment the action should be brought by the corporation and cancellation should not be permitted.[44] In cases where cancellation will not defeat creditors' rights, whether the action may be brought by corporation or shareholder or by each does not, from a practical standpoint, matter except where security-for-expenses statutes are applicable in derivative actions. The shares are cancelled and the certificates returned to the company in any case. And the asset value and participating rights of fewer outstanding shares are thereby increased.

§ 26. The Promoter under the Federal Securities Act of 1933

By the requirement of full disclosure of essential information concerning securities publicly offered or sold in interstate commerce or through the mails, and not exempted under the Act, the promoter finds himself in a tight spot insofar as concealment of profits is concerned. The registration statement and prospectus must contain a full disclosure of any compensation to be received by him for his services, or which has been received within two years preceding the filing of the registration statement, the values of property to be acquired by the issuer, and if the assets were acquired by the promoter within two years of their transfer to the issuer, there must be a statement of their cost to the promoter. There are other protective requirements. The term "promoter" is broadly defined in Rule 405, General Rules and Regulations of the Securities and Exchange Commission,[45] as including one who, acting alone or with others, directly or indirectly takes initiative in founding and organizing the business of an issuer or who directly or indirectly receives for services and/or property in connection with such organizing and founding 10% or more of any class of securities of the issuer or 10% or more of the proceeds from the sale of any class of securities of the issuer. The underwriter who takes commissions in securities or the proceeds therefrom is excepted as is a seller of property

---

44. Ballantine, Corporations 852 (Rev. ed. 1946).

45. 17 C.F.R., Rule 230.405 (1949 ed.) and see the provisions of similar character in the new Uniform Securities Act, § 304, as approved on August 25, 1956. There are also other protective provisions which would be applicable to promoters in the process of promotion; the Act is now printed in the Handbook of the National Conference of Commissioners on Uniform State Laws, 182–238, plus several appendices (1956); also in 9C U.L.A. 86 et seq. (1957). See the volume written by the draftsmen of the Uniform Securities Act, Loss and Cowett, Blue Sky Law, pp. 230 et seq., on the Act itself (1958). For an excellent discussion of Blue Sky laws, including the Uniform Securities Act, see Jennings, The Role of the States in Corporate Regulation and Investor Protection, 23 Law and Contemp.Prob. 193, at 207 et seq. (1958).

who takes in payment securities or the proceeds from their sale where he does not otherwise participate in founding and organizing the enterprise.

The effectiveness of the Act depends upon the administrative controls, chief of which is the use of the stop order to prevent the issue and sale until a full disclosure which is true and not misleading is made. The Commission has made special efforts to reduce excessive appraisal values upon properties promoters have sold to their companies. This has sometimes resulted in a like increase in "organization expenses" which the Commission apparently originally thought would put a prospective purchaser of securities on his guard. But where the item listed as "organization expenses" was so clearly out of line with the services rendered, a stop order has been justified.[46] ". . . Control by the commission . . . at least has the advantage of attacking the problem at the outset, before complicated questions of causation arise, and, being administrative, it has the further advantage of being better fitted than a cumbersome judicial machinery to handle a problem that is essentially one of accounting." [47]

The requirement of a statement of the cost to the promoter of property acquired within two years of its transfer to the issuer recognizes the ineffectiveness of the common law view that if the property was purchased with no intent of promoting a company at the time of acquisition the only fiduciary duty of the promoter is to disclose that he is selling to the company later formed.[48] Since the Act, prior to a sale of securities, requires the furnishing of a prospectus containing information about the promoters' activities, the subscriber has the opportunity of notice which the *Lewisohn* holding denied him.

46. See Note, Promoters' Profits: Control by Court and Commission, 49 Harv.L.Rev. 785 (1936); MacChesney, The Securities Act and the Promoter, 25 Calif.L.Rev. 66 (1936); McGowan, Legal Controls of Corporate Promoters' Profits, 25 Geo.L.J. 269 (1937).

47. Note, 49 Harv.L.Rev. 785 at 792 (1936).

48. See page 131, supra, and footnote 8.

Chapter 4

EVOLUTION AND FORMATION OF CORPORA-TIONS; LEGAL EFFECTS WHEN DEFECTIVELY FORMED

§ 1. Evolution of Anglo-American Corporations; Origin of the "Concession" Theory

In a short work on the law of modern corporations little can be done on historical matters except to summarize briefly those events which make for a better understanding of present-day law. The student of history in this area must be sent to the source material or to texts and articles, some of the more important of which are listed below.[1]

The origin of the English business corporation is uncertain. Within the past half-century or so a number of fine historical treatises on this subject have been written and some excellent chapters in works devoted generally to the history of the law have appeared. The customs and traditions of the merchant and craft guilds in feudal England and their relationship to the towns in which they functioned have given an insight into some of the management procedures of later corporations formed by Crown charter or Parliamentary grant. It is not definitely known whether the guilds evolved from Anglo-Saxon religious guilds or whether they were imports from the continent. And uncertainty exists as to whether the merchant guilds by their presence in a town or borough contributed something of a corporate quality to the borough or town or whether the town or borough could independently claim a corporate existence with the guild as something incidental thereto. However, the guilds did acquire the control and a substantial monopoly of the trade

---

1. Gross, The Gild Merchant (1890); Scott, The Constitution and Finance of English, Scottish and Irish Joint-Stock Companies to 1720 (1910–1912); DuBois, The English Business Company After the Bubble Act, 1720–1800 (1938); Davis, Essays in the Earlier History of American Corporations (1917); Williston, A History of the Law of Business Corporations Before 1800, 2 Harv. L.Rev. 105, 149 (1888); Dodd, The First Half Century of Statutory Regulation of Business Corporations in Massachusetts, Harvard Legal Essays 65 (1934); Dodd, American Business Association Law a Hundred Years Ago and Today, 3 Law; A Century of Progress, 1835–1935, 254 (1937); Dodd, American Business Corporations Until 1860 (1954); Livermore, Early American Land Companies: Their Influence on Corporate Development (1939). And see the excellent chapters by Gower, Modern Company Law, Chapters 2 and 3 (1954); ibid., Chapters 2 and 3 (2d ed. 1957).

though this control and monopoly were not for the common benefit of the guild members, as in case of shareholders in more modern corporations, but for the members individually. The members had the privilege of trading on their own account and had
the advantage of the monopoly which was the guild's. The guild
regulated the trade of the town, made and enforced rules governing its members in their trading, and assured them of the monopoly when non-members attempted to intrude. Many of the guilds
eventually obtained Crown charters to secure for their members
a monopoly of the particular commodity or trade.

There is doubt whether the craft guilds, through a struggle
with the merchant guilds, finally won out and superseded them,
and the problem is unimportant here. What is important is
that the merchant guilds through management (i.e., by a governing body consisting of a "governor and assistant governors"
which later became "directors") and other procedures had set
the pattern for later trade organization development. But trade
was carried on by the members individually and not jointly.
The guild assured them protection and a monopoly within the
area of guild operation.

During the period of merchant guilds a monopoly grew up
in "staple" towns where English goods were exported, the monopoly resulting in the organization of the Company of the
Staple and the Company of the Merchant Adventurers, the former handling raw materials, the latter, manufactured products.
While these companies were for the purpose of exporting goods
they no doubt also imported goods from those countries to which
English goods were being sent. Other companies with similar
purposes developed contemporaneously with these for trading
in specially designated countries, such as the Andalusia Company
for trading with Spain, the Eastland Company for operations
in Norway, Sweden and Denmark, and the Prussia Company.
"These seem to have been the beginnings of the 'regulated company', originating in the realm of foreign trade." [2] Subsequent
to the formation of these companies, Queen Mary in 1555 granted
a charter to the Russia Company to trade with that country.
This company seems to have been the first to have been formed
with the intention that the trade was to be conducted by the
members on a joint-stock basis, a characteristic which is universal today. Other companies, later formed, notably the African
Company chartered in 1619 whose charter was later revoked,
and the Royal African Company of England, chartered in 1672,
also appear to have proceeded on a joint-stock basis, though
funds seem to have been raised for each voyage, the proceeds of

----

2. Dodd and Baker, Cases and Materials on Corporations 8 (2d ed.
   1951).

each being distributed to the members and a new subscription taken for the next voyage. The famous East India Company was chartered in 1600 to trade with the Indies on a joint-stock and, while its early trading was through subscriptions for a single voyage, in 1613 an important change occurred which slanted toward a permanent joint-stock, namely, the subscription was for four successive voyages (years), and in 1617 the period was extended to eight years. Thus, permanent joint-stock was on its way and in 1657, by virtue of a new charter, permanent capital was provided for. The trend toward permanent joint-stock also proceeded in companies chartered for domestic operations. Thus the corporation born by Royal charter had, three centuries ago, the earmarks of modernity through the operation of a permanent joint-stock.

Proceeding along in the development of trade was another business association whose characteristics have been considered in Chapter 1, the unincorporated joint stock company. This organization was formed by contract and needed no aid from the Crown or from Parliament though frequently it was formed of royal patent or grant chiefly because of the fear of encountering the Royal prerogative. But substantial capital was frequently set to work in such associations with no aid from King or Parliament unless a charter was required for other reasons. Royal charters were expensive and in the seventeenth and early eighteenth centuries and beyond there was not the feeling that the corporation was so much more effective for carrying on a business than the unincorporated joint stock association.

There is some question whether the unincorporated joint stock associations were the real forerunners of the modern business corporation rather than these large Crown chartered trading companies—monopolies—of the sixteenth and seventeenth centuries.[3] It is probable that each gathered characteristics from the other as they developed more or less side by side. One may point to the articles of association of the joint stock company as following closely the form of the corporate charter. Since the lawyer was attempting to give to the unincorporated association as many of the qualities of the corporation as were possible,

---

3. Ballantine, Corporations 33 (Rev. ed. 1946) gives credit to the unincorporated joint stock associations created by contract. In agreement with Ballantine is Palmer, Company Law 4 (19th ed. 1949). On the other hand, Professors Dodd and Baker state: "It does not seem that the unincorporated association contributed more to the corporate form than the latter did to the former." Dodd and Baker, Cases and Materials on Corporations 14 (2d ed. 1951). Horrwitz, Historical Development of Company Law, 62 Law Q.Rev. 375 (1946), concludes that large joint stock companies of the sixteenth century obtained crown charters primarily for special powers and privileges that could be gained only by crown charter, and not particularly to receive limited liability for the members.

this was a natural thing for him to do. We have already seen another instance of the lawyer's ingenuity in devising the business or "Massachusetts" trust from the combination of corporation, contract and trust provisions but steering clear of the threat of partnership liability.[4] While many of the features of the modern corporation such as transferable shares, continuity of life, management by a managing group comparable to directors in a corporation, could be obtained by agreement, it was not found possible for the joint stock company to obtain limited liability, or for it to hold its property in the association name and own it as such, or sue or be sued as if it were a separate legal personality through agreement or provisions in the articles of association without the aid of statute. And, while limited liability was a late comer in the corporation's list of attributes, it eventually became one of the leading characteristics which made incorporation so desirable.[5]

By the passing of the so-called "Bubble Act" in 1720 which was phrased in ambiguous terms, sometimes described as "incoherent," the promotion of joint stock associations was retarded because of the doubt cast upon the issue of transferable shares by such companies. The South Sea Company chartered in 1711 had speculated in and manipulated its own shares which resulted in a great rise in their market value. This led to numerous promotions and speculation. In 1719 this company encouraged investors to sell or exchange their government bonds and annuities and invest in or exchange for South Sea stock. The South Sea Company, it has been stated, encouraged the passing of the Bubble Act so that more funds might be used to purchase South Sea shares. This company and some others were excepted from the provisions of the Act.[6] While the Crown was still able to grant charters, it apparently did so sparingly and while Parliament shortly thereafter might have incorporated by special act, there was still a slowing down of the incorporating of companies for some time. However, in the last 65 years of the operation of the Act, many corporations were formed by Crown charter or Parliamentary special act to carry on canal, water and gas companies.

The Bubble Act was repealed in 1825.[7] Thereafter followed a series of acts which eventually resulted in the Companies Act

---

4. See Ch. 1, supra, page 49 et seq.

5. Limited liability, however, was an incident of Crown charter companies. Palmer, Company Law 2 (19th ed. 1949).

6. See Ballantine, Corporations 33–34 (Rev. ed. 1946).

7. Because of the Bubble Act of 1720, for more than a century English industry was deprived of capital otherwise procurable. Furthermore, it has been stated that this legislation exercised "a deterrent psychological effect upon company promotion even after its repeal under the pressure of a rising industrialism a century later." Hunt, The Development of the Business Corporation in England, 1800–1867, at page 9 (1936).

of 1862, the forerunner of the Companies (Consolidation) Act of 1908 and the Companies Act of 1929 and that of 1948,[8] acts which permitted all who complied with them to incorporate upon equal terms set forth by a general law and which gave limited liability to the shareholders. It should be said that the first *general* joint stock company act came in 1844 when the Joint Stock Companies Registration Act was passed. It was described as "An Act for the registration, incorporation and regulation of joint stock companies," and while joint stock companies might be incorporated under this act, in fact were compelled to if there were more than twenty-five members with the capital comprised of freely transferable shares, there was no provision for limited liability, though creditors were required to proceed against the company assets first, and such limited liability could not be gained by placing a provision in the articles. The Act did permit suit by or against the association in the association name. However, by virtue of the Limited Liability Act of 1855 [9] this privilege, upon the named conditions in the statute, was offered for the first time in England under a general act.

While an organization coming pretty close to the corporation could be formed by contract, complete corporateness could not be acquired except through sovereign grant. In England there are still three methods of incorporation: (1) by compliance with the Companies Act of 1862 and its successors; (2) by act of Parliament in which case certain standarized provisions contained in a series of acts are applicable, depending upon the purpose for which the corporation is formed; and (3) by Royal charter by virtue of the Crown's prerogative and supplemented by the Chartered Companies Act of 1837. Thus, the privilege to be a corporation is considered a franchise and is traceable to those corporations early formed under Crown charters.

The impact of the "concession theory" that corporate powers were derived from the state resulted in a social control over the activities of corporations and substantial revenue for the Crown. "Other elements of sovereign power could be called upon to support the choice; to grant monopolies, to prohibit claim of right to establish local government, and to control to some extent the right of assembly, perhaps in an early period to create new or extend forms of tenure, to have the precious minerals of the realm or tare therefrom and the benefit of fisheries, to grant monopolies and covertly or otherwise the right of privateering on enemies or even ostensible friends, to prohibit

8. Companies Act of 1862, 25 and 26 Vict., c. 89, with its many amendments resulting in the Companies Act of 1948, 11 and 12 Geo. VI, c. 38, the latest enactment to date.

9. 5 Halsbury's Laws of England 86 (2d ed. 1932).

the subject leaving the realm or exporting bullion, to exact customs and to control and to grant rights of trade in foreign parts." [10]

In America, Royal charter companies were used to develop many of the original settlements and for trading with them. After the Revolution when states were formed corporations were created first by special act of the legislature. The states had the local example of the special charter granted by the Continental Congress in 1781 to the Bank of North America. The corporation was needed for the development of roads, bridges, ferries and wharfs, and for supplies of water, as well as for the banks to supply short term credit in various trade, manufacturing, stage and navigation projects that were obtaining special charters.

But special charters granted by state legislatures were subject to the same political pressures that existed in case of other legislation, and incorporation by this method which frequently resulted in favoritism for one wielding the most political power was soon questioned. In 1811 New York adopted a general corporation act under which any five or more persons might become incorporated to engage in definitely specified types of manufacturing, by signing, acknowledging and filing with the secretary of state a certificate of incorporation setting forth the corporate name, its location, objects, capitalization and number of shares, and the names and addresses of its first board of directors.[11] The Act of 1811 limited the capital to $100,000, the life of the corporation to 20 years, and imposed additional liability upon shareholders for the benefit of creditors upon dissolution if the corporate assets could not pay them. By legislation in 1825 and a few years later, other corporate characteristics were added.

By the middle of the nineteenth century the corporation by special act was on its way out. By constitutional provision in many states, or by legislation, corporations by special act except in rare instances were prohibited. Hence, today, incorporation by general act in the United States is the almost exclusive method of forming corporations. There are, however, other general acts for the creation of corporations carrying on businesses such as banking, insurance, utilities, cooperatives, loan associations, etc., businesses which for the most part carry with them rather significant social aspects. But these too are general acts and pre-

---

10. Dodd and Baker, Cases and Materials on Corporations 2 (2d ed. 1951).

11. N.Y.Laws 1811, c. 67. There was a general "Manufacturing Corporations Act" passed in Massachusetts in 1809 which provided for regulations to apply to all manufacturing corporations formed thereafter by special charters, something quite different from the New York act. See Dodd, American Business Corporations Until 1860, 228 et seq. (1954).

sumably political pressure and favoritism have no place in their functioning. Controls are usually kept over such corporations after birth by additional legislation not appearing in the particular general incorporation statute and by the use of administrative bodies set up for the specific purpose. And prior to the incorporation of banks, building and loan associations, insurance companies, and public utilities, many states require the approval of the proposed incorporation by the administrative body or its officials.

Really comprehensive general corporation acts came during the last quarter of the nineteenth century and the first quarter of the twentieth, the Pennsylvania act in 1874, the New Jersey act or revision of 1896 (though in 1875 New Jersey had brought most corporations under its general act), and the very liberal Delaware act. This last act with its later amendments became and remained popular as an act under which to incorporate and one which offered many suggestions to those engaged in the study and drafting of the modern statutes enacted in the second quarter of the present century.[12] Useful, too, chiefly for suggestions in the drafting of modern statutes, was the Uniform, now designated "Model," Corporation Act of 1928.[13] Quite recently a committee of the American Bar Association has completed a Model Business Corporation Act which, due to its source, has already had some influence and is likely to have more on future legislation, though one writer has questioned it as an invitation to irresponsibility.[14]

The earlier corporation laws in the United States generally restricted the amount of authorized capital the corporation might have, put limitations upon the scope of its powers and activity—permission to incorporate for "any lawful purpose" not being common until about 1875—, limited corporate life to 20, 30 or 50 years, required the incorporators, or a majority of them, to be citizens or residents of the incorporating state, sometimes required this of directors also, gave no power to hold stock in

12. Now the Delaware General Corporation Law of 1953.

13. See 9 U.L.A. 49 et seq. (1951).

14. A late draft was published in 6 The Business Lawyer (1950); it was revised in 1953 and published by the Committee on Continuing Legal Education of the American Law Institute. See Harris, The Model Business Corporation Act— Invitation to Irresponsibility? 50 Nw.U.L.Rev. 1 (1955); on the new Ohio Act of 1955, see Emerson, The New Ohio General Corporation Law: Some Comments and Some Comparisons, 24 U. of Cin.L.Rev. 463 (1956). Professor Emerson compares the provisions of the Ohio act with those of the recent North Carolina Business Corporation Act passed in 1955 which became effective in 1957 and the Model Act of the American Bar Association, now known as the A. L. I. Model Business Corporation Act (Rev. 1953). Slight revision, with optional sections, was accomplished in 1955. For further criticism of this Model Act, see Jennings, The Role of the States in Corporate Regulation and Investor Protection, 23 Law and Contemp.Prob. 192, at 197 et seq. (1958).

other corporations and the power was not implied except in quite unusual cases—thus holding companies were not possible—, and generally showed their "fear of encroachment upon the liberties and opportunities of the individual." [15]   Seldom are any of the restrictions mentioned in force anywhere today, nor were they when Mr. Justice Brandeis wrote [16]: "The typical business corporation of the last century, owned by a small group of individuals, managed by their owners, and limited in size by their personal wealth, is being supplanted by huge concerns in which the lives of tens or hundreds of thousands of employees and the property of tens or hundreds of thousands of investors are subjected, through the corporate mechanism, to the control of a few men. Ownership has been separated from control; and this separation has removed many of the checks which formerly operated to curb the misuse of wealth and power. And, as ownership of the shares is becoming continually more dispersed, the power which formerly accompanied ownership is becoming increasingly concentrated in the hands of a few. The changes thereby wrought in the lives of the workers, of the owners and of the general public, are so fundamental and far-reaching as to lead these scholars to compare the evolving 'corporate system' with the feudal system; and to lead other men of insight and experience to assert that this 'master institution of civilized life' is committing it to the rule of a plutocracy . . .. Such is the Frankenstein Monster which states have created by their corporation laws."

The same year that Mr. Justice Brandeis wrote his dissenting opinion in *Louis K. Liggett Co.* v. *Lee* [17] there was passed by Congress the first of a series of important regulatory acts, the Securities Act of 1933 followed the next year by the Securities Exchange Act of 1934—these two acts being the most important ones at this point—aimed at some of the abuses of which this great justice wrote,[18] but legislating more widely than the field of corporate securities, their issue and sale upon national exchanges. It is no doubt better that legislation purporting to correct economic and social abuses should come through special statutes rather than through the general incorporation statutes

---

15. Mr. Justice Brandeis in his dissenting opinion in Louis K. Liggett Co. v. Lee, 288 U.S. 517, at 550 et seq., 53 S.Ct. 481, at 490 et seq., 77 L.Ed. 929, 85 A.L.R. 699 (1933).

16. Ibid. 288 U.S. at 565, 567, 53 S.Ct. at 496, 497. The reference to "these scholars" is to Professors Berle and Means, authors of The Modern Corporation and Private Property (1932). The court's footnotes point also to Veblen, Absentee Ownership and Business Enterprise (1923) and Wormser, Frankenstein, Incorporated (1931).

17. Supra, note 15.

18. The Securities Act of 1933 will be found in 15 U.S.C.A. §§ 77a et seq., as amended; the Securities Exchange Act of 1934 in 15 U.S.C.A. §§ 78b et seq.

which we have today.   These latter statutes are "enabling acts,
to authorize business men to organize and operate their business,
large or small, with the advantages of the corporate mechanism." [19]   However, in a general act, much can be said for better protective devices for the owners against the managers and
for minority owners against majority owners.   These are things
pertaining to the running of the corporation and the so-called
liberal provisions of many of the general corporation statutes
today have a tendency to subordinate the rights of owners
to those of their trustees by making it too difficult to pursue the
remedy available or by permitting exculpatory clauses of great
breadth as well as by giving insufficient protection to minority
owners against majority ones.[20]   The trend has been toward
ease of corporate functioning from management's standpoint by
removing the obstacles which formerly slowed down or stopped
management from pursuing its own corporate policy in the face
of strong owner opposition or lethargy.

Three factors have contributed to the frequently "over-lib-
eral" provisions of many of the general corporation statutes enacted since around 1925:   (1) the lack of interest on the part of
shareholders in participating in corporate meetings; (2) the fact
that the draftsmen and committees that have revamped the
older statutes have, for the most part, been lawyers who have
represented corporations, large or small, and who have had little
patience with protective devices which might delay the smooth
functioning of the corporate machinery even when such devices
were for the protection of the true owners; and (3) the lack of
knowledge and of time of legislative committees, which have
thrown into their legislative laps a draft of a new corporation
code, to examine carefully every section of the draft, call in
disinterested corporate experts for advice, and then redraft if
necessary or send it back to the original draftsmen for revision
in accordance with the recommendations made by these committees.   Model codes may be excellent, but they too should be
fine-combed for possible inequities to shareholders or creditors.

At many points in this book modern corporation statutes on
specific corporate problems must be examined.   They will be
discussed, as they have been thus far, in connection with particu-

---

19. Ballantine,   Corporations   41
(Rev. ed. 1946).

20. See Emerson, The New Ohio
General Corporation Law: Some
Comments and Some Comparisons,
24 U. of Cin.L.Rev. 463, at 473–474,
476–477, 496–497, 499, 502, 505, 515–
518 (1956); Emerson, Vital Weak-
nesses and the New Virginia Stock
Corporation Law and the Model
Act, 42 Va.L.Rev. 489, at 497, 498–
499, 507, 513–514, 518, 519, 521–
522, 525, 527, 528 (1956); Emerson
and Latcham, Shareholder Democracy: A Broader Outlook for Corporations (1954);   Harris,   The
Model Business Corporation Act—
Invitation to Irresponsibility? 50
Nw.U.L.Rev. 1 (1955).

lar topics.   At the present moment we are concerned with the requirements set up by modern general corporation statutes to become a corporation and what legal results occur when there is not substantial compliance with the conditions precedent which the statute requires.

§ 2.   Conditions Precedent to Incorporation under General Statutes

The traditional method prescribed by general statutes is for the specified number of properly qualified incorporators, usually three,[21] to sign and acknowledge a document variously described as "articles of incorporation" or "certificate of incorporation" or "articles of association" or "charter" containing information required by the statute and a generous amount that is permitted though not required, and to file the document with the secretary of state and frequently with a local officer, the filing also being required by the statute.   Some statutes require an official, usually the secretary of state, to issue a certificate as evidence that the statute has been complied with, while a few prescribe letters patent signed by the governor under the state's seal, a really formal document, granting corporateness.   The better modern statutes contain provisions that upon the filing of the certificate or articles of incorporation at the designated office or offices the persons so associating, their successors and assigns, shall be and constitute a body corporate.

Conditions precedent to filing, that is, the facts which must be stated in the certificate or articles, are discernible by the usual statement in the statute that "The Certificate of Incorporation shall set forth:" followed by a number of requirements.   The Delaware statute is illustrative.   It requires (1) the name of the corporation which must contain one of the words "association," "company," "corporation," "club," "foundation," "incorporated," "institute," "society," "union," "syndicate," or "limited," or "co.," "corp.," "inc." or "Ltd."   The name must be such as to distinguish it from the names of other corporations organized under the laws of Delaware and recorded with the Secretary of State; (2) the name of the county and city, town or place in which the principal office or place of business is to be located in the state, and the name and address of the corporation's resident agent who

---

21.   One natural person 21 years or more, and any corporation, may be sole incorporators under Ky.Rev. Stat.1953, § 271.025, as amended by L.1954, c. 33.   And see Mich.Gen. Corp.Act § 2 and § 3 as amended by L.1949, Act 229 [15 Mich.Stat.Ann., 1957 Cum.Supp. § 21.3], which provides that one or more incorpora- tors may incorporate under this act."   Under Iowa Code Ann. § 491.1, "any number of persons" may be incorporated.   See also Wis.Bus.Corp.Law of 1951, § 180.- 44.   The Michigan Act, § 2, defines incorporator to include a corpo- ration.

may be an individual or corporation, and where the city or town contains 6,000 or more inhabitants, the street and number must be stated in either case; (3) the nature of the business, or objects or purposes; (4) a detailed statement of the stock authorized to be issued with a setting forth of the minimum amount of capital with which the corporation will commence business, "which shall not be less than $1,000"; (5) the names and places of residence of each of the incorporators (any number of persons not less than three); (6) whether the corporation is to have perpetual existence, and if not, then the time when its existence is to commence and cease; (7) whether or not the private property of the stockholders shall be subject to the payment of corporate debts, and if so, to what extent.[22] Then follow several paragraphs of matters which *may* be set forth in the articles but need not be.

Under the Delaware statute the certificate must be signed and sealed by the incorporators individually and acknowledged as the act and deed of the signers and that the facts stated are true. "The certificate shall be filed in the office of the Secretary of State, who shall furnish a certified copy of the same under his hand and seal of office, and the certified copy shall be recorded in the office of the recorder of the county where the principal office of the corporation is to be located in this State, in a book kept for that purpose." [23]

§ 3. Failure to Comply with Statutory Requirements—Mandatory and Directory Provisions

The preceding section has pointed out the conditions precedent which one modern statute requires in order to obtain corporateness. If there has been substantial compliance with these conditions precedent a de jure corporation results. No one, not even the state, may then question its existence. But if there is a failure substantially to comply with one or more of the mandatory conditions precedent or perhaps the entire failure to perform one of the conditions, real problems arise. And they arise in a number of ways. The state itself may bring an action in the nature of quo warranto to take the life of an organization parading as a corporation without complying with what the legislature has clearly stated must be there if the incorporating group is to be recognized as a separate legal personality. Or a party who has contracted with what appeared to him to be a corporation or who has been tortiously injured by a servant of what appears to be a corporation sues the supposed corporation and finds it defending on the ground that it is no corporation. Or the suit

22. § 102(a), Del.Gen.Corp.Law of   23. § 103(b), ibid.
     1953.

may be by the "corporation" and the defense raised by the defendant may be nul tiel corporation. Or the plaintiff may bring his action in tort or contract against the associates of what was thought to be a corporation in order to hold them personally on obligations they did not have the slightest cause to suspect were theirs. Whatever failure there was in complying with the statute may have been due to the negligence or inadvertence of the attorney who drew up the articles and failed to comply with all of the conditions precedent or who failed to file the articles in the proper place or places; or it may have been due to the innocent mistake of business men who themselves attempted to draft and file the articles; or it may have occurred with full knowledge of the failure to comply. And cases have occasionally arisen where there was full compliance with a statute which was later held unconstitutional or where the statute did not authorize the type of business for which the corporation was organized, or, though there was full compliance, the limited corporate life granted by the statute has run out and the associates have continued the corporate business without realizing this.

While the failure to comply substantially with a mandatory provision will prevent a corporation from being de jure, a failure to comply with a directory provision does not have that consequence.[24] While what is mandatory and what is directory depends primarily upon the legislative intent (which is never quite fully disclosed even by the use of the word "shall") those matters which are insignificant and which have little or no bearing on protecting shareholders, creditors or the public are usually classified as directory merely. Failure of subscription and payment of all or a proportionate part of capital required to be paid in before incorporation, or failure of the articles to state the principal place of business, the duration of the corporate life, or the minimum amount of capital, which has been paid in may well warrant the determination, in a proper case, that there has been a violation of mandatory provisions.[25] But even where mandatory provi-

24. In Peo. v. Ford, 294 Ill. 319, 128 N.E. 470 (1920), the then statute required the incorporators to sign, seal and acknowledge the articles. The failure to affix their seals was held not to prevent the corporation from becoming de jure as the provision concerning sealing was considered a directory provision. Failure to file the duplicate "certificate of organization" where the original was properly filed in county clerk's office was held in Cross v. Pinckneyville Mill Co., 17 Ill. 54 (1855), to be a violation merely of a directory provision. And where statute required no-

tice to be given shareholders in a certain manner but persons attended the meeting and waived notice, this was held to be a mere violation of a directory matter. J. W. Butler Paper Co. v. Cleveland, 220 Ill. 128, 77 N.E. 99 (1906). Statute required affidavit stating that 10% of the stock subscription had been paid "in good faith." Affidavit failing to state "in good faith" was held a substantial compliance. Peo. v. Stockton & Visalia R. Co., 45 Cal. 306, 13 Am.Rep. 178 (1873).

25. In action to forfeit charter, so held: State ex rel. Sanche v. Webb,

sions are in issue and it is claimed that substantial compliance has not occurred, courts have recognized (or better, created) an organization which the statutes have not expressly sanctioned called a de facto corporation provided certain judge-made requirements have been met. And, even when such requirements have not been met, the common law has frequently reached into the doctrine of estoppel where the parties in good faith had dealt on a corporate basis to find what has been loosely called a "corporation by estoppel." We shall now examine these common law creations to discover their legal incidents and their importance in a world where men make mistakes.

§ 4.   De facto Corporations—What are—Incidents of

The first question that arises is why should the courts recognize a "corporation" that falls short of being what the legislature has so specifically commanded? Presumably, the legislature has required those matters to be done which it has thought wise should be done prior to granting the privilege of being a corporation. Perhaps the best answer to the question is that men frequently make mistakes in drawing up the certificate or articles of incorporation or in the filing thereof, business is transacted by associates and third parties on what is innocently thought by all to be a corporate basis, and much injustice would result if, upon discovery of defective compliance, innocent persons should be held on the basis of some other relationship, that of partners or agents who have no principals, for example. But, as we shall see, when the failure to comply exceeds the reasonable bounds set up by the common law, innocent persons are sometimes held to a greater liability than they had reason to expect. Furthermore, the assumption that the legislature has carefully weighed the conditions precedent to becoming a corporation and has made each condition precedent, however small, a mandatory one puts an undue accent upon legislative efficiency and acumen. If the public interest is not jeopardized by the particular noncompliance and can be protected sufficiently by a colorable compliance, there would seem to be no very good reason why collateral attack should be permitted to oust the corporation as party-plaintiff or -defendant or to hold the associates to liability other than that of shareholders in a corporation. There may be some reason for permitting a direct attack by the state in a quo warranto or similar proceeding in order to keep the record straight or to head the corporation in when it attempts to con-

97 Ala. 111, 12 So. 377, 38 Am.St. Rep. 151 (1893); Peo. v. Montecito Water Co., 97 Cal. 276, 32 P. 236, 33 Am.St.Rep. 172 (1893); State ex rel. Howe v. Shelbyville & Chapel Turnpike Co., 41 Ind. 151 (1872); in a condemnation proceeding, so held: Kinston & Carolina R. Co. v. Stroud, 132 N.C. 413, 43 S.E. 913 (1903).

demn land—if it has that power—or to enforce subscriptions to its shares until it has acquired de jure status, but in the last two instances the arguments are not strong and rarely is a state interested in ousting a corporation whose only defect is a failure to comply substantially with the incorporating statute.

Once it has been determined that there has been a substantial compliance with the statutory mandatory conditions precedent to becoming a corporation, a corporation de jure results.[26] The statute may require other conditions precedent to doing business, such as subscription to and payment of a certain proportion of the corporation's capital stock, but such a condition is not, though it might have been made, a condition to becoming a corporation.[27] Four essential factors are said to be necessary for the existence of a de facto corporation: (1) a valid law under which the corporation could have been formed; (2) a good faith attempt to comply with the law; (3) a "colorable" or apparent compliance with it; and (4) user of the corporate powers.[28] Except in a direct attack by the state to take the life of a corporation de facto, such an organization is usually treated, except for a few minor purposes, as if it were de jure. The incidents of limited liability, continuity of life, manner of holding property and of conveying it, manner of bringing and defending suits, of making contracts and of the exercise of corporate powers are, by the great weight of authority, exactly the same as in case of a de jure corporation.

It seems doubtful whether the first requirement of a valid law under which a de jure corporation might have been formed is a just one. Until the high court has spoken on the constitutionality of a statute it is often difficult to determine its constitutional validity. Certainly it is placing a big burden upon organizers of a corporation to ascertain at their peril whether the corporation statute is a valid one for, if it is not, the association they have raised is likely to be considered a general partner-

---

26. Martin v. Deetz, 102 Cal. 55, 36 P. 368, 41 Am.St.Rep. 151 (1894); Moe v. Harris, 142 Minn. 442, 172 N.W. 494 (1919).

27. See Beck v. Stimmel, 39 Ohio App. 510, 177 N.E. 920 (1931), where statute provided for corporate existence upon filing of articles with the secretary of state and also required that the capital stock specified in the articles as that amount with which the corporation would commence business must be subscribed and paid in. The amount set forth in the articles was neither subscribed nor paid in.

The incorporators who had opened for business were held liable as if they had been joint enterprisers. See Ohio Gen.Corp.Law of 1955, Rev.Code § 1701.12, which purports to change this result.

28. Inter-Ocean Newspaper Co. v. Robertson, 296 Ill. 92, 129 N.E. 523 (1921); Culkin v. Hillside Restaurant, Inc., 126 N.J.Eq. 97, 8 A. 2d 173 (1939); Baker v. Bates-Street Shirt Co., 6 F.2d 854 (1st Cir. 1925); Wilkin Grain Co. v. Monroe County Co-Operative Ass'n, 208 Iowa 921, 223 N.W. 899 (1929).

ship with unlimited liability in its members.[29]   The basis of the rule is that corporations can be formed only by statutory fiat and if the statute is unconstitutional there is actually no statute at all; hence, the state's authorization is lacking.

Good faith is essential if the court is to find a de facto corporation.   Thus, if the associates know of the failure to comply substantially with the statute they are in no position to argue that the organization should be treated as if it were a corporation even though third parties may have dealt with them on a corporate basis, nor can they avoid unlimited liability in such a case.[30]

But if there has been a good faith attempt to comply with the statutory "musts" and this has resulted in "colorable" compliance, a term which has never been adequately explained by the courts but meaning roughly that there has been reasonable closeness to substantial compliance, and there has been an exercise of the corporate powers ("user") a corporation de facto results.   And, of course, if there has been no exercise of corporate powers no problem can arise.

§ 5.   What is "Colorable Compliance" with the Mandatory Conditions Precedent?

Cases where the state has sued to compel a forfeiture of a corporate charter are of little aid in this area for, unless there has been substantial compliance with mandatory conditions precedent, the state in a direct action is entitled to forfeiture. Colorable compliance is no defense against the direct action.

There has been no general agreement as to what performance will qualify as "colorable compliance" and in some cases where de facto corporations were found to exist there is no mention made of this requirement.[31]   One would think that the filing requirement is as important to the public interest as any

29.   Eaton v. Walker, 76 Mich. 579, 43 N.W. 638 (1889) (held as partners, the statute being unconstitutional).   In Davis v. Stevens, 104 F. 235 (D.Ct.S.D.1900), there was no law under which the corporation could be formed.   The "corporation" was bankrupt and the associates were held as partners.

30.   Culkin v. Hillside Restaurant, Inc., supra, note 28; Harrill v. Davis, 168 F. 187, 22 L.R.A.,N.S., 1153 (8th Cir. 1909).

31.   See on this last statement Frawley v. Tenafly Transportation Co., 95 N.J.L. 405, 113 A. 242 at 245 (1921): "It (the trial court) included a finding that the three individual defendants had attempted bona fide to form a corporation, and that they had likewise done acts which amounted to the exercise of corporate powers."   The court held there was a de facto corporation, holding it to a tort committed prior to the recording and filing of its certificate of incorporation.   See also Petition of Planz, 282 App.Div. 552, 125 N.Y.S.2d 750 (1953); Paper Products Co. v. Doggrell, 195 Tenn. 581, 261 S.W.2d 127, at 129, 42 A.L.R.2d 651 (1953).

of the mandatory conditions precedent set up by these statutes, and that a complete failure to file, whether filing is required in one or more places, would be considered so vital a failure that all courts would agree that there has been no "colorable compliance." While a sizeable majority holds such failure to be fatal, there is respectable authority to the contrary.[32] Where filing is required in two places, a quite usual statutory requirement, it would seem that if filing has taken place in one of the designated offices and all other conditions of the statute have been met the colorable compliance requirement, if argued not to exist, would be given short shrift by the courts. Probably a majority of the courts which have had the problem before them hold that filing in one of two designated public offices constitutes colorable compliance and that there can be no collateral attack on the ground of non-filing.[33]

---

32. Baker v. Bates-Street Shirt Co., 6 F.2d 854 (1st Cir. 1925) (only shareholders actively engaged in the business were held unlimitedly liable); Harrill v. Davis, 168 F. 187, 22 L.R.A.,N.S., 1153 (8th Cir. 1909) (debts were incurred prior to filing of articles and associates were held as if partners); Bigelow v. Gregory, 73 Ill. 197 (1874) (collateral attack was permitted where contract was entered into before articles were filed and published as required by statute); Bergeron v. Hobbs, 96 Wis. 641, 71 N.W. 1056, 35 Am.St.Rep. 85 (1897) (articles had been recorded but not filed). *Contra:* Tarbell v. Page, 24 Ill. 46 (1860); Frawley v. Tenafly Transportation Co., 85 N.J.L. 405, 113 A. 242, 22 A.L.R. 369, Ann. at 376 (1921); Tisch Auto Supply Co. v. Nelson, 222 Mich. 196, 192 N.W. 600 (1923); Petition of Planz, 282 App.Div. 552, 125 N.Y.S.2d 750 (1953).

As to effect of non-filing in one or more offices on the attainment of de facto existence, see Annotations in 22 A.L.R. 376 (1923) and 37 A. L.R. 1319 (1925); Warren, Corporate Advantages Without Incorporation 816 et seq. (1929). See also Frey, Cases and Materials on Corporations and Partnerships 31 (1951), containing a chart-analysis of cases concerning individual liability of members of defectively incorporated associations.

33. Cross v. Pinckneyville Mill Co., 17 Ill. 54 (1855) (Statute required

recording in county clerk's office and a duplicate certificate of organization had to be filed with the secretary of state. The former had, but latter had not, been done. *Held:* In suit against stock subscriber to recover calls on his stock, failure to file was not fatal—provision for filing was merely directory); McCarter v. Ketcham, 72 N.J.L. 247, 62 A. 693 (1905) (held a corporation de facto where certificate was filed in county clerk's office but not in the secretary of state's); Bushnell v. Consolidated Ice-Machine Co., 138 Ill. 67, 27 N.E. 596 (1891) (Suit to have company declared a partnership and to have its affairs settled. Certificate had not been recorded in office of recorder of deeds. *Held:* A corporation de facto and there could be no partnership liability); and see later case of Inter-Ocean Newspaper Co. v. Robertson, 296 Ill. 92, 129 N.E. 523 (1921), where the secretary of state had issued a certificate of complete organization but corporation's secretary, though instructed to have a copy recorded with the recorder of deeds, failed to do so. Statute read: "Upon the recording of the said copy, the corporation shall be deemed fully organized and may proceed to business." It was held a de facto corporation since there had been colorable compliance plus the other three requirements. See Frey, supra, note 32, page 31.

A recent case illustrates the minority doctrine.[34] The articles were filed with the secretary of state but not with the county clerk which the Arkansas statute also required. The statute stated that "Upon the filing with the Secretary of State of articles of incorporation, the corporate existence shall begin." One of the three shareholders of the corporation—the two remaining shareholders were Tennessee residents and could not be served in Arkansas—was sued upon a "corporate" contract and was held to the liability of a partner, as filing in one of the two required public offices was not considered colorable compliance. The other two shareholders were sued in Tennessee and that court, while recognizing the doctrine that the liability of shareholders is to be determined by the law of the state in which the corporation is domiciled unless the law is contrary "to the legislation or public policy of Tennessee, or is penal in nature," felt that the Arkansas statute "establishes a 'penalty'" and that the full faith and credit clause of the federal constitution did not require Tennessee to enforce it.[35] The court stated that the Arkansas rule is "contrary to the public policy of Tennessee." [36] Strangely enough, the federal court (later, on rehearing, reversing itself) in litigation covering the same problem with the same shareholders had held that the Arkansas statute was not penal,[37] and the Tennessee court cited the case. Seeing the injustice of holding shareholders as partners when they had in good faith done everything but file in the second public office, the Tennessee court held that the imposition of unlimited liability under these circumstances was contrary to the public policy of Tennessee, that all who dealt with the associates on a corporate basis were aware that corporations are used to obtain limited liability, and that the Tennessee rule forwards the accomplishment of this objective. Hence, the court concluded, Tennessee need not give full faith and credit to the Arkansas law.

Another provision in the statutes requires a certain number of incorporators to subscribe and (frequently) to acknowledge the articles or certificate of incorporation. Some of the statutes still require that a certain proportion of these be citizens of the incorporating state or of the United States; occasionally

34. Whitaker v. Mitchell Mfg. Co., 219 Ark. 779, 244 S.W.2d 965 (1952). See later case to same effect. Burks v. Cook, 225 Ark. 756, 284 S.W.2d 855 (1955), noted in 10 Ark.L.Rev. 217 (1956).

35. Paper Products Co. v. Doggrell, 195 Tenn. 581, 261 S.W.2d 127, at 130, 42 A.L.R.2d 651 (1953).

36. Ibid. 261 S.W.2d at 129.

37. Doggrell v. Great Southern Box Co., Inc., of Mississippi, 206 F.2d 671 (6th Cir. 1953), held the two remaining shareholders to partnership liability. Judge McAllister wrote a strong dissent at page 679 et seq. On petition for rehearing, this case was reversed in id. v. id., 208 F.2d 310 (6th Cir. 1953), with a strong dissent by Judge Martin who wrote the majority opinion in the first hearing of the case.

there is a specific statement that the incorporators must be "adult persons," and it is certainly the general understanding that this must be so even though the statute does not mention the fact. Suppose that fewer incorporators sign than are required; or that one or more signs but fails to acknowledge, when this is specified; or that there is a smaller proportion than permitted of citizens of the state or of the United States signing; or that an infant or mentally incompetent person is among those signing. If all has been done in good faith and the remaining statutory conditions precedent commanded are performed is it just that collateral attack be permitted? Is not this a colorable compliance with the statutory provision? In a recent Iowa case collateral attack was made by a judgment creditor who had levied upon property which the defectively organized corporation had mortgaged to another, the plaintiff's argument being based upon the invalidity of the mortgage because of the non-existence of the corporation since there were some incorporators who were infants. The statute stated that any number of persons, without specifying adults, might incorporate for lawful purposes. The court held that there had been colorable compliance and that, while the state might have an action directly attacking the corporation's existence, collateral attack would not be permitted. Said the court: "The reason a collateral attack by a third person will not avail against a corporation de facto is that, if the rights and franchises have been usurped, they are the rights and franchises of the state, and it alone can challenge the validity of the franchise. Until such interposition, the public may treat those in possession and exercising corporate powers under color of law as doing so rightfully. The rule is in the interest of the public and is essential to the safety of business transactions with corporations." [38]

It would seem that if there has been performance of the mandatory conditions precedent to the extent that the public interest is protected, the requirement of colorable compliance has been met. And if the court, for any reason, finds that something less than colorable compliance exists there is still a chance that if the parties have dealt with each other on a corporate basis, the corporate associates believing that they are a cor-

---

38. Thies v. Weible (Farmers' Union Live Stock Credit Ass'n, Intervenor), 126 Neb. 720, 254 N.W. 420, at 423 (1934). Would not the quoted portion be applicable also in a case where the parties dealt on a corporate basis but the incorporation was so defective as to result in no corporation? In Bond & Braswell v. Scott Lumber Co., 128 La. 818, 55 So. 468 (1911), one incorporator was legally incompetent. The associates were held not individually liable on the corporation's contracts on the basis of estoppel. In American Salt Co. v. Heidenheimer, 80 Tex. 344, 15 S.W. 1038, 26 Am.St.Rep. 743 (1891), two of the incorporators did not qualify as citizens under the statute. Innocent shareholders were held not to be partners.

poration and the other contracting party believing that he is dealing with a corporation, the judicial mind will accept an argument that there should be no collateral attack because of an estoppel raised by such dealing.

§ 6. Corporations by "Estoppel"

The term *"corporations by estoppel"* is not a happy one because, actually, when estoppel is properly used to deny collateral attack there is neither a corporation de jure nor de facto in existence. Some courts have talked of estoppel in cases clearly indicating that all the elements of a de facto corporation were present, but there is no need of using the estoppel argument if the court recognizes the de facto corporation fully as having, for most purposes, the characteristics of a de jure corporation. However, some of the earlier cases particularly required the setting up of the requirements for de facto existence before the estoppel argument was permitted.[39] Majority opinion is *contra* and does not require de facto elements in order to raise an estoppel. The justification of this view may well be that the state is not as much concerned with a good faith assumption of corporateness as it is in seeing that justice is done between the parties concerned. And if the parties who have dealt on a corporate basis obtain the same remedies they would have obtained had the corporation been de jure, justice is done.

The term "estoppel" has been used to deny the right to deny corporateness. It is apparent that the only situation where a true estoppel in pais is involved is where the party contracting or dealing with the corporation is the plaintiff. If the "corporation" through the use of a corporate name or by other representation has led the other party to believe that he is dealing with a corporation and he has so dealt, the association cannot deny that it is a corporation. But if the "corporation" is the plaintiff and the defendant hopes to oust the plaintiff on the ground that it has no capacity to sue because it is not a corporation, the better and majority of cases hold there is an estoppel, not in pais, true, but a loose estoppel, because the parties have dealt on a corporate basis.[40]

39. Callender v. Painesville R. Co., 11 Ohio St. 516 (1860). "[U]ntil comparatively recently it was contended by some that, with one or two exceptions, the de facto doctrine did not prevent collateral attack except in cases where there had been a mutual assumption of corporateness." Stevens, Corporations 152–153 (2d ed. 1949), citing Warren, Collateral Attack on Incorporation, 20 Harv.L.Rev. 456, 479 (1907), and Warren, Corporate Advantages Without Incorporation 792 (1929).

40. One of the leading cases is Lowell-Woodward Hardware Co. v. Woods, 104 Kan. 729, 180 P. 734 (1919), where the "corporate"-promisee of a note sued the promisor upon it. The promisor contended the promisee was not a corporation. The court held that

Not all courts have been willing to recognize the loose estoppel argument, some insisting upon finding the elements which form the basis of estoppel in pais. Said Sanborn, Cir. J., in a leading case taking this view:[41] "The fact that the plaintiff dealt with and treated the Coweta Cotton & Milling Company as a corporation did not estop it from denying that it was such before the defendants filed their articles of incorporation, because it was not a corporation de facto before that time and because the indispensable elements of an estoppel in pais, ignorance of the truth and absence of equal means of knowledge of it by the party who claims the estoppel, and action by the latter induced by the misrepresentation of the party against whom the estoppel is invoked, do not exist in the case at bar." The associates, all of whom were actively engaged in prosecuting the business, were held to partnership liability. The result has been explained by pointing out that "The defendants did not understand and could not have understood that they were a corporation duly organized, and that they were conducting the business under such organization, and the only question was whether, on the facts, they could be held jointly liable."[42] In any case where the associates realize that their association is less than de jure and yet operate on a corporate basis, it cannot be said that they are acting in good faith and it is not unjust that they be held as if they were partners. This is even clearer if they knowingly operate under conditions indicating lack of corporateness de facto. But there is no good reason why the party who has dealt with an organization known by its associates not to have reached the de facto or de jure corporation stage should be barred from suit against the "corporation" so represented by the associates to him if he has relied upon the representation. He should have the choice of suing the organization as if it were a

---

since the parties had dealt on a corporate basis the defendant was estopped to deny the plaintiff's corporate existence, saying: "We agree that no full, formal, technical estoppel to deny corporate existence arises from such state of facts, but we think it accords with modern views of good practice and tends to promote substantial justice . . ." 180 P. at 734. See also Commercial Bank v. Pfeiffer, 108 N.Y. 242, 15 N.E. 311 (1888), where dealing was with the Commercial Bank of Keokuk, "evidently the name of a corporate institution." The plaintiff who had dealt with the bank was held estopped to deny its corporate existence. But see Retail Merchants Service v. John Bauer & Co., 124 Neb. 360, 246 N.W. 726, aff'd on rehearing, 125 Neb. 61, 248 N.W. 813 (1933). Person dealing with the Retail Merchants Service was held not estopped to deny its corporateness. Did the name indicate non-corporateness? Compare Société Titanor v. Paxton & Vierling Iron Works, 124 Neb. 570, 247 N.W. 356 (1953). See notes on the basis of corporation by estoppel in 7 Minn.L.Rev. 42 (1922); 14 Calif.L.Rev. 486 (1926); 84 U. of Pa.L.Rev. 514 (1936).

41.   Harrill v. Davis, 168 F. 187, at 195, 22 L.R.A.,N.S., 1153 (8th Cir. 1909).

42.   Baker v. Bates-Street Shirt Co., 6 F.2d 854, at 858 (1st Cir. 1925).

corporation or of pursuing the associates as partners. And if the statute makes shareholders liable beyond their contractual liability to pay for their shares, such a plaintiff, if he chooses, should have full advantage of such provisions if he elects to pursue the corporate remedy. His is a true estoppel in pais case.

§ 7.   Liability of Shareholders Where Organization is Neither De Jure nor De Facto

This situation may have arisen because there was no statute under which the corporation could have been formed, or there was a statute but it was unconstitutional, or there was a failure to comply to the extent that a corporation de facto resulted, or the corporate life had ended and the associates carried on thereafter in innocent ignorance of the fact, or though the parties dealt on a corporate basis and estoppel would seem to apply the court, when posed with the problem of whether the associates should be held as partners, accepts the view that, at least in this situation, estoppel does not apply.

If there was no statute under which the corporation could have been legally formed the necessary legislative fiat is lacking and the associates have been held as partners.[43] However, where a statute exists at the time suit is brought, though not at the time of the formation of the corporation, it has been held that the defect having been cured, collateral attack will not be permitted.[44] The state has shown that it has no policy against a corporation formed for similar purposes so that nothing but a technical argument against corporateness remains. Hence, the parties are treated exactly as they had expected to be at the time they dealt on a corporate basis.

Should good faith incorporation under a statute which turns out to be unconstitutional be treated as if no statute existed or as if one existed at least until the discovery of its unconstitutionality? Some courts have treated this situation as if no statute existed and have permitted collateral attack even by the associates, and have held the associates as partners when sued by a creditor of the "corporation."[45] This is harsh doctrine for whether a corporation statute is unconstitutional or not is usual-

43. Davis v. Stevens, 104 F. 235 (D.C.S.D.1900); Imperial Bldg. Co. v. Chicago Open Board of Trade, 238 Ill. 100, 87 N.E. 167 (1909).

44. Baum v. Baum Holding Co., 158 Neb. 197, 62 N.W.2d 864 (1954), noted in 53 Mich.L.Rev. 283 (1954); Lewis v. West Side Trust & Savings Bank, 376 Ill. 23, 32 N.E.2d 907 (1941); Jennings v. Dark, 175 Ind. 332, 92 N.E. 778 (1910), a negli-

gence action; Mason v. Stevens, 16 S.D. 320, 92 N.W. 424 (1902). See notes on problem of Mason v. Stevens in 16 Harv.L.Rev. 362 (1903); on Jennings v. Dark, 11 Col.L.Rev. 160 (1911).

45. Brandenstein v. Hoke, 101 Cal. 131, 35 P. 562 (1894); Eaton v. Walker, 76 Mich. 579, 43 N.W. 638, 6 L.R.A. 102 (1889).

ly not easy of determination and furthermore there is always a presumption that statutes are constitutional. Better opinion, fortunately, respects the presumption and the difficulty, holding that a de facto corporation is possible under such circumstances and that the usual incidents of corporate liability follow.[46] Again, the expectation of the parties when they dealt on a corporate basis is respected. Estoppel is another valid argument in such cases.

The earlier statutes did not grant perpetual life to corporations but usually stated a time limit with perhaps a privilege of renewal for a like or different period. Some of the present-day statutes permit the incorporators, if they wish, to state in the certificate or articles a time limit on the life of their corporation. Suppose the corporation continues functioning without renewal because the directors have not realized that the corporate life has ended. Contracts are entered into and torts are committed against and by the "corporation." If there is no provision, for renewal, then there is no statute under which the corporation can function and one of the elements of a de facto corporation is missing. The problem is handled in a manner similar to that in which no corporation statute existed under which the particular type of corporation could be legally formed. With a statutory provision for renewal of the corporate life the better opinions hold that the former corporation de jure is now one de facto or by estoppel with the incidents, with few exceptions, of a corporation de jure.[47] While there has been no color-

46. Gardner v. Minneapolis & St. Louis Ry. Co., 73 Minn. 517, 76 N. W. 282 (1898), aff'd 177 U.S. 332, 20 S.Ct. 656, 44 L.Ed. 793 (1900). Statutory liability of shareholders was imposed in favor of a creditor. Gwynne v. Board of Education, 259 N.Y. 191, 181 N.E. 353 (1932). See Dodd, Partnership Liability of Stockholders in Defective Corporations, 40 Harv.L.Rev. 525 (1927); Field, The Status of a Private Corporation Organized Under Unconstitutional Statute, 17 Col.L.Rev. 327 (1917).

47. Thompson v. Park Savings Bank, 77 F.2d 955 (D.C.Cir., 1935), cert. denied 296 U.S. 592, 56 S.Ct. 104, 105, 80 L.Ed. 419 (1935); id. v. id., 96 F.2d 544 (D.C.Cir., 1938), cert. denied 305 U.S. 606, 59 S.Ct. 66, 83 L.Ed. 385 (1938); Detroit Trust Co. v. Allinger, 271 Mich. 600, 261 N.W. 90 (1935). *Contra:* Bonfils v. Hayes, 70 Colo. 36, 201 P. 677 (1921), active managers were held personally liable in tort;

Jones v. Young, 115 W.Va. 225, 174 S.E. 885 (1934), a case where corporation functioned after a forfeiture of its charter for non-payment of taxes, the court holding shareholders liable in tort.

In Thompson v. Park Sav. Bank, (above) 77 F.2d 955, at 959 (D.C. Cir., 1935), where the bank's charter had expired, Martin, C. J., stated: "The persons thereafter dealing with the corporation as depositors were charged with a knowledge of the corporate charter. They therefore knew, either actually or constructively, that the bank was not then authorized by its charter to proceed with a general banking business. Therefore they are estopped to deny the legality of the bank's actions and cannot hold the directors or stockholders individually or as partners." Continuance of its business after expiration of its charter was held ultra vires. But the directors, as trustees under the laws of Alabama

able compliance with the renewal provisions and thus on a strict application of the usual four requirements for a corporation de facto such a corporation has not been born, there would seem to be no particular legislative policy to support by holding otherwise. And by a finding of a corporation de facto tort cases are taken care of as well as those cases where the parties have dealt on a corporate basis. Of course, if a statute prohibits a corporation whose charter has been forfeited for any reason to continue functioning during the period of forfeiture, corporate contracts will be subject to collateral attack and estoppel will not be available in the face of the legislative command.[48]

In any case where the failure to meet corporation de facto standards occurs an estoppel argument is possible provided the associates acted in good faith in their attempt to comply with the statute's mandatory conditions precedent and the "corporation" and other contracting party dealt on a corporate basis. Courts have had little trouble when the suit has been by third party against the corporation or vice versa. An estoppel has generally been recognized in both cases. But where the third party sues the associates claiming that, since no corporation de jure or de facto exists, the associates should be held as partners, diverse holdings appear. It would seem that the same estoppel argument should cover this type of case, for then the parties obtain the legal redress, and only the legal redress which each anticipated when dealing on a corporate basis. Is it unjust to tell the parties who have dealt in this manner that an implied promise will be raised that, if it turns out there is no corporation recognized by the law, their rights will be settled in the same manner as if a corporation de jure actually existed?[49] Does the state have such a vital interest in keeping its incorporators and shareholders within rather narrowly defined corporate grooves that its interest outweighs the injustice of holding all or a part of the officers and shareholders unlimitedly liable as if they had intended to carry on as co-owners a business for profit, that is, a partnership?

Three factual situations suggest the variations to be expected in this area: (1) where associates combine to carry on

where the banking corporation was formed, cannot avoid their duties as such even though directors and depositors both had equal opportunity of knowing the effect of the statute. A waiver or ratification by the beneficiaries (depositors) requires full knowledge of all the material circumstances and full apprisal of the effect of the acts waived or ratified. Id. v. id., 96 F. 2d 544, at 548 (1938).

48. Van Landingham v. United Tuna Packers, 189 Cal. 353, 208 P. 973 (1922), noted in 11 Calif. L.Rev. 40 (1922).

49. Gartside Coal Co. v. Maxwell, 22 F. 197 (C.C.Mo.1884). And see Warren, Collateral Attack on Incorporation, 20 Harv.L.Rev. 456, 475–476 (1907).

as a corporation but with no intent of complying with the requirements of the corporation statute or, at least, with knowledge that they have not complied with them; (2) the same facts as in (1) but with the additional fact that shareholders with no knowledge of the facts in (1) have been brought into the picture; and (3) where all the shareholders thought the corporation was properly incorporated. One fact is common to these three factual situations, namely, neither a corporation de jure nor de facto exists. The additional fact of dealing on a corporate basis with parties who now hope to hold the associates as if they were partners should be noted for any estoppel raised must be based upon such dealing. In (1) all courts would agree that there is no injustice in holding those to partnership liability who had no intent to incorporate or who, while they may intend to do this later, carry on as a corporation prior to perfecting its organization.[50] As to (2), all courts would have no difficulty in imposing partnership liability upon those who participated in carrying on as a corporation when they knew such was not the case, but courts split on the liability of the innocent shareholders. The better holdings, but probably the minority in number,[51] are that the innocent shareholders may be held only to the extent that they might have been held had the corporation been de jure. In (3) where neither the shareholders, whether inactive or managing, know of the defect which makes the association less than a de facto corporation, the better decisions hold the inactive innocent shareholders to the limited liability which would have been theirs had the attempted incorporation resulted in a corporation de jure.

One of the strongest statements on this point was made by Bigelow, J., over a century ago in a case frequently referred to today, *Fay* v. *Noble*:[52] "We are not aware of any authority, . . . that, in consequence of an omission to comply with the requisitions of law in the organization of a corporation, by which its proceedings were rendered void, persons who had subscribed

---

50. Harrill v. Davis, 168 F. 187, 22 L.R.A.,N.S., 1153 (8th Cir., 1909). At page 193 the court stated: "The defendants cannot escape individual liability for the $4700 on the ground that the . . . company was a corporation de facto when that portion of the plaintiff's claim was incurred, because it then had no color of incorporation, and they knew it and yet actively used its name to incur the obligation." The same would be true where shareholders learn of their defectively organized corporation and do nothing about curing the defect.

Magruder, A Note on Partnership Liability of Stockholders in Defective Corporations, 40 Harv.L. Rev. 733, at 746 (1927).

51. See Professor Frey's chart, "Analysis of Cases Concerning Individual Liability of Members of Defectively Incorporated Associations," in his Cases and Materials on Corporations and Partnerships 31 (1951).

52. 7 Cush. (61 Mass.) 188, at 192 (1851). See also Kinney v. Bank of Plymouth, 213 Iowa 267, 236 N.W. 31 (1931).

for and taken stock in the company, thereby became copartners. The doctrine seems to us to be quite novel and somewhat startling. Surely it cannot be, in the absence of all fraudulent intent, (and none was proved or alleged in this case,) that such a legal result follows as to fasten on parties involuntarily, for such a cause, the enlarged liability of copartners; a liability neither contemplated nor assented to by them. The very statement of the proposition carries with it a sufficient refutation." But the court held that those who had acted or purported to act for the association as its agents were acting without authority as there was no principal who could appoint an agent. Consequently, such purported agents were principals and liable as such. Thus innocent persons—quite as innocent as the inactive shareholders— were to be held because of an agency doctrine which the court thought applicable.[53] But is it applicable? Whatever authority the board of directors of this defective corporation possessed came from its members; and whatever powers its contracting officers and agents had stemmed from the board. Logically, then, if anyone is to be held it should be the principals, that is the shareholders, rather than the agents whose contracts clearly showed that they were not dealing on their own behalf. And of course if they too are shareholders they could be held as principals. But if it is unjust to hold the inactive innocent shareholders to unlimited liability, is it not also unjust to hold unlimitedly liable the active innocent members? Under this doctrine if any or all of the agents who made contracts for the supposed corporation owned not a share of stock they would be individually liable for contracts thus made because of the lack of a principal. There would be something to be said for this doctrine if the party dealing with the "corporation" were confined to remedies less valuable than those available when the association turns out to be a corporation de jure or de facto. But if he is allowed to pursue such remedies he, the corporation, its shareholders, whether active or inactive, and the corporate officers and agents would then be treated according to their original expectation and no one would be obtaining a windfall. The only valid arguments against such an approach are (1) that the state has a vital interest in having its specifications of corporate existence complied with even where there has been innocent noncompliance, and (2) that the now plaintiff who claims that some or all of the associates are unlimitedly liable has been misled by the representatives of the associates into dealing on a corporate basis. If

53. *Accord*: Baker v. Bates-Street Shirt Co., 6 F.2d 854 (1st Cir. 1925). But that the majority rule holds inactive shareholders to unlimited liability, see Dodd, Partnership Liability of Stockholders in Defective Corporations, 40 Harv.L. Rev. 521, at 560 (1927). But see Magruder, A Note on Partnership Liability in Defective Corporations, 40 Harv.L.Rev. 733 (1927).

(2) can be proved, then unlimited liability should follow. But it seems doubtful whether (1) can be supported in this late period of corporation law except upon arguments that seemed pretty weak a century ago and are much weaker today.

A century ago there was a fear of business and manufacturing expansion through the use of the corporate form, a fear which no longer exists. Incorporation by special act was fast being superseded by the enactment and use of general statutes which, at that time, contained many restrictions. It is not surprising that, at that time, much emphasis was placed upon complying substantially with the statutory requirements. But today, except where the innocent failure to comply with mandatory conditions precedent may have a serious tendency to thwart a known legislative policy, there would seem to be little reason for imposing unlimited liability upon those believing themselves to be shareholders in a corporation properly formed, whether they be inactive or active, or upon officers and agents who had no intimation that they were acting for anything less than a corporation de jure.[54]

But suppose there has been no dealing between the parties on a corporate basis. Let us assume that an employee in the course of his employment with the "corporation" negligently injures the plaintiff and upon discovery that it is not a corporation de jure or de facto, he brings an action against the associates, whether inactive or active, on the claim that they are actually partners. Professor Frey analyzed all the cases he could find where there had and had not been corporate dealings and of the thirty-two cases in the latter category, fifteen held the inactive associates liable, fifteen held the managing associates liable while two held them not liable, and not one held the inactive associates not liable.[55] There can be, of course, no estoppel in such cases. And it seems just that the injured party should not be confined to the usual remedies available in case of a tort committed by a corporation de facto or de jure. The equities in his case would seem to far outweigh those of even the inactive and innocent shareholders.

54. See Staver & Abbott Mfg. Co. v. Blake, 111 Mich. 282, 69 N.W. 508, 38 L.R.A. 798 (1896); Carpenter, Are Members of a Defectively Organized Corporation Liable as Partners, 8 Minn.L.Rev. 409 (1924). "If they were acting in good faith for a supposed corporation, there might well be found an implied contractual limitation of liability which would permit remedies only as if they were incorporated." Ballantine, Corporations 96 (Rev. ed. 1946).

55. Frey, Cases and Materials on Corporations and Partnerships, chart on page 31 (1951). Professor Frey found 211 cases in both categories. His chart referring to cases where there were dealings on a corporate basis is not nearly as positive as to what may be expected from courts in these cases as is the chart where dealings were not on a corporate basis.

From his examination of "all the ascertainable cases" involving the individual liability of associates of defectively organized corporations Professor Frey concluded: "These conclusions are evident: (1) the utter impossibility of formulating a brief proposition, such as the orthodox statements as to 'de jure' and 'de facto' corporations, that will adequately set forth what the courts are actually doing in this field; (2) the extreme importance of the factor 'dealing on a corporate basis' . . . ; and (3) the activity or inactivity of the defendants in the management of the association is, surprisingly, an unimportant factor in determining their personal liability." [56]

It is obvious that this area needs considerable rethinking with an emphasis upon desirable results rather than upon what many courts have too hastily assumed, namely, that persons associating together in good faith for the purpose of becoming incorporated are in fact a partnership when they fail to meet the standards of de facto corporateness; or upon the assumption that only those members passively engaged in the business should be treated as if they were shareholders in a de jure corporation.[57] If all has been done in good faith and whatever dealings are in issue have been on a corporate basis, there is no valid reason today for holding active or inactive members or the officers or agents, always assuming that they have no knowledge of the defective incorporation and have not been negligent in contributing to their ignorance or in organizing the "corporation." The state's interest today is negligible and justice is carried out by giving all parties what they assumed they had, rights and liabilities on a de jure corporate basis.

§ 8. Statutes Bearing upon the Problems of Defectively Formed Corporations

Recent statutes have usually been in terms of making the certificate or articles of incorporation either presumptive or conclusive evidence of corporateness or that all conditions precedent have been met. Some of the statutes also specifically reserve the right of the state to terminate the corporate life for failure to comply substantially with the statutory requirements. The California statute is illustrative: "In any action at law, other than

---

56. Frey, Cases and Materials on Corporations and Partnerships 29–30 (1951), which note relates the editor's study for the American Law Institute in 1932 brought up to the date of Professor Frey's casebook. His chart-analysis of the 211 cases studied is interesting and illuminating. And see Dodd, Partnership Liability of Stockholders in Defective Corporations, 40 Harv. L.Rev. 521, at Appendix A (1927), where he lists the authorities state by state.

57. See particularly Magruder, A Note on Partnership Liability in Defective Corporations, 40 Harv.L. Rev. 733 (1927). He suggests an interesting solution at 748.

one in the nature of quo warranto, the original articles or certificate of incorporation, or a copy of either thereof, duly certified by the Secretary of State, shall be *conclusive* evidence of the formation of the corporation and prima facie evidence of its corporate existence." [58]   Another type of statute prohibits collateral attack, the Delaware statute being illustrative: "No corporation organized under this chapter or existing under the laws of this State, shall be permitted to set up, or rely upon the want of legal organization as a defense to any action against it, and no person transacting business with the corporation, or sued for injury done to its property, shall be permitted to rely upon such want of legal organization as a defense." [59]   This section is badly framed if it was meant to cover the case of a suit by a person transacting business with the supposed corporation against the individual members of the defectively formed corporation.   But the statutes generally show a trend away from overly strict judicial construction to something more lenient and indicate that legislative policy is protected if the quo warranto possibility is kept alive.   Furthermore, it should be noted that these statutes do not foreclose a possible successful argument, that, even where there has been no filing at the designated place or places, or administrative approval has not been obtained, there may still be a corporation de facto or perhaps a mutual dealing on a corporate basis which warrants an estoppel.   And if the statute merely makes the filing with an administrative official, such as the secretary of state, or the obtaining of a certificate presumptive or prima facie evidence of corporateness, the whole business of de facto corporations and of estoppel remains except that the burden of proof has been shifted.

A third type of statute which should not be confused with the others places a liability upon directors and/or participating officers and shareholders for debts of the company to the extent of the minimum amount of capital stock required to be subscribed and paid in before starting business, or for a greater amount, if the business is started before this condition precedent has been met.   Or the statute may set up other conditions precedent before commencing business with the imposition of a penalty if the condition is violated.[60]   Under these statutes the corporation al-

---

58. West's Ann.Cal.Corp.Code § 313. See also Ill.Business Corp.Act § 49; Minn.Business Corp.Act § 301.08; N.Y.Gen.Corp.Law § 12; English Companies Act of 1948, § 15.

59. Del.Gen.Corp.Law of 1953, § 329 (a).   Subpar. (b) preserves the right judicially to inquire into the validity of corporate existence and its lawful possession of any cor-

porate power.   See also South Dakota Code of 1939, § 11.0108.

60. Fair examples are: Ohio Rev. Code § 1701.12 (liability of participating incorporators and directors who commence business before the minimum capital stated in the articles has been subscribed and paid in cannot exceed the minimum stated); Ark.Stat.1947,

ready has acquired its legal existence, or should have. If it has not acquired legal existence de jure or de facto, or if the statute has not raised a conclusive presumption of corporateness or has not prohibited collateral attack, the problems of de facto corporateness or of estoppel must be fought over again.[61]

§ 64.607 (liability of directors and shareholders to extent of minimum capital); 5 Idaho Code Ann. 1948, § 30–110 (liability of directors and officers who participate is unlimited); Wis.Stat.Ann., § 180.-40(1) (e).

61. See Beck v. Stimmel, 39 Ohio App. 510, 177 N.E. 920 (1931), discussed in Note, Corporations De Facto Under the Ohio Act, 7 Ohio St.L.J. 71 (1941). The holding has now been cured by a 1955 change. Ohio Rev.Code § 1701.12. Compare Moe v. Harris, 142 Minn. 442, 172 N.W. 494 (1919) which case has lost its importance since 20 Minn.Stat. Ann., § 301.13. Moe v. Harris was badly decided in the first instance and an abler court would have done better with Beck v. Stimmel had it analogized the situation to that of directors who started the business before the minimum capital had been subscribed and paid in. In Automotriz Del Golfo de California, S. A. De C. V. v. Resnick, 47 Cal.2d 792, 306 P.2d 1 (1957), the court stated at page 4: "The failure to issue stock or to apply at any time for a permit, although not conclusive evidence, is an indication that defendants were doing business as individuals." Another basis for holding the incorporators individually was the incorporation with little or no capital. Carter, J., dissented on both points.

Chapter 5

THE PURPOSE CLAUSE AND ITS IMPORTANCE; "AVOIDING THE ULTRA VIRES PITFALL"[1]

§ 1. Function of the Purpose Clause

Whether the corporation be an English Crown charter one or one formed under a special legislative act or a general act there will be a clause setting forth the purpose or purposes for which the corporation was formed. Modern general acts usually provide that corporations may be formed under them for any lawful purposes for which natural persons may associate themselves except for carrying on a profession or for purposes for which special provisions have been made to incorporate in a different manner.[2]

The requirement that the objects or purposes be stated in the certificate or articles of incorporation is to inform those who contemplate investing their money in corporate shares of the field of activity in which it is to be put at risk and to give notice to others who care to investigate, particularly those intending to deal with the corporation, of the general area in which the corporate officers have been authorized to function.[3] The statement of purposes is also a guide to management in carrying on the business and a warning that its measure of authority is to be gauged from the purposes stated and from what is reasonably necessary or incidental to carry out these purposes. The state, too, has an interest, for the described purposes may not be legitimate ones under the general act although perhaps perfectly legitimate under some other statutory provisions, or the purposes stated may actually be illegal.[4]

---

1. A term invented by Professor Richard W. Jennings for use as a partial chapter heading in Ballantine, Lattin and Jennings, Cases and Materials on Corporations 138 (2d ed. 1953).

2. See Ohio Rev.Code (Ohio Gen. Corp.Law of 1955) § 1701.03; Del. Gen.Corp.Law of 1953, § 101.

3. Cotman, Liquidator of the Essequibo Co. v. Brougham, Liquidator of the Anglo-Cuban Co., [1918] A.C. 514.

4. Central Transportation Co. v. Pullman's Palace Car Co., 139 U.S. 24, 11 S.Ct. 478, 35 L.Ed. 478 (1891) (contract to prevent competition and create monopoly). In State ex rel. Church v. Brown, Sec'y of State, 165 Ohio St. 31, 133 N.E.2d 333 (1956), relators brought mandamus to compel the secretary of state to file and record articles of incorporation for a non-profit corporation to be known as "National Nudist Council, Inc.," to practice and promote nudism. A criminal statute made nudist activities illegal. Mandamus was denied.

§ 2. Corporate Authority—"Powers" of a Corporation

Lawyers and judges frequently use the term "authority" and "powers" in the same breath to mean the same thing, corporate authority. And the term corporate authority "signifies the authorized scope of the corporate business as indicated by the statement of objects and purposes (usually in verbose and general form) in the articles or certificate of incorporation" [5] or, in the English law, in the memorandum of association. "Powers" are used to carry out the corporate purposes and, within reasonable bounds, the directors may use their own discretion as to the means used to accomplish these purposes just so long as they are reasonably conducive to the attainment of the purposes. As Lord Wrenbury has put it: [6] "The objects of the company and the powers of the company to be exercised in effecting the objects are different things. Powers are not required to be, and ought not to be, specified in the memorandum. The Act intended that the company, if it be a trading company, should by its memorandum define the trade, not that it should specify the various acts which it should be within the power of the company to do in carrying on the trade . . ." However, he had to admit that a "pernicious practice" had grown up of using "paragraph after paragraph not specifying or delimiting the proposed trade or purpose, but confusing power with purpose and indicating every class of act which the corporation is to have power to do." [7] The same practice has grown up in the United States with the same result complained of by Lord Wrenbury, namely, that "the function of the memorandum is taken to be, not to specify, not to disclose, but to bury beneath a mass of words the real object or objects of the company with the intent that every conceivable form of activity shall be found included somewhere within its terms . . ." [8] And this is true even though the incorpora-

---

5. Ballantine, Lattin and Jennings, Cases and Materials on Corporations 138 (2d ed. 1953).

6. Cotman, Liquidator, etc. v. Brougham, Liquidator, etc., supra, note 3, at page 522.

7. Ibid. at page 523. After setting forth eleven specific powers, Okl. Bus.Corp.Act § 1.19, provides: "It shall not be necessary to set forth in the articles of incorporation any of the corporate powers enumerated in this section, and the enumeration of powers herein shall not limit or exclude the exercise of others." And see Pa.Bus.Corp. Law § 302 as amended in 1957, and Ga.Corp.Act of 1938 § 10(j), to the

same effect as the Oklahoma statute.

8. Ibid. at page 523. In Lois Grunow Memorial Clinic v. Davis, 49 Ariz. 277, 66 P.2d 238, at 243 (1937), the court states: "But of more recent times, for some reason, the charters of corporations organized under general statutes usually attempt to include the right to do everything which a private individual can do, and many things which he cannot, although the incorporators have no intention of ever exercising a tithe of the powers conferred by the charter and, as a matter of fact, limit their activities to one or two of those powers."

tors intended not to use more than a small fraction of the purposes and powers stated.

If this is so, why should not the purpose clause be phrased something like this: "To carry on any business whatever which the board of directors determines would be profitable to the shareholders?" The few cases which have considered this possibility have rejected the suggestion. The statutory requirement is not met by such a broad statement of corporate purposes. It anticipates some degree of definiteness "not by simply declaring that its purpose is to manufacture and sell every article known or at present unknown to mankind." [9]

However, better practice favors a more conservative handling of the purpose clause by including only those purposes which are presently intended to be within the area of the particular business and those which may reasonably be anticipated in the foreseeable future. The few powers that are unusual and difficult for a court to imply from the purposes stated should be spelled out with clarity. Modern corporation statutes frequently grant some of these powers so that they need not be stated in the articles though they may be included there for ready reference.

Since corporations can only incur obligations and liabilities through the acts of their representatives the word "powers" has reference to the authority of these representatives. In appropriate cases, such representatives may be the directors, officers, agents, or all or a majority or some other proportion of the shareholders. If the limits of charter authority are exceeded the result is termed ultra vires. While an act or transaction may be beyond the powers of a corporation, that is beyond the charter and statutory authority, the result in a proper case may be charged to the corporation for it has the "capacity" or "ability" to do many things not authorized by its charter. And while courts have frequently stated that corporations possess only such powers and capacities as the state has granted in the corporate charter and that, consequently, a corporation has no "capacity" to commit ultra vires acts, it is believed that Professor Ballantine is a keener analyst when he states: "It is . . . the view of the present writer that the law on this topic (ultra vires) cannot be expressed in terms of capacity or incapacity . . . The result is that in general the objects and purposes clause of the articles should operate simply like by-laws or articles of partnership, as limitations on the actual authority of the directors and officers to bind the corporation, but not upon their ostensible

9. Imperial Trust Co. v. Magazine Repeating Razor Co., 138 N.J.Eq. 20, 46 A.2d 449, at 451 (1946). See also In re Crown Bank, 44 Ch. Div. 634, at 644 (1890).

or apparent authority, unless reasonably to be inferred or actually known. Their ostensible authority to bind the corporation would then depend upon the nature of the business, banking, insurance, etc., according to the actual course in which it is carried on by similar concerns, or by that concern, very much as in the case of partnerships." [10]

§ 3. Corporate Authority in Special Situations not Readily Implied from the Purposes Stated

While powers implied to carry out the charter purposes are not confined to those which are indepensable to reach that result, they should have more than a slight, indirect or remote relation to the charter purposes.[11] It has been said that such powers comprise all "that are necessary in the sense of (being) appropriate, convenient and suitable, including the right of reasonable choice of means to be employed." [12] But whatever adjectives are used they fall far short of explaining differences in holdings upon approximately similar factual patterns. Differences of opinion are bound to exist as to what is "reasonably incidental" or "reasonably necessary" or "appropriate, convenient and suitable" to accomplish the purposes outlined in the charter. And a reading of the American cases convinces one that rough justice is at work in an attempt to solve by vague and conflicting ultra vires principles a problem which, had it been approached by agency principles as in case of partners in a partnership, would have been much simpler.

There are some powers, however, not easily implied as reasonably incidental to the pursuit of charter objectives. Such are contracts of suretyship and guaranty, the purchase of shares in other corporations or the purchase of its own shares, the carrying on as a member of a partnership either with a natural person or another corporation or other business association, the making of gifts to charitable or educational institutions, the building of homes for corporate employees or the financing of the same for them, or the building of entire villages with banking, educational, religious and recreational facilities for employees as well as other facilities necessary or convenient for the running of a municipality. Powers have been implied in appropriate cases to permit all of the above activities but they have not been

---

10. Ballantine, Proposed Revision of the Ultra Vires Doctrine, 12 Cornell L.Q. 453, at 455 (1926). But compare Dodd and Baker, Cases and Materials on Corporations, Introductory Note 312, at 313 (2d ed. 1951).

11. People ex rel. Moloney v. Pullman's Palace Car Co., 175 Ill. 125, 51 N.E. 664, 64 L.R.A. 366 (1898).

12. Central Ohio Natural Gas & Fuel Co. v. Capital City Dairy Co., 60 Ohio St. 96, at 104, 53 N.E. 711, 712 (1899).

easily implied and more often have most of such powers been denied unless statutory or charter authorization is shown.

Without statutory or charter aid it is clearly outside ordinary corporate business to indorse a note or guarantee the payment of a debt as an accommodation of a natural person, association or other corporation.[13]   However, if such an accommodation indorsement or guaranty has a reasonable connection with the accomplishment of the corporate purposes—if it is reasonably incidental to such accomplishment—the implied power is recognized.[14]

When a corporation purchases shares in another corporation it risks its assets so invested in another venture whether of a like or different nature from its own.   If the business is different from that authorized by its charter, it is doing indirectly that which would not qualify as intra vires if done directly. There is also the chance that it may speculate in other corporations' shares or that purchases of shares in competitor corporations will be made to stifle competition, both having policy implications.   Thus, without statutory or charter aid, an implied power to purchase shares in other corporations has not been easily implied although, if such purchases are reasonably incidental or conducive to carrying out the objects of the purchasing corporation, as for example the purchase by a railroad corporation of shares in a coal mine whose coal is used by the corporation or of shares in a grain elevator in which it stores customers' grain for shipment, they may be recognized as intra vires purchases.[15]   Such holdings may be justified on the ground that if it is lawful for the corporation to own outright its coal mines and grain elevators, indirect ownership through the purchase of some, a majority or all of the stock of corporations organized to carry on such businesses is quite as legitimate.[16]

The power to purchase its own shares by a corporation when there are proper funds for the purchase has been more readily implied than the power to purchase other corporation's shares. The English law, however, recognizes neither an implied power

13.   Brinson v. Mill Supply Co., 219 N.C. 498, 14 S.E.2d 505, at 508 (1941); William Filene's Sons Co. v. Gilchrist Co., 284 F. 664 (1st Cir. 1922); Davis v. Old Colony Ry. Co., 131 Mass. 258, 41 Am.Rep. 221 (1881).

14.   Woods Lumber Co. v. Moore, 183 Cal. 497, 191 P. 905, 11 A.L.R. 549 (1920); Timm v. Grand Rapids Brewing Co., 160 Mich. 371, 125 N.W. 357, 27 L.R.A.,N.S., 186 (1910). But see Northside Ry. Co. v. Worthington, 88 Tex. 562, 30 S.W.

1055 (1895); Globe Indemnity Co. v. McCullom, Rec'r, 313 Pa. 135, 169 A. 76 (1933), and Note, 47 Harv.L.Rev. 1437 (1934).

15.   State ex inf. Atty. Gen. v. Missouri Pacific Ry. Co., 237 Mo. 338, 141 S.W. 643 (1911).

16.   But see decision contra to State ex inf. Atty. Gen. v. Missouri Pacific Ry. Co., supra, note 15. People ex rel. Moloney v. Pullman's Palace Car Co., 175 Ill. 125, 51 N.E. 664, at 676, 64 L.R.A. 366 (1898).

to purchase nor an express power contained in its memorandum of association.[17] The English cases proceed on the theory that if the company purchases its own shares for the purpose of resale it is trafficking in its shares and if it purchases and retains its shares it is an indirect way of reducing its capital, neither of which powers to do may be implied from or even derived through a statement in its memorandum. The strict English rule does not apply to "unlimited companies" in which the members are unlimitedly liable for in such companies there is no requirement that the capital be kept intact and members may freely withdraw from membership.[18]

Two valid reasons have been assigned to the failure of courts to readily imply that a corporation may become a member of a partnership. First, the corporation's assets would be subjected to the unlimited liability of a partner; and second, the statutory provision which places the management of the corporate affairs in a board of directors would be violated since partners in a general partnership are general agents of the partnership business. Even if the agreement placed the entire management in the board of directors the other partners could bind the partnership by dealing with third parties who had no notice of their actual lack of authority to bind the partnership.[19] But this objection has not seemed too strong and membership in partnerships thus managed has been held to be within the implied powers of a corporation.[20] Partnerships—usually described as joint ventures—of which one member at least is a corporation have been recognized where the use of the partnership device is reasonably incidental to accomplishing a corporate purpose such as attempting to recoup a debt or save the corporate partner from a loss.[21] It is

17. Trevor v. Whitworth, 12 App. Cas. 409 (1887).

18. In re Borough Comm'l and Building Society, [1893] 2 Ch. 242, at 252.

19. See Mallory v. Hanour Oil-Works, 86 Tenn. 598, 8 S.W. 396 (1888), and Whittenton Mills v. Upton, 10 Gray (Mass.) 582, 71 Am. Dec. 681 (1858), for the usual argument that management of a corporation must be separate and exclusive. But see Bates v. Coronado Beach Co., 109 Cal. 160, 41 P. 855 (1895), where A entered into a partnership (joint venture) with B Corporation, the latter to have entire control over the partnership business. The court held that this arrangement was legitimate. In Universal Pictures Corp. v. Roy Davidge Film Laboratory, Ltd., 7

Cal.App.2d 366, 45 P.2d 1028 (1935), it was held that a corporation could become a member of a partnership when its articles permitted it. The court mentioned estoppel as being applicable where all shareholders had consented to the partnership agreement. And see 2 Fletcher, Cyc. of Corporations § 2520 (Perm. ed. 1931) where it is stated that "If the agreement does not take the direction of the corporate affairs out of the hands of the corporate officers, it is not objectionable."

20. See note 19, supra.

21. Clinchfield Fuel Co. v. Henderson Iron Works Co., 254 F. 411 (5th Cir. 1918); Snow Hill Banking & Trust Co. v. D. J. Odom Drug Co., 188 N.C. 672, 125 S.E. 394, 37 A.L.R. 1101 (1924). See Rowley,

highly questionable whether a banking corporation in order to try to save itself from a loss should be allowed to risk its depositors' money in this manner as was permitted in *Snow Hill Banking & Trust Co.* v. *D. J. Odom Drug Co.*[22] Traditional banking practice has long favored methods more conservative than this to accomplish the legitimate purpose of saving itself from a loss.

Whether a business corporation should have an implied power to make gifts to charitable or educational institutions where there is no or very little chance of benefiting the corporation or its employees is a live question at the present time. Reasonable contributions to Community Fund or United Appeal Associations, the Red Cross, the local hospital and library, and similar organizations which indirectly, but rather intimately, benefit the employees of the corporation, may be sustained as being impliedly authorized because of the possible benefits which may accrue therefrom to any of the company's employees. As gifts go farther afield in aid of national projects such as fund raising for cancer or heart research, or for the support of colleges and universities hard pressed for survival, it becomes more difficult to sustain as intra vires such gifts on the more ancient bases. Indirect benefits may eventually result but, even so, they remain a remote possibility. However, the test has never been whether actual benefits result but whether the particular power used is reasonably calculated to further the corporation's objectives. Every business corporation must in some way advertise its products if it hopes to sell them to the best advantage and no corporation would deny that the building up of good will is a legitimate and worthy objective. Furthermore, enlightened public opinion not only favors corporate and other gifts to worthy causes [23] but, indeed, exerts pressure at times to encourage not only the gift but that it also be a generous one. The recognition that corporations have a social responsibility extending beyond their membership and employees has been a long time in the making but it is gradually emerging through liberal common law holdings and statutory provisions. Additional impetus to liberal holdings is the fact that corporate giving to charitable and educational ventures has become so customary that one court has recently stated "it is estimated that annual corporate contributions throughout the nation aggregate over 300 million dollars, with

---

The Corporate Partner, 14 Minn.L. Rev. 769 (1930); Note, Power of Corporation to Become Partner, 25 Tulane L.Rev. 272 (1951).

22. Supra note 21. But see Merchants Nat. Bank v. Wehrmann, 202 U.S. 295, 26 S.Ct. 613, 50 L.Ed. 1036 (1906), where the court held that a national bank was not liable for firm or association debts where, to salvage a bad debt, it took an interest in a partnership or joint stock company.

23. Dodd, For Whom Are Corporate Managers Trustees? 45 Harv.L. Rev. 1145, at 1158 (1932).

over 60 million dollars thereof going to universities and other educational institutions. Similarly, it is estimated that local community chests receive well over 40% of their contributions from corporations; these contributions and those made by corporations to the American Red Cross, to Boy Scouts and Girl Scouts, to 4-H Clubs and similar organizations have almost invariably been unquestioned." [24] But, apart from any argument of social responsibility, the advertising and good will values are direct enough for the most conservative minds to conclude that such gifts are reasonably ancillary to a corporation's objectives to qualify as intra vires.[25]

One of the most important cases involving a gift to educational institutions was *Evans* v. *Brunner, Mond & Company.*[26] The directors of a chemical manufacturing corporation had passed a resolution to distribute £100,000 to universities for the furtherance of scientific research without further restrictions. A shareholder brought an action to restrain the anticipated action of the board, arguing that the money might be used for scientific education in astronomy or some other branch not useful to the chemical trade and that, besides, the benefit if any was too remote; in fact, competitors might get the benefit. At the time of the gift there was a shortage of scientists and of chemists in particular. The court followed the usual rule that the contemplated act must be one which can fairly be regarded as incidental or conducive to the paramount purpose for which the company was formed, namely, for the purpose of manufacturing chemicals. It found that men trained in other sciences would be useful in a branch in which they had not been trained by virtue of their knowledge of scientific methods and procedures and the acquisition, through such training, of a scientific attitude of mind. While the donor corporation might not acquire any of the scien-

---

24. Jacobs, J., in A. P. Smith Mfg. Co. v. Barlow, 13 N.J. 145, 98 A. 2d 581, at 586 (1953), appeal dismissed 346 U.S. 861, 74 S.Ct. 107, 98 L.Ed. 373 (1953). Justice Jacobs' opinion is a brilliant and illuminating one. See Rohr, Corporate Philanthropy: The Changing Law, 33 Mich.St.Bar J. 14 (1954).

25. "It was also considered, in making the subscriptions or donations (to the University of Buffalo and Canisius College), that the company would receive advertisement of substantial value, including the good will of many influential citizens and of its patrons, who are interested in the success of the development of these branches of education, and, on the other hand, suffer a loss of prestige if the contributions were not made, in view of the fact that business competitors had donated and shown a commendable public spirit in that relation. In the circumstances the rule of law that may fairly be applied is that the action of the officers of the company was not ultra vires, but was in fact within their corporate powers, since it tended to promote the welfare of the business in which the corporation was engaged." Armstrong Cork Co. v. H. A. Meldrum Co., 285 F. 58, at 58–59 (D.C.N.Y.1922).

26. [1921] 1 Ch. 359, 90 L.J.Ch.Div. 294.

tists trained through its gifts, it had the opportunity of acquiring them and with the shortage of scientifically trained men this was the best way to relieve the shortage. The court held the gift to be within the corporate powers and denied the injunction. Similar arguments are available today, the shortage of scientists being a daily complaint of both the state and industry. And would not similar arguments be effective in sustaining gifts for training in the arts? The college or university trained employee has proved his greater worth to business and industry by virtue of his general training and there seems to be no end to the demand by corporations for educated minds in this ever-expanding economy.

One need only recall the admonition of the court given to Mr. Henry Ford, owner of 58% of the then capital stock of $2,000,-000 of the Ford Motor Company, when through his control of the board a large program of expansion was being planned and a reduction of the price of each car from $440 to $360 was being contemplated at a time when the 600,000 cars which could be produced annually by the existing plant could have been sold for $440, to realize that there are limits to which corporate philanthropy may be extended in the face of minority shareholder objection. In his testimony, Mr. Ford made it clear that the shareholders had been generously treated in the past by a 5% monthly dividend and year-end special dividends and that in the future only the regular dividend of 5% monthly would be forthcoming, this in spite of an enormous surplus much of which was not necessary for expansion purposes. Concerning the expansion program, Mr. Ford, declared, "My ambition is to employ still more men; to spread the benefits of this industrial system to the greatest possible number, to help them build up their lives and their homes. To do this, we are putting the greatest share of our profits back into the business." [27]

With reference to the reduction in the price of cars, Mr. Ford was of the opinion that his company had made too much money and that, although large profits might still be made, they should be shared with the public by reducing the price of the car. The court permitted the contemplated expansion through the use of the corporate surplus. But with reference to the lowering of the price of cars to give the public a "break" the court said: "There should be no confusion (of which there is evidence) of the duties which Mr. Ford conceives that he and the stockholders owe to the general public and the duties which in law he and his codirectors owe to protesting, minority stockholders. A business corporation is organized and carried on primarily for the prof-

27. Dodge v. Ford Motor Co., 204 Mich. 459, 170 N.W. 668, at 671, 3 A.L.R. 413 (1919).

it of the stockholders. The powers of the directors are to be employed for that end. The discretion of directors is to be exercised in the choice of means to attain that end, and does not extend to a change in the end itself, to the reduction of profits, or to the nondistribution of profits among stockholders in order to devote them to other purposes." [28]

It would have been interesting to know what the court would have done with the case had Mr. Ford and members of his board testified that the reason for the price reduction was to gain the good will of the public so that when the company really needed public support (as it shortly did) it would not forget this gesture of corporate magnanimity; and, furthermore, by increasing the plant and producing more cars on the assembly line, substantial profits would be made on the larger turnover, an objective sought by modern business in a competitive profit-making economy. The *Ford* case was decided nearly a half-century ago. Today, profit-sharing beyond the salaries and wages of officers and employees is a common incentive for the production and sale of more goods at cheaper prices. May it not be said that a legitimate corporate objective at the present time is a sharing also with the public of some of the profits which the same public has made possible? Not to the extent of conducting "the affairs of a corporation for the merely incidental benefit of shareholders and for the primary purpose of benefiting others," [29] but to increase the good will of the company through the advertising potential of such action.

Statutes have been passed in at least thirty-eight states, the District of Columbia and Hawaii giving specific authority to a corporation formed under them, or to which such statutes apply, to make gifts for charitable, scientific or educational purposes.[30]

28. Ibid. 170 N.W. 668, at 684. But see Fischer, The Lost Liberals, 194 Harper's Magazine 385 (1947), a part of which will be found in Berle and Warren, Business Organizations 1106(C) (1948).

29. Ibid. 170 N.W. 668, at 684.

30. For a discussion of the New Jersey statute, see A. P. Smith Mfg. Co. v. Barlow, 13 N.J. 145, 98 A.2d 581, at 586–587 (1953), appeal dismissed 346 U.S. 861, 74 S.Ct. 107, 98 L.Ed. 373 (1953). Justice Jacobs held that the corporation had, under the common law, the power to make the gift ($1,500 to Princeton University) but that the statute also authorized it. West's Ann.Cal.Corp.Code § 802(g) as amended in 1949 (no restrictions as to amount); Del.Gen.Corp.Law of 1953, § 122(9) (no restrictions as to the amount that may be donated); Ohio Gen.Corp.Law of 1955 (Ohio Rev.Code) § 1701.13(D), which provides: "Unless otherwise provided in the articles, a corporation . . . may make donations for the public welfare or for charitable, scientific, or educational purposes." The Ohio statute immediately preceding the 1955 statute carried restrictions upon the amount of the gift and, if the directors authorized a greater amount, the shareholders had to be notified and if those holding 25% of the voting shares objected in writing the contemplated gift had to be submitted to the shareholders for a vote. See Ohio Rev.

Some of these statutes have restrictions upon the amount that the directors may authorize as contributions for such purposes without shareholder aid or, at least, where a given proportion of the shareholders object to a larger gift. These statutes quite clearly indicate a trend toward an enlightened public policy which favors the distribution of some of the corporate profits for worthy purposes. As Jacobs, J., has so aptly put it: [31] "It seems to us that just as the conditions prevailing when corporations were originally created required that they serve public as well as private interests, modern conditions require that corporations acknowledge and discharge social as well as private responsibilities as members of the communities within which they operate. Within this broad concept there is no difficulty in sustaining, as incidental to their proper objects and in aid of the public welfare, the power of corporations to contribute corporate funds within reasonable limits in support of academic institutions." [32]

The building of homes or the financing of the same by a corporation for its employees is not difficult to support on the usual grounds of implied powers reasonably incidental to the purposes of the corporation, at least where the building and loan and banking facilities usually performing such services are not reasonably adequate to do the job. Problems will arise where such facilities are not readily available or, if available, where the terms are too rigorous for some of the employees. Satisfied employees presumably do better work than their opposite numbers and thus a corporate objective is being served in a manner seemingly not too indirect or remote. And even though building and loan facilities are reasonably available, the corporation may wish to keep some control over possible harsh foreclosures in a time of economic distress and to keep available for other employees desiring to purchase homes those which may revert to the corporation upon resignation, death or removal from the community of employees purchasing their own homes.

There was grave question originally of whether a corporation might purchase a large tract of land, build its factory there-

---

Code § 1702.26, effective Oct. 1, 1953 (H.B. 1, Laws of 1953). And see the New Jersey statute, above, for restrictions somewhat similar, and Vt.Laws 1955, Act 81, § 1. Few statutes have any restrictions on the amount.

See Note, Corporate Charitable Contributions, 24 U. of Cin.L.Rev. 572, at 578 (1955), where various state statutes are listed.

31. A. P. Smith Mfg. Co. v. Barlow, supra, note 30, 98 A.2d at page 586.

32. Some of the recent articles on this question are: deCapriles and Garrett, Legality of Corporate Support to Education, 38 A.B.A.J. 209 (1952); Bell, Corporate Support of Education, 38 A.B.A.J. 119 (1952); Bleichen, Corporate Contributions to Charity, 38 A.B.A.J. 999 (1952); Cousins, How Far Corporations May Contribute to Charity, 35 Va. L.Rev. 401 (1949); Rohr, Corporate Philanthropy: The Changing Law, 33 Mich.St.Bar J. 14 (1954).

on and a community of homes, banking, educational, religious and recreational facilities for its employees besides the necessary facilities like sewers, waterworks and mains, power plants, etc., for the town or village so built. The great piano manufacturing firm of Steinway and Sons finding itself expanding at a rate which justified moving from its then crowded quarters and thinking it desirable to locate where its many expert workmen might find greater happiness in a bit of blue sky and green grass was permitted to do just this toward the end of the last century.[33] The court wisely recognized that business methods change as industrial progress is made and acts which earlier had been considered beyond the implied powers of a corporation became permissible and within such powers. The field of corporate action, felt the court, as it pertained to incidental powers was an expanding one. Would not an elephant hunt organized for the purpose of obtaining ivory for the white piano keys, or the purchase of a forest of ebony trees in Africa from which to manufacture the black keys or of a mahogany forest in tropical America from which to make the casing and legs of the piano, or of a steel mill from which to fashion the frame and manufacture the wire for its strings, and many more activities be within the implied powers of such a corporation?

§ 4. Importance of Modern Statutes in Granting Powers

Without any statement in statute, articles or by-laws, a corporation has implied powers (better called incidents of the corporate form) to sue and be sued in its corporate name, to hold and convey corporate property in the same manner, to have continuity of existence though its shareholders or members die or transfer their shares to others, to have and use a corporate seal, and to make by-laws for its internal management.[34] Frequently, modern statutes spell these powers out and lawyers often draft them into the articles of incorporation thus cluttering the articles with superfluous verbiage for whose benefit it is hard to conceive.[35] However modern statutes have, in large part, added to

---

33. Steinway v. Steinway & Sons, 17 Misc. 43, 40 N.Y.S. 718 (Sup.Ct. 1896). Accord: State ex inf. Atty. Gen. v. Long-Bell Lumber Co., 321 Mo. 461, 12 S.W.2d 64 (1928). But see People ex rel. Moloney v. Pullman's Palace Car Co., 175 Ill. 125, 51 N.E. 664, 64 L.R.A. 366 (1898).

34. In re Sutton's Hospital, 10 Coke 23a, at 30b, 77 Eng.Rep. 960, at 970 (1612).

35. See Del.Gen.Corp.Law of 1953, § 122(1), (2), (3), (4) and (6), which state the general powers just dis-

cussed. § 122(5) grants the power to appoint company officers and agents and to compensate them for their services, another general power which the law would imply. Other powers are stated in subsections (7) through (10) of § 122, § 123, § 121, § 143, § 242, and § 271. § 283 provides for revocation or forfeiture of charter for misuse or non-use of its powers. Similarly, Ohio Rev. Code (Ohio Gen.Corp.Law of 1955) § 1701.13 lists general powers, stating additional ones. Both the Delaware and Ohio statutes granting the list of powers which the law implies from the mere fact of being a corporation other powers not easily implied to accomplish the purposes set out in the articles, such as the power to purchase and hold shares in other corporations, the power to enter into suretyship and guaranty agreements, the authority to make gifts for charitable and other purposes, to enter into partnership agreements and to function as a partner, and, very recently, to grant from corporate funds indemnification for legal and other expenses incurred by directors and officers, or former directors and officers, in connection with the defense of litigation in which they were charged with misconduct in carrying on the corporate business but were adjudged not liable or, under some statutes, when the case is compromised with no determination of liability for wrongdoing. The latter type statutes go much too far for, "By so avoiding being 'adjudged' liable for their wrong-doing they may still be indemnified by their fellow directors in spite of their wrongful conduct." [36]

But, even with additional powers provided by statute, a warning should be given that, unless the statutory authority is broad enough to cover the particular act for which the power is used, the usual interpretation by courts is that the power stated is merely a means by which the purposes set forth in the articles are to be carried out, and not an end in itself. For example, a statutory power to purchase shares in other corporations does not give a corporation *carte blanche* to purchase for the purpose of speculation or to purchase when there is no reasonable expectation of benefit and no reasonable connection between the corporate purposes and the purchase. It would be proper to use idle funds to make such purchases for temporary investment, or to accept shares of other corporations in compromise of a claim, or to purchase shares where such purchase was reasonably conducive to carrying out some corporate objective. But neither the statement in a statute of the *power* to purchase shares in other corporations, nor in the articles of incorporation, can be regarded as an end in itself. An important distinction between

powers include a broad one to indemnify directors and officers for expenses incurred in defense of certain judicial proceedings unless found liable for negligence or misconduct. For criticism of this section (§ 1701.13(E)), see Emerson, The New Ohio General Corporation Law: Some Comments and Some Comparisons, 24 U. of Cin.L.Rev. 463, at 472–474 (1955).

36. See note 35, supra, and Emerson, The New Ohio General Corporation Law, etc., cited there, at pages 472–

473. The California section is more protective (West's Ann.Cal.Corp. Code § 830) and is at a more proper place in the statute than the Ohio and Delaware provisions which are included under a general section on authority or power of a corporation. The California provision is under the subject "Directors and Management." See Ballantine, Lattin and Jennings, Cases and Materials on Corporations, Note on General Powers and Contract Powers: Relation Between Purposes and Powers, at 142 et seq. (2d ed. 1953).

purposes and powers should be noticed at this point for, if the articles state as a *purpose* the purchasing of shares in other corporations, this becomes one of the ends of the corporation rather than a means, but such a statement in the articles should leave no doubt that it is a purpose rather than a power.[37] Good draftsmanship should not confuse the two, but poor draftsmanship frequently does out of ignorance or carelessness. If there is any doubt as to the extent of the power (or purpose) it should be set out so specifically that a court, in examining it, will be able to see that the act complained of is or is not within its intended area.

Some of the more recent statutes are so stating some powers that there can be little if any confusion as to their scope. For example, the new Ohio statute provides: "In carrying out the purposes stated in its articles and subject to limitations prescribed by law or in its articles, a corporation may: . . . Form or acquire the control of other corporations, whether nonprofit or for profit . . ."[38] Another provision permits a corporation to invest its funds, not currently needed, in any shares or securities of "another corporation, business, or undertaking" the activities of which are not incidental to the purposes stated in the purchasing corporation's articles, but not to acquire control of such corporation, business or undertaking in whose shares the funds are invested, and subject to any limitations expressed in the purchasing corporation's articles.[39] Section 13.1–3 (f) of the new Virginia Stock Corporation Law which became effective as law on January 1, 1957, is another example. This section provides that the corporation has power "to lend money to its employees, officers and directors, and otherwise assist them," a power which is not easily implied from a business corporation's articles and one which, in case of directors and officers, is usually specifically prohibited by statutes.

Another type of provision which has recently made its appearance is the "all-purpose" clause which calls for a brief statement of purposes and provides, in effect, that the corporation may do anything which a natural person may do.[40] Such powers

---

37. Edward Hines Western Pine Co. v. First Nat. Bank, 61 F.2d 503 (7th Cir., 1932). See also Ballantine, Corporations 237 (Rev. ed. 1946); Ballantine, Lattin and Jennings, Cases and Materials on Corporations, Note on Limits of Power to Bind Corporation in Particular Transactions, 145 et seq. (2d ed. 1953); Dodd and Baker, Cases and Materials on Corporations, Note on Distinction Between Powers and Purposes, 344 (2d ed. 1951).

38. Ohio Rev.Code (Ohio Gen.Corp. Law of 1955) § 1701.13(F) (3).

39. Ohio Rev.Code (Ohio Gen.Corp. Law of 1955) § 1701.13(G).

40. Nevada Rev.Stat. § 78.035 as amended in 1957: ". . . It shall be a sufficient compliance with this subsection to state, either alone or with other purposes, that the corporation may engage in any lawful activity, subject to expressed limitations, if any. Such statement shall make all lawful activities within the objects or purposes of the corporation." Wis.Bus.Corp.Law of 1951, § 180.45(1) (c). See Luce, Trends in Modern Corporate Legis-

have been interpreted as present from time immemorial in English Crown charter corporations, sometimes called corporations at common law, but not in corporations formed under special or general corporation acts. The "all-purpose" clause legislation gives the draftsman an advantage for he need not spell out ad infinitum every conceivable purpose and power to reach the same result. On the other hand, it places in the board of directors unlimited power to determine what acts are within the scope of the corporate venture, a thing which persons dealing with a corporation should be able to rely upon in any case where the purposes stated are more limited. Limitations upon the directors' authority may be placed in the articles containing an all-purpose clause and, if the limitations are known by one who deals with the corporation, such limitations will be as effective as in other agency cases. Furthermore, if the directors exceed their thus limited authority, they will be liable for loss or damage therefrom to the corporation though the person dealing with the corporation will be protected because of his lack of knowledge of such limitations.

§ 5. Legal Effect of Acts and Transactions outside the Scope of the Authorized Business

With the growth of the law through a more liberal construction of powers which may be implied from the purposes stated in the articles together with statutes conferring powers not easily implied from the purposes stated and, finally, by the enactment of statutes shortly to be discussed which place the defense of ultra vires in all but a few instances beyond the pale of the law, this topic has become one of minor importance. The trend has been toward corporate liability for acts and transactions set in motion by the board of directors to whom are entrusted the powers, though such acts and transactions be outside the scope of the authorized business, on the very reasonable basis that no one is better able to determine the scope of the business than the directors and, upon their judgment, persons dealing with the corporation should be able to rely. It seems probable that within the next quarter-century the subject of ultra vires will be of historic value only.

(a) **English law.** Concerning Crown charter corporations, the law is indeed simple. These corporations have such general capacity, as an incident given by law, to contract as have natural persons.[41] So firm is the established rule that Blackburn, J., was

lation, 50 Mich.L.Rev. 1291, at 1301 (1952).

41. Bonanza Creek Gold Mining Co., Ltd. v. Rex, [1916] 1 A.C. 566;

British South Africa Co. v. De Beers Consolidated Mines, Ltd. [1910] 1 Ch. 354.

able to state that he was aware of no decision by which a chartered corporation or the persons who contract with it could say that the contract was void as beyond its capacity.[42] And this is so even if the act performed is prohibited by its charter.[43] Such a violation, however, may be a ground upon which a proceeding for the forfeiture of the charter may be based.

But a similar rule was not adopted in case of corporations formed either under a special or general act. In the great case that settled the English law a corporation formed under the Companies Act of 1862 had exceeded both its express and its implied powers by entering into a contract with the plaintiff which, after partial performance, the corporation repudiated. In an action to recover damages for this, the Court of Exchequer held that the contract was ultra vires but that, as it had been ratified by all of the shareholders, it was a binding and valid contract. On appeal to the Exchequer Chamber, three of the judges agreed with the lower court and three dissented, thus making necessary an affirmance of the trial court.[44] It should be noted that at the time of suit there was no provision in the Companies Act of 1862 for the amendment or alteration of the objects clause of a memorandum. Blackburn, J., one of the judges agreeing with the trial court recognized the general capacity of a Crown charter corporation but questioned: "But if a body corporate has, as incident to it, a general capacity to contract, the question is, Does the statute creating the corporation by express provision, or necessary implication, shew an intention in the legislature to prohibit, and so avoid the making of a contract of this particular kind?" Since, under the then Act, the objects of the company must always remain the same, Blackburn concluded that if a single shareholder objected to the corporation's proceeding beyond its powers he might prevent its doing so. Furthermore, thought Blackburn, no one could claim a valid contract with the company "on the ground that the board had an ostensible or apparent authority to make contracts of that kind," but must prove

42. Riche v. Ashbury Ry. Carriage & Iron Co., Ltd., L.R. 9 Ex. 224, at 264 (1874), rev'd in Ashbury Ry. Carriage & Iron Co., Ltd. v. Riche, L.R. 7 H.L. (E. & I. App.) 653, 33 L.T.,N.S., 450 (1875).

43. British South Africa Co. v. De Beers Consolidated Mines, Ltd., [1910] 1 Ch. 354; Jenkin v. Pharmaceutical Society of Great Britain, [1921] 1 Ch. 392, 398; Bonanza Creek Gold Mining Co., Ltd. v. Rex, [1916] 1 A.C. 566; Edwards v. Blackmore, 12 Ont.L.R. 105, 42 D.L. R. 280, 289 (Sup.Ct. of Ontario, App.Div.1918). In the last case a corporation whose object was to carry on a real estate business was sued upon a note given on account of the purchase of machinery and patent rights for the manufacture of machines for pressing clothes. The Canadian statute gave corporations organized under it the general capacity of crown charter corporations. It was held that the corporation had the capacity of a natural person and that the purchase was not ultra vires.

44. Riche v. Ashbury Ry. Carriage & Iron Co., Ltd., L.R. 9 Ex. 224 (1874).

an actual authority. However, contracts beyond the scope of the memorandum of association were capable of ratification if all of the shareholders agreed. Blackburn argued the possible hardship to the shareholders if they could not, on occasion, do this. Thus the "actual authority" of which Blackburn spoke seems to exist, or at least this defect is cured, when the shareholders unanimously agree to ratify the ultra vires contract.

In the House of Lords Blackburn's approach was rejected. If the contract under review was beyond the powers of the company, wrote The Lord Chancellor (Lord Cairns), it was void from the beginning and could not be ratified even by unanimous vote of the shareholders. "If every shareholder of the company . . . had said, 'That is a contract which we desire to make, which we authorize the directors to make, to which we sanction the placing the seal of the company,' the case would not have stood in any different position from that in which it stands now. The shareholders would thereby, by unanimous consent, have been attempting to do the very thing which, by the Act of Parliament, they were prohibited from doing." [45] Thus, the English courts were committed to what is known as the special or limited capacities doctrine in case of companies created under Parliamentary grant, whether special or general, which meant that such a company had neither the power nor the capacity to act or bind itself outside the area of statutory authorization and the objects clause in its memorandum.

Why was it that the English courts as a common law matter decided that the powers of a Crown charter corporation were coextensive with those of a natural person insofar as they were compatible with their physical differences? Was not the King as interested in keeping his Crown charter corporations within the objects stated in such charters as Parliament was in companies formed under its legislation? There is no ready answer for these questions. Lord Cairns stated that by the Act of Parliament corporations formed thereunder were *prohibited* from exceeding the powers granted. But there was nothing in the Companies Act of 1862 setting forth any express prohibition. [46] And

45. Ashbury Ry. Carriage & Iron C., Ltd. v. Riche, L.R. 7 H.L. (E. & I. App.) 653, at 672, 33 L.T.,N.S., 450 (1875). As to companies incorporated by special act, the law was settled to the same effect in East Anglican Rys. Co. v. Eastern Counties Ry. Co., 11 C.B. 775 (1851). See Horrwitz, Company Law Reform and the Ultra Vires Doctrine, 62 L.Q.Rev. 66 (1946).

46. Dean Stevens states that "The limited capacity doctrine is the

corollary of the theory that a corporation is a fictitious entity created by law," which theory has two distinct sources: (1) Pope Innocent IV who, in deciding a point of ecclesiastical law, declared that ecclesiastical corporations were soulless entities; and (2) the English Crown which, in defense of the growing power of such units, invented the notion that corporations are created by sovereign power. "The entities existed; they had to

the company which had exceeded the scope of its authority as projected in its memorandum of association was not one operating in a field in which the public at large might have an interest. Hence, unless the state had some interest to protect, the only other conceivable present interests were those of the shareholders—and they had unanimously ratified the contract made by the directors—and those of the corporation's creditors who apparently were not injured or, at least, were not complaining.[47] Had the corporation been formed under a special or general act to carry out some public or semi-public purpose the special capacities doctrine might well have had an appeal for the protection of the public interest.

Under the English common law constructive notice of the provisions of the memorandum of association and of the articles of association (termed by-laws in the United States), which articles as well as the memorandum are filed, is charged to persons who deal with the corporation even to the extent of understanding the provisions contained in these documents according to their proper meaning.[48] "It follows that there can be no apparent authority and in any departure from the lines of the authorized business the excess of actual authority by the directors, officers or agents must always be considered as disclosed."[49] This is contrary to the great weight of authority in the United States where the rule is that no constructive notice is given by the mere filing of the articles of incorporation.

The English rule that one who has dealt with a corporation may not plead ultra vires when suit is brought against him by the corporation, such defense being solely for the protection of the corporate interests,[50] is also contrary to the rule in the United

---

be subdued, not created. Therefore, it was established that they could not exist legally without a sovereign grant of authority." Stevens, Corporations 332–333 (2d ed. 1949).

47. Lord Cairns stated that the statutory provisions providing for limited liability were not mainly for the benefit of the present shareholders but for those who might succeed them and for the "outside public," and "more particularly those who might be creditors of companies of this kind." Ashbury Ry. Carriage & Iron Co., Ltd. v. Riche, L.R. 7 H.L. (E. & I. App.) 653, at 667, 33 L.T.,N.S., 450 (1875).

48. Palmer's Company Law 32 (19th ed. 1949); British Thomson-Houston Co., Ltd. v. Federated European Bank, Ltd., [1932] 2 K.B. 176, at 179. See also Montrose, The Ap-

parent Authority of an Agent of a Company, 50 L.Q.Rev. 224, at 236–237 (1934), where the writer points out that the Act itself has no statement concerning notice to those dealing with the corporation. The great weight of authority in the United States does not charge a third person who deals with the corporation with notice of what the articles contain.

49. Ballantine, Corporations 254 (Rev. ed. 1946).

50. Street, The Doctrine of Ultra Vires 30 (1930). However, some early American cases were in accord with the English doctrine. Chester Glass Co. v. Dewey, 16 Mass. 94 (1819); Steam Navigation Co. v. Weed, 17 Barb. (N.Y.) 378 (1853); Bank of South Carolina v. Hammond, 1 Rich.L. (S.C.) 281

States which, in proper cases, permits the defense by either.

But what are the rights of a third person who has fully performed his part of an ultra vires contract and all that remains is performance by the corporation? Since the contract is considered void, the court will not order specific performance in a case otherwise warranting this remedy; nor will it enforce the payment of the contract price, if that is what constitutes corporate performance. The ultra vires borrowing cases perhaps point the way to an answer. Where the corporation has no power to borrow but nevertheless does, if the company still retains the money in its coffers, since the money belongs to the lender, he may recover it. Or, if the loan has been invested or used to purchase property, it should be recoverable in its new form if it can be traced into it.[51] For any part of the ultra vires loan that has been expended in paying off legitimate debts of the corporation, that is intra vires debts for which the company could be held liable, recovery has been permitted on a half-hearted quasi-contractual theory.[52] If a true quasi-contractual theory were followed, the money loaned and received by the company *is the benefit received,* and, no matter how later used, should be recoverable.[53]

(b) Ultra vires principles as developed in the federal and a few state courts. The English special capacities doctrine has, with some variations, been accepted by the federal courts and a small minority of state courts. But the development of the doctrine can hardly be attributed particularly to the influence of English decisions for the case law here was already well seasoned before the land-mark decisions of the English courts. However,

---

(1845). And it was suggested by Magruder, Cir. J., in his dissenting opinion in Herbert v. Sullivan, 123 F.2d 477 (1st Cir., 1941), cert. denied 315 U.S. 803, 62 S.Ct. 632, 86 L.Ed. 1203 (1942), that, as the Massachusetts law was not clear on this point, "It does not necessarily follow that ultra vires may be invoked as a defense when the corporation is suing the other party to a bilateral contract."

51. See 2 Machen, Modern Law of Corporations § 1031 (1908).

52. Blackburn & Dist. Ben. Bldg. Society v. Cunliffe, Brooks & Co., L.R. 29 Ch.Div. 902 (1885); Baroness Wenlock v. River Dee Co., L.R. 36 Ch.Div. 674, 19 Q.B.D. 155 (1887); In re Wrexham, Mold and Connah's Quay Ry. Co., [1899] 1 Ch. 440 (recovery based upon the principle that the corporation's debts had not been increased by the borrowing). In the last case Vaughan Williams, L.J., at page 457 wrote: "But, if the company, instead of either refraining from adopting the loan, or applying it in such a manner as that their total indebtedness shall remain unchanged, apply it, say, to the purchase of new property, the company cannot, after so doing, be sued in any form for a return of the money, since the money had been dealt with under the contract of loan, and to allow the company to repay it would simply be to allow them to carry through an ultra vires transaction." And see In re Birbeck Permanent Benefit Bldg. Society, [1912] 2 Ch. 183, at 232.

53. Compare Woodward, Quasi-Contracts §§ 158 and 159 (1913).

it has been stated that "The decision of the House of Lords in Ashbury Railway Carriage & Iron Co. v. Riche was influential in bringing about the adoption by the Supreme Court of the United States of the so-called 'federal rule' that ultra vires contracts are void because the corporation does not have legal capacity to make them." [54]

It has frequently been pointed out that the courts have failed to discriminate clearly between those acts which are legal but simply go beyond what was authorized by statute and articles and consequently exceed the authority of the corporate agents, and acts which are prohibited by statute or charter, or are condemned by the common law as illegal, the doing of which violates some policy concept. These latter acts are not only ultra vires but are accurately described as illegal and it is the function of the courts to adopt such rules as will best sustain the policy intended. As Machen earlier stated, "The illegality of *ultra vires* contracts depends upon no policy of the law as to the subject matter to which they relate, but solely upon the fact that they are not within the company's powers as defined in its act of incorporation or incorporation paper. To apply to them precisely the same rules that have been deemed necessary in order to discourage illegal contracts in general and to relieve the courts from the disagreeable task of nicely adjusting equities between various parties all of whom have been acting contrary to good morals or to the policy of the law, would be both illogical and unjust." [55] Because of this lack of precision in the use of the word "illegal" care should be exercised in accepting the rationale of a holding which points to lack of capacity, power or authority to do the act when, in fact, the act is truly opposed to policy and would

---

54. Dodd and Baker, Cases and Materials on Corporations 355 (2d ed. 1951). Some of the early cases are set out in Ibid., Note on Early American Cases, 355, and in 2 Machen, Modern Law of Corporations 826 in footnote 5 (1908). Professor Dodd, in his book published after his tragic death, American Business Corporations Until 1860, at 42–43 (1954), states: "On the other hand, Marshall's (i. e., Mr. Chief Justice Marshall) repeatedly stated proposition that a corporation can do nothing not authorized by its charter—a proposition which was echoed by federal and state judges in several nonconstitutional cases—was not one which had at that time been established by English law or which was necessarily implied in that law's theory of corporations. It is a proposition which, at least in the view of some commentators, has had a baneful influence on the development of the American law of ultra vires. . . ." And, at page 105: "In the absence of any known rule of the common law vesting corporations with general contractual capacity, both the traditional theory of corporations as legislatively created artificial persons and the early-nineteenth-century tendency to view business corporations with considerable suspicion as forms of special privilege made it very natural for American lawyers to regard contracts which were not within the scope of a business corporation's charter powers as wholly void."

55. 2 Machen, Modern Law of Corporations § 1020 (1908).

not have been permitted even if the company's objects clause had included it.[56]

What are the rights and liabilities, under this minority doctrine, of the corporation and persons dealing with it or tortiously injured by it when the corporation has exceeded its statutory and charter powers and has dealt with such person or injured him while engaged in an ultra vires venture? Such problems arise when ultra vires contracts are executory, when partially or fully performed by one or both parties or, indeed, during the preliminary stages prior to entering into a contract or transaction when shareholders seek to enjoin the contemplated ultra vires action. Torts may be committed upon the person who has so contracted or upon his property during the execution of the contract or upon one who is a stranger to the ultra vires act being performed by the corporation. And, under similar circumstances, torts may be committed by the person or stranger upon the corporation.

It is a well established principle that an executory ultra vires contract cannot be enforced by either party and that neither party may have a suit for damages for its repudiation or breach.[57] The doctrine applies as well to the majority holdings to be discussed shortly as to the minority holdings represented by the federal view and that of a few states. At this stage, or the prior stage where negotiations are going forward in anticipation of an ultra vires transaction, a shareholder who has not by his own acts estopped himself may bring an action to enjoin the entering into or the performance of an ultra vires transaction. The basic reason is that the corporate funds are authorized to be used only for the purposes of its business and each shareholder is vitally concerned that they not be used otherwise.

Where an ultra vires transaction has been consummated by both parties, the court will not disturb either nor will it force a

56. See, for example, Texas & Pacific Ry. Co. v. Pottorff, 291 U.S. 245, 54 S.Ct. 416, 78 L.Ed. 777 (1934), where a bank pledged part of its assets to secure a private deposit. The court held the pledge ultra vires and stated that, though the contract had been performed, no rights could arise from it. The bank could have given this security to a public depositor and it is difficult to see why the contract to secure the private depositor was not reasonably incidental to the banking business. (But see Baltimore & Ohio R. Co. v. Smith, 56 F.2d 799, at 802 (3d Cir., 1932).) The case can be sustained, however, on the public policy argument that depositors should be treated equally and that one should

not be permitted a preference by obtaining security. The result is no more uncertain under the policy reasoning than it would be under the "reasonably incidental or conducive" rule.

57. There is one notable contrary common law decision and that is by the Kansas court in Harris v. Independence Gas Co., 76 Kan. 750, 92 P. 1123, 13 L.R.A.,N.S., 1171 (1907), a very able opinion being written by Mason, J. Today there are several statutes reaching the same result and the California statutory provisions, in effect, adopted the Kansas court's suggestions. Ballantine, Corporations 249, note 3 (Rev. ed. 1946).

rescission at the request of one party. At this point, "The usurpation is at an end. Each party has received from the other what he bargained for. Neither of them has any cause to complain. The contract has ceased to be a living thing. The courts will leave it in its grave."[58] Such holdings depart widely from the English law which, even in completely executed transactions by both parties, considers the result void. Thus where an ultra vires contract to purchase land is made by an American corporation and a deed has conveyed the land to the corporate grantee, a valid title passes to the corporation, and the grantee can reconvey it and give a valid title to the new grantee. Under the English law, the execution of the contract gives no validity to it and title does not pass by virtue of this.[59] The English law squares up logically with its theory of special capacities; but to hold that a corporation may acquire title to a thing which it had no capacity to acquire, as do the American holdings, is clearly in direct conflict with the limited capacity doctrine. However, this does not mean that better and more just results are not obtained under the American view.

While the rule that an ultra vires transaction fully performed by both parties will not be disturbed is disarmingly simple in statement, the determination of what constitutes full performance in some transactions has been troublesome. The ultra vires transfer of land or of personalty and payment for the same is the simplest and easiest case of full performance by both parties. But what of a loan by a corporation with an ultra vires mortgage given as security for the loan? Or the loan to the corporation secured by an ultra vires mortgage given on its property? Are these transactions fully executed by both parties or must the remedies be examined in order to make a determination one way or the other? The American cases have permitted the corporation to enforce the mortgage where the corporation is a lender-mortgagee.[60] And where the corporation is a borrower-mortgagor and for some reason the corporate mortgage is ultra

---

58. Alabama Consolidated Coal & Iron Co. v. Baltimore Trust Co., 197 F. 347, at 358 (D.C.Md.1912).

59. Street, The Doctrine of Ultra Vires, 119 et seq. (1930). Ayers v. The South Australian Banking Co., L.R. 3 P.C. 548 (1871), seems to have been a Crown charter company and the case can be explained because of this. Furthermore, it was decided prior to Ashbury Ry. Carriage & Iron Co., Ltd. v. Riche, L.R. 7 H.L. 653 (1875). See 2 Machen, Modern Law of Corporations § 1030 (1908). For the American view, see Kerfoot v.

Farmers' & Merchants' Bank, 218 U.S. 281, 31 S.Ct. 14, 54 L.Ed. 1042 (1910); Lord v. Schultz, 115 Neb. 33, 211 N.W. 210, 62 A.L.R. 489 (1926) (corporation having acquired title to land which it had no power to purchase was allowed specific performance of a contract to sell it). The rule also applies to a purchase of personalty. Prescott National Bank v. Butler, 157 Mass. 548, 32 N.E. 909 (1893).

60. Silver Lake Bank v. North, 4 Johns.Ch. (N.Y.) 370 (1820). And see Union Nat. Bank v. Matthews, 98 U.S. 621, 25 L.Ed. 188 (1879).

vires, "The general tendency is to hold that where the corporation has received substantial benefits in connection with the execution of an ultra vires mortgage, neither it nor its creditors may attack the mortgage." [61] It would seem that in both situations the remedies available due to the "ownership" of the property are something apart from the consummated transaction by which the interest in property was acquired. In other words, rights and liabilities are acquired through such ownership, though a conditional one, and these should accompany such consummated transactions as incidents of ownership and not be considered as an unexecuted part of the transaction. Thus, where a corporation makes an ultra vires purchase of shares of stock in another corporation the shares of which carry additional liability under stated conditions, it should be clear (though it has not been) that as an incident of ownership the corporation should be under the same obligation to meet the additional liability as if the purchase had been intra vires. It has been held that, by such a consummated ultra vires purchase of shares, the corporation obtains a good title which it can convey to others and which entitles it to dividends,[62] but that it cannot be held liable for the additional assessments.[63] It is submitted that cases so holding run counter to the accepted doctrine that consummated transactions will not be disturbed, and that the courts so holding have failed to distinguish between consummation and remedy. The cases in which banks have been ultra vires holders of corporate shares carrying additional liability may be explained by the ever-present policy of protecting depositors from extrahazardous risks of various sorts.

Difficulties comparable to those mentioned in case of ultra vires mortgages and shareholdings are also encountered in case of ultra vires leases which have not run their term, and pledges. Rights and liabilities arising from the execution of and entry under the lease, and possession under the pledge, should not be confused with the enforcement remedies provided by the law. The lease is a conveyance for the time-period stated and the pledge is somewhat analogous to it in giving a right of possession in the thing pledged until the condition of the pledge is met. In either case a breach affords certain remedies which should be clearly distinguished from the "title" obtained by consummating

61. Dodd and Baker, Cases and Materials on Corporations 374 (2d ed. 1951) and cases cited. But there are holdings contra. Ibid. at 375.

62. Compare Shaw v. National German-American Bank, 132 F. 658, (8th Cir., 1904), aff'd 199 U.S. 603, 26 S.Ct. 750, 50 L.Ed. 328 (1905).

63. California Bank v. Kennedy, 167 U.S. 362, 17 S.Ct. 831, 42 L.Ed. 198 (1897), is the leading case. An earlier case contained a dictum that such an ultra vires holding subjected the holder to the liabilities of a shareholder. Germania Nat. Bank v. Case, 99 U.S. 628, at 633, 25 L.Ed. 448 (1879).

such transactions in the first instance.   Neither party should lose the rights nor escape the liabilities provided by the law.[64]

But suppose that both parties have not fully performed the ultra vires contract but that one has fully or partially performed when the other breaches or repudiates the same.   The view of the federal courts and of the few state courts following it has permitted recovery on a quantum meruit or quasi-contractual basis.   Since the ultra vires agreement is considered beyond the authority and capacity of the corporation, no contractual action may be brought.[65]   However, in a recent case, Magruder, Cir. J., in a dissenting opinion, suggested that "It does not necessarily follow that ultra vires may be invoked as a defense when the corporation is suing the other party to a bilateral contract . . . .," at the same time pointing out that cases in which the other party has successfully pleaded this defense are few.   He was recommending a view which, if accepted, would have justified recovery on the contract itself, since the party dealing with the corporation could not have raised the ultra vires defense.[66]   But, as stated above, the American cases have permitted the defense both in aid of the corporation and of the other party.

Torts committed by corporate agents in carrying on the intra vires business of the corporation while the agents are acting within the scope of their authority are chargeable to the cor-

---

64. It is believed that the approach in Mutual Life Ins. Co. v. Stephens, 214 N.Y. 488, 108 N.E. 856, L.R.A. 1917C, 809 (1915), and in St. Louis, V. & T. H. R. Co. v. Terre Haute & I. R. Co., 145 U.S. 393, 12 S.Ct. 953, 36 L.Ed. 748 (1892), is correct, although Machen feels that the St. Louis, etc., R. Co. case is of "doubtful consistency" with some of the other Supreme Court holdings.   2 Machen, Modern Law of Corporations § 1039 (1908).   The plaintiff had leased to defendant its railroad and franchises for 999 years and defendant had possessed them under the lease for 17 years.   Plaintiff prayed for a cancellation and surrender of the lease.   The court refused to disturb the lease stating that if "illegal" or simply ultra vires, it was fully executed and would not be set aside.   As a dictum, the shareholders were barred because of laches.   But compare Pullman's Palace Car Co. v. Central Transportation Co., 171 U.S. 138, 18 S.Ct. 808, 43 L.Ed. 108 (1898).

65. Citizens Nat. Bank of New York v. Appleton, 219 U.S. 196, 30 S.Ct. 364, 54 L.Ed. 443 (1909); Brunswick Gas Light Co. v. United Gas, Fuel & Light Co., 85 Me. 532, 27 A. 525, 35 Am.St.Rep. 385 (1893); Herbert v. Sullivan, 123 F.2d 477 (1st Cir., 1941), cert. denied 315 U.S. 803, 62 S.Ct. 632, 86 L.Ed. 1203 (1942); Commercial Casualty Ins. Co. v. Daniel Russell Boiler Works, 258 Mass. 453, 155 N.E. 422 (1927) (if no benefit has been received, then no recovery); Nat. Shawmut Bank of Boston v. Citizens Nat. Bank of Boston, 287 Mass. 329, 191 N.E. 647 (1934) (defendant, found the court, received no benefit.   Sed quaere?); Western Maryland Ry. Co. v. Blue Ridge Hotel Co., 102 Md. 307, 62 A. 351, 2 L.R.A.,N.S., 887 (1905); Norton v. Derby Nat. Bank, 61 N.H. 589, 60 Am.Rep. 334 (1882).   See Peairs, Corporate Powers in Massachusetts, 28 B.U.L.Rev. 301 (1948).

66. Herbert v. Sullivan, 123 F.2d 477, at 478 (1st Cir., 1941), cert. denied 315 U.S. 803, 62 S.Ct. 632, 86 L.Ed. 1203 (1942).   Massachusetts takes the minority or federal view on ultra vires contracts, and the case concerned its law.

poration as in other cases involving principals and agents. There has been little dissent from this doctrine when applied to torts committed during the pursuit of ultra vires transactions, the only inquiry allowed being whether the corporate agent committed the tort while operating within the scope of his authority or the employee while acting within the course of his employment. If the special capacity doctrine had been carried to its logical end the lack of capacity to commit torts as well as to enter into ultra vires contracts would have supported holdings of non-liability in the tort area.[67] Fortunately, the federal courts and those espousing its doctrine of special capacities saw the anomaly of permitting a corporation to defend by arguing that since its business was not authorized therefore torts committed by it in the pursuit of its unauthorized business were not chargeable to it.[68]

The extension of the tort doctrine into the area of criminal liability has been a gradual but an expanding one so that today a corporation may be held for a large variety of criminal acts of its agents and servants where such acts were authorized or committed by those acting within the scope of their authority or employment. However, Professor Ballantine has suggested that "Normally, if an unauthorized crime is committed by an employee while acting in the course of the corporate business, the individual so acting and not the corporation should be punished. This is based on a proper distinction between innocent shareholders and guilty actors."[69] Some criminal acts are thought to be so personal in character that a corporation should not be charged with them, and if the punishment is one not capable of being applied, such as imprisonment or death by electrocution,

67. See Dodd, American Business Corporations Until 1860, at 190–191 (1954) where he states: "In addition to such torts as negligent injuries to persons or property, corporations were held liable for nuisance, trespass, patent infringement (a parent corporation being held liable for infringement by a subsidiary), defamation, assault and battery, willful injury to a passenger, and false imprisonment. A Connecticut court even held a bank liable for malicious prosecution, untroubled by the supposed difficulty of imputing malice to a corporation, a difficulty which continued to trouble the English courts until a much later period. A Mississippi case held it proper to inflict exemplary damages on a corporation; and the Rhode Island court said that that could be done if, but only if, the tortious act was authorized or ratified by some high official of the company."

68. See N. Y., L. E. & W. R. Co. v. Haring, 47 N.J.L. 137, 54 Am.Rep. 123 (1885). In Merchants' Nat. Bank v. State Nat. Bank, 10 Wall. (77 U.S.) 604, at 645, 19 L.Ed. 1008, at 1018 (1871), it is stated: "Corporations are liable for every wrong of which they are guilty, and in such cases the doctrine of ultra vires has no application." Probably the leading early case holding a corporation for a tort committed while in the execution of an ultra vires contract is Bissell v. Michigan Southern & Northern Indiana R. Co., 22 N.Y. 258 (1860).

69. Ballantine, Corporations 278 (Rev. ed. 1946).

hanging or the gas chamber, it is obvious that the legislature could not have intended to include corporations as criminal defendants.[70]

Since *Erie Railroad Co.* v. *Tompkins*,[71] it has been clear that the federal courts, in diversity of citizenship cases, must take the law of the jurisdiction under which the corporation was organized in making determinations on ultra vires issues. Corporations formed under federal acts, such as national banks, are still subject to the federal doctrine of ultra vires.

(c) Ultra vires principles as developed in the majority of American courts. The major differences between the special capacities doctrine as it developed in the federal courts and those rules applied in the majority of state courts are that under the latter (1) the shareholders, by unanimous action, may authorize or ratify ultra vires transactions so as to make them valid; and that (2) once an ultra vires transaction has been fully performed by one of the parties, the other may sue upon the contract and does not have to rely upon a quasi-contractual remedy.[72]

In case of an ultra vires executory contract, neither party may enforce it nor may either recover damages for its breach or repudiation, which is the same as the federal rule. And, of course, fully executed contracts, as in the federal courts, will not be disturbed. Thus, the majority of state courts feel that ultra vires rules are for the protection of the shareholders and if they do not object others may not attack collaterally except in case of the executory ultra vires contract. The only loss at that point is the loss of a contract, and, as between third party and the shareholders, it is perhaps better policy—though this is doubtful —to protect the shareholders. On the other hand, where the third party by furnishing property or services to the corporation has fully performed and the corporation has not, the conflict of interests would seem clearly to favor the third party

---

70. The type of act of the personal sort which it is thought corporations cannot commit is perhaps illustrated by the crime of rape. May a corporation commit rape? Professor Edgerton, now the federal circuit court chief judge of the District of Columbia Circuit, wrote an article, Corporate Criminal Responsibility, 36 Yale L.J. 827, at 842 (1927) in which he saw no reason why a corporation, under proper circumstances, could not be held liable criminally for rape. So long as fines are provided as sanctions for criminal violations, or money penalties for criminal contempt, there is no difficulty in imposing such sanctions upon a corporation.

71. 304 U.S. 64, 58 S.Ct. 817, 82 L.Ed. 1188, 114 A.L.R. 1487 (1938).

72. Bath Gas Light Co. v. Claffy, 151 N.Y. 24, 45 N.E. 390, 36 L.R.A. 664 (1896); Denver Fire Ins. Co. v. McClelland, 9 Colo. 11, 9 P. 771, 59 Am. Rep. 134 (1885) (estoppel was an additional argument used to support these decisions as is usually the case); Schlitz Brewing Co. v. Missouri Poultry & Game Co., 287 Mo. 400, 229 S.W. 813 (1921) (case also relied upon the estoppel argument).

rather than the shareholders.[73] There are also valid arguments for supporting the third party in the executory contract situation as well as in case of the executed contract, for, barring some actual notice that the third party may have of the lack of corporate authority to enter into the particular contract, the corporate executives and their legal advisers are in a much better position to know what contracts are within and what without the four corners of the corporate articles. Thus, should not third parties be permitted to rely upon their determination? While constructive notice of what the articles contain has been charged against third parties dealing with the corporation in some federal and minority cases,[74] the majority opinions usually do not recognize this as a defense.

It has sometimes been argued that intra vires creditors should be protected against any inroads made upon the corporate treasury through ultra vires expenditures. There is very little support for this and, as a practical matter, the chances are small that the intra vires creditor has seen the articles and dealt on the basis of what they contain any more than the ultra vires creditor who dealt honestly and in the belief that the corporation had the power to enter into the agreement with him. However, there are a few cases involving insolvent banks where intra vires creditors were given priorities.[75]

A distinction has sometimes been made between the abuse of a general power which the corporation has and the exercise of a power not conferred upon the corporation. Where the person dealing with the corporation has no knowledge of the abuse of a power conferred, it is said "the doctrine of ultra vires does

---

73. Whether property or services have been received by the corporation should not be the test of recovery upon the contract. Many courts mention it and some specifically require it but do not satisfactorily explain the requirement. See Maren v. Calmenson, 158 Minn. 282, 197 N.W. 262 (1924); Brinson v. Mill Supply Co., Inc., 219 N.C. 498, 14 S.E.2d 505 (1941). Under the federal doctrine where the action is in quasi-contract and benefit must be shown, the requirement is understandable as a usual quasi-contract rule. The cases accepting the majority doctrine seem to have confused the two. See Dodd and Baker, Cases and Materials on Corporations 363–365 (2d ed. 1951).

74. McCormick v. Market Nat. Bank, 165 U.S. 538, at 550, 17 S.Ct. 433, at 436, 41 L.Ed. 817 (1897), which

charges those dealing with a corporation with constructive notice of what the articles contain. But the majority view is well expressed in Denver Fire Ins. Co. v. McClelland, 9 Colo. 11, 9 P. 771 at 777, 59 Am.Rep. 134 (1885): "Every one may have access to the statutes of the states affecting companies incorporated thereunder, and to their articles of incorporation; but to impute a knowledge of the probable construction the courts would put upon these statutes and articles of incorporation to determine questions raised upon a given contract proposed, is carrying the doctrine of notice to an extent which can only be denominated preposterous."

75. Ballantine, Corporations 259 (Rev. ed. 1946).

not apply." [76]   But the true explanation of the difference is that in the abuse of a power which the corporation has a third person may rely upon the apparent authority of the corporate agent, and, by doing so, obtain a valid contract untainted by any of the principles of ultra vires. It is by virtue of an authority which, upon its face, is sufficient to justify the reliance placed upon it by the other party. A fact peculiarly within the knowledge of the corporation, or of its agent, and which has not been disclosed or discovered by the other party, cannot be the basis of limiting the wider authority which has been disclosed. This agency doctrine is quite as applicable in jurisdictions accepting the limited capacity doctrine as in those which deny this doctrine. Thus, in an English case where a railroad corporation had authority to purchase land for its own purposes, but land was purchased for an undisclosed ultra vires purpose, it was properly held that the other contracting party had a valid contract. [77]   Somewhat comparable to this type of case is that in which the articles are sufficient to justify the corporate agent's action but the by-laws, unknown to the party dealing with the agent, limit his authority to something less. Such limitations if unknown to the other party have no effect on him.

But some American cases have permitted recovery against a corporation when benefits have been conferred in the performance of an intra vires contract where the plaintiff knew that the consideration he furnished would be used by the corporation in an ultra vires venture. The few cases reported have usually involved intra vires loans which were made with actual knowledge that the funds would be used in a venture outside the powers of the corporation. If the corporate borrower is left free to use the money at its discretion, mere knowledge by the lender that the borrower intends to use it for an ultra vires purpose

---

76. See, for example, Monument Nat. Bank v. Globe Works, 101 Mass. 57, 3 Am.Rep. 322 (1869); Bissell v. Michigan Southern & Northern Indiana R. Co., 22 N.Y. 289, 290 (1860). In City Coal & Ice Co., Inc. v. Union Trust Co., 140 Va. 600, 125 S.E. 697 (1924), noted in 10 Cornell L.Q. 498 (1925), 9 Minn.L.Rev. 478 (1925), and 11 Va.L.Rev. 406 (1925), a corporation gave its negotiable promissory note in payment of an ultra vires purchase of shares of stock in another corporation. The note was later transferred to the plaintiff bank as collateral for a loan, the bank having actual notice of the fact that the note was given to purchase shares but no actual notice that such purchase was ultra vires. The court held that the corporation was bound upon its note. It had general power to issue negotiable paper and plaintiff was not under a duty to make further inquiry.

77. Eastern Counties Ry. Co. v. Hawkes, 5 H.L.Cas. 331, at 373, 10 Eng.Rep. 928, at 944 (1855). And see Mayor, etc., of Norwich v. Norwalk Ry. Co., 4 E. & B. 397, at 443, 119 Eng.Rep. 143, at 160 (1855); In re David Payne & Co., Ltd., [1904] 2 Ch. 608; J. P. Morgan & Co., v. Hall & Lyon Co., 34 R.I. 273, 83 A. 113 (1912); 2 Machen, Modern Law of Corporations § 1061 (1908).

will not bar recovery.[78] But if, as part of the lending agreement it is stipulated that the loan shall be used for such a purpose, or if the lender actively participates in the ultra vires purpose, recovery will not be allowed.[79] The mere lending with knowledge of the intended use is not considered participation which will bar recovery, though in a real sense it is. The reasoning is a bit artificial: A contract's validity depends upon its terms and the consideration behind it. This contract was for the lender to lend money and for the corporation-borrower to pay it back. Knowledge of how the money is to be used forms no part of the consideration—the consideration is distinct from the motive behind it. Therefore, recovery is allowed on the contract. It should be noticed that recovery under such circumstances is somewhat comparable to quasi-contractual recovery under the federal doctrine for, under that doctrine, the third party is charged with constructive notice of the ultra vires character of the transaction. Here, of course, the lending is intra vires and the intended use of the money loaned is ultra vires, a fact which the lender knows. It is apparent that courts have not been too interested in discouraging ultra vires acts when they have allowed recovery in cases where a plaintiff has actual knowledge of the ultra vires use to which the consideration he furnished was to be put.

§ 6.   Liability of Corporate Directors, Officers and Agents to Other Party or to Corporation on Ultra Vires Contracts

For a variety of reasons it is generally held that directors, officers and agents of a corporation are not liable to the other contracting party who, through their supposed authority, has entered into an ultra vires contract with the corporation. In a case in which the court takes the view that a third party dealing with a corporation has constructive notice of the extent of the corporate powers, such notice should bar a suit against corporate officers based upon the theory that they have warranted their authority to execute the contract, for the other contracting party theoretically, at least, knows that their authority is non-

---

78. Franklin Co. v. Lewiston Institution for Savings, 68 Me. 43, 28 Am.Rep. 9 (1877).

79. Ibid.;   Marion   Trust   Co.   v. Crescent Loan & Investment Co., 27 Ind.App. 451, 61 N.E. 688, 87 Am.St.Rep. 257 (dictum) (1901); Nat. Shawmut Bank v. Citizens' Nat. Bank, 287 Mass. 329, 191 N. E. 647 (1934), noted in 48 Harv.L. Rev. 681 (1935). The Massachusetts case involved an ultra **vires** loan, the proceeds of which were directly used by the lender to make an immediate distribution in liquidation of $75 per share among the borrower's shareholders. The case was decided upon the basis that no benefit was received by the borrower. Active participation in the ultra vires act of paying off the borrower's shareholders might better have been emphasized.

existent.[80] It has also been held that there is no warranty by an agent that his principal has the *legal* power to enter into the contract.[81] And, as another reason for not holding the corporate officer, it has been held that if the contract is not one that can be enforced against the principal, it may not be enforced against the agent.[82]

But there are better reasons for not holding the board, the officers or agents when the corporation is suing them for losses brought about by virtue of ultra vires contracts entered into and performed or partially performed. Directors and officers are under a duty to use reasonable care in corporate matters and, if the duty is breached, they are liable for losses traceable to their lack of care.[83] It is frequently no easy matter to determine whether a particular act comes within the corporate purposes or powers. That is one reason why courts have become increasingly liberal in interpreting statutes and corporate articles so that, if there is doubt, the transaction will be held valid. Since what is reasonably incidental or conducive to carrying out the purposes of the corporation is an elastic principle, much leeway should be given directors and officers in making this determination and, if they have used reasonable care in arriving at the conclusion that the contract or transaction is within the scope of the principle, their due care and good faith should protect them. And it does, although there is some conflict in the books.[84] If management intentionally exceeds its authority or, through negligence, does the same and enters into ultra vires transactions which bring losses upon the company, there is no reason for exculpation, and management will be liable for such losses.

§ 7. Modern Statutes Concerning the Ultra Vires Doctrine

It has been said that "A modern corporation does not have limited powers; where it acts *ultra vires,* the usual reason is bad draftsmanship on the part of the lawyer drawing the certificate of incorporation." [85] And, " 'Ultra vires' was the result of

---

80. Sanford v. McArthur, 18 B.Mon. (Ky.) 411 (1857). *Contra*: Seeburger v. McCormick, 178 Ill. 404, 53 N.E. 340 (1899), based on warranty of authority by agent. In the same year Nat. Home Bldg. Ass'n v. Home Savings Bank, 181 Ill. 35, 54 N.E. 619, 64 L.R.A. 399 (1899), held that all who contracted with a corporation must take notice of its powers.

81. McCarty v. Love, 145 Miss. 330, 110 So. 795 (1927).

82. Browns v. Hare, 112 W.Va. 648, 166 S.E. 362 (1932).

83. For problems involving management, see Chapter 6, infra.

84. See Ballantine, Corporations §§ 65 and 106 (Rev.ed. 1946). See Litwin v. Allen, 25 N.Y.S.2d 667 (Sup.Ct. 1940) and authority cited in court's footnote 2.

85. Berle and Warren, Cases and Materials on Business Organization (Corporations), Note on The

an attempt to limit the corporation as a matter of social policy. It failed: corporations today are substantially unlimited. There remains merely the occasional case which may occur in a lawyer's practice . . . But *ultra vires,* once the principal preoccupation of corporation lawyers, is today confined to the occasional anachronism which one finds where an ancient corporate charter has been carried forward from an earlier year." [86] A lawyer's poor draftsmanship, however, may be aided by the more liberal interpretation of the purpose clause whereby more is included within the ambit of "reasonably incidental or conducive to accomplish the purposes set out" than was included at an earlier period. Modern statutes granting powers not easily implied at an earlier date have also made it easier to reach conclusions that corporate action is intra rather than ultra vires. And the very recent all-purpose-clause statutes are giving to the modern corporation the powers of the English Crown charter corporations.

But progress in the law of ultra vires has not stopped with more liberal interpretations, more statutory powers, or even with the statutory all-purpose clause.[87] The trend has been toward statutes which in effect make corporate transactions binding, whether executory or executed, if they have been authorized or ratified by the board and/or executed by a corporate officer or agent within the scope of his authority even though the transaction was not within the area of the objects clause or within the powers of the corporation.[88] Several recent statutes give the corporation the "power and capacity" of a natural person or the "capacity" of a natural person but "authority" only to do such acts as are necessary or proper to accomplish the corporate pur-

---

Doctrine of "Ultra Vires", 45 at 48 (1948).

86. Ibid.

87. See Nev.Rev.Stat. § 78.035 as amended in 1957 (all-purpose clause); § 78.135 (ultra vires to third persons abolished; this provision is necessary where the all-purpose clause section is not used).

88. See Vt.Gen.Corp.Law of 1947, § 5789; Okl.Bus.Corp.Act of 1947, § 1.29. The Oklahoma provision in § 1.29(a) (1) reads: "a. In no event shall it be asserted in any action that any contract, conveyance, undertaking, or tortious act, executed or executory, is beyond the purposes of a corporation expressed in its articles of incorporation, if: (1) Such contract, conveyance, undertaking, or tortious act was authorized or ratified by its board of directors or shareholders; . . ."

Ohio Gen.Corp.Law of 1955 (Rev. Code) § 1701.13(H) states: "No lack of, or limitation upon, the authority of a corporation shall be asserted in any action except (1) by the state in an action by it against the corporation, (2) by or on behalf of the corporation against a director, an officer, or any shareholder as such, (3) by a shareholder as such or by or on behalf of the holders of shares of any class against the corporation, a director, an officer, or any shareholder as such, or (4) in an action involving an alleged overissue of shares. This division shall apply to any action brought in this state upon any contract made in this state by a foreign corporation."

poses,[89] this latter type originating in the Model Business Corporation Act of 1928.[90] In either type it would seem that the only defense open would be the lack of authority of the corporate agent to bind the corporation, a pure agency problem.

Most of the statutes so far enacted make no reference to one who deals with the corporation with actual notice of the ultra vires nature of the transaction entered into with it. While it is doubtful whether those who have actual notice should obtain a good contract or valid transaction, the difficult determination of what constitutes actual notice in a particular set of facts is avoided. Some statutes, however, make an exception where the third party has actual notice.[91]

A few of the statutes have an additional provision that the articles constitute an agreement by the directors and officers with the corporation that they will confine their activities to those authorized by the articles and the statute.[92] The California statute states that the purposes and powers constitute an authorization to the directors and a limitation upon the actual authority of the corporate representatives; that such limitations may be pleaded by a shareholder or the state to enjoin the doing or continuation of unauthorized acts where third parties have not acquired rights thereby, or to dissolve the corporation, or in a suit by the corporation or a representative suit brought

89. Ariz.Rev.Stat. § 10–152(6) (1956): Power . . . "to make contracts, acquire and transfer property, possessing the same powers in such respects as private individuals now enjoy." § 10–171 reads: "No corporation shall engage in any business other than that expressly authorized in its articles of incorporation or by the law under which it is organized." Idaho Bus.Corp.Act (Idaho Code Ann.1949) § 30–114, subd. 1 (capacity of natural persons but authority only to do such acts as are necessary or proper to accomplish its purposes). Similar to Idaho provision are: Ind.Gen.Corp.Act § 3; La.L.S.—Rev.Stats. § 12:12; Wash. Rev.Code of 1951, § 23.08.070. In Kan.Gen.Stats.1949, § 17–3001 the corporation is given the power and capacity of natural persons and in Minn.Stat.Ann. § 301.12 the corporation has the capacity possessed by natural persons, but a person having actual knowledge of the lack of authority is not protected.

90. § 11, subsec. 1, Model Business Corporation Act of 1928, 9 U.L.A.

75 (1951). § 10 provides that no person dealing with the corporation shall be charged with constructive notice of the contents of articles or other corporate papers filed.

91. Mich.Gen.Corp.Act § 11 as amended by P.A.1935, No. 194: "The plea of ultra vires shall not be made by anyone except by (1) the corporation in an action between it and a director or officer thereof or a person having actual knowledge of the ultra vires character of the act or (2) by either party in an action between a shareholder and the corporation. The foregoing provision shall be construed as a limitation on the power of a corporation." The second unnumbered paragraph of this section applies similarly to a foreign corporation sued or suing in Michigan. See also Minn.Stat.Ann.1953, § 301.12 (a person having actual knowledge of the lack of corporate authority is not protected).

92. For example: Kan.Gen.Stats. 1949, § 17–3001(J); West's Ann. Cal.Corp.Code § 803(a).

by a shareholder against officers or directors who have violated their authority.[93]   Such provisions are codifications of the partnership-agency principle and open the way for the application of agency doctrine in the confused area of ultra vires.   Apparent authority of corporate agents which many courts have held not applicable to widen the horizon of corporate authority is, under such provisions, warranted.

A considerable number of statutes today spell out the legal results when an ultra vires transaction is either executory or consummated.   Limitations upon the purposes or powers of the corporation, or upon the powers of shareholders, officers or directors may not be asserted as between the corporation or any shareholder and any third person.   Contracts or conveyances made in the name of the corporation which have been authorized or ratified by its directors, or done within the scope of authority, whether actual or apparent, given by the directors, bind the corporation, and rights are acquired whether the contract is executory or partially or wholly executed.[94]   While these statutes are fairly similar some of them provide for injunctions when acts are about to be or are being performed in pursuance of an ultra vires contract if all parties to the contract are made parties and if the court deems the injunction to be equitable; the court may allow the corporation or the other party compensation for loss or damage which may result from the injunction, but may not award loss of anticipated profits.[95]   Suits by the corporation against the directors, officers and agents who may be liable in proper cases for losses occasioned by ultra vires acts authorized or accomplished by them and suits by the state to take the corporate life or to enjoin further exercise of ultra vires powers are usually expressly reserved in these statutes.

93. West's Ann.Cal.Corp.Code § 803 (a). "In view of the customarily general and vague statement of purposes, and as a matter of legislative policy, the draftsmen of the California General Corporation Law considered it advisable to give the directors power to decide what is within the scope of the business of the corporation and what is covered by the articles as far as outsiders are concerned. The shareholders entrust the management of the business to the directors as general agents. Public policy, business convenience, and fairness to those dealing with corporations require that the power of the directors should not be treated as a mere question of agency but that for some purposes the directors should be treated as being the corporation itself."   Ballantine, Corporations 266–267 (Rev.ed. 1946).

94. West's Ann.Cal.Corp.Code § 803. And see Ohio Rev.Code (Gen.Corp. Law of 1955) § 1701.13(H) quoted in note 83 above.

95. Wis.Bus.Corp.Law § 180.06(1); Pa.Bus.Corp.Law § 303(1); Tex. Bus.Corp.Act of 1955, Art. 2.04(1); D.C.Bus.Corp.Act of 1954, § 7(a) as amended in 1957; Ill.Bus.Corp.Acts of 1933, § 8(a) as amended by L. 1945, p. 544; Flack's Ann.Code of Md.1951, § 120(1), Art. 23; Or.Rev. Stats.1953, § 57.040(1).   See also A.L.I.Model Business Corporation Act § 6(a) (Rev.1953).

Thus, statutes are gradually eliminating ultra vires as a defense either for the corporation or ones dealing with it. Injunctions to prevent contemplated ultra vires acts or to stop the corporation from further ultra vires transactions together with the possibility of holding the corporate representatives who have intentionally or negligently bound the corporation to an ultra vires contract sufficiently protect the shareholders. The state may always take the life of such a corporation or enjoin it from further pursuit of ultra vires projects, so the public interest, if such there be, is protected. Third persons dealing with a corporation must, as in other agency cases, find out at their peril whether the corporate representative is acting within the scope of his authority, express, implied or apparent. But he need not go further. Thus, charter limitations are, as Professor Ballantine has stated, "a matter of 'indoor management.' " "Responsibility for exceeding the charter bounds should be placed on the directors." [96] By these statutes we have come reasonably close —in some, the mark has been hit—to giving the corporation the capacities and powers of the English Crown charter companies, having sought ancient doctrine as a satisfactory solution of our modern problems of ultra vires.

96. Ballantine, Corporations 267 (Rev. ed. 1946).

Chapter 6

POSTINCORPORATION MANAGEMENT: DIRECTORS, OFFICERS, AGENTS

§ 1. In General

The management of the modern corporation is almost exclusively in the hands of the board of directors. Unusual powers such as those of amending the corporate charter, the sale of all or a large part of the corporate assets, merger and consolidation, and dissolution belong to the shareholders. Likewise, the making of by-laws is a shareholder function unless a statutory provision gives this power to the board as well as to the shareholders, which modern statutes frequently do especially for the purpose of enacting by-laws in the interval between shareholder meetings.

Control by the shareholders over directorial action is a difficult thing where such action comes within the area of usual corporate functioning, for, in a rather true sense, the directors are more nearly principals than agents. While the shareholders have at common law the right to remove directors for cause, a right which exists for all types of corporations, and under some modern statutes the authority to remove with or without cause, their protection from action which they disapprove is primarily through the use of their voting power at the next election of directors. In a large corporation with widely dispersed stockholding where management has a pretty complete throttle-hold on proxy solicitation a change in management through the use of the ballot requires concentrated effort and a considerable expenditure of funds.

For practical reasons, the board of directors may legally delegate much of their authority to executive committees and officers. More frequently than not all or some of the officers are members of the board and are thus in close contact with their "principals" and know their desires and policies. But whether the officers are members of the board or not, the supervisory function of the board and the power of removal keep executive committees and officers within the actual control of their superiors, the board.

§ 2. Top Echelon, the Board of Directors—How Chosen—Qualifications—Pay—Removal

Except where the corporation statute requires the initial board of directors to be designated in the articles or certificate

211

of incorporation,[1] the board is elected by the shareholders who have voting rights. The usual term provided by statutes is one year or until another board is chosen and takes office. The number of board members may vary but nearly all of the statutes provide that there may not be less than three.[2] The great majority of statutes provide that, unless the articles or by-laws provide otherwise, the directors need not be shareholders in their company.[3] There is generally no requirement that directors be residents or citizens of the state of incorporation, but an occasional statute requires one or more directors to be citizens of the United States.[4] It is anticipated, and some statutes specifically provide, that directors must be adults.

There seems to be a movement toward statutory authorization to classify directors so that if there are nine, for example, one group of three may be chosen for three years, another for two and another for one, but after the two lower-termed directors have served their terms their successors are chosen for three years.[5] The argument of those who sponsor such laws is that the longer term gives directors a chance to become expert and always gives the inexperienced director the opportunity to learn his job from those who have had service on the board. Experience has shown, however, that boards are almost always re-elected if the members desire re-election and they have served with reasonable (sometimes with abominable) efficiency. There is a danger in such classification procedures that minority representation obtained by cumulative voting may be lost. This problem is discussed in the following chapter.

1. Examples of statutes requiring first board of directors to be named in the articles: West's Ann.Cal. Corp.Code § 301, as amended by L. 1957, c. 2261, § 2.5; Ind.Gen.Corp. Act § 17 as amended by L.1949, c. 194, § 4a; Flack's Ann.Code of Md., Art. 23, § 4(8); N.Y. Stock Corp. Law § 5–8 as amended.

2. Iowa apparently has no provision concerning number, terms, qualifications, etc. See Iowa Code Ann. § 491.5–5.

3. Me.Rev.Stat.1954, c. 53, § 32, as amended in 1955 and 1957, states: "Directors must be and remain stockholders . . .", with one exception.

4. Ark.Stat.1947, Ann. § 64–401 requires "at least one" to be a citizen of the United States. Accord: Fla.Stat.Ann. § 608.09(1). Ind.Gen. Corp.Act § 9, as amended by L.1953, c. 19, § 2, provides that a majority of directors must be citizens of the United States. N.Y.Gen.Corp.Law § 27 requires at least one director to be a citizen of the United States and a resident of New York.

5. See Ohio Rev.Code (Ohio Gen. Corp.Law of 1955) § 1701.57(B) which reads: "The articles or the regulations may provide for the classification of directors into either two or three classes consisting of not less than three directors each, and that the terms of office of the several classes need not be uniform, except that no term shall exceed the maximum period (3 years) specified in division (A) of this section." Conn.Gen.Stat.1949, § 5165 as reenacted in 1957; Ga. Corp.Act 1938, § 30; Ind.Gen.Corp. Act 1929, § 9, as amended by L. 1953, c. 19, § 2.

A director need not be an expert in the business which, as one member of a board, he directs. However, he must inform himself sufficiently about the business so that he may act with intelligence in supervising the activities of the officers who carry on the actual day-to-day transactions. He is entitled to rely upon their expert advice where he has no notice of irregularities or knowledge of facts which raise suspicions of irregular or negligent conduct.

Board members in America are usually not paid but are given their expenses and, at times, a small gratuity for their services. If the members hold offices in their company, they are paid as officers and not as board members. From an early period a tradition has existed that board members, frequently large stockholders, should obtain their compensation through the normal channels of dividends. However, there has recently been a "noticeable trend" toward paying directors salaries which, in a few companies, are substantial.[6] In England it is customary to pay "managing" directors for their services and so there has grown up a professional class of "managing directors" which does not yet exist in this country. It is probably true that salaries for directors have produced officials who actually direct rather than sit as dummies for whatever esteem the community entertains for men holding such positions. Board members are in a position to obtain inside information which they sometimes use for their own personal benefit but frequently with unanticipated dire consequences to themselves.

In the preceding section some mention was made of the fact that directors may be removed for cause. During their term of office, however, neither a majority nor all of the board, nor a majority or all of the shareholders may remove a director except for cause, that is, without statutory or charter aid. Professor Ballantine has called this an "unsound rule" for it denies the "sovereign owners" the right to remove their agents, although they may have become "entirely unsatisfactory."[7] The justification for it is that, unlike ordinary agents, they occupy a unique position as top echelon officers of the corporation and that the statutory command that corporations shall be managed by their directors would be meaningless if they were subject to the ever-present threat of removal at the whim of the shareholders. They would be mere puppets of the shareholders, a position they could not attain by a written agreement with their shareholders, a topic discussed a little later in this book. Strangely enough today, statutory permission has been given in some states for a majority or other pro-

6. Washington and Rothschild, Compensating the Corporate Executive 231 (Rev.ed. 1951).

7. Ballantine, Corporations 434 (Rev.ed. 1946).

portion of shareholders to remove directors without cause, or to provide for this in charter or by-laws, with no apparent recognition of fact that puppets are thereby created whereas they could not be so created by agreement.[8] These statutes evidence the growing feeling that while the state has formally declared that directors shall be the corporate managers, in the last analysis it is the shareholders who are the principals, and if for any reason they wish to change their agents before their elected terms have been served, they may do it; the state has no interest to protect. These statutory provisions should be critically examined in connection with problems to be considered presently where fewer than all the shareholders, by agreement, have attempted to create a "sterilized" board of directors.

§ 3. Top Echelon, the Board of Directors—Functions—Powers

The directors of a corporation are the managing group possessed with broad powers to run the business and to form its policies. They are limited in their authority only by reservations made by statute, articles or by-laws, or by the common law upon a determination that the authority is basicly one which belongs to the shareholders.

Corporation statutes are uniform in providing in essence that the corporate business shall be managed by the board of directors. However, a common provision permits the articles and/or by-laws to limit, define or regulate the powers of the corporation, or of its directors or shareholders.[9] It seems obvious that some reasonable limitations must be placed upon the authority to "limit, define or regulate" the powers of the directors; otherwise, directors could easily be made puppets by limit-

---

8. Ohio Rev.Code (Ohio Gen.Corp. Law of 1955) § 1701.58(C); West's Ann.Cal.Corp.Code § 810, as amended by L.1947, c. 1232; La.S.A.— Rev.Stat. § 12:34(C) (4); Minn.Stat. Ann. § 301.29. All of the above statutes qualifiedly protect minority shareholders. Idaho Code Ann. § 30–139, subpar. 4; Flack's Ann. Code of Md.1951, Art. 23, § 48(d). Chancellor Kent noted that shareholders at common law could remove directors at will. See Berle and Means, The Modern Corporation and Private Property 139 (1933).

The English Companies Act of 1948, § 184, permits shareholders by ordinary resolution, to remove directors and appoint new ones in their places. The director is entitled to notice and a hearing at the meeting. See Gower, Modern Company Law 127–130 (1954).

9. For example, see Mass.Gen.Laws 1932, c. 156, §§ 6 and 25, the latter providing: "The board of directors may exercise all the powers of the corporation, except such as are conferred by law, or by the by-laws of the corporation, upon the stockholders." The Ohio Rev.Code (Ohio Gen.Corp.Law of 1955) § 1701.59 states: "Except where the law, the articles, or the regulations require action to be authorized or taken by shareholders, all of the authority of a corporation shall be exercised by its directors. For their own government the directors may adopt by-laws not inconsistent with the articles or the regulations."

ing their authority to that which a majority of shareholders at any time should determine. Modern statutes delineate the specific corporate action requiring shareholder authorization and this, impliedly at least, gives the board of directors authority to act in the remaining corporate areas. But there are often important areas which, apart from the specific statutory inclusions, would have been considered at common law as within the province of the shareholders. These, certainly, are within the control of the shareholders through provisions in articles and/or by-laws limiting the authority of the board. In fact, since directorial authority is primarily for the purpose of managing the regular business of the corporation, unless authority beyond this is expressly provided, it is reasonable to conclude that restrictions through articles and/or by-laws outside these areas and those which pertain to indoor management of the others are within the control of the shareholders.

The directors are responsible for the selection of the executive officers and for establishing their salaries and retirement benefits. They have power to delegate much of their authority to the officers they have chosen, and statutes usually specifically empower them to appoint from their members executive committees having the authority of the board during the intervals between board meetings. Policy matters concerning the retention of earnings for future corporate operations, the payment or nonpayment of dividends, labor relations, prices, development of new products and of territorial expansion for the sale of products, the building of new plants when expansion seems advisable, determining the method of financing, and other policy matters, with the over-all supervision of the business, are functions of the directors. Since the board is the source of authority to carry on the corporate business, contracts and other transactions entered into by the corporation should derive their origin from the board rather than from the shareholders, except where statutory or legitimate provisions of articles or by-laws provide otherwise.

Modern statutes frequently give the board the function of appointing new members to its body upon the death or resignation of a director, the new member to serve until the next annual meeting of the shareholders when directors will again be elected. More extensive provisions appear in some of the statutes. The board may be given the power to remove a director upon his insanity established by a court, or upon his bankruptcy, or if he does not acquire the qualifications set up in articles or by-laws, and for other stated reasons.[10] Without statutory aid, such rea-

10. See Ohio Rev.Code (Ohio Gen. Corp.Law of 1955) § 1701.58(B).

sonable provisions of appointment and removal by the board may be provided for in articles or by-laws. They constitute regulations for inside management rather than encroachments upon shareholder rights.

§ 4. Top Echelon Procedures—Requirement of Notice of Meetings and of Quorum—Directors Must Operate as a Board—Legal Effect of Informal Board Action

Every director is entitled to have personal notice, unless some other type of notice is provided by custom, statute, articles or by-laws, in advance of a directors' meeting of the time and place of the meeting and, if the meeting is for the transaction of other than ordinary business, should be given notice of business of an extraordinary character.[11] Statute or by-law will usually provide for the giving of such notice a few days in advance of the meeting, or at least in time for the directors to make arrangements to attend it. Where the board meets without having been given the prescribed notice, if all members are present and no member objects, notice will be considered waived and the meeting held valid. Or if the formal notice prescribed has not been given but directors have been notified in some other manner, they may waive the prescribed notice and if a quorum appears it may function as a board. However, it has been held that where no notice has been given to one or more directors who do not appear at the meeting such director or directors may not waive notice after the meeting and thus make it a valid meeting.[12] This seems like an unduly narrow refinement and some statutes now permit waiver of notice either before or after a directors' meeting.[13] In any case where notice has not been

11. Bank of Little Rock v. McCarthy, 55 Ark. 473, 18 S.W. 759, 29 Am.St.Rep. 60 (1892) (as to personal notice); Compagnie de Mayville v. Whitney, [1896] 1 Ch. 788 (extraordinary business permitted though no notice of it in notice to directors); Mercantile Library Hall Co. v. Pittsburgh Library Ass'n, 173 Pa. 30, 33 A. 744 (1896) (on necessity of notice of extraordinary business).

12. United States v. Interstate R. Co., 14 F.2d 328 (D.Va.1926). In Holcombe v. Trenton White City Co., 80 N.J.Eq. 122, at 134, 82 A. 618, at 624 (1912), aff'd without opinion 82 N.J.Eq. 364, 91 A. 1069 (1913), the reason for the rule is stated: "The reason and principle underlying these decisions is this: Each member of a corporate body has the right of consultation with the others, and has the right to be heard upon all questions considered, and it is presumed that, if the absent members had been present, they might have dissented, and their arguments might have convinced the majority of the unwisdom of their proposed action, and thus have produced a different result. If, however, they had notice and failed to attend, they waived their rights, likewise if they signed a waiver of notice prior to the meeting; but consent given subsequent to the meeting, looking to ratification of what was done, is without force to validate the action taken."

13. Ohio Rev.Code (Ohio Gen.Corp. Law of 1955) § 1701.42; West's Ann.Cal.Corp.Code § 814.

given and waiver is not legally possible, any action taken by the board at such a meeting, which action was within the scope of the board's authority, may be ratified at a subsequently held meeting where notice was given. And in the case of regular periodic meetings of which the board has had notice there is no legal necessity of giving further notice before each meeting unless, as is sometimes the case, a statute or by-law requires it. Whether required or not, as a matter of good business practice notice should be given of these meetings, especially if scheduled at long intervals.

It has been stated that "a special meeting, held without due notice to all the directors, is not lawful, and all acts done at such meetings are void." [14] A more accurate statement is that they are voidable and it should be added that several exceptions and curative devices exist. For example, where notice would be futile as where a meeting must be held immediately or promptly and the director not notified is abroad or perhaps not within range to bring him to the meeting if the prescribed notice is given, there is no need to notify him. [15] Or, where a quorum of the board meets and authorizes a contract with a third person who, without notice that some members of the board have not been notified, enters into the contract with the corporation, it has been held that such a person cannot be expected to ascertain, at his peril, whether this bit of inside management has been complied with. [16] The notice requirement is usually through a by-law provision, and, by the overwhelming weight of authority, persons dealing with a corporation are not charged with constructive notice of what the by-laws contain. "It would be inequitable and unjust to place upon third persons, dealing with a corporation, the duty of first ascertaining whether the directing officers had complied with its own regulations adopted for its own convenience and safety," as was stated in one case. [17] Furthermore, if the board has customarily met without complying with a formal written notice requirement, the fact of notice given in some other less formal manner cannot be raised. [18] And a contract entered into or act done at an illegal board meeting may be ratified at a subsequently legally held meeting of the board [19] and, by better opinion, upon the unanimous vote of the

14. United States v. Interstate R. Co., 14 F.2d 328 (D.Va.1926).

15. Sherman v. Fitch, 98 Mass. 59 (1867); Nat. Bank of Commerce v. Shumway, 49 Kan. 224, 30 P. 411 (1892); Chase v. Tuttle, 55 Conn. 455, 12 A. 874 (1888).

16. Colcord v. Granzow, 137 Okla. 194, 278 P. 654, 64 A.L.R. 699 (1929).

17. Ibid. 278 P. at 662.

18. Ibid. at 661–662.

19. Meyers v. El Tejon Oil & Refining Co., 29 Cal.2d 184, 174 P.2d 1 (1946); United States v. Interstate R. Co., 14 F.2d 328 (D.Va.1926).

shareholders.[20]   Ratification need not be by formal resolution
but may be as informal as inaction under circumstances known
or that should have been known by the director who had not
been notified of the first meeting.[21]

By the common law a quorum of directors is a majority of
the board. If the meeting was properly notified those present
constituting a quorum may carry on the corporate business by a
majority of the quorum's voting in favor of a resolution. Thus,
in a board of five directors, three constitute a quorum and, three
only being present, two voting for a resolution may carry it.
There are some exceptions to these rules in case a director is
interested personally in a transaction with his corporation or
where he sits upon the board of another corporation which is
dealing with the one he now represents as a board member.
These exceptions will be discussed in due time. As in so many
other situations, statutes are making inroads on this common
law rule. The California statute, for example, provides: "A
majority of the authorized number of directors constitutes a
quorum of the board for the transaction of business unless the
articles or by-laws provide that a different number, which in no
case shall be less than one-third the authorized number of directors, nor less than two, constitutes a quorum." [22] And further:
"Every act or decision done or made by a majority of the directors present at a meeting duly held at which a quorum is present
is the act of the board of directors, unless the law, the articles,
or the by-laws require a greater number." [23]

If the number of directors is stated to be a definite number,
as 5 or 8 or 15, a majority constituting a quorum is a simple
matter of arithmetic; in our case, 3, 5, and 8 respectively. But
suppose a by-law provides that the board shall consist of from
three to seven persons and the shareholders elect seven but five
only accept their directorates. These five proceed to carry on
the business of the corporation. If, after proper notice of a
board meeting, three only appear for the meeting, is there a
quorum or must there be four present under these circum-

20. Vawter v. Rogue River Valley
     Canning Co., 124 Or. 94, 257 P. 23
     (1927), 262 P. 851 (1928). See Land-
     strom, Ratification by Majority
     Shareholders, 31 B.U.L.Rev. 165
     (1951).

21. See, for a good example, Meyers
     v. El Tejon Oil & Refining Co., su-
     pra note 16.

22. West's Ann.Cal.Corp.Code § 816.
     Conn.Gen.Stat.1949, § 5165, as reen-
     acted in 1957, provides: "A major-
     ity of the directors shall constitute
     a quorum . . . unless it is

provided in a by-law adopted by
a stockholders' meeting that more
or less than a majority shall constitute a quorum." Since a board
may be composed of three members, may not a by-law effectively
make one director a quorum? See
also Ohio Rev.Code (Ohio Gen.Corp.
Law of 1955) § 1701.62, where the
articles or regulations (by-laws
elsewhere) may designate less than
a majority as a quorum, with no
minimum stated.

23. West's Ann.Cal.Corp.Code § 817.

stances? It was argued in a recent case that by electing seven directors the shareholders had indicated their intent to make their board one of seven members as they might have by proper resolution or by-law. The court thought not and held that it was not the number elected but the number who accepted, in this case five, who constituted the board. "Acceptance by the selectee after notice of his election is as essential as the election itself," said the court. Acceptance may be presumed after the passage of a reasonable time during which the selectee has notice of his election, but should not be otherwise indulged. The failure of two shareholders to accept their offices nullified the shareholders' action in respect to each and, thought the court, the full board was composed of five members three of whom would constitute a quorum.[24] The reasoning is not too impressive for what is more indicative of the shareholders' intent to create a 7-member board than by nominating seven and voting for seven candidates unless it be a resolution stating that the board shall consist of seven persons to be chosen, etc.? At the time of the decision in this case a statute provided that "Vacancies shall be filled by a majority of the remaining directors, though less than a quorum, unless it is otherwise provided in the Certificate of Incorporation or the by-laws." [25] If the court had concluded that the board consisted of seven members *and* if the five had then proceeded to name two additional members they would have been met by the argument that the statute did not encompass newly created directorships, which these were, and that additional statutory aid would be necessary to give this power.[26] A layman would probably not be impressed by the idea that an office provided for contains no vacancy until it has had a previous occupant.[27] But there were other statutory provisions which the court thought could not be ignored in reaching its conclusion.

That the directors must operate as a board is a requirement which is primarily for the benefit of the shareholders. Thus the general rule has been established that corporate acts must be done or authorized at a meeting of directors at which all are

24. Blish v. Thompson Automatic Arms Corp., 30 Del.Ch. 538, 64 A. 2d 581 (1948).

25. Former Del.Gen.Corp.Law § 30. The interesting question of the possibility of changing the number of directors required by a by-law through the customary practice of carrying on the corporate business with a fewer or larger number acquiesced in by the shareholders is discussed in Belle Isle Corp. v. MacBean, 29 Del.Ch. 261, 49 A.2d 5 (1946).

26. Belle Isle Corp. v. MacBean, 30 Del.Ch. 373, 61 A.2d 699 (1948); Automatic Steel Products, Inc. v. Johnston, 31 Del.Ch. 469, 64 A.2d 416, 6 A.L.R.2d 170 (Sup.Ct.1949). See Comment, 47 Mich.L.Rev. 378 (1949). By a 1949 amendment the Delaware statute was changed to cover newly created directorships. See Del.Gen.Corp.Law of 1953, § 223.

27. See also McWhirter v. Washington Royalties Co., 17 Del.Ch. 243, 152 A. 220 (1930).

present or have the opportunity to be present by due and proper notice of the meeting.[28] The reason assigned for the rule is that the corporation is entitled to the benefit of the conflicting views, if any, and of the advice of the board members as a group. But no special formality is necessary to constitute a meeting of the board and if all members are present, whether notified or not, and if they participate, the meeting will be considered valid. Furthermore, since the rule is for the protection of the shareholders, they may by unanimous action, according to some cases, waive the necessity of a meeting of the board.[29] Informality in corporations where the shares are closely held is so common that, were a rigid rule to apply, much injustice would result. As was well stated by Gourley, Ch.J.:[30] "The doctrine of permitting close corporations to act informally is recognized as an exception to the general rule that directors must act as a board at duly convened meetings. The exception is founded upon principles of equitable estoppel and is limited to instances in which the custom or usage of the directors is to act separately or informally and not as a board." Thus, by establishing that the customary directorial procedures are informal ones, perhaps by agreeing individually on the street or over the telephone to the proposed corporate action, such action forms the basis of an estoppel against the corporation. This is analogous to the additional authority which an agent may acquire by acting outside his express or implied authority to the knowledge of his principal who ignores it, and thereby establishes the basis of an apparent or ostensible authority to bind the principal to what had previously been an unauthorized act. Corporate agents form no exception to this rule and the top echelon of corporate "agents" acquires ostensible authority to act informally by acting without restraint

28. Merchants' & Farmers' Bank v. Harris Lumber Co., 103 Ark. 283, 146 S.W. 508, Ann.Cas.1914B, 713 (1912); Baldwin v. Canfield, 26 Minn. 43 (1879). The fact that majority directors are also majority shareholders does not alter the rule: Mosell Realty Corp. v. Schofield, 183 Va. 782, 33 S.E.2d 774 (1945). But see Buckley v. Jennings, 95 Vt. 205, 114 A. 40 (1920), where it is stated: "The action of a majority of the directors though acting separately, if within the scope of their powers as directors, binds the company."

29. Merchants' & Farmers' Bank v. Harris Lumber Co., supra, note 28; Murtland Holding Co. v. Egg Harbor Comm'l Bank, 123 N.J.Eq. 117, 196 A. 230 (1938) (no formal meeting of board but all the shareholders assented to the assignment of a stock certificate which was held a valid assignment).

30. Sharon Herald Co. v. Granger, 97 F.Supp. 295, at 301 (D.Pa.1951). *Accord:* Holy Cross Gold Mining & Milling Co. v. Goodwin, 74 Colo. 532, 223 P. 58 (1924); Forrest City Box Co. v. Barney, 14 F.2d 590 (8th Cir., 1926); Brainard v. De La Montanya, 18 Cal.2d 502, 116 P.2d 66 (1941). But the rule has been applied rigorously in some, particularly early, cases: Baldwin v. Canfield, 26 Minn. 43 (1879); Gashwiler v. Willis, 33 Cal. 11 (1867); Branch v. Augusta Glass Works, 95 Ga. 573, 23 S.E. 128 (1895); Hamlin v. Union Brass Co., 68 N.H. 292, 44 A. 385 (1895); Chavelle v. Washington Trust Co., 226 F. 400 (9th Cir., 1915).

from its own members or from the shareholders.[31] Some of the cases are based on the theory that the top echelon may determine its own means of carrying on the business;[32] others that, through the open use of informal procedures, the shareholders have consented to what they have seen or should have seen of actual board action,[33] a theory pointing toward apparent authority conferred by inaction.

But informal action of the kind discussed above should be distinguished from informal action by fewer than those sitting on the board at any particular time. A majority of the board, acting without the knowledge of the remaining members, cannot by informal action *alone* bind the corporation. Thus, where one board member, on behalf of the corporation, agreed to an accord and satisfaction with the defendant, and a second board member later agreed to the same and told the defendant of his agreement but the remaining board member knew nothing of this agreement, it was held that the corporation was not bound by it. "There is nothing . . . to show any knowledge of or ratification by acquiescence or otherwise of the alleged accord and satisfaction by the third member of the board of directors," said the court.[34] Actual knowledge is probably not necessary if the board member ought to have known of the agreement had he paid proper attention to the corporation's business.[35] And acceptance and retention of the benefits of a contract, with the full knowledge of the board, has rightly been held to be "as complete a ratification as would have resulted from any formal all-inclusive resolution" of the contract entered into by informal action of the board.[36]

---

31. Directors are not agents in the ordinary sense. They represent the corporation which, when we go behind this entity, means the shareholders. But the directors represent the minority as well as the majority shareholders and cannot favor one group over the other. And, thus, when the majority shareholders voted to sell the assets of the company over the dissent of a minority and the directors refused to make the sale, the court rightly held that the board could not be compelled to sell. Automatic Self-Cleansing Filter Syndicate Co., Ltd. v. Cuninghame, [1906] 2 Ch. 34.

32. Buckley v. Jennings, 95 Vt. 205, 114 A. 40 (1921).

33. Gorrill v. Greenlees, 104 Kan. 693, 180 P. 708 (1919).

34. Hurley v. Ornsteen, 311 Mass. 477, 42 N.E.2d 273, at 276 (1942). There is not unanimous agreement, even, on this point. See authorities cited in Dodd and Baker, Cases and Materials on Corporations, Note on Effect of Acquiescence of Directors, 165 et seq. (2d ed. 1951).

35. See Baltimore & O. R. Co. v. Foar, 84 F.2d 67 (7th Cir., 1936), where the whole board was charged with notice of what a corporate agent had, without authority, agreed to.

36. Bayer v. Beran, 49 N.Y.S.2d 2 (Sup.Ct.N.Y.1944). This case involved informal board action of the Celanese Corporation of America which had 1,375,000 shares outstanding, 10% of which were held by officers and directors. Expenditures for radio advertising had been made without a formal meet-

A few statutes specifically authorize informal directorial action if the directors consent in writing to the same.[37]

§ 5. Top Echelon Operation Through Executive Committee of Board—Necessity to Act as a Committee—Limitation on Powers the Board may Delegate

It is not customary for directors, as such, to carry on the day-to-day business of the corporation. At an earlier date when corporations were formed by special act many charters failed to state that the corporation was to be managed by a board of trustees or directors. As Professor Dodd has shown the implication of such cases as reached the courts "seems to be that in the absence of such a provision a shareholders' meeting could do any ordinary business act other than those which it was impracticable to do at a meeting." [38] Where the charter or general law vested the directors with general managerial powers, a few of the early cases indicated that such powers were exclusive and that attempts by the shareholders to exercise such powers through shareholders' meetings would not be effective.[39]

But even the directors of the early American corporations of which Professor Dodd wrote had, by virtue of their managerial powers, the power to appoint agents "even for terms which would outlast the directors' term of office," [40] and with broad powers, though a few decisions stated that the directors' discretionary powers could not be delegated.[41]

The usual statutory statement that the business and affairs of a corporation shall be managed by a board of directors or that the property and business of a corporation shall be controlled and managed by its board of directors places large discretionary powers in the directors. Implied is the power to appoint officers and agents and to give them large powers, not coextensive with directorial powers but sufficiently broad to carry on the day-to-day business which may include the making of important contracts. By-laws and statutes give directors specific

ing of the board but had been approved by the members individually. And see Hannigan v. Italo Petroleum Corp. of America, 4 Terry 333, 47 A.2d 169 (Del.Sup.Ct.1945); id. v. id., 6 Terry 593, 77 A.2d 209 (Del.Sup.Ct.1950).

37. Mich.Gen.Corp.Act § 47–4(c) as amended by L.1943, Act No. 160, provides: ". . . if the director shall severally and/or collectively consent in writing to any action to be taken by the corporation such action shall be as valid corporate action as though it had been authorized at a meeting of the directors." Similar is Pa.Bus.Corp. Law of 1933, § 402(5) as amended by 1949 P.L. 1773; 1951 P.L. 1475, § 4. And Minn.Stat.Ann. § 301.28–4(7), provides for board action without a meeting "if done in writing signed by all of the directors."

38. Dodd, American Business Corporations Until 1860, at 191 (1954).

39. Ibid. at 193.

40. Ibid. at 193.

41. Ibid. at 193.

power to appoint from their number executive and other committees and many of these statutes, in words at least, purport to permit the board to pass on all the authority they possess in the management of the property and affairs of the corporation. But there are limits beyond which the top echelon of corporate authority may not go.

No court has yet said, nor is it likely to say, that the directors may pass on to an executive committee their complete powers. The power and duty to supervise the various operations of the corporation come within the class of non-delegable functions. The selection of the superior officers, the determination of their salaries, of profit-sharing additional compensation, of length of term of employment, of dismissal, and other vital matters pertaining to the operation of these upper echelon employees would all seem to be matters of managerial discretion which only the top echelon may exercise, unless the authority delegated clearly permits these things and even then, it seems doubtful whether such important items should be passed on to an executive committee. Whether and when dividends should be declared, their amount, time of payment and to shareholders of record of what date are also top management problems. Should money be borrowed and upon what terms; should unissued shares be sold and for what purposes; should by-laws be amended (when the board has the power of amendment) and how; should suits be defended or brought—all are likewise highly discretionary matters and unusual enough to warrant action by the board rather than its executive committee.

Just where the line should be drawn in permitting the delegation of powers by the board to an executive committee has not been definitely decided. In a case where the by-laws permitted the board to appoint from its membership an executive committee with "full powers of the board of directors when said board is not in session," it was stated that it was intolerable to maintain that the words "full powers" meant more than full powers to carry on the ordinary business transactions of the corporation. The defendant had argued that the by-law had no limitations. In response to this argument the court stated that "Such an assumed absorption of the powers of the creator by the created is too absurd to receive the approbation of any court of law." [42] Since there are many matters involving discretion coming within the scope of "ordinary business operations" of

---

42. Hayes v. Canada, Atlantic & Plant S. S. Co., Ltd., 181 F. 289 at 293 (1st Cir., 1910). Such a by-law was held invalid in Temple v. Dodge, 89 Tex. 68, 32 S.W. 514, 33 S.W. 222 (1895), but the decision carries a dictum that managerial operations of the board involving discretion might be validly delegated in the charter. Compare De Pova v. Camden Forge Company, 254 F.2d 248, at 252 (3d Cir., 1958).

the particular corporations, it seems clear that whether or not the delegated power involves discretion is not the test.[43] If it involves an extraordinary power which, by reasonable interpretation, is outside the ambit of ordinary business operations in the particular business, the delegation is vulnerable.

Yet there is no doubt that in many corporations executive committees take over wider managerial powers than those usually permitted by courts and, by later ratification by the directors, the determination of such committees becomes binding and legally enforceable. So prevalent has the use by "giant" corporations of various committees with what purports to be unlimited power in the field of their appointment become that it has been said:[44] "Board committees . . . are often more active and of more positive influence than the boards as a whole. Their power, of course, stems from the tendency of boards to approve the recommendations of their committees, but this does not destroy their influence. Approval is typically almost routine in nature. As a consequence a small group on a strategic committee may wield a great deal of influence, particularly in the field of its specialty. A small finance committee, for example, was considered the main power in Armour & Co. of Illinois for a decade.[45] There are two influential committees in the board of Du Pont: The finance committee has supervision of the extensive investments of the company and the executive committee concerns itself with the operative side." It may well be that the

43. See Haldeman v. Haldeman, 176 Ky. 635, 197 S.W. 376 (1917), where the court held that matters of discretion might be delegated. It is doubtful whether the case goes any further than the *Hayes* case, supra, note 42.

44. Temporary National Economic Committee, Monograph No. 11, "Bureaucracy and Trusteeship in Large Corporations" at page 25 (1940). See Drucker, Management Must Manage, 28 Harv.Bus.Rev. 80 (1950). Directors cannot escape liability for neglect or maladministration by allowing the corporation to be run by an executive committee. Lane v. Bogert, 116 N.J.Eq. 454, 174 A. 217 (1934). This is sometimes specifically provided in statutes. See Mo.Rev.Stat.1949, V.A.M.S., § 351.330; Burns' Ann.Ind.Stat.1933, § 25–208 (Ind.Gen.Corp.Law, § 9) as amended by L.1953, c. 19, § 2; Ill.Bus.Corp.Act of 1933, § 38, as amended by L.1957, S.B. 266. On the subject of the general delegation of powers to an executive committee, see Note, 42 Mich.L.Rev. 133 (1943).

45. In Smith v. California Thorn Cordage, Inc., 129 Cal.App. 93, 18 P.2d 393 (1933), a finance committee of shareholders was appointed by agreement with the shareholder members "to take complete charge and control of the finances of the corporation, to raise funds for the development of the corporation, either by sale of its capital stock or a bond issue, and to become guarantors upon its notes." When all the obligations of the company had been discharged, the committee was to cease to exist and "its powers shall thereafter be exercised" by the directors. The court held the agreement invalid, and stated that "it was a bald attempt to usurp the powers and duties of the directors." Problems of agreements between shareholders and the board to control corporate activity are discussed at page 331 and following.

time has arrived when statutes should recognize these customary procedures, particularly in large corporations, and place these expert committees on a plane with boards of directors concerning action within their specialties. Many of the statutes now in force are so broadly stated that it is difficult to believe that the legislature did not so intend.

The requirements of notice and of quorum which are applied in board-of-directors cases are likewise applicable to committees. If no time for notice is specified, reasonable notice to enable committee members to attend the meeting is required.[46] Committees, like boards, are useful in obtaining the viewpoints and advice of the members and, as agencies of the board, the board is entitled to this exchange of ideas before committee determination of the business at hand. In other words, the committee, like the board, can ordinarily act only as a body.[47]

Because of the uncertainty of what powers are actually conferred by a delegation of "all the powers of the board" a wise draftsman will be careful to spell out in the by-laws the exceptions or state specifically the powers intended to be delegated to the particular committee. This would seem desirable even where the statute itself permits a delegation of what appears to be the full authority of the board but states specifically a few exceptions.[48]

§ 6. Top Echelon Operation Through Management Contracts— Limitation on Power to Delegate

The problem of delegating broad powers of management to a natural person or other corporation is analogous to that of delegation to an executive or other committee, or to a general manager. There is one essential difference, however, for management contracts anticipate the turning over of the business to outsiders whereas a delegation of powers to a committee of the board or to the corporate officers keeps the authority in the

---

46. Hayes v. Canada, Atlantic & Plant S. S. Co., Ltd., supra, note 42; Close v. Brictson Mfg. Co., 43 F.2d 869 (D.Neb.1930).

47. Peurifoy v. Loyal, 154 S.C. 267, 151 S.E. 579 (1930).

48. West's Ann.Cal.Corp.Code § 822 provides: "The by-laws may provide for the appointment by the board of directors of an executive committee and other committees and may authorize the board to delegate to the executive committee any of the powers and authority of the board in the management

of the business and affairs of the corporation, except the power to declare dividends and to adopt, amend, or repeal by-laws. The executive committee shall be composed of two or more directors." And see Flack's Ann.Code of Md. 1951, Art. 23, § 55(a); Ohio Rev. Code (Ohio Gen.Corp.Law of 1955) § 1701.63(A), which gives the board the authority to appoint executive and other committees. § 1701.11(A) (5) pertains to shareholder authorization through a "regulation" (by-law).

family and gives the board the opportunity to supervise and control the activities of committees and officers. In a recent case [49] all of the shareholders of Trenton-New Brunswick Theatres Co. and their corporation had contracted that for a period of 19 years the B. F. Keith Corporation should manage all the theaters owned or leased by Trenton with full authority and power to supervise the operation and management of these theaters. The only provision for a change of management during that period was by joint submission of the holders of Class B and C stock of Trenton (the plaintiff owned Class B, while Trenton Theatres Building Company owned Class C) to the American Arbitration Association of the question as to whether or not the management should shift from the holders of Class A–1 and A–2 stock (i.e., B. F. Keith Corporation) to the holders of the B and C stock jointly. After a period of time during which the contract was carried out, the plaintiff tired of the contract and brought an action for a declaratory judgment to determine the validity of the contract. The agreement was held valid in the Special Term and in the Appellate Division of the Supreme Court of New York. But the Court of Appeals held the contract in violation of the statutory provision that "The business of a corporation shall be managed by its board of directors" stating: "We are not confronted with a slight impingement or innocuous variance from the statutory norm, but rather with the deprivation of all the powers of the board insofar as the selection and supervision of the management of the corporation's theatres, including the manner and policy of their operation, are concerned." This is an extreme holding as the delegation of authority was not only made by the board of the corporation but sanctioned by unanimous action of its shareholders. And one is led to ask whether the state, by virtue of its statute placing corporate management in directors, has indicated a wider policy than one to protect minority shareholders from majority activity, and to protect all shareholders against unreasonable delegation by a board of its authority. Had the agreement been a lease of the theaters for the same period on a profit-sharing rental basis the court, no doubt, would have supported it even though for the period the directors of the lessor corporation would have no control over its properties.[50]

There is much less to be said for an extreme delegation of its powers by the board when there has not been unanimous consent

49. Long Park v. Trenton-New Brunswick Theatres Co., 297 N.Y. 174, 77 N.E.2d 633 (1948), discussed in Note, 43 Ill.L.Rev. 561 (1948); Note, 61 Harv.L.Rev. 1251 (1948); Comment, 17 Ford.L.Rev. 95 (1948). Compare Clark v. Dodge, 269 N.Y. 410, 199 N.E. 641 (1936), with the principal case.

50. Schneider v. Greater M. & S. Circuit, Inc., 144 Misc. 534, 259 N. Y.Supp. 319 (1932).

of the shareholders. The board is the representative of all shareholders. The statute creating the board and giving it the power to manage is for the protection of the owners of a business corporation and the holder of one share may insist that his directors keep within the statutory norm. Thus, where the directors agreed to turn over the management of their company for 20 years to another company which was expert in the particular business, the court refused specific performance of the contract, admitting that no bright line could be drawn between cases which had permitted certain managerial powers to be delegated to strangers and those which denied the authority to so delegate. "That corporations may, at least for a limited period, delegate to a stranger certain duties usually performed by the officers, is clear . . . On the other hand, it is equally well settled that there are duties, the performance of which may not be indefinitely delegated to outsiders . . ."[51] The court pointed to *Jones* v. *Williams*[52] where the board of directors gave an outsider the editorship and management of a newspaper for the period of 5 years during which he was to determine the editorial policy of the paper. The fact that the period was much shorter and that "a large part of the board's official duties was undelegated" was thought important in distinguishing the two cases. The length of time during which powers are to be exercised by outsiders is important as well as the retention of supervisory control and the power to terminate such management contracts when, in the directors' judgment, outside management should be terminated.

Management contracts have been used in the public utility field though at times they have been abused, especially through the use of managing subsidiaries and the charge of exorbitant management fees for the purpose of obtaining higher rates from the commission. Expert part-time management contracts can be of advantage to small corporations unable to pay for full-time performance of an expert more competent than the company's board or officers.[53]

§ 7. How Top Officers are Chosen—What Authority do they have from their Offices as Such—Importance of Adequate By-laws

The traditional officers of business corporations are the president, vice-president, secretary and treasurer. General

---

51. Sherman & Ellis, Inc. v. Indiana Mutual Casualty Co., 41 F.2d 588, 590 (7th Cir., 1930), cert. denied 282 U.S. 893, 51 S.Ct. 107, 75 L.Ed. 787 (1930).

52. 139 Mo. 1, 39 S.W. 486, 40 S.W. 353, 37 L.R.A. 682, 61 Am.St.Rep. 755 (1897).

53. See Dodd and Baker, Cases and Materials on Corporations, footnote 8, pp. 196–197 (2d ed. 1951).

managers are frequently appointed and, in the case of banks, a cashier with one or more assistant cashiers. The president or other officer of a business corporation is frequently given the powers of a general manager through a by-law or resolution of the board. These officers are usually appointed by and remain under the direct control of the directors. Thus, through the power of removal, the board is able to control the operation of the corporate business and keep the officers within the particular areas of operation to which their express authority confines them. Persons dealing with these corporate agents are under the same duty to ascertain the extent of their authority as in other agency cases. And the authority which they possess is derived in the same manner as that of other agents, by express delegation through by-law or resolution of the board, by authority implied as in other agency cases and by authority arising out of appearances created by the board or assumed by the corporate agent without rectification or protest by an informed board.

But, apart from authority arising from express, implied or apparent sources, what does the office itself connote in terms of authority? What powers does the president possess from the office itself? Very few, according to the strict view which is represented by the rule that the president of a private corporation has little or no authority to bind the corporation by virtue of his office.[54] This view recognizes no inherent authority in the president to buy, sell or contract for his corporation. And though he be a director as well, which is customary, this does not add to his authority to bind the corporation unless the board has authorized him to do this.[55] His office, under this view, gives him the position of presiding officer at meetings but little else.[56]

Fortunately, by force of what authority is usually delegated to the president, or assumed by him and not objected to by the board, there has been a tendency to imply the powers of a general manager from the office alone, some courts stating that there is the prima facie authority for the president "to enter into such ordinary contracts as the custom and necessities of the business would justify," [57] other courts not mentioning "prima facie authority" but placing their decision squarely upon an

54. Black v. Harrison Home Co., 155 Cal. 121, 99 P. 494 (1909); dictum in Italo-Petroleum Corp. of America v. Hannigan, 40 Del. 534, 14 A. 2d 401 (1940), which accepted the modern and liberal rule.

55. Hurley v. Ornsteen, 311 Mass. 477, 42 N.E.2d 273 (1942).

56. Black v. Harrison Home Co., supra, note 54.

57. Learned Hand, J., in Schwartz v. United Merchants & Manufacturers, Inc., 72 F.2d 256 (2d Cir., 1934), noted in 35 Col.L.Rev. 112 (1935). The quotation was from another New York case.

implied authority basis as in *Joseph Greenspon's Sons Iron and Steel Co. v. Pecos Valley Gas Co.*[58] where it is stated: "Corporations have assumed and acquired such a position in the business world that the office of president carries with it certain implied powers of an agency. He is usually either expressly or by implied consent made the chief executive officer, [and] without special authority or explicitly delegated power he may perform all acts of an ordinary nature which by usage or necessity are incidents to his office and by virtue of his office he may enter into a contract and bind his corporation in matters arising from and concerning the usual course of the corporation's business. These are the implied powers of the president of the corporation and they inhere in him by virtue of the position itself. Beyond these powers—beyond the carrying out of the usual and proper functions of the corporation necessary for the proper and convenient management of the business of the corporation, the president remains as any other director of the company, and other and further powers must be specifically conferred." That the authority is to be implied from the position, rather than prima facie implied, removes the uncertainty of what must be proved and by whom and supports the general understanding of businessmen that the president is the executive head of the business and has the authority to carry on the business in its usual course. Where extraordinary powers are exercised by the president or any other officer, one who deals with him is put on his notice and should insist upon having evidence of his authority or he should obtain a certificate of authority from the secretary under the seal of the company certifying that at a legal meeting of the board whose members had been properly notified, a quorum of the board being present, there was passed the following resolution, quoting it, specifying the authority conferred upon the officer. It is generally held that such a certificate will estop the corporation from denying the statements contained in it.[59]

But whether the president is given the authority of a general manager by provision in the by-laws, a resolution, or through

58. Rodney, J., in 34 Del. 567, 156 A. 350, at 352 (Super.Ct.1931). The principle was well stated over a century ago in Baltimore & P. Steamboat Co. v. McCutcheon & Collins, 13 Pa. 13, 15 (1850). But as to extraordinary contracts such as a contract of guaranty, see Atlantic Refining Co. v. Ingalls & Co., 37 Del. 503, 185 A. 885 (Super.Ct. 1936). But in Italo-Petroleum Corp. v. Hannigan, 40 Del. 534, 546, 14 A.2d 401, at 406 (Sup.Ct.1940), the court held there was a "rebuttable presumption" that the president had authority to bind the corporation by the execution of negotiable paper for ordinary corporate business purposes. See Note, Inherent Power as a Basis of a Corporate Officer's Authority to Contract, 57 Col.L.Rev. 868 (1957).

59. See Ballantine, Lattin and Jennings, Cases and Materials on Corporations 239–240 (2d ed. 1953), for a note on this subject and a form of a certificate.

the uncontrolled assumption of the powers of a general manager, or by a common law decision to that effect, any actual or implied authority may be terminated by action of the board.[60] While apparent authority may also be restricted, third parties who have no notice of the restriction may deal with safety with the officer. Thus, where a president with broad powers presented to the board, as a part of its business, the question of whether suit should be brought against another company for breach of contract and the board of four members was evenly split on the matter, the president was held without authority to bring suit since the board, by failing to have a majority vote, had refused to sanction the suit. Any actual or implied authority the president may have had to bring the suit was held terminated by the board's action and, since third parties were not involved, apparent authority was out of question. There is a suggestion in the case that had evidentiary facts been alleged to indicate that a crisis was at hand or that immediate or vital injury threatened the corporation, the case might have been handled differently. While the suggestion was a faint one, there is more merit to it than at first appears. Is it true that because it takes a majority to pass a resolution an equally divided vote means a majority is opposed to bringing suit? If vital injury to the corporation is threatened but the board by a tied vote refuses to act, may it not be the duty of the president to protect the interest represented by the other fifty percent? The formal logical argument that, whatever authority the president possessed prior to submitting the problem to the board, he has lost because the board split 50–50, is not too convincing especially under emergency circumstances.

Where a president with authority to manage the business has defended or brought suits knowing that the board was equally divided, but not having presented the problem to the board, some decisions have sustained the presidential authority.[61] And

60. Sterling Industries, Inc. v. Ball Bearing Pen Corp., 298 N.Y. 483, 84 N.E.2d 790, 10 A.L.R.2d 694 (1949). On the problem of authority of the president to institute suits, see 52 Harv.L.Rev. 321 (1938).

61. Regal Cleaners & Dyers, Inc. v. Merlis, 274 F. 915 (2d Cir., 1921) (two director-creditors had filed a petition in bankruptcy against the corporation and the president filed an answer in defense); Elblum Holding Corp. v. Mintz, 120 N.J.L. 604, 1 A.2d 204 (Sup.Ct.1938) (president brought suit to recover rent from a member of one faction which controlled half of the board without consulting the board and was sustained by the court). See also Ly-

dia E. Pinkham Medicine Co. v. Gove, 298 Mass. 53, 9 N.E.2d 573 (1934); id. v. id., 305 Mass. 213, 25 N.E.2d 332 (1940); Rothman & Schneider v. Beckerman, 2 N.Y.2d 493, 161 N.Y.S.2d 118, 141 N.E.2d 610 at 613 (1957), stating that "Where there has been no direct prohibition by the board of directors, the president has presumptive authority in the discharge of his duties to defend and prosecute suits in the name of the corporation." A contrary view is expressed in Fanchon & Marco, Inc. v. Paramount Pictures, Inc., 107 F.Supp. 532, 538 (D.N.Y.1952). Note, The Role of the Corporation in Litigation Caused by Factional

it has been held that the rule applies to suits thus brought by the president on behalf of the corporation against one faction represented by an equal number of a divided board to redress wrongs done the corporation by that faction.[62]   Furthermore, where the president has been authorized to exercise general supervision and control over the business, and he exercises his authority by increasing the salaries of important employees, the fact that the board was evenly divided on the matter of ratifying his action has been held not to affect the validity of his action.[63]   His authority was also held to include the retaining of general counsel at a sizeable, but reasonable, retainer and to contract generally with counsel for services beyond what the retainer called for. "The retaining of general counsel for a corporation of the magnitude of the petitioner cannot be said to be beyond the ordinary scope of the business of which the president was to 'exercise general supervision and control.' " [64]

While the law is probably moving toward a rule which recognizes the president's authority to appoint counsel both for the defense and the bringing of suits as an incident to his authority to manage the business, many decisions while seeming to go this far have emphasized particular facts such as an evenly divided board, the president's share in ownership as well as in management, the type of corporation—is it likely to be more easily injured if authority to appoint counsel is withheld—, the reasons for employing counsel, previous customary practice, and the fact that previously the same attorney had been used by the company.[65]   Such uncertainty as to the real basis of a decision should spur the draftsman to include in the by-laws specific authority on this and other extraordinary matters or to exclude them specifically, whichever is intended.

Where a president, either by virtue of an express delegation of authority or by a holding that he has the inherent or implied

Disputes Among Directors, 48 Yale L.J. 1082 (1939).

62. 1st Lydia E. Pinkham case cited in note 61, supra. In Kelly v. Citizens Finance Co. of Lowell, Inc., 306 Mass. 531, 28 N.E.2d 1005, 130 A.L.R. 890 (1940), the president, one of two living directors, not having the authority of a general manager, hired counsel to defend a suit by a shareholder who sought the appointment of a receiver and a dissolution of the corporation. The court held that he had no such authority even in what appeared to be an emergency. See Note, 89 U. of Pa.L.Rev. 386 (1941), and criti-

cism of the holding in Ballantine, Corporations 141 (Rev.ed. 1946).

63. 2d Lydia E. Pinkham case cited in note 61, supra. Where the president is merely carrying out an existing agreement that all disputes under a contract would be submitted to arbitration, he may submit as provided without board action. In re Paloma Frocks, Inc. v. Shamokin Sportswear Corp., 3 N.Y.2d 572, 147 N.E.2d 779 (1958).

64. Lydia E. Pinkham Medicine Co. v. Gove, 305 Mass. 213, 25 N.E.2d 332 at 336 (1940).

65. See Note, 89 U. of Pa.L.Rev. 386 (1941).

authority to carry on the business in its ordinary course, ventures into extraordinary and unusual transactions, he and those dealing with him run the risk of having the court decree that the authority is not that extensive. Take the conveyance of a part or all of the company's realty, for example. Or the purchase of real estate for his company which is not engaged in the real estate business. Or the mortgage of the corporate property. All are "extraordinary and unusual" transactions not coming within the authority to manage the business.[66] What powers are usual in the business may be assumed to have been granted, but the extraordinary and unusual ones may not.[67]

But business in its ordinary course may require the procuring of temporary loans and the giving of negotiable paper for the same. In an important recent case it was said: "It is not unreasonable to presume that the president has the authority to bind the corporation by executing and transferring negotiable paper to pay the debts of the corporation; and the more reasonable view, proceeding from realistic considerations, is that presumption should be indulged that the president has the authority to bind the corporation by the execution and transfer of negotiable paper in the ordinary course of the corporation's business." [68] On the other hand, the treasurer does not have that authority from his office alone, but must acquire it through one of the methods by which authority can be acquired.[69]

The vice-president of a business corporation has little authority unless (as is usually the case) a by-law or resolution of the board delegates it. Not infrequently a vice-president is given the authority of a general manager and the descriptive term of "executive vice-president" is sometimes assigned to him. In such a case, of course, he would possess all the powers necessary to carry on the usual business of the corporation. However, in

---

66. Mosell Realty Corp. v. Schofield, 183 Va. 782, 33 S.E.2d 774 (1945) (purported brokerage contract to sell corporation's only piece of realty upon which were a theater and four stores, the corporation not being one dealing in real estate); Edelstone v. Salmon Falls Mfg. Co., 84 N.H. 315, 150 A. 545 (1930) (a treasurer with powers of a general manager, and with shareholder-authorization, employed a broker to negotiate a sale of the entire business); Sherman v. Fitch, 98 Mass. 59 (1867) (president executed and delivered a mortgage on the company's property).

67. Schwartz v. United Merchants & Manufacturers, Inc., 72 F.2d 256

(2d Cir., 1934). See Comment, Inherent Powers of Corporate Officers: Need for a Statutory Definition, 61 Harv.L.Rev. 867 (1948); Ballantine, Lattin and Jennings, Cases and Materials on Corporations, Note on Inherent Powers of the Corporate President, 263–265 (2d ed. 1953).

68. Italo-Petroleum Corp. of America v. Hannigan, 1 Terry (40 Del.) 534, 14 A.2d 401, at 406 (Sup.Ct. 1940). See notes on this case in 29 Geo.L.Rev. 782 (1941) and 50 Yale L.J. 348 (1940).

69. Jacobus v. Jamestown Mantel Co., 211 N.Y. 154, 105 N.E. 210 (1914).

the absence of the president, he substitutes for him as chairman of the board unless other provisions are made therefor, and generally takes on the duties of the president's office.[70]

The secretary is the keeper of the corporate records and of the seal. He has no implied authority to enter into contracts for the corporation unless authority has been derived by express delegation or through the exercise of powers openly used and knowingly consented to or not checked by the board after receiving notice. While he is the keeper of the seal, his authority to place it upon a company document must come from the board or from an officer with authority to command it. He keeps the minutes of the board and of shareholders' meetings. Usually the by-laws or a resolution of the board will assign to him rather limited powers though, occasionally, he is given the authority of a general manager which is perfectly proper.

The treasurer has authority by virtue of his office to receive moneys and to bank them and to give receipts for moneys received. From his office alone he derives no implied powers to borrow for his corporation, or to make and issue promissory notes or bills of exchange, or to compromise debts, or to do a host of other things which are frequently done by treasurers through the delegation of powers by the board.[71] He is usually given the express power to sign or countersign checks, notes and at times other instruments, and to execute them. But, like the offices already discussed, carefully drawn provisions should always be used to inform him and those who must rely upon him of the exact powers which it is intended he should have.

The implied powers of a general manager are those sufficient to carry on the ordinary operations of the business.[72] The discussion above indicates the extent of his authority for the president or some other officer is usually given the powers of a general manager without the use of the descriptive term. Functions expressly intrusted to another officer, which functions are normally part of the general manager's, are no longer his;[73] but persons dealing with him may rely upon powers normally his if they have no notice of their delegation to another officer. This

---

70. See Ballantine, Corporations 142 (Rev.ed. 1946).

71. See 2 Machen, Modern Law of Corporations § 1671 (1908). "A treasurer is bound to disburse the corporate funds under, and only under, the orders of the directors or other officers in charge of the corporate business." Lydia E. Pinkham Medicine Co. v. Gove, 305 Mass. 213, 25 N.E.2d 332, at 334 (1940).

72. Memorial Hospital Ass'n v. Pacific Grape Products Co., 45 Cal.2d 634, 290 P.2d 481 (1955); Wells-Dickey Co. v. Embody, 82 Mont. 150, 266 P. 869, 874 (1928); Miller v. Wick Bldg. Co., 154 Ohio St. 93, 93 N.E.2d 467 (1950); Diederich v. Wisconsin Wood Products, Inc., 247 Wis. 212, 19 N.W.2d 268 (1945); Restatement, Agency § 73 (1933).

73. 2 Machen, supra, note 71, § 1672.

is comparable to the case where secret restrictions on the authority of a general manager are imposed by resolution or by-law. One who deals without notice of the restrictions may rely upon authority which is normally there.

In some, particularly large, companies an officer known as the chairman of the board of directors is employed. The title implies no more than that he is the presiding officer at board meetings. He may be given the powers of the chief executive officer of his company or be given special authority over a part of the business, but whatever powers he possesses must be by delegation rather than implied from his office. As to the actual practice from company to company, there is substantial variation on functions delegated to board chairmen.

From what has been stated above, it is apparent that the drafting of by-laws and resolutions delegating authority to the various corporate officers is an extremely important function which ought not to be tossed aside by the use of ready-made by-laws which can be purchased from any legal stationer for a nominal sum. One illustration will suffice. A by-law read: "All checks, drafts or orders for the payment of moneys and all notes and acceptances shall be signed by the President, Vice-President or Manager, and also by the Secretary or Assistant Secretary, unless the power to sign the same shall have been duly delegated by the Board of Directors to some other officer or officers of the corporation." Notes were thus signed and executed. In a suit upon the notes it was held that the by-law related only to the formalities of execution and was not a grant of power. Said the court: "It is unreasonable to suppose that it was intended to lodge the power to bind the corporation by notes and acceptances indiscriminately in the president, vice-president and manager." [74] It is doubtful whether "it is unreasonable to suppose" any such thing, but all doubt could have been removed had the draftsman been more circumspect in his approach.

§ 8. De Facto Directors and Officers

It sometimes happens that boards of directors and officers who reasonably assume that they have been properly elected or appointed to their positions actually have not been, due to the failure of some legal requirement. Acts are done, and contracts made by such officials with third parties who have no reason to suspect that there is any deficiency in the officers with whom they deal. For the same reasons that the common law has recognized corporations de facto it has recognized directors and officers de

---

74. Italo-Petroleum Corp. of America v. Hannigan, 1 Terry (40 Del.) 534, 14 A.2d 401, at 405–406 (1940).

facto as well, though at times, the supporting reason assigned is estoppel. Two basic requirements have been laid down as essential: (1) color of authority by election or appointment—not mere usurpation of office—and (2) exercise of the assumed authority. If these requirements are present and the person dealing with the de facto official has no knowledge of his deficiency, a contract made or a conveyance executed will be given the same weight as if the official were de jure. And other acts—torts, for example, committed within the scope of the de facto officer's authority—will create liability to the same extent as acts performed by a de jure official.

It has generally been held that an office must exist to which a de jure officer might have functioned if elected, otherwise there is no office to occupy. But in the case of boards of directors where more have been elected than the by-laws call for, it has been held that the directors are de facto. If all have been elected on one ballot, it would appear that all are de facto directors. But if the number called for by the by-laws are elected and there is a tie as to the unauthorized remainder, which are again balloted upon and chosen, it would seem that the whole board is not de facto but simply the ones chosen last.[75]

Where, by virtue of authority to fill vacancies on the board, de facto directors have appointed members to fill vacancies, courts have held that such members are also de facto directors— that de facto directors cannot create de jure directors by appointment.[76] A dubious and unjust principle has been recognized that an officer appointed from de facto directors is not entitled to the salary provided for him although had the services been rendered by a de jure officer, the reverse would have been true.[77] There is no good reason for such a holding provided the officer has performed his services in good faith believing that he had de jure status.

By statute, articles or by-law, it is usually provided that the directors carry over in their offices if, for any reason, at the periodic election, a board is not chosen. Some decisions have considered the directors in this hold-over period as de facto, others saying "de facto, at least." There ought to be no doubt as to the intent of such provisions—they were to keep alive the de jure status of the directors. The fact that they are au-

75. See McWhirter v. Washington Royalties Co., 17 Del.Ch. 243, 152 A. 220 (1930). Generally, on de facto directors and officers, see Ballantine, Lattin and Jennings, Cases and Materials on Corporations, Note on De Facto Directors and Officers, 228–231 (2d ed. 1953).

76. Matter of George Ringler & Co., 204 N.Y. 30, at 42, 97 N.E. 593, at 597–598, Ann.Cas.1913C, 1036 (1912).

77. Waterman v. Chicago & Iowa R. Co., 139 Ill. 658, 29 N.E. 689, 15 L. R.A. 418, 32 Am.St.Rep. 228 (1892).

thorized to act during the hiatus between the end of their terms and a new election should be enough to indicate this.[78]

De facto directors or officers cannot plead their lack of de jure status to defeat liability which would have been theirs had they been de jure, or to avoid their duty to use reasonable care in the performance of their functions, or to escape the fiduciary obligations owed by de jure directors and officers to their company, to their fellow officers or to the shareholders.[79]

§ 9.   Compensation of Board and Officers

It is generally recognized that directors have no right to compensation for services rendered as directors unless payment is authorized by statute, charter, by-law or resolution of the shareholders.   As to services rendered by directors outside their duties as directors, some courts have held that there must be an express contract for the same; others, and better authority, that if such services are rendered under circumstances sufficient to show that both the director claiming compensation and those who might properly have authorized payment understood that the services were to be paid for, the right to payment exists.[80] Where a contract is made by a director with his corporation, his personal interest disqualifies him from participating either to fill out a quorum or to carry the resolution by his vote.[81]   And if he does participate under such circumstances the majority rule holds the contract voidable, the minority holds it void.[82] Likewise, where two or more directors are interested in salary contracts and one's presence is necessary to constitute a quorum or his vote to constitute a majority for his fellow director's contract, such reciprocal action is not considered disinterested and the contract of each may be avoided.[83]   A disinterested board

78. In re Crozer's Estate, 296 Pa. 48, at 54, 145 A. 697, at 699 (1929) (holding that such a director is both a de facto and a de jure officer); Baker v. Smith, 41 R.I. 17, 32, 102 A. 721 (1918) ("de facto, if not de jure"); Russian Reinsurance Co. v. Stoddard, 211 App.Div. 132, at 142, 207 N.Y.S. 574 (1925) ("de facto, at least"), rev'd 240 N.Y. 149, 160, 147 N.E. 703 (1925).

79. See Ballantine, Corporations 149 (Rev.ed. 1946).

80. Lofland v. Cahall, 13 Del.Ch. 384, 118 A. 1 (1922), discusses both rules.

81. Briggs v. Gilbert Grocery Co., 116 Ohio St. 343, 156 N.E. 494 (1927).   But see recent statute which permits directors who have a personal interest to participate in setting their own salaries unless the articles or regulations (by-laws elsewhere) provide otherwise. Ohio Rev.Code (Ohio Gen.Corp. Law of 1955) § 1701.60.

82. Ballantine, Lattin and Jennings, Cases and Materials on Corporations 316 (2d ed. 1953). But even where the resolution is invalid because of the lack of a disinterested majority, quasi-contractual recovery has been allowed. Thwing v. Weibatch Liquid Scale Co., 233 Mich. 87, 206 N.W. 320 (1926).

83. Stoiber v. Miller Brewing Co., 257 Wis. 13, 42 N.W.2d 144 (1950), quoting from Ballantine, Corporations § 74, p. 190 (Rev.ed. 1946);

or the shareholders may, however, ratify a voidable contract of this kind and the interested director may vote his shares in aid of ratification.[84]

Some recent authority has recognized a contract, voidable in most jurisdictions because of the interested director's necessary presence or vote, as valid if reasonable and fair, putting the burden upon him to prove its reasonableness and fairness.[85] But where the officer-director's salary is determined without his participation by disinterested members of the board, wide scope is given to the discretion of this disinterested group, as it should be. Under such circumstances, the burden is upon one attacking the salary to show that it was so unreasonable as to be deemed fraudulent.[86] Or, as it is sometimes stated, if the directors have exercised their unbiased judgment uninfluenced by the officer-director whose salary is being voted upon, a court will not disturb the determination made through managerial discretion unless "there has been so clear an abuse of discretion as to amount to legal waste." [87] While the directors have wide discretion in entering into contracts for officer-services, there must be some reasonable connection between the services rendered and the quid pro quo to be paid. Gifts which are labeled salaries, bonuses, retirement annuities or pensions, or options to purchase stock, are gifts nevertheless and directors have no authority to make

Sagalyn v. Meekins, Packard & Wheat, Inc., 290 Mass. 434, 195 N.E. 769 (1935). Professor Ballantine has called this "mutual back-scratching." Ballantine, Corporations § 74 (Rev.ed. 1946).

84. Russell v. Henry C. Patterson Co., 232 Pa. 113, 81 A. 136 (1911); Kerbs v. California Eastern Airways, Inc., 33 Del.Ch. 69, 90 A.2d 652 (Sup.Ct.1952), opinion on denial of reargument, 33 Del.Ch. 174, 91 A.2d 62 (Sup.Ct.1952), on further hearing before the Chancellor, 33 Del.Ch. 395, 94 A.2d 217 (Ch. 1953). But in McKey v. Swenson, 232 Mich. 505, 205 N.W. 583 (1926), the directors' action was held void and not subject to ratification by the shareholders.

85. Church v. Harnit, 35 F.2d 499 (6th Cir., 1929), cert. den. 281 U.S. 732, 50 S.Ct. 247, 74 L.Ed. 1148 (1930). See Note, Problems in Fixing or Increasing Compensation of Officer-Directors, 38 Calif.L.Rev. 906 (1950).

86. Seitz v. Union Brass & Metal Co., 152 Minn. 460, 189 N.W. 586, 27 A.L.R. 293 (1922); Ann., 27 A.L.R. 300 (1923); Gallin v. Nat. City Bank of New York, 152 Misc. 679, 273 N.Y.S. 87 (1934); Note, 32 Mich. L.Rev. 839, at 845 (1934). But the influence of non-participating directors may be so great as to warrant close scrutiny and, in a proper case, rescission. See Globe Woolen Co. v. Utica Gas & Electric Co., 224 N.Y. 483, 121 N.E. 378 (1918).

87. See discussion of Swan, Cir. J., in Fogelson v. American Woolen Co., Inc., 170 F.2d 660 (2d Cir., 1948), where a plan involving retirement annuities had been ratified by the majority shareholders. Wrote Judge Swan: "A plan which provides a very large pension to an officer who has served to within one year of the retirement age without any expectation of receiving a pension would seem analogous to a gift or bonus." See 79 F. Supp. 291 (D.N.Y.1948), the opinion in the trial court which the Second Circuit reversed, for interesting factual material.

them without the unanimous consent of the shareholders, nor have officers any legal right to keep them.

Salaries plus bonuses and/or options to purchase shares have been used to keep key officers and employees interested in retaining their positions with the company and to lure able executives from other companies less able to meet this kind of competition. By spreading bonuses out over a period of years, perhaps into years after retirement, and by provisions through which the employee forfeits future payments if he resigns to accept other employment, a company may be able to keep its key employees until they retire. At the same time, because of heavy income surtaxes, the employee, by virtue of the distribution of bonuses over a long period, may be able to avoid some of the very heavy taxes he would have to pay if the bonuses were distributed during the years when earned, provided the plan is carefully designed to avoid an argument of constructive receipt of the bonus when declared.[88] In case of options to purchase shares, he is given the opportunity to acquire an interest in the company, take advantage of market conditions and, if he does not sell his shares on the short swing after purchase, he obtains another tax advantage via the capital gains route.[89] Pension plans, too, can be a means of spreading earnings over a long period and can be advantageous tax-wise. Needless to say, tax experts should be consulted on such plans for dangerous pitfalls exist.

Bonuses, pension plans and options to purchase shares are legitimate devices for compensating corporate officers. It is in their abuse that difficulties arise. Neither the action of disinterested directors nor the ratification by majority shareholders can justify the payment of bonuses as salaries when the amounts are so large "as in substance and effect to amount to spoliation or waste of corporate property." [90] In the case cited the Supreme Court accepted the principle which Judge Swan had projected in his dissenting opinion in *Rogers* v. *Hill*: [91] "If a

88. See Washington and Rothschild, Compensating the Corporate Executive 168 et seq. on deferred compensation (Rev.ed. 1951).

89. A good example recognizing specifically this fact is Eliasberg v. Standard Oil Co., 23 N.J.Super. 431, 92 A.2d 862, at 869 (1952), aff'd without opinion, 12 N.J. 467, 97 A.2d 437 (1953).

90. Mr. Justice Butler in Rogers v. Hill, 289 U.S. 582, at 591, 53 S.Ct. 731, 77 L.Ed. 1385, 88 A.L.R. 744 (1933), sustaining Swan, Cir. J., in his dissenting opinion in id. v. id.,

60 F.2d 109 (2d Cir., 1932). See Ann., Corporation's payment of bonus to officers or employees, 88 A. L.R. 751 (1933); Ann., Power of corporation or its officers with respect to payment of bonus or pension to officers or employees, 164 A.L.R. 1125 (1946).

91. 60 F.2d 109, at 113–114 (2d Cir., 1932). "In my opinion a bonus of $840,000 to an officer receiving a fixed salary of $168,000 is presumptively so much beyond fair compensation for services as to make a prima facie showing that the cor-

bonus payment has no relation to the value of services for which it is given, it is in reality a gift in part, and the majority stockholders have no power to give away corporate property against the protest of the minority." And the fact that the bonus provisions were valid at the time of their adoption, does not mean that they will remain valid if bonuses under them later are so large that they fall within the rule stated.[92]

Pensions and annuities for executive officers represent a comparatively new device to keep them happy in their present positions or to lure them from other pastures. The use of pension and annuity plans for executives, however, is fast becoming standard procedure. No more than bonus payments may pensions or annuities be used when they have no relation to the consideration given for them. It has been said that "The real question as to corporate power to grant pensions arises when they are granted after employment has ceased, or granted so shortly prior to retirement that the services still to be rendered are clearly not worth the amount of the proposed payments," [93] and that the attack upon such plans may be based upon arguments of past consideration, inadequate consideration, and that the corporation is making a gift which, without unanimous consent of its shareholders, it may not do. As was also said by Judge Swan in one of the most important recent cases involving a retirement income plan,[94] where the plan was to be put into effect a short time prior to the president's eligibility for retirement: "A retirement plan which provides a very large pension to an officer who has served to within one year of the retirement age without any expectation of receiving a pension, would seem analogous to a gift or bonus." It was claimed that the purpose of the plan to set aside immediately in a trust fund more than $4,500,000 was to secure to the president his pension of over $54,000 a year "free from the hazard of future business vicissitudes to which the corporation will be subject," and that the

poration is giving away money, and a by-law which sanctions this is prima facie unreasonable, and hence unlawful." Swan, Cir. J., at 114, supra.

92. Ibid., which was just such a case. As to the final result in the compromise resulting from the Supreme Court opinion, see Haller v. Boylan, 29 N.Y.S.2d 653, at 666–667 (Sup.Ct.1941), aff'd 263 App.Div. 815, 32 N.Y.S.2d 131 (1941), reargument denied 263 App.Div. 852, 32 N.Y.S.2d 1011 (1941).

93. Washington and Rothschild, supra, note 88, at 197.

94. Fogelson v. American Woolen Co., Inc., 170 F.2d 660, at 663 (2d Cir., 1948). The plan was to pay into a trust immediately the sum of $4,657,292 "to fund that part of the pension based on past services of employees." The president was to receive an annual pension (at age 65) of $54,220 for life. The next highest pension was for $7,-285. See Henderson, A Better Pension Program, 30 Harv.Bus.Rev. 67 (1952); O'Neal, Stockholder Attacks on Corporate Pension Systems, 2 Vand.L.Rev. 351 (1949).

directors voting for the plan did not exercise their honest business judgment but were motivated by favoritism for the president. The court held that there was a triable issue on whether the directors had used their honest business judgment. But Judge Swan indicated the traditional reluctance of courts to interfere with the business judgment of directors, laying down the usual rule that "they do so only if there has been so clear an abuse of discretion as to amount to legal waste." [95] But the size of a pension or annuity may justify a court in pursuing an inquiry into whether it amounts to spoliation or waste of the corporate property.

The giving of options to purchase shares must also be supported by consideration and not be granted as gifts. Sufficient consideration to the corporation may be the retention of the services of the employee, or the acquiring of the services of a new employee, "provided there is a reasonable relationship between the value of the services to be rendered . . . and the value of the options granted as an inducement or compensation." [96] The mere desire to give an interest through stock ownership has been held not to qualify as consideration.[97] And recently an option plan has been disapproved because it was not reasonably calculated to insure that the corporation would receive the contemplated benefits.[98] If the agreement provides for and guarantees the retention of the employee's services for a period before the option may be exercised, and further provides that it may not be exercised except while he is in the service of the company, it would seem that the two requirements have been met, that is, (1) consideration and (2) some assurance that the consideration will be received.[99]

95. 170 F.2d 660, at 662 (2d Cir., 1948). See also McQuillen v. National Cash Register Co., 112 F.2d 877, at 884 (4th Cir., 1940), cert. den. 311 U.S. 695, 61 S.Ct. 140, 85 L.Ed. 450 (1940), cited by the court. See the unique plan in Berkwitz v. Humphrey, 163 F.Supp. 78, and discussion at 90 et seq. (N.D.Ohio, 1958). Failure of the plan to equate compensation with the value of the services rendered made it vulnerable.

96. Kerbs v. California Eastern Airways, 33 Del.Ch. 69, 90 A.2d 652, at 656 (Sup.Ct.1952), opinion on denial of reargument, 33 Del.Ch. 174, 91 A.2d 62 (Sup.Ct.1952), on further hearing before the Chancellor, 33 Del.Ch. 395, 94 A.2d 217 (Ch. 1953). See Comment, 52 Col.L.Rev. 1003 (1952) on employee stock option plans, and recent case of Mc-

Phail v. L. S. Starrett Co., 157 F. Supp. 560 (D.Mass.1957).

97. Rosenthal v. Burry Biscuit Corp., 30 Del.Ch. 299, 60 A.2d 106 (1948); Gottlieb v. Heyden Chemical Corp., 33 Del.Ch. 82, 90 A.2d 660 (Sup.Ct. 1952), 33 Del.Ch. 177, 91 A.2d 57 (Sup.Ct.1952).

98. Kerbs case supra, note 96.

99. See P-H Students' Corporation Law Service Par. 25,084, Notes and Problems; ibid. Par. 25,085, Notes and Problems. These Notes and Problems follow the reports of the Kerbs and Gottlieb cases, cited in notes 96 and 97, supra. See also Holthusen v. Edward G. Budd Mfg. Co., 53 F.Supp. 488 (D.Pa.1943). See Scott, Developments in Corporate Law, 8 The Business Lawyer 24 (1953).

Thus, there would seem to be two basic rules concerning salaries for the board or for officers: (1) They must be authorized by the proper body and (2) they must be fair and reasonable for the services rendered. Concerning the matter of fairness and reasonableness a good deal of leeway is permitted, for men will differ in their business judgment on the worth of a corporate officer. As to the proper body or official to authorize and execute a salary contract, a number of statutes already give the directors, whether interested or not, the power to set their own compensation as directors or as officers;[1] and other statutes, while not mentioning compensation, are broad enough to have that effect when contracts of any kind are made between the corporation and members of the board.[2] But such authorization is not the grant of a power to mulct the corporation. Even though the requirements of these statutes are technically met, transactions that are unfair and unreasonable to the corporation may be avoided as was held in a recent case involving the broad California statute.[3]

§ 10. Liability of Directors for Failure to use Care Required of Directors

The language used to describe the duty of care owed by the directors to their corporation has varied a bit but it is believed that, for the most part, the same result would have been reached under any of the tests save perhaps one. The common expression of duty of care is that care which a reasonably prudent director of a similar corporation would have used under the circumstances of the particular case.[4] In some jurisdictions, it has been described as that care and skill which ordinarily prudent men would exercise under similar circumstances in their own personal business affairs.[5] The "business judgment rule"

---

1. Burns' Ind.Ann.Stat.1933, § 25–208 (Ind.Gen.Corp.Act of 1929, § 9, as amended by L.1953, c. 19, § 2) (interest of director not mentioned); Ohio Rev.Code (Ohio Gen. Corp.Law of 1955) § 1701.60; Wis. Bus.Corp.Law of 1951, § 180.31 as amended by L.1953, c. 399, § 16.

2. West's Ann.Cal.Corp.Code § 820 (interest must be disclosed and other conditions required); Mich.Gen. Corp.Act § 13–5, as amended by L. 1949, Act 229.

3. Remillard Brick Co. v. Remillard-Dandini Co., 109 Cal.App.2d 405, 241 P.2d 66 (1952). As to the effect of shareholder ratification, see Eliasberg v. Standard Oil Co., 23 N.J. Super. 431, 92 A.2d 862, at 871

(1952), aff'd without opinion 12 N. J. 467, 97 A.2d 437 (1953).

4. Briggs v. Spaulding, 141 U.S. 132, 11 S.Ct. 924, 35 L.Ed. 662 (1890); Anderson v. Akers, 7 F.Supp. 924 (D.Ky.1934), modified in 86 F.2d 518 (6th Cir., 1936), rev'd 302 U.S. 643, 58 S.Ct. 53, 82 L.Ed. 500 (1937), on other grounds. The case was finally determined in Atherton v. Anderson, 99 F.2d 883 (6th Cir., 1938). The opinion in this last case is a fine one on analyzing facts upon which the directors were held liable.

5. Otis & Co. v. Pennsylvania R. Co., 61 F.Supp. 905 (D.Pa.1945), aff'd 155 F.2d 522 (3d Cir., 1946), by statute in Pennsylvania.

of New York asks whether the corporate action is the result of
the exercise of the directors' unbiased judgment in determining
whether their action will promote the corporate interests. Or,
as stated by Justice Shientag:[6] "The law will not interfere
with the internal affairs of a corporation so long as it is managed
by its directors pursuant to a free, honest exercise of judgment
uninfluenced by personal, or by any considerations other than
the welfare of the corporation." Directors, stated Justice Shientag, are expected to have initiative, daring and vision, and they
may take the same chances that they might take in their own
business as far as commercial corporations are concerned. That
directors are not liable for mere errors of judgment is a rule
of long standing, but where the line is to be drawn between such
errors and negligent operation is not clear. If the board has
several choices and reasonable care has been used to select the
choice finally made, that is probably a matter of poor judgment
if the choice turns out badly.[7] But there is no need of talking
about "errors of judgment" it would seem, for the basic test is
one of due care.

6. Bayer v. Beran, 49 N.Y.S.2d 2 at
6 (Sup.Ct.1944). In almost the
same breath Justice Shientag (at
page 5) stated that the director "is
called upon to use care, to exercise judgment, the degree of care,
the kind of judgment that one
would give in similar situations to
the conduct of his own affairs."
This is sometimes described as the
New York rule. Ballantine, Corporations, 158 (Rev.ed. 1946). How
does the "business judgment rule"
tie in with the concept of negligence? In Casey v. Woodruff, 49
N.Y.S.2d 625, at 643 (Sup.Ct.1944),
Justice Shientag wrote: "When
courts say that they will not interfere in matters of business judgment, it is presupposed that judgment—reasonable diligence—has in
fact been exercised." See also
Chelrob, Inc. v. Barrett, 293 N.Y.
442, at 460, 57 N.E.2d 825, at 833
(1944), and interesting case of
Abrams v. Allen, 297 N.Y. 52, 74
N.E.2d 305, 173 A.L.R. 671 (1947)
rehearing denied 297 N.Y. 604, 75
N.E.2d 274 (1947), noted in 15 U.
of Chi.L.Rev. 423 (1948); 48 Col.
L.Rev. 290 (1948); 33 Corn.L.Q.
421 (1948); 61 Harv.L.Rev. 541
(1948); 46 Mich.L.Rev. 683 (1948);
23 N.Y.U.L.Q. 209 (1948); 96 U. of
Pa.L.Rev. 418 (1948); 57 Yale L.J.
489 (1948). On the business judgment rule, see also Carson, Current

Phases of Derivative Actions
Against Directors, 40 Mich.L.Rev.
1125 (1942); Carson, Further Phases of Derivative Actions Against
Directors, 29 Cornell L.Q. 431
(1944); Uhlman, The Duty of Corporate Directors to Exercise Business Judgment, 20 B.U.L.Rev. 488
(1940).

7. See Casey v. Woodruff, 49 N.Y.S.
2d 625, at 642–643 (Sup.Ct.1944),
where Justice Shientag states:
"Mistakes in the exercise of honest
business judgment do not subject
the directors to liability for negligence in the discharge of their fiduciary duties. The standard is one
of reasonable diligence, not the utmost amount of diligence . . .
[Authorities are omitted.] . .
The directors are entrusted with the
management of the affairs of the
railroad. If in the course of management they arrive at a decision
for which there is a reasonable basis, and they act in good faith, as
the result of their independent
judgment, and uninfluenced by any
consideration other than what they
honestly believe to be for the best
interests of the railroad, it is not
the function of the court to say that
it would have acted differently and
to charge the directors for any loss
or expenditures incurred."

Occasional opinions have declared that directors are not liable unless their lack of care constitutes gross negligence.[8] Or put a little differently, "If directors, acting in good faith, nevertheless act imprudently, they cannot ordinarily be held to personal responsibility for loss unless there is a 'clear and gross negligence' in their conduct."[9] Any court taking such a view has a heart too tender for the hard-headed business men who usually sit upon boards of directors. There is no valid reason why directors should not pay sufficient attention to the business of the corporations upon whose boards they sit so that they will qualify under any of the tests in the paragraph above. If they cannot pay that much attention to the corporate business, they should not be sitting upon the board. Courts have been far too lenient in their treatment of directors who do not direct under whatever rule they adopt as a test of liability.

When directors have been charged with negligence in handling the company's affairs, the facts usually show one of three types of inactivity: (1) the director has not attended board meetings as he should and has had no valid excuse for being absent; or (2) he has not taken the time to acquaint himself with the general aspects of the business so that he is qualified to act upon propositions when they are discussed at board meetings; or (3) he has sat quietly at board meetings when there were indications of bad management by the officers, or perhaps downright crookedness, and has been so unconcerned or perhaps unaware of what was in the offing that he did not object or did not suggest an investigation or did not do something else that a director reasonably capable, under similar circumstances, would have done.[10]

Directors are supposed to attend meetings of the board or have valid excuses for being absent, such as sickness, a death in the family, temporary absence from the state or country, or some other important event that keeps them from attending. The question whether non-resident directors should come under the same rule was raised in *Wallach* v. *Billings*[11] where the de-

---

8. Swentzel v. Penn Bank, 147 Pa. 140, 23 A. 405, 15 L.R.A. 305, 30 Am.St.Rep. 718 (1892) ("only liable for fraud, or such gross negligence as amounts to fraud"); Murphy v. Hanlon, 322 Mass. 683, 79 N.E.2d 992 (1948).

9. Spiegel v. Beacon Participations, Inc., 297 Mass. 398, 8 N.E.2d 895, at 904 (1937).

10. For an example of (1), see Bowerman v. Hamner, 250 U.S. 504, 39 S.Ct. 549, 63 L.Ed. 1113 (1919); of

(2), see Barnes v. Andrews, 298 F. 614 (D.N.Y.1924) ("[T]hey have an individual duty to keep themselves informed in some detail . ."); of (3), see Atherton v. Anderson, 99 F.2d 883 (6th Cir., 1938).

11. 277 Ill. 218, 115 N.E. 382, L.R.A. 1918A, 1097 (1917), cert. den. 244 U.S. 659, 37 S.Ct. 745, 61 L.Ed. 1376 (1917). See Note, 12 Ill.L.Rev. 356 (1918), criticising this holding. But see Note, A Defense of Non-Managing Directors, 5 U. of Chi.L.Rev. 668 (1938).

fendant, a resident of New York, was a director for a number of years on the Chicago National Bank board. The president was permitted by the directors to run the bank as he saw fit and he wrecked it by the misuse of funds which, if reasonable care had been used by the directors, would have been discovered. The defendant failed, without excuse except his non-residence, to attend board meetings. The court, in a dubious opinion, held that he was not liable except as he may have been negligent in his duties of non-resident director, not because of his continued absences from board meetings. He could not be held for the negligence of the resident directors whose duty it was to supervise loans and the immediate conduct of the bank's business. But shortly thereafter, in *Bowerman* v. *Hamner*,[12] it was held that the fact that the director lived some 200 miles from the board's meeting place was no excuse for failing to attend the meetings of the board and for not paying attention to the corporate business. And in an important New York case, the court took the reasonable view that neither custom nor practice could relieve a director from his duty to attend board meetings.[13] At a period when transportation was slow there was less reason for a non-resident director's accepting his office unless he intended to take with it the inconvenience of slow travel and loss of time; with the greatly stepped-up tempo of transportation, there is no good reason for excusing a director from attending from afar unless he has a better excuse than mere distance from his residence to board-meeting place.

The English have not felt the same necessity of requiring attendance at board meetings that has been apparent in most of the American cases. The most recent English text [14] states: "It is true that Romer, J. says that a director should attend meetings whenever he can, but the cases tend to suggest that this is little more than a pious hope." And, as the writer points out, Stirling, J., in *the Marquis of Bute's Case,*[15] said that "Neglect or omission to attend meetings is not, in my opinion, the same thing as neglect or omission of a duty which ought to be performed at those meetings." Both statements were aimed at the ordinary director rather than at "managing directors" who are paid for their services.[16]

---

12. 250 U.S. 504, 39 S.Ct. 549, 63 L. Ed. 1113 (1919). See also Michelson v. Penney, 135 F.2d 409, at 418 (2d Cir., 1943).

13. Kavanaugh v. Commonwealth Trust Co. of New York, 223 N.Y. 103, 119 N.E. 237 (1918).

14. Gower, Modern Company Law 142 (1954). But see Palmer's Company Law 190 (19th ed. 1949), concerning continuous non-attendance.

15. [1892] 2 Ch. 100, at 109.

16. A managing director "is essentially different (from "service directors") in that his function is to exercise some or all of the directors' powers of managing." Gower, supra, note 14, at 134.

But even if sufficient proof is produced to place a director under one of the several rules discussed above, there is a second hurdle that must be taken before he can be held, that is, the loss to the corporation must be traced to the director's negligent act or omission. In case of banks where loans, overdrafts and embezzlements are the chief causes for proceedings against directors, there is always a reasonable chance of proving that director A's negligence, along with that of some or all of the remaining directors, was the legal cause of the loss.[17] But where a business collapses because of lack of directorial supervision, it has been difficult to trace the failure to the particular directors charged. As able a judge as Learned Hand, after finding that the defendant had been negligent to a degree which would have made him liable if his negligence could have been shown to be the legal cause of his corporation's collapse, felt obliged to state: [18] "When the corporate funds have been illegally lent, it is a fair inference that a protest would have stopped the loan, and that the director's neglect caused the loss. But when a business fails from general mismanagement, business incapacity, or bad judgment, how is it possible to say that a single director could have made the company successful, or how much in dollars he could have saved? Before this cause can go to a master, the plaintiff must show that, had Andrews done his full duty, he could have made the company prosper, or at least could have broken its fall. He must show what sum he could have saved the company. Neither of these has he made any effort to do." The burden was thus placed upon the plaintiff to show the causal connection between the defendant's negligence and the corporate injury, the usual burden of proof in tort.

But is there not a fallacy in this reasoning? If this is a case of joint or concurrent tortfeasing, as it generally is, proof of the negligent act of the several tortfeasors with proof of the indivisible loss caused by them is sufficient to place the burden of going forward with proof of their due care upon them, rather than keeping the burden upon the plaintiff.[19] From the practical standpoint, it is much easier for the delinquent directors to produce proof that they used due care or that, no matter what care might have been used it was impossible, under the circumstances, for them to have prevented the injury or collapse, than it is for

---

17. See, for example, Atherton v. Anderson, supra, note 10, and the penetrating dissenting opinion of Hart, C. J., in the all too lenient case of Sternberg v. Blaine, 179 Ark. 448, 17 S.W.2d 286 (1929).

18. While he was a trial judge in Barnes v. Andrews, 298 F. 614, at 616–617 (D.N.Y.1924). Accord:

Murphy v. Hanlon, 323 Mass. 683, 79 N.E.2d 292 (1948).

19. See Prosser, Torts 226, 232 et seq. (2d ed. 1955); Prosser, Joint Torts and Several Liability, 25 Calif.L.Rev. 413, 418, 433 (1937); 3 Fletcher Cyc. of Corporations § 1002 (Perm. ed. 1947).

the plaintiff to produce proof that, between two negligent directors, one or the other is responsible for the indivisible corporate loss. Perhaps the error in *Barnes* v. *Andrews* was in the plaintiff's failure to bring into the case as defendants other members of the board so that those charged jointly or concurrently with having committed the tort could have been required to go forward with proof of their non-liability.[20]

The supporting arguments that men would not take directorships if the law put them under a guaranty of the general success of their companies because of their negligence, that directors are not to be charged as specialists like lawyers and doctors, and that "After all, it is the same corporation that chose him which now seeks to charge him," should have some influence on decisions in this area, but their influence should be secondary and subordinate to considerations long entertained that directors are fiduciaries in a real sense to their corporation and its shareholders and that reasonable care under the circumstances is not too heavy a burden to place upon one who accepts membership on a board. Directors are not going to be placed under a "guaranty" of the general success of their companies in any case; but they ought to be kept under a guaranty of using reasonable care in the conduct of the business. And, since the trend has been toward boards composed partly or entirely of officers of the company,[21] it is even more obvious that such directors should be held to a strict accountability to keep their trust and exercise that degree of care which reasonably prudent directors under similar circumstances would exercise. Perhaps the day will come when, contrary to what Judge Learned Hand stated in *Barnes* v. *Andrews* about directors not being held as specialists, they will be so held by virtue of their assumption of dual roles. And contrary to his disagreement with *Hun* v. *Cary* [22] which in effect held that one who assumes the position of director impliedly warrants "that he possesses at least ordinary knowledge and skill, and that he will bring them to bear in the discharge of his duties," it will be held, because of the partial or total composition of the board of trained experts, that there is an implied warranty of special fitness. And such special circumstances are, of

20. Wormser's understatement is significant: "Whether this suggestion (that the plaintiff must accept the burden of showing that defendant's performance of his duties would have prevented the loss and what loss it would have prevented) is not unduly lenient is a debatable point." 1 Brooklyn L.Rev. 28, 34 (1932).

21. "Of 535 corporations participating in a survey in 1945 by NICB, approximately 45% had an 'officer' board (50% or more officers), approximately 30% had a mixed board (30% to 50% officers), and approximately 25% had a non-officer board (less than 30% officers)." Washington and Rothschild, Compensating the Corporate Executive 236 (Rev.ed. 1951).

22. 82 N.Y. 65, at 74, 37 Am.Rep. 546 (1880).

course, to be considered when the question is raised whether the board member has exercised the duty of care required to give him immunity from corporate loss.

In supervising the business, directors may rely upon reports of their officers as to the progress being made by their corporation, its financial condition, its probable earnings and a host of other things upon which tabs should be kept but about which no director would be expected to do the leg-work.[23] But once they have knowledge of corporate irregularities or of facts that carry with them a reasonable inference that all is not well with the management under the board's control, reasonable diligence requires action.[24] This has been particularly true in banking corporations. Where national or state bank examiners have, by their periodic reports, disclosed that the accounts are badly kept or that the capital is impaired, or some other fact which points toward lax management, a failure to follow up the disclosure promptly and to exercise reasonable care in remedying it has resulted in directorial liability.[25] On the other hand, it has been held that directors cannot rely entirely upon bank examiners who have examined the bank's affairs and not found defects. Bank examiners can also be negligent in carrying on their functions and employees bent upon embezzling bank funds have on occasion used such clever means of covering up for the moment their defalcations that the usual bank examination may fail to discover that funds are missing or even to find suspicious circumstances to report to the bank's board.[26] That such periodic examinations by government officials are prescribed does not relieve the directors of institutions so examined from exercising reasonable care. And where any special procedures are provided by the by-laws or resolution of the shareholders, such as appointing auditing committees or engaging outside accountants to examine the books periodically and the like, a failure to comply with such commands may be a legitimate basis for a find-

23. See Bates v. Dresser, 251 U.S. 524, 40 S.Ct. 247, 64 L.Ed. 388 (1920), where the president and cashier made honest reports to the board who had no reason to suspect that they were inaccurate. But the president, though honest, knew enough about the employee who embezzled a large sum to have put him on his guard. The board was not held to be negligent but the president was.

24. See, for a good example, Atherton v. Anderson, 99 F.2d 883 (6th Cir., 1938).

25. Ibid.; Ford v. Taylor, 176 Ark. 843, 4 S.W.2d 938 (1928); Prudential Trust Co. v. McCarter, 271 Mass. 132, 171 N.E. 42 (1930); Gamble v. Brown, 29 F.2d 366 (4th Cir., 1928), cert. den. 279 U.S. 839, 49 S.Ct. 253, 73 L.Ed. 986 (1928).

26. Broderick v. Horvatt, 148 Misc. 731, 266 N.Y.S. 341 (Sup.Ct.1933) (such reliance, however, may be one circumstance to be considered along with the rest); Van Schaick v. Cronin, 237 App.Div. 182, 261 N.Y. S. 358 (1932) (superintendent of insurance had made the examination of a surety company in this case).

ing that there was negligence.[27] Periodic audits and examinations are traditional procedure in corporations of any size and the tendency of decisions has been to place responsibility upon directors "to investigate and to check the possible wrongdoing of co-directors, officers and subordinates." [28] Thus, the tendency of courts is merely bringing into the law the better business practice already established.

What has been said above indicates the difficulties encountered in holding directors for corporate injury due to their negligence. To protect themselves against liability, they should inform themselves of the business generally, should attend board meetings with regularity and, when absent, have a valid excuse therefor and have it put on the record. When in disagreement with board action, they should register a dissent and see that the minutes show this, and they should always inform themselves of the by-laws and charter provisions for there may be limitations upon board action in them which, if violated, will be the basis of liability.

A number of statutes now provide that a director who is present at a board meeting shall be presumed to have assented to whatever action the board may have taken unless he shall have had his dissent entered in the minutes of the meeting or have given prompt written notice of his dissent after the meeting.[29] And, of course, the director should inform himself of any other statutory provisions bearing on his office, for many statutes today specify certain prohibited acts he must not join in and, in case of banks, building and loan associations, insurance companies and perhaps other corporations having specialized functions, statutes specify certain duties that must be performed and prohibit some activities.

Like other agents, directors may be indemnified out of the company's assets for liabilities properly incurred in carrying on the authorized business. But for expenses incurred in successfully defending suits brought against them by the corporation or derivatively, by a shareholder, for malfeasance or misfeasance in office, the courts are not agreed. Some have assumed that the risk of suit is in the nature of an occupational hazard and, where no benefit results to the company—which is usually, if not always the case—neither the expenses of suit nor reasonable

27. Atherton v. Anderson, supra, note 24; Gamble v. Brown, supra, note 25; Campbell v. Watson, 62 N.J.Eq. 396, 50 A. 120 (1901).

28. Ballantine, Corporations 164 (Rev.ed. 1946).

29. See, for examples, Or.Rev.Stat. 1953, § 57.231(2); Ohio Rev.Code (Ohio Gen.Corp.Law of 1955) § 1701.95(B); D.C.Bus.Corp.Act 1954 § 42(b) (a conclusive presumption unless placed in the minutes or written dissent is made).

attorney's fees have been allowed the director.[30] There are few cases on the point and the better ones hold that the successful director is entitled to indemnification for his expenses and reasonable counsel fees.[31] "This right of reimbursement has its foundation in the maintenance of a sound public policy favorable to the development of sound corporate management as a prerequisite for responsible corporate action." [32]

Statutes are gradually giving directors and officers a specific right to be reimbursed for expenses incurred in successfully defending suits brought against them for acts done while serving in these capacities.[33] By-laws are now frequently used for the same purpose. Some of the statutes, and likewise by-laws, are not adequately protective of the corporation in case of a compromise of claims settled out of court and requiring no court approval.[34] Other reimbursement-for-expenses statutes are sure to appear in the near future. Legislatures should be careful to provide that delinquent directors do not benefit from these and that, in any case, a court should make the final determination of whether reimbursement should be made and for how much. Otherwise, the statutory command that corporations shall be managed by a board of directors will not be worth the printing cost of the statement. The shareholders may, by unanimous vote, decide to pay counsel fees and other expenses of suit after the event, but anything short of unanimous consent would seem like bargaining away the shareholders' protection against negligent and wilful activity of their top echelon agents. If such bargaining away can be legitimately done, it would be much simpler to place in the articles or by-laws a provision to the effect that no director shall be liable for damage "which shall happen in the execution of the duties of his office or in relation thereto, unless the same happen through his own dishonesty." [35]

30. New York Dock Co. v. McCollom, 173 Misc. 106, 16 N.Y.S.2d 844 (Sup.Ct.1939) (but see present New York statute in note 33, infra); Griesse v. Lang, 37 Ohio App. 553, 175 N.E. 222 (1931).

31. In re E. C. Warner Co., 232 Minn. 207, 45 N.W.2d 388 (1950); Figge v. Bergenthal, 130 Wis. 594, 109 N.W. 581 (1906), 110 N.W. 798 (1907); Solimine v. Hollander, 129 N.J.Eq. 264, 19 A.2d 344 (1941).

32. In re E. C. Warner Co., supra, note 31, 45 N.W.2d at 393. And see for a fine statement of the reasons, Solimine v. Hollander, supra, note 31, 19 A.2d at 348.

33. Good examples are: West's Ann. Cal.Corp.Code § 830; Minn.Stat.

Ann. § 301.09(7); Mo.Rev.Stat.1949, V.A.M.S., § 351.355; N.J.S.A. 14:3-14, added by L.1942, c. 124; N.Y. Gen.Corp.Law § 63, as amended by L.1949, c. 811; Ohio Rev.Code (Ohio Gen.Corp.Law of 1955) § 1701.13(E).

34. See page 382, infra; Ballantine, California's Statute as to Directors' Litigation Expenses, 31 Calif. L.Rev. 515, at 521 (1943); Ballantine, Corporations 373 (Rev.ed. 1946).

35. The provision was contained in In re Brazilian Rubber Plantation & Estates, Ltd., [1911] 1 Ch. 425, and was held to protect the director against losses due to his negligence. And see In re City Equita-

Since 1929 such exculpatory clauses have been prohibited in England though they were considered standard clauses to be included in every memorandum or articles of association prior to that time.[36] It took the English Parliament to express a policy which should have been apparent to the keepers of the King's conscience without a statutory prohibition.

§ 11.   Liability of Directors and Officers for Taking Advantage of Corporate Opportunities

Directors are often held as fiduciaries of their corporations. Conflicts of interest arise when they take advantage of corporate opportunities, contract or deal with the corporations upon whose boards they sit, when as directors of two or more corporations such corporations deal with one another, when directors use confidential information which they have derived from their corporations to their own advantage, and when they deal with shareholders in matters usually pertaining to shares of stock. In this section we are concerned with directors who have taken advantage of corporate opportunities.

The problem is simple when a director has been chosen by the board to buy or sell property, to enter into a lease for his company, or to do anything else as agent for the corporation. If he takes advantage of his agency to make a profit for himself, he will have to disgorge it under the usual agency rule. Likewise, if he buys property or leases it by virtue of such a mandate, he cannot keep it as his own but holds it in trust for his principal, the corporation.

But suppose a director, because of his position, (1) learns that the company is interested in purchasing a certain piece of property; or (2) the board talks over the possibility of expanding by acquiring property in a named city and building a factory on the site; or (3) the board discusses the possibility of purchasing a large block of its own shares on the market to retire them. May the director in (1) purchase the property for himself or dicker with the owner for a slice of the purchase price when the purchase is eventually made? May he in (2) organize a corporation to purchase property and erect a factory to manufacture the same type of product manufactured by his present company to compete in the same markets with it? Or in (3)

able Fire Ins. Co., [1925] Ch. 407. But the Brazilian Rubber case is the only one cited by Fletcher (3 Fletcher, Cyc. of Corporations § 1047 (Perm. ed. 1947)), supporting this proposition and it is certainly dubious from the moral angle. Such exculpatory provisions are expressly prohibited in England to-day, and have been since 1929. Companies Act of 1929, § 152; now § 205 of the Companies Act of 1948. See Palmer's Company Law 192 (19th ed. 1949); Gower, Modern Company Law 143 (1954).

36.   See note 35, supra.

may he purchase stock and on a rising market caused by company purchases sell his shares to third parties and keep the profit he has made? In each case he will be taking advantage of information which came to him by virtue of his position as board member, and in the first two he will be taking advantage of corporate opportunities which are seriously being considered by the board. In the third, if his purchases of shares have not disturbed the market in such a way that his corporation will be unable to purchase the number of shares anticipated or will have to pay more for the shares it purchases than it would otherwise have had to pay, it can hardly be said that he has taken advantage of a corporate opportunity. But he has taken advantage of information which was confidential and personal to the company, and which was obtained only by virtue of his position, and has made a profit on the strength of it.

The rule may be simply stated: A director or officer must account to his corporation for profits or other benefits received in violation of a fiduciary duty owed to his corporation.[37] The difficulty comes in defining the duty. Where a director sells to his corporation at a secret profit property which he might have retained for himself or sold to a stranger, it has been held that while the company may rescind the sale by tendering the property and demanding the price paid for it, there may be no recovery of the profit.[38] While a director owes a duty of undivided loyalty to his corporation, he is under no obligation to sell any of his own property to the corporation and if he does he may set his own terms, subject to the rules which courts have laid down to protect corporations against dealings of any sort with their directors and against the undue influence which some directors exert over their fellow directors to make a deal.[39] If he purchases property knowing that his company is in the market for it and with the intent of reselling it to his company, or keeping it for himself, he stands in no better position than an agent with a mandate—his company may insist that his title is held for its benefit.[40] And the price it will pay is the cost to the director.[41]

---

37. New York Trust Co., Trustee v. American Realty Co., 244 N.Y. 209, 155 N.E. 102 (1926). But where there is no conflict of interest, a director has no duty to refrain from taking a profit. Reliance upon the advice of counsel, especially corporate counsel, has been effective in some cases. See Spirt v. Bechtel, 232 F.2d 241 (2d Cir., 1956), noted in 66 Yale L.J. 611 (1957).

38. Ibid.; Burland v. Earle, [1902] A.C. 83 (the case goes further than the New York and Massachusetts cases, for the director had apparently purchased the property with the intent of selling it at a profit to his company).

39. See § 12, infra, for a discussion of these rules.

40. New York Trust Co., Trustee v. American Realty Co., supra, note 37; Guth v. Loft, Inc., 23 Del.Ch. 255, 5 A.2d 503 (Sup.Ct.1939); Durfee v. Durfee & Canning, Inc., 323 Mass. 187, 80 N.E.2d 522 (1948);

41. See Note 41 on page 252.

Or, if he has purchased under such circumstances and sold the property to others at a profit, he will be required to disgorge it as legally belonging to the corporation.[42]   Or if a business opportunity is "so closely associated with the existing and prospective activities of the corporation that the defendants (directors, here) should fairly have acquired that business for or made it available to the corporation," he cannot acquire it for his own benefit.[43]   The conflict between self-interest and integrity in such a case is still too great to permit a less rigid rule.

Yet, some courts have held that a breach of duty does not exist unless the property acquired is "property wherein the corporation has an interest already existing, or in which it has an expectancy growing out of an existing right, or . . . where the officers' interference will in some degree balk the corporation

Production Machine Co. v. Howe, 327 Mass. 372, 99 N.E.2d 32 (1951) and note in 50 Mich.L.Rev. 471 (1952).

41.   Hauben v. Morris, 161 Misc. 174, 291 N.Y.S. 96, 107–108 (1936), s. c. 255 App.Div. 35, at 46, 5 N.Y.S.2d 721 (1938) (the Appellate Division recognized Burland v. Earle as settled law but the case was enough different to justify the result). *Contra:* Burland v. Earle, supra note 38, which held that "a commission or mandate to purchase on behalf of the company" was a requirement if the profits were to be recovered.

42.   Irving Trust Co. v. Deutsch, 73 F.2d 121 (2d Cir., 1934), cert. den. 294 U.S. 708, 55 S.Ct. 405, 79 L.Ed. 1243 (1935), rev'g 2 F.Supp. 971 (1932), rehearing den. 294 U.S. 733, 55 S.Ct. 514, 79 L.Ed. 1262 (1935). In this case the A Corp. had an option to purchase 200,000 shares of stock for $100,000 in a company which owned patents needed in A Corp.'s business. Deutsch, a director and president of A Corp. reported to the directors that A Corp. could not finance this purchase. At the time, Deutsch owed his company a disputed claim of $125,000 and no effort was made to collect it. But see the interesting case of Dravosburg Land Co. v. Scott, 340 Pa. 280, 16 A.2d 415 (1940), where the director who was also president owned a piece of land which, together with his corporation's larger tract, another corporation desired. Representing his compa-

ny, he was able, by the leverage of the desired two-piece sale, to obtain for his property $40,000, whereas his corporation, for its piece of land worth four times as much, received but $35,000. Should he not have been held for a proportionate part of the $40,000? The court did not think so.

43.   Rosenblum v. Judson Engineering Corp., 99 N.H. 267, 109 A.2d 558, at 563 (1954). In Lutherland, Inc. v. Dahlen, 357 Pa. 143, 53 A. 2d 143, at 147 (1947), it is stated: " . . . [I]f there is presented to him (the officer or director) a business opportunity which is within the scope of its (the corporation's) own activities and of present or potential advantage to it, the law will not permit him to seize the opportunity for himself; if he does so, the corporation may elect to claim all the benefits of the transaction." Three facts were emphasized in Johnston v. Greene, 121 A.2d 919, at 923 (Del.Sup.Ct.1956), rev'g Greene v. Allen, 114 A.2d 916 (Del.Ch.1955), which were held to justify the accepting of the opportunity (patent rights): (1) The opportunity had been offered the director individually and not as director or officer; (2) the manufacture of the thing patented had no direct or close relationship to any business the corporation was engaged in or had ever engaged in; and (3) the corporation had no interest or expectancy in the patent rights. See Note, The Doctrine of Corporate Opportunity, 26 U. of Cin.L.Rev. 104 (1957), on this case.

in effecting the purposes of its creation." [44]   And the Arizona court has required a corporate interest, "actual or in expectancy" in the property or a showing that the director's or officer's purchase "may hinder or defeat the plans and purposes of the corporation in the carrying on or development of the legitimate business for which it was created." [45]   The alternative in either of the above statements of the rule should not be too serious an obstacle in protecting the corporation against the self-interest of its fiduciary.   It would be a rare case, indeed, where the officer's act will not "in some degree" balk or hinder the corporation in carrying out some of its purposes.   And where the purchase has no reference to corporate purposes, it would be ultra vires the corporation and hence unenforceable against its officer.

A few cases have gone further and held that to constitute a breach of fiduciary duty, the officer's purchase must have been of property "highly desirable if not absolutely necessary to the furtherance of" a corporate purpose.[46]   Since the proof must show that there was an interference with a corporate opportunity, the extent of the opportunity would seem to be a minor matter.   On the other hand, whether or not the corporation is financially capable of taking advantage of it is a matter of high importance, for directors and officers should not be held to a duty which cannot actually be performed for their corporation. If they have made an honest effort on behalf of the corporation to finance an intended purchase and have been unable to do this, they should be able to operate without fear of reprisal later.[47]

44. Lagarde v. Anniston Lime & Stone Co., 126 Ala. 496, at 502, 28 So. 199, at 201 (1900), quoted in Durfee v. Durfee & Canning, Inc., supra, note 40. Lincoln Stores v. Grant, 309 Mass. 417, 34 N.E.2d 704 (1941), noted in 55 Harv.L.Rev. 866 (1942), seems to have accepted this rule. But Durfee v. Durfee & Canning, Inc., supra, specifically rejects this test or rule and agrees with Ballantine, Corporations 204–205 (Rev.ed. 1946), which it cites. Where the opportunity is not essential to the corporation and is one in which it has no interest or expectation, the officer may seize it. Gottlieb v. McKee, 107 A.2d 240 (Del.Ch.1954).

45. Zeckendorf v. Steinfeld, 12 Ariz. 245, 262, 100 P. 784 (1909), modified in 225 U.S. 445, 32 S.Ct. 728, 56 L. Ed. 1156 (1912). See also Westerly Theatre Operating Co. v. Pouzzner, 162 F.2d 821 (1st Cir., 1947).

46. Golden Rod Mining Co. v. Bukvich, 108 Mont. 569, 92 P.2d 316 (1939) (A dissenting opinion by Morris, J., emphasizes the fact that the defendant was a dummy director and had never attended a directors' meeting; thus, he should not be denied the right to acquire part of the public domain open to everyone else); Carper v. Frost Oil Co., 72 Colo. 345, 211 P. 370 (1922); Colorado & Utah Coal Co. v. Harris, 97 Colo. 309, at 313, 49 P. 2d 429, at 431 (1935).

47. In Zeckendorf v. Steinfeld, supra, note 45, the corporation was found financially unable to take advantage of the purchase of adjoining mining property.   Compare with the Zeckendorf case News-Journal Corp. v. Gore, 147 Fla. 217, 2 So.2d 741 (1941). The effort to find finances for the corporation must be a bona fide one. Electronics Development Co. v. Robson, 148 Neb. 526, 28 N.W.2d 130 (1927). It

The same should be true when it clearly appears that the third person would not have dealt directly with the corporation, whatever his reason may have been.[48] In either case the good faith of the fiduciary should be beyond any reasonable doubt of the same.

It has been stated that "Directors or officers of a corporation are not, by reason of the fiduciary relationship they bear toward the corporation, necessarily precluded from entering into an independent business in competition with it, but, in doing so, they must act in good faith." [49] It is difficult to imagine how directors may enter into an "independent business," at least as owners and managers of the business, after their acceptance of membership on the board and during their service as directors, in competition with their corporation without acting in bad faith. Would not their integrity be so exposed to their own self-interest that the result would most surely be foreseen? And should a court have to weigh the matter of self-interest and fiduciary obligation to ascertain whether the balance tips one way or the other? If the director accepts a position in a competing business there is some danger that knowledge gained from his directorship will be used by him to the advantage of his competing employer. Or if he accepts membership on the board of a competing corporation, there is some chance of his favoring one over the other, particularly if he owns a large interest in one. In the case of the employee, equity has the means of restraining him in the use of information he has gained, and his employer would

---

was not that in Irving Trust Co. v. Deutsch, supra, note 42. There may be bona fide reasons other than the lack of finances which justify a holding that the fiduciary duty is not violated as in Blaustein v. Pan American Petroleum & Transport Co., 293 N.Y. 281, 56 N. E.2d 705 (1944) (dissent by two judges), noted in 58 Harv.L.Rev. 125 (1944). If the corporation is unable to take advantage of the opportunity, should the shareholders be given the chance? Young v. Columbia Oil Co. of West Virginia, 110 W.Va. 364, 158 S.E. 678 (1931), discussed in 45 Harv.L.Rev. at 1389 (1932); 38 W.Va.L.Q. 158 (1931).

48. Pioneer Oil & Gas Co. v. Anderson, 168 Miss. 334, 151 So. 161 (1934); Crittenden & Cowler Co. v. Cowles, 66 App.Div. 95, 72 N.Y.S. 701, at 702 (1901). See Durfee v. Durfee & Canning, Inc., supra, note 40, where it was argued by the di-

rector who, through his self-formed $40-capital-stock corporation, profited, that the seller would not have dealt with the plaintiff-corporation. The $40 corporation had purchased some 60,000,000 gallons of "natural gasoline" and sold 45,000,000 gallons to the plaintiff-corporation at a profit of nearly $200,000.

The English rule does not permit the director to keep a profit made where the opportunity came from information derived from sitting on the board, even though the corporation was financially unable to take advantage of the deal. Regal (Hastings), Ltd. v. Gulliver, [1942] 1 All.E.R. 378 (House of Lords).

49. Lincoln Stores, Inc. v. Grant, 309 Mass. 417, 34 N.E.2d 704, at 707 (1941), citing Red Top Cab Co. v. Hanchett, 48 F.2d 236, at 238 (D. Cal.1931) "and cases cited," and Golden Rod Mining Co. v. Bukvich, 108 Mont. 569, at 576, 92 P.2d 316 (1939) "and cases cited."

be in jeopardy if he knowingly used certain types of information —lists of customers, for example—gained from his employee's service on the board of the competitor.[50]   Legal controls over interlocking directors are well enough established to guarantee just results.   The dangers in competitor-employee and competitor-director cases are perhaps more imaginary than real though some types of information, such as costs of production, extent of business, advertising experience and costs, salaries of officers, and lists of customers and, perhaps, of shareholders could prove of much value to a competitor.   And since a director has virtually an absolute right to examine the books and records of his corporation so long as he remains a director, and this irrespective of his motive, he is in a position to obtain most of the corporate secrets.[51]   Fortunately, if it can be shown that he desires his information to aid the corporation's competitors, access to the records can, by the better view, be restricted.[52]

In *Lincoln Stores* v. *Grant,*[53] two directors and an important employee of the plaintiff-corporation secretly purchased all of the shares of a non-competing corporation whose business was located within ninety feet of the plaintiff's business property, with the intent of carrying on a business similar to that of the plaintiff.   They had used information gained from confidential records of the plaintiff to determine the inventory and capital necessary for similar departments they were to establish in their new business.   The plaintiff had previously considered expanding its own business but found the rents of adjoining property too high to warrant expansion.   The important employee resigned to manage the newly acquired business and, eventually, the plaintiff discovered that its two director-officers were co-owners of the competing business and discharged them from their company offices and demanded that they resign their directorships.   The latter they refused to do but did not actually participate in any later board meetings.   In a suit brought to enjoin them from

50. In E. I. Du Pont de Nemours Powder Co. v. Masland, 244 U.S. 100, 37 S.Ct. 575, 61 L.Ed. 1016 (1917), a former employee was restrained from using the former employer's trade secrets. For a case in which there was a mass exodus of employees, high and low, with the taking over of a large part of the corporate employer's advertising business, see Duane-Jones Co. v. Burke, 306 N.Y. 172, 117 N.E.2d 237 (1954), modifying and affirming, 281 App.Div. 622, 121 N.Y.S.2d 107 (1953), and notes in 54 Col.L.Rev. 994 (1954); 38 Minn.L.Rev. 661 (1954); 22 U. of Chi.L.Rev. 278 (1954).

51. Wilkins v. M. Ascher Silk Corp., 207 App.Div. 168, 201 N.Y.S. 739 (1923), aff'd without opinion, 237 N.Y. 574, 143 N.E. 748 (1924) (He has the right irrespective of motive which, in this case, was one of hostility to his corporation, being a competitor with it. His hostility may be so extreme as to be the basis of removal for cause).

52. Ballantine, Corporations 383–384 (Rev.ed. 1946); Stevens, Corporations 497 (2d ed. 1949).

53. Supra, note 49.

operating a store similar to that of the plaintiff, for an accounting for damage sustained due to the unfaithful acts of the defendants, and to have a constructive trust declared of the shares owned by the three defendants, the court sustained a master's report which (1) found that the two directors were, as directors, and the employee who had joined them, under a duty not to engage in competition with the company nor to acquire interests conflicting with its interests; (2) that the plaintiff had sustained damages due to the loss of profits caused by the competition and that these profits were recoverable; and (3) that the plaintiff should be reimbursed for the salaries paid to the three defendants from the date they had agreed with a broker to purchase the shares until they left the plaintiff's employ, together with some expenses charged to the plaintiff by them which arose out of the negotiations resulting in the purchase of the shares. The prayer that a constructive trust be raised of the stock in the competitor was denied because there was no showing that the plaintiff was interested in acquiring the competitor's stock or of expanding prior to its purchase by the defendants; and, further, that the competing store "was not essential to the company, and that it was something in which the company had no interest or expectancy." In the acquisition of the store, thought the court, as distinguished from its operation, there had been no violation of duty. The relief granted the plaintiff was limited to damages sustained through loss of profits to the date the plaintiff claimed and its proof supported plus a return of the salaries paid the defendants after their secret purchase of shares and their start to change the non-competitive business into a competitive one.[54]

Any emphasis upon the essentiality of the property to the company or upon an interest or expectancy in it would seem to be a misconception as to the real basis of a fiduciary's liability to his beneficiary, in this case to his corporation. The real basis upon which the better holdings rest is that, under the particular circumstances, the possible conflict between the director's or officer's self-interest and his duty of self-disinterested service to his company is sufficiently apparent to warrant a prohibition against his dealing except with full notice to his company and with its consent. And, as was said in *Guth* v. *Loft, Inc.:* [55] "The

54. See Dodd and Baker, Cases and Materials on Corporations 538, footnote 2 (2d ed. 1951). And see, for similar result, where directors formed a competing corporation, Coleman v. Hanger, 210 Ky. 309, 275 S.W. 784 (1925). For annotation on the right of stockholders, directors, officers, etc., to compete with their corporations, see 64 A.L. R. 782 (1929). And see Fuller, Restrictions Imposed by the Directorship Status on the Personal Business Activities of Directors, 26 Wash.U.L.Q. 189 (1941).

55. 23 Del.Ch. 255, at 270, 5 A.2d 503, at 510 (Sup.Ct.1939). And see Durfee v. Durfee & Canning, Inc., 323 Mass. 187, 80 N.E.2d 522 (1948),

rule, inveterate and uncompromising in its rigidity, does not rest upon the narrow ground of injury or damage to the corporation resulting from a betrayal of confidence, but upon a broader foundation of a wise public policy that, for the purpose of removing all temptation, extinguishes all possibility of profit flowing from a breach of the confidence imposed by the fiduciary relation."

Confidential information may be of various sorts and offer greater or lesser possibilities of profit when used. Its use may or may not injure the corporation; it may simply benefit the user. Earlier the question was asked whether a director who had used confidential information that his corporation was about to purchase for retirement a large block of stock, and who had then purchased on the market his corporation's shares and had sold them at a profit upon a rise in their market price due to the corporate purchase, could retain the profit so made if his corporation insisted upon having that profit. In a case where a confidential secretary of a director-officer obtained his information by virtue of his position and proceeded to use it in the manner described above, the court held that he was accountable to his corporation for the profit made though there was no injury to the corporation.[56] Injury is not the test—secret information acquired by an employee in the course of his employment cannot be used as a means for personal profit. When so used he is accountable to his employer for any profit made. He holds the profit as a constructive trustee for his employer.

§ 12. Transactions between Corporation and Director, or between Corporations Having Common Directors

Courts have struggled hard with the problem of how best to handle transactions between the director and his corporation and those between corporations having one or more common directors. The struggle has centered around the director's duty as a fiduciary to his corporation and his conflicting self-interest, with the recognition of a practical fact of corporate life that such transactions are frequent and often to the advantage of the corporation. Then, too, there has been the surprising discovery in some quarters that directors, for the most part, are not bent on skullduggery.

The English rule makes voidable by the company any transaction with a director, whether fair or unfair, unless the articles

---

where this later Massachusetts case specifically rejected the essential-property, interest-or-expectancy concept.

56. Brophy v. Cities Service Co., 70 A.2d 5 (Del.Ch.1949).

confer upon him an express power to deal with it.[57] And it does not matter how many disinterested directors vote for it. The same strict rule has been applied to transactions between corporations having one or more common directors.[58] This rule removes all temptation from directors to deal with their corporations and relieves a court from determining the fairness or reasonableness of the transaction, the influences that might have been present to encourage it, the motives of the directors who voted for it, and other pertinent factors. Its main value is certainty.

Where the director's presence is not necessary to constitute a quorum and his vote is not required to carry the resolution, most courts hold the transaction valid if fair to the corporation, and the burden is upon him to show its fairness.[59] This rule is practical and tends to produce the sort of contract or other transaction which strict adherence to directorial duty, in other circumstances, tends to produce—that is, a fair contract. It gives the corporation protection in case of an unfair contract which is all the protection it needs.

If the director's presence is necessary to make a quorum or his vote is essential to pass the resolution, by the prevailing rule the contract or other transaction is voidable at the election of the company.[60] The director's self-interest in such a case perhaps warrants this view, though some courts recognize that even under these circumstances the transaction, if fair, is binding.[61] Provisions are frequently made in the articles of incorporation

57. The leading case is Aberdeen Ry. Co. v. Blaikie Bros., 1 Macq. 461 (House of Lords, 1854). Subscribing for shares or debentures in his company are exceptions to the rule. Palmer's Company Law 175 (19th ed. 1949). A few early cases in America took the English view, for example, Metropolitan Elevated Ry. Co. v. Manhattan Elevated Ry. Co., 11 Daly (N.Y.) 373, 14 Abb. N.C. 103 (Ct. of C.P.1884), which is no longer the law in New York.

58. Metropolitan Elevated Ry. Co. v. Manhattan Elevated Ry. Co., supra, note 57.

59. Globe Woolen Co. v. Utica Gas & Electric Co., 224 N.Y. 483, 121 N.E. 378 (1918); Twin-Lick Oil Co. v. Marbury, 91 U.S. 587, 23 L. Ed. 328 (1876). The minority view is expressed in Stewart v. Lehigh Valley R. Co., 38 N.J.L. 505 (1875), where such a contract was held voidable by the corporation (but not by others) whether fair or not,

if avoided within a reasonable time. A later recognition of this rule is found in Cuthbert v. McNeill, 103 N.J.Eq. 199, 142 A. 819 (1928). However, the shareholders, by majority vote, may ratify such a contract. U. S. Steel Corp. v. Hodge, 64 N.J.Eq. 807, 54 A. 1 (Ct. Err. & App.1903).

60. Hotaling v. Hotaling, 193 Cal. 368, 224 P. 455 (1924); Cathedral Estates v. Taft Realty Corp., 228 F.2d 84 (2d Cir., 1955) (Connecticut law applied); Federal Mtg. Co. v. Simes, 210 Wis. 139, 245 N.W. 169, at 173 (1932), noted in 8 Wis.L.Rev. 342 (1933); Mobile Land Improvement Co. v. Gass, 142 Ala. 520, 39 So. 229 (1905).

61. Ransome Concrete Machinery Co. v. Moody, 282 F. 29 (2d Cir., 1922). See Note, The Fairness Test of Corporate Contracts With Interested Directors, 61 Harv.L.Rev. 335 (1948); Ann., 175 A.L.R. 577, 596 (1948).

or by-laws whereby transactions between the corporation and its directors or officers are not to be affected or invalidated by virtue of the self-interest of these officials or the fact that their presence is necessary to make a quorum or that their vote is required to carry the resolution. There is not yet much law on these clauses and some clauses are broad enough to include, as excusable, fraud or unfairness.[62] "In a few cases they have been construed to absolve the directors of the charge of bad faith and shift the burden of proof as to fairness from the director or the one claiming under the contract to the complainant." [63] In a case involving statutory authorization for a director or officer to so deal with his company, it was rightly held that the broad authorization did not warrant transactions that were unfair or unreasonable—that full compliance with the provisions of the statute could not justify the mulcting of the corporation by its officials. There was still the duty of exercising their powers in good faith and for the benefit of the corporation.[64] There would seem to be no good reason for interpreting charter or by-law provisions with any greater breadth.

Statutes vary on whether the interested director may be part of a quorum, whether he may cast his vote when necessary to carry the resolution, or whether he may do neither.[65] The Rhode Island statute does not permit him to do either, and if he complies and enters into a contract in good faith, the contract having been approved by a majority of the directors at any board meeting, it is voidable only if it would have been, had the contract been with a stranger.[66] These statutes also cover, in like manner, transactions between corporations having common directors.

62. In Sterling v. Mayflower Hotel Corp., 33 Del.Ch. 20, 89 A.2d 862 (1952), aff'd 33 Del.Ch. 293, 93 A. 2d 107 (Sup.Ct.1952), an exculpatory provision, excluding fraud, was inserted in the articles. There was no fraud or unfairness and the court held the provision valid against the contention that it was "contrary to the law of the state," i. e., the common law as there was no statute prohibiting such clauses.

63. Ballantine, Lattin and Jennings, Cases and Materials on Corporations, 300, Note on Charter Provisions Authorizing Directors' Contracts (2d ed. 1953). See Spiegel v. Beacon Participations, Inc., 297 Mass. 398, 8 N.E.2d 895, at 907 (1937); Everett v. Phillips, 288 N. Y. 227, 43 N.E.2d 18 (1942).

64. Remillard Brick Co. v. Remillard-Dandini Co., 109 Cal.App.2d 405, 241 P.2d 66 (1952), interpreting West's Ann.Cal.Corp.Code § 820. *Accord:* Kennerson v. Burbank Amusement Co., 120 Cal.App.2d 157, 260 P.2d 823 (1953).

65. West's Ann.Cal.Corp.Code § 820; Mich.Gen.Corp.Act § 13–5, as amended by L.1949, Act 229; W. Va.Code of 1931, c. 31, Art. 1, § 69, as amended by L.1937, c. 22.

66. Gen.Laws R.I.1938, ch. 116, § 21, as amended L.1956, c. 3785. See Duncan Shaw Corp. v. Standard Machinery Co., 196 F.2d 147 (1st Cir., 1952), and 51 Mich.L.Rev. 705 (1953).

Without benefit of statute, the rules having reference to transactions between corporations with interlocking boards are the same as set forth above where directors have dealt with their own corporations with the exception that, where interlocking board members must sit to form a quorum or must vote to pass the resolution, the majority holdings recognize the validity of the transaction if the directors acted in good faith and the transaction is a fair one.[67] The burden of proof as to fairness is, as it was in the director-corporation transactions, usually upon the party (in this case, corporation) claiming the validity of the transaction.[68]

Since, in any case, the fairness of the transaction will be an issue and may always be questioned, whether the fiduciary's vote or presence was necessary ought not to be of importance. The problem is a practical one and deserves a practical solution. By leaving the question of fairness always open, the corporation obtains the protection it needs and contracts will have at least fair stability. Directors and officers, too, have their warning that any benefit they receive must be accompanied by fairness to their corporation.

As long as courts hold that transactions between directors and their corporations are voidable for reasons other than their unfairness it should be remembered that such voidable contracts can be ratified by the majority vote of the shareholders and that the interested director may vote his shares in aid of ratification.[69] However, it should not be forgotten that a majority may not ratify an unfair contract so as to make it free from attack, whether that majority includes the interested director and his shares or not. The fiduciary obligation of the majority shareholders to the minority enters at this point to prevent the unfair contract from acquiring validity from the vote alone.[70]

---

67. Robotham v. Prudential Ins. Co. of America, 64 N.J.Eq. 673, 53 A. 842 (1903); Chelrob, Inc. v. Barrett, 293 N.Y. 442, 57 N.E.2d 825 (1944), motion for reargument denied, 293 N.Y. 859, 59 N.E.2d 446 (1944) (innocent mistake caused the contract to be unfair in this case); South Side Trust Co. v. Washington Tin Plate Co., 252 Pa. 237, 97 A. 450 (1916).

68. This is usually so. Everett v. Phillips, 288 N.Y. 227, 43 N.E.2d 18 (1942); Geddes v. Anaconda Copper Mining Co., 254 U.S. 590, 41 S.Ct. 209, 65 L.Ed. 425 (1921). But see Spiegel v. Beacon Participations, Inc., supra note 63, 8 N.E.2d at 905. See Dodd and Baker, Cases and Materials on Corporations 474–476, Note on Contracts Between Corporations Having Common Directors (2d ed. 1951).

69. U. S. Steel Corp. v. Hodge, 64 N.J.Eq. 807, 54 A. 1, 60 L.R.A. 742 (Ct.Err. and App.1903); Gamble v. Queens County Water Co., 123 N. Y. 91, 25 N.E. 201 (1890); Bjorngaard v. Goodhue County Bank, 49 Minn. 483, 52 N.W. 48 (1892); North-West Transportation Co., Ltd. v. Beatty, L.R. 12 App.Cas. 589 (Privy Council 1887) (director was majority shareholder and voted his shares to ratify his contract which was a fair one).

70. Pepper v. Litton, 308 U.S. 295, 306, 60 S.Ct. 238, 245, 84 L.Ed. 281

§ 13.　Directors' use of inside Information for Personal Profit in Purchase and Sale of Corporation's Securities

The directors are in the best position of all corporate officers to obtain information which, if used by them, may result in profit from the purchase and sale of the corporation's shares. Information so gained can also be the means of saving them from financial loss. There is no longer any dispute over the contention that directors occupy the status of fiduciaries of their corporation. They are not considered in quite the same position as trustees of a trust, but they are said to approximate, by frequent analogies, that position. The preceding sections are illustrative of this statement. However, when it is said that the directors of a business corporation are also fiduciaries of the shareholders, notice must be taken of the type of factual situation which has given rise to such a statement. They are definitely not violating any trust to their shareholders when they, as members of the board, drive a hard bargain in a contract between a shareholder and their corporation. They have no duty, in such a situation, to make a fair contract for their shareholder.[71] But when they deal individually with a shareholder in the purchase of corporate shares from him, or they recommend that the shareholder sell his shares to a third person who has promised them a higher price if he, the purchaser, can acquire not only the directors' shares but more, perhaps for the purpose of gaining control of the corporation, or where the directors act in such a way as to prefer one group of shareholders over another, it is not improper to classify such directors as fiduciaries and hold them to strict accountability. And while directors who own shares may, as shareholders, vote their shares in any way they see fit, if the shares are voted for personal contracts which for some reason are voidable, they will not be permitted to ratify an unfair contract by exercising their shareholders' prerogative. As shareholders they owe a fiduciary duty to the remaining shareholders not to take advantage of their more powerful position.[72]

(1939); Southern Pacific Co. v. Bogert, 250 U.S. 483, 487, 488, 39 S.Ct. 533, 535, 63 L.Ed. 1099 (1919); Zahn v. Transamerica Corp., 162 F.2d 36 (3d Cir., 1947). See Lattin, The Minority Stockholder and Intra-Corporate Conflict, 17 Iowa L.Rev. 313, 335 et seq. (1932).

71. This is true even where they purchase shares from individual shareholders for their corporation. Gladstone v. Murray Co., 314 Mass. 584, 50 N.E.2d 958 (1943).

72. This last statement takes us into a yet undiscussed area, namely, the fiduciary duty of majority to minority shareholders. It is a large subject and is discussed in Lattin, Equitable Limitations on Statutory or Charter Powers Given to Majority Stockholders, 30 Mich. L.Rev. 645 (1932) and in the article cited in note 70, supra. For the discussion in this book, see p. 511 et seq., infra.

Whenever by contract a shareholder is entitled to full information of transactions having a bearing on the value of his shares, or by the course of dealing with the purchaser he has been led to believe that such information would be given prior to the sale of his shares, the director or officer who purchases without supplying the information is in a position similar to that of a fiduciary in his dealings with his beneficiary and must disgorge any profit made from his purchase or return the shares so purchased when proper demand and tender is made for rescission.[73]

There is a conflict of authority as to whether a director, in purchasing shares from individual shareholders, owes them a duty to disclose information not accessible to them, which information has come to the director by virtue of his position on the board. The older, and what is still perhaps the majority rule, considers the purchase of stock by a director or officer not to be within the area of corporate business and that, consequently, there is no fiduciary duty owed a shareholder to disclose inside information to him. A director or officer may thus deal with individual shareholders at arms' length barring fraudulent misstatements or, when an inquiry has been made by the shareholder, concealments, without fear of later successful attack upon his purchase of the shares. Harsh results have frequently resulted under this rule. In one case, for example, a director was able to purchase for approximately $27,000 shares of stock which he knew to be grossly undervalued on the market and which were actually worth $342,000.[74] Even in a freely competitive economy, this seems highly outrageous, especially since the information leading to the purchase came from the opportunity furnished him through an office to which the shareholder-seller and others—the real owners of the business—elected him.

The fairer rule, and the one which has steadily been gaining recognition due to the injustice of the earlier established rule

---

73. Sher v. Sandler, 325 Mass. 348, 90 N.E.2d 536 (1950). There was a contract between directors to supply full information, but it would seem that directors are always entitled to full information from fellow-directors without a contract. (But on this point, see contrary dictum in Broffe v. Horton, 172 F.2d 489 (2d Cir., 1949).) The purchasing director concealed the fact that the important lease which he was negotiating was a certainty. The value of the corporate stock depended upon this. Notes on the case are in 63 Harv.L.Rev. 1463 (1950) and 45 Ill.L.Rev. 510 (1950).

74. Board of Commissioners of Tippecanoe County v. Reynolds, 44 Ind. 509, 15 Am.Rep. 245 (1873), which Professor Ballantine uses in his text as one illustration of the injustice of the rule. Ballantine, Corporations 212 (Rev.ed. 1946). A fair expression of the non-fiduciary doctrine will be found in Gladstone v. Murray Co., 314 Mass. 584, 50 N.E.2d 958 (1943), where the purchaser was director, president, treasurer, and majority shareholder of a small corporation.

and to the continued criticism of it, holds that there is a fiduciary duty imposed by virtue of the director's office of trust to disclose facts which came to him because of his position, and which facts have a material bearing on the value of the corporate shares, to a shareholder with whom he is negotiating for the purchase of his shares.[75]   A failure to disclose this inside information may form the basis for a rescission or for the recovery of the difference between the purchase price and the actual value of the shares.[76]

But the rule which imposes a fiduciary obligation to disclose material facts can also be carried to an unwarranted extreme as happened in *Hotchkiss* v. *Fischer*,[77] a case where the plaintiff-shareholder had inquired of the purchasing-director who was also president whether a dividend was about to be declared and he answered honestly that he did not know but showed her the most recent corporate financial statement which, had she understood its significance, should have told her that the stock she was about to sell was of much more book value than the suggested selling price.   She also made inquiry of the value of her shares and the director told her that she would have to make that determination herself.   Special findings were returned by the jury that, upon the plaintiff's request, the defendant had disclosed the financial condition of the company by showing the plaintiff the company's financial statement, that upon inquiry he told the plaintiff he did not know the value of her stock, that he showed her the financial statement of another company in which his company owned one-half of the capital stock, and that there was no fraud imposed upon the plaintiff.   The judgment of the lower court for the defendant was reversed and the case was remanded for a new trial.   While the upper court found that the financial statement of the company did not disclose "the true book value" of the shares and contained some other discrepancies, it felt that full disclosure required interpretation of the financial statement plus other information on the likelihood of the company's declaring a dividend.

It turned out that five days after the defendant's purchase of plaintiff's $1-par-value shares at $1.25 each, the directors did declare a dividend of $1 per share.   The secretary-treasurer of the company testified that the book value was $3.85 a share.

---

75. The leading case is, perhaps, Oliver v. Oliver, 118 Ga. 362, 45 S.E. 232 (1903).

76. Hotchkiss v. Fischer, infra, note 77; Sautter v. Fulmer, 258 N.Y. 107, 179 N.E. 310 (1932), reargument denied 259 N.Y. 508, 182 N. E. 157 (1932).   But it has been held that a profit made by the buyer on resale is not recoverable. Bisbee v. Midland Linseed Products Co., 19 F.2d 24 (8th Cir., 1927), cert. den. 275 U.S. 564, 48 S.Ct. 121, 72 L.Ed. 428 (1927); Steven v. Hale-Haas Corp., 249 Wis. 205, 221–222, 23 N.W.2d 620 (1946).

77. 136 Kan. 530, 16 P.2d 531 (1932), noted in 46 Harv.L.Rev. 847 (1933).

Brokers testified that during the year the market price had ranged from $1 to $1.15 per share. The court confined itself chiefly to the failure of the defendant to interpret the financial statement to the plaintiff, an inexperienced widow who needed money, using these significant words:[78] "The director could not say to a shareholder: Here is the financial statement of the corporation; it shows these current and working assets of so much, these fixed assets of so much, these investments, etc.; shows these current liabilities, shows this contingent liability, shows this surplus, etc.; and in that manner qualify himself as a purchaser of the shareholder's shares. Without being analyzed and interpreted, the statement would convey little information respecting financial condition to a shareholder who did not acknowledge competency to interpret such a document. When interpreted, the statement would reflect book value of shares. Book value might have little relation to market value, and might have still less relation to actual value." It should be added that the court in *Hotchkiss* v. *Fischer* quoted from the Restatement of Trusts (§ 165) on the duty of loyalty and then stated that the principles are applicable to fiduciaries other than trustees, the section stating the rule supported by the weight of authority, but added, "The rule in this state is more strict." It might be asked: What director or officer would venture to interpret a balance sheet as minutely as the Kansas court required with any assurance that he had included a sufficient statement of each item to make his purchase of shares invulnerable?

What might be described as an intermediate position (and quite possibly the prevalent one today) in this area was taken nearly a half-century ago by the United States Supreme Court in the well-known case of *Strong* v. *Repide*.[79] Sometimes known as the "special facts" or "special circumstances" doctrine, the rule recognizes that one in the position of a director or officer may possess special facts upon which a duty to disclose is raised, although acknowledging that generally there is no such duty. The defendant-director in *Strong* v. *Repide* owned three-quarters of the corporation's shares and was also the company's agent and "administrator general." He himself was dickering for his company with the United States government which was seeking

---

78. Ibid., 16 P.2d at 534. The case on appeal from retrial is reported in 139 Kan. 333, 31 P.2d 37 (1934). The jury actually gave the plaintiff the difference between $1.68 and $1.25 per share she had received. The balance sheet shows the book value to have been substantially more than $1.68. The second case is instructive in stating the manner in which the value should be determined. It is interesting to speculate on what advantage she would have obtained had she sought rescission. Could she not have recovered the $1 per share dividend as well as her stock?

79. 213 U.S. 419, 29 S.Ct. 521, 53 L.Ed. 853 (1909).

to buy the corporate property. Concealing the fact that there was an excellent chance that the government would purchase at a substantial figure, and concealing his identity as a prospective purchaser of the plaintiff's shares, he was able to purchase through his agent the plaintiff's shares at one-tenth their later value, that is, their value after the government purchased the property some three months later. Rescission was granted as requested by the plaintiff. There also seems to be no good reason why the director, or officer, or other insider who has knowledge of the precarious financial condition of his corporation, should not be liable when he sells to an outsider to save himself from a loss without disclosing these special facts.[80]

The special facts doctrine has been accepted by many cases since its formulation in 1909 although, in most of these, the courts have been firm in their assertion that the duty is not the strict one owed by a trustee to his cestuis. Special facts warranting a duty to disclose have usually been in the form of the extraordinary, such as a prospective sale of all or of some of the company's assets, as in *Strong* v. *Repide*, anticipated mergers or consolidations, or a dissolution from which, due to an advantageous disposal of the corporate property, the shareholder can expect more than the sale of his shares will bring. And usually, if not always, the special facts known by the director are ones which are practically impossible of discovery by a shareholder unless he, too, has been in a position of trust where the information was available.[81] This doctrine offers substantial protection to the selling shareholder but carries with it the uncertainty of what facts a court may or may not classify as "special."

Many purchases will be made through brokers on a stock exchange where the only practical disclosure, if required in such a case, would open the field for broker-speculation. Should the director or officer who would be required to disclose his inside information were he dealing personally with a shareholder be required to keep out of the market until the information he has becomes generally known? In a practical world the answer

80. See Judge Learned Hand in Gratz v. Claughton, 187 F.2d 46, at 49 (2d Cir., 1951), cert. denied 341 U.S. 920, 71 S.Ct. 741, 95 L. Ed. 1353 (1951).

81. See interesting example of extraordinary facts concealed in Nichol v. Sensenbrenner, 220 Wis. 165, 263 N.W. 650 (1935); Broffe v. Horton, 172 F.2d 489 (2d Cir., 1949). A combination of concealment and misleading statements where there was a preconceived intent of the majority shareholder to capture through its control, an inventory appreciation, led the court to conclude that the count for fraud and deceit at common law was valid. This gives an additional possibility in many cases. Speed v. Transamerica Corp., 99 F.Supp. 808 (D.Del., 1951). The Speed case and related cases are discussed in notes in 59 Yale L.J. 1120, at 1150 et seq. (1950); 36 Calif.L.Rev. 325 (1948); 46 Mich. L.Rev. 1061 (1948); 96 U. of Pa. L.Rev. 276 (1947); 61 Harv.L.Rev. 359 (1948).

should be "no." Rugg, C. J., in *Goodwin* v. *Agassiz*,[82] states the reasons well: "Purchases and sales of stock on the stock exchange are commonly impersonal affairs. An honest director would be in a difficult situation if he could neither buy nor sell on the stock exchange shares of stock in his corporation without first seeking out the other actual ultimate party to the transaction and disclosing to him everything which a court or jury might later find that he then knew affecting the real or speculative value of such shares. Business of that nature is a matter to be governed by practical rules. Fiduciary obligations of directors ought not to be made so onerous that men of experience and ability will be deterred from accepting such office. Law in its sanctions is not coextensive with morality. It cannot undertake to put all parties to every contract on an equality as to knowledge, experience, skill and shrewdness. It cannot undertake to relieve against hard bargains made between competent parties without fraud." But wilful failure to disclose information to which shareholders as a class are entitled for their own protection, or the intentional manipulation of corporate affairs in such a way as to produce a false impression that the corporation is not doing well, in each case with the intent of purchasing shares at a bargain, would not be tolerated even if the purchases were made on the market.[83]

There are other circumstances where directors, through stock purchases, have been held to be fiduciaries of their shareholders, as where they use corporate funds to purchase some of the corporation's shares to be held by the corporation as treasury shares but with the intent of changing, and actually changing, the control to themselves (or others) by decreasing outside ownership. Manipulation of control by taking advantage of their official positions constitutes not only a breach of their fiduciary obligations to their corporation, but to their remaining shareholders as well.[84] In the case cited, a derivative action had been brought by a shareholder and the court rightly held that in

82. 283 Mass. 358, 186 N.E. 659 (1933). See Note, Duty of Director to Stockholder in Stock Exchange Sales, 32 Mich.L.Rev. 678 (1933).

83. Coronado Development Corp. v. Millikin, 175 Misc. 1, 22 N.Y.S.2d 670 (Sup.Ct.1940), but complaint was dismissed for insufficient allegation of damages in 262 App. Div. 504, 30 N.Y.S.2d 548 (1941) (see discussion at pp. 62–64, 346, supra of this text); Von Au v. Magenheimer, 126 App.Div. 257, 110 N.Y.S. 629 (1908), aff'd without opinion, 196 N.Y. 510, 89 N.E. 1114 (1909) (directors cut down

dividends, increased salaries, and represented that the corporation was in a bad condition); Backus v. Kirsch, 264 Mich. 73, 249 N.W. 469 (1933); Walsham v. Stainton, 1 De G. & S. 678, 46 Eng.Rep. 268 (1863).

84. Andersen v. Albert & J. M. Anderson Mfg. Co., 325 Mass. 343, 90 N.E.2d 541 (1950). See also Lawrence v. I. N. Parlier Est. Co., 15 Cal.2d 220, 100 P.2d 765, at 770 (1940); Yasik v. Wachtel, 23 Del. Ch. 247, 17 A.2d 309, at 313 (1941), noted in 40 Mich.L.Rev. 313 (1941).

such an action the corporation was not only a proper party but also an indispensable one. Since the company's treasury shares were involved, it would seem that had a personal action been brought the corporation would likewise be a necessary party, particularly when the remedy sought is a return of the control existing prior to the corporate purchase of its own shares.

Directors have sometimes issued to themselves or others treasury shares to change the voting control but, again, their fiduciary obligations to the whole shareholding group make the issue vulnerable.[85]   And, where statutes or articles have abolished a shareholder's pre-emptive right to a new issue of shares, the directors or officers may not legally favor themselves by issuing shares for their own profit or control, or discriminate between shareholders for similar purposes.[86]

While normally a director who is a majority or controlling shareholder may sell his shares to whomever he will and for whatever a purchaser is willing to pay, if he sells to persons he knows will plunder the corporate assets, or if he sells under circumstances that fairly put him on his guard that the purchase is for that purpose, he may be held by his corporation for damage done it by the purchasers. Those who control corporations through majority shareholding, or through minority stock ownership which is able to control, owe a duty to their corporations not to transfer control to outsiders "if the circumstances surrounding the proposed transfer are such as to awaken suspicion and put a prudent man on his guard—unless a reasonably adequate investigation discloses such facts as would convince a reasonable person that no fraud is intended or likely to result." [87] Some of the factors considered as important in awakening suspicion are the nature of the corporate assets—are they fairly liquid as in the case of an investment company—, the method by which the purchase is to be consummated—are the corporate assets to be used as a means of financing the purchase—, the relation of the price to be paid to the value of the stock—is the price excessive, and whether the agreement provides that the present directors resign before or just after the sale and that

85. Elliott v. Baker, 194 Mass. 518, 80 N.E. 450 (1907); Borg v. International Silver Co., 11 F.2d 147 (2d Cir., 1925). Compare Witherbee v. Bowles, 201 N.Y. 427, 95 N. E. 27 (1911).

86. Schwab v. Schwab-Wilson Machine Corp., Ltd., 13 Cal.App.2d 1, 55 P.2d 1268 (1936).

87. Insuranshares Corp. of Delaware v. Northern Fiscal Corp., 35 F.Supp. 22, at 25 (D.Pa.1940), dis-

cussed in notes in 26 Cornell L.Q. 325 (1941); 39 Mich.L.Rev. 650 (1941); 25 Minn.L.Rev. 525 (1941); 8 U. of Chi.L.Rev. 335 (1941); and 27 Va.L.Rev. 546 (1941). Some courts seem to require more than knowledge of suspicious circumstances. See Levy v. American Beverage Corp., 265 App.Div. 208, 38 N.Y.S.2d 517 (1942), which seems to require knowledge of purchaser's intent to loot or of his previous looting.

the resigning directors appoint, when they have the power, successors designated by the purchasers.[88]

While directors usually may resign at will, they may not do this if the immediate consequence is to leave the corporation without reasonable protection, nor may they accept compensation for the promise to resign. If the court finds the price received for their shares was excessive and that resignation, followed by appointment of the purchaser's nominees, occurred, it may conclude that part of the price was for the directors' resignations and this may be recovered by the corporation. "The basis of their liability for its return is their participation in a breach of fiduciary duty, and their liability is joint and several."[89]

It cannot now be as emphatically stated, as it was by Professor Berle nearly a quarter-century ago, that "the law thus far has been unable to deal with" the sale of control as a valuable property interest to its holder, whose "value arises out of the ability which the holder has to dominate property which in equity belongs to others."[90] The conventional approach, though there is very little direct authority for it, is "to regard controlling shares as an ordinary asset which corporate managers may buy and sell with the same freedom which the law permits with respect to other kinds of property."[91] The trend of the law seems to be toward holding control as a corporate asset in which all shareholders have an equitable interest and in which they are entitled to share. That there is a difficulty in separating the investment value of the shares sold from their control value has been solved in a recent case by putting the burden upon the seller, which seems fair enough.[92]

88. See Gerdes v. Reynolds, Ballantine v. Ferretti, 28 N.Y.S.2d 622 (Sup.Ct.1941); Ballantine v. Ferretti, 28 N.Y.S.2d 668 (Sup.Ct. 1941); Gerdes v. Reynolds, 30 N. Y.S.2d 755 (Sup.Ct.1941).

89. Ibid. 28 N.Y.S.2d at 661. Justice Walter concluded that $791,-250 was paid for the stock and $1,318,750 as the price of the directors' resignations and the election of the purchasers' nominees. The latter amount was the company's property and could be recovered. See also Bosworth v. Allen, 168 N. Y. 157, 61 N.E. 163 (1901). And see generally, Stickells, Stockholders' Duty in Sale of Stock, 31 B. U.L.Rev. 191 (1951); Notes, Duties of Controlling Shareholders in Transferring Their Shares, 54 Harv.L.Rev. 648 (1941); Sale of

Corporate Control, 19 U. of Chi. L.Rev. 869 (1952).

90. Berle and Means, The Modern Corporation and Private Property 244 (1932).

91. Jennings, Trading in Corporate Control, 44 Calif.L.Rev. 1, at 5, 7–8, 31–32 (1956); Hill, The Sale of Controlling Shares, 70 Harv.L. Rev. 986, at 986 (1957).

92. Perlman v. Feldmann, 219 F.2d 173 (2d Cir., 1955), cert. den. 349 U.S. 952, 75 S.Ct. 880, 99 L.Ed. 1277 (1955), Judge Swan writing a strong dissenting opinion; Zweifach v. Scranton Lace Co., 156 F. Supp. 384 at 397 (D.Pa.1957). See Hill, The Sale of Controlling Shares, 70 Harv.L.Rev. 986, at 989 (1957), where the writer classifies the Perlman decision as falling es-

In the case cited, the owner of 37% of the corporation's shares which actually controlled the election of directors refused $18 a share offered, asked $22, agreed finally to take $20, the book value being $17 and the over-the-counter price not above $12. The purchasers were a syndicate of manufacturers of finished steel products who, due to tight markets in steel, wished to assure themselves of an uninterrupted supply of the raw product for their own use. The corporation was a marginal sheet steel producer which, in periods of shortages in steel, got along well enough but, in normal times, could not compete with other steel manufacturing companies except in a small area near its manufacturing base. However, due to shortages in steel, the company had built up a good business, its purchasers of steel being willing to pay in advance without charging interest for commitments in the future. By virtue of these advance payments and the profits made from these sources which were fairly stable, the corporation was able to refurbish its plant and acquire new ones. Upon consummation of the sale, the seller, as part of the agreement, delivered the resignations of all the members of the board and elected nominees chosen by the buyer. Outside shareholders brought a derivative action to recover for the "unlawful" sale of control asserting that the seller, as director and dominating shareholder, had a fiduciary obligation to the corporation and to the outside shareholders, that the price paid for the stock included an additional amount for the sale of a corporate asset, namely, the power to fix the allocation of the corporate output in a tight market. The defense contended that the transaction was merely a sale of controlling shares with the usual incidents which shares carry with them. The trial court gave judgment to the defendants, rejecting the corporate asset theory and holding that the power of control to transfer management was a quality, characteristic of majority stock, which if it affected value was an inseparable factor entering into the stock's value.[93] The court of appeals, one judge dissenting, held that the price received by the seller was separable and that the burden was upon him to establish that it contained no premium for control. The case was remanded to the district court with instructions to find what part of the price was to be assigned to the power to control the management, and whatever that was should be shared, in proportion to their stockholdings, by the

sentially within the category of the "looting" cases. On remand by the Court of Appeals for a determination of the value of the defendants' stock, the court found the difference between $14.67 and the $20 per share received by the defendants constituted a premium or bonus for control. Perlman v. Feldmann, 154 F.Supp. 436 (D. Conn.1957).

93. Perlman v. Feldmann, 129 F. Supp. 162, at 183 (D.Conn.1952). See the analysis of Leech in his article, Transactions in Corporate Control, 104 U. of Pa.L.Rev. 725, at 809–820 (1956).

plaintiffs and defendants. Contrary to the judgment expected in a derivative action, recovery was not to be a corporate one but the plaintiffs were to recover individually; otherwise, if corporate recovery were had, the purchasers or their successors would be returned a part of the purchase price which they were not entitled to.[94] This perhaps indicates that the action really belongs to the outside shareholders on the theory that the fiduciary duty of not selling control without permitting them to participate in the premium paid for it is a fiduciary duty owed to the outside shareholders rather than to the corporation.[95]

Control is purchased for a variety of reasons besides that of acquiring a business and running it with new management in the hope of making a greater success than its previous owners and managers had. In *Tryon* v. *Smith* [96] controlling shares were apparently purchased honestly to acquire a successful banking business and the seller of control, the president who was also a director, and his associates, would have nothing to do with acquiring or making recommendations concerning the outside shares. He did tell the buyer that the shares were worth more than the book value ($200) and that the outside shareholders should obtain at least $220 per share, although sales on the market had been made for $160 and $170 per share. The seller and his associates received $460 per share against the $220 per share received by the outside shareholders. The court held that there was no fiduciary relationship between stockholders so far as the sale of individual stock was concerned, and no duty by the seller of control to inform the outside shareholders of the price he was getting for his shares. Stock of the majority is generally of more value than that of the minority, thought the court, and the fact that the seller is also a director did not, in itself, make a difference. If there were fraud, duress, domination or interference on the part of the seller with the sale of outsiders' shares, then a basis would exist for holding the seller of the controlling shares. As Professor Jennings points out: [97]

94. But there is some good authority for personal recovery in derivative actions in certain factual situations which Professor Jennings, op. cit. supra, note 91, cites in footnote 98, page 28.

95. Jennings, op. cit. supra, note 91, at 28, suggests this and advises: "Until this question is ultimately resolved a plaintiff, in a proper case, where local procedure so permits, should join an individual or class action against the individual defendants for redress of a grievance personal to himself as a stockholder with a count which asserts a corporate right of action, in which he also asks for personal recovery." He cites Benson v. Braun, 286 App.Div. 1098, 145 N. Y.S.2d 711 (1955), affirming 141 N. Y.S.2d 286 (Sup.Ct.1955) "now pending in the New York courts" where essentially this was done. Upon trial, the plaintiffs failed to prove their case. Id. v. id., 155 N.Y.S.2d 622 (Sup.Ct.1956).

96. 191 Or. 172, 229 P.2d 251 (1951).

97. Jennings, op. cit. supra, note 91, at 25.

"The result in *Tryon* appears dubious unless a distinction is to be drawn between the situation where the purchaser desires to acquire the assets of the corporation and where he desires to acquire all the stock (as in *Tryon*) or a controlling interest (as in *Feldmann* [98]) with a view to controlling the underlying assets. Further, even if the court had been willing to frown on defendant's course of action, the corporate asset theory would not have furnished an appropriate basis for a recovery and again would have revealed itself as only a half truth. Only the selling shareholders had been injured; they, however, would not have benefited by a corporate recovery if the court had accorded them standing to maintain the action." It would seem that such causes of action are more naturally those of the shareholders than of the corporation; that the seller of control, especially when he is a director or officer, has a fiduciary duty to the shareholders as such in the matter of shareholder-control, and that the court in *Perlman* v. *Feldmann* [99] was correct, from a practical standpoint, in giving personal recovery in a derivative action which, from the technically accurate legal standpoint, requires a judgment for the corporation.

In a now famous case,[1] it was alleged that after the purchase of the majority of two classes of common stock, control was exercised by puppet directors acting for the purchaser to call for redemption one class of common shares for the purpose of dissolving the company to realize upon an asset carried on the books of the company at $6 1/3 million which, unknown to the minority shareholders, had attained a value of about $20 million. Redemption was alleged to have been made at $80.80 per share, whereas if the outside shareholders had been permitted to participate in the dissolution they would have obtained $240 per share. The trial court dismissed the petition for not stating a cause of action. The court of appeals reversed, holding that if the directors, as they were charged, acted as puppets of the majority shareholder, not using an impartial judgment in calling the shares for redemption, they had breached their fiduciary duty to the minority shareholders thus making the call for redemption voidable in equity. As the court pointed out, there was no reason for the redemption followed promptly by liquidation of the company except to enable one class of shares to profit at the expense of another. The action was a class action, not a derivative one, in which there was a prayer that those who had not sur-

98. Perlman v. Feldmann, supra, note 92.

99. Supra, note 92. See also Porter v. Healy, 244 Pa. 427, 91 A. 428 (1914), where plaintiffs who had parted with their shares were held proper parties to sue. Since they were not then shareholders, they could not have sued derivatively.

1. Zahn v. Transamerica Corporation, 162 F.2d 36, 172 A.L.R. 495 (3d Cir., 1947).

rendered their stock be paid the liquidation value, and that those who had surrendered it for $80.80 per share be paid the difference between that amount and the liquidation value of $240 per share.

Until recently under the federal income tax provisions, the sale of control in a corporation with substantial operating loss carry-overs, with some property whose value had diminished below cost, and with perhaps other attributes which, upon merger with another corporation, would result in tax benefits, offered subtle opportunities for profit.[2] With the increasing sensitiveness of courts to the profit-making possibilities of trading in control, and to the ever present danger of majority action whenever this profit-making opportunity presents itself, one may predict a closer scrutiny in any case where control is sold, whether through a sale of a majority or controlling interest by directors or officers, or simply by shareholders occupying no office in their companies, or whether, as a part of the contract, board members resign and appoint or elect the purchasers' nominees in their places. As Professor Jennings concludes:[3] "It is to be hoped that either now or eventually the courts will give legal recognition to the widespread belief in the business community that a sale of control shares should be accompanied by a general offer, and thus reject the philosophy that, in this situation, the right to a special profit is simply a perquisite of control."

A number of cases have arisen where majority shareholders have induced the minority to sell their shares to a purchaser without disclosing that they were receiving from the purchaser a higher price than that quoted to the minority, or by the disclosure of a fictitious offer. In such cases a cause of action may exist based upon misrepresentation or the failure to disclose facts which, under the circumstances, ought to have been disclosed.[4] Many of these cases have involved majority shareholders who were also directors and/or officers, and the courts have stressed the fiduciary obligation owed by directors and officers to their companies as the ground, or one ground, for imposing liability. Thus the sale has been considered one which, fundamentally, was a sale of a corporate asset, the profits from which should be shared by all.[5]

2. See hypothetical case along these lines and discussion of the possibilities in Jennings, op. cit. supra, note 91, at 29–31. But see Hill, The Sale of Controlling Shares, 70 Harv.L.Rev. 986, at 1007 (1957). The use of the device of the purchase of a loss corporation has been considerably restricted by I. R.C.1954 (26 U.S.C.A.) § 382.

3. Op. cit. supra, note 91, at 39.

4. Sautter v. Fulmer, 258 N.Y. 107, 179 N.E. 310 (1932), reargument denied 259 N.Y. 508, 182 N.E. 157 (1932); Mayflower Hotel Stockholders Protective Committee v. Mayflower Hotel Corporation, 173 F.2d 416 (D.C.Cir., 1949), second appeal, 193 F.2d 666 (D.C.Cir., 1951).

5. Dunnett v. Arn, 71 F.2d 912 (10th Cir., 1934); American Trust Co. v. California Western States Life

Unless a corporation has indicated that it is in the market to purchase its obligations, such as bonds and notes, directors and officers may purchase obligations of a solvent corporation at whatever discount they are selling and enforce payment at their face value plus interest, or profit on a resale of these securities.[6] Under such circumstances, there is no fiduciary obligation to anyone to share in any profit made. When the corporation is insolvent, but still a going concern, directors and officers, by purchasing corporate obligations, may be able to stave off impatient creditors who threaten to file petitions in bankruptcy or to ask for a receivership, by purchasing such obligations. In fact, the corporation may be saved from bankruptcy or receivership through purchases by those most likely to have a vital interest in saving the corporation, that is, the directors and officers; and if the officers succeed, creditors may be able to collect the full amount of their claims. But if they fail and the corporation is unable to pay the full amount of its debts, should directors and officers who have purchased corporate claims at a discount be barred from competing with the creditors, and if the obligations are such as to be secured on the corporate property, should such purchasers be excluded as secured creditors? Such officials have been allowed to compete when their purchases have been made in good faith. Even in the bankruptcy court, claims of corporate officials arising out of transactions such as these have been enforced when good faith and fairness were found.[7] By purchasing corporate obligations when there is insolvency, there is danger, because of the conflict of interests inconsistent with the directors' role of fiduciary to the creditors of the corporation. It has been argued that a director would be tempted "to postpone the adjustments of claims or the institution of proceedings for relief when such action would serve the interests of the corporation and its creditors, in order to continue his own purchase of corporate obligations at a market price lower than the valuation which he has made with the benefit of inside in-

Ins. Co., 15 Cal.2d 42, 98 P.2d 497 (1940).

6. Seymour v. Spring Forest Cemetery Ass'n, 144 N.Y. 333, 39 N.E. 365, 26 L.R.A. 859 (1895). The early rule was contra: Ballantine, Corporations 209 (Rev.ed.1946).

7. Manufacturers Trust Co. v. Becker, 338 U.S. 304, 70 S.Ct. 127, 94 L.Ed. 107 (1949), and cases there cited. Purchases of corporate debentures of a face value of $147,-300 were acquired for approximately $10,000. Claimants were allowed to compete with other debenture holders and received, as their share of the corporate assets in the bankruptcy court, approximately $64,250. Justices Burton and Black dissented, Justice Douglas taking no part in the case. For notes on the case, see: 19 Ford.L. Rev. 220 (1950); 25 Ind.L.J. 208 (1950); 18 Geo.Wash.L.Rev. 492 (1950); 62 Harv.L.Rev. 1391 (1950); 4 Miami L.Q. 386 (1950); 48 Mich. L.Rev. 1194 (1950); 23 So.Calif. L.Rev. 392 (1950); 1 Syracuse L.Rev. 509; 17 U. of Chi.L.Rev. 675 (1950); 98 U. of Pa.L.Rev. 751 (1950).

formation." [8]   But the majority of the court felt that in the case of a "technically insolvent" but nevertheless "going concern" the possible conflict, without more, was not sufficient to bar the purchasers from competing with outside security holders on an equal basis.

Where the line should be drawn in the purchase-of-obligation cases has not been definitely determined. But the conflict of interests becomes more intense as the corporation becomes less of a going concern. The lower federal courts have held that the director may not purchase after judicial proceedings for the relief of a debtor are expected or have begun.[9]

§ 14.   Additional Aid to Security Holders Where Insiders Profit from Purchases or Sales of Securities but Violate § 10 (b) and Rule X–10B–5, Securities Exchange Act of 1934

This section with the rule adopted by the Commission (now Rule 10b–5 or, as it appears in the Code of Federal Regulations, § 240.10b–5) makes it unlawful for any person, directly or indirectly, to use the means or instrumentalities of interstate commerce, the mails or the facilities of national securities exchanges to employ any device, scheme, or artifice to defraud, to make any untrue statement of a material fact or omit statements of material facts which make misleading other statements made, or to engage in any act, practice, or course of business which operates or would operate as a fraud or deceit upon any person, in connection with the purchase or sale of any security. § 10(b) applies to securities whether or not registered on any exchange, its terms being specific on this.[10]   And it is significant that the word "security" was used instead of "equity security" which latter term is defined, in part, as "any stock or similar security; or any security convertible, with or without consideration, into such a security." [11]

§ 10(b), in part, with its complementary Rule 10b–5, has practically codified the "special facts" doctrine of *Strong* v. *Re-*

8. Ibid. where the S.E.C. as amicus curiae so argued. See 338 U.S. at 312, 70 S.Ct. at 132.

9. Monroe v. Scofield, 135 F.2d 725 (10th Cir., 1943); In re Los Angeles Lumber Products Co., 46 F. Supp. 77 (D.Cal.1941). The lower court opinion in the Manufacturers Trust Co. case, supra, note 7, sub. nom, In re Calton Crescent, Inc., Manufacturers Trust Co. v. Becker, 173 F.2d 944, at 951, 13 A.L.R. 2d 1161 (2d Cir., 1949), states: "Although the debtor had long been insolvent in the bankruptcy sense, it does not appear that the bankruptcy proceedings were at any time contemplated before the filing of the arrangement petition in May 1946. Prior to that time the appellees acquired debentures from owners who were willing to sell and were not overreached."

10. 15 U.S.C.A. § 78j(b); Robinson v. Difford, 92 F.Supp. 145 (D.Pa. 1950).

11. § 3(a) (11), Securities Exchange Act of 1934; 15 U.S.C.A. § 78c(a) (11). This subsection contains more than has been quoted.

pide [12] discussed in the preceding section. In a case where the majority shareholder had secret plans to dissolve the company in order to capture for itself a large portion of the increased value of a tobacco inventory, the failure to disclose the company's increased earnings and the increased value of the inventory was held to be a violation of all three subsections of Rule 10b–5 warranting a class suit by former shareholders who had accepted the offer of the defendant in reliance upon the company's annual report and its accompanying letter which, it was alleged, the defendant had caused to be mailed to the company's shareholders. The accompanying letter showed a decline in sales and net income and the inventory was carried at much less than its actual value with no narrative of its actual value. The court sustained the count based upon a common law action for fraud and deceit and also the counts based upon Rule 10b–5, stating with reference to the latter: "The rule is clear. It is unlawful for an insider, such as a majority stockholder, to purchase the stock of minority stockholders without disclosing material facts affecting the value of the stock, known to the majority stockholder by virtue of his inside position but not known to the selling minority stockholders, which information would have affected the judgment of the sellers. The duty of disclosure stems from the necessity of preventing a corporate insider from utilizing his position to take unfair advantage of the uninformed minority stockholders. It is an attempt to provide some degree of equalization of bargaining position in order that the minority may exercise an informed judgment in any such transaction. Some of the courts have called this a fiduciary duty while others state it is a duty imposed by the 'special circumstances.' One of the primary purposes of the Securities Exchange Act of 1934, 15 U.S.C.A. § 78a et seq., was to outlaw the use of inside information by corporate officers and principal stockholders for their own financial advantage to the detriment of uninformed public security holders." [13] And as the court later stated, " . . . under the unambiguous provisions of the Act it covers the sale or purchase of a security on a doorstep as well as the trading of a professional securities broker." [14]

---

12. See discussion of doctrine at pp. 264–265, supra.

13. Leahy, Dist. J., in Speed v. Transamerica Corp., 99 F.Supp. 808, at 828–829 (D.Del.1951). And see Kardon v. National Gypsum Corp., 73 F.Supp. 798 (D.Pa.1947). Compare the factual situation of Kardon with that of Sher v. Sandler, 325 Mass. 348, 90 N.E.2d 536 (1950).

14. Speed v. Transamerica Corp., supra, note 13, at 830. But see Stephens, Cir. J., in Fratt v. Robinson, 203 F.2d 627, at 630–631 (9th Cir., 1953). See Note, The Prospects for Rule X–10B–5; An Emerging Remedy for Defrauded Investors, 59 Yale L.J. 1120, 1149 (1950); Note, Application of SEC Rule X–10B–5 to Prevent Non-Disclosure in the Sale of Corporate Securities, 39 Calif.L.Rev. 429

The fraud anticipated by § 10(b) and Rule 10b–5 is that which is perpetrated upon a buyer or seller of securities rather than that involving mismanagement of the corporation.[15]

There is considerable flexibility in bringing civil actions to enforce liabilities or duties created by the Act or the rules and regulations promulgated under it. § 27 of the Act provides that actions may be brought in any district where the act or transaction occurred, or where the defendant is found or is an inhabitant or transacts business, "and process in such cases may be served in any other district of which the defendant is an inhabitant or wherever the defendant may be found." By this section the federal courts are given "exclusive jurisdiction" in cases arising under the Act or under the rules and regulations thereof.[16] This wide choice of venue is desirable and important in order not to handicap the security holder in his enforcement of this and other sections of the Act.

§ 15. Corporate Recovery of Profits made by Insiders on "Short-Swing" Purchases and Sales or Sales and Purchases under the Securities Exchange Act of 1934

Other protection is given against the possible use of inside information under § 16 of the Act. Under § 16(a), every person who is directly or indirectly the beneficial owner of more than ten percent of an equity security which is not exempted and which is registered on a national securities exchange, or one who is a director or an officer of the issuer, must file, at the time of the registration of the security or within ten days after he has become the beneficial owner of it, or has become a director, or officer, a statement with the exchange (with a duplicate original to the Commission) of his holdings and must report periodically, as required, any changes in his holdings. Since these records are public ones, the publicity which is likely to be given to a change in holdings of any size informs the public shareholders of what their officers and major shareholders are doing with their corporate stock.[17]

(1951); Loss, Securities Regulation 827–844 (1951).

15. Augustus N. Hand, Cir. J., in Birnbaum v. Newport Steel Corp., 193 F.2d 461, at 462–463 (2d Cir., 1952), stated: "The district court . . . viewed the Rule [X–10B–5] in question as aimed only at 'a fraud perpetrated upon the purchaser or seller' of securities and as having no relation to breaches of fiduciary duty by corporate insiders resulting in fraud upon those who were not purchasers or sellers. We are in accord with the district court's interpretation of the Rule."

16. See American Distilling Co. v. Brown, 295 N.Y. 36, 64 N.E.2d 347 (1945), where the court held that suit under § 16(b) of the Act could not be maintained in state courts because § 16(b) must be read with § 27, the jurisdiction and venue section.

17. For an example of what can happen, see Jefferson Lake Sulphur

§ 16(b) gives a corporate cause of action, and if not taken advantage of by the corporation within the period stated, or if not diligently prosecuted, it gives a right to any security owner on behalf of the issuer to recover any profit made by a director, officer or better-than-ten-percent beneficial owner on a purchase and sale or sale and purchase of any equity security which is not exempt, provided these transactions have occurred within less than six months of each other, unless such security was acquired in good faith in connection with a debt previously contracted. The section specifically states that these remedies are given to prevent the unfair use of inside information and that they are given irrespective of any intent the insiders may have had not to make short-swing deals. "Suit to recover such profit may be instituted at law or in equity in any court of competent jurisdiction by the issuer, or by the owner of any security of the issuer in the name and in behalf of the issuer if the issuer shall fail or refuse to bring such suit within sixty days after request or shall fail diligently to prosecute the same thereafter; but no such suit shall be brought more than two years after the date such profit was realized."

§ 16(b) is based upon the theory that short-swing trading by insiders would be discontinued if all possibility of profit were removed by permitting corporate recovery of such profits no matter whether an insider intended to hold his shares for longer than six months after purchase or remain out of the market for longer than that period after a sale, or whether or not he actually had inside information upon which his sale or purchase was made. Subsection (b) has some of the elements of a shareholder's derivative suit for damages based upon a breach of fiduciary duty, some aspects of a punitive damage action, and some of an informer's statute.[18] But an action to recover profits made in violation of § 16(b) differs from an ordinary derivative action, for any security holder may bring it—not simply a shareholder—and, since the action is based upon a federal statute, jurisdiction is in the federal courts on this basis and not upon the diversity of citizenship of the parties, and consequently Rule 23(b) of the Federal Rules of Civil Procedure does not apply.[19]   Congres-

Co. v. Walet, 104 F.Supp. 20, at 22 (D.La.1952): "The transactions . . . were duly reported to the Commission in accordance with the requirement of Section 16(a) of the Act. Whereupon the company was advised by the Commission of the possible liability of the defendant to it under Section 16(b) as a result of his trading activities. This suit (to recover short-swing profits) followed   .   .   .." This case

was aff'd, 202 F.2d 433 (5th Cir., 1953), cert. den. 346 U.S. 820, 74 S.Ct. 35, 98 L.Ed. 346 (1953).

18. Cook and Feldman, Insider Trading Under the Securities Exchange Act, 66 Harv.L.Rev. 385, at 408; 612 (1953).

19. Benisch v. Cameron, 81 F.Supp. 882 (D.N.Y.1948); Dottenheim v. Murchison, 227 F.2d 737 (5th Cir., 1956), cert. denied 351 U.S. 919, 76

sional intent is further shown, from the reasons set forth in § 2 and in the preamble to § 16(b), to have been to make the general public the ultimate beneficiary of the statutory policy and not to permit procedural restrictions to hamper such policy. The insider not only has to make periodic reports of his change in position in shareholding but, if proxies are solicited, directors and officers must state their indebtedness to their company and short-swing profits must be stated as such.[20]

It has been pointed out that " . . . although common law liability does not usually extend to transactions on an exchange, Section 16(b) is applicable to such transactions even though the sales may be made to persons not previously shareholders." [21] The sixty-day period, in the portion of the statute quoted above, has been held to be for the benefit of the corporation and not the profiting insider who may not raise the question when a security holder has brought the action before that period has passed. This, of course, is important when the statute of limitations is about to run and the corporation has not acted.[22]

The Act defines "buy" and "purchase" to "include any contract to buy, purchase, or otherwise acquire." [23] And the terms "sale" and "sell" include "any contract to sell or otherwise dispose of." [24] The last clauses of these definitions are broad enough to include all kinds of acquisitions or disposals but the intent of the Congress was definitely aimed at transactions in which an insider might profit by the use of confidential information to the possible detriment of other shareholders and the corporation. Thus, it has been held that a bona fide gift, whether charitable or private, does not come within the intended prohibition, and that neither the donor, nor the donee who disposes of the gift within the six-month period, comes within the bounds of the defini-

S.Ct. 712, 100 L.Ed. 1451 (1956). Kogan v. Schulte, 61 F.Supp. 604 (D.N.Y.1945). Rule 23(b) reads: "In an action brought to enforce a secondary right on the part of one or more shareholders in an association, incorporated or unincorporated, because the association refuses to enforce rights which may properly be asserted by it, the complaint shall be verified by oath and shall aver (1) that the plaintiff was a shareholder at the time of the transaction of which he complains or that his share thereafter devolved on him by operation of law and (2) that the action is not a collusive one to confer on a court of the United States jurisdiction of any action of which it would not otherwise have jurisdiction. The complaint shall also set forth with particularity the efforts of the plaintiff to secure from the managing directors or trustees and, if necessary, from the shareholders such action as he desires, and the reasons for his failure to obtain such action or the reasons for not making such effort."

20. Cook and Feldman, op. cit. supra, note 18, at 410.

21. Ibid. at 409–410.

22. Benisch v. Cameron, supra, note 19; Grossman v. Young, 72 F.Supp. 375 (D.N.Y.1948).

23. § 3(a) (13), 15 U.S.C.A. § 78c(a) (13).

24. § 3(a) (14), 15 U.S.C.A. § 78c(a) (14).

tions.[25] Nor does the devisor or devisee of shares come within the policy behind § 16(b).[26] And " 'Purchase' is not an apt word to describe the receipt by a stockholder of shares representing a stock dividend or of warrants representing his preemptive right to subscribe for new shares." [27] Hence, a sale of these within six months by an insider is not within § 16(b).[28] But shares acquired by the exercise of such warrants representing preemptive rights is a "purchase," and a sale of such shares within the six months period by an insider which results in a profit comes within the forbidden area of the section. Likewise, it has been held that the voluntary conversion of preferred stock into common, under an option thus to convert, is an initial "purchase" and that any profit made upon a sale of the common thus acquired on the short-swing is recoverable by the corporation.[29] In the case cited, the profit was figured as the difference between the selling price of the block of common acquired on conversion and

25. Shaw v. Dreyfus, 172 F.2d 140 (2d Cir., 1949), cert. den. 337 U.S. 907, 69 S.Ct. 1048, 93 L.Ed. 1719 (1949), with strong dissent by Clark, Cir. J., who stated at 143: "If these transactions are without the scope of the Act, we have an area of considerable inducement to the insider to play for the short swing." Truncale v. Blumberg, 80 F.Supp. 387 (D.N.Y.1948) (All "acquisitions" are not "purchases" and all "disposals" not "sales." A gift "is the very antithesis of a sale; and there is no reason to suppose that the Congress intended the statute to apply to gifts." Medina, Dist. J., at 391); id. v. id., 83 F. Supp. 628 (D.N.Y.1949) (Sale by donee within 6 months of date of gift is not within the prohibition. "Such liability should not be imposed unless it appeared that the donee was, in effect, the alter-ego of the donor and that the sale was really made by the latter." Rifkind, Dist. J., thus accepted Judge Medina's statement in the first Truncale case in note.) In Truncale v. Blumberg, 88 F.Supp. 677 (D.N.Y.1950), aff'd sub nom. Truncale v. Scully, 182 F.2d 1021 (2d Cir., 1950), the director who made the gifts above sold warrants within six months of their issue for less than their market price at date of issue. See p. 281 of text, infra. This exception (of gifts) is recognized in Rule 16a–9(a) (1) and (2) (C.F.R. § 240.16a–9(a) (1) and

(2)) where a limit is put upon the amount of gifts that may be so made. See also Rule 16a–10.

26. Judge Medina in the first Truncale case in note 25, supra, at 390. A good discussion of the meaning of "sale" and "purchase" is contained at 389–391 of this opinion.

27. Shaw v. Dreyfus, supra, note 25, at 142.

28. Ibid.

29. Park & Tilford, Inc. v. Schulte, 160 F.2d 984 (2d Cir., 1947), cert. den. 332 U.S. 761, 68 S.Ct. 64, 92 L.Ed. 347 (1947). Swan, Cir. J., on petition for rehearing, dissented on the matter of how the profit should be figured. He contended that it should be the difference between the market value of the common at the time of conversion and its selling price at the date of sale. It happened that the market price of the preferred on the day of conversion was $364,871 but the common shares acquired through the conversion had a market value of $480,853.75. The price acquired for the common on the short-swing was $782,999.59. See Smolowe v. Delendo Corp., 136 F.2d 231, 148 A.L.R. 300 (2d Cir., 1943), on the method of computing "any profit realized" on a § 16(b) transaction. Also, Loss, Securities Regulation 570 (1951); and see pp. 281–282, this text, infra.

the market value of the preferred on the date of its conversion into common.

"Similarly receipt of stock in a parent corporation in exchange for stock in a subsidiary pursuant to a plan of corporate simplification has been held a 'purchase' where the insider had an option to dissent from the plan and receive cash instead." [30] And receipt of stock purchase warrants by an officer under his contract of employment has been held to be a "purchase," [31] though it would seem that the problem is somewhat complicated by the fact that the warrants may not, by agreement, be exercisable until a later time, in which case it is reasonably arguable that the "purchase" does not take place until the warrants are exercisable. And, more recently, the court "found a 'sale' in an exchange of stock of the issuer for stock of a holding company where substantial quantities of the stock received were publicly held and had an established market, despite the fact that the insider's control of and proportional interest in the issuer remained unchanged." [32] On the other hand, the same case also held that an identical exchange was not a "sale" when there was no public ownership and no established market for the stock received. In the most recent important case further pinpointing the area covered by "purchase" and "sale" [33] a reclassification of shares where all shareholders participated on the same basis, there being no discrimination between shareholders or classes of shareholders, and where there was no pre-existing market value for the securities received, was held not to be a "purchase" under § 16(b). Such a reclassification, felt the court, could not possibly

---

30. Clark, Cir. J., in Roberts v. Eaton, 212 F.2d 82, at 83–84 (2d Cir., 1954), citing and approving Blau v. Hodgkinson, 100 F.Supp. 361 (D.N.Y.1951).

31. Ibid., in reviewing the previous cases; and Cook and Feldman, op. cit. supra, note 18, at 621, citing Blau v. Hodgkinson, supra, note 30. These authors conclude (at page 618) that the cases are not clear whether the "purchase" is on the accrual date of the option which, if the right to exercise the option accrues on the date of issue, is immediately; but otherwise if the option is not exercisable until a later date. It might be asked whether a warrant which is not exercisable until later has any present value in the hands of the owner. Compare MacDonald v. C. I. R., 230 F.2d 534 (7th Cir., 1956), where, for income tax purposes, it was held that a restriction on the taxpayer's right to sell his shares for the time agreed upon had an important relation to what economic gain the taxpayer realized upon the purchase of the shares. The court rejected the Commissioner's contention that the gain was the difference between the fair market value of the shares when purchased and the price paid under the option. The case was sent back to the tax court with the statement that "Whether there is some other formula by which such gain can be ascertained, either in 1949 or some other year, we are not called upon to decide." (Page 541.)

32. Blau v. Mission Corp., 212 F.2d 77 (2d Cir., 1954), cert. den. 347 U. S. 1016, 74 S.Ct. 872, 98 L.Ed. 728 (1954). The quoted words are Judge Clark's in Roberts v. Eaton, supra, note 30, at 84.

33. Roberts v. Eaton, supra, note 30.

lend itself to the speculation anticipated by § 16(b). Professor Jennings who comments on *Roberts* v. *Eaton* [34] states: " . . . [T]he Court raises a doubt as to whether all compulsory exchanges incident to reclassifications, mergers and consolidations will be exempt, even though the volitional element (usually regarded as a technical requirement of a sale) be absent. The SEC has issued rules exempting certain of these transactions (Rule X–16B–7), but the precise scope of these rules is by no means clear." But the court recognized that "the lines to be drawn" to effectuate the statutory command to curb insider short-swing speculation were becoming "increasingly fine," and that there may be differences of opinion as to what transactions offer insiders the opportunity to so speculate, as there was over the charitable and private gift cases.

It has been unsuccessfully argued that by granting as compensation an option to purchase stock the corporation estops itself from recovering short-swing profits gained from using the options to purchase. It was held that there could be no waiver of this statutory right by the corporation even if there was shown an intent that the options were to be used for short-swing purposes. [35]

Where there is a market value of options on the date of their receipt (or upon the date of their accrual so that they may be exercised, if this view be taken), the cost basis of the option is established by it. But where there is no market value, this complication "has been resolved by simply taking as the value of the option the difference between the exercise price and the market value of the stock underlying the option." [36] Where a director resold warrants issued to him under a contract of employment within six months of their receipt by him, at a price less than their market value when issued to him, it was held that there was no profit to recover. The plaintiff had argued that "profit is the excess of selling price over cost and that here cost was zero." But the court pointed out that, under the defendant's contract, warrants were issued annually and that, according to the plaintiff's argument, no matter when the defendant exercised them he would always be within six months of the past previous receipt or of the next succeeding one and consequently would thus forfeit the whole of the selling price. The court accepted the rule which Clark, Cir.

34. P-H Students' Corporation Law Service Par. 25,131, at page 25,405.

35. Jefferson Lake Sulphur Co. v. Walet, 104 F.Supp. 20 (D.La.1952), aff'd Walet v. Jefferson Lake Sulphur Co., 202 F.2d 433 (5th Cir., 1953), cert. den. 346 U.S. 820, 74 S.

Ct. 35, 98 L.Ed. 346 (1953). It was also unsuccessfully contended that treasury stock is not an equity security but the court held it qualified as "stock or similar security."

36. Cook and Feldman, op. cit. supra, note 18, at 621.

J., had suggested in his dissenting opinion in *Shaw* v. *Dreyfus*,[37] in these words: "It seems to me but the ordinary task of valuing the security at its fair market price at the crucial dates of its acquisition and disposition."[38]

When several purchases and sales or sales and purchases at different prices occur during one six-months' period, or perhaps over a greater period where there is no interval of at least six months between transactions, a question of how to determine the "profit realized" arises. In the first case in which this question was raised the defendant argued alternatively that the profit realized should be figured on a first-in, first-out basis, or on an average cost basis. The court rejected both contentions and determined the profit realized by matching the lowest purchases against the highest sales within six months.[39] Otherwise the short-swing speculative possibility would be a temptation likely to be taken advantage of. Hence, "The lowest purchase was subtracted from the highest sale within six months, then the next lowest purchase subtracted from the next highest sale, and so on until all of the shares purchased or all of the shares sold, whichever was less, had been included in the computation. All the differences in the subtractions were then totalled, and the resulting sum was considered the 'profit realized.'"[40]

§ 16(d) excepts arbitrage transactions, whether foreign or domestic, unless contrary to rules and regulations which the Commission may legitimately set up, from the profit-recovery possibilities of § 16(b), although the Act does not define the term "arbitrage." In *Falco* v. *Donner Foundation, Inc.*[41] a more than ten percent owner of the corporation's preferred stock simultane-

37. 172 F.2d 140, at 143 (2d Cir., 1949), cert. den. 337 U.S. 907, 69 S.Ct. 1048, 93 L.Ed. 1719 (1949).

38. Truncale v. Blumberg, 88 F. Supp. 677, at 678 (D.N.Y.1950), aff'd 182 F.2d 1021 (2d Cir., 1950), noted in 62 Harv.L.Rev. 706 (1949). Medina, Dist. J., in Steinberg v. Sharpe, 95 F.Supp. 32 (D.N.Y.1950), aff'd, without opinion, 190 F.2d 82 (2d Cir., 1951), applied the same rule where warrants were issued periodically, namely, "lowest price in, highest price out." But see SEC Rule 16b–6, which was not applicable in the Steinberg case, but which exempts, under the conditions there stated, long term profits incident to sales within six months of the exercise of an option.

39. Smolowe v. Delendo Corp., 136 F.2d 231, 148 A.L.R. 300 (2d Cir.,

1943), cert. den. 320 U.S. 751, 64 S.Ct. 56, 88 L.Ed. 446 (1943). Accord: Gratz v. Claughton, 187 F. 2d 46 (2d Cir., 1951), cert. den. 341 U.S. 920, 71 S.Ct. 741, 95 L.Ed. 1353 (1951). In the Gratz case, Learned Hand, Ch. J., at page 52, stated: "It is true that this means that no director, officer or 'beneficial owner' may safely buy and sell, or sell and buy, shares of stock in the company except at intervals of six months."

40. Cook and Feldman, Insider Trading Under the Securities Exchange Act, 66 Harv.L.Rev. 385; 612, at 612 (1953).

41. 208 F.2d 600, 40 A.L.R.2d 1340 (2d Cir., 1953), noted in 67 Harv.L. Rev. 1277 (1954).

ously sold his shares with dividend attached and purchased shares of the same class ex-dividend in order to avoid the payment to him of a large arrearage dividend which would have to be reported as income for federal tax purposes. By doing this the selling price of the shares with dividend exceeded by a small amount the price of the shares ex-dividend, plus the value of the dividend. The court held that the "simultaneous matched purchase and sale of identical or equivalent securities is arbitrage within the meaning of § 16(d) and hence removed from the thrust of § 16(b)." [42]

As to what officers are insiders under the Act, the Commission has defined "officer" as meaning "a president, vice-president, treasurer, secretary, comptroller, and any other person who performs for an issuer, whether incorporated or unincorporated, functions corresponding to those performed by the foregoing officers." [43] In *Lockheed Aircraft Corporation* v. *Rathman*,[44] an "assistant treasurer" was included in a stock option plan which excluded the president, vice-president, treasurer, secretary and comptroller because it was thought that these officers were within § 16(b) and could not take advantage of a short-swing sale intended for the assistant treasurer and others. The assistant treasurer in this case did not have the functions of the treasurer, that is, the functions did not correspond to those performed by the treasurer. And the court held that the term "other person" did not relate to an employee who assists one of the named officers or performs the functions of named officers during their absence, but related to an officer, no matter what his title, "the functions of whose office correspond to those performed by one of the enumerated officers." [45] There is thus a loophole of considerable size through which officers close enough to the enumerated officers to acquire much inside information useful for short-swing transactions may safely operate.[46]

---

42. Ibid. at 604. At 603 the court discusses generally the meaning of "arbitrage."

43. SEC Rule 3b–2.

44. 106 F.Supp. 810 (D.Cal.1952). And see companion case of Lockheed Aircraft Corp. v. Campbell, 110 F.Supp. 282 (D.Cal.1953). Reliance upon SEC Rule X–16B–3 was held a defense against recovery of profits in Greene v. Dietz, 247 F.2d 689 (2d Cir., 1957).

45. Ibid. at 813.

46. Compare Frank, Cir. J., in Colby v. Klune, 178 F.2d 872, at 873, where he states: "It (the word "officer") includes, inter alia, a corporate employee performing important executive duties of such character that he would be likely, in discharging these duties, to obtain confidential information about the company's affairs that would aid him if he engaged in personal market transactions," the label of his office being immaterial. And see Cook and Feldman, op. cit. supra, note 40, at 397 and 407. In the companion case of Lockheed Aircraft Corp. v. Campbell, 110 F. Supp. 282 (D.Cal.1953), the defendant was an assistant treasurer *and* an assistant secretary, and had also the title of "Manager of the Finance Department." The court concluded that whether the sub-

The rules promulgated by the Commission having reference particularly to § 16(a) and (b) are important but lack of space does not permit their discussion. What constitutes ownership of more than 10 percent of an equity security [47] and the exemptions from operation of this section are of particular interest.[48]

jective test as laid down by Judge Frank or the objective one of the regulation were applied, the defendant was not an "officer" within either meaning. Some of the chief functions of the treasurer were to make financial forecasts, to determine what the company's cash position would be in the future, what need there might be for money, and to forecast the anticipated profit and loss. These functions were not those of the defendant.

47. Rule 16a–2. "The total amount of the issue, including unregistered securities and treasury shares, is used as the basis of the ten per cent calculation." Cook and Feld-man, op. cit. supra, note 40, at 401. See Stella v. Graham-Paige Motors Corp., 232 F.2d 299 (2d Cir., 1956), cert. denied, 352 U.S. 831, 77 S.Ct. 46, 1 L.Ed.2d 52 (1956), and Note, Purchase of Stock by Which Shareholder Becomes a 10% Beneficial Owner is Covered by § 16(b), 70 Harv.L.Rev. 1312 (1957).

48. Rules 16a–4, –5, –6, –9, –10; 16b–1, –2, –3, –4, –5, –6, and –7. And see generally, Ann. 40 A.L.R. 2d 1346 (1955), "Securities Exchange Act provisions regarding liability of directors, officers, and principal stockholders for profits on short-swing speculation in corporation's stock."

Chapter 7

POSTINCORPORATION MANAGEMENT: SHAREHOLDERS' AMBIT OF ACTION

---

§ 1. In General

While the board of directors has the general authority to carry on the business of the corporation and to initiate its policies, with wide discretion as to the means to be employed, the shareholders who are the real owners have, through their voice in choosing the board, a weapon of control which can be effective if strategically used. Since, in most states, both non-voting and voting stock may be created legal counsel has the means to assure effective control from the beginning and, with wise drafting of the stock provisions and of supplementary agreements, if these seem necessary, a limited perpetuity of control can be guaranteed to the parties who are most interested in the new corporation.

Modern statutes have codified rather large areas which the common law had ruled belonged to the shareholders or, in some cases, did not exist at all without the aid of a statute, such as dissolution, merger, consolidation, sale of all or a large part of the corporate assets, and these areas belong only to the shareholders. Frequently, these statutes require board action recommending that the shareholders act upon the matter, but in the end it is shareholder action that counts. And in these major determinations such statutes usually require more than a majority vote, frequently setting up a two-thirds or larger vote approving the action. Wise draftsmen, again, will study these provisions carefully for many of them provide for the better-than-majority vote "unless the articles otherwise provide." And such provisions are the cue for solving a good many mean problems that may arise in the future if one fails to take advantage of them. In these large policy areas reserved for the shareholders provision is usually made for shareholders who do not agree with the required majority to dissent and demand the fair value of their shares, a thing which can embarrass a company not able to scrape up funds to pay the dissenters' appraisal value. Here, once more, is a chance for good draftsmanship for some statutes giving appraisal rights also include the proviso "unless otherwise provided in the articles." Since the articles constitute a contract between shareholders and corporation, even without the aid of a

285

statute many limitations and restrictions upon common law rights may, by contract, be reshaped to give greater flexibility and protection to majority shareholder action.

But the appraisal right is one protective device against major changes which the statutory majority may want to make. The minority shareholders may not wish to risk their capital after the change is made. Even if the statute permits the wiping out of this protection by a provision in the articles, this should be done only after careful study as to the probable necessity for such drastic action, and its probable effect on prospective shareholders.

Besides the control exercised through the voting franchise, and the protection it offers in the selection of board members and in the choice of major change, the shareholder obtains some further protection through his right to inspect the corporate books and records for legitimate purposes and, by virtue of another right, under limited circumstances, to bring a derivative action for certain types of corporate injury. And he has several devices which he can use in conjunction with other shareholders to secure a continuity of management through the exercise of voting control which such devices are able to secure. This chapter is devoted to these problems.

§ 2. Shareholders' Right to Inspect the Books and Records; Financial Reports

At common law, a shareholder has the right to inspect the corporate books and records for a legitimate purpose and he may send his accountant or lawyer to do the job for him. He is regarded as an owner and as such he seeks to inspect property held by his agents.[1] But, unless he owns all of the company's shares, there are other "owners" whose interests must be protected. Hence the requirement that his purpose be a legitimate one, for an unlimited right to inspect for any purpose would open wide avenues to abuse, for example to aid competitors or to supply a stock broker with a list of possible customers.[2]

The English common law did not compel the corporation to open its books and records to a shareholder on mere suspicion

1. William Coale Development Co. v. Kennedy, 121 Ohio St. 582, 170 N.E. 434 (1930). In Feick, Executrix v. Hill Bread Co., 91 N.J.L. 486, 103 A. 813 (Sup.Ct.1918), aff'd on opinion below in 92 N.J.L. 513, 105 A. 725 (Ct.Err. & App.1919), the owner of shares sent her accountant to represent her; in Crouse v. Rogers Park Apartments, Inc., 343 Ill.App. 319, 99 N.E.2d 404 (1951), the owner sent her lawyer.

2. Chas. A. Day & Co., Inc. v. Booth, 123 Me. 443, 123 A. 557, 43 A.L.R. 780 (1924); Capron v. Pacific Southwest Discount Corp., 6 Cal. App.2d 436, 44 P.2d 629 (1935). But a broker may inspect for a proper purpose, for example, to ascertain the condition of the company. Kemp v. Sloss-Sheffield Steel & Iron Co., 128 N.J.L. 322, 26 A.2d 70 (1940).

that the company was being mismanaged, but before mandamus would be granted required that there be some matter in dispute between the shareholder and his company.[3] But in the United States the shareholder has usually been given the right, enforceable by mandamus, to inspect the books and records of his corporation, at reasonable times, if he acts in good faith either to advance some corporate interest or to protect his own.[4] To inspect for possible or suspected mismanagement, to determine the corporation's financial condition, to ascertain whether dividends may be declared, to obtain a list of shareholders in order to solicit their proxies, to ascertain the value of his shares, to obtain information to aid in litigation or anticipated litigation with the corporation, its officers and directors, as to corporate acts which he hopes to attack, and other purposes aimed at protecting his corporation or his own rights and interests, are legitimate reasons for a shareholder to demand his right to inspect the books and records.[5] But hostile purposes such as seeking inspection to obtain information to use in a competing business, or to obtain a shareholders' list in order to seek their business (a shareholder-broker to sell shares, for example), or simply to embarrass the management are not legitimate reasons for demanding an inspection.[6] Where a shareholder is a member of a competing firm, courts have protected the corporation by withholding records containing trade secrets from inspection, by selecting neutral parties to inspect on behalf of the shareholder, and by supporting the

---

3.   Rex v. Master & Wardens of Merchant Tailors' Co., 2 B. & Ad. 115 (K.B.1831), which involved members in a non-stock corporation. For the present English rule see Companies Act of 1948, 11 & 12 Geo. 6, c. 38, Table A, § 125, which reads: "The directors shall from time to time determine whether and to what extent and at what times and places and under what conditions or regulations the accounts and books of the company or any of them shall be open to the inspection of members not being directors, and no member (not being a director) shall have any right of inspecting any account or book or document of the company except as conferred by statute or authorized by the directors or by the company in general meeting." But see also §§ 113, 146 and 158 of the Act itself, which sections provide for inspection of the register of members (shareholders), minutes of proceedings of general meetings, and the right to receive copies of balance sheets and auditor's reports, all three sections providing sanctions in case of violation.

4.   Albee v. Lamson & Hubbard Corp., 320 Mass. 421, 69 N.E.2d 811 (1946).

5.   See authorities cited in Ballantine, Lattin and Jennings, Cases and Materials on Corporations 397–398 (2d ed. 1953); Dodd and Baker, Cases and Materials on Corporations 674–676 (2d ed. 1951). As to whether inspection in furtherance of speculation in the corporation's stock is a legitimate reason, see Crouse v. Rogers Park Apartments, Inc., 343 Ill.App. 319, 99 N. E.2d 404 (1951). See Annotation, Shareholder's or officer's right to inspect books and records of corporation, 174 A.L.R. 262 (1948).

6.   Ballantine, Lattin and Jennings, op. cit. supra, note 5, at 398; Sawers v. American Phenolic Corp., 404 Ill. 440, 89 N.E.2d 374, 15 A.L. R.2d 1 (1949), and Annotation in 15 A.L.R.2d 1 (1951).

corporation when it requests an order protecting its trade secrets.[7]

The common law right to inspect includes all records relevant to show the true condition of the company and whether it is being mismanaged or not. Thus, in a recent case, the court granted the right to inspect not only the books of account and other standard records, but also the corporation's contracts and data with reference thereto, plus pertinent information concerning its assets and liabilities, its operations and practices.[8] Modern statutes usually state that the shareholders have the right to inspect named records such as books and records of account, minutes and records of shareholders' meetings, register or list of shareholders with addresses, voting trust agreements, if any, on file with the company.[9] A question arises whether the shareholder is entitled to go beyond the named list of records or whether the statute has limited him to the records named. The answer becomes important when the statute names a minimum of records, or where the statute permits inspection by a shareholder holding a stated percentage of the corporate shares. In a case interpreting a statute permitting a 10% shareholder to inspect the named records, it was held that the common law right was still available to any shareholder with a legitimate purpose of inspecting.[10] By analogy, it would seem that a shareholder would not be confined to the records stated in the statute but would retain his com-

---

7. Ballantine, Lattin and Jennings, op. cit. supra, note 5, at 398.

8. Kemp v. Sloss-Sheffield Steel & Iron Co., 128 N.J.L. 322, 26 A.2d 70 (1942).

9. Examples are Ohio Rev.Code (Gen.Corp.Law of 1955) § 1701.37 (C) (Written demand stating the specific purpose of inspection is required. Records mentioned are: articles, regulations (by-laws), books and records of account, minutes and records of shareholders, and voting trust agreements on file); West's Ann.Cal.Corp.Code § 3003 (Records mentioned are the share or duplicate share register, books of account, minutes of shareholders', board's and executive committee's meetings. Written demand by shareholder or holder of a voting trust certificate is necessary and it must be "for a purpose reasonably related to his interests as a shareholder or as a holder of such voting trust certificate"). Other important provisions are contained in this section.

10. Soreno Hotel Co. v. State, 107 Fla. 195, 144 So. 339 (1932). For present Florida statute, see Fla. Stat.Ann. § 608.39, as amended by L.1955, c. 29.886, § 13. But see Neiman v. Templeton, Kenly & Co., Ltd., 294 Ill.App. 45, 13 N.E.2d 290 (1938), for a contrary result, and criticism of the case in 5 U. of Chi.L.Rev. 684 (1938); 32 Ill.L. Rev. 988 (1938). In State ex rel. Cochran v. Penn-Beaver Oil Co., 34 Del. 81, 143 A. 257 (1926), it is stated: "Because the Legislature saw fit to expressly give stockholders the right to examine certain records of the company, it cannot be inferred that the stockholders' common law right to examine any other records, under proper conditions and for a proper purpose, was thereby taken away. The statute granting the power to examine the stock ledger at any time during business hours did not expressly, or by necessary implication, give the corporation the power to prevent examination of other pertinent records at proper times and under reasonable conditions."

mon law right to the rest unless the statute specifically stated as much.[11]   It seems like pretty poor policy for a statute to limit a shareholder beyond the common law requirements laid down for inspection of the records.   While there is a certain nuisance value to the exercise of the right to inspect, it would seem much better to sacrifice the inconvenience and keep intact one of the few protective devices which the owners possess.   Owners have a right to know whether their trustees are faithful to their trust and whether there has been mismanagement.

Due chiefly to the persistent refusal of corporate managers to permit the reasonable inspection of records when a shareholder made his demand, which refusal meant that the shareholder had to proceed by suit to compel management to permit an inspection, statutes for a while gave an absolute or almost absolute right of inspection to the shareholder.   Thus, under such statutes, it has been held that the writ of mandamus will issue as a matter of course, that the right of the shareholder is absolute and he cannot be met with the defense that his motives are improper, that the only requirement that must be met is that he qualifies by his ownership of stock.[12]   Some cases, however, while admitting that the right to inspect was absolute, held that the writ of mandamus was discretionary with the court and would not be issued to enforce the right except for a just cause and proper purpose.[13]   A common interpretation was that the statute put upon the corporation the burden of asserting and proving that the purpose of the shareholder was an improper one rather than requiring the shareholder, as at common law, to assert and prove a proper purpose.[14]   After holding that mere allegations of improp-

---

11. That this is the common law rule, see Holdsworth v. Goodall-Sanford, Inc., 143 Me. 56, 55 A.2d 130, 174 A.L.R. 257 (1947).

12. State ex rel. Dempsey v. Werra Aluminum Foundry Co., 173 Wis. 651, 182 N.W. 354, 22 A.L.R. 1 (1921) (But the court intimated that he might be prevented from using the information thus gained for an unlawful purpose); Pick v. Wesbar Stamping Corp., 238 Wis. 93, 298 N.W. 58 (1941); Johnson v. Langdon, 135 Cal. 624, 67 P. 1050, 87 Am.St.Rep. 156 (1902); Furst v. W. T. Rawleigh Medical Co., 282 Ill. 366, 118 N.E. 763 (1918). The statutes in these states now require a proper purpose for inspection.   See Wis.Bus.Corp.Law of 1951, § 180.43(2), as amended by L. 1953, c. 399, § 32; West's Ann.Cal. Corp.Code § 3003 (see note 9,

supra); Ill.Bus.Corp.Act of 1933, § 45, as amended by L.1947, p. 678.

13. Guthrie v. Harkness, 199 U.S. 148, 26 S.Ct. 4, 50 L.Ed. 130 (1905); State ex rel. Theile v. Cities Service Co., 31 Del. 514, 115 A. 773, 22 A.L.R. 8 (Sup.Ct.1922); Slay v. Polonia Publishing Co., 249 Mich. 609, 229 N.W. 434 (1930).

14. Dines v. Harris, 88 Colo. 22, 291 P. 1024 (1930); Slay v. Polonia Publishing Co., supra, note 13. Both involved competitor-shareholders who were looking for trade secrets to aid them in their competition.   And see Insuranshares Corp. of Delaware v. Kirchner, 40 Del. 105, 5 A.2d 519 (1939); Application of Joslyn, 191 Misc. 512, 78 N.Y.S.2d 183 (1948), aff'd 273 App.Div. 945, 78 N.Y.S.2d 923 (1948).

er motives or bad faith are not enough, one interpretive decision continued: [15] "Their independent investigations as stockholders should be encouraged, and the writ should go ordinarily as a matter of course; in fact it should generally not be necessary to invoke the office of such a writ at all. A complete investigation by stockholders or stockholders' committees would naturally lead to either praise or blame of the actions of corporate directors or employees. On the other hand, when petitioner entertains a destructive purpose, hostile to the interests of the corporation as a whole, or the interests of other stockholders, whose rights are as sacred as his own, certainly the writ in his favor ought to be denied. He is then a trespasser, even on ground which otherwise would be his own domain; he has made himself an avowed enemy to be repelled."

Recent statutes have tended to return to the common law concept with further restrictions, chiefly by requiring a certain period to pass before a shareholder is entitled to demand an inspection and/or by requiring the ownership or the holding of proxies of a named percentage of the corporate shares. The California statute also provides for an inspection of not only the records, but of the property and funds of a corporation, by a court-appointed inspector or inspectors where there has been a refusal of a lawful demand for inspection or upon petition of the holders of ten percent of the stock issued and outstanding.[16] This is somewhat comparable to the inspection which may be made under the English Companies Act by inspectors appointed by the Board of Trade,[17] an inspection first made possible by provisions in the Companies Act of 1908, later amended and repeated in the Act of 1929 and by amendment and extension in the Act of 1948.

The fact that a corporation gives its shareholders complete periodic reports concerning its progress and condition is usually held to be no ground for refusing a shareholder his right to inspect.[18] To ascertain whether the reports are accurate would

There is a conflict of authority on whether the shareholder who requests inspection must allege and prove a proper purpose or whether the corporation must allege and prove an improper one. That shareholder must: Albee v. Lamson & Hubbard Corp., 320 Mass. 421, 69 N.E.2d 811 (1946); Sawers v. American Phenolic Corp., 404 Ill. 440, 89 N.E.2d 374, 15 A.L.R.2d 1 (1949). That corporation has the burden: State ex rel. Grismer v. Merger Mines Corp., 3 Wash.2d 417, 101 P.2d 308 (1940).

15. Adams, J., in Dines v. Harris, 88 Colo. 22, 291 P. 1024, at 1029 (1930).

16. West's Ann.Cal.Corp.Code § 3005.

17. See Palmer, Company Law 213–214 (19th ed. 1949). Palmer states, at 213: "This is a power which has been very rarely used, owing no doubt partly to the risk that the applicants may incur heavy expenses." See also Gower, Modern Company Law 515–517 (1954).

18. William Coale Development Co. v. Kennedy, 121 Ohio St. 582, 170 N.E. 434 (1930). But see State ex rel. Miller v. Loft, Inc., 34 Del. 538, 156 A. 170 (Super.Ct.1931) (mandamus denied where corporate financial statements sent to share-

seem to be sufficient reason for an inspection, and there are many other legitimate purposes which would lead to the same result. It would indeed be an unusual corporate report that gave the shareholders all the information they are entitled to through their right to inspect the corporate books and records. However, full reports to the shareholders make it much less probable that demands will be made to examine the corporate records and recent statutes, some requiring important periodic reports to be made to the owners, tend to fulfil the shareholders' natural inquisitiveness for information they are entitled to.

The shareholder's right to examine his own company's records will not aid him in his demand to examine the records of his company's subsidiary unless he has special grounds warranting such an inspection.[19] If his company happens to be a subsidiary and the parent company is so managing it that he can show a relationship akin to that of a principal and agent, or closely approaching such a relationship, mandamus will issue to compel an inspection of the parent company's records.[20]

It sometimes happens that the books of a domestic company are outside the state of origin and a shareholder inside such a state is demanding his right to inspect. If undue hardship will not be caused by requiring the books to be brought back so that the shareholder may examine them in the corporate birthplace, a court may order them returned.[21] Otherwise, it will not. A shareholder of a foreign corporation, without the aid of a statute, may obtain aid through a writ of mandamus to examine the books of the corporation in the state where the books are and his demand is made.[22] While the law of the corporate domicile is usually applied in such a case, if a local statute is interpreted as being applicable to the foreign corporation, the local law will be applied.[23] This may well make a difference as to what conditions precedent must be met before an inspection will be forced upon the corporation.

holders were considered adequately complete).

19. State ex rel. Rogers v. Sherman Oil Co., 31 Del. 570, 117 A. 122 (1922).

20. State ex rel. United Brick & Tile Co. v. Wright, 339 Mo. 160, 95 S.W.2d 804 (1936); Bailey v. Boxboard Products Co., 314 Pa. 45, 170 A. 127 (1934).

21. Ross v. Robinson, 185 N.C. 548, 118 S.E. 4 (1923). But where undue hardship will be caused, mandamus will not be issued. Ruby v.

Penn Fibre Board Co., 326 Pa. 582, 192 A. 914 (1937).

22. See discussion and citations in Note, Right of Stockholders in a Foreign Corporation to Inspect Books, 31 Ill.L.Rev. 677 (1937); Note, Shareholders' Right to Inspect Books of Foreign Corporations, 39 Calif.L.Rev. 133 (1951).

23. State ex rel. Grismer v. Merger Mines Corp., 3 Wash.2d 417, 101 P. 2d 308 (1940). Statute of the forum was involved in Kahn v. American Cone & Pretzel Co., 365 Pa. 161, 74 A.2d 160 (1950).

Any shareholder of record is in a position to demand the right to inspect even though he is a mere nominee of the true owner. But by transferring his shares, a shareholder loses his right of inspection.[24] Whether the beneficial owner of shares registered in a nominee's name, or in the name of a trustee or pledgee should be entitled to the inspection right is a debatable question and cases have gone both ways upon it. The usual holding denies the right to one who is not a registered owner, but there are some holdings recognizing the beneficial, though unregistered, owner. Statutes have often dictated the results, or at least the courts have thought so.[25] The difficulty, of course, is that of identification of the beneficial owner with perhaps the thought that if he is not a registered holder his reason for inspecting may be for ulterior purposes. Where the corporation itself is the pledgee, there is no difficulty of identifying the pledgor as owner and inspection has been allowed in such a case.[26] And the right of inspection accorded an executor or administrator has been supported on the ground that he is the successor to the deceased or that the right exists to determine the value of the shares in marshalling the assets for creditors and devisees.[27] Identification in such a case is not difficult and ulterior motives are hard to imagine in this situation. In fact, barring statutes to the contrary, should not the unregistered owner who produces a stock certificate properly indorsed to him, upon a showing of his legitimate purpose, be entitled to inspect whether or not he has had the opportunity to have his stock recorded? Honest shareholders frequently have reasons for not recording their shares for a period and yet have the same necessity for protection through inspection that registered shareholders have.

Statutes have been previously mentioned which are returning to the common law concept that shareholders must have a proper purpose and must allege and support it by proof before mandamus will issue. But, whereas the holder of one share at common law might have access to important corporate records, and his right accrued the moment he acquired ownership, recent statutes have tended to require that he own his shares for a time

24. S. F. Bowser & Co. v. State ex rel. Hines, 192 Ind. 462, 137 N.E. 57 (1922).

25. State ex rel. Manlin v. Druggists' Addressing Co., 113 S.W.2d 1061 (Mo.App.1938) (transferee who had not had stock registered was denied right of inspection). In Brentmore Estates v. Hotel Barbizon, Inc., 263 App.Div. 389, 33 N.Y. S.2d 331 (1942), a holder of a voting trust certificate, though denied a shareholder's statutory right to inspect stock books, was given a common law right of inspection of the stock list.

26. Booth v. Consolidated Fruit Jar Co., 62 Misc. 252, 114 N.Y.S. 1000 (Sup.Ct.1909).

27. Application of Schnepf, 84 N.Y. S.2d 416 (Sup.Ct.1948); Feick, Executrix v. Hill Bread Co., 91 N.J.L. 486, 103 A. 813 (Sup.Ct.1918), aff'd 92 N.J.L. 513, 105 A. 725 (Ct.Err. & App.1919).

period, perhaps six months, before he has the right and/or that he own a specified proportion of the company's shares. Some of these statutes are cited below.[28] The statutory trend has been to require the corporation to give him more information concerning his company in the form of balance sheets and profit and loss statements periodically, and corporations with real vision have been supplying their shareholders with a good deal of information without any prodding from shareholders or statutes. And, of course, where a corporation has had to comply with the several federal acts beginning with the Securities Act of 1933, thorough disclosure of important information which may guide shareholders and prospective purchasers of shares is required. Officers who have nothing to conceal have no valid reasons for keeping important corporate information from their shareholders.

Attempts have been made to limit the right of inspection through provisions in articles or by-laws. In the most important case yet decided a statutory provision gave authority to insert in the certificate of incorporation provisions "creating, defining, limiting and regulating the powers   .   .   .   of the stockholders   .   .   ." provided such provisions were not contrary to the laws of the state. A provision was placed in the certificate and in the by-laws to the effect that no shareholder had the right to inspect except as conferred by statute "or authorized by the board of directors, or by a resolution of the stockholders." A shareholder was refused the right to inspect and petitioned for mandamus to compel the corporation and its officers to permit an inspection for proper purposes. The court held that the statute merely provided for reasonable regulations such as limiting inspection to reasonable times and under proper conditions so as not unreasonably to interfere with the company's business. The court was firm in its statement that the right to examine the books and records of a corporation was a right which could not be

---

28. Colo.Rev.Stat.1953, § 31-2-10 (court may refuse mandamus unless shareholder demands in good faith and "has a substantial interest"); D.C.Bus.Corp.Act of 1954, § 45, in which subsections (b) and (d) refer to 5% owners but subsection (f) reserves the common law right to even one shareholder; Ill. Bus.Corp.Act of 1933, § 45, as amended by L.1947, p. 678 (shareholder of record or holder of voting trust certificate for 6 months, or a "holder of record of at least 5% of all outstanding shares of a corporation"); La.S.A.–Rev.Stat. § 12:38E (except competitors, holders of at least 2% of all outstanding shares for at least 6 months; 2 or more shareholders who have between them owned for at least 6 months at least 2% of all outstanding shares; and for competitors they must have owned 25% of all outstanding stock for at least 6 months); Flack's Md.Ann.Code 1951, Art. 23, § 47 (Subsection (b) which pertains to inspecting the really useful corporate records requires one or more persons who were stockholders of record for at least 6 months with at least a 5% aggregate ownership of the outstanding shares of any class). There are other fairly similar statutes in Florida, Michigan, New York and a few other states.

taken away except by express provision or necessary implication of a statute, thus invalidating both the charter and by-law provision.[29]

In the case just cited it was also contended that a demand to inspect made upon the president at the company's Philadelphia office or upon the company's resident agent at its home office in Wilmington, Delaware, was not sufficient, that it must be made upon the board of directors. The court quite properly held that demand upon either the president or resident agent was sufficient. "It was the duty of the president or resident agent to submit the relator's demand to the directors." [30] A demand made upon anyone who has legal charge of the books and records should be sufficient, and for the same reason.

While a shareholder who is wrongfully refused his right to inspect has a cause of action for damages resulting therefrom, it is by no means an adequate remedy,[31] for usually there is no way of determining what actual damage accrues by his inability to inspect. Modern statutes, however, provide for rather substantial penalties for wrongful refusal of inspection and usually provide that the aggrieved shareholder may recover the penalty, either against the officer refusing or the corporation, plus any other damages caused by the refusal. A few of these statutes are cited in the note below.[32]

29. State ex rel. Cochran v. Penn-Beaver Oil Co., 34 Del. 81, 143 A. 257 (1926). In accord, inferentially: Holdsworth v. Goodall-Sanford, Inc., 143 Me. 56, 55 A.2d 130, 174 A.L.R. 257 (1947). And as to records other than those named in the statute, the court stated that ". . . it cannot be inferred that the stockholders' common law right to examine any other records . . . was thereby taken away." Compare Davids v. Sillcox, 272 App.Div. 54, 69 N.Y.S.2d 63 (1947), which involved a "membership corporation." A by-law provided that a list of members should not be furnished to anyone without the authorization of the corporation's council. A per curiam 3–2 decision upheld the by-law.

30. State ex rel. Cochran v. Penn-Beaver Oil Co., supra, note 29, 143 A. at 260.

31. See Ballantine, Corporations 387 (Rev. ed. 1946).

32. Alaska Bus.Corp.Act § 46 (10% of the value of the shares owned by such shareholder in addition to any other damages); Ariz.Rev. Stat. § 10–195 makes refusal of lawful demand to inspect a misdemeanor; West's Ann.Cal.Corp.Code § 3015 (Corporation is subject to penalty of $10 per day for continued refusal beginning 30 days after receipt of written request with maximum of $1,000. Penalty is payable to shareholder or shareholders making request who are damaged by such refusal if suit is started within 90 days after written request is made, with maximum penalty per day of $100 for failure to comply with any number of separate requests. See also § 3017); Colo.Rev.Stat.1953, § 31–2–9 (Wrongful refusal is a misdemeanor with penalty of $200 and person aggrieved has a cause of action against person offending to recover that amount "or less" as a jury or court may find. § 31–2–10 provides other money penalties); D.C. Bus.Corp.Act of 1954, § 45(e) ($50 penalty to aggrieved shareholder, in addition to any other damages afforded by law); Ill.Bus.Corp. Act of 1933, § 45, as amended by L.1947, p. 678 (wrongful refusal

§ 3. Shareholders' Voting Rights and Meetings

At an earlier time it was natural for the common law to adopt rules developed for non-stock corporations for the business corporation with shares. Thus, originally, each shareholder had one vote no matter how many shares he held, and he had to vote, if at all, in person for he could not appoint a proxy to do this for him any more than he could send his agent to vote at the public polls for him. Voting was considered personal and the shareholder's interest and that of his co-shareholders was thought to be of sufficient importance to demand his personal attention. There was also a fear of large shareholders which is evidenced in the early charters granted corporations in the United States by the limitation upon the number of votes a shareholder might have no matter how many shares he held.[33]

Both the privilege of voting by number of shares and of using proxies for this purpose may be acquired by statute, by provision in the charter, and, by the weight of authority, simply by by-law without the aid of statute or charter. It is now practically universal that shares whose voting rights have not been limited by contract carry one vote per share. While in a few states there are constitutional or statutory provisions which prevent the use of nonvoting shares, articles of incorporation elsewhere may provide for classes of shares without a vote, a common method of control even in small corporations,[34] and numerous modern statutes expressly, or by implication, authorize the issue of nonvoting shares. It is fairly customary not to give preferred shareholders the voting right except upon the failure to declare and pay the preferred dividend for a stated period whereupon the right accrues and remains until all back dividends have been paid. A good deal of variation in voting rights may thus be provided in the certificate or articles of incorporation which is the normal document setting forth the shareholders' contracts.

In voting for directors, each voting share has as many votes as there are directors to be elected, i. e., if five directors are to be elected, each share has five votes. Unless the cumulative voting right has been given shareholders by constitution, statute, charter or by-law, the five votes in our illustration can be voted one each for five nominees but cannot be cumulated so as to give more

---

makes officer refusing liable to shareholder [or holder of certificate of voting trust] for 10% of the value of his shares [or 10% of the value of his beneficial interest where voting trust certificates are concerned] plus any other damages recoverable at law).

33. Dodd, American Business Corporations Until 1860, 203, 231 (1954).

34. In the Illinois Constitution § 3, Art. XI, shareholders of no class may be deprived of the vote. People ex rel. Watseka Tel. Co. v. Emmerson, 302 Ill. 300, 134 N.E. 707 (1922), and see Ill.Bus.Corp.Act of 1933, § 28, as amended by L.1941, p. 421.

than one vote per nominee. If the shareholders have the cumulative voting right each shareholder may multiply the number of shares (votes) he is entitled to cast by the number of directors to be elected and may then give the total votes to one or more nominees in any proportion he desires.

The right to vote cumulatively is a special right not recognized by the common law as incidental to the right to vote. In some states it has been provided by a constitutional provision, in many by statutory fiat, and even where not authorized by statute may be acquired through a provision in the articles or by-laws. In *Maddock* v. *Vorclone Corporation* [35] shareholders had the right to vote cumulatively by virtue of a provision in the certificate of incorporation. Later, the certificate was amended, as the statute and also the certificate permitted, to take away the right to cumulate one's votes. It was held that the right was a matter of contract, to be distinguished from cases where constitutions or statutes guaranteed the right, and could be taken away by an amendment to the certificate which amendment could also be anticipated because of the shareholder's contract evidenced by certificate and statute. The right of cumulative voting belongs to no group as such, but to all of the shareholders. The court reasoned that "When   .   .   .   a majority of the shares outstanding vote to take away the right of one share to vote with cumulative strength, those who compose that majority take from themselves as well as from those who compose the then minority a right which is common to all. The deprivation of the right is not partial in its operation. It is visited on all alike." [36] However, there is much to be said for creating this right by statute in terms which permit of no alteration by articles or by-laws, and some statutes so provide.[37] Minority representation on the board is a thing which irks some directors who fear watch-dogs of any type. If, by virtue of their failure to live up to their fiduciary obligations or duty of reasonable care, their fears are well-grounded, and there is all the more reason for minority representation. In any case where directorial duties are honestly performed with the reasonable care which the law commands, minority representation can be useful in reassuring its constituents of the fact and in presenting views at variance with those of the majority but some of which may turn out to be quite as valuable. This latter is no doubt the reason for a number of statutes which now provide for employee representation on boards of directors.[38]

---

35. 17 Del.Ch. 39, 147 A. 255 (1929).

36. Ibid. 147 A. at 257.

37. West's Ann.Cal.Corp.Code § 2235 as amended by L.1951, c. 1178; Ohio Rev.Code (Gen.Corp.Law of 1955) § 1701.55(D).

38. See N.J.S.A. 14:9–1(d); Mass. Gen.Laws, 1932, c. 156, § 23. These statutes give a corporation the power to provide for employee representation on the board.

A shareholder in voting his shares must act fairly and in good faith toward other shareholders and may not legally enter into an agreement with other shareholders to so vote his shares as to perpetrate a fraud upon another shareholder. For example, he may not contract to vote his shares a certain way in order privately to benefit another or himself. Thus where a shareholder's vote to sell all the assets of a corporation was given in reliance upon a promise of the cancellation of a debt owing to the shareholder who needed the additional votes to pass the resolution, it was rightly held that this consideration could not support the agreement as to make it binding.[39] If he happens to be the majority shareholder, he may not legally use his voting power to advance his own interests at the expense of the minority, nor may he create proxies to use this power for their own personal gain.[40] He may, however, vote his shares in support of the ratification of a personal contract or other transaction with his corporation where good faith and fairness of deal are present, though there be a personal benefit to himself. And his good faith will protect him if he happens to have voted into office a board of directors who prove faithless or incompetent, or to have voted for resolutions which, when set in motion, prove disastrous to his corporation.

Shareholders entitled to be present and to vote at shareholders' meetings are those who are legal owners of shares. This is the general rule. But if by statute, articles or by-law, a particular method of transfer of title or the evidence thereof is required, such as transfer or registration on the corporate books, one who has acquired the certificate of stock would have to comply with the stock transfer or registration provision before he could qualify as a voting shareholder.[41] From practical necessity, modern statutes and articles have provided a record date reasonably prior in time to the date of the meeting, or have provided for the closing of the stock transfer books during that period, so as to enable the inspectors of election, or the chairman if inspectors are not provided, to be able to determine those entitled to vote. The present Delaware statute, for example, permits the directors to close the stock transfer books for a period not exceeding 50 days prior to the date of a meeting or, in lieu thereof through a by-law provision, to authorize the board to fix a record date with similar time restrictions. The latter is preferable for then stock presented for transfer during the 50-or-less-day period may be transferred on the books but this does not permit the new owner to vote except as he may have a proxy from the

---

39. Palmbaum v. Magulsky, 217 Mass. 306, 104 N.E. 746 (1914); Stott v. Stott, 258 Mich. 547, 242 N. W. 747 (1932).

40. Cone's Executors v. Russell, 48 N.J.Eq. 208, 21 A. 847 (1891).

41. See Ballantine, Corporations 397 (Rev. ed. 1946).

record owner on the record date.[42]   Another section of the Delaware statute provides that, "except where the transfer books of the corporation have been closed or a date has been fixed as a record date for the determination of its stockholders entitled to vote . . . no share of stock shall be voted on at any election for directors which has been transferred on the books of the corporation within 20 days next preceding such election of directors," thus disenfranchising, under the named circumstances, some of the shareholders.[43]

The fixing of a record date or the closing of the stock transfer books during the stated period is for the benefit of the corporation and based, as stated above, on practical considerations. Notwithstanding such provisions, the legal title of the transferor passes to the transferee but "So far as the corporation is concerned, until such a by-law is complied with, the record owner must . . . be regarded as the real owner of the stock, with the consequent general right to vote it by proxy, or otherwise." [44]   But since the record owner under such circumstances is a mere nominal owner, the true owner may compel the record owner to give him a proxy so that he may vote the stock which is now his.[45]   And while, ordinarily, the record owner's right to vote cannot be questioned by the inspectors of election, "if inequitable circumstances appear making it improper for the record owner, having the bare legal title, to vote the stock standing in his name," he may be refused that right.[46]

Pledgees or trustees of shares properly registered in their own names, as if general owners, in the absence of statutory provisions to the contrary, are entitled to vote them.   Even if the pledgee is registered as holding the shares as collateral, he may vote them if the pledgor does not claim the right.   If the shares pledged remain in the name of the pledgor on the company's books, or if the pledgee, without authority, registered them in his own name, the pledgor is entitled to vote them unless, by agreement, the pledgee was to have this right.   And, of course, the statutory provision that only shareholders of record may vote will apply here as in other cases if registration has been in accordance with the agreement of the parties, subject always to the right to compel a proxy where the vote was reserved or to refuse the registered holder the vote, in a proper case, because of in-

---

42. Del.Gen.Corp.Law 1953, § 213.

43. Ibid. § 212.

44. In re Giant Portland Cement Co., 26 Del.Ch. 32, 21 A.2d 697, at 701 (1941); In re Canal Construction Co., 21 Del.Ch. 155, 182 A. 545 (1936).

45. In re Giant Portland Cement Co., supra, note 44.

46. Ibid. 21 A.2d at 702; Lawrence v. I. N. Parlier Est. Co., 15 Cal.2d 220, 100 P.2d 765 (1940), although West's Cal.Corp.Code § 2215 makes stock records final. See also Tracy v. Brentwood Village Corp., 30 Del. Ch. 296, 59 A.2d 708 (1948).

equities.[47] As a common law matter, a pledgor remains the "owner" in the sense that he is entitled to vote the shares in the hands of the pledgee.

Modern statutes frequently have provisions concerning pledgors and pledgees, beneficiaries and trustees. The California statute, for instance, provides, in part: "Shares standing in the name of any person as pledgee, trustee, or other fiduciary may be voted and all rights incident thereto may be exercised only by the pledgee, trustee, or other fiduciary, in person or by proxy, and without proof of authority." [48]

Shares registered in the names of shareholders now deceased may be voted by the administrator or executor of the deceased's estate since these representatives are considered successors in interest to the deceased. Proof by letters of administration from a proper court is conclusive evidence of the representative's right to vote the shares though not registered in his name.[49] Modern statutes have generally codified this common law concept. Cases analogous to that just mentioned are those where legally appointed guardians of infants or incompetents, or the receiver of an insolvent, proceed to vote the shares of their wards or insolvent person in whose names such shares are registered. Statutes are gradually making specific provision to the effect that such representatives may vote the shares registered in the names of those they represent.[50]

47. See, generally, Ballantine, 399–400 (Rev. ed. 1946).

48. West's Ann.Cal.Corp.Code § 2218, as amended by L.1947, c. 101, § 2. See also Ill.Bus.Corp.Act 1933, § 30; Mass.Gen.Laws 1932, c. 155, § 21; Ohio Rev.Code (Gen.Corp. Law of 1955) § 1701.46. Compare California provision with that of § 1.64 of the Okl.Bus.Corp.Act which provides: "A shareholder of a domestic corporation whose shares are pledged shall be entitled to vote such shares until they have been transferred to the pledgee upon the books of the corporation. Such transferee shall thereafter be regarded by the corporation as the owner thereof unless the instrument of transfer discloses the pledge. If such instrument discloses the pledge, the transferor shall be entitled to vote such pledged shares unless, in the instrument of transfer, the pledgor shall have expressly empowered the pledgee to represent the shares. If the pledgee is thus empowered, he or his proxy, shall be exclusively entitled to represent such shares." And see § 1.63 of the Oklahoma statute concerning fiduciaries.

49. Stevens, Corporations 526 (2d ed. 1949). See Albert E. Touchet, Inc. v. Touchet, 264 Mass. 499, 163 N.E. 184 (1928), where a special administrator holding the majority of shares which were registered in the name of the deceased was held capable of demanding a shareholders' meeting which the board had refused to call. Under the by-laws holders of the majority of the shares could call a meeting.

50. Okl.Bus.Corp.Act § 1.63–b: "Such shares standing in the name of any deceased person, person adjudged incompetent, or minor may be represented only by his administrator, executor, or guardian as the case may be, either in person or by proxy." Ibid. § 1.63–c: "Such shares may be represented by receiver in case authority to represent such shares be contained in an appropriate order of the court by which such receiver was

A corporation which owns shares in another corporation which is not its parent may vote the shares in accordance with the determination made by its board of directors. But a corporation may not vote its own shares which have acquired a treasury-share status, nor may its subsidiary vote shares of the parent held by it. Nor may such shares be counted for quorum purposes. For all practical purposes in the area of voting, the parent corporation is the owner of its shares in the hands of its subsidiary. And if either a corporation could vote its own shares held in its treasury or a subsidiary vote its parent's shares held by it, management could easily intrench itself permanently by the subterfuge of buying in, through the use of corporate funds, outstanding shares of its own stock or by using a subsidiary and its funds for the same purpose. Statutes generally provide that a corporation may not vote its own shares either directly or indirectly which, of course, would include a subsidiary's voting its parent's shares.[51] Some statutes specifically provide, as they should, that shares of its own stock held in a fiduciary capacity may be voted and counted as part of a quorum and in determining the total number of outstanding shares at any given time.[52]

Shares held jointly, whether by owners or by fiduciaries, are voted in accordance with the majority's desires; but if there is an even division of joint owners or holders, one faction desiring to vote one way, the second faction wanting to vote contrariwise, it has been held that no vote can be cast.[53] This seems wrong, for shares of stock like fungible goods, are easily divisible; and a just decision would let each faction vote half the shares the way it desires. Some statutes have seen this difficulty and made pro-

---

appointed." Wis.Bus.Corp.Law of 1951, § 180.25(5), as amended by L.1953, c. 399, §§ 13 and 14: "Shares held by an administrator, executor, guardian, conservator, trustee in bankruptcy, receiver or assignee for creditors may be voted by him, either in person or by proxy, without a transfer of such shares into his name. Shares standing in the name of a fiduciary may be voted by him, either in person or by proxy." Other statutes along the same lines are: Or.Rev.Stat.1953, § 57.170(6) and (7); Ohio Rev.Code (Gen.Corp.Law of 1955) § 1701.46(C). There are many more of them.

51. Italo Petroleum Corp. of America v. Producers' Oil Corp. of America, 20 Del.Ch. 283, 174 A. 276 (1934). Dean Stevens asks:

"If the voting of those shares is done in a manner compatible with the interests of all shareholders, can there, in the absence of an expressed statutory provision, be any objection to such voting?" Stevens, Corporations 529 (2d ed. 1949). Statutes: Ohio Rev.Code (Gen. Corp.Law of 1955) § 1701.47(C); Pa.Bus.Corp.Law of 1933, § 508, as amended by L.1957, Act 370; N.M.Stat.1953, § 51–6–9; N.J.S.A., § 14:10–8. There are many others which are similar.

52. See Pa.Bus.Corp.Law of 1933, § 508, note 51, supra. But see A.L.I., Model Bus.Corp.Act (Rev.1953), § 31 specifically prohibiting this.

53. Tunis v. Hestonville, M. & F. Pass. R. Co., 149 Pa. 70, 24 A. 88, 15 L.R.A. 665 (1892).

vision for it in the suggested manner,[54] while other statutes provide for the appointment of a disinterested party to cast his vote to create a majority.[55] Liberality in interpretation should be the rule, and not the exception, in order to allow the shareholder his franchise whenever possible.

Formalities required for shareholders' meetings are often prescribed by modern statutes, such as what notice must be given, how many shares are necessary to constitute a quorum, the manner of determining shareholders of record entitled to vote, the duties of the inspector or inspectors of election, and other questions involving such meetings. Usually, the formalities of such meetings are set forth in the by-laws of the corporation and should appear there with such definiteness that, for the major questions that may arise, there is an answer. And, while statutes frequently spell out the formalities, they usually provide the customary elasticity provided in many other areas by qualifying the prescription by the usual phrase, "Unless otherwise provided by the articles or by-laws."

Where statutes, articles or by-laws fail to provide a time and place to hold shareholders' meetings, the power and duty to call such meetings and to name a place and time is in the governing authority of the corporation, that is, in its board of directors.[56] And personal notice, under such circumstances, should be furnished each shareholder,[57] although this is not necessary at common law where a time and place have been set for regular meetings in the articles or by-laws. In case of special meetings, the time, place and purpose of the special meeting must be set forth.[58] And the better practice, whether required or not, is to set forth any extraordinary matter that is to be considered at a regular meeting. With such notice, the shareholder has the opportunity to think upon, and discuss with other shareholders, the matter and be prepared to vote intelligently upon it. Perhaps the severest criticism concerning shareholders' meetings is that, unless compelled by statute, directors do not furnish their shareholders with the information they are enitled to, as owners, to use their voting franchise with real discrimination. A by-law,

54. Ohio Rev.Code (Gen.Corp.Law of 1955) § 1701.46(E); Pa.Bus.Corp. Law of 1933, § 507, as amended by 1951 P.L. 1475, § 8; Okl.Bus.Corp. Act § 1.61 (joint owners vote in proportion to their interests and, when fiduciaries cannot agree, they vote as if they were joint owners).

55. N.J.S.A. § 14:10–7, as amended by L.1953, c. 14, § 8, pertaining to shares held jointly by fiduciaries, which seems fair enough for fiduciaries.

56. Commonwealth ex rel. Jackson v. Smith, 45 Pa. 59 (1863). But see Stebbins v. Merrill, 10 Cush. (Mass.) 27 (1852), where a general agent was held to have the authority to call the meeting.

57. Stowe v. Wyse, 7 Conn. 214 (1828).

58. Atlantic De Laine Co. v. Mason, 5 R.I. 463 (1858).

carefully drafted to include the various types of information which the board must disclose at the regular or special meetings, can go far toward curing this defect.

Unlike a quorum for a board or executive committee meeting which requires the presence of a majority of members, a quorum for a shareholders' meeting at common law existed if two shareholders were present no matter what their quantum of shareholding might be.[59] Barring statutory or charter provisions setting the quorum requirement, a provision in the by-laws may designate any proportion of shares or of shareholders as constituting a quorum. While most states now have statutes specifying the manner in which quorums are to be ascertained, there are still a few states that have no provisions at all on this subject. A common provision found in a number of statutes is that unless the articles, or the articles or by-laws, otherwise provide, the holders of a majority in interest of voting shares issued and outstanding shall constitute a quorum.[60] Some statutes providing as above also contain a prohibition that the quorum provisions must not go below a certain minimum of shares, such as not less than a third or a majority.[61] A number of statutes spell out meticulously that, once a quorum has been established at a meeting, the withdrawal of shares from the meeting shall not break the quorum, thus incorporating the better common law on this subject.[62] There are a few statutes that prescribe what the quorum shall be and leave no opening for such a determination through articles or by-laws.[63] The Delaware

---

59. Palmer, Company Law 148 (19th ed. 1949), states: "At common law one member prima facie cannot constitute a meeting", citing Sharp v. Dawes, 2 Q.B.D. 26 (1876), and Re Sanitary Carbon Co., [1877] W. N. 223. See also Gower, Modern Company Law 469 (1954); Companies Act of 1948, § 134 (quorum under the Act). And see Sylvania & G. R. Co. v. Hoge, 129 Ga. 734, 59 S.E. 806 (1907). But in Morrill v. Little Falls Mfg. Co., 53 Minn. 371, 55 N.W. 547, 21 L.R.A. 174 (1893), the court stated (55 N.W. at 549): "It is immaterial whether the number is only one or more than one."

60. Examples are: Mass.Gen.Laws 1932, c. 156, § 28; Mich.Gen.Corp. Act § 38 as amended by L.1951, Act No. 239 (unless otherwise provided by law, articles or by-law); Minn.Stat.Ann. § 301.25–7.

61. Mo.Rev.Stat.1949, V.A.M.S., § 351.265 (in no case less than a ma-

jority); Ill.Bus.Corp.Act of 1933, § 31 (not less than one-third); D.C. Bus.Corp.Act of 1954, § 31(a) (not less than one-third).

62. West's Ann.Cal.Corp.Code § 2212; D.C.Bus.Corp.Act of 1954, § 31(b); Idaho Code Ann. 1949, § 30–136–2a; Ky.Rev.Stat., 1953, § 271.335(2) (a); La.S.A.—Rev.Stat. § 12:31B(1). And see, for the common law rule in accord: Duffy v. Loft, Inc., 17 Del.Ch. 140, 151 A. 223 (1930), aff'd 17 Del.Ch. 376, 152 A. 849 (1930). The English rule is contra, providing that unless the articles otherwise provide, a quorum must exist throughout the meeting. Gower, Modern Company Law 469 (1954).

63. West's Ann.Cal.Corp.Code § 2211 ("The presence in person or by proxy of the persons entitled to vote a majority of the voting shares at any meeting constitutes a quorum for the transaction of business unless, in the case of a

statute provides that the certificate of incorporation or the by-laws may fix the quorum with no mention of what constitutes a quorum if there is an absence of such provisions, while the Ohio statute provides that unless the articles or regulations (by-laws) otherwise provide, the shareholders present in person or by proxy shall constitute a quorum for that meeting except for action specifically requiring a larger vote.[64] It would seem that, by a provision in the certificate or by-laws under the Delaware statute, and without any provision under the Ohio statute, one shareholder with one share (if he is the only one to appear at the meeting) would constitute a quorum.   Under the majority of statutes now existing, the same result could be reached by a provision in articles or by-laws restating the Ohio statutory provision.   Or does the term "shareholders" mean more than one?

With the variety of statutes existing, one is led to recommend the practical approach (as always) to the draftsman. Where he has discretion in stating what the quorum shall be, he should not put it so low as to make a possible farce of shareholders' meetings nor so high as to make it difficult to obtain, either in person or by proxy, a quorum for these meetings. Shareholders are notoriously delinquent in appearing at meetings and in returning proxy forms properly signed to their proxy solicitors. This is the really important consideration. And what the quorum should be will depend much on whether the corporate voting stock is closely or widely held and, if closely held, the danger that eventually it may have this position reversed.

Whether or not a quorum is present is to be figured on the number of shares entitled to vote at the meeting which are present in their owners' or proxies' possession with some purpose of their possessor other than presenting them only to protest against the legality of the meeting. If they are there for some other purpose whether yet counted or not, they may be counted as a part of the total shares present at the meeting.[65] And if a quorum is once present but the meeting for some reason is adjourned to a future day, the later meeting may proceed even though at that time a quorum is not present.[66] The two sessions

nonprofit corporation, the by-laws provide a different number"); Colo.Rev.Stat.1953, § 31–2–4.

64. Del.Gen.Corp.Law of 1953, § 216; Ohio Rev.Code (Gen.Corp. Law of 1955) § 1701.51(A).

65. Duffy v. Loft, Inc., supra, note 62. One present solely to protest the meeting's legality and who departs immediately thereafter cannot be counted for quorum pur-

poses. Leamy v. Sinaloa Exploration & Development Co., 15 Del. Ch. 28, 130 A. 282 (1925).

66. Atterbury v. Consolidated Mines, 26 Del.Ch. 1, 20 A.2d 743 (1941). Some of the statutes also codify this principle. See, for example, West's Ann.Cal.Corp.Code § 2212. See notes in 39 Calif.L.Rev. 127 (1951); 11 B.U.L.Rev. 267 (1931); 4 So.Calif.L.Rev. 222 (1931); 79 U. of Pa.L.Rev. 223 (1930).

are considered a part of the same meeting and, as in case of an attempted withdrawal from a quorum once established, the withdrawal or abstention is not legally effective to break the quorum. The rules in this area have been established, where at all possible, for convenience and for the purpose of aiding shareholders in having their meetings rather than having them fail on technical grounds. This approach is well illustrated in a case where the results of an annual election of directors prescribed by statute were in issue. Said the court: "So important is the direction (of the statute) that this duty be performed that in some instances courts have brushed aside all strictness and technicality of view in the interest either of securing a statutorily commanded election or, if one has been sought and held, in sustaining its results." [67]

The requirements of notice and of a quorum, and of a meeting where there may be an exchange of ideas, are for the same purpose for which similar requirements have been laid down for board and executive committee meetings, that is, for the protection of the shareholders. If all those entitled to vote attend a meeting where no formal notice was given or a quorum attends after all have waived whatever formal notice was required, the meeting will be considered a legal one.[68] Or if the notice of a special meeting was defective in not stating the purpose or purposes of the meeting, unanimous waiver will cure the defect and the meeting may proceed as if proper notice had been given. A vote of the majority of all shares present at a properly called and attended meeting will carry a resolution unless a larger vote is required by statute, articles or by-laws.[69] And, unless statute, articles or by-laws require a majority vote of those *present* to pass a resolution, majority votes of those *actually cast* upon a resolution will pass it.[70] Modern statutes are tending to make action without a meeting valid if authorized in writing by all the shareholders entitled to vote at the meeting in question.[71] And statutory provisions permitting shareholders to waive notice before or after a meeting have aided in making formalities of somewhat less importance than formerly.[72] Such provisions are particularly useful in case of corporations having a small number of shareholders where formalities are sometimes cut down to a minimum.

67. Duffy v. Loft, Inc., supra, note 62, 151 A. at 227.

68. Scranton Axle & Spring Co. v. Scranton Board of Trade, 271 Pa. 6, 113 A. 838 (1921).

69. State ex rel. Martin v. Chute, 34 Minn. 135, 24 N.W. 353 (1885).

70. Ballantine, Corporations 395–396 (Rev. ed. 1946).

71. Ohio Rev.Code (Gen.Corp.Law of 1955) § 1701.54; A.L.I. Model Business Corporation Act § 138 (Rev.1953).

72. Ohio Rev.Code § 1701.42; Minn. Stat.Ann. § 301.25–6; West's Ann. Cal.Corp.Code § 2209; A.L.I. Model Business Corporation Act § 137 (Rev.1953).

It was originally held in the United States that meetings of shareholders must be held in the state under whose laws the corporation got its existence, the reason usually assigned being that a corporation had no legal existence outside the borders of the sovereignty creating it.[73]   This erroneous idea has long since evaporated and, today, most statutes make specific provision for meetings outside the state if provided for in articles or by-laws. Suggestions are sometimes made today by shareholders that some of the meetings should be held in places other than the home office of the company, because of the inconvenience of going to the home office when the bulk of the shareholders may be in New York, Chicago, or elsewhere.   In large corporations where stock ownership may be concentrated mainly in a few financial centers, there is much to be said for an occasional meeting outside the locus of the home office in order to give the democratic process a wider range in which to operate.   In large publicly held corporations this procedure might well stimulate an interest in shareholders which, in the past, has too frequently been lacking.

Statutes commonly provide for an annual election of directors.   This should also be provided for in the by-laws of the company.   The shareholders have this right to have the annual meeting called and if the directors fail or refuse to call such a meeting, a shareholder, by writ of mandamus, may compel the calling of it.[74]   Otherwise, the board could perpetuate itself by this kind of inaction.[75]

Except as to meetings required by statute, articles or by-laws—that is, regular meetings—it is doubtful whether shareholders may compel a special meeting to be called.[76]   However, it would seem that extraordinary circumstances might well be the basis of a court's sustaining mandamus by a shareholder seeking a special meeting where his board unreasonably refused to call one.   Where statutory provisions do not exist, or where a statute provides for a call of a special meeting by a certain percentage of qualified shareholders but allows a smaller or larger percentage to be named in articles or by-laws, provisions should

---

73.   2 Machen, Modern Law of Corporations § 1212 (1908).

74.   Albert E. Touchet, Inc. v. Touchet, 264 Mass. 499, 163 N.E. 184 (1928); People ex rel. Miller v. Cummings, 72 N.Y. 433 (1878).

75.   See Gries v. Eversharp, Inc., 31 Del.Ch. 489, 69 A.2d 922 (Sup.Ct. 1949), where directors attempted to manipulate annual meeting by postponement.

76.   West's   Ann.Cal.Corp.Code   § 2202(c) provides that shareholders holding one-fifth of the voting power may call a special meeting. Ohio Rev.Code (Gen.Corp.Law of 1955) § 1701.40(A) (3) provides for a calling of a special meeting by 25% of shares outstanding and entitled to vote at the meeting, but articles or regulations (by-laws) may provide for smaller or larger, but not in excess of 50%, proportion.   A.L.I. Model Business Corporation Act § 26 (Rev.1953) provides that holders of not less than one-tenth of all shares entitled to vote at the meeting may call a special meeting.

be made for a call by a reasonably low percentage of the voting shares.[77]   However, if the percentage is placed too low the result may be the creation of a nuisance value to the shares of a small minority, a thing which should be avoided.

§ 4.   Voting by Proxy and its Importance in Contests for Control

Where voting shares are widely dispersed the only practical way that the voting franchise can be exercised is through the appointment of agents, called proxies,[78] who will be personally present to vote the shares of absent owners at the meeting. Without the use of this device, many corporations would find it impossible to obtain a quorum to hold a meeting.   And where major changes requiring a two-thirds or even a majority affirmative vote of the company's outstanding shares are being contemplated, if it were not for the proxy process it would be impossible to obtain such a vote.

While it is a useful device to get things done it is also a device which favors management, in its operation, more than the corporation's shareholders.[79]   Management selects its slate of nominees for the board, makes its recommendations concerning them and any resolutions to be passed upon by the shareholders, uses the company's funds to solicit proxies and, unless compelled by statute, articles or by-laws, gives the owners whatever information it pleases to make them cognizant of how their corporation is being run.   Since it is difficult to prove that management is seeking proxies for selfish personal reasons, it is seldom that a court can find that it is not legitimate to charge the printing, mailing and other expense to the corporation.   This is on the assumption that it is a corporate advantage to have as large a representation of shares at shareholders' meetings as possible, and even when there is a vigorous contest by shareholders to overthrow the present management the argument is strong that man-

---

77.   See Weisblum v. Li Falco Mfg. Co., Inc., 193 Misc. 473, 84 N.Y.S.2d 162 (Sup.Ct.1947), where such a provision was under construction.

78.   The term "proxy" is also used to designate the written or printed instrument by which the agency is created.   It is also used as the term "authority" is used in creating an agency.   The term "proxy" is a contraction of "procuracy" which means, among other things, the act of officiating as an agent for another.

79.   Berle and Means, The Modern Corporation and Private Property

245 (1933), state: "Legally, the proxy is an agent for the shareholder; and necessarily under a duty of fidelity to him.   Factually, he is a dummy for the management, and is expected to do as he is told.   Indeed, proxies are often clerks in the management, perhaps assisted by the company's attorney. The vote when mobilized really represents the will of the Directors." Ballantine, Corporations 412 (Rev. ed 1946) states: "In practice . . proxy voting has operated to enable the management in office to perpetuate itself and control the corporation."

agement's expense should come out of the corporate coffers in order that the shareholders be fully informed of their corporation's position as represented by their freely chosen board.

Those who seek to overthrow the present management must first obtain a list of the corporation's shareholders with their addresses and this any shareholder is entitled to for the purpose is a legitimate one. But delaying tactics can and have been used by an intrenched management with the effect that the voting is over before the attacking group has obtained the list or had time to get its materials to the shareholders whose proxies are being solicited. Furthermore, a proxy contest is an uncertain and expensive thing. If the insurgents lose, there will be no chance to charge the expenses to the company. If they win, there is still the somewhat uncertain answer to the question of whether the elected board may legitimately charge the expenses of the winning dissident shareholders to the corporation, either without or with ratification short of unanimity.[80] Dissident shareholders who are willing to risk their money in what may turn out to be a losing venture do not ordinarily take the risk except for the good of their company, or at least their good faith belief that a change is for the company's good. If they win, reasonable expenses incurred in proxy solicitation should be chargeable, at the option of the new directors, to the corporation. Recent cases have permitted this, and rightly. Analogy suggests the case of the successful shareholder in a derivative action, although in most of such cases money or property is brought back into the corporate treasury against which the reasonable costs of suit may be charged.[81] Possible benefit which may result by virtue of a change of management should be a sufficient argument to support the successful insurgents.

Since proxies are agents, the law of agency prevails when problems arise concerning who may vote, what may be voted upon, whether there has been a revocation of the agency, etc. A

---

80. See Steinberg v. Adams, 90 F. Supp. 604 (D.N.Y.1950) (insurgents won and court held they might be reimbursed by the corporation) and notes on the subject in 61 Yale L. J. 229 (1952) and 36 Cornell L.Q. 558 (1951). See article by Friedman, Expenses of Corporate Proxy Contests, 51 Col.L.Rev. 951 (1951). In accord with Steinberg case is Rosenfeld v. Fairchild Engine and Airplane Corp., 116 N.Y.S.2d 840 (Sup.Ct.1952), aff'd 284 App.Div. 201, 132 N.Y.S.2d 273 (1954), aff'd 309 N.Y. 168, 128 N.E.2d 291 (1955). "[W]ith the official reporting of the *Steinberg* case . . . and the litigation that followed over the *Fairchild* case it became increasingly apparent . . . that insurgents' proxy contest expenses could be recovered if they were successful." Emerson, Congressional Investigation of Proxy Regulation: A Case Study of Committee Exploratory Methods and Techniques, 2 Villanova L.Rev. 75, at 89–90 (1956).

81. Compare Holthusen v. Edward G. Budd Mfg. Co., 55 F.Supp. 945 (D.Pa.1944) which was, apparently, a representative (but not a derivative) suit.

proxy not coupled with an interest may always be revoked at any time by the principal. And the mere agreement that the proxy is irrevocable is not enough to make it so unless actually coupled with an interest. Unless a statute provides that certain formalities have to be complied with in order to revoke a proxy, it may be revoked informally as, for example, by appearing at the meeting and voting the shares in person, or by the giving of a later proxy to another, by the sale of the shares, or by the death of the principal or his proxy or the loss of capacity of either, revocation thus resulting from the application of traditional agency rules.

While it has sometimes been argued that the interest which, coupled with a power in a proxy, creates an irrevocable agency must be an interest in the shares themselves, it is believed that this concept is too narrow.[82] Thus, if a proxy is given in connection with an option, authority or contract to buy or sell the shares or a part thereof; or if given in connection with a pledge of the shares to secure the performance of an act, such as repayment of a loan for which the shares were pledged, or for the nonperformance of an act; or for the performance or nonperformance of any act, or agreement for an act, by the corporation issuing the shares, there seems no doubt that in each case there is a power coupled with an interest.[83] Texts on agency should be consulted when a problem of powers coupled with an interest arises. A proxy is merely a special type of power which may, or may not, be coupled with an interest.

Proxies, like other agencies, may be general or limited in the authority granted. And, whether the authority is specific and limited, or general, it is expected that a proxy will be present and vote the shares he represents with the same good faith to be expected from the principal-owner were he present and voting the shares in person. If the proxy attends the meeting at which he has authority to vote his principal's shares, it is anticipated that his votes, whether tendered or not, are to be counted to determine

---

82. Ballantine, Corporations 410 (Rev. ed. 1946). And see Deibler v. Chas. H. Elliott Co., 368 Pa. 267, 81 A.2d 557 (1951), where a proxy, given for the life of the agent based upon an agreement of payment for the shares under proxy and the agreement that the seller be employed for life at a named salary, was held valid and irrevocable. The court also held that the interest need not be in the stock itself to make the proxy irrevocable.

83. The Ohio Rev.Code (Gen.Corp. Law of 1955) § 1701.49(B) contains

similar provisions which the code says "shall be deemed coupled with an interest" in cases of voting trusts. As agency propositions, they are adequately stated. See annotation on this subject (powers coupled with an interest) in 97 A.L. R. 923 (1935); 64 A.L.R. 380 (1929). The Restatement, Agency, § 138 (1933) makes powers of attorney irrevocable if given as security for the performance of a duty or to protect a title, either legal or equitable, for the benefit of a person other than the power gives.

whether a quorum is present.[84] Having accepted the agency, he has the legal duty of voting the shares as his authority permits and will be held responsible to his principal, as in other agency cases, where he violates his trust. "An agent can always abandon his agency at the expense of assuming the risk of liability if the circumstances are such that the law attaches liability." [85] But abandonment should not be easily assumed and, as stated in an important case, ". . . relatively slight circumstances ought to justify the conclusion that a solicited agency when granted was assumed and acted on when the occasion for its exercise arises and the agent is present participating in some way in the business with which the proposed agency is concerned." [86] Thus the proxies held by the corporation's president were counted to obtain a quorum when he departed from the meeting in a huff because he had not been chosen its chairman.

It has been held that even a general authority given a proxy does not permit him to vote for the unusual, such as a fundamental change in the charter or the sale of all of the assets or dissolution.[87] If the shareholder desires his proxy to have the authority to vote for such unusual things, he should make his intention specific in his power of attorney. This is especially true when the proxy is for a regular meeting where the common law rule permitted extraordinary action without notice to the shareholders that it was to be taken. The same difficulty is not apparent in the special meeting for notice must be given of the purpose for which the special meeting is called and if the proxy is given after the notice has been received, there is no doubt as to what authority is meant to be given.

(a) Proxy regulation under the federal acts. Under three of the acts administered by the Securities and Exchange Commission, the Commission has the duty to prescribe rules and regulations, and has so prescribed them, concerning the solicitation of proxies in corporations whose securities, other than exempted securities, are registered on any national securities exchange.[88]

84. Duffy v. Loft, Inc., 17 Del.Ch. 140, 151 A. 223 (1930), aff'd 17 Del.Ch. 376, 152 A. 849 (1930).

85. Ibid. 151 A. at 227.

86. Ibid. at 227.

87. McKee v. Home Savings & Trust Co., 122 Iowa 731, 98 N.W. 609 (1904).

88. These acts are: The Securities Exchange Act of 1934 (§ 14(a), 15 U.S.C.A. § 78n(a)), the Public Utility Holding Company Act of 1935 (§ 12(e), 15 U.S.C.A. § 79*l*(e)), and the Investment Company Act of 1940 (§ 20(a), 15 U.S.C.A. § 80a–20(a)). § 14(a) of the first named act provides: "It shall be unlawful for any person, by the use of the mails or by any means or instrumentality of interstate commerce or of any facility of any national securities exchange or otherwise to solicit or to permit the use of his name to solicit any proxy or consent or authorization in respect of any security (other than an exempted security) registered on any national securities exchange in contravention of such rules and regulations as the Com-

Section 14(a) of the Securities Exchange Act of 1934, in general, makes it unlawful to solicit by the use of the mails, the facilities of interstate commerce or of a national securities exchange or otherwise, a proxy, consent or authorization with respect to securities listed on a national securities exchange otherwise than in accordance with the rules and regulations set up by the Commission for the protection of investors. Since 1938 such rules have been in effect, the regulation X-14 known as the "proxy rules" containing them. The solicitation of proxy rules will be found in 17 Code of Federal Regulations § 240.14a–1 through § 240.14a–11, Schedule 14A which follows immediately after § 240.11 listing the information required in a proxy statement, and Schedule 14B, following immediately after Schedule 14A, listing the information to be included in statements filed by or on behalf of a participant (other than the issuer) in a proxy solicitation pursuant to § 240.14–11(c).

Apart from the few types of solicitation excepted [89] by Regulation 240.14a–2, persons solicited for proxies must be furnished with the detailed information specified in Schedule 14A, information which will give the persons solicited a basis upon which to make an intelligent decision. The purpose of this regulation is "to protect investors by means of disclosures of material facts important to an analysis of matters presented to shareholders for their vote. The theory of the rules is that if all such facts are clearly presented to the investor or shareholder he will be capable of arriving at his own decisions."[90]

Recently, new regulations have been promulgated by the Commission to better take care of proxy contests, some of which have been carried on through procedures highly questionable. At times in the past, participants in such contests have tried to conceal their backgrounds, financial interests in the corporation and their solicitation activities. The new rules bring out into the open the activities of the participants such as the methods of solicitation, the material features of solicitation contracts, the probable expense of solicitation and whether reimbursement will be sought from the corporation. But behind all of this is the basic idea that material facts must be stated and explained, when necessary, so that the shareholders who are solicited will be able to judge, from the materials used to gain their proxies, information concerning the solicitors, the exact purpose for which solici-

---

mission may prescribe as necessary or appropriate in the public interest or for the protection of investors." Regulation § 240.14a–1 et seq. and Schedule 14A requiring the disclosure of certain information when proxies, consents and authorizations of security holders are solicited apply to all three acts.

89. See Regulation 240.14a–2, formerly X–14A–2.

90. 22nd Annual Report, Securities and Exchange Commission 33 (1956).

tation is made, what interest the solicitors have in making their solicitation, and other important facts upon which an intelligent judgment may be based.[91]

Some of the more important provisions of the rules which the Securities and Exchange Commission has set up are, in essence: making unlawful a solicitation which is false or misleading as to any material fact or which omits a material fact necessary to make statements already made not false or misleading; in case of proxies solicited for the election of directors, the requirements that the solicitor must state whom he represents, must furnish the name and security holdings of each nominee, the nominee's remuneration from the company, if any, and any "inside" transactions between the nominee and the company; if management solicits proxies for use at an annual meeting where directors are to be elected, it must send out, with its solicitation or beforehand, a copy of its annual report containing financial statements adequately reflecting the financial position and operations of the issuer, "in any form deemed suitable by the management"; for other corporate action, the proposal must be fully described, its purpose and effect stated, the interest, if any, of the officers and directors and their associates in the proposal—whether because of their holding of particular classes of securities or otherwise—must be set forth; that the form of the proxy sent out permit the solicited person to indicate the action he desires on each separate matter to be voted upon thus permitting him to approve or disapprove it. There are also rules which permit non-management solicitors, when management is seeking proxies, to get in touch with other security holders, and management may not solicit unless it undertakes to forward, at the expense of the security holder involved, soliciting material which such security holder may wish to submit for transmission to those being solicited by management. However, Regulation 240.-14a-7(c) gives the corporation an alternative by permitting it to supply the security holder with a reasonably current list of shareholders and their addresses in lieu of the above. Proposals submitted by nonmanagement shareholders may also be included in the management's soliciting material if proper subjects for shareholder action, together with a brief statement in support of the proposal. Thus a minority proposal must be presented to those solicited before management may vote proxies in favor of the proposal.[92]

If the proxy rules are not complied with by proxy solicitors coming within the area of required compliance, they may be en-

91. Ibid. pp. 34–42.

92. See 10th Annual Report, Securities and Exchange Commission

51–53 (1945), and Regulations 240.-14a-1 through 240.14a-11 and Schedules 14A and 14B.

joined from using the mails or other means of interstate communication to solicit proxies,[93] and may be prosecuted criminally for wilful violations. And where management has solicited and obtained proxies it may not order its proxy agents to remain away from the meeting to defeat a quorum requirement and thus prevent the holding of the meeting.[94] And it would seem to follow that a proxy solicitor may be forced to vote the proxies obtained by his solicitation in accordance with the promise which he must make in his proxy statement or form of proxy submitted to the solicited security holder.[95]

What is "a proper subject for action by the security holders" [96] so that a shareholder's proposal may be entitled to inclusion in management's proxy solicitation materials? In *Securities and Exchange Commission* v. *Transamerica Corp.*,[97] the owner of 17 out of nearly 10 million shares in a Delaware corporation distributed among some 151,000 shareholders submitted to the management four proposals: (1) to have independent auditors of the corporate books, such auditors to be elected (annually) by the shareholders, a representative of the auditing firm last chosen to attend the annual meeting each year; (2) to amend a present by-law to eliminate a requirement that notice of any proposed alteration or amendment of the by-laws be contained in the notice of meeting (over which the directors had control); (3) to change the place of the annual meeting from Wilmington, Delaware, to San Francisco, California (this became moot because the directors amended the by-laws without further encouragement); and (4) to require a report of the annual meeting to be sent to all the shareholders.

The management of the corporation argued that "a stockholder may interest himself with propriety only in a subject in respect to which he is entitled to vote at a stockholders' meeting when every requirement of Delaware law and of the provisions

93. S. E. C. v. O'Hara Re-Election Committee, 28 F.Supp. 523 (D.Mass. 1939).

94. See 10th Annual Report, Securities and Exchange Commission 53 (1945); Ballantine, Lattin and Jennings, Cases and Materials on Corporations 435, containing excerpt from same report (2d ed. 1953).

95. S. E. C. Regulation 240.14a–4(e) provides: "The proxy statement or form of proxy shall provide, subject to reasonable specified conditions, that the shares represented by the proxy will be voted and that where the person solicited specifies by means of a ballot provided pursuant to paragraph (b) of this section a choice with respect to any matter to be acted upon, the shares will be voted in accordance with the specifications so made."

96. The phrase contained in Regulation 240.14a–8.

97. 163 F.2d 511 (3d Cir., 1947), cert. den. 332 U.S. 847, 68 S.Ct. 351, 92 L.Ed. 418 (1948), noted in 96 U. of Pa.L.Rev. 286 (1947) and 57 Yale L.J. 874 (1948). See Caplin, Annual Meetings and Corporate Democracy: The Lawyer's Role, 37 Va.L.Rev. 653, at 671 (1951).

of the charter and by-laws, including notice, has been fulfilled."
The S.E.C., as amicus curiae, contended that "a proper subject"
for stockholder action "is one in which the stockholders may
properly be interested under the law of Delaware," and that all
three proposals, only one of which (the first) had been supported
by the District Court, came within the phrase. The Circuit Court
of Appeals upheld the contentions of the S.E.C., holding that
management could not use the notice requirement of the by-law
in question "as a block or strainer to prevent any proposal to
amend the by-laws, which it may deem unsuitable, from reaching
a vote at an annual meeting of stockholders," that shareholders
as beneficial owners of the corporate property may prefer independent auditors of their own choosing to audit the books and
make a report of their managers' trusteeship, and that shareholders are entitled to a report of their annual meeting (at least
where they vote for it)—that accurate information of what
transpires there respecting the corporation is a necessity if
shareholders are to act for their best interest. Had the court
supported management's contention, the federal statute and the
rules promulgated under it would have been a practical nullity,
for boards are frequently given the power to enact by-laws, as
in the principal case, and since the notice provision was, under
the by-law, within the discretion of the board, it could, as the
court states, use it as a "strainer" or a "block" to prevent proposals which it did not favor from getting before the shareholders. But in another case it was held that a proposal that
segregated seating used in the South by the corporation be
abolished was not a proper subject of shareholder action.[98] It
might be asked whether such a matter involving a determination
of grave public policy should not be one in which shareholders
"may properly be interested" under the laws of any state.

Since the great majority of corporations do not have their
shares registered on a national exchange, the benefits obtainable
by virtue of the proxy requirements are not available to the
shareholders of most corporations. And, even if a corporation's
shares are so registered, unless management seeks proxies it need
not comply with the proxy regulations—thus, the great benefit
through disclosure and minority proposals at the corporation's
expense is not possible. It has been pointed out by two men who
have been actively engaged in encouraging shareholder participation in corporate meetings and who have been fighting vigorously
what appears to be a winning battle to force management to give

98. Peck v. Greyhound Corp., 97 F.Supp. 679 (D.N.Y.1951). The court based its holding on fact that the Commission's rule did not support the plaintiff. But Regulation 240.14a–8(c) (2) now states that management may omit a proposal if it is primarily for the purpose of promoting general economic, political, racial, religious, social or similar causes.

more information to their owners than they have done in the past that "At the present time some 8% of the corporations on the New York Stock Exchange still do not solicit proxies, thus failing to give full disclosure on the part of these managements when time for election comes." [99] This loophole is being closed for new listings, as the New York Stock Exchange makes proxy solicitation for such listings mandatory. Commenting upon this change, Mr. Keith Funston, President of the Exchange, recently stated: "The Exchange has taken these steps believing firmly that shareholders are entitled to adequate information about the affairs of their companies and should have an opportunity to voice their opinions on important corporate matters." [1] It seems certain that the time is near when all corporations, large and small, will be required by law to give complete reports of the activities of their corporate agents to the real owners, the shareholders. Too long has the practice been otherwise.

§ 5. Cumulative Voting and its Importance to Minority Representation

Some mention has already been made of the cumulative voting possibility. Mandatory provisions for cumulative voting are provided by both constitution and statute in thirteen states; in eight states by statute alone mandatory provisions exist; seventeen states have statutes which permit cumulative voting if provided for in articles or by-laws; ten states have no statutes or constitutional provisions one way or the other. [2]

Cumulative voting, though not invented by the common law, is the only method by which a minority group may obtain recognition by representation upon the board of directors. Even a group holding 49% of the voting shares could not elect a single director though it seems obvious even to the most naive that they are entitled to representation. The only damage minority representation can possibly do on a board is to report back to the shareholders the manner in which the corporation is being managed, and all shareholders have the right to know this. The board members elected by the majority will always control in the sense that they have the votes necessary to do this. Hence, the real objection which management has had to cumulative voting is the fear that a representative of a minority group will report majority misdoings to the group and that then there will follow derivative actions to recover for the corporation losses

---

99. Lewis D. and John J. Gilbert, Sixteenth Annual Report of Stockholders' Activities at Corporation Meetings 184 (1955).

1. Ibid. at 185.

2. See Note, The Conflict of Cumulative Voting and Staggered Directorships, 24 U. of Cin.L.Rev. 560, at 562 (1955) where the statutes and constitutional provisions are enumerated.

attributable to directorial misconduct, which is just what should happen when management breaches its trust. The right to vote cumulatively should be provided by statute and should be absolute and so protected by statutory provisions that it will not be defeated by staggered elections, as has been the case recently. Opposition on a corporate board can be as healthful as that in a state or national legislature. Not all of the best ideas, by any means, come from the majority.

Cumulative voting permits a shareholder to multiply the number of votes his total shares give him by the number of directors to be elected and to cast the total for one nominee or split the total in any proportion he sees fit for two or more nominees. Whether he owns or has control of enough votes to obtain representation may be ascertained by formulas designed for that purpose. There are two in common use:

Under Method A:[3]

Let X = number of shares needed to elect a given number of directors.

Let Y = total number of shares at the meeting (5,000 in this example).

Let N' = number of directors desired to elect (2).

Let N = total number of directors to be elected (3).

$$X = \frac{Y \cdot N'}{N + 1} + 1 \text{ share}$$

$$X = \frac{5,000 \times 2}{3+1} + 1 \text{ share}$$

$$X = 2501 \text{ shares}$$

Under Method B:[4]

Assuming there are 5,000 shares at the meeting:

Let D = number of directors to be elected (3).

Let X = percentage of necessary voting shares to elect one director.

$$X = \frac{100\%}{D+1} + 1 \text{ share}$$

$$X = \frac{100\%}{3+1} + 1 \text{ share}$$

$$X = 25\% + 1 \text{ share}$$

$$2X = 50\% + 1 \text{ share}$$

$$2X = 2501 \text{ shares}$$

And, using the formula to ascertain how many shares it will take to elect one director, assuming each share has one vote, it will take 1251 shares, if cumulated. The three directors receiving the highest number of votes in our illustration will be elected.

In order to avoid a possible tied vote one who cumulates his votes over two or more directors will be wise to give one less vote to each succeeding nominee voted upon, that is, an uneven number of votes to each candidate. If there is a tied vote among some who otherwise might have been elected, one court has stated that those receiving the highest number of votes are elected and that another vote must be taken and in that vote one may cumu-

3. Williams, Cumulative Voting for Directors, pp. 40–46 (1951).

4. Note, 24 U. of Cin.L.Rev. 560, at 561 (1955), using the illustration thus set out.

late just as before.   Hence, a minority might get a greater representation than it was entitled to if this occurred.[5]   It is also possible for a minority which properly cumulates its shares to obtain more representation than it is entitled to if the majority does not cumulate its shares or if it cumulates them badly.[6]

It is possible to defeat the effectiveness of cumulative voting by reducing the number of the board members to a point, if that is statutorily possible, where the minority has insufficient cumulated votes to elect one member to the board, or by staggering board elections by providing, say, that one, two or three directors shall be elected annually for three year terms, the first board being composed of members with one, two and three year terms in order to start the sequence.   In Ohio, where the cumulative vote is secured by mandatory provision in the corporation statute, an attempt was recently made to stagger the terms of a three-member board so that but one should be elected annually.   This would prevent any minority, no matter how large, from obtaining representation by cumulating its votes, thus emasculating the mandatory provision of the statute.   Tested in court, the code of regulations (by-law) provision was held invalid; the statutory provision permitting staggered elections can be allowed only if it does not nullify the mandatory right of cumulative voting.[7]   However, this well-considered opinion in the Ohio Court of Appeals was later reversed by the Ohio Supreme Court in a badly reasoned opinion, two able judges dissenting.[8]   The new Ohio General Corporation Law enacted in 1955 permits staggered elections if the articles or regulations (by-laws) so provide but not less than three directors may be chosen at any one time and the term of none can be more than three years.[9]   Thus the cumulative voting provision has no meaning to minorities unless they hold at the meeting 25% of the voting shares present plus 1 share, in accordance with the formulas set out above.

In the recent contest for control in Montgomery-Ward & Co., Inc., the mandatory constitutionally provided cumulative voting right was tested against a statutory staggered-directors provision which this company had taken advantage of through a provision in its by-laws.   The by-laws provided for nine directors divided into classes of three each for purposes of elec-

---

5. A dictum in State ex rel. Price v. Du Brul, 100 Ohio St. 272, 126 N. E. 87 (1919).

6. A good illustration is Pierce v. Commonwealth, 104 Pa.St. 150 (1883).   Other examples are: Schwartz v. State ex rel. Schwartz, 61 Ohio St. 497, 56 N.E. 201 (1900); Chicago Macaroni Mfg. Co. v. Boggiano, 202 Ill. 312, 67 N.E. 17 (1903).

7. Humphrys v. The Winous Co., 57 Ohio Opinions 44, 125 N.E.2d 204 (Ct.App.1955).

8. Humphrys v. The Winous Co., 165 Ohio St. 45, 133 N.E.2d 780 (1956).

9. Ohio Rev.Code § 1701.57 (A) and (B).   This was not in effect when the Humphrys case arose.

tions staggered over a period of three years. In a declaratory judgment action, the Illinois court held that the statute subverted the constitutional intent which guaranteed proportional representation and must fail as a device which impairs the rights of minority shareholders.[10]

The argument for staggered directors is that there will always be some experienced directors on the board to train junior directors later elected. This is a pretty weak argument as the company records will show. Directors are usually reelected year after year so that there are few vacancies and when they are filled there are old performers on the board without the aid of the staggering device. The practice of staggering the election of directors limits and frequently defeats the cumulative voting right so that a minority, otherwise assured of representation, loses this valuable right. It is surprising that legislatures have not been better informed of the possible effects of staggered elections on the cumulative voting provisions in the same statutes.

There is, of course, need of protecting the majority against a surprise vote cumulative-wise which might obtain a larger percentage of representation than the minority is entitled to. The Ohio statute does this by providing that a shareholder give written notice not less than 48 hours prior to the meeting, if the corporation has given notice of the meeting at least ten days prior thereto, that he desires the voting to be cumulative. He is required to give at least 24 hours' notice if the corporation's notice of meeting is less than 10 days prior to it. The statute contains another proviso, namely, "if an announcement of the giving of such notice is made upon the convening of the meeting by the chairman   .   .   .", etc. All shareholders present may then vote their shares cumulatively.[11]

§ 6. Control Exercised Through Shareholders' Pooling Agreements and Voting Trusts

It is legally proper for shareholders to combine in order to control, for legitimate purposes, their corporation. In a frequently cited case,[12] three individuals purchased a block of stock

10. Wolfson v. Avery, 6 Ill.2d 78, 126 N.E.2d 701 (1955). Compare Janney v. Philadelphia Transportation Co., 387 Pa. 282, 128 A.2d 76 (1956), which reached an opposite conclusion, distinguishing Wolfson v. Avery. In Application of New York Hanseatic Corp., 200 Misc. 530, 103 N.Y.S.2d 698 (1951), a permissive cumulative voting right had been eliminated by charter amendment. It was held that the amendment eliminated a substantial right and entitled the common shareholders thus affected to an appraisal of their shares and payment therefor.

11. Ohio Rev.Code § 1701.55(C).

12. Smith v. San Francisco & N. P. Ry. Co., 115 Cal. 584, 47 P. 582, 35 L.R.A. 309, 56 Am.St.Rep. 119 (1897).

under a pooling agreement that for five years the block would be voted as the majority of the three should determine. One of the three attempted to vote the shares registered in his name contrary to the agreement. His vote was rejected and the vote of the block as determined by the other two was accepted. The court held the pooling agreement to be a valid contract, calling it a proxy, and holding that it was irrevocable as a power coupled with an interest. There was no joint interest in the shares, each shareholder owning his own and having them registered as such on the company's books. If in fact it was a proxy, it was of an unusual sort but perhaps might be loosely supported upon an implied agreement to constitute one or both of the majority as proxies in case of disagreement. The agreement was in writing so that if all three were present a simple determination could be made as to who might vote the shares. All three had an interest in the shares and their voting power to keep the corporation in grooves which all hoped would make for success, and it is probable the three would not have purchased the shares had they not been able to exact from each other the promise that the block would be voted as the majority wished. The case has been criticised for rather picayunish reasons such as there was no joint ownership or voting trust but each party held his shares individually and they were registered thus; [13] that the decision was, in effect, one which specifically enforced a voting contract; [14] that since no particular agent was appointed it is difficult to see a proxy; [15] and that the interest of each in the shares of the others also "seems doubtful." [16] The most serious criticism to such an arrangement would seem to be the possible confusion at a meeting to determine just who is entitled to vote the shares. Registered holders are, or should be, not hard to determine. Proxies, by their written powers of attorney, are also not difficult to ascertain. But it does seem like an unusual burden to place upon inspectors of election or the chairman the responsibility of determining how the shares are to be voted and who may vote them. If fewer than all had turned up at the meeting the question of who could vote the block and for what nominees or resolutions would involve matters of veracity which could cause greater confusion.

However, pooling agreements similar to the one described above have generally been recognized if the purpose is a legiti-

13. Note, 56 Am.St.Rep. 138 (1897).

14. Note, 3 U. of Chi.L.Rev. 640, 644 (1935).

15. Ballantine, Corporations 411 (Rev. ed. 1946).

16. Ibid. But see Ecclestone v. Indialantic, Inc., 319 Mich. 248, 29 N.W.2d 679 (1947), where a president (who was also a director) transferred his stock but retained, by contract, the voting rights. It was held that the power to vote was coupled with an interest, continuous management being a benefit to both the corporation and its shareholders.

mate one.   In the recent well-known case of *Ringling Bros.-Bar-num & Bailey Combined Shows, Inc. v. Ringling,*[17] Mrs. Ringling and Mrs. Haley, each owning 315 shares in this family-owned corporation whose only remaining outstanding shares, 370 in number, were owned by Mr. North, joined in an agreement whose duration was stated to be ten years, unless terminated by mutual agreement.   Each was to have an option to buy the other's shares at stated terms if such shares were proposed to be sold, and the 630 shares were to be voted as mutually agreed, any disagreement to be submitted to Mr. Loos, an attorney, as arbitrator "and his decision thereon shall be binding upon the parties hereto."   The purpose of the agreement was to secure good management and the participation therein by members of the Ringling family insofar as their experience, capacity and ability might warrant, certainly worthy objectives and legitimate legally.   The time arrived when the two ladies could not agree upon how the vote should be cast at a directors' election.   Of the seven-member board, they could always, by cumulating their vote, be sure of electing five of the seven directors.   Mrs. Ringling requested the arbitrator to decide how the votes should be cast.   After some preliminary voting upon a resolution for adjournment, the arbitrator directed that the two vote their shares cumulatively for five named nominees, and the chairman of the meeting ruled that these five, with two of three voted for by Mr. North, had been elected.   The trial court held the stock pooling agreement lawful and not opposed to any public policy of Delaware; that the arbitrator, when he acts under the agreement, is "an implied agent possessing the irrevocable proxy of the recalcitrant party for the purpose of casting the particular vote," and that in a new election to be held before a master the votes be recognized in accordance with the agreement of the parties.[18]

In reviewing the lower court's determination, the Delaware Supreme Court held that the agreement to arbitrate did not give the arbitrator authority to command compliance with his recom-

---

17.   29 Del.Ch. 610, 53 A.2d 441 (Sup. Ct. 1947), directing a modification of the order of the Court of Chancery whose opinion was reported in 49 A.2d 603 (Del.Ch.1946).   See notes on the principal case in 36 Calif.L.Rev. 281 (1948); 60 Harv. L.Rev. 651 (1947); 46 Mich.L.Rev. 70 (1947); 15 U. of Chi.L.Rev. 738 (1948); 96 U. of Pa.L.Rev. 121 (1947).   Besides the several cases cited in *Ringling* which sustain pooling agreements, see these: State ex rel. Everett Trust & Savings Bank v. Pacific Waxed Paper Co., 22 Wash.2d 844, 157 P.2d 707, 159 A.L.R. 297 (1945) (a two-shareholder agreement, each having a 25-year option to buy the other's shares if offered for sale, the survivor to have an irrevocable proxy to vote the deceased shareholder's shares, was held valid and irrevocable as against the executor of one); White v. Snell, 35 Utah 434, 100 P. 927 (1909).   However, some cases are contra: Roberts v. Whitson, 188 S. W.2d 875 (Tex.Civ.App.1945).

18.   See citation to lower court's opinion in note 17, supra.

mendations and to carry his recommendations into effect; that the agreement contemplates that "at least one of the parties must determine that such decision shall be carried into effect;" that the parties themselves could override the arbitrator's recommendations. The court modified the order of the trial court, holding that Mrs. Ringling's votes should be counted, that Mrs. Haley's votes should not be, and that Mr. North who was not bound by the agreement should have his votes counted, as tendered. Thus, Mrs. Ringling obtained recognition for the three directors for whom her votes had been cumulated, Mr. North for the three directors for whom his votes had been cumulated, and the court left in the air, so to speak, what was to be done concerning the seventh director but indicated that another election was about due and that this might make a determination of that question unimportant. However, the court indicated that any of the parties could raise the question in the Court of Chancery after the mandate of the Supreme Court had been received there.

The reasoning of the lower court in *Ringling* seems more in accord with the intent of the parties and more reasonable since Mrs. Ringling was in agreement with what the arbitrator had commanded. In fact, did not the arbitrator stand in Mrs. Ringling's shoes thus fulfilling the upper court's determination that "the arbitrator's decision cannot be enforced unless at least one of the parties (entitled to cast one-half of their combined votes) is willing that it be enforced?" [19] In light of the upper court's holding, a wise draftsman will make specific provision that the parties agree that the arbitrator shall have the authority to cast their combined vote whenever, by referral of a disagreement to him by one of the parties, he shall have concluded how the shares should be voted.

Agreements *not* to vote shares have been sustained when made for a valid purpose, such as the furnishing of new capital by subscribing for shares, thereby putting into the hands of the new subscribers or shareholders subscribing for additional shares a higher percentage of voting power than they would otherwise have had. Such an agreement was sustained in *Trefethen v. Amazeen*.[20] The agreement was to continue as long as the two new subscribers, or either of them, held any shares in the company. By virtue of the agreement the two subscribers obtained a 50% voting power in a closely held corporation thus giving

19. 53 A.2d 441, at 445 (Del.Sup.Ct. 1947).

20. 93 N.H. 110, 36 A.2d 266 (1944). Compare Creed v. Copps, 103 Vt. 164, 152 A. 369 (1930), where one shareholder agreed to vote his shares as the other directed him to, and this was held invalid; and Nickolopoulos v. Sarantis, 102 N.J. Eq. 585, 141 A. 792 (1928), where by agreement the holder of 25% of the shares was to have 50% of the voting power.

them a voice in its management and the protection which this afforded their investment. This result might well be reached by a pooling agreement of some or all of the shareholders in order to obtain further capital, or for some other legitimate reason, such as procuring a corporate loan or securing a high-powered executive who would not otherwise come to the company except with this additional security.

(a) Control through voting trusts. The use of the voting trust device by which shareholders transfer their shares to voting trustees under an agreement that the trustees shall have the right to vote the shares for the period and in the manner stated in the agreement, the other rights such as that to dividends to be retained by the transferors, with the usual provision that the trustees shall issue to the transferors voting trust certificates with earmarks of negotiability, is another common method of control. The device has been used occasionally by promoters who have offered to the public voting trust certificates in the first instance, thus securing and retaining control from the beginning with little investment.[21] Voting trust agreements were recognized by the common law in the majority of states when the purpose for which they were designed was a legitimate one. In a minority of the states the device was held to be invalid because of the separation of the beneficial interest from the voting right, of a supposed conflict between other statutory provisions such as those providing for annual elections and voting by proxy, and of a supposed violation of the reason and spirit of the statute's use of the term "stockholders" which, according to this view, means *"actual* stockholders"—*"real* stockholders"—"and not those who, from the fortuitous circumstance that they hold stock certificates without ownership of or interest in the stock itself, assume to vote in respect thereto." [22] Thus, no matter how worthy the purpose, the voting trust was ruled out as a possible device for control purposes, and was considered invalid not only when the question was raised by the shareholders who were parties to the agreement but also when their transferees or those not parties to the agreement raised it.[23]

The weakness of the proxy as a practical device for keeping control for any length of time is that it is revocable at any time

21. Carnegie Trust Co. v. Security Life Ins. Co., 111 Va. 1, 68 S.E. 412 (1910), is a good illustration of this. The trust in issue was created for a period of 25 years.

22. Pitney, J., in Warren v. Pim, 66 N.J.Eq. 353, 59 A. 773, at 783 (Ct. Err. & App. 1904). See also Shepaug Voting Trust Cases, 60 Conn. 553, 24 A. 32 (1890). These are the

two leading cases expressing the minority view. By N.J.S.A. 14:-10–10 voting trusts are now legalized, and the same is true in Connecticut by Conn.Gen.Stat.1949, Supp. § 504a.

23. Warren v. Pim, supra note 22, included complainants who were transferees and holders of shares outside the voting trust.

unless coupled with an interest. The same is true of a pooling
agreement if the court insists upon an interest in the shares
pooled in order to find a power coupled with an interest. Fortunately, for those who seek control, courts have usually been
satisfied if each in the pool has an interest in the manner in which
the shares are to be voted and in the results to be thus achieved.[24]
In fact, it should be apparent that the agency coupled with an interest is a bit of machinery in the realm of legerdemain invented
to give the agent specific performance without a showing that
the remedy at law is inadequate. And agreements to vote shares
for legitimate purposes, based upon a valid consideration, ought
to be enforceable by specific performance as there is no way of
showing that the remedy at law is sufficient. That is what courts
are apparently doing when they are able to analyze the particular set of facts as constituting a proxy coupled with an interest.

Where voting trusts have been recognized as legitimate devices for pooling votes, the voting trustee is given title and he
votes as any other title holder. In truth, he is little more than a
proxy for his only purpose is to vote on behalf of those who have
made him trustee albeit that the creation of the trust was for
the protection, perhaps, of a lender or another class of shareholders or even of the trustee himself. It has been said that a
voting trustee is "only a sham owner vested with a colorable and
fictitious title for the sole purpose of voting upon stock that (he)
does not own." [25] However, the voting trust "is the only sure
method of binding shareholders to vote as a unit and thus (of)
assuring a desirable stability and continuity in management in
situations where that is needed." [26] Thus the practical reason
for voting trusts has been supported and, at the present time,
many statutes exist which authorize their use for respectable
business purposes and for reasonable time periods during which
such agreements are irrevocable. Originally there was a good
deal of criticism made of voting trusts which purported to be irrevocable for an unreasonable length of time. The statutes, as
we shall presently see, have incorporated the universal feeling
that the beneficial owners should periodically reexamine their
position as beneficiaries under voting trusts with the opportunity, under most statutes, of withdrawing at the end of the period.

24. In Deibler v. Chas. H. Elliott
Co., 368 Pa. 267, 81 A.2d 557, at
561 (1951), the court stated: "We
know of no decision in Delaware,
nor has any been cited, which
holds that the interest necessary to
make a proxy irrevocable must be
in the stock itself rather than a
general interest in the corporation
or in what the exercise of the
proxy may accomplish or secure."

25. Pitney, J., in Warren v. Pim, 66
N.J.Eq. 353, 59 A. 773, at 785 (Ct.
Err. & App.1904).

26. Ballantine, Corporations 426
(Rev. ed. 1946).

While it is not possible to specify all of the purposes for which a voting trust may be legally formed, it may be stated generally that any purpose which is aimed at the common good of all shareholders and within the ambit of shareholder action will qualify, as well as action which a majority or minority, whichever is the case, may legitimately take though there may be some question whether it is for the best interests of all, as where a majority under statutory authority votes to dissolve a prosperous corporation and go out of business. Equality of treatment, however, can be insisted upon with the playing of no favorites. Creating voting trusts by agreements with creditors, senior shareholders, or a combination of both in order to give them security in their loans or investments, separately or as part of a reorganization plan, is not only legitimate but laudable.[27] To secure continuity in management, to enable a group to obtain representation on the corporation's board of directors, to further some plan or policy of the company, to prevent competitors from obtaining control, to assure impartial choice of directors where stock is closely held and equally balanced—all are legitimate purposes aimed at the common good or within the sphere of legitimate shareholder action. But voting trusts created for personal benefit at the expense of shareholders outside the trust whether that personal benefit be for shareholders within the trust, persons outside the trust such as promoters or other third parties, or for the trustees themselves, are clearly outside the area of legitimate purposes for which such trusts have been permitted.

It is usual to give the trustees of a voting trust full power to vote the shares in the trust and frequently, through their use of this power, they elect themselves members of the board. If they have sufficient votes to elect a majority of the board they may legitimately take their seats and function like any other majority, but with the same limitations. By becoming members of the board they do not lose their identity as trustees, and they retain the strict fiduciary obligations and duties of trustees. In *Brown v. McLanahan*,[28] voting trustees of all the preferred and common shares with very broad specific powers including the right to vote for certain amendments to the corporate charter "as well as every other right of an absolute owner of said shares" proceeded, by amendment, to eliminate the arrearage dividend clause providing for exclusive voting rights in the preferred

27. Bullivant v. First Nat. Bank, 246 Mass. 324, 141 N.E. 41 (1923) (voting trust originally made to comply with demands of a large creditor); Mackin v. Nicollet Hotel, Inc., 25 F.2d 783 (8th Cir. 1928), cert. den. 278 U.S. 618, 49 S.Ct. 22, 73 L.Ed. 541 (1928) (voting trust to secure bondholders and preferred shareholders in the financing of the corporation).

28. 148 F.2d 703 (4th Cir. 1945).

stock, to create 221,000 new votes by granting voting rights to the debenture holders, a thing which the Virginia statute permitted, and to deprive the common shareholders of their exclusive right to elect one director. This was done shortly before the expiration of the voting trust which had a term of ten years and it was alleged that the reason for these changes was to give the trustees in their individual capacities control of the business and affairs of the company after the expiration of the voting trust. In a class action brought by an owner of voting trust certificates representing preferred shares for a breach of fiduciary duty by the trustees, in which one remedy sought was the setting aside as unlawful the granting of votes to the debenture holders, it was held that the power to amend the charter granted in the trust indenture did not authorize an amendment in derogation of the trust reposed in the trustees; that the trust agreement was not intended to vest the trustees with power either to impair the voting power of the preferred stock or to use the power for the benefit of debenture holders to the detriment of the preferred shares. Furthermore, it is fundamental that a trustee may not exercise powers granted in a way that will injure the beneficiary nor may he favor one beneficiary over another. "Even if we assume that the trustees' voting power was without substantial limitation, legal phraseology may never serve as a cloak for a breach of fiduciary duty," concluded the court.[29] But, without reference to their breach of duty, the court held that the authority granted, broad as it was, did not warrant the action taken by the trustees even if they had, in good faith, taken it.

The voting trust agreement in *Brown v. McLanahan* came out of a reorganization proceeding, as many voting trusts do, and was for the particular protection of those who, prior to the reorganization, had held first lien bonds or were unsecured creditors. The purpose for which the voting trust is set up may, and should play an important part in determining how far the voting trustees may legitimately go in carrying out their powers. If a voting trust of common shares is set up for the purpose of protecting senior security holders, such as holders of debentures or of preferred shares carrying preferences upon dissolution, a good faith determination that a sale of all the assets with eventual dissolution may well be supported by a court against the attack of a voting trust certificate holder who has no other claim than lack of power in the trustees.[30] But if the contemplated sale were for

---

29. Ibid. at 709. Berle and Means, The Modern Corporation and Private Property 78 (1932), cite the case of the Interborough Rapid Transit Company voting trust agreement which was for five years but renewable without action by the holders of voting trust certificates for five successive periods of five years each.

30. See Gottschalk v. Avalon Realty Co., 249 Wis. 78, 23 N.W.2d 606 (1946). Compare Matter of Bacon, 287 N.Y. 1, 38 N.E.2d 105 (1941).

an unfair price or to one of the trustees, a voting trust certificate holder would have a just cause for complaint. And a shareholder not within the voting trust could enjoin a sale at an unfair price though he would be in no position to prevent a sale at a fair price.

While voting trustees owe strict fiduciary duties to their certificate holders the other side of the coin should also be mentioned. There is another fundamental principle that those who induce management to act make themselves liable as managers. In such a case, the duties and obligations of directors will be theirs though they do not hold the office.[31] Control through the voting trust is easily traceable; and, while the mere election of directors outside their own group would not make them liable as directors any more than a similar election by a majority shareholder or even a sole shareholder, the temptation of "inducing" management action is always a present one. Thus trustees under a voting trust cannot avoid their duties as shareholders, as trustees, or as managers if they elect themselves to the board or if, without membership on the board, they induce board action. Gilbert and Sullivan could find no better material for a parody on paradoxes.

At the present time statutes in 35 states and the District of Columbia specifically authorize the use of voting trusts, while in 13 states and Hawaii there are no statutes on this subject.[32] The majority of the statutes provide for irrevocable voting trusts for a period of not over 10 years, many of them with renewal provisions either upon a vote of the majority in interest in the voting trust or upon the consent of those who wish to renew for another ten years and for like periods later. The California statute[33] specifies a period of 21 years which is the longest of any statute, but it also contains a provision that the trust may be terminated by the holders of a majority in interest

---

31. The classic statement is that of Justice Brandeis in Southern Pacific Ry. Co. v. Bogert, 250 U.S. 483, at 487, 39 S.Ct. 533, at 535, 63 L.Ed. 1099 (1919): "The majority has the right to control; but when it does so, it occupies a fiduciary relation toward the minority, as much so as the corporation itself or its officers and directors." Later, the opinion discusses the problem on the basis of majority "domination."

32. States with voting trust statutes are: Arizona, Arkansas, California, Colorado, Connecticut, Delaware, Florida, Georgia, Idaho, Illinois, Indiana, Kansas, Kentucky, Louisiana, Maryland, Michigan, Minnesota, Nebraska, Nevada, New Hampshire, New Jersey, New Mexico, New York, North Carolina, North Dakota, Ohio, Oklahoma, Oregon, Pennsylvania, Tennessee, Texas, Virginia, Washington, West Virginia, and Wisconsin.
States with no statutes on voting trusts are: Alabama, Iowa, Maine, Massachusetts, Missouri, Mississippi, Montana, Rhode Island, South Carolina, South Dakota, Utah, Vermont, and Wyoming.

33. West's Ann.Cal.Corp.Code §§ 2230 and 2231. Minnesota and Nevada state 15 years.

of the beneficial interests unless otherwise specified. A few statutes permit irrevocability for 5 years, with renewal for like periods in some cases,[34] while the Wisconsin statute mentions no time limit on irrevocable voting trusts.[35] An occasional statute, while naming a maximum for which an irrevocable voting trust may be created, adds that the period may be longer if coupled with an interest in the shares.[36] The policy indicated by these statutes is that a reasonable time only should be available for irrevocable voting trusts and that if, upon reconsideration at the end of the period named, the beneficial owners desire to keep the trust alive they may do so in the manner set forth in the statute.

Some of the other provisions in the statutes are that, under some, a specific right is given the beneficial owners to examine the books and records of the company; under a few the voting may be by the trustee in person or by proxy; under several all shareholders of the class or classes in the voting trust are entitled to place their shares in the trust also; and under a fair number there is a specific provision that the trustee shall issue certificates of voting trust which shall be transferable in the same manner as certificates of stock under the Uniform Stock Transfer Act in force in the state.

It should be said that these statutes do not give permission to create voting trusts for every purpose. They have, when they have spoken at all, codified the common law in requiring a legitimate purpose. They are useful in pointing the way to those who draft voting trust agreements in states not having statutes and which have not called such devices illegal, for they express rather uniform policies that such trusts should not be made irrevocable for more than a reasonable length of time, say ten years with provisions for renewal by those who desire another term and that, perhaps, they should be open to all shareholders who wish to come into the trust. A number of them specify interests which, joined with the voting power, will create a power coupled with an interest, and these may be useful where the local law is short on such matters.[37] A few of the statutes have indicated specifically that voting trust agreements may not be created for shares in banks, insurance companies, building and loan asso-

---

34. Neb. Reissue Rev.Stat.1943, § 21–139 (5 years but may be extended another 5 years); N.M.Stat.Ann. 1953, § 51–3–22 (5 years, apparently no longer).

35. Wis.Bus.Corp.Law 1951, § 180.27 as amended by L.1953, c. 399, § 15.

36. Ariz.Rev.Stat. § 10–302 (1956); Burns' Ind.Ann.Stat. § 25–256 (1933); Kan.Gen.Stat.1949, § 17–3307 and –3308.

37. See Ariz. statute, supra note 36; Ohio Rev.Code (Gen.Corp.Law of 1955) § 1701.49(B). Actually, there is no need of talking of powers coupled with an interest. The trustee has title and votes as titleholder, not as a proxy.

ciations and similar institutions.[38]   Apparently the feeling is
that what is good for General Motors is not fit for its Acceptance Corporation.   Regardless of these limitations, it is doubtful
whether good reasons exist for their enactment.

The statutes concerning voting trusts have, as a rule, been
rather strictly interpreted and, when there is doubt as to their
application in a particular case, it would seem wiser to use another device, for example, a pooling agreement.   In *Smith* v.
Biggs Boiler Works Co.[39] a voting trust agreement purported to
place within the hands of its trustees shares which, for the moment, were in escrow with a bank, part of them being optioned
for sale.   The agreement was challenged as being invalid as a
voting trust when one shareholder in the "trust" was ousted by
the majority vote of the trustees from his position on the board
and his office as president.   The court held that there was no
valid voting trust and that the action of the trustees was void
and the ouster of no effect.   Though it was physically impossible
to deposit the shares in escrow with the trustees, the court held
that the legislative intent was not to permit shares in pledge or
escrow to qualify in a voting trust, stating that, "since the owners of shares in pledge or escrow may, in general, accomplish
the same purpose contemplated by the Voting Trust Statute by
other legally permissible methods, then the Legislature could not
have intended that shares of stock, which could not be physically deposited with Voting Trustees as required by the provisions
of Section 18, could ever become the subject of a valid Voting
Trust."[40]   A pooling agreement by the registered owners of the
shares would have been valid although the certificates evidencing the shares were in escrow and optioned for sale.   And there is
an advantage which has not as yet been mentioned which favors
the pooling agreement where courts sustain its irrevocability
for reasonable periods.   It has not been taxable whereas the federal stock transfer tax statute has been held applicable to voting
trust certificates.[41]   And it is probable that many state securities acts require compliance for the issue of voting trust certificates.[42]

38. Conn.Gen.Stat.1949, Supp. §
504a; W.Va.Code of 1931, c. 31,
Art. 1, § 73.

39. 32 Del.Ch. 147, 82 A.2d 372 (Del.
Ch.1951).   The Delaware statute
was interpreted.

40. Ibid. 82 A.2d at 376.   And see
In re Chilson, 19 Del.Ch. 398, 168
A. 82 (1933), Perry v. Missouri-
Kansas Pipe Line Co., 22 Del.Ch.
33, 191 A. 823 (1923), and Belle

Isle Corp. v. Corcoran, 29 Del.Ch.
554, 49 A.2d 1 (1946), all of which
are strict interpretations.

41. It was held in Orpheum Bldg.
Co. v. Anglim, 127 F.2d 478 (9th
Cir., 1942) that such transfers were
taxable as representing shares in
an "association."

42. So held in California in Barney
v. First Nat. Bank of Monterey, 90
P.2d 584 (Cal.App.1939).

(b) Open-end voting trusts and the Securities Act of 1933.
§ 2(1) of the federal act includes in its definition of "security"
the voting trust certificate, and § 2(4) defining "issuer" specifically mentions voting trust certificates, the trustee being the "issuer" in such cases.[43] Thus it has been held that an open-end
voting trust whereby all shareholders of a class may deposit
their shares and receive voting trust certificates, where interstate facilities are used, is subject to the federal act unless exempt under § 4(1) as not constituting a public offering.[44]

(c) Position of holders of voting trust certificates. When a
shareholder transfers his shares to a voting trustee and accepts
in return a voting trust certificate does he lose all of his shareholder rights or is he still entitled to those rights not granted
by the voting trust agreement? We have already seen that a
voting trustee with the broadest of powers has been held without legal authority to use his powers in derogation of his trust.[45]
The beneficiaries may always restrain the trustee from violating
his trust and may have an accounting for damages incurred by
such a breach of trust. It has been argued that the trustee,
since he is the legal and registered owner of the shares should
be treated like any other owner with a full owner's rights but
accountable to the beneficial owners for any breach of trust as
in other trust cases.[46] Does it necessarily follow that a voting
trust, which is merely a device for a quite special purpose,
should possess all of the characteristics of an active trust for
other purposes? Where the voting trust is set up with the distinct purpose of controlling the election of directors or for
minority representation or for the protection of stated security
holders or creditors, does it follow that the trustee's powers
should extend to fundamental matters not essential to the job
for which the voting trust was formed? Unless the trustee is
given specific authority to vote for an amendment to the corporate charter, or for a merger or consolidation, or for anything
else which is fundamental in the sense that it requires shareholder action to give it validity, should a voting trustee simply
by virtue of his legal ownership have these additional voting
rights? If he has such extensive voting power he may even de-

---

43. Securities Act Release 97, De-
cember 28, 1933.

44. Corporation Trust Co. v. Logan,
52 F.Supp. 999 (D.Del.1943), where
the voting trust was open to "any
present or future holder of Class
'B' stock of the corporation," and
there were some 3,500 existing
shareholders holding 800,000 shares
and thousands of others who might
acquire 4,200,000 as yet unissued

shares, and interstate facilities
were being used to carry out the
exchange, it was held that non-
compliance with the act justified
rescission.

45. Brown v. McLanahan, 148 F.2d
703 (4th Cir., 1945), and discussion
of case at pages 323–324, supra.

46. See Gose, Legal Characteristics
and Consequences of Voting Trusts,
20 Wash.L.Rev. 129 (1945).

prive his beneficiaries who, in several fundamental changes, have a dissenting appraisal right, of this important protection as well as the protection offered through voting down a resolution of the type described. As Professor Ballantine has stated: "There is ordinarily no justification for such a complete stripping of the shareholder of all the safeguards provided by law for his protection." [47]

While the law seems to be in a formative stage concerning the voting trust certificate holder's right to participate as a shareholder in areas not necessary to accomplish the purpose of the voting trust, there are strong indications that he retains some of the protective coloring of a shareholder. He has been held entitled to his dissent and his appraisal right which follows from it in a case which required the vote of the shareholders to sell all of the corporate assets, and the trustee was held to have no power to vote the dissenter's stock for that purpose. [48] He has been allowed to contest a corporate election. [49] He has been permitted to compel an inspection of the list of voting trust certificate holders, [50] but there is a conflict as to whether he, or any other unregistered shareholder, whether a legal or equitable owner, may have the inspection rights of a registered shareholder. [51] Many of the statutes authorizing voting trusts carry a specific provision that a list of voting trust certificate holders be kept at the office of the corporation within the state and be open to inspection by shareholders, and by some statutes, voting trust certificate holders. While in the main the remedies which the certificate holder has are against the trustee to remove him for breach of fiduciary duty or because his interests conflict with those of the corporation, [52] or for an accounting, [53] or to terminate the trust if there is a basis for it, or to enjoin the trustee from

---

47. Ballantine, Corporations 431 (Rev. ed. 1946).

48. Matter of Bacon, 287 N.Y. 1, 38 N.E.2d 105 (1941), noted in 55 Harv.L.Rev. 868 (1942). This holding is "indefensible" says Gose, op. cit. supra note 46, at 141. But is it, except upon interpreting the voting trust as if it were an active trust for some other purpose? Compare Salt Dome Oil Corp. v. Schenck, 28 Del.Ch. 433, 41 A.2d 583 (1945), and Gottschalk v. Avalon Realty Co., 249 Wis. 78, 23 N.W.2d 606 (1946).

49. Chandler v. Bellanca Aircraft Corp., 19 Del.Ch. 57, 162 A. 63 (1932), noted in 18 Cornell L.Q. 274 (1933), 46 Harv.L.Rev. 333 (1932).

50. Brentmore Estates v. Hotel Barbizon, 263 App.Div. 389, 33 N.Y.S. 2d 331 (1942).

51. See discussion at page 292, supra.

52. Moore v. Bowes, 8 Cal.2d 162, 64 P.2d 423 (1937); Lippard v. Parish, 22 Del.Ch. 25, 191 A. 829 (1937).

53. Overfield v. Pennroad Corp., 42 F.Supp. 586 (D.Pa.1941), rev'd because statute of limitations had run, id. v. id., 146 F.2d 889 (3d Cir., 1944). And see Perrine v. Pennroad Corp., 29 Del.Ch. 531, 47 A.2d 479 (Del.Sup.Ct.1946), in which a settlement was approved, the same facts being involved.

exercising powers which he does not possess, there would seem to be good reasons for liberal treatment of the voting trust certificate holder when he needs the protection which his prior shareholder status gave him. The voting trust agreement should make clear just what the voting trustee may vote for and should reserve, when not necessary to carry out the purpose of the voting trust, for shareholder action through the trustee the fundamental changes of various sorts, amendments to the by-laws, and the exercise of appraisal rights which the statute gives to dissenting shareholders. If the voting trust agreement permits the trustee to vote the total shares held for fundamental changes upon a majority vote of the certificate holders, it may mean that less than the majority required by statute (usually two-thirds) may actually approve such a change. It seems probable that the requirement of the statute has not, under such circumstances, been met. Certainly, the spirit of the statute has been violated. Care should be taken in the drafting of such agreements to make specific provisions for the voting of fundamental changes with a spelling out of dissenters' rights if the trustee is to be directed by a certificate holders' vote.[54] The statutes generally suggest or imply limitations which the shareholders may place upon the trustee's power to vote the shares so deposited with him.

§ 7. Dead-Hand Control Through Testamentary Directions to Trustees

Shares devised by will to trustees may contain directions as to how the shares shall be voted and, at times, such directions have been aimed at tying the directors' discretionary authority so that they must act in accordance with the directions. How far the dead hand of a deceased shareholder should be allowed to control the action of his testamentary trustee concerns a matter of policy which ought to be recognized for what it is. The analogies offered by the voting trust device and by cases involving attempts of living shareholders to tie the hands of their directors in discretionary matters offer aid in solving problems of shares in the hands of testamentary trustees with similar mandatory functions.

Where testamentary trustees of a majority of the corporation's stock had directions to vote the stock for themselves as directors with the expressed desire of the testator that they would retain named persons as officers of the company, it was held that such directions were valid,[55] the latter request being

---

54. For some excellent material on the drafting problems in voting trust agreements, see Burke, Voting Trusts Currently Observed, 24 Minn.L.Rev. 347, 373 et seq. (1940).

55. In re Pittock's Will, 102 Ore. 159, 199 P. 633, 17 A.L.R. 218 (1921).

valid as it did not conflict with the trustees' discretion as directors, since it had been expressed as a wish rather than a command. The direction that the shares be voted for the trustees as nominees for the board would have been valid had there been a pooling of shares by living shareholders; thus, there seems no valid reason why the dead hand should have less force. Where trustees held all the shares of the corporation and the testator had directed that the shares be voted as named persons should direct, the court held the trustees who assumed their duties under the will took the shares with the condition attached and that there was no rule of law or of policy which conflicted with the testamentary direction.[56] This is comparable to a voting trust created by living shareholders who have directed how the trustees shall vote the shares in the trust, perhaps by the majority vote of the voting trust certificate holders. There would seem to be no good reason why the dead hand should not have the same privilege. But where the testator has not only directed how the shares shall be voted but has attempted to emasculate the board of its powers of discretion in determining whether dividends shall be declared and paid or whether, irrespective of its own judgment, an officer or employee shall be elected or retained in his job, the courts have generally followed the line of holdings in similar cases where living shareholders have agreed upon such procedures, a topic to be discussed shortly.[57] It would seem, however, that to the extent that by-laws under modern statutes permit the limitation of the powers of directors, a testator who had a controlling interest in a corporation might, by testamentary directions, proceed as far as a by-law might.[58] Such statutes indicate that policy-wise there is no objection to limiting the powers of directors to that extent.

§ 8.   Control Through Agreements Limiting the Discretionary Powers of the Board of Directors

While there is general agreement that shareholders may combine for the purpose of electing a board of directors, wheth-

56. Elger v. Boyle, 69 Misc. 273, 126 N.Y.S. 946 (1910). But see William Randall & Sons, Inc. v. Lucke, 123 Misc. 5, 205 N.Y.S. 121 (1924), which seems contra to Elger v. Boyle, a case not cited by the later court.

57. Boyle v. John Boyle & Co., 136 App.Div. 367, 120 N.Y.S. 1048 (1910), aff'd without opinion, 200 N.Y. 597, 94 N.E. 1092 (1911) (trustees tried to force the corporation to declare dividends from its surplus earnings); Billings v. Marshall Furnace Co., 210 Mich. 1, 177 N.W. 222, 9 A.L.R. 1239 (1920) (testamentary directions provided, in part, for the voting of the shares annually for two sons of the testator and one trustee (unnamed) for positions on the board, but the court had other reasons, also); D'Arcangelo v. D'Arcangelo, 137 N. J.Eq. 63, 43 A.2d 169 (1945) (testamentary directions to employ testator's brother).

58. It was so argued, and sustained in Farmers' Loan & Trust Co. v. Pierson, 130 Misc. 110, 222 N.Y.S. 532 (1927).

er the combination is evidenced by one or more proxies, or a pooling agreement or a voting trust, and that these devices may be used for collective action for any legitimate business purpose, the attempt by majority shareholders to bind their elected officials by agreements of any sort has not fared so well. The reasons usually given are two: (1) all statutes provide that the corporation shall be managed by a board of directors, and those who carry on business in the corporate form must comply with the statutory command; and (2) the minority shareholders would lose much of their protection if the board could, by agreement, abandon its discretionary powers. As to the statutory command, it has been said that ". . . the powers of the board of directors are, in a very important sense, original and undelegated. The stockholders do not confer, nor can they revoke, those powers. They are derivative only in the sense of being received from the state in the act of incorporation." [59] The second reason is the sounder of the two and recognizes the fact that the board represents the entire group of shareholders who comprise the corporation and it must act for the good of all with equality of treatment and without special favors to anyone. Thus, where majority shareholders have agreed to elect each other to the board and as board members to vote to employ one or each other as officers of the company, or to employ some third person, thus purporting to surrender their discretionary power to appoint others who may be worthier, courts have with fair consistency held the agreement of the board members invalid with no cause of action for its breach. While shareholders may unite to elect stated directors, including themselves, to the board, "The power to unite is . . . limited to the election of directors and is not extended to contracts whereby limitations are placed on the power of directors to manage the business of the corporation by the selection of agents at defined salaries." [60] And, of course, the agreement of board members to abdicate and permit full reign by other company officers is invalid for the same reason.[61]

59. Manson v. Curtis, 223 N.Y. 313, 119 N.E. 559, at 562 (1918).

60. McQuade v. Stoneham, 263 N.Y. 323, 189 N.E. 234, at 236 (1934). Plaintiff argued he had been removed from his office because he had acted to protect minority shareholders, but the court found no outside shareholders complaining. And see Seitz v. Michel, 148 Minn. 80, 181 N.W. 102, 12 A.L.R. 1060 (1921): "Defendant would no longer be free to exercise his judgment with sole regard to the interests of the corporation and the entire body of its stockholders."

61. Manson v. Curtis, supra, note 59, was such a case. Judge Collin wrote a sentence which has frequently been quoted: "Clearly the law does not permit the stockholders to create a sterilized board of directors." 119 N.E. 559, at 562. And see Ray v. Homewood Hospital, Inc., 223 Minn. 440, 27 N.W.2d 409 (1947).

A distinction should be made between agreements entered into by majority or controlling shareholders and members of the board and those entered into by unanimous agreement of the shareholders. In the latter type of agreement, the shareholders have waived the protection of the board by contracting that certain of its powers shall be controlled by their agreement. The remaining and opposing argument is the one already mentioned: that the statute has set up the machinery of corporate government from which there may be no extraordinary deviation. The legislative purpose, however, may well have been something more than the formality of carrying on the corporate business. Legislative permission to delegate to executive and other committees and to corporate officers large areas of directorial power and to limit board powers through the by-laws indicates that board formality is not of prime importance. The recognition by the common law that corporations are frequently run as informally as partnerships and that, consequently, a course of informal action may lead to the same results as formal board action, points also to the unimportance of an exact formality through board action. The emphasis is usually placed upon the very practical side of corporate life, that corporations can act only through agents because of the very nature of this business device and, due to the diverse interests of the corporate owners, protection is needed by a board whose discretion may not be bartered away. If all shareholders agree that Smith shall be elected a director and that others of the directorate shall use their powers to keep Smith in his position as president at a stated salary for the rest of his life, as long as he is "faithful, efficient and competent," is there any reason for judging a contract to this effect invalid?

In what is perhaps the leading case answering the above question, the plaintiff who was owner of 25% and the defendant who owned 75% of the stock of the corporation had an agreement, based upon a valid consideration, which bound the defendant (and his testamentary trustee) to so vote his stock that plaintiff would be elected a director, and to so vote as a director that plaintiff would continue as the corporation's general manager "so long as he should be 'faithful, efficient and competent,'" that during the plaintiff's life he should receive one-fourth of the net income of the corporation as salary or dividends, and that no unreasonable or incommensurate salaries should be paid to other officers or agents as to materially dilute the plaintiff's profits. The defendant later failed as a director to use his power to keep him in the general manager's position. Specific performance was sought by the plaintiff and granted by the court.[62]   A dictum in *McQuade v. Stoneham* [63] was rejected and the court pointed to the fact that all shareholders were not under the agreement in that case.   Stated Crouch, J.: [64] "Are we committed by the McQuade Case to the doctrine that there may be no variation, however slight or innocuous, from that norm, where salaries or policies or the retention of individuals in office are concerned?   There is ample authority supporting this doctrine . . . [Authorities omitted] . . . and something may be said for it, since it furnishes a simple, if arbitrary, test.   Apart from its practical administrative convenience, the reasons upon which it is said to rest are more or less nebulous.   Public policy, the intention of the Legislature, detriment to the corporation, are phrases which in this connection mean little.   Possible harm to bona fide purchasers of stock or to creditors or to stockholding minorities have more substance; but such harms are absent in many instances.   If the enforcement of a particular contract damages nobody—not even, in any perceptible degree, the public—one sees no reason for holding it illegal, even though it impinges slightly upon the broad provision of section 27 (providing that the business shall be managed by the board)."

The New York court in a later case [65] had occasion to refer to the "slight impingement" or "innocuous variance" as justification of the earlier decision but refused to sustain a deprivation of the powers of supervision and management, including the manner and policy of running the business, although the shareholders had unanimously agreed that this should be so.   Thus

62. Clark v. Dodge, 269 N.Y. 410, 199 N.E. 641 (1936), noted in 5 Brooklyn L.Rev. 336 (1936) and 36 Col.L. Rev. 836 (1936). Unanimity is required and if but one shareholder remains out of the agreement, the court will hold it invalid. Odman v. Oleson, 319 Mass. 24, 64 N.E.2d 439 (1946).

63. Supra note 60 and quotation in text, supra, page 332. And see West v. Camden, 135 U.S. 507, 10 S.Ct. 838, 34 L.Ed. 254 (1890); Jackson v. Hooper, 76 N.J.Eq. 592, 75 A. 568, 27 L.R.A.,N.S., 658 (1910) (that even all the shareholders cannot agree that the corporate business and property are to be treated as if they were a partnership's business and property). But compare Mansfield v. Lang, 293 Mass. 386, 200 N.E. 110 (1936).

64. Clark v. Dodge, 269 N.Y. 410, 199 N.E. 641, at 642 (1936). *Ac-*

cord: Hayden v. Beane, 293 Mass. 347, 199 N.E. 755 (1936); Kantzler v. Benzinger, 214 Ill. 589, 73 N.E. 874 (1905).

65. Long Park v. Trenton-New Brunswick Theatres Co., 297 N.Y. 174, 77 N.E.2d 633 (1948), discussed in 43 Ill.L.Rev. 561 (1948), 61 Harv. L.Rev. 1251 (1948), 17 Ford.L.Rev. 95 (1948). And see discussion of this case at page 226, supra, this text.

Compare Schneider v. Greater M. & S. Circuit, Inc., 144 Misc. 534, 259 N.Y.S. 319 (1932), which was a lease to an individual of the assets of subsidiaries on a profit-sharing rental basis, the assets and credit of the subsidiaries being available to the lessee for the purpose of operation. The agreement was sustained by the court.

the court sustained the statutory provision as a command that a corporation must be managed by its board of directors except as to minor encroachments which, of course, leaves much uncertainty as to what powers the board may relinquish by agreement.[66]

Irrespective of the language used in *Clark v. Dodge* the variation from the norm in that case was more than a slight or innocuous one for it anticipated the surrender for a long period of a major function of the board, namely, the selection of the general manager whose duty it was to carry on the day-to-day business of the company. A possible line that might be drawn between powers that may and those that may not be surrendered by the board or any of its members is that those powers which the law permits to be passed on to an executive or other committee of the board and those which may be legitimately restricted by the enactment of by-laws may be contracted away; others may not. If, as many courts believe, the statutory enactment that corporations are to be managed by their board of directors is a statement of general policy rather than one of protection to the minority owners, it is difficult to see why even slight encroachments are permitted. If management by a board is simply for the protection of the shareholders, it is also difficult to understand why a unanimous waiver of the protection should not be respected by the courts. If there were the slightest indication that the requirement of this managing group is for the benefit of the public, or of those with whom the corporation deals, or with its employees, such a policy should also be preserved by prohibiting even slight encroachments upon the board's authority. An explanation, but not a very satisfactory one, of why courts have hesitated to hold that by unanimous action the shareholders may waive the necessity of a board is that by such a holding an incorporated partnership could carry on in corporate form as if it were still a partnership,[67] thus ob-

---

66. See Matter of Hega Knitting Mills, Inc., 124 N.Y.S.2d 115 (Sup. Ct.1953). All shareholders had agreed that, upon a certain contingency, they would vote that the corporation be dissolved. The contingency happened. The court held that the agreement was valid, following Clark v. Dodge, supra, note 64.

67. See the leading case of Jackson v. Hooper, 76 N.J.Eq. 592, 75 A. 568, 27 L.R.A.,N.S., 658 (1910). At p. 598 of 76 N.J.Eq., at p. 571 of 75A., it is stated: "An agreement or course of dealing by which corporations are organized for the purpose of using them merely as agencies or instrumentalities, or forms in the conduct of a copartnership or joint business, and by the consent of the parties in interest to be independent of statutory control cannot be recognized, enforced or perpetuated by the court of chancery in this state . . ." And see Seitz v. Michel, 148 Minn. 80, 181 N.W. 102, 12 A.L.R. 1060 (1921).

The recently operative North Carolina statute has some fine provisions for the "close corporation," sometimes called an "incorporated partnership." N.C.Gen.Stat.Cum.

taining the limited liability and other benefits of a corporation while the owners were essentially partners. Actually, that is what many closely held corporations are doing without benefit of any formal agreements emasculating the powers of the board. And, as we have already seen, their informal action is usually given legal significance.

§ 9. The Enactment of By-Laws as a Means of Controlling Directorial Action

Closely related to the subject matter of the preceding section is the use of by-laws to limit the powers of the board; likewise, to limit the powers of the shareholders themselves. The enactment of by-laws is a shareholder function and, unless authorized by law, by the articles or by shareholder resolution, the directors have no power to enact them.[68] A by-law is a rule for the government of the corporation and its officers, and the shareholders' primary right to legislate in this manner is an important one. Modern statutes sometimes specify a number of proper objectives which by-laws may prescribe or limit in addition to the more general statement that by-laws may define, limit, or regulate the exercise of the authority of the corporation, the directors, the officers, or all the shareholders.[69] And, as if to supplement or make clear the shareholders' power of legislating in the area of directorial action, some statutes also provide that "Except where the law, the articles, or the regulations (by-laws) require action to be authorized or taken by shareholders, all of the authority of a corporation shall be exercised by its directors." [70] Modern statutes frequently authorize the directors to adopt, alter or repeal by-laws provided the articles so provide, a power that is convenient especially between shareholders' meetings, but one which has sometimes been abused by directors.[71] There should be, and sometimes is a pro-

Supp.1957, § 55–73(b); § 55–24(a). See article by Latty, The Close Corporation and the New North Carolina Business Corporation Act, 34 N.C.L.Rev. 432 (1956); Symposium on the Close Corporation, 52 Nw.U.L.Rev. 345, at 397–413 (1957).

68. North Milwaukee Town-Site Co. No. 2 v. Bishop, 103 Wis. 492, 79 N.W. 785 (1899).

69. Ohio Rev.Code (Gen.Corp.Law of 1955) § 1701.11(B) (9). Eight specific objectives are stated in this subsection (B). And see §§ 1701.-56, 1701.57, 1701.59, 1701.60. In Ohio by-laws as generally understood are called "regulations." Al-

so, in Ohio, the term "by-laws" is used to designate rules enacted by the board for its own government. See § 1701.59 authorizing such "by-laws."

70. Ohio Rev.Code § 1701.59, first of two sentences.

71. A good example is S.E.C. v. Transamerica Corp., 165 F.2d 511 (3d Cir., 1947), cert. den. 332 U.S. 847, 68 S.Ct. 351, 92 L.Ed. 418 (1948), discussed in this text supra at page 312. A few modern statutes provide that the power to enact by-laws is in the directors unless the power is reserved to the shareholders in the articles. See

vision that by-laws thus adopted by the directors must be submitted to the shareholders at the next annual meeting for their approval.

By-laws, however, must not conflict with statutory or charter provisions of the corporation. If they do, they are invalid. This rule is beautifully illustrated by an attempt of two shareholders who owned, in unequal amounts, all of the stock in a corporation to equalize their positions through by-laws which provided (1) for shareholder action only when unanimous, (2) for a board of three directors to be elected only by unanimous vote, (3) for action by the directors only when in unanimous agreement, and (4) for amendment to the by-laws only upon the unanimous vote of the shareholders. In an action by one shareholder to have these by-laws adjudged valid and to enjoin the doing by the other of anything inconsistent therewith, the court struck down all but (4) on the ground that they conflicted with statutory provisions. The by-law requiring unanimous agreement for shareholder action violated statutory provisions permitting certain fundamental changes by a two-thirds vote, conflicted with other provisions giving a majority the right to force the directors to dissolve the corporation, and with a section which gave to holders of half the stock the power to dissolve the corporation when there was a deadlock. To require unanimity to elect the board of directors, a provision in the statute stating that directors shall be chosen "by a plurality of the votes at such election" would be violated. Requiring unanimous directorial action would be in opposition to the statutory quorum requirement—". . . the very idea of a 'quorum' is that, when that required number of persons goes into session as a body, the votes of a majority thereof are sufficient for binding action." [72] The requirement of unanimous shareholder action to amend the by-laws, the court found not contrary to statute or to any policy. Conway, J., who wrote a dissenting opinion joined in by two other judges, agreed with the majority on (1), (2) and (4), but thought there was nothing in the statutes which conflicted with a by-law requiring unanimous directorial action, pointing to the phrase "unless otherwise provided" as giving the necessary leeway, and he felt that equity should enjoin the other contracting

Ill.Bus.Corp.Act of 1933, § 25; Ind. Gen.Corp.Act of 1929, § 7 (Burns' Ind.Ann.Stat.1933, § 25–206).

72. Benintendi v. Kenton Hotel, 294 N.Y. 112, 60 N.E.2d 829, 159 A.L.R. 280, Ann. at 290 (1945), noted in 45 Col.L.Rev. 960 (1945), 20 N.Y.U.L.Q. Rev. 513 (1945), 19 St. John's L. Rev. 144 (1945), which was a 4–3 decision in which Conway, J.,

wrote a strong dissenting opinion. And see Kaplan v. Block, 183 Va. 327, 31 S.E.2d 893 (1944); Prigerson v. White Cap Sea Foods, Inc., 100 N.Y.S.2d 881 (Sup.Ct.1950). But see DeMarco v. Paramount Ice Corp., 102 N.Y.S.2d 692 (Sup.Ct. 1950), where a voting trust agreement was used successfully to obtain objectives similar to those of Benintendi v. Kenton Hotel.

shareholder from voting his stock contrary to his *agreement* with the plaintiff "even though validity may not be accorded to the first two attempted amendments."

By an amendment to the New York Stock Corporation Law enacted in 1948, the certificate of incorporation as originally filed or as amended may contain provisions that both the quorum and votes of the directors necessary to pass a resolution may be "such number greater than a majority as may be specified in such certificate," and the number of shares of the corporation or the number of shares the holders of which must be present in person or by proxy to constitute a quorum may be greater than a majority or plurality required by law in the absence of such a provision, and the number of votes required may be a number greater than the proportion prescribed by law in the absence of such a provision. Hence, under the New York provision (§ 9) what was attempted in the case above under discussion is today legally possible, but not through a by-law.[73]

Restrictions upon the powers of directors and officers which are contained in the by-laws are binding upon them, though not upon third parties who act upon the reasonable assumption of implied authority or upon appearances indicating apparent authority, unless such persons have knowledge of the by-law limitation. The rule that by-law limitations of authority must not conflict with statutory or charter provisions is quite as applicable to the statutory provision that a corporation shall be managed by its directors. Otherwise, by-law provisions could strip the directors of every vestige of authority, a thing which has not yet been permitted by unanimous agreement of the shareholders; and by-laws are, unless otherwise provided by statute or articles, enacted by majority vote of the shareholders. A similar rule is applicable to the amendment of the corporate charter—such amendments must not conflict with statutory or constitutional provisions. If they do, they are invalid.

§ 10. The Combination of Voting and Non-voting Stock as a Control Device

Under most modern statutes it is possible to create a class of common shares with voting rights and a class without such rights, this being the only difference between the two classes. Thus, if buyers can be found for the non-voting class of shares, control can be had and kept in the holders of the voting shares. By using the non-voting shares in large quantities and keeping

---

73. This is the first statutory provision of its kind. It goes far toward recognizing the "incorporated partnership." It also evidences the feeling that the closely held corporation should have different statutory treatment from that of the publicly held one. But see the North Carolina statute and law review citations in note 67, supra.

the voting shares at a minimum, control by those with a small investment is possible, that is, by the holders of 51% of the voting shares.   Thus, one of the chief protective devices of the shareholder is lost when his common shares carry no votes, and his risk is the same as those with the additional voting right. Non-voting preferred stock had been permitted and used for a considerable period before non-voting common made its appearance toward the end of the first quarter of the present century.   Thus, by holding common voting shares of an investment of less than $2,250,000 an investment banking institution in 1925 was able to control the great automotive industry of Dodge Brothers, Inc., with assets of more than $130,000,000.   Neither the preferred nor four-fifths of the common shares of this company carried voting rights.[74]

Generally, it may be stated that unless there is a constitutional or statutory prohibition against the use of non-voting shares, it is within the power of a corporation to create them. Their use is far more common in case of preferred issues than in case of common, but even in the preferred issues a reservation is usually made for the voting right in case of the passing of a stated number of consecutive dividends.   And, in case of fundamental changes in the preferred shareholder's contract, statutes usually give him a vote on the matter though, for other purposes, his contract limits his voting rights.

§ 11.   Restrictions on Stock Transfers as a Method of Control

Reasonable restrictions upon the transfer of shares in a close corporation can be used effectively to keep control within the group most interested in continuity of management or to keep shares out of unfriendly hands.   Too confining a restraint upon the alienation of shares, however, is as obnoxious to the law as unreasonable restraints upon the alienation of real or personal property.   Restrictions may be contained in the articles (which is a proper place for them) or in the by-laws (which have frequently been held to be contracts not subject to change by amendment to the by-laws by majority vote) [75] or in mutual agreements of the shareholders not appearing in either place. If restrictions are contained in the articles, they also constitute

---

74.   Berle and Means, The Modern Corporation and Private Property 75–76 (1932). Chrysler Corporation later acquired the Dodge stock.

75.   Bechtold v. Coleman Realty Co., 367 Pa. 208, 79 A.2d 661 (1951). And see Note, Restriction Upon Transfer of Stock, While Not a Valid By-Law, Is Nonetheless Binding Upon the Parties as a Contract, 38 Va.L.Rev. 103 (1952).   A by-law giving the corporation first right to purchase its shares at a price to be fixed by appraisers was held valid in Shumaker v. Utex Exploration Co., 157 F.Supp. 68 (D. Utah 1957).

contracts between the corporation and its shareholders and between the shareholders themselves.

An agreement of shareholders that, in case of a contemplated sale, the shares will first be offered to the company and/or to the shareholders, with perhaps a provision that in the latter case the shares shall be offered in proportion to the offeree-shareholders' interests in the corporation, the offer to remain open for a reasonable time, has been considered a reasonable one except in a few early cases, and is binding upon the shareholders; and, if contained in the articles or if it is a term in the share-contract appearing elsewhere, is binding upon the transferees.[76] However, restrictions upon the transfer of shares should also appear on the stock certificate and must so appear in a state having the Uniform Stock Transfer Act if, without more, they are to bind the parties and their transferees.[77] However, even when the restriction is not noted on the certificate, it has been held valid as against a shareholder who agreed to it or a transferee with notice.[78]

A restriction which makes the transfer of shares dependent upon the will of the directors or upon a vote of the shareholders has usually been held to be within the area of undue restraint upon alienation and, consequently, invalid.[79] However, there are a few cases which have sustained this type of restraint in closely held corporations.[80] The tendency of recent decisions is to sustain such provisions.[81] Such holdings may be justified on

76. Bechtold v. Coleman Realty Co., supra note 71; Elson v. Schmidt, 140 Neb. 646, 1 N.W.2d 314 (1941); Lawson v. Household Finance Corp., 17 Del.Ch. 343, 152 A. 723 (Sup.Ct.1930). Some of the older cases were contra: Victor G. Bloede Co. v. Bloede, 84 Md. 129, 34 A. 1127 (1896); Ireland v. Globe Milling & Reduction Co., 19 R.I. 180, 32 A. 921, 29 L.R.A. 429, 61 Am.St. Rep. 756 (1895).

77. § 15 U.S.T.A., provides that restrictions on transfers are not valid unless stated on the certificate.

78. Doss v. Yingling, 95 Ind.App. 494, 172 N.E. 801 (1930); Baumohl v. Goldstein, 95 N.J.Eq. 597, 124 A. 118 (1924). But in Costello v. Farrell, 234 Minn. 453, 48 N.W.2d 557 (1951), a purchaser with notice of the restriction which did not appear on the certificate was protected.

79. McNulta v. Corn Belt Bank, 164 Ill. 427, 447, 45 N.E. 954, 56 Am.St.

Rep. 203 (1897); Victor G. Bloede Co. v. Bloede, supra note 76.

80. Mason v. Mallard Telephone Co., 213 Iowa 1076, 240 N.W. 671 (1932), noted in 18 Iowa L.Rev. 88 (1932); Longyear v. Hardman, 219 Mass. 405, 106 N.E. 1012 (1914) (charter provision that shares could not be transferred "without the consent of three-fourths of the capital stock" was held valid but statute was emphasized).

81. See O'Neal, Restrictions on Transfer of Stock in Closely Held Corporations: Planning and Drafting, 65 Harv.L.Rev. 773, at 780 (1952). The author quite rightly asserts that "in view of the early decisions, the validity of such restrictions is still doubtful in many jurisdictions." But Professor O'Neal concludes that "The underlying test seems to be whether the restraint is sufficiently needed by the particular enterprise to justify **overriding** the general policy

the ground that it is particularly undesirable in close corporations to have participating owners who are objectionable to the group.   The decisions turn upon a matter of policy—whether to permit this much restraint upon the transfer of shares in order to give the owners something comparable to the right of *delectus personarum* in the partnership.   The purpose for which a restriction is placed upon the transfer of shares ought, in the last analysis, to have a strong bearing on how imposing the restriction may be.[82]

Draftsmen should make restrictions on stock transfers a part of the share-contract which provisions, under the better modern statutes, are required to be in the certificate or articles of incorporation.   The articles should provide not only for restrictions against the transfer by the owner and his transferee, but against the sale by a pledgee, a purchaser at a judicial sale, and the administrator or executor of a deceased shareholder. The option to purchase should not be to the corporation alone, for it may not have a fund out of which the purchase may be legally made;   many jurisdictions require a surplus for this purpose.   The provision should be clear as to whether the shares must be offered to the other shareholders on a pro rata basis or just offered to any shareholders.   It is proper to have the option extended to the directors also although, in a close corporation, they would normally be shareholders as well.   The restrictions, as indicated, should not be too tightly drawn for the policy against unreasonable restraints against alienation of property of all kinds is a strong one.[83]

§ 12.   Control Through Pyramiding of Corporations

Prior to the enactment of statutes permitting corporations to own shares in other corporations, there was no problem of parent and subsidiary to any substantial degree.   True, there were cases where the purchase and ownership of shares in other corporations were held to be reasonably incidental to the powers of the purchasing corporation, but such purchases were made in good faith and without the primary purpose of control.   It is

against restraints on alienation." Furthermore, courts more willingly sustain restraints on stock transfers in closely held corporations than in case of publicly held ones. Ibid. 778–779.

82. Greene v. E. H. Rollins & Sons, Inc., 22 Del.Ch. 394, 2 A.2d 249 (1938) is suggestive.   At the demurrer stage the court held a restriction invalid unless, at this stage, there was a showing that the restriction was so related to the successful operation of the company as to be reasonable.   And see O'Neal, supra, note 81, at 778–779.

83. See the draft set forth in Lawson v. Household Finance Corp., 17 Del.Ch. 343, 152 A. 723 (Sup.Ct. 1930), and O'Neal, Restrictions on Transfer of Stock in Closely Held Corporations: Planning and Drafting, supra, note 81.

reported that of the 573 corporations whose securities were listed and active on the New York Stock Exchange in 1928, 92 were holding companies, 395 were both holding and operating companies, and 86 were purely operating companies. Of the purely holding companies, 69 were industrial, 21 were public utilities and 2 were railroads; of those companies which were both operating and holding, 338 were industrials, 13 were public utilities and 44 were railroads. "Thus in the overwhelming majority of instances, there was at least a double mechanism interposed between the public investor and at least some of the properties represented by his securities, with a consequent increase of the legal powers which could be called into play by the persons managing the corporations." [84] As Berle and Means show there was a very rapid growth of holding companies from about 1910 onward.

By pyramiding corporations with the operating company at the base it is possible for a very small investment in the top company of the pyramid to control the large investment at the base. And by combining one or more of the devices for control already discussed the possibilities of control with little financial interest become fantastic. In fact, the device of pyramiding has been called "the most important among the very large companies" to maintain control without the ownership of the majority of voting stock.[85] In developing the great public utility systems of the United States pyramiding was extensively used and abused; in fact, the major criticism of this device was aimed at its use in the public utility field. Holding companies of shares in gas and electric utilities, insofar as they function between states in interstate commerce, are now subject to the Public Utility Holding Company Act of 1935.[86] This Act requires such holding companies to register with the Securities and Exchange Commission, giving the Commission power to direct reorganization or dissolution when in the public interest or the interest of investors or consumers of gas and electricity. The topic is too specialized to be pursued here. However, the Act has been used to simplify the holding company systems, to confine their individual operation to a single integrated public utility system, and to provide for a fairer distribution of voting power in the system.[87]

---

84. Berle and Means, The Modern Corporation and Private Property, footnote 18, page 205 (1932).

85. Ibid. at 72. For a good example of how pyramiding worked for the Van Sweringen interests in controlling several major railroad systems, see Chart 111 at page 74. And see North American Co. v. S.

E. C., 327 U.S. 686, 66 S.Ct. 785, 90 L.Ed. 945 (1946).

86. 15 U.S.C.A. § 79 et seq.

87. For helpful literature, see: Comment, Geographical Integration Under The Public Utility Holding Company Act, 50 Yale L.J. 1045 (1941); Meck and Cary, Regulation

Other federal legislation [88] prohibits the acquisition of shares in a competing corporation by a corporation engaged in interstate commerce when the effect may be to substantially decrease competition or tend to create a monopoly.

The illustration concerning the control obtained by the use of voting and non-voting shares in the *Dodge Brothers, Inc.,* case [89] by which a less than 2% investment ruled a great industry is not more startling than what can be done through the use of the holding company device. In large publicly owned corporations where the stock is widely diffused a very small proportion of the outstanding shares will actually control though all of the shares may carry voting rights. A holding company which acquires shares to the extent of this small proportion will have a working control and, of course, those with the voting control of the holding company will command the votes constituting the working control of the operating company, thus further diluting the process. This well-known fact is recognized in a provision of the Public Utility Holding Company Act mentioned above that "any company which directly or indirectly owns, controls, or holds with power to vote, 10 per centum or more of the outstanding voting securities of a public-utility company . . ." is a holding company for purposes of the Act unless, by order of the Securities and Exchange Commission, such a company is declared not to be a holding company.[90]

The holding company may also serve the same purposes as a pooling agreement of shareholders or a voting trust and avoid any dispute as to whether there is or is not a power coupled with an interest, a problem which has troubled some courts because of their failure to discern the real reason behind the invention of the power coupled with an interest.[91] The directors of the holding company will vote the shares owned by it while the shareholders of the holding company will elect its own board, an indirect control over how the directors will vote but with the

---

of Corporate Finance and Management Under the P.U.H.C.Act of 1935, 52 Harv.L.Rev. 216 (1938); Forer, Divestment of Utility Properties, 42 Col.L.Rev. 232 (1942). The 21st Annual Report, S. E. C. 1955, pp. 51–88 will give an insight into the importance of this Act. The P.U.H.C.Act § 7(c), 15 U.S.C.A. § 79g(c) contains provisions which guarantee that the holding company's issue and sale of common stock shall have "at least equal voting rights with any outstanding security" of the company. Protective provisions which guarantee representation on the board in case of

the issue of senior securities and which require voting rights in all stock issued having equal voting rights with every other outstanding stock are contained in § 18(a) (2) (C) and § 18(i) of the Investment Company Act of 1940, 15 U.S.C.A. § 80a–18.

88. Clayton Act § 7; 15 U.S.C.A. § 18.

89. See page 339, supra.

90. P.U.H.C.Act § 2(a) (7); 15 U.S. C.A. § 79b(a) (7).

91. See discussion at page 322, supra.

same restrictions on limiting the board's discretion as exist in other cases.

§ 13.   Control Through the Removal of Directors

The possibility of removing directors with or without cause through the action of shareholders or directors has been discussed earlier and need not be repeated here.[92]   However, their removal through court action warrants additional discussion at this point.

The theory that directors are fiduciaries to their corporation offers the starting point from which courts may confidently proceed in quite the same manner as in the removal of trustees for a breach of their fiduciary obligations.[93]   Yet it has been stated that "A court of law or equity has no inherent power to remove for misconduct a director who has been duly elected and who is qualified according to law and the regulations of the corporation   .   .   . "[94]   But, as Professor Ballantine has vigorously replied to a similar statement by Morawetz, "This is a surprising doctrine in view of the well established power of equity to remove trustees for substantial cause, such as misappropriation, long continued absence, antagonism of interest and other grounds."[95]   A good deal of water has flowed over the dam since Machen and other early writers on corporations expounded in this manner.   A much stronger feeling exists today that directors are in a real sense fiduciaries to their corporations and to their shareholders than was apparent at the time Machen wrote his classic work.   There were cases at the time of these earlier texts which supported the ridiculous rule that the shareholders themselves could not remove directors for cause unless the company's articles or by-laws contained a provision to that effect.[96] But if the shareholders had exercised this so-called illegal power and removed a director for cause, a court of equity would "refuse to lend its aid to force upon an unwilling company a director whom the shareholders have pronounced unacceptable, even though he may be legally entitled to the office."[97]   The more drastic and expensive remedy of a receivership on a shareholder's bill was said to be the proper remedy, the appointment of the receiver to take charge of the business until honest and/or

---

92. See pages 211, 213–214, supra.

93. See, for example, Shuster v. Ventnor Gardens, Inc., 103 N.J.Eq. 93, 141 A. 457 (1928). But compare Hollander v. Breeze Corporations, Inc., 131 N.J.Eq. 585, 26 A. 2d 507 (1941), aff'd 131 N.J.Eq. 613, 26 A.2d 522 (1942) ; s. c., sub nom. Hollander v. Mascuch, 136 N.J.Eq. 215, 40 A.2d 637 (1945).

94. 2 Machen, Modern Law of Corporations § 1432, page 1184 (1908).

95. Ballantine, Corporations 438 (Rev. ed. 1946).

96. 2 Machen, op. cit. supra, note 94, § 1432.

97. 2 Machen, op. cit. supra, note 94, § 1509.

capable directors should be elected.[98]   All of which adds up to a good deal of nonsense.

There are times when a court is needed to act in the removal or suspension of directors from their offices.   If the majority shareholders happen to be the directors themselves, as is often the case in small corporations, and they are grossly mishandling the business or are raiding its treasury for their own benefit, even a statute, or a provision in the articles or by-laws permitting the holders of a majority or two-thirds of the voting shares to remove directors with or without cause would not suffice.   It is then that equity should take over and, upon the petition of a minority shareholder who is able to prove the facts, remove the director or directors before more damage is done. There are surprisingly few statutes which specifically authorize the removal of directors in this manner.   However, the statutes of Alaska until recently provided for court action to suspend directors for "abuse of trust" and to remove them for "gross misconduct." [99]   And both California and Pennsylvania permit a suit by holders of at least 10% of the outstanding shares, with or without voting rights, for fraudulent or dishonest acts and for "gross abuse of authority or discretion with reference to the corporation." [1]   Except for some early badly decided cases and a not too vigorous criticism of them in early texts, it is submitted that there is no need for such statutes—that a court of equity does have the power, if it will use it, to suspend or remove delinquent directors.

98.   2 Machen, op. cit. supra, note 94, § 1161.

99.   Alaska Comp.Laws Ann.1949, § 36–1–94, III and IV.   The section seems to have been omitted from the new, 1957, statute.   See Alaska Bus.Corp.Act § 45 (1957).

1.   West's Ann.Cal.Corp.Code § 811; Pa.Bus.Corp.Law of 1933, § 405 (C).   New York provides for a suit by the attorney-general.   N.Y.Gen. Corp.Law § 60, as amended by L. 1944, c. 727, and § 61, as amended by L.1946, c. 162.

Chapter 8

SHAREHOLDERS' PROTECTION AGAINST ACTS OF MANAGEMENT: SHAREHOLDERS' INDIVIDUAL AND DERIVATIVE ACTIONS

§ 1. Distinguishing Individual from Derivative Actions

At an earlier point, while discussing the meaning of the concept of separate personality, an attempt was made to distinguish between tortious injuries to individual members of a corporation and to the corporation itself which, indirectly, injured the members.[1] It was discovered that no bright line could be drawn between the two and that there were some types of cases which warranted actions by both. Where management has embezzled company property or where it has negligently caused losses, not only is the corporation injured but also the shareholder who suffers a decrease in the value of his stock. But the remedy available to the corporation in such cases is supposed to be sufficient for the protection of both; corporate recovery, theoretically at least, results in a return of the lost value to the stock. In the great majority of cases, the only cause of action for damages is in favor of the corporation.

In extreme cases, there may exist two causes of action, one for the corporation and the other for the shareholder individually. If the directors carry on the business with the intent of causing corporate losses, or disseminate false information concerning the financial condition of the corporation, both with the objective of purchasing shares on a market influenced by their action, there would seem to be two distinct causes of action, that is, if injury has been caused thereby to both the corporation and the shareholder.[2] Or, "Suppose, as a result of a conspiracy of insiders against P and the corporation, P has been 'frozen out' and deprived of part of his shares and the remainder have been greatly impaired in value by wrongful manipulation of the conspirators, such as by an issue of new shares to themselves without adequate consideration. May not P bring a suit either on the theory of a personal wrong or on the theory of enforcing a right of action for a corporate wrong?"[3] In such cases, if he has sold his shares and taken his loss, a corporate recovery could

1. See Chapter 2, pages 61–64, supra.

2. See discussion at page 62, supra, and Lesnik v. Public Indus-

trials Corp., 144 F.2d 968 (2d Cir., 1944).

3. Ballantine, Lattin and Jennings, Cases and Materials on Corpora-

not possibly benefit him, and an individual cause of action has been held proper.[4] But even if he retains his shares, the damage done by such intentionally tortious acts should be compensable even if there is some chance that two causes of action may spell double recovery. While there is considerable authority to the effect that even though there was malicious action toward the shareholder, the depreciation of his stock due to the corporate injury gives him no personal cause of action against the tort-feasor,[5] the facts of each case should be scanned to ascertain whether or not corporate recovery will place the shareholder in the same position he occupied prior to the corporate injury, for that is one basis upon which the cases rest. It was suggested earlier that injury caused to shareholders by the intentional acts of management, where such can be proved, should be handled differently from those caused by unintentional but negligent acts of mismanagement; the equities are all in favor of the sharehold-er when intentional indirect injury is caused to his shares and the fact that a judgment in his favor (and one in favor of his cor-poration) may result in double recovery should be considered in somewhat the same light as a punitive damage case.[6]

The clear cases giving an individual cause of action are those where some relationship other than that of shareholder and director or officer exists, such as the relationship derived from a pledging of his shares with the directors, or where the directors, or some of them are trustees of the shareholder,[7] or where there is a duty arising from contract or otherwise owing the shareholder by the directors and this has been violated.[8] Where the wrongful act of those in control of the corporation does not injure the corporation but does injure innocent share-holders, there is clearly an individual cause of action.[9] And

---

tions 520–521 (2d ed. 1953). And see Southern Pacific Co. v. Bogert, 250 U.S. 483, 39 S.Ct. 533, 63 L.Ed. 1099 (1919), where majority share-holders put through a reorganiza-tion of the corporation which froze out and eliminated the minority shareholders.

4. See discussion at page 62, and citations there set out, and Raf-ferty v. Donnelly, 197 Pa. 429, 47 A. 202 (1900).

5. See discussion and citations at page 63, supra.

6. See page 64, supra. That the same act may be the basis for an individual and a corporate cause of action, see Ann., **167** A.L.R. 279 (1947).

7. The classic example of a relation-ship apart from shareholding is: General Rubber Co. v. Benedict, 215 N.Y. 18, 109 N.E. 96, L.R.A. 1915F, 617 (1915). See also Cutler v. Fitch, 231 App.Div. 8, 246 N.Y.S. 28 (1930); In re Auditore's Will (Parascandola v. National Surety Co.), 249 N.Y. 335, 164 N.E. 242, 62 A.L.R. 551 (1928).

8. Ritchie v. McMullen, 79 F. 522 (6th Cir., 1897), cert. denied 168 U.S. 710, 18 S.Ct. 945, 42 L.Ed. 1212 (1897)—the case involved a pledge of stock in certain corporations with the defendants who were of-ficers of the corporation.

9. Southern Pacific Co. v. Bogert, supra note 3. The corporation was actually benefited by the wrongful

where the wrongful act, or one connected with it, has ended the corporate life as in case of a consolidation with another corporation where the valuations in the first were deliberately set low in order to favor the majority shareholders who owned stock in the second corporation, the cause of action is personal.[10] However, this last would seem to depend upon whether the corporate life had been kept lingering by statute for the purpose of suit, as is frequently the case today.

Of course, where the corporation, through its directors or shareholders, is about to do something not within the scope of its purpose clause or powers, either a shareholder in a suit personal to himself or in a derivative action may enjoin such unauthorized act whether it is simply beyond the corporate purposes and powers or is illegal in the sense of being unlawful. Every shareholder has a personal contractual right to have the corporation keep within the area of its operation. And, as we shall later see, in exceptional circumstances a shareholder is sometimes permitted to obtain a personal judgment in what would normally be considered a derivative action, the exceptions being based upon equitable principles. Other cases clearly giving the shareholder a personal action are where he is deprived of rights under his shareholder's contract,—deprived of preemptive rights, for example, or where the corporation fails to pay him dividends after a declaration, or makes fraudulent representations inducing him to purchase its shares or to part with them.[11]

Whether the corporation has a cause of action will depend upon whether or not its assets have been lost or destroyed or depreciated or its business interfered with by the wrongful act of the parties charged, whether they be insiders or outsiders. The bulk of the cases, as already stated, will fall within the corporate cause of action area with indirect injury to the shares and will, therefore, warrant but one cause of action and that one by the corporation.

action of the majority shareholders. And see Lebold v. Inland S. S. Co., 82 F.2d 351 (7th Cir., 1936); s. c. sub nom. Lebold v. Inland Steel Co., 125 F.2d 369 (7th Cir., 1941); Zahn v. Transamerica Corp., 162 F.2d 36 (3d Cir., 1947); Overfield v. Pennroad Corp., 42 F. Supp. 586 (D.Pa.1941), rev'd on ground of statute of limitations, 146 F.2d 889 (3d Cir., 1944).

10. Jones v. Missouri-Edison Electric Co., 144 F. 765 (8th Cir., 1906),

cert. denied 229 U.S. 615, 33 S.Ct. 774, 57 L.Ed. 1352 (1913). The opinion in the district court is in 135 F. 153 (D.Mo.1905); second appeal in 199 F. 64 (8th Cir., 1912); third appeal, 233 F. 49 (8th Cir., 1916); last appeal, Thompson v. Bomar, 258 F. 339 (8th Cir., 1919), which pertains to the fees of successful counsel.

11. See Note, 40 Calif.L.Rev. 127 (1952).

§ 2.   Theories of the Nature of Shareholders' Derivative Actions

There is no general agreement as to the nature of the share-holders' action called a derivative suit. The action itself is one brought by one or more shareholders on behalf of the plaintiffs and all others similarly situated against individual defendants who will normally be the directors and/or officers whose tortious acts are the bases of the action, the corporation being made a party-defendant as a procedural matter although it is the real party-plaintiff and any judgment given will normally be in its favor.[12] As a first requirement, there must be a cause of action in favor of the corporation; if the cause of action is personal to the plaintiffs it should be brought as a personal action and, if the plaintiffs are numerous, a class or representative action as recognized in equity may be brought. Certain conditions precedent must be present before the shareholder acquires the right to bring a derivative action, and these will be discussed shortly. Since the cause of action is the corporation's, it should be the party to bring it. But, due to the directors' personal interests or, perhaps, their abuse of discretion in failing to bring it, the action would be lost if the shareholders were not given this equitable right. And, if the majority shareholders are personally interested, unless a minority shareholder could bring it, the action would be lost to the damage of the corporation and, indirectly, its shareholders.

As to theories, it has been suggested that the shareholder's right to sue for the enforcement of a corporate right of action is based upon a special injury to him which, if he were not permitted to sue, would leave him remediless. Another theory is that the shareholder does not sue in his own right but as a representative of the company—a volunteer representative, which raises a question of whether this is so or whether he is actually the representative of the shareholders for whom he sues. The true basis, however, is that the shareholders have a right in equity to force the assertion of the corporate right against the corporate managers or other parties when these top echelon officers wrongfully refuse to sue. "The suit is thus an action for specific enforcement of an obligation owed by the corporation to the shareholders to assert its rights of action when the corporation has been put in default by the wrongful refusal of the directors or management to take suitable measures for its protection." [13]

12. This statement will have to be qualified a bit for, under unusual circumstances to be discussed, an occasional judgment has been given to the plaintiffs individually. See page 378, infra.

13. Ballantine, Lattin and Jennings, Cases and Materials on Corporations 521 and authorities cited (2d ed. 1953).

But, whatever theory is accepted, the derivative action is in some measure an instrument of control and at the same time a weapon of self-defense, a very necessary one although it can be used, though not legitimately, for its nuisance value.

§ 3. Some Basic Considerations in Shareholders' Derivative Actions

Basic, and already stated, is that the cause of action is the corporation's and not that of the shareholder who appears as plaintiff, really a nominal plaintiff. Hence, when recovery is allowed, the judgment is entered for the corporation, not the plaintiff-shareholder, although occasionally there has been encroachment upon this rule. One of the basic reasons why courts have not permitted direct proportionate recoveries in derivative actions is that creditors have first claim upon the judgment and a proportionate reward to shareholders leaving creditors unpaid would be fraudulent as to them. More recently another reason has been given: "Another matter of increasing importance in recent years is the matter of state and federal taxes. Apart from the question of the recovery being needed to pay the unpaid claims of the state and federal government, is the fact that in a good many cases a substantial recovery by the corporation will require changes in tax reports previously made and result in additional tax liability." [14]

A derivative action is an invention of courts of equity and may be brought only in equity whether the corporate cause of action be in law or not.[15] As far as corporate rights and defenses available against it are in issue, these issues are decided exactly as if the corporation were the plaintiff except the matter of jury trial, for the case being in equity there is no right to jury trial. Any defense available against the corporation had it sued is thus available to the defendant in the derivative action. If the statute of limitations has run against the corporate cause of action, the claim would be barred when asserted in its behalf in a derivative action. And in equity cases in the federal courts where jurisdiction is based upon diversity of citizenship of the parties, the state statutes of limitations are applicable.[16]

Basic, too, is the equity rule which turns away plaintiffs who do not come into court with clean hands. Thus, while the corporation may bring the action without regard to the conduct

---

14. Graven, Dist. J., in Liken v. Shaffer, 64 F.Supp. 432, at 441 (D. Iowa 1946).

15. Rettinger v. Pierpont, 145 **Neb.** 161, 15 N.W.2d 393 (1944).

16. Guaranty Trust Co. v. York, 326 U.S. 99, 65 S.Ct. 1464, 89 L.Ed. 2079 (1945).

of one or more of its shareholders, the same is not true when a shareholder brings the action derivatively. If the shareholder has participated or acquiesced in, or has ratified the action which he now claims as a basis of the suit, he will be barred if this defense is raised, and if no other shareholder brings the action the case may never materialize. On the other hand, if another shareholder who has not acquiesced in or ratified the action brings the suit, any recovery, since it is corporate recovery, will benefit indirectly those who have acquiesced or ratified as well as the others. Likewise, a plaintiff-shareholder who has had knowledge of the wrong but has been guilty of laches in failing to seek rectification thereof may be barred from bringing the suit though shareholders not delinquent in this respect may bring it. It should be noted that the corporation does not lose its cause of action because of the conduct or situation of one or some of its shareholders. In an important case, it was said: "In stockholder's derivative suits, matters in bar relate only to the claim of the corporation itself. Matters in abatement can relate to both the claim of the corporation and the particular stockholder instituting the action. A stockholder's derivative suit may be abated so far as the corporation itself is concerned because of lack of jurisdiction or because the claim was not due. A stockholder's derivative suit may also be abated because of the conduct or situation of the particular stockholder or stockholders instituting the action. However, the claim of the corporation cannot be barred by the conduct or situation of the particular stockholder or stockholders instituting the proceedings." [17]

In spite of the clean hands doctrine, it has been held in a number of cases that the shareholder's motive in bringing a derivative action, though it be highly improper, will not be questioned, provided he brings the action in his own interest.[18] But if it appears that he has brought the suit for another, for example, on behalf of a non-shareholder competitor of the corporation, this is a good defense.[19] Apparently a puppet's hands

---

17. Liken v. Shaffer, supra, note 14, at 442.

18. Eshleman v. Keenan, 21 Del.Ch. 116, 181 A. 655 (Del.Ch.1935); Johnson v. King-Richardson Co., 36 F.2d 675, 67 A.L.R. 1465 (1st Cir., 1930). See Rohrlich, Suits in Equity by Minority Stockholders as a Means of Corporate Control, 81 U. of Pa.L.Rev. 692, at 719 (1933); Note, Extortionate Corporate Litigation: The Strike Suit, 34 Col.L.Rev. 1308, at 1309–1311 (1934).

19. Breeze v. Lone Pine-Surprise Consol. Min. Co., 39 Wash. 602, 81 P. 1050 (1905); Manchester, Sheffield & Lincolnshire Ry. Co., 4 deG., F. & J., 126, 30 Beav. 40, 45 Eng. Rep. 1131 (1861). But where the plaintiff is himself a competitor, his motive to drive the corporation out of business has been held no defense. Johnson v. King-Richardson Co., supra, note 18 and Note criticising the case in 16 Va.L.Rev. 716 (1930). And see Rohrlich, op. cit. supra, note 18, at 719.

are always less clean than those of a corporate blackmailer; at least the chancellor sees them that way.

§ 4. Conditions Precedent to Bringing the Action

A plaintiff-shareholder must allege, with the same particularity required of the corporation had it brought the suit, the facts constituting the corporate cause of action; and, further, he must allege facts which entitle him to bring the action on behalf of the corporation.[20] The facts he must allege to entitle him to bring the action are that he has demanded that the board of directors bring it and that they have wrongfully refused or failed to bring it, or show a sufficient reason for not making the demand, such as, that a majority of the board are subject to the suit or that there is a conspiracy among innocent and guilty board members who, together, constitute a majority.[21] If the action is one that might have been ratified by the shareholders because of its voidability, he is usually required to allege that he has sought shareholder action and they have refused or failed to ratify the voidable act, or he must state a valid reason for not putting the case to the shareholders, for example, that the majority are benefiting from the wrongful action of the board or that they have conspired with the board in the matter, or that they are defendants in the suit.[22]

The shareholders have no authority to ratify (or initiate, for that matter) that which is prohibited by law or is against public policy. Stockholders who ratify a directorial fraud or misappropriation of funds can not, short of unanimous action,

20. Continental Securities Co. v. Belmont, 206 N.Y. 7, 99 N.E. 138 (1912). The leading case is Hawes v. Oakland, 104 U.S. 450, 26 L.Ed. 827 (1882).

21. Continental Securities Co. v. Belmont, supra, note 20; Cathedral Estates v. Taft Realty Corp., 228 F.2d 85 (2d Cir., 1955); Daniels v. Briggs, 279 Mass. 87, 180 N.E. 717 (1932).

22. Continental Securities Co. v. Belmont, supra, note 20, for an excellent discussion. See also Cathedral Estates v. Taft Realty Corp., supra note 21. In Fisher v. National Mortgage Loan Co., 132 Neb. 185, 271 N.W. 433, at 439–440, modified in 133 Neb. 280, 274 N.W. 568 (1937), it is stated: "The theory of the rule, and the exception, seems to be that the individual stockholder must exhaust all means of redress within the corporation itself before bringing such an action. Some examples wherein such a demand for action by the body of the stockholders is not necessary are where it is made clear that such demand would meet refusal, or that the litigation following would naturally be under control of persons opposed to success, or where the governing body is the wrongdoer, or where the appeal to the stockholders would be unavailing for want of time or for lack of authority to act or other cause, or where the corporation has gone out of existence." In Campbell v. Loew's Inc., 134 A.2d 565, at 567 (Del.Ch.1957), it is said: "A demand upon stockholders implies that legally they can do something about it. Where they cannot, the Rule does not contemplate that such a useless act must nevertheless be performed."

prevent a derivative suit;[23] however, those who have participated in the attempt to ratify, will be barred from bringing the action though they may benefit through a recovery in a derivative action brought by an innocent shareholder. It would seem futile to require a plaintiff to pursue the shareholders in a case where they have no authority to ratify whatever acts are the basis of the suit. But some cases have not discriminated, as they should, concerning this requirement and consequently there are holdings and numerous dicta to the effect that the plaintiff must allege that he has sought relief through the shareholders or state an adequate excuse for not having done so.[24] If he has actually presented a state of facts to the shareholders which they have no authority to ratify, their affirmative vote to ratify will have no legal effect upon the bringing of the derivative action which, as clearly as anything, is a valid reason for not requiring an approach to the shareholders when their ratification would be meaningless.[25] The most convincing reason yet given for requiring an approach to the shareholders in a case where they have no authority to ratify is that they may be encouraged to remove their delinquent directors and replace them with others who will decide whether or not to start a corporate cause of action against the delinquents.[26]

It should be added that there are many cases where the plaintiff has alleged only that he has approached the board, made his demand, and been refused or that the stated reasons excuse a lack of demand upon the board where the case has gone to trial and to an upper court without any discussion of the further requirement of seeking out the shareholders.[27] It may be that courts of equity—such as these are—have seen the obvious conflict between the approach-to-shareholder requirement and the long standing equity principle that equity will not require the doing of an idle act. The rule should be universal that a plaintiff-shareholder need not allege that he has presented the facts to the shareholders except in a case where they have authority to ratify and bind the corporation thereby.

One of the more sensitive problems concerns the discretion of the board in determining whether or not suit should be brought in a particular case. Matters of policy, particularly when the suit may have a tendency to injure the good will of

23. But see Claman v. Robertson, 164 Ohio St. 61, 128 N.E.2d 429 (1955), and Note, Shareholders' Ratification of Directors' Frauds, 24 U. of Cin. L.Rev. 612 (1955).

24. Hagood v. Smith, 162 Ala. 512, 50 So. 374 (1909).

25. Keenan v. Eshleman, 23 Del.Ch. 234, 2 A.2d 904, 120 A.L.R. 227 (Sup.Ct.1938).

26. See, for example, Rathbone v. Gas Co., 31 W.Va. 798, 8 S.E. 570 (1888).

27. Eston v. Argus, Inc., 328 Mich. 554, 44 N.W.2d 154 (1950).

the company, will play an important part in this determination. It may be better not to bring the suit if the community has strong feelings about it, or it may be preferable to compromise a claim though there may be a sacrifice in the amount which a suit might have brought in, or there may be other reasons considered adequate by the board. And, of course, similar arguments may be raised for the failure to defend a suit brought against the company. Where a disinterested board has made its determination should any shareholder be able to bring the suit on behalf of the corporation? [28] Of if the shareholders have, through their by-laws, reserved the right to make the determination of whether suit should be brought, once a majority of disinterested shareholders has made the determination not to sue, should a minority shareholder be allowed to bring a derivative suit? On the other hand, if the board or the shareholders have abused their discretion, is there any good reason why a minority shareholder should not be able to bring it?

We start with the principle that the board and the majority shareholders are presumed to be acting in good faith, with fair discretion, and with a consciousness of duty toward the corporation and all its shareholders. In every intra vires matter, the board or the majority shareholders when operating within the area of their authority must govern so long as their discretion is not abused. This is as true of bringing or not bringing suit as in case of carrying on the ordinary or extraordinary business of the company. But if either group abuses its discretion—and there are limits of credulity in any case—a minority shareholder may still bring the derivative action for this very reason.[29]

---

28. See the discussion in Swanson v. Traer, 249 F.2d 854 (7th Cir., 1958).

29. Groel v. United Elect. Co. of New Jersey, 70 N.J.Eq. 616, 61 A. 1061, at 1064 (1905), where promoters were alleged to have taken a $20,000,000 profit in shares of the company but the directors deemed it "inexpedient" to bring suit. It was there stated: "Would it not clearly be held by any court to be a breach of trust for directors to neglect or refuse to recover, or seek to recover, such an amount of stock improperly obtained from it by a promoter? It is perfectly clear that, if the complainant sets forth a good cause of action and there is a right in the corporation to recover $20,000,000 of stock from the promoter, it is a clear breach of trust on the part of the directors not to proceed to recover the same. For them to reply that it is by them deemed inexpedient to do so is only to emphasize the breach of trust they are committing by not doing so." But see S. Solomont & Sons Trust, Inc. v. New England Theatres Operating Corp., 326 Mass. 99, 93 N.E.2d 241 (1950), where neither the directors' nor the shareholders' discretion was abused. In Post v. Buck's Stove & Range Co., 200 F. 918, at 921 (8th Cir., 1912), the court stated: "The directors of the Stove Company did nothing more, save to yield an unliquidated claim for damages. It was their province to determine the wisdom or expediency of the course adopted. They did not act oppressively or fraudulently, and no stockholder gained or lost more or less than another. They acted in good faith,

Furthermore, where the question of whether suit should or should not be brought is submitted to the shareholders for affirmation by an inquiring board and the majority shareholders decide, in good faith, that suit ought not to be brought, that should end the matter. The principle is well stated in a recent case:[30] "On principle, we perceive no reason why the usual rule recognizing that it is for the corporation to decide questions of business policy should be subject to an exception limiting the corporate power where a charge is made against an officer or director but where an independent, disinterested majority of the stockholders acting reasonably and in good faith have voted that in their judgment it is not in the best interest of the corporation to sue." And the frequently stated principle that an honest mistake of business judgment is not reviewable by the courts is quite as applicable here as elsewhere.

But the discretion of the board and its apparent proper exercise have not always prevailed. This has been particularly true in the failure to resist tax claims where some valid argument existed to the effect that the tax was unconstitutional or not applicable or for some other apparently persuasive reason. In the most famous of these cases the shareholder was permitted to sue derivatively because, thought the court, the directors' refusal to resist the collection of the tax when they considered it illegal amounted to a breach of trust.[31] In some of the cases such failure to act has been considered an ultra vires gift of corporate assets. It seems senseless to treat such cases differently from the ordinary run. If the directors have not abused their discretion in deciding not to resist the tax, and if the shareholders when given the opportunity to ratify the board's action have done so, no minority shareholder should be permitted to litigate on behalf of the corporation. If, however, there has been an abuse of discretion by the board, or by the shareholders if the issue has been submitted to them, the minority shareholder should have his day in court as in other cases.

according to the lights given them, and for the welfare of all the interests in their charge."

30. S. Solomont & Sons Trust, Inc. v. New England Theatres Operating Corp., supra, note 29, 93 N.E.2d at 249; Karasik v. Pacific Eastern Corp., 21 Del.Ch. 81, 180 A. 604 (1935). See Landstrom, Ratification by Majority Stockholders—A Problem in Corporate Democracy, 31 B.U.L.Rev. 165 (1951); Notes, 39 Calif.L.Rev. 268 (1951); 64 Harv.L.Rev. 334 (1950); 49 Mich. L.Rev. 898 (1951).

31. Dodge v. Woolsey, 18 How. (U.S.) 331, 15 L.Ed. 401 (1856). The reason given for their nonaction was that there were too many obstacles in the way of testing the law. And see Helvering v. Davis, 301 U.S. 619, 57 S.Ct. 904, 81 L.Ed. 1307 (1937). But compare Norman v. Consolidated Edison Co., 89 F.2d 619 (2d Cir., 1937), cert. denied 300 U.S. 673, 57 S.Ct. 612, 81 L.Ed. 879 (1937), where a shareholders' suit was dismissed on the ground that the corporation had four years to claim a refund if the tax proved to be unconstitutional.

§ 5. Parties to a Derivative Action

The party-plaintiff must be a shareholder but, as is usual, the simple statement needs explanation. For purposes of voting, the payment of dividends, and in appraisal proceedings there is much more necessity for a rather inflexible basis of shareholder identity than there is in the derivative action. There is no undue burden placed upon the corporation to let an equitable owner of shares bring the action (and he is permitted to bring it) for he must, in any case, prove his ownership to maintain the action. The same is true of an unregistered owner, and he too has been permitted to bring the action.[32]

By a rule of long standing in the federal courts a shareholder-plaintiff in a derivative action must have been a shareholder at the time of the events which are alleged to give the corporation a cause of action unless his shares have devolved upon him later than these events by operation of law.[33] This rule which was shortly adopted as an equity rule of procedure by the Supreme Court exists today as Rule 23(b) of the Federal Rules of Civil Procedure, and is set forth in the note below.[34] As originally established, and as it exists today, the rule aims at preventing collusive share-transfers to obtain federal jurisdiction on diversity of citizenship grounds. A number of states have accepted as common law the conditions precedent of the federal holdings and a few states have changed their previous common law rule by adopting the basic requirements (with some variations) of the federal rule by statute.[35] A contrary rule

32. Hall v. O'Reilly Realty & Investment Co., 306 Mo. 182, 267 S.W. 407 (1924) (if trustee fails to bring suit, after demand, the beneficiary may sue); Goodliffe v. Colonial Corp., 107 Utah 488, 155 P.2d 177 (1945) (where former owners who had been fraudulently deprived of their shares were allowed to sue); Rosenthal v. Burry Biscuit Corp., 30 Del.Ch. 299, 60 A.2d 106 (1948) (suit was brought by owner who was not registered).

33. Hawes v. Oakland, 104 U.S. 450, 26 L.Ed. 827 (1881), was the starting point of this rule.

34. Originally adopted as Equity Rule 94, it is now Rule 23(b), F.R. C.P., and reads: "In an action brought to enforce a secondary right on the part of one or more shareholders in an association, incorporated or unincorporated, because the association refuses to enforce rights which may properly be asserted by it, the complaint shall be verified by oath and shall aver (1) that the plaintiff was a shareholder at the time of the transaction of which he complains or that his share thereafter devolved on him by operation of law and (2) that the action is not a collusive one to confer on a court of the United States jurisdiction of any action of which it would not otherwise have jurisdiction. The complaint shall also set forth with particularity the efforts of the plaintiff to secure from the managing directors or trustees and, if necessary, from the shareholders such action as he desires, and the reasons for his failure to obtain such action or the reasons for not making such effort."

35. Jepson v. Peterson, 69 S.D. 388, 10 N.W.2d 749, 148 A.L.R. 1087 (1943). For samples of the recent statutes, see N.Y.Gen.Corp. Law § 61; West's Ann.Cal.Corp. Code § 834(1); Del.Gen.Corp.Law of 1953, § 327; Ohio Rev.Code § 2307.311.

prevails in most states, thereby permitting a shareholder who acquired his shares other than by operation of law subsequent to the events upon which suit is based to bring the action even in a case where he had knowledge of the transaction at the time he purchased the shares.[36] Thus, in the absence of special circumstances about to be discussed, a shareholder is not barred simply by looking at the time when he acquired his shares. This rule is thought to be the sounder of the two and the reasons for so considering it have been explained as follows:[37] "A stockholder has an indivisible interest in the property and assets of a corporation subject to the discharge of its obligations. This indivisible interest generally speaking is represented by certificates of stock and is transferred by their transfer. . . . As an original proposition it would seem to be clear that a right of action by or in behalf of the corporation for fraud to set aside a conveyance of its assets or to avoid obligations imposed upon it is part of its rights, property and assets in which a stockholder has this indivisible interest transferable by the transfer of his certificates. I am unable to see any real or substantial distinction by virtue of which a stockholder transferring his certificates would transfer all of his indivisible interest in bonds or real estate on hand, but would not transfer his interest in a right of action to recover bonds or real estate which had been fraudulently withdrawn from the possession of the corporation, and which it was entitled to recover. And if the subsequent holder by acquiring the certificates does not acquire such latter interest, it seems to follow that he may if necessary, in behalf of the corporation, assert and prosecute an action to protect and enforce the same." Arguments of the practical inconvenience of determining whether the transferor had participated in or ratified the transaction sued upon, or that a shareholder buys shares subject to transactions preceding his purchase, or that the price of the share has been adjusted to take into consideration prior transactions which are the foundation of suits were rejected by the court.

The special circumstances mentioned above are that a shareholder who has participated in or ratified the acts which are the subject of suit, or who has been guilty of laches in failing to take action after discovery of them, is barred from being a plaintiff in a derivative action. Some of the cases hold that a transferee of such a shareholder, even though he has no notice of what the previous owner has done, is barred from suit be-

36. The leading case is Pollitz v. Gould, 202 N.Y. 11, 94 N.E. 1088 (1911), which, by § 61, N.Y.Gen. Corp.Law, enacted in 1944, accepts the federal doctrine.

37. Hiscock, J., in Pollitz v. Gould, supra, note 36, 94 N.E. 1088, at 1089.

cause the shares carry with them the taint which would have barred the former owner. Another line of cases believed to be preferable permits the transferee, who has no notice at the time of acquiring his shares of the events upon which successful suit depends, to bring the action.[38] The innocent transferee ought not to be barred from bringing what, after all, is a corporate cause of action; and, if the shares are negotiable which is usually the case, one who purchases them without notice of what the previous owner has done should have all the advantages that negotiability gives in other negotiable instrument legal controversies.

If, for some reason, no shareholder is qualified to bring the action it has been properly held that the corporation itself may not bring it, as for example where there was unanimous ratification of the acts which are alleged to be the basis of the suit by those who owned the shares at the time these acts occurred.[39] The same would be true if all the shareholders were willing beneficiaries of the wrongful act or all were guilty of laches in seeking redress after discovery of the act. Whether later transferees of shares may be plaintiffs in a derivative suit for such prior acts will depend upon the principles already discussed and, in any case where the shareholders can legitimately authorize or ratify the particular act so as to bind the corporation, and have so done, no transferee could successfully prevail in such an action. Any ratification by the shareholders or the board in the area of their authority to act would naturally bind the corporation, thus preventing suit by it or on its behalf derivatively. In a jurisdiction now having (by statute) the requirement that a shareholder bringing a derivative suit must have been such at the time of the transaction of which he complains or be an owner by operation of law, it was argued that the corporation might bring the action as the statute applied only to derivative suits. In a split decision, the majority held otherwise, Van Voorhis,

38. Russell v. Louis Melind Co., 331 Ill.App. 182, 72 N.E.2d 869 (1947), noted in 46 Mich.L.Rev. 429 (1948) (innocent transferees of guilty shares may not bring the action—the traditional, and majority, view); Parsons v. Joseph, 92 Ala. 403, 8 So. 788 (1890) (such a transferee may sue—which is the preferable view). See Rohrlich, Suits in Equity by Minority Stockholders as a Means of Corporate Control, 81 U. of Pa.L.Rev. 692, at 721 (1933). The problem should be examined in the light of the Uniform Stock Transfer Act and the negotiability of shares thereunder. See Note, Uniform Stock Transfer Act —Right of Subsequent Transferee to Sue, 23 Minn.L.Rev. 484 (1939).

39. Home Fire Insurance Co. v. Barber, 67 Neb. 644, at 664–665, 93 N. W. 1024, 60 L.R.A. 927, 108 Am.St. Rep. 716 (1903), in which Commissioner Roscoe Pound (later dean of Harvard Law School) wrote: "If they have no standing in equity to entitle them to the relief sought for their benefit, they cannot obtain such relief through the corporation or in its own name. It would be a reproach to courts of equity if this were not so."

J., writing:[40] ". . . [J]ust as the courts of this state have long held that a corporation cannot sue where recovery would inure only to the benefit of stockholders none of whom could institute a derivative action due to ratification or estoppel, so now, under the same principle, a corporation cannot prosecute an action in which recovery would be for the sole benefit of stockholders all of whom would be precluded from instituting a derivative action by section 61 of the General Corporation Law." The Court of Appeals of New York in sustaining the Appellate Division held that the section was a bar to the maintenance of the action by the corporation itself.[41]

It is usually stated that the plaintiff need not own a substantial interest in the company for which he brings suit. This is certainly true in cases where the real defendants have been guilty of illegality or fraud, for in such cases, this factor alone outweighs any argument that the plaintiff is bringing a "strike suit" to compel a payoff.[42] Theoretically, it would seem to make no difference whether the plaintiff owned one or a large number of shares but the fact must be recognized that, in the past, there have been many suits where the plaintiff's sole motive was to blackmail the real defendants so that they would settle with him rather than defend in court. That courts frequently mention the small interest of the plaintiff-shareholder "especially in consideration of discretionary matters" is indicative of the fact that some weight is attached to the size of his interest.[43]

An existing corporation, although the real party-plaintiff in a derivative suit, is the formal party-defendant and a necessary

---

40. Capitol Wine & Spirit Corp. v. Pokrass, 277 App.Div. 184, at 189, 98 N.Y.S.2d 291 (1950), two judges dissenting on the ground that § 61 did not apply to corporate suits but only to derivative actions. Judge Peck also felt the same way but believed the circumstances here present justified affirming the motion for summary judgment as modified. Creditors (who were the United States and the State of New York, for taxes) were otherwise protected and hence were out of the picture. The Court of Appeals affirmed the Appellate Division, holding that § 61 of the General Corporation Law was a bar to the maintenance of the action. 302 N.Y. 734, 98 N.E.2d 704 (1951). And see Diamond v. Diamond, 307 N.Y. 263, 120 N.E.2d 819 (1954).

41. See note 40, supra.

42. Rohrlich, Suits in Equity by Minority Stockholders as a Means of Corporate Control, 81 U. of Pa.L. Rev. 692, at 719 (1933). "[I]t is irrelevant that plaintiff owns but a few shares" and that he is a competitor of the corporation for which the action to restrain is brought. Subin v. Goldsmith, 224 F.2d 753 (2d Cir. 1955), per Frank, Cir. J.

43. Ibid. And see Note, Extortionate Corporate Litigation: The Strike Suit, 34 Col.L.Rev. 1308, at 1314 and 1318–1319 (1934). That the motive of corporate blackmail may sometimes save "numerous small and impecunious stockholders" from serious injustice, see Simpson, Fifty Years of American Equity, 50 Harv.L.Rev. 171, at 190–191 (1936), quoted from by Frank, Cir. J., in Subin v. Goldsmith, supra, note 42.

defendant in any case. The real party- or parties-defendant are those against whom the corporate cause of action is alleged, and they are likewise necessary parties to such a suit. Equity practice as it exists in America has been found sufficiently flexible to permit affirmative judgments in such cases to be entered in favor of one defendant against other defendants. And, since a recovery in a derivative suit runs in favor of the formal corporate-defendant, it has been held that there must be in personam jurisdiction over the corporation for whom the action was brought.[44] "Justice," as one court has stated, "requires that the corporation itself be bound by the result of such a suit and be not left free to bring its own suit later against the same defendants for the same alleged wrongs." [45]

But injustice has been caused by the rule when the real parties-defendant are in a jurisdiction in which the corporation itself cannot be personally served.[46] The appointment of a receiver or trustee by a court having jurisdiction over the corporation, with an order or authority to prosecute the action against the real defendants to prevent the loss of the corporate cause of action, has been suggested as one way to overcome this difficulty,[47] but the practical difficulties through this route are formidable,[48] including the reluctance of courts to appoint receivers when other remedies are available. As a second possi-

44. Carruthers v. Jack Waite Min. Co., 306 N.Y. 136, 116 N.E.2d 286 (1953); Dean v. Kellogg, 294 Mich. 200, 202 N.W. 704 (1940); Turner v. United Mineral Lands Corp., 308 Mass. 531, 33 N.E.2d 282 (1941). "The reason is apparent; the decree must protect the directors against any further suit by the corporation; and this will not be true unless it be a party to the suit." L Hand, Cir. J., in Philipbar v. Derby, 85 F.2d 27, at 30 (2d Cir. 1936). But a dissolved corporation, not kept alive by statute for purposes of suit, is not an indispensable party for the shareholders are the equitable owners of such corporation's property, including its causes of action. Weinert v. Kinkel, 296 N.Y. 151, 71 N.E. 2d 445, 172 A.L.R. 688 (1947). See Ann., 172 A.L.R. at 691 (1948). Compare Cohen v. Dana, infra, note 47, where it was found not necessary to determine whether the dissolved corporation was an indispensable party.

45. Turner v. United Mineral Lands Corp., 308 Mass. 531, 33 N.E.2d 282, at 286 (1941).

46. Such was the case in Freeman v. Bean, 243 App.Div. 503, 276 N.Y.S. 310 (1934), two judges dissenting, aff'd without opinion in 266 N.Y. 657, 195 N.E. 368 (1935).

47. See the following sequence starting with a suggestion of the New York court: Cohen v. Dana, 287 N. Y. 405, 40 N.E.2d 227 (1942); Levin v. Fisk Rubber Corp., 27 Del.Ch. 200, 33 A.2d 546 (1943); id. v. id., 30 Del. Ch. 31, 52 A.2d 741 (1947); and Cohen v. Dana, 83 N.Y.S.2d 414 (Sup.Ct.1948), aff'd mem. 275 App. Div. 723, 87 N.Y.S.2d 614 (1949).

48. Note, Necessity of Joinder of Corporation in Representative Suit Against the Directors, 44 Yale L.J. 1091, at 1092–1093 (1935). This note properly points out the necessity of an ancillary receiver in the jurisdiction where suit is brought, and the expense of action for this purpose as well as for bringing the final suit on behalf of the corporation.

bility, a mandatory injunction sought at the corporate domicile to compel the corporation to enter an appearance in the foreign suit to satisfy the requirement of joinder has been suggested.[49] The matter of proving sufficient facts in the court of the corporate domicile in order to obtain a mandatory injunction and again proving them in the foreign court to establish the corporation's case offers practical objections similar to those in the receivership case, including the initial expense to the shareholder. A third possibility has been proposed by way of analogy to the garnishment proceeding where the principal debtor with property within the jurisdiction may be constructively served. The cause of action is a corporate asset within the state where suit is brought.[50] ". . . [T]he corporation may be analogized to the principal debtor, whose 'debt' may be regarded as the breach of its duty to the representative stockholder of pressing the litigation against the directors; the status of the representative shareholders, in turn, is similar to that of the garnishor, whose right to have the corporation prosecute the suit has been violated; and the defendant directors are in the position of garnishees who hold a corporate asset in the property they have allegedly misappropriated." [51] Thus, with all necessary parties before the court, the real parties-defendant will be unable to argue that they may be later pursued by the corporate defendant for it, too, will be bound by the proceedings.

While this is a simpler theory than the two mentioned above, the analogy seems a bit far-fetched, particularly in considering the corporation as in the position of the principal debtor of the plaintiff-shareholder. But analogies in the common law have frequently been stretched to reach desirable ends, and there is no merit to an argument which permits delinquent directors or others to avoid their just obligations to the equitable owners of the corporation, that is, to the shareholders. The criticism, that "this analogy is invalidated by the fact that a judgment absolving the garnishee of indebtedness could not bind an absent principal debtor," [52] is a bit picayune for the cause of action is the property with which a court will deal under this theory and, to the extent of the property involved, a decision will bind the corporation—no personal judgment is involved in dealing with this property interest whether the court concludes that the prop-

---

49. Ibid. at 1093–1094, and Cohen v. Dana, supra, note 47.

50. See Kidd v. New Hampshire Traction Co., 72 N.H. 273, 56 A. 465, at 469 (1903). But see note 54, infra.

51. Note, 44 Yale L.J. 1091, at 1095 (1935).

52. Note, Joinder of Foreign Corporations in Stockholders' Derivative Suits, 50 Yale L.J. 1261, footnote 7 at p. 1262 (1941), which discusses Report of the New York Law Revision Commission, pp. 209–236 (1941), suggesting a solution despite non-joinder of the corporation.

erty interest does not exist, that is, that there is no cause of action, or that it exists to the extent of X-dollars instead of the Y-dollars claimed. The fact that usually a shareholder's derivative action lies in tort makes the analogy to garnishment proceedings even more remote, for such proceedings have been held inapplicable to tort claims.[53] But, perhaps, not too remote when one considers the equitable purpose of its application. Since derivative actions are in equity, the court has discretionary power to insist upon devices which will protect the absent corporation which cannot be personally served. If the above analysis of the cause of action as a property interest is correct,[54] then the real defendants will be protected to the extent that, once litigated, the defense of res adjudicata will be available if other suits are brought based upon the litigated facts. There is room for experimentation and a factor not yet mentioned should be emphasized—namely, that the corporation in a derivative action will be the beneficiary in case of recovery. Furthermore, the shareholder bringing the action will not obtain his costs of suit and of attorney's fees unless the suit is successful which, in large measure, assures vigilant prosecution of the suit. And, with its equitable powers, the court has the means of heading in the "strike" suit before it becomes troublesome.[55]

It has been suggested that the court of chancery at the corporate domicile or at its principal place of business should act as a clearing house for shareholders of all states who wish to prosecute the action. An appropriate order would then be issued to compel by mandatory injunction or refuse to compel the corporation's appearance in the foreign jurisdiction where the real defendants may be personally served.[56] A trustee for the sole purpose of suit would be appointed by the court to bring the action. Thus, the litigation would lose its character as a strike suit, if such it started to be, or would be thrown out by the court

---

53. Winer, Jurisdiction Over the Beneficiary Corporation in Stockholders' Suits, 22 Va.L.Rev. 153, at 159 (1935).

54. Unable to obtain jurisdiction over his corporation in New York where the principal defendants were domiciled, the plaintiff-shareholder argued that the cause of action was a corporate asset for which a receiver should be appointed to take action and to collect it. His argument was rejected in Application of Burge, 282 App.Div. 219, 122 N.Y.S.2d 232 (1953), aff'd 306 N.Y. 811, 118 N.E.2d 822 (1954), noted in 66 Harv.L.Rev. 1130 (1953) —note on trial court's decision;

51 Mich.L.Rev. 1239 (1953); 40 Va.L.Rev. 63 (1954). And see, in accord, Dean v. Kellogg, supra, note 44. Compare Kidd v. New Hampshire Traction Co., supra, note 50.

55. But see Winer, supra, note 53, at 165–166.

56. Winer, supra, note 53, at 167 et seq. At 169, Mr. Winer states: "The adequate and desirable solution seems to be for the Chancellor to appoint a trustee or receiver for the cause of action, or to represent the corporation in the stockholder's action." Further, at page 173, he states the items to be weighed in determining whether suit should, in this manner, be brought.

after hearing the parties urging suit. This procedure, as stated above, contains some practical difficulties, including judicial reluctance to make such appointments when other remedies are available. But this method does have the merit of ironing out differences at the source and presumably reaching a just solution of whether suit should be brought or the appearance of the corporation be ordered as requested.

§ 6.   Jurisdiction and Venue in the Federal Courts

Where diversity of citizenship exists in derivative suits— i.e., where the plaintiff is a citizen of a state different from that of all the defendants—the federal statutes provide for the prosecution of such suits in any judicial district where the corporation might have sued the same defendants,[57] process being servable "upon such corporation in any district where it is organized or licensed to do business or is doing business." [58] Diversity of citizenship is a requisite and the plaintiff-shareholder must be of a citizenship different from his corporation-defendant and the individual defendants.[59]

While, normally, derivative suits will concern corporations which have a majority of directors who are antagonistic to bringing the action, it occasionally happens that this is not so. Until June of 1957 it was thought that the law was well-settled and in this manner: If it appeared that the corporation was in hands not antagonistic to the action, the federal court would realign the parties and make, for purposes of jurisdictional determination, the corporation the plaintiff. If, then, there was no diversity of citizenship between the now plaintiff-corporation and the defendants, the case would be dismissed for lack of jurisdiction.[60] Thus the rule of *Doctor* v. *Harrington* [61] and the decisions following it in point of time prevailed. However, it had been suggested quite recently by Circuit Judge Learned Hand

57. 28 U.S.C.A. § 1401. For diversity jurisdiction generally, see Chapter 2, § 12, supra.

58. 28 U.S.C.A. § 1695.

59. Tucker v. New Orleans Laundries, Inc., 188 F.2d 263 (5th Cir., 1951), cert. den. 342 U.S. 828, 72 S.Ct. 52, 96 L.Ed. 627 (1951); Lavin v. Lavin, 182 F.2d 870, 18 A. L.R.2d 1017 (2d Cir., 1950), noted in 39 Calif.L.Rev. 138 (1951) and 49 Mich.L.Rev. 1070 (1951). See also Braunstein v. Devins, 136 F. Supp. 156 (D.Mass.1955).

60. See 39 Calif.L.Rev. 138, at 140 (1951); and Smith v. Sperling, 117 F.Supp. 781 (D.Cal.1953), noted in 38 Minn.L.Rev. 877 (1954). While Smith v. Sperling was affirmed in 237 F.2d 317 (9th Cir., 1956), the two were reversed in 354 U.S. 91, 77 S.Ct. 1112, 1 L.Ed.2d 1205 (1957), a 5 to 4 decision. See also Swanson v. Traer, 230 F.2d 228 (7th Cir., 1956), rev'd in 354 U.S. 114, 77 S.Ct. 1116, 1 L.Ed.2d 1221 (1957), a companion case of Smith v. Sperling. For an interesting interpretation of these cases, see Kartub v. Optical Fashions, Inc., 158 F.Supp. 757 (D. N.Y.1958).

61. 196 U.S. 579, 25 S.Ct. 355, 49 L. Ed. 606 (1905).

that "It may indeed be doubted whether as an original question the Supreme Court would not today align the corporation as a party plaintiff in all cases; nevertheless it has shown no disposition to change the rule in Doctor v. Harrington . . . but has recognized its continued authority." [62]   The decision of the Supreme Court on June 10, 1957, in *Smith* v. *Sperling*, may well have settled his doubt and, at the same time, have changed the supposed effect of *Doctor* v. *Harrington*.[63] It was there held that whether antagonism exists is not to be tried preliminarily to determine whether the parties should be realigned. This, felt the majority of the court, would be delving into the merits of the action. "There is antagonism," wrote Mr. Justice Douglas, "whenever the management is aligned against the stockholder and defends a course of conduct which he attacks." Whether there is antagonism is to be determined from the face of the pleadings and from the nature of the controversy. "The bill and the answer normally determine whether the management is antagonistic to the stockholder . . ." Whether the management has fraudulently refused to sue, or has been reluctant because the defendant is a close business associate, or has had an honest belief that suit is not for the best interests of the company, there is antagonism. "Whenever the management refuses to take action to undo a business transaction or whenever . . . it so solidly approves it that any demand to rescind would be futile, antagonism is evident." [64] As Mr. Justice Frankfurter who wrote the dissenting opinion, which was joined in by three other members of the court, states: "The Court, purporting to interpret this half-century of precedents, sweeps them away. In doing so, it greatly expands the diversity jurisdiction." [65] However, collusion to satisfy jurisdictional requirements may always be shown to defeat jurisdiction.

Under the federal statutes in force prior to 1948, a shareholder could bring his derivative action in the district where he resided, or where the corporation or the offending directors resided. However, it might happen that when the action was brought at the residence of the shareholder, personal service could not be made on the corporation in that district. Since the

62. Lavin v. Lavin, supra, note 59, at 871, citing Koster v. American Lumbermen's Mutual Casualty Co., 330 U.S. 518, 522, 533, 67 S.Ct. 828, 91 L.Ed. 1067 (1947), a 5 to 4 decision involving the doctrine of *forum non conveniens* in derivative suits in the federal courts.

63. Smith v. Sperling, 354 U.S. 91, 77 S.Ct. 1112, 1 L.Ed.2d 1205 (1957), rev'g 237 F.2d 317 (9th Cir., 1956). Notes in 68 Harv.L.Rev. 193 (1954);

54 Col.L.Rev. 629 (1954); 38 Minn. L.Rev. 87 (1954); 40 Va.L.Rev. 492 (1954)—all in the lower court.

64. Ibid., quoted portions 354 U.S. at 95–97, 77 S.Ct. 1114–1116, 1 L.Ed. 2d at 1210 and 1211.

65. 354 U.S. 98, at 105, 77 S.Ct. 1119, at 1123, 1 L.Ed.2d 1212, at 1216. Justices Burton, Harlan and Whittaker joined in the dissent.

corporation is an indispensable party in such actions, the share-holder found himself effectively barred from bringing the action in the forum where it was most convenient and least expensive for him. As a practical matter, the action could be brought only at the residence of the corporation (if personal service upon the real defendants could be had there) or of the real parties-defend-ant and not at the residence of the plaintiff-shareholder unless his residence happened to be at one of these two points.[66] If brought at the residence of the delinquent directors, the statute provided for extraterritorial service upon the corporation, that is, service outside the district in which the directors resided.

There is some doubt as to whether the revision of 1948 may not have extended the venue possibilities. It has been suggested, for example, that Section 1695 of Title 28 U.S.C.A. applies to all shareholders' derivative suits and not merely to those brought in a district in which the injured corporation might have brought them.[67] And Circuit Judge Learned Hand who wrote the opin-ion in *Greenberg* v. *Giannini* has more recently written: "There remains the question whether the recension of 1948 changed the law. We leave open, (as the Third Circuit suggested in Schoen v. Mountain Producers Corporation . . .), whether § 1695 may not have overruled Greenberg v. Giannini, supra; perhaps a shareholder, who is a citizen of one state, may now sue direc-tors who are citizens of another state in his own state and fetch in the corporation, organized in still a third state, although the corporation could not have sued the directors in the district which the shareholder has chosen . . ."[68] These sugges-tions have real merit. They are, perhaps, somewhat aided by Section 1391(c) of revised Title 28 (the general venue statute of the Revision of 1948) which substantially enlarges the venue as to corporate defendants and which reads: "A corporation may be sued in any judicial district in which it is incorporated or licensed to do business or is doing business, and such judicial dis-trict shall be regarded as the residence of such corporation for

66. Greenberg v. Giannini, 140 F.2d 550, at 552, 152 A.L.R. 966 (2d Cir., 1944). And see, Barron and Holt-zoff, Federal Practice & Procedure, § 569 at note 24; 3 Moore, Federal Practice, at page 3536 (2d ed. 1948).

67. Maris, Cir. J., in Schoen v. Mountain Producers' Corp., 170 F. 2d 707, at 712, footnote 9 (3d Cir., 1948). See page 363, supra, for the phrasing of § 1695. Montro Corp. v. Prindle, 105 F.Supp. 460 (D.N.Y.1952), contains an excellent discussion, with diagrams, of the venue possibilities of derivative suits in the federal courts.

68. Lavin v. Lavin, supra, note 59. at 873. But see Barron & Holtzoff, Federal Practice and Procedure, § 569 at note 24, and 3 Moore, Fed-eral Practice, pages 3542–3543 (2d ed. 1948). There is also the prob-lem of *forum non conveniens*. See Koster v. American Lumbermen's Mutual Casualty Co., 330 U.S. 518, 67 S.Ct. 831, 91 L.Ed. 1073 (1947), Barron & Holtzoff, § 569 at note 34, and 3 Moore, op. cit. supra at 3541.

venue purposes." [69]   The doctrine of *forum non conveniens* is sufficient to protect the parties in a proper case.[70]   Under the 1948 statute an action brought in a *forum non conveniens* is not dismissed for this reason if there is "a district or division in which it could have been brought," and it will be transferred for trial at such place.[71]

There are other problems of jurisdiction and venue in derivative actions too specialized to warrant discussion in a short work on corporations and, for these, works on local and federal practice should be consulted.[72]

§ 7. Double and Multiple Derivative Actions

A problem arises when a shareholder of a corporation which owns shares in one or more other corporations complains that causes of action in favor of such other corporations exist but that their directors and his have wrongfully failed to prosecute them. Or there may be a chain of corporations, each owning shares in the other. The corporate shareholder may, of course, bring the derivative action in favor of the corporation in which it owns shares. But, upon wrongful refusal of his own corporation to bring an action, may the shareholder of the shareholding company then bring a derivative action? And if he may, does his right extend to B and C corporations when his corporation, A, owns shares in B, and B owns shares in C? It has been held that such suits will lie and the term applied to them is double or multiple derivative suits depending upon the number of corporations involved in the line. Thus, where the plaintiff owned a minority interest in the N Corporation and it owned a one-half interest in the PN Corporation and PN, in turn, owned a one-third interest in MP Corporation, the plaintiff was allowed to bring this multiple derivative action to enforce claims of all three corporations against numerous defendants alleged to have received "unconscionable and excessive compensation under certain management contracts" with these corporations.[73]   Thus a share-

---

69. But see 3 Moore, op. cit. supra, note 68, at pages 3543–3544; Barron and Holtzoff, § 569.

70. See note 62, supra.

71. 3 Moore, op. cit. supra, note 68, at 3541; Barron and Holtzoff, § 569.

72. See excellent Note, Federal Courts: Diversity Jurisdiction and Venue in Shareholders' Derivative Suits, 39 Calif.L.Rev. 138 (1951); 3 Moore, op. cit. supra, note 68, page 3530 et seq. with a discussion of the changes brought about by the Judicial Code and Judiciary Re-

vision Act of 1948 at page 3541 et seq. with a short summary at page 3544.

73. S. Solomont & Sons Trust, Inc. v. New England Theatres Operating Corporation, 326 Mass. 99, 93 N.E. 2d 241 (1950). The case went in favor of the defendants but the right of the plaintiff to bring the suit was thoroughly recognized as it has been in other cases. The plaintiff's corporation need not be a majority shareholder as this case illustrates. Also, see U. S. Lines, Inc. v. U. S. Lines Co., 96 F.2d 148 (2d Cir., 1938).

holder is permitted to enforce a right twice or more derived, and whether or not his immediate corporation dominated the rest is not important in determining his right.[74] Only sporadic dicta and a few cases which should have been narrowly construed have questioned this right to bring a double or multiple derivative action.[75]

Since the failure to bring the action is charged to be a wrongful one of the directors and/or shareholders, the right to bring a double derivative suit offers complications not present in a single derivative suit. There must first be a wrongful refusal on the part of the corporation whose cause of action is in question and, second, a wrongful refusal by the corporation some of whose shares the plaintiff owns. However, where it is alleged that the parent corporation is controlling the action of the subsidiary in not bringing the action, it would appear that a demand upon the parent alone and a refusal to act thereafter would supply this necessary condition precedent. It would be futile to request the board of the subsidiary to bring the suit when its board members were controlled by the board of the parent.

There are other complications inherent in the double or multiple derivative suit in a jurisdiction having the rule that the plaintiff-shareholder must have possessed his shares prior to the events which he alleges are the basis of the corporate right, or should have acquired his shares by operation of law. The reason supporting the prior acquisition rule is to prevent the bringing of vexatious suits by a shareholder's purchasing a few shares for this purpose; and, in the federal courts, the additional reason of obtaining federal jurisdiction on diversity of citizenship grounds. If both the plaintiff-shareholder and his corporation must have possessed their shares in their respective corporations prior to the events upon which suit depends, there will be cases where valid claims may not be litigated because of the inelasticity of the basic rule. The plaintiff-shareholder may have acquired his shares, but his immediate corporation may not have, prior to the wrong upon which suit is based. Unless it appears that the reasons for the prior acquisition rule in the particular case justify requiring both to have been prior shareholders, the rule in all its strictness ought not to be applied.

It has been pointed out that, while the corporation is an indispensable party in the ordinary derivative suit, the same rule should not be extended to apply in double or multiple derivative suits to require the several corporations to be parties, since the

74. Note, Suits by a Shareholder in a Parent Corporation to Redress Injuries to the Subsidiary, 64 Harv.L.Rev. 1313, 1314 (1951).

75. Ibid. at 1315–1316.

ultimate cause of action belongs to the corporation which has wrongfully refused to bring the action for its own benefit.[76] There is merit to this suggestion. Any decree will bind the corporation-defendant having the primary right to sue and that would seem sufficient reason for not requiring the plaintiff-shareholder's corporation to be brought in as a party-defendant.[77] In fact, the plaintiff-shareholder's corporation (not having the primary right to sue) has indicated its unwillingness to bring the action which, if successful, will result only in indirect benefit to itself as in other single derivative actions.

There are other problems such as that of the jurisdiction and venue in diversity of citizenship cases in the federal courts, and of venue in the state courts if judicial insistence makes necessary the joinder of the several corporations involved in a multiple derivative action. The discussion in the preceding section points the way toward possible solutions in this area. However, one should not ignore the possibility of defeating the reasonable purpose of the federal rule if the court concludes that the corporation having the derivative right but failing to use it need not be brought in as a party-defendant.

Quite as troublesome may be the application of the security-for-expenses statutes in double or multiple derivative actions unless these statutes are liberally interpreted in favor of the plaintiff-shareholder, for multiple defendants in these cases do not necessarily create extraordinary expenses because of their numbers alone. Probably the draftsmen of these statutes did not have in mind the special problems of the multiple derivative suit.[78]

§ 8. The Corporation's Role in Derivative Suits

May the corporation which must be, under our procedural holdings, a nominal party-defendant in a derivative action file an answer to the plaintiff shareholder's complaint setting forth affirmative defenses? Or must the corporation be neutral or, if it acts, proceed as if it were the real party-plaintiff which, had it elected to bring the action, would have been the case and which, in effect, is the case? There is little helpful authority on this point or, indeed, little authority of any kind. Defenses made by the corporate defendant have frequently not been questioned at all perhaps due to counsel's lack of knowledge as to the possibilities.

A clear case where a corporation should not be permitted to defend affirmatively is where its officers have been charged with

---

76. Ibid. at 1320.

77. But see Busch v. Mary A. Riddle Co., 283 F. 443 (D.Del.1922).

78. Note, supra footnote 74, at 1320–1321.

wrongdoing—misappropriation of corporate funds, for example, —and the corporation seeks to shield the wrongdoers.[79] A case similarly clear where the corporation should be permitted to defend is that in which a shareholder seeks to have a receiver of the corporate assets appointed.[80] It would be difficult to lay down a principle which would be useful and practical for all derivative suits, for the remedies sought by the shareholder are so varied. Furthermore, there is not unanimous agreement as to what are and what are not within the classification of derivative suits. New York, for example, has considered an action by a shareholder to compel the declaration and distribution of a dividend as a derivative, rather than personal, suit.[81] Yet, in such a case, the corporation may have valid reasons for passing a dividend and, thus, should be able to defend affirmatively.

Defenses such as that the conditions precedent to bringing suit have not been met,[82] or that the shareholders have ratified the board's action in a case where such ratification is binding upon the corporation,[83] or that the court has no jurisdiction to hear and decide the case, are legitimate areas of corporate defense. The corporation, too, may be entitled to insist upon the plaintiff's compliance with a security-for-expenses statute before the case proceeds beyond the pleading stage, and his inability to comply may be the equivalent of a perfect defense if no other shareholder can be found to bring the action or join with him in an effort to comply with the statute.[84] Thus, it is obvious that a rigid rule to the effect that a corporation in a derivative suit may not step in and frustrate what is, in effect, its own suit is too narrow; whereas one which purports to permit the corporation

79. Meyers v. Smith, 190 Minn. 157, 251 N.W. 20 (1933). In Groel v. United Electric Co. of New Jersey, 70 N.J.Eq. 616, 61 A. 1061 (1905), the directors thought it inexpedient to bring an action against promoters to recover $20,-000,000 of the corporation's stock. The court thought this was a breach of trust by the directors and had "grave doubt" whether the defendant should be able to raise the issue.

80. Godley v. Crandall & Godley Co., 181 App.Div. 75, 168 N.Y.S. 251 (1917), aff'd without opinion, 227 N.Y. 656, 126 N.E. 908 (1920).

81. Gordon v. Elliman, 306 N.Y. 456, 119 N.E.2d 331 (1954)—a 4 to 3 decision; *contra*, and better opinion, Knapp v. Bankers' Securities Corp., 230 F.2d 717 (3d Cir., 1956).

Lattin Corporations F.P.Inc.—24

82. Note, 38 Va.L.Rev. 676 (1952).

83. S. Solomont & Sons Trust, Inc. v. New England Theatres Operating Corp., 326 Mass. 99, 93 N.E.2d 241 (1950). See Landstrom, Ratification by Majority Stockholders— A Problem in Corporate Democracy, 31 B.U.L.Rev. 165 (1951).

84. Cohen v. Beneficial Industrial Loan Corp., 337 U.S. 541, 69 S.Ct. 1221, 93 L.Ed. 1528 (1949), involving the constitutionality of the New Jersey Act and its applicability to diversity cases in the federal courts. "It is urged that such a requirement will foreclose resort by most stockholders to the only available judicial remedy for the protection of their rights." Mr. Justice Jackson at page 552 of 337 U.S., at p. 1228 of 69 S.Ct.

to dictate what defenses shall or shall not be made is much too broad.[85]

It has been suggested that when the directors' fraud is the basis of a derivative action, the ascertainment of the truth and recovery of funds or property so acquired should normally demand that the corporation not defend affirmatively. But when a cause of action endangers, rather than advances corporate interests, corporate defenses would seem proper.[86] Thus, since whether or not suit should be brought in a particular case is within the discretion of the board of directors, it is within their right affirmatively to answer for their corporation on the basis of their good faith determination and use company counsel at company expense to present the defense.[87] But a defense upon the merits of an alleged cause of action against a third-party defendant goes right to the heart of a matter for which derivative suits were invented and such defense should not be allowed.

It may be that a rule which looks primarily to the party whom the particular defense is designed to protect and which limits the defense to that party is as near to a basic and practical rule as is possible.[88] There will be a few factual situations where doubt may exist as to what party the rule was intended to protect, but even there the possible choices will normally reveal the probable party designed to be protected.[89]

§ 9. May Shareholders Intervene on Behalf of Corporation in Derivative Actions?

Occasions have arisen where the shareholder-plaintiff and the corporation-defendant have seemingly worked together for a result contrary to the best interests of the corporation and its non-suing shareholders. Intervention by other shareholders may be necessary in order to obtain an adequate (or any) defense by the corporation in the area of legitimate corporate defenses in such cases. It has been rightly held that when the corporation wrongfully refuses to defend or, having proceeded to defend, does not press its defense in good faith a shareholder, upon application to intervene, will be permitted to do so upon a showing of corporate non-action and that the shareholder has been unable

85. Compare Meyers v. Smith, supra, note 78, 251 N.W. at 21, with McHarg v. Commonwealth Finance Corp., 44 S.D. 144, 182 N.W. 705, at 706 (1921).

86. Otis & Co. v. Pennsylvania R. Co., 57 F.Supp. 680 at 682 (D.Pa. 1944).

87. See Otis & Co. v. Pennsylvania R. Co., supra, note 86. But their discretion must not have been abused as in Groel v. United Electric Co. of New Jersey, supra, note 78. Also see Note, Defenses in Shareholders' Derivative Suits —Who May Raise Them, 66 Harv. L.Rev. 342 (1952).

88. Note, 66 Harv.L.Rev. 342, at 343 and 346 (1952).

89. See ibid. at 346–347.

to obtain action by the plaintiffs to do what is fair and just.[90] But mere disagreement as to how the corporation should carry on its defense, that is, disagreement concerning the manner of presentation, or whether certain defenses thought to be unwise by the directors because of their public relations implications should be used, are beyond the pale of shareholder intervention.[91]

No demand upon the board of directors prior to intervention is necessary in any case where the facts alleged show that such a request would be useless, as where the majority of the board members are conspiring with the plaintiffs' counsel to secure a judgment favorable to the plaintiffs.[92]

There are differences between the bringing of a derivative suit which may result in corporate benefit and the intervention on behalf of the corporate defendant so that it is adequately defended which warrant discussion. The reason for the rule requiring the plaintiff to have been a shareholder at the time of the events upon which his suit is based is not present when he intervenes to defend his corporation. Vexatious litigation, if such there be, has been brought by the plaintiff. Hence, even if the intervenor's shares have been acquired after the corporate defendant has lost its case, there is no good reason for barring him on this ground alone from pursuing possible remedies to reopen the judgment.[93]

As far as the security-for-expenses statutes are concerned, their language and the reasons for their enactment would appear to be inapplicable to intervening shareholders whether intervention be to defend or prosecute on behalf of the corporate defendant.[94] These statutes were aimed at discouraging plain-

90. Eggers v. National Radio Co., 208 Cal. 308, 281 P. 58 (1929); Fitzwater v. Nat. Bank of Seneca, 62 Kan. 163, 61 P. 684 (1900); Thorman v. Dome Producing & Developing Co., 50 Cal.App.2d 201, 122 P.2d 927 (1942); First Merchants Nat. Bank & Trust Co. v. Murdock Realty Co., 111 Ind.App. 226, 39 N. E.2d 507 (1942).

91. Atlanta Laundries, Inc. v. National Linen Serv. Corp., 81 F. Supp. 650 (D.Ga.1948).

92. Eggers v. National Radio Co., supra, note 90. But Continental & Commercial Trust & Savings Bank v. Allis-Chalmers Co., 200 F. 600 (D.Wis.1912), holds that the usual requirements in derivative suits are applicable in cases of intervention to defend. Hence, the shareholder complains that he is

not satisfied with the corporate conduct in defending the suit and demands that the directors assert and press the defenses. Upon their failure to comply with the shareholder's request intervention is based. See Note, Shareholder Intervention in Corporate Litigation, 63 Harv.L.Rev. 1426, 1427 (1950).

93. That there may still be a basis of requiring compliance with Rule 23(b) of the Federal Rules of Civil Procedure in a diversity of citizenship case, see Piccard v. Sperry Corp., 36 F.Supp. 1006 (D.N.Y.1941), aff'd 120 F.2d 328 (2d Cir., 1941). See Rules 24(a) (2) and 24(b) of the Federal Rules of Civil Procedure which relate to intervention.

94. Note, 63 Harv.L.Rev. 1426, at 1428 (1950).

tiffs from bringing "strike" suits, not at intervention which
normally works toward frustrating such motives.

While normally intervention will be sought after the pleadings have been filed and before the case goes to trial, there will
be times when intervention will be necessary during trial or
after judgment.[95] This is apparent when the corporation's directors collude with the plaintiffs and the corporate defense is
carried on in a luke-warm manner, or not at all. Collusion, or
the appearances of collusion, would seem to warrant intervention
at any stage of the proceedings[96] as would an exhibition or dem-
onstration of incompetent counsel representing the corporation.
Statutes vary as to when intervention is permitted and these
will have to be consulted along with the case-law to ascertain the
local rule and its interpretation. The phrase "on timely application" appearing in Rule 24 of the Federal Rules of Civil Procedure gives much leeway and, even where the statute or rule
of court permits intervention "before trial" a liberal interpretation that this applies only when the intervenor was aware of inadequate representation before trial would be justified.[97] There
are other problems such as who may control the course of
litigation after the admission of intervenors and whether the
intervenor, when successful, is entitled to the expenses incurred
by his intervention, including counsel fees,—topics to be discussed shortly.

§ 10.   Control, Settlement, Compromise and Dismissal of De-rivative Actions

A settlement of a derivative action which took the form
of a purchase by the corporation of the plaintiffs' stock at approximately seven times its market value was followed by a stipulation of discontinuance of the action and a consent order by
the court. All expenses of settlement and of defending the action were paid by the corporation or its subsidiaries without any
contribution from the delinquent director-defendants. The settlement had neither been submitted for approval to shareholders
not parties to the suit nor to the court for approval. In a motion
by other shareholders to vacate and set aside the stipulation of

---

95. See Park & Tilford, Inc. v.
Schulte, 160 F.2d 984 (2d Cir.,
1947), cert. denied 332 U.S. 761,
68 S.Ct. 64, 92 L.Ed. 347 (1947),
where a shareholder was denied intervention at the trial stage but
was allowed to intervene on appeal. The legal point which the
shareholder was not permitted to
present in the lower court due to
the court's denial of her request
to intervene resulted in a much
larger judgment dollar-wise than
if her argument had not been allowed.

96. See Pyle Nat. Co. v. Amos, 172
F.2d 425 (7th Cir., 1949), where intervention was allowed to set aside
an alleged fraudulent settlement.

97. Note, 63 Harv.L.Rev. 1426, at
1433 (1950).

discontinuance, the court held that under the New York law a shareholder-plaintiff in a derivative action may discontinue his action at any time before another shareholder has intervened or judgment has been entered.[98] This holding was in the face of a local rule of civil practice which authorized discontinuance "in the subject matter of which no person not a party has an interest." Justice Shientag indicated that if the case had been one of first impression his conclusion "might be otherwise," but the New York authority, mostly in the form of dicta,[99] was too strong to hold otherwise. Thus, the shareholder-plaintiff in a derivative action was held to have exclusive control of the action and to be able to settle his individual damages leaving his fellow shareholders to seek their remedy in a new action. A discontinuance of a suit does not bar a later one by other shareholders as it is not *res adjudicata* as to them. But it may be that the statute of limitations has run thus making the later suit valueless.

The New York doctrine which is followed in some other jurisdictions has been severely criticized for its possible harsh effects upon innocent shareholders and for the encouragement it gives to collusive settlements. However, the effect of the doctrine has been softened and collusive settlements discouraged by a rule laid down in a later New York case,[1] to the effect that a shareholder who discontinues a derivative action because of a personal settlement with the defendants holds the moneys so received impressed with a trust in favor of his corporation. In the particular case the settlement involved the sum of $9,000 given for the plaintiff's stock which had a market value of but $51.88, the amount held in trust being $8948.12 which he was compelled to return to the corporation.

The New York approach is also softened by the generally recognized doctrine that other shareholders who desire may be joined, as parties-plaintiff, at the discretion of the court, to aid in the prosecution of the suit and that they may, if ignorant of a prior action, prosecute separate actions in which case the court may consolidate the several actions or let them stand for the present denying motions to dismiss merely because of the pend-

98. Manufacturers Mutual Fire Ins. Co. of Rhode Island v. Hopson, 176 Misc. 220, 25 N.Y.S.2d 502 (Sup. Ct.1940), aff'd 262 App.Div. 731, 29 N.Y.S.2d 139 (1941), aff'd 228 N.Y. 668, 43 N.E.2d 71 (1942).

99. These apparently got their start from statements in, but not necessary for the decision of Brinckerhoff v. Bostwick, 99 N.Y. 185, 1 N. E. 663 (1885).

1. Clarke v. Greenberg, 296 N.Y. 146, 71 N.E.2d 443 (1947), discussed in Notes, 47 Col.L.Rev. 684 (1947); 32 Cornell L.Q. 564 (1947); 32 Minn. L.Rev. 180 (1948); 23 N.Y.U.L.Q. Rev. 192 (1948); 33 Va.L.Rev. 512 (1947); 14 U. of Chi.L.Rev. 673 (1947). Compare Young v. Higbee Co., 324 U.S. 204, 65 S.Ct. 594, 89 L.Ed. 890 (1945), which is based upon the same philosophy but is in another area of corporate and bankruptcy (reorganization) law.

ency of one or more similar actions.[2] The latter type of approach keeps the case alive in situations where another case is discontinued, and gives protection against a failure of the action due to the running of the statute of limitations, and has other practical advantages.[3]

Where a compromise or settlement has been presented for judicial approval, or is entered in the course of a trial, the court may (and ought when reasonably practical) require notice to all shareholders that they may be given the opportunity to be heard before final settlement of the action is approved and entered by the court, for this constitutes *res adjudicata* which will bar other shareholders from bringing subsequent suits or from prosecuting pending actions for the same injury.[4]

Fortunately, other jurisdictions do not hesitate to set aside stipulations for discontinuances in derivative actions where court approval has not been first obtained. And if, as the New York court in *Clarke* v. *Greenberg*[5] states, the shareholder-plaintiff holds compromise funds as trustee for the corporation on whose behalf he has sued, he is virtually suing as if he were in the position of a guardian *ad litem* of the corporation. That, in itself, would warrant future determinations in accord with the better view requiring judicial sanction to discontinuances of derivative suits and supervision over compromises and settlements. The Supreme Court of California saw the problem and its ramifications clearly when it wrote, through Justice Henshaw:[6] "What is the exact situation of a plaintiff in such an action? He is a trustee pure and simple, seeking in the name of another a recovery for wrongs that have been committed against that other. His position in the litigation is in every legal sense the precise equivalent of that of the guardian *ad litem* . . . The principles governing the conduct of a guardian *ad litem* are in full strictness applicable to the conduct of such a plaintiff stockholder. Not only should a plaintiff in such a fiduciary capacity be willing to take no act that did not first receive the sanction of the court of equity to which he has appealed, but, more than this, he is not permitted to take any act without such sanction . . . It is the right and duty of the court to protect the interests of the incompetent represented by the guardian *ad litem* and to exercise supervision over the conduct of that guardian."

2. Dresdner v. Goldman Sachs Trading Corp., 240 App.Div. 242, 269 N.Y.S. 369 (1934).

3. Ibid. 240 App.Div. at 246 and 247.

4. Stevens, Corporations 825 (2d ed. 1949).

5. Supra, note 1.

6. Whitten v. Dabney, 171 Cal. 621, at 630–631, 154 P. 312 (1915). And see Spellacy v. Superior Court of Los Angeles County, 23 Cal.App.2d 142, 72 P.2d 262 (1937); National Power & Paper Co. v. Rossman, 122 Minn. 355, 142 N.W. 818, Ann. Cas.1914D, 830 (1913).

Federal Rule 23(c) of the Federal Rules of Civil Procedure requires, in case of dismissal or compromise of a shareholder's derivative action, the approval of the court after notice to other shareholders in such manner as the court directs.[7] This method brings the compromise plan or settlement offers out in the open where they may be contested for their fairness in the light of what results might have been obtained had the case gone to trial.

Since compromise and settlement of corporate suits are within the province of the members of the board of directors (who are not parties defendant) acting impartially and in good faith, some courts have held, or agreed in dicta, that there is no legal requirement for submitting the settlement agreed upon to the shareholders.[8] Where this rule prevails close scrutiny should be made of the settlement especially where fellow-directors are involved, which is usually the case.[9]

While a great disparity in value between the amount of the settlement and what the corporation is giving up in exchange therefor raises a prima facie inference of fraud, it is not conclusive.[10] The disparity may be consistent with honesty in spite

7. See Note, Settlement of Derivative Suits Under the Federal Rules, 52 Mich.L.Rev. 748 (1954).

8. Karasik v. Pacific Eastern Corp., 21 Del.Ch. 81, 180 A. 604 (Del.Ch. 1935), contains a strong dictum to this effect. The settlements had been submitted to the shareholders and overwhelmingly approved although the suit was for $100,000,000, and the net yield from the agreement would be about $250,000 though, depending upon what value was set upon shares returned by the settlement, the gross return might be from $385,000 to $585,000. This, of course, is a far cry from the $100,000,000 claimed, but was justified on several reasonable bases.

9. In Karasik v. Pacific Eastern Corp., supra, note 8, only one of the defendants was a director at the time of the negotiation of the settlement and he did not participate on the corporation's side. In Perrine v. Pennroad Corp., 29 Del.Ch. 531, 47 A.2d 479 (Sup.Ct. 1946), cert. denied 329 U.S. 808, 67 S.Ct. 620, 91 L.Ed. 690 (1947), after the trial of a later filed case in the federal court had resulted in a large judgment for the plaintiff shareholders, the board of the corporation-defendant actively en-

gaged in supporting the plaintiffs when the real party defendants appealed. The appeal was in defendants' favor (one judge dissenting) and the board continued to aid the plaintiffs in obtaining a substantial settlement. None of the directors of Pennroad Corp. who executed the settlement agreement with the Pennsylvania Railroad, with perhaps one exception, was a director of Pennroad at the time of the events leading to directorial liability. As one of the conditions for accepting the settlement, the federal Third Circuit required the settlement to be submitted to the Delaware court (where the first derivative suit had been brought) for shareholder notice and for that court's approval.

10. Karasik v. Pacific Eastern Corp., supra, note 8. The difference between the amount sued for and the settlement was over $99,000,000, an amount greatly in excess of what the defendants could pay if a judgment were obtained. In Perrine v. Pennroad Corp., supra, note 9, a judgment for approximately $22,000,000 was obtained, but was reversed, and a settlement without further trial was negotiated for $15,000,000 which, under the circumstances, was held not fraudulent. And see Masterson v. Perg-

of it. What might have been recovered had the case gone to trial is not as important as what might have been collected from the defendants by enforcing such a judgment. "No judgment is worth more than it can be made to yield." [11]   Uncertainties as to whether the suit may stand up in court have their bearing as do the possible loss of witnesses over a long trial or retrial period, the expenses of suit plus counsel fees, the effect of the publicity of suit upon the public relations of the corporation, and the usual exaggeration in petitions as to the amount sought as damages.

The interesting procedure worked out in *Perrine* v. *Penn-road Corporation* [12] is worth noting. A derivative action had been filed in Delaware seven years prior to an action based on the same facts filed in the federal District Court in Pennsylvania. The latter was tried and one defendant adjudged liable for approximately $22,000,000.   The Third Circuit reversed on grounds that the claims were barred by the statute of limitations, the ground upon which several other defendants were relieved in the District Court, but one judge dissented and thought all defendants were liable. At this point settlement negotiations started and finally resulted in an agreement to pay to the injured corporation the sum of $15,000,000 under conditions which (1) required the approval of the Delaware Chancery Court where the first case was filed, (2) the issuance by the Third Circuit of an order to the District Court staying further proceedings, and (3) the expiration of the time for applying for certiorari. Upon petition for approval of the settlement, the Delaware Chancery Court, after notice of the hearing was given to the shareholders, heard the evidence concerning the fairness of the settlement and approved it. On appeal, the court held that where another court, having jurisdiction, has fully heard the case and settled the controversy, it is competent for a court of chancery to entertain a petition for approval of a settlement agreement reached in the first court. The chancellor's problem in such a case is to satisfy himself that the settlement agreement is for the best interests of all the shareholders. The case also held that the chancellor is not required to retry the case which is to be settled, and he is under no duty under due process concepts to admit all the evidence offered by objecting shareholders on the merits of the case being settled.

ament, 203 F.2d 315, at 335–336 (6th Cir., 1953), cert. denied 346 U.S. 832, 74 S.Ct. 33, 98 L.Ed. 355 (1954), where the court presents matters to be considered in the appraisal of the consideration for settlement. This case is noted in 52 Mich.L.Rev. 748 (1954).

11. Karasik v. Pacific Eastern Corp., supra note 8, 180 A. at 610.

12. Supra, note 9.

§ 11. Control of Conduct of Suit When Other Shareholders Intervene

Whether or not a shareholder will be permitted to intervene as an additional plaintiff is generally considered a matter within the discretion of the court, depending upon whether the intervenor's interest is being adequately protected. Once the court has consented to intervention, the problem of the control over the litigation in its various stages becomes important. Usually the shareholder originally bringing the action retains his right to control the proceedings and his counsel will be "chief of staff" as the suit progresses. It has been stated that ". . . counsel for an intervenor may not participate in the presentation of the main case save as counsel for plaintiff may consent or the court otherwise order . . . Even if counsel for plaintiff is agreeable to their active participation in the case, they nevertheless do not by such participation become entitled to any fee out of any recovery that ensues as a result of the action, unless it be affirmatively shown that their contribution is separate, distinct and of a character which was not, could not or would not have been made by counsel of the original plaintiff." [13] However, if the suit is not prosecuted vigorously or with reasonable capability and efficiency, the court has the power to transfer the prosecution to an intervenor.[14]

In the federal courts, intervention is likewise ordinarily a matter of the court's discretion,[15] and is non-appealable.[16]

If, instead of seeking permission to intervene, the shareholder brings a second derivative action based upon the same subject matter as the pending suit, the court has the discretionary power to grant a stay of the later action without prejudice to vacate the stay upon later motion of the shareholder if the first action is discontinued or unreasonably delayed in going to trial.[17] The court also has the discretionary right to consolidate pending suits of this kind if they are in the same court,[18] and in such a case the New York court has appointed what it considered the best qualified counsel to conduct the suit.[19]

13. Mann v. Superior Court of Los Angeles County, 53 Cal.App.2d 272, at 281, 127 P.2d 970 (1942).

14. Mann v. Superior Court of Los Angeles County, supra, note 13; White v. British Type Investors, Inc., 130 N.J.Eq. 157, 21 A.2d 681 (1941).

15. See Rule 24, Federal Rules of Civil Procedure.

16. Thompson v. Broadfoot, 165 F.2d 744 (2d Cir., 1948).

17. Schwartz v. Kaufman, 46 F. Supp. 318 (D.N.Y.1940); Dresdner v. Goldman Sachs Trading Corp., 240 App.Div. 242, 269 N.Y.S. 360 (1934). See this text at pages 373–374, supra.

18. Dresdner v. Goldman Sachs Trading Corp., supra, note 17.

19. And, in general, see Hornstein, Problems of Procedure in Stockholders' Derivative Suits, 42 Col. L.Rev. 574 (1942). And note Breswick & Co. v. Briggs, 135 F.Supp.

§ 12. Basic Rule Regarding Damages Recoverable—Exceptions to the Rule

Since a derivative suit is brought on behalf of a corporation and for its benefit when the directors have wrongfully refused to bring a direct action, damages recoverable in such a suit belong to the corporation as such and not to the plaintiff shareholders. Were the rule otherwise, creditors would frequently find the corporate coffers empty. Furthermore, since the cause of action is the corporation's, had the shareholder brought the action as one personal to himself he would have been told that, while his shareholder's interest was indirectly injured, his remedy came through corporate, not individual, recovery.

In the now famous case of *Old Dominion Copper Mining & Smelting Co.* v. *Lewisohn* [20] one of the practical reasons assigned by Mr. Justice Holmes for supporting the case for no corporate recovery was the fact that, were it permitted, $13/15$ of the guilty participating shares in the promotion scheme would benefit as well as the remaining $2/15$ of non-participating shares. It was considered unjust that the promoter, if he were held at all, should be compelled to disgorge more than the $2/15$ of the secret profits taken and these should be distributed to the holders of the non-participating shares. In derivative suits, the argument that only non-participating or non-ratifying shares should participate in the fund recovered has generally been rejected. Creditors may be injured if the bars are let down and innocent shareholders have a right to expect that the corporation will use funds so acquired in the business until the board legitimately declares a dividend or there is a capital reduction made through the usual shareholders' vote and the fund realized is distributed pro rata.

In one of the leading cases where an overwhelming majority of shareholders had voted to release the wrongdoing directors from accountability, it was argued that the complainants should be limited in their recovery to a sum which the proportion of their shares bore to the total number of shares outstanding, and this sum should be distributed to them individually. The court held that such an individual recovery could not be justified in a derivative action; that, if it were, it would be comparable to compelling the board to declare and distribute a dividend, a thing within their discretion and certainly not possible unless a legal fund existed from which a dividend could be declared and

397 (D.N.Y.1955), where Walsh, D. J., denied an application for consolidation of the federal court action with several actions already consolidated in the state court on the ground that general counsel in the consolidated actions "showed less than a full comprehension of the proceedings which plaintiffs have conducted."

20. 210 U.S. 206, 28 S.Ct. 634, 52 L.Ed. 1025 (1907).

paid.[21]   It was brought out that it was not the complainants who were seeking individual compensation but the defendants who were attempting to force the complainants to receive individual recompense.   The court, perhaps with tongue in cheek, suggested that once the judgment was satisfied and the corporation had received the benefit of it the directors, if a proper fund existed, might declare a dividend equal to the judgment and the ratifying shareholders, if they then wished, might make a gift of their dividend to the directors who had been required to pay for their misdeeds, poetic justice to say the least.

While the normal remedy discounts the notion that guilty as well as innocent shares will benefit if the judgment recovered must go to the corporation,[22] exceptions have been made.   Where a large proportion of the shares are in the possession of those against whom a judgment is sought, or in possession of their transferees, some courts have held that a judgment personal to the plaintiff is justified.[23]   And where the corporation had no shareholders other than the plaintiff and the defendants, and no creditors, it was held proper to decree a proportionate part of the property misappropriated by the defendants to the plaintiff.[24] Where the financial condition of the company was such that recovery by the company would "clearly call for the declaration of

21. Eshleman v. Keenan, 22 Del.Ch. 82, 194 A. 40 (Ch.Ct.1937), aff'd Keenan v. Eshleman, 23 Del.Ch. 234, 2 A.2d 904, 120 A.L.R. 227 (Sup.Ct.1938).   The company was solvent and its capital unimpaired, but it did not appear of record that the company was in a financial condition to warrant a disbursement of the recoverable amount as a dividend.

22. Old Dominion Copper Mining & Smelting Co. v. Bigelow, 203 Mass. 159, 89 N.E. 193 (1909) (Here, a promoter was held for secret profits made by him and by Lewisohn, a joint promoter tortfeasor, although $13\%_{15}$ of the shares had been held by these promoters when they took their secret profit and all these shares were apparently in other hands at the time of the suit.   Furthermore, it did not appear whether any of the original shareholders who took $2\%_{15}$ of the shares and who had no notice of the promoters' profit now held these shares).

23. Matthews v. Headley Chocolate Co., 130 Md. 523, 100 A. 645 (1917) (the defendants who were officers had owned 75% of the company's shares but had sold to third parties a majority of their holdings, so that recovery in favor of the corporation would, in effect, reduce the price paid by the third parties for their stock; May v. Midwest Refining Co., 121 F.2d 431 (1st Cir., 1941) (the plaintiff and but one other shareholder who could not be found were apparently the only ones in a position to sue derivatively); Di Tomasso v. Loverro, 250 App.Div. 206, 293 N.Y.S. 912 (1937), aff'd 276 N.Y. 551, 12 N.E.2d 70 (1937) (a somewhat similar case to the May case); Chounis v. Laing, 125 W.Va. 275, 23 S.E.2d 628 (1942) (95% of the shares had participated in or assented to the plan causing corporate injury).   And see the holding in Perlman v. Feldmann, 219 F.2d 173 (2d Cir., 1955), cert. denied 349 U.S. 952, 75 S.Ct. 880, 99 L.Ed. 1277 (1955), and Jennings, Trading in Corporate Control, 44 Calif.L.Rev. 1, 27–28 (1956).

24. Peoples State Bank v. Jacksonian Hotel Co., 261 Ky. 166, 87 S.W.2d 111 (1935).

a dividend," it was held proper to award the plaintiffs their proportionate part of the decree.[25]

An occasional case has sanctioned recovery in a class action (not derivative in character) by injured shareholders [26] or by the corporation as trustee for the injured shareholders.[27] The theory behind such holdings seems to be that the promoters or officers who are being sued occupy a fiduciary relation towards the subscribers or shareholders as such, emphasizing this rather than their fiduciary obligations to the corporation.[28] As Dean Stevens has recently written: "This is, in effect, a shortcut designed to route the recovery directly to those entitled to it; but this shortcut will not be employed if the rights of creditors of the corporation would thereby be prejudiced." [29]

And, of course, in the special case where the corporation has been dissolved and has but a formal existence, conditions at that time may well warrant individual recovery.[30]

In any case where special facts may justify the bringing of an individual action as, for example, in the sale of control by a shareholder, or in the special situations discussed above, until the law has been definitely shaped toward personal recovery or toward corporate recovery, the plaintiff should join, where possible, an individual or class action against the individual defendants based upon a cause of action personal to the plaintiff or his class with a separate count based upon the derivative action.[31]

---

25. Baillie v. Columbia Gold Mining Co., 86 Or. 1, 166 P. 965, petitions for rehearing denied, 167 P. 1167 (1917).

26. Downey v. Byrd, 171 Ga. 532, 156 S.E. 259 (1930), noted in 31 Col.L. Rev. 890 (1931); 19 Geo.L.J. 495 (1931); 26 Ill.L.Rev. 340 (1931); 17 Va.L.Rev. 713 (1931); Brown v. De Young, 167 Ill. 549, at 557, 47 N.E. 863 (1897); Mason v. Carrothers, 105 Me. 392, 74 A. 1030 (1909). But see Barrett v. Shambeau, 187 Minn. 430, 245 N.W. 830 (1932); Voorhees v. Mason, 245 Ill. 256, 91 N.E. 1056 (1910).

27. Hyde Park Terrace Co. v. Jackson Bros. Realty Co., 161 App.Div. 699, 146 N.Y.S. 1037 (1914); Matthews v. Headley Chocolate Co., 130 Md. 523, 100 A. 645 (1917).

28. See particularly Downey v. Byrd, supra, note 26, 171 Ga. at page 544, 156 S.E. at 265; Remillard Brick Co. v. Remillard-Dandani Co., 109 Cal.App.2d 405, 419, 241 P.2d 66, 74 (1952). Compare Tryon v. Smith, 191 Or. 172, 180, 229 P.2d 251, 254 (1951).

29. Stevens and Larson, Cases and Materials on Corporations 702 (2d ed. 1955). See Note, Individual Pro Rata Recovery in Stockholders' Derivative Suits, 69 Harv.L.Rev. 1314 (1956).

30. See Bailey v. Jacobs, 325 Pa. 187, 189 A. 320 (1937). In Ruplinger v. Ruplinger, 154 Nev. 394, 48 N.W.2d 73 (1951), noted in 50 Mich.L.Rev. 609 (1952), the corporate life was extended after dissolution by statutory provision. A derivative suit was held proper.

31. See Jennings, Trading in Corporate Control, 44 Calif.L.Rev. 1, at 29, and footnote 100 of the article (1956). And see Note, Policy Considerations Leading to Choice of Derivative Form: Individual Recovery in Derivative Action, 40 Calif.L.Rev. 127 (1952).

§ 13. Reimbursement for Litigation Expenses

A successful shareholder-plaintiff in a derivative suit, where a tangible corporate benefit has been derived therefrom, has uniformly been granted reimbursement for his reasonable expenses including accountant's and attorney's fees.[32] And where a shareholder has made his investigation and his demand upon the defendants and this has resulted in some real benefit to his corporation without the necessity for litigation, he has been granted indemnity for his expenses in connection with his successful preliminaries.[33] Even where no tangible benefit has resulted, a shareholder who, whether in a derivative or a class action, has been able to restrain his corporation from action which might reasonably have led to loss or a wasting of corporate assets, or has brought about the cancellation of a disadvantageous contract, is entitled to reimbursement for his reasonable costs.[34]

Courts generally have been generous in the matter of counsel fees on the theory that derivative suits successfully waged are to be encouraged for their corporate therapeutic value,[35] and for "the socially desirable purpose of affording practical protection to minority stockholders against corporate abuses by the management." [36] Such suits, for the most part, are taken by lawyers on the expectation that their remuneration will come from the corporation if the suit is successful. If unsuccessful, they obtain nothing unless, perhaps, some financial gain resulted or some needed protection was brought about.[37]

The real controversy has been waged over compensating defendant-directors when they successfully defend derivative actions.[38] While there is a conflict, the better holdings have permitted reimbursement after successful defense, whether or not any tangible benefits have resulted, "the policy of the law [being] to encourage directors to resist unjust charges in the confidence that ultimately, if their innocence be judicially estab-

32. Neuberger v. Barrett, 180 Misc. 222, 39 N.Y.S.2d 575 (1942). The court set aside $200,000 of a recovery of about $650,000 for distribution among the attorneys and accountants who had, through their efforts, brought about a settlement on the eve of trial. In Murphy v. North American L. & P. Co., 33 F.Supp. 567 (D.N.Y.1940), $200,000 in fees was awarded to two attorneys whose suit had produced for the corporation about $900,000. Other instances of like liberal treatment could be cited.

33. Kaufman v. Shoenberg, 33 Del. Ch. 282, 92 A.2d 295 (Ch.Ct.1952); Dottenheim v. Emerson Elect.

Mfg. Co., 77 F.Supp. 306 (D.N.Y. 1948).

34. See Holthusen v. Edward G. Budd Mfg. Co., 55 F.Supp. 945 (D.Pa.1944).

35. Woolsey, J., in Murphy v. North American L. & P. Co., supra, note 32, at page 571.

36. Holthusen v. Edward G. Budd Mfg. Co., supra, note 34, at page 946.

37. Gottlieb v. Heyden Chemical Corp., 105 A.2d 461 (Del.Sup.Ct. 1954).

38. See this text at pp. 248–249, supra.

lished, they will be reimbursed for their necessary expenses of defense." [39] If the rule were otherwise, men of substance might hesitate to assume the responsibility of directors. Furthermore, the right to reimbursement, it is thought, has the virtue of being conducive to discouraging derivative suits of the strike variety.[40]

By the adoption of by-laws giving directors who successfully defend such suits a right to indemnification, corporations are able to spell out the protection needed. A tendency all too prevalent is to provide for reimbursement under circumstances which indicate major directorial fault, thus purporting to protect such fiduciaries where the chancellor would have condemned them. It took Parliamentary action in 1929 to cure the then customary English practice of inserting in memorandum or articles an exculpatory provision which purported to relieve directors from damage caused by their fault except by their dishonesty.[41]

Modern statutes are gradually specifically providing for indemnification of directors and officers who are sued for acts done while they occupied these positions.[42] Under the California statute [43] the court is given discretion to grant indemnification in case the director, officer or employee successfully defends himself "in whole or in part" and "the court finds that his conduct fairly and equitably merits such indemnity," this remedy being exclusive, the statute not permitting contrary provisions in the articles or by-laws or by resolution or agreement. This statute applies also to trials terminated by settlement or dismissal.

The New York sections authorize provisions in the certificate of incorporation, by-laws, or resolutions in a specific case giving those sued because of their corporate positions (or because of

---

39. In re Dissolution of E. C. Warner Co., 232 Minn. 207, 45 N.W.2d 388 (1950); Figge v. Bergenthal, 130 Wis. 594, 109 N.W. 581 (1906), 110 N.W. 798 (1907); Solimine v. Hollander, 129 N.J.Eq. 264, 19 A. 2d 344 (1941). In Griesse v. Lang, 37 Ohio App. 553, 175 N.E. 222 (1931), recovery was denied, the principal reason being that no benefit was received by the corporation through the vindication of its directors. To the same effect is New York Dock Co., Inc. v. Mc-Collom, 173 Misc. 106, 16 N.Y.S.2d 844 (Sup.Ct.1939). The legislature has rectified this in N.Y.Gen.Corp. Law § 63 as amended by L.1949, c. 811.

40. Solimine v. Hollander, supra, note 39. Shortly thereafter Minne-sota amended its statute to permit indemnification. Minn.Stat.Ann. § 301.09(7).

41. Companies Act of 1929, § 152, now § 205 of the Companies Act of 1948. Such provisions are now prohibited.

42. See footnote 33, p. 249, supra, for some examples. About a third of the states now have them. Comment, Indemnification of Management for Litigation Expenses, 52 Mich.L.Rev. 1023 (1954).

43. West's Ann.Cal.Corp.Code § 830, as amended by L.1957, c. 2261, § 3. See Ballantine, California's 1943 Statute as to Directors' Litigation Expenses, 31 Calif.L.Rev. 515 (1943).

their testator's or intestate's corporate position) indemnification for expenses, including attorneys' fees, necessarily incurred by them "except in relation to matters as to which it shall be adjudged . . . that such officer, director or employee is liable for negligence or misconduct in the performance of his duties." [44]   Another section supplements § 63, making no reference to articles, by-laws or resolutions, but giving a statutory right to have expenses assessed, with the same limitation concerning negligent or intentional misdeeds.[45]   Under this latter section, by the successful defense of the directors and officers who pleaded the statute of limitations, such officers were allowed reimbursement.[46]   And in a later case, the defendants obtained reimbursement when the action was dismissed because of the plaintiff's failure to comply with a security-for-expenses order.[47] This statute has been held to apply to civil cases and not to indictments for crimes which have been successfully defended.[48]

Not all of the indemnification statutes are as protective as the two discussed above.   The Model Business Corporation Act (Revised, 1953) in § 4(*o*), for example, gives the corporation "power" to indemnify directors and officers for their necessary expenses except where they are adjudged liable for negligence or misconduct in the performance of their duties.   But the indemnification so provided is not exclusive "of any other rights to which such director or officer may be entitled, under any by-law, agreement, vote of shareholders or otherwise." [49]   This leaves wide open the matter of providing for indemnification even where the officers have caused loss due to their own fault, something which should not be permitted except upon unanimous vote of the shareholders, whether entitled or not to vote.   And statutes should also make clear that where settlements are in-

44.   N.Y.Gen.Corp.Law § 63.

45.   Ibid. § 64. See also § 67.   For a critical examination of the New York sections see Joseph W. Bishop, Jr., Current Status of Corporate Directors' Right to Indemnification, 69 Harv.L.Rev. 1057, 1068 et seq. (1956).

46.   Dorman v. Humphrey, 278 App. Div. 1010, 106 N.Y.S.2d 142 (1942), noted in 37 Cornell L.Q. 78 (1951); 2 Syracuse L.Rev. 386 (1951).

47.   Tichner v. Andrews, 275 App. Div. 749, 90 N.Y.S.2d 920 (1949).

48.   Schwarz v. General Aniline & Film Corp., 305 N.Y. 395, 113 N.E. 2d 533 (1953), a 4–3 decision.   See Notes in 67 Harv.L.Rev. 514 (1954);

29 N.Y.U.L.Rev. 748 (1954); 40 Va. L.Rev. 65 (1954).

49.   Provisions similar to those in the Model Business Corporation Act are: Conn.Gen.Stat.1949, § 5129; D.C.Bus.Corp.Act § 4(p);   Flack's Ann.Code of Md.1951, Art. 23, § 60; Minn.Stat.Ann. § 301.09(7);   Ohio Rev.Code § 1701.13 [E];   Pa.Bus. Corp.Law § 410, as added by 1949 P.L.1773, § 7;   R.I.L.1948, c. 2154; Wis.Bus.Corp.Law § 180.04.

See the opinion of the Attorney General of New York on an indemnification provision in a charter which was broader than the New York statute provided for.   N.Y.Att'y Gen.Ann.Rep. 182 (1953).

volved the defendant-officers should not be granted reimbursement without a finding of no guilt of misconduct.[50]

There is little doubt that many of the exculpatory clauses inserted in articles and by-laws which purport to exonerate directors and officers for losses caused by their malfeasance or misfeasance are couched in such broad terms that, when litigated, they will be held void as a common law matter because of their conflict with a policy which discourages anything but a reasonable and honorable standard of performance by directors and officers. The day of the "robber barons" is gone. There is no more reason why directors and officers should be protected for their actionable negligence than there is for their intentional misdeeds, and certainly no good reason for providing reimbursement for defending in such cases.

§ 14. Security-for-Expenses Statutes

The effect of common law holdings and of provisions in articles, by-laws, resolutions or statutes permitting indemnification for expenses and lawyers' fees to officer-defendants who successfully defend a derivative suit, is to place a heavy financial burden upon the corporation. While losing parties are usually charged with the legal costs, these do not include such things as accountants' and lawyers' fees and other necessary expenses incurred in preparing and making the defense through which victory is possible. It was thought, too, that many derivative actions were actually strike suits not brought to benefit the corporation but to blackmail the directors into settling with the plaintiffs at a handsome profit to themselves.

Thus, after considerable research on behalf of the Chamber of Commerce of the State of New York which resulted in findings that in a ten-year period 693 such suits relating to closely held corporations and 573 relating to publicly held corporations had been brought in New York, and that recoveries by the corporations as a result of judgments or settlements approved by the court were had in but 8% of the cases involving publicly held corporations and that such recoveries through suit amounted to less than 5% of the amounts sued for and in court-approved settlements less than 3% of the amounts sued for, 215 of the cases being dismissed, and that in cases involving closely held corporations recoveries were had in but 5% of the cases, settlements made in 28% of the cases, 122 of the cases being dismissed

---

50. Ky.Rev.Stat.1953, § 271.375. See also for comparable statutes: Mich. Gen.Corp.Act § 10(*l*), as amended by L.1953, Act No. 156; Rev.Codes of Mont.1947, § 15–412; Mo.Rev. Stat.1949, V.A.M.S., § 351.355; N.J. S.A. 14:3–14, added by L.1942, c. 124 (the last sentence in the section, somewhat uncertain as to its meaning, offers some possible dangers of agreements to indemnify delinquent officials).

and the remainder being discontinued or showing no court disposition, the New York legislature enacted in 1944 the first security-for-expenses statute.[51]   The large number of suits settled out of court or discontinued had apparently not resulted in any substantial corporate benefit, the conclusion being that the plaintiffs and their lawyers were the chief beneficiaries if beneficiaries there were.   There was a further finding that in most of the actions brought the plaintiff-shareholder's interest in the corporation was small.

Under the New York statute plaintiffs who are holders of less than 5% of the outstanding shares of any class of stock or of voting trust certificates, unless these have a market value of more than $50,000, must furnish security upon the corporation's request at any stage of the proceedings before final judgment, for the reasonable expenses, including attorneys' fees, that may be incurred by the corporation (and by other parties defendant pursuant to section 64 for which the corporation may be liable) [52] in connection with such an action.   The amount of the security may be increased or decreased during the progress of the suit upon a showing that it is inadequate or excessive. Upon the termination of the suit "the corporation shall have recourse in such amount as the court having jurisdiction shall determine." [53]

The California act of 1949 [54] eliminated the worst features of the New York act.   The corporation or any defendant (including one not connected with the corporation) may move, within 30 days after the service of summons upon the movant, for security for costs upon the basis that there is no reasonable probability that the prosecution of the action will benefit the corporation or its security holders *or* that the movant, if other than the

---

51. Wood, Survey and Report Regarding Stockholders' Derivative Suits, 6–7 (1944). With duplicating actions the total cases examined amounted to 1,400. § 61–b of N.Y.Gen.Corp.Law is the security-for-expenses statute. "An examination of New York cases resulting in court approval of a settlement indicates that the amount paid to the corporation averages 3% of the amount sued for." Hornstein, Legal Control for Intracorporate Abuse—Present and Future, 41 Col.L.Rev. 405, 426 (1941).

52. See § 13 this chapter discussing this section of the New York statute. As to the date of the determination of the market value of

Lattin Corporations F.P.Inc.—25

the shares, see Dalva v. Bailey, 158 F.Supp. 204 (D.N.Y.1957).

53. N.Y.Gen.Corp.Law § 61–b; N.J. Stat.Ann. 14.3–15, added by L.1945, c. 131, is essentially like the New York statute as is Pa.P.L. 253, 1945, § 2. See criticism of § 180–405(4), West's Wis.Stat.Ann., in Note 1956 Wis.L.Rev. 322. The Wisconsin statute requires holders of less than 3% of any class of outstanding shares (of whatever value) to put up security when a defendant moves for it. This may mean that 3% of the outstanding shares of a corporation with substantial shareholdings may amount to a half-million or so dollars' worth.

54. West's Ann.Cal.Corp.Code § 834.

corporation, did not participate in the transaction complained of in any capacity. A hearing is had upon the motion and evidence, written or oral, by witnesses or affidavit, must be presented to support the motion and upon the matter of probable reasonable expenses if the court determines that there is no reasonable probability of successful action. Thus the burden is upon the movant to establish his case of no reasonable probability. If he establishes it, the court then fixes the kind and amount of security that the plaintiff must furnish for expenses of litigation including those provided for by § 830 of the act.[55] While, in a rather true sense, this requires a trial of important issues upon the motion, which if decided in favor of the movant may discourage the plaintiff in proceeding further, its real effect is to discourage strike suits, not legitimate ones. As Professor Ballantine has written: "The primary inquiry is whether the maintenance of the suit will probably produce more harm than good to the corporation and the persons having a real financial stake in it." [56] Recourse to the security is all that the winning defendants can have no matter what their necessary expenses may have been, and the court determines the amount they may obtain upon termination of the action. This also seems to be the limit under the New York statute which, in part, was borrowed by the California legislature. Certain preliminaries must also be carried out by the plaintiff [57] if he hopes to keep his cause in court. While the motion for security must be made within 30 days of the service of summons, the court, on application and for good cause shown, may extend this period for an additional period or periods not exceeding 60 days. This differs materially from the New York type of legislation which allows the defendants at any stage of the proceedings to move for security, even after the plaintiff may have expended much time and money in carrying on the trial.[58] The California statute provides for dismissal of the action against any of the movants whom the court finds entitled to security when the security ordered is not produced. Thus, the plaintiff may decide to dismiss the action against some defendants and not against others supplying only the security required of the defendants who remain in the suit.[59]

55. West's Ann.Cal.Corp.Code § 830, as amended by L.1957, c. 2261, § 3, provides for the indemnification of a director, officer or employee sued for misfeasance or nonfeasance who successfully defends or where there is a settlement of the case with the approval of the court, and the court finds that his conduct fairly and equitably merits such indemnity.

56. Abuses of Shareholders' Derivative Suits: How Far is California's New "Security For Expenses" Act Sound Regulation? 37 Calif.L.Rev. 399, at 405 (1949).

57. See West's Ann.Cal.Corp.Code § 834(a) (1) and (2).

58. Ballantine, supra, note 56, at 407.

59. Ibid. at 410.

However, there are other provisions of the California act which Professor Ballantine has severely criticised.[60]

The New Jersey act, which is similar to that of New York, was sustained constitutionally by the Supreme Court of the United States, Mr. Justice Jackson writing: [61] "The very nature of the stockholder's derivative action makes it one in the regulation of which the legislature of a state has wide powers. Whatever theory one may hold as to the nature of the corporate entity, it remains a wholly artificial creation whose internal relations between management and stockholders are dependent upon state law and may be subject to most complete and penetrating regulation, either by public authority or by some form of stockholder action." In the same decision the court held that " . . . this statute is not merely a regulation of procedure" and that in a derivative suit in the federal court based on diversity of citizenship of the parties the court must apply the state security expense statute, if there is one.[62]

The New York court has somewhat softened the application of the statute by applying a long-recognized rule of practice permitting the plaintiff leave to vacate an order requiring security if, within the time set for filing the bond, additional shareholders should join the plaintiff in sufficient number or dollar-amount to qualify under § 61–b.[63] And it has been held that shareholders permitted to intervene to avoid the giving of security need not have owned their shares at the time of the events sued upon where the rule required this for the *plaintiff* to be eligible to bring the suit.[64] The value of an intervenor's

---

60. Ibid. at 414–416.

61. Cohen v. Beneficial Industrial Loan Corp., 337 U.S. 541, at 549, 69 S.Ct. 1221, at 1227, 93 L.Ed. 1528 (1949). The New York court held its statute constitutional in Lapchak v. Baker, 298 N.Y. 89, 80 N.E. 2d 751 (1948), noted in 24 N.Y.U. L.Q.Rev. 395 (1949).

62. See Notes in 62 Harv.L.Rev. 309 (1948); 48 Col.L.Rev. 435 (1948); 40 Calif.L.Rev. 433 (1952); 16 U. of Chi.L.Rev. 738 (1949); 35 Va.L.Rev. 789 (1949).

63. In the Matter of Baker v. Macfadden Publications, Inc., 300 N.Y. 325, 90 N.E.2d 876 (1950).

64. Noel Associates, Inc. v. Merrill, 184 Misc. 646, 53 N.Y.S.2d 143 (Sup. Ct.1944); Fuller v. American Machine & Foundry Co., 95 F.Supp. 764, 97 F.Supp. 742 (D.N.Y.1951). But see Kaufman v. Wolfson, 136 F.Supp. 939 (D.N.Y.1955), noted in 25 Ford.L.Rev. 140 (1956); 44 Geo. L.J. 334 (1956); 69 Harv.L.Rev. 1504 (1956). Contra to the Fuller case, Dimock, Dist. J., in Kaufman stated: "The 'time of ownership' provision of Rule 23(b) must be applied in federal court . . . even if no such provision is part of the state law which is being enforced." (Page 940.) And, further, "Fuller v. American Machine & Foundry Co. . . . holds that the rule of the Noel case must be applied in federal court. I regret that, for reasons hereinafter stated, I cannot agree." (Page 941.) Judge Dimock pointed to Mr. Justice Jackson's dictum in Cohen, supra, note 61, 337 U.S. 541, at 556, 69 S.Ct. 1221, at 1230 that Rule 23(b) must be observed by a federal court "even if not applicable in state court." To the effect that such a holding tends to deny any

shares in order to meet the $50,000 requirement is to be figured
as of the time of intervention or "at the very earliest, [when] he
applied for leave to intervene as a plaintiff." [65]

For the moment the urge to enact statutes similar to the
above seems to have abated. The criticism that the existing statutes have engendered should be seriously considered by any legislature before imposing the drastic conditions of the New York
type of statute. It is, of course, debatable how far a statute
should go in discouraging such suits. The "strike suit," which
is the reason for such statutes, can be prevented by a modification of the gentler approach of the California statute and in
great measure by the adoption of the basic elements of the approach of the federal rules.[66] The derivative suit is the minority
shareholders' one effective remedy against management's abuse
of its trusteeship. The cleansing effect of the threat of such
suits would seem to an impartial observer to far outweigh the
possible abuse through strike suits.

§ 15. Statutes of Limitation as Applied to Derivative Actions

It is apparent from an examination of case authority in this
area that confusion has for a long time existed. The difficulty

right to the plaintiff who, under
the rule of Noel, could have prosecuted his case in the state court
except for diversity of citizenship,
a court in which he could meet
the percentage or dollar requirement by counting shares acquired
by intervenors after the events upon which the suit is based, see
Note in 69 Harv.L.Rev. 1504, at
1506 (1956). In Kaufman, supra,
the plaintiffs were given more time
to comply and were able to assert
that the new intervening shareholders were such at the time of the incidents sued upon. Kaufman v.
Wolfson, 137 F.Supp. 479 (D.N.Y.
1956). Judge McGohey in Fuller
had emphasized the idea that the
Noel rule not requiring contemporary ownership (New York's statute requires it for the plaintiff)
was part of the rule regarding security-for-expenses and as such
came in under Justice Jackson's
opinion.

65. Weinstein v. Behn, 68 N.Y.S.2d
199 (Sup.Ct.1947).

66. See, for valid criticism, the following: Pierce, Security for Expenses in Stockholder's Derivative
Actions, in Current Trends in State
Legislation (1952), Legislative Re-

search Center, University of Michigan, pp. 388–440; Note, 1956 Wis.
L.Rev. 322 for criticism of the Wisconsin statute and for some helpful
suggestions; Note, Security for
Expenses Legislation; Summary,
Analysis and Critique, 52 Col.L.
Rev. 267 (1952); Ballantine, supra,
note 56; Hornstein, The Death
Knell of Stockholders' Derivative
Suits in New York, 32 Calif.L.Rev.
123 (1944). Hornstein, New Aspects of Stockholders' Derivative
Suits, 47 Col.L.Rev. 1, at 3 (1947),
was able to say: "The New York
state legislation, since aped in other commercial states, was clearly
designed to insulate corporate management from investors who discovered that the corporation had
been looted." And, at page 5: "In
the two and a half years since the
enactment of the law, there appears to have been started in the
Supreme Court, New York County, only four stockholders' suits involving widely-held corporations,
three of which have been dismissed
for non-compliance with the new
laws. These four suits amounted
to less than two a year, as contrasted with an annual average of over
fifty a year in the preceding decade."

stems from a failure to apply with any consistency the basic philosophies underlying statutes of limitations with their particular bearing on the problems peculiar to the derivative action. Until comparatively recently, such statutes have been primarily addressed to the cause of action, whether contract or tort, and the remedy, whether legal or equitable, and have not been specifically aimed at suits against directors for their negligent or wilful acts which cause injury to the corporation and its shareholders. It seems probable that the policy factors of statutes of limitation to insure the security of transactions and to protect defendants from producing evidence (if at all produceable) long after the events upon which suit is brought have stronger claim to liberal treatment in derivative actions than in most other cases.[67] The ease with which directors and officers can cover up their delinquencies and the difficulties and expense that shareholders have in uncovering them warrant careful weight by a court when pressed to make a choice between two theories under one of which suit is barred because of a short statute of limitations and under the second of which suit may still be possible.

The derivative suit itself is an equitable one and, as we have already seen, the shareholder-plaintiff has imposed upon him a number of equitable principles.[68] If the fact that the action itself is equitable were the important one, then the statute of limitations for equitable actions (if one exists) should be applied. But more is involved. The suit is generally against directors or officers who, in the corporate realm, are considered fiduciaries of a special sort, at times being called trustees.[69] If this were the real point of emphasis, a statute limiting actions to a stated time period in case of suits against trustees or in equitable actions generally would seem to be the one applicable.[70] But, again, the

---

67. See Note, Statute of Limitations and Shareholders' Derivative Actions, 56 Col.L.Rev. 106, 110–111 (1956).

68. See §§ 2, 3 and 4, this chapter, supra.

69. Directors are not usually as strictly treated as are true trustees. Some cases, however, have placed them in a position comparable to trustees under an express trust. Felsenheld v. Bloch Bros. Tobacco Co., 119 W.Va. 167, 192 S.E. 545, 123 A.L.R. 334 (1937). See Ann., 123 A.L.R. 346. In Bovay v. H. M. Byllesby & Co., 27 Del.Ch. 381, 38 A.2d 808, 174 A.L. R. 1201 (Sup.Ct.1944), the court distinguishes between injuries due

to negligence and those due to intentional directorial action.

70. Such has been the holding or dictum in a few such suits. Brinckerhoff v. Bostwick, 99 N.Y. 185, 1 N.E. 663 (1885); Coane v. American Distilling Co., 298 N.Y. 197, 81 N.E.2d 87 (1948) (N.Y.Civ. Prac.Act § 48, subd. 8, was not applied, the Act having been enacted in 1942 after the suit was started in that year); Heller v. Boylan, 29 N.Y.S.2d 653 (Sup.Ct.1941), aff'd without opinion in 263 App.Div. 815, 32 N.Y.S.2d 131 (1941) (excessive bonuses—10-year statute applied). "After Brinckerhoff v. Bostwick, 88 N.Y. 52, was decided in 1882, it was generally thought that the ten year statute of lim-

real point of emphasis is not (or should not be) here. The derivative action is one which equity devised for minority shareholder protection and the action is really one between the corporation and the delinquent directors. Hence, the corporate remedy sought is the determinative factor of whether one statute of limitations or another applies.[71] If the corporate cause of action is one for damages in tort or in contract, the remedy at law being adequate, the appropriate statute of limitations applies as in other cases of legal remedies in tort and contract.[72] If the corporate cause of action is equitable in nature, such as specific performance or for an accounting, then the appropriate statute of limitations in equitable actions will apply. If the litigious facts present the double possibility of suing in tort or waiving tort and seeking an accounting or suing in quasi-contract, a choice will have to be made. And it is here that the importance of realizing that the derivative suit differs from most others because of the factors mentioned above comes into play. It is at this point that danger exists for, without a sensitive regard for the differences between the derivative action and, say, a straight corporate action, meritorious causes may well be lost.

Under the general rule, the period of limitations starts running when the cause of action accrues.[73] But where the directors are charged with fraud, statutes of limitation have often made knowledge of such fraud the point at which the statute starts running and, if no specific provision has been inserted, traditional interpretation has required knowledge or facts indicating that by the use of reasonable diligence such knowledge would have resulted. The problem here centers around the charging of knowledge to the corporation through innocent directors, or, perhaps, through the shareholders as a class, for it is obvious that knowledge of one or several shareholders would not have

---

itations governed. . . . The rationale was that corporate assets constituted a trust fund." Heller v. Boylan, 29 N.Y.S.2d 653, at 698.

71. Potter v. Walker, 276 N.Y. 15, 11 N.E.2d 333 (1939). "Potter v. Walker . . . did not decide that the ten-year Statute of Limitations (Civil Practice Act, § 53) is necessarily applicable to all cases in which corporate directors have profited in any degree through a breach of their fiduciary duties. In such a case an action for an accounting may be brought only for the recovery of gains received by the directors beyond the amount of losses caused to the corporation by their wrong. Where, as in the present case, the gains received by the directors do not exceed the correlated losses suffered by the corporation, no accounting is necessary and the Statute of Limitations, Civil Practice Act, § 48, which controls the remedy at law is to be applied." Jno. Dunlop's Sons, Inc. v. Dunlop, 285 N.Y. 333, 34 N.E.2d 344, at 344 (1941).

72. Statutes of limitations frequently distinguish written from oral contracts and between various kinds of torts.

73. See Dawson, Undiscovered Fraud and Statutes of Limitation, 31 Mich.L.Rev. 591, at 602 et seq. (1933) concerning the phrase "cause of action."

this effect.   Professor Ballantine has pointed out that some cases have gone to an "unjust extreme" in charging the corporation through the constructive knowledge of shareholders as a class "of matters which impractical vigilance might have revealed." [74] These were cases where constructive knowledge was implied because, through an examination of the corporate records or otherwise, the directors' frauds would (or might have been) discovered.[75]   Fortunately, other courts have not imposed the duty of examining corporate books and other records or sources of information upon the shareholders under penalty of implying constructive knowledge of the discoverable facts.[76]   The extreme advantage which delinquent directors have over shareholders in concealing from them facts upon which corporate recovery may be based warrants a cautious application of the doctrine of constructive notice in derivative actions of this sort, at least.   Where there is active effort by the defendants to prevent discovery, a court is justified in tolling the statute for this reason.[77]   If the particular shareholder-plaintiff bringing the action has had notice and has been guilty of laches in seeking a remedy, he may be barred, on equitable grounds, from bringing such an action.[78] But another shareholder, not so notified or, if so, acting with promptness, may bring the action.   This may, as we have already seen, result in benefit to those disqualified for some reason to bring the suit.

A number of statutes relate specifically to the limitation of actions brought against directors or shareholders for their activities as directors and as shareholders, which activities are the bases of suit.   The more common statutes are aimed at the recovery of "penalties" or "forfeitures imposed" or "to enforce a liability created by law," leaving suits based upon negligent or intentional act outside the prescribed statutory areas to statutes of limitation more general in their application.[79]

74. Ballantine,   Corporations   360 (Rev. ed. 1946).   And see Note, Constructive Notice to Shareholders of Fraud from Corporate Records, 30 Calif.L.Rev. 589 (1942).

75. See Bainbridge v. Stoner, 16 Cal. 2d 423, 106 P.2d 423 (1940); Note, 30 Calif.L.Rev. 589 (1942).

76. Lenhart v. Lenhart Wagon Co., 210 Minn. 164, 298 N.W. 37 (1941); Ballantine, supra note 74, at 360.

77. Ebbert v. Plymouth Oil Co., 338 Pa. 272, 13 A.2d 42 (1940) (comparable case where court refused to find laches on plaintiff's part); Bailey v. Jacobs, 325 Pa. 187, 189 A. 320 (1937) (statute of limitations tolled because of active concealment by directors).

78. Baker v. Spokane Sav. Bank, 71 F.2d 487 (9th Cir., 1934).

79. See, for example, West's Ann. Cal.Code of Civ.Proc. § 359 (three years after discovery by the aggrieved party); 2 Idaho Code Ann. § 5–237 (1948) (three years); a cause of action for loss of profits realized by a director-general manager due to breach of fiduciary relationship was held not a suit for "liability created by law." Melgard v. Moscow Idaho Seed Co., 73 Idaho 265, 251 P.2d 546 (1952); 7 Rev.Codes of Mont.1947, § 93–2715

In an attempt to end the confusion and uncertainty [80] in the New York law, the legislature enacted in 1942 an amendment to its Civil Practice Act which prescribes specifically for actions, legal or equitable, against directors, officers or stockholders, limiting the period during which suit may be brought to six years where the action is for an accounting, or based upon fraud, or to recover a penalty or forfeiture imposed or "to enforce a liability created by common law or by statute unless such action is one to recover damages for waste or for an injury to property or for an accounting in connection therewith in which case such action shall be subject to the provisions of subdivision seven of section forty-nine," which prescribes a three-year limitation.[81] Thus, it has been stated that this section "has eliminated any ten-year statute where an accounting is sought in an action of this nature, and has substituted six or three year statutes, the latter period being applicable when the accounting relates to a claim of waste or injury to property." [82] "If, however, money or its equivalent has been received by the officers or directors, and the allegations of the complaint were sufficient to make defendants liable for moneys had and received, this court has held that a six-year statute of limitations would apply to such a claim." [83] "Furthermore, if a complaint alleges facts to show that the gravamen of the action is to recover a judgment on the ground of actual fraud, a period of six years from the discovery of the fraud would be available" under this section, subdivision 5.[84] The statute has been interpreted to apply to transactions occurring after the effective date (September 1, 1942) of the legislation, prior statutes and interpretations being applicable to causes of action founded upon transactions occurring before its effective date.[85] Where the shareholder's derivative action has not been barred by the six or three year statute, it has been held that the defense of laches is no longer available.[86]

(three years); 3 N.D.Rev.Code § 28–0133 (1943) (six years); 9 Utah Code Ann. § 78–12–27 (1953) (three years); 3 Code of Va.1950, § 13.1–44 (1956 Replacement Volume) (two years). Another similar type of statute makes directors liable for unlawful dividends, withdrawals or decreases of capital and usually prescribes a short period of limitations. See Ark.Stat. of 1947, § 64–606 (two years).

80. There is a résumé of the New York law in Heller v. Boylan, 29 N.Y.S.2d 653, 698–700 (Sup.Ct.1941).

81. N.Y.Civ.Prac.Act § 48, subd. 8.

82. Gottfried v. Gottfried, 50 N.Y.S. 2d 951 (1944), modified in 269 App.

Div. 413, 56 N.Y.S.2d 50, at 55 (1945).

83. Myer v. Myer, 271 App.Div. 465, 66 N.Y.S.2d 83, at 93 (1946), aff'd in memo. opinion, 296 N.Y. 979, 73 N.E.2d 562 (1947), citing Gottfried v. Gottfried, supra note 82.

84. Ibid. at 93, citing Brundige v. Bradley, 294 N.Y. 345, 62 N.E.2d 385 (1945) (a true trust case).

85. Myer v. Myer, supra, note 83, at 93–94. See also Equity Corp. v. Groves, 294 N.Y. 8, 60 N.E.2d 19 (1945), holding that the amendment of 1942 did not affect action commenced prior to the amendment.

86. Gross v. Price, 128 N.Y.S.2d 209 (Sup.Ct.1953), modified in 284 App.

The Michigan statute provides, in part, that "No director or directors shall be held liable for any delinquency under this section after 6 years from the date of such delinquency, or after 2 years from the time when such delinquency is discovered by one complaining thereof, whichever shall sooner occur." [87]

Statutes specifically providing for derivative actions are sorely needed but they should be framed with special reference to the problems and the difficulties inherent in such actions.

Div. 964, 134 N.Y.S.2d 649 (1953). Accord, under Michigan statute: Koppitz-Melchers, Inc. v. Koppitz, 315 Mich. 582, 24 N.W.2d 220 (1946), but Michigan statute has specific provision that aggrieved party must bring the action within two years of discovery of the delinquency.

87.   Mich.Gen.Corp.Act § 47.   12 Purdon's Pa.Stat.Ann. § 41 provides that no suit at law or in equity shall be brought more than 6 years after the date of accrual.

Chapter 9

THE USE OF SHARES TO ACQUIRE
CORPORATE ASSETS

§ 1. Shares and Their Significance in Corporate Financing

Ownership in a corporation is represented by shares [1] which, due to the variety of contractual possibilities offered, give great elasticity to the financing of this business association. Through a wise use of the varied possibilities of distributing claims against the income and assets of the corporation, funds and property may be acquired to finance the corporate business often not obtainable through the use of common shares alone which carry the burden of highest risk. Retained earnings are also a source frequently made use of for expansion purposes either with, or without, a share dividend to freeze the earned surplus so used. While expansion through the use of long term (bonds, debentures or long term notes) or short term loans (loans evidenced by promissory notes payable within a year or less) is a third possibility, this subject is so specialized that it is treated only incidentally in this book. The owners of bonds, debentures, long or short term notes, are creditors of the corporation, while the shareholders, whether preferred or common, are considered owners of the enterprise. However, the preferred share contract is sometimes so drafted as to lead the layman to believe that he is more nearly a creditor than an owner with an owner's risk.

§ 2. When are Shares Issued?

The American cases have used the term "issue" in two connections. The first speaks of the "issue of shares"; the second, of "certificates" evidencing share ownership. The distinction is important in determining at what point a shareholder's liability as such begins. In an earlier chapter, the matter of subscriptions to shares was discussed. [2] The problem to be solved was when did the subscriber become a shareholder obligated to pay, in accordance with his subscription agreement, the subscription price, and liable to satisfy creditors should other corporate assets be insufficient for that purpose. At the point when the subscriber reaches shareholder status it is proper to say that "shares" have

---

1. " 'Shares' means the units into which the proprietary interests in a corporation are divided." A.L.I.

Model Business Corp. Act § 2(d) (Rev. 1953).

2. See Chapter 3, 109 et seq., supra.

been issued to him. The further act of issuing a "certificate" is not necessary for this purpose. He is, of course, entitled to a share certificate as this is evidence of his ownership in the company and is the instrument by which he is able to transfer his ownership to another either by endorsement thereon or by written assignment or power of attorney accompanying the certificate itself.[3]

An interesting illustration of the distinction between the issue of shares and of certificates arose under a provision of the Federal Banking Act of 1933. Section 32 [4] removed the double liability imposed upon shareholders of national banks stating that the additional liability provisions "shall not apply with respect to shares in any such associations issued after the date of the enactment of this Act." After this date, the X Bank twice reclassified its stock, first reducing its $100 par value to $70 par value without calling in its shares and, second, by calling in its $70 par value stock and substituting therefor 7 shares of $10 par value stock. The X Bank's capitalization remained the same after the reclassification. It was held that this was not an "issue" of shares which would free the shareholders of the additional liability. There was, of course, an issue of new certificates. Other provisions of the statute, it should be added, also supported the holding.[5] But where an apparently insolvent bank called in its outstanding shares and canceled them, reduced its common capital stock under a plan in which the Reconstruction Finance Corporation purchased all of the bank's preferred stock, new common shares being issued to old and new subscribers of the bank upon payment of their par value, it was held that this was a new "issue" and, since it came after the effective date of the statute, the shareholders were not subject to double liability.[6]

Statutes frequently prohibit the issue and delivery of stock certificates until full payment has been received by the issuing corporation, but authorize or anticipate the issue of shares before payment.[7]

The conditions precedent to the issue of shares are important in determining whether shares have been "issued," as where

---

3. See § 1, Uniform Stock Transfer Act.

4. 12 U.S.C.A. § 64a.

5. Federal Deposit Ins. Corp. v. Apfelbaum, 268 App.Div. 455, 52 N.Y.S.2d 110 (1944), aff'd in memo. op., 294 N.Y. 780, 62 N.E.2d 230 (1945), cert. denied 326 U.S. 724, 66 S.Ct. 54, 90 L.Ed. 443 (1945).

6. Federal Deposit Ins. Corp. v. Gunderson, 106 F.2d 633 (8th Cir., 1939).

7. Ohio Rev.Code § 1701.24(B), in part, provides: "Each holder of shares is entitled to one or more certificates . . . which shall certify the number and class of shares held by him in such corporation, but no certificate for shares shall be executed or delivered until such shares are fully paid." And see A.L.I. Model Business Corp. Act § 21 (Rev. 1953): "No certificate shall be issued for any share until such share is fully paid."

the statute requires that the articles state the *number* of no par value shares authorized and the draftsman, after providing a statement concerning the authorized preferred par value shares, concluded with the description that the no par common shares were "the remaining seventy-five thousand dollars" of the "capital."[8] How many shares of no par common were authorized under such a description, no one could tell. Hence, the attempted issue of no par shares was held to be of no effect. In an attempt to remedy this defect, a proper statement of the *number* of no par shares authorized was inserted by amendment but the draftsman failed to comply with a further requirement that the consideration for such shares was to be fixed by a two-thirds vote of shareholders of each class entitled to vote, unless the articles conferred this power on the directors, which they did not do. The directors, nevertheless, fixed the selling price of these shares. The court held that, under the circumstances, the directors did not have this power and that the shares purporting to be so issued were of no effect, that they could not be considered as outstanding. Thus, it is important that the shares be properly authorized in the first instance if they are to be considered properly issued in the second.

§ 3. The Quality of Consideration for Which Shares may be Issued

The privilege of carrying on business in the corporate form and thereby escaping full personal liability is conditioned upon the supplying of a substitute for personal liability in the form of "capital stock," "stated capital" or "legal capital," some of the terms used for this substitute.[9] It must be, in quality, money or money's worth in property or services. And it is acquired by the issue of shares, the units into which the proprietary interests in a corporation are divided.

Modern statutes frequently spell out in some detail the quality or type of consideration that must be given for shares. The New York statute[10] provides, in part, that "No corporation shall issue either shares of stock or bonds, except for money, labor done or property actually received for the use and lawful purposes of such corporation."[11] Some statutes specify the

---

8. Rice & Hutchins, Inc. v. Triplex Shoe Co., 16 Del.Ch. 298, 147 A. 317 (1929), aff'd 17 Del.Ch. 356, 152 A. 342, 72 A.L.R. 932 (1930).

9. Limited liability, even where the original capitalization was adequate, has not always been a characteristic of corporations. Dodd, American Business Corporations Until 1860, at 258 (1954), states: "As in the case of contemporary

(circa 1817) manufacturing corporations, the shareholders were made liable for the corporation's debts."

10. N. Y. Stock Corp. Law § 69, as amended by L.1954, c. 799.

11. N.J.S.A. § 14:8-9 is somewhat comparable: "Only cash or its equivalent and property, including stock of another corporation, and

medium of payment with more particularity, confining the issue of par or no par shares to "money paid, labor done, services actually rendered, debts or securities canceled, tangible or intangible property actually received . . . , and amounts transferred from surplus to stated capital upon the issue of shares as a dividend." [12] And, while statutes and constitutional provisions customarily limit the issue of shares to money, labor, services and property *actually received,* some statutes do not mention the actual receipt requirement.[13] But even under such provisions, it has been held that while shares may be issued, they may not be issued *as fully paid* except where the consideration so required has actually been furnished as distinguished from the promise to furnish.[14] This conclusion is well illustrated where the statute prohibits the issue except upon the actual receipt of the consideration and, in the next breath, states that every holder of shares not fully paid shall be personally liable to creditors to an amount equal to the amount unpaid on his shares.[15]

The *quality* of consideration applies equally to the issue of par and no-par shares except where the statute differentiates the two.

Where shares may only be issued for money or property, the latter term has usually been interpreted broadly to include much more than property which is "visible and tangible." [16] In *Thoms v. Sutherland* [17] a going business was held to be within the term "property" though trade in the form of satisfied customers, good will, a far-flung sales organization, rights in patents and secret processes, a record of consistent earnings over a long period, as well as tangible property, were accepted for the issue of shares "to the amount of the value thereof." The court pointed out that

labor as in section 14:3–9 of this title is specified (i. e., "for the amount it actually pays for labor performed"), shall be considered as payment of any part of the capital stock of any corporation organized under this title." See also A.L.I. Model Business Corp. Act § 18 (Rev. 1953).

12. E. g., West's Ann.Cal.Corp.Code § 1109. But see last paragraph of this section which provides for a procedure by which shares or certificates may be issued prior to full payment. See Ballantine and Sterling, California Corporation Laws, 147–148 (1949 ed.) Other sections also anticipate the issue of partly paid shares.

13. For example, Nev.Rev.Stat. § 78.210.

14. Diamond State Brewery, Inc. v. De La Rigaudiere, 25 Del.Ch. 257, 17 A.2d 313 (1941).

15. N. Y. Stock Corp. Law § 69 and § 70.

16. Examine See v. Heppenheimer, 69 N.J.Eq. 36, 61 A. 843 (1905), which must be read critically to obtain the meaning of "visible and tangible" as used in this case. There was a capitalization of a mere "hope"—the capitalization of future profits anticipated to be realized as a result of suppressing competition.

17. Also sub nom. Eastman Kodak Co. v. Sutherland, 52 F.2d 592 (3d Cir., 1931).

the same statute had previously been interpreted by the local court to include as "property" such intangibles as work and labor done, leases and contracts, name and trade of a partnership business, inventions, patents, licenses under patents, trademarks, and good will.   However, where there is no substantial value to the thing given, courts have not hesitated at times to hold that it does not qualify as property.   It would seem, however, that the quality of the consideration is present where the thing furnished has any value.   The quantity, naturally, may be short of that required and so be questioned.[18]   On the other hand, it has been held that shares given as a bonus to secure a loan could not qualify as shares issued for "services" or property.[19]   And the Vermont court, construing the Maryland statute, held that shares issued for underwriting services were not issued for the "services" meant by the statute.[20]   Better opinion respects the lending of money or credit as proper consideration but leaves the quantity of consideration as a proper matter to contest.[21]

Payment in shares for selling them or underwriting an issue would both seem to be legitimately within the area of compensation for services.[22]   However, for reasons that are not clearly demonstrable, underwriting commissions payable in shares have been held vulnerable in a number of cases.[23]   Since payment in cash for such services would be permitted and a purchase of shares for cash thus received would be valid there is no good reason why this roundabout route may not be shortened by the

---

18.   In Scully v. Automobile Finance Co., 12 Del.Ch. 174, 109 A. 49 (1920), a plan of doing business which had no novelty was held not to be property.   But the holding is somewhat weakened by a dictum that the issue would have been legal had the shares not been marked as fully paid.   And see See v. Heppenheimer, supra note 16; Diamond State Brewery, Inc. v. De La Rigaudiere, supra, note 14; Trotta v. Metalmold Corp., 139 Conn. 668, 96 A.2d 798, 37 A.L.R.2d 906, Ann. at 913 (1953).

19.   Hopper v. Brodie, 134 Md. 290, 106 A. 700 (1919); Schroeder v. Edwards, 267 Mo. 459, 184 S.W. 108 (1916).

20.   International Products Co. v. Vail's Estate, 97 Vt. 318, 123 A. 194 (1924).   Said the court at page 197 of 123 A.: "It is apparent from the decision (Hopper v. Brodie, supra) that under the law of Maryland a corporation cannot issue its stock in return for mere financial aid whether the stock is issued as a bonus or in payment for services."

21.   A good example is: J. F. Lucey Co. v. McMullen, 178 Cal. 425, 173 P. 1000 (1918).   And see Lamprecht v. Swiss Oil Corp., 32 F.2d 646 (6th Cir., 1929).

22.   Yasik v. Wachtel, 25 Del.Ch. 247, 17 A.2d 309 (1941).

23.   A leading case is Australian Investment Trust, Ltd. v. Strand & Pitt Street Properties, Ltd., [1932] A.C. 735, holding that payment in shares of a commission for underwriting was an issue at a discount.   See also International Products Co. v. Vail's Estate, supra, note 20. The payment for underwriting services in treasury shares has been allowed.   Positype Corp. v. Flowers, 36 F.2d 617 (7th Cir., 1929), cert. denied 281 U.S. 762, 50 S.Ct. 461, 74 L.Ed. 1170 (1930).   Since treasury shares of the par value variety may be sold at any price, the quantity given would seem immaterial.

payment in shares initially. The quantity of consideration given for such services, however, may well be questioned as in other cases where the quality qualifies under the law.

With reference to the modern underwriter who purchases an issue, or part of an issue, of shares from the issuer to market them, the price below par he pays is the measuring base of his profit for services in connection with the distribution. And there is no good reason why such compensation in shares should not qualify as payment for services.[24] However, the quantity of consideration given in shares is always contestable as in other cases. And, with underwriting, factors such as the effort required to sell the shares in the particular market, the size of the issue, the earning prospects of the issuer, and other relevant factors incident to marketing shares are all pertinent to a determination of what is reasonable compensation.[25] ". . . [T]he more speculative the corporation the greater is the underwriting risk and the selling effort required, and therefore the higher the reasonable value of these services."[26]

Whether a promissory note is money or property has caused considerable controversy as well as whether, if secured, such notes should be treated differently. The usual holding is that the unsecured note of the subscriber is not "property" which will support an issue of shares as fully paid. A note is a mere promise to pay, and a check merely a demand upon another, usually a bank, to pay—in a sense another promise to pay—and neither warrants the description of "property." [27] However, even where the statute prohibits the acceptance of notes or checks for shares, the corporation, except occasionally, has been permitted to enforce such promises.

§ 4. The Quantity of Consideration for Which Shares may be Issued

Prior to 1912 shares were of the par value variety, carrying a dollar sign upon them.[28] If they were $100-par-value shares, the layman was led reasonably to believe that value to that extent had been received by the corporation in "meal or malt." And creditors of the corporation were permitted to rely upon the capitalization of shares at par, if so carried on the balance

---

24. See, for example Gruenwald v. Moir Hotel Co., 96 F.2d 932 (7th Cir., 1938), cert. denied 305 U.S. 615, 59 S.Ct. 74, 83 L.Ed. 392 (1938), where such an underwriting profit was permitted on a transaction in bonds. And see Weichel v. Jones, 109 S.W.2d 332 (Tex.Civ.App.1937), rehearing denied in 109 S.W.2d 1097.

25. See Note, 55 Harv.L.Rev. 1365, at 1371–1372 (1942).

26. Ibid. at 1372.

27. Ballantine, Corporations 793 (Rev. ed. 1946).

28. New York enacted the first no-par statute. Laws of N.Y.1912, c. 351.

sheet (or elsewhere), as a representation that money or money's worth to the aggregate amount of stated capital had been or would be contributed for the purpose of carrying on the business. The consideration paid for shares constitutes an important "cushion" for creditors, gives protection to senior shares, if any, and furnishes the corporation with the means of reaping profits. Difficulties would have been few had the courts required the full par value to be paid to the corporation in money, property or services and had they outlawed provisions in initial subscription agreements or sales of shares by the corporation by which the shareholder agreed to give less than par value. Reasonable exceptions could have been made for expenses in the sale of shares through investment bankers and underwriters. And at a later date, if unissued shares could not be sold at par, reasonable exceptions could have been made and a sale below par been permitted, with capitalization at the price for which sold rather than at the par value.[29] An equally efficacious method would have been through a reduction of the par value of the old unissued shares to, or authorization of new shares at, a par value at which they could be sold, all other provisions remaining the same.

But the early statutes usually contained no provisions specifically requiring full payment for par value shares. And when the statutes began to appear requiring the payment of the par value in money, services or property, for the most part there was no provision stating the legal consequences of their violation. Furthermore, when statutes projected the legal consequences, creditors were mentioned as entitled to the difference between par and the amount paid for the shares when the corporate assets were insufficient. The courts assumed that the corporation could collect no more for its own account than the contract for discount shares called for, and nothing for bonus shares. Thus watered stock became, in a limited sense, "legal" by virtue of this customary treatment by the courts. True, if a shareholder brought an action to restrain his corporation from issuing its shares at less than par, an injunction would issue. And a corporate or derivative action to cancel bonus shares was possible.[30] An occasional successful suit resulted in the cancellation of a sufficient number of shares issued for cash at a discount to take care of the difference between par and the amount the shareholder had contracted to pay, thus making him end up with shares only for which he had fully paid.

---

29. Handley v. Stutz, 139 U.S. 417, 11 S.Ct. 530, 35 L.Ed. 227 (1891), was such a case. As to the limitations of the common law rule, see Harman v. Himes, 64 App.D.C. 252, 77 F.2d 375 (1935), noted in 22 Va. L.Rev. 350 (1936).

30. Diamond State Brewery, Inc. v. De La Rigaudiere, 25 Del.Ch. 257, 17 A.2d 313 (1941).

The issue of shares for intentionally overvalued property or services results in discount shares and, while honest valuation of property or services accepted for shares may result in overvaluation, problems in this category caused serious controversy whether "true value" must be there or whether good-faith valuation by the board tested the validity of the issue for all time. The problem is always difficult because of honest differences of opinion regarding the value of property or services.

When statutes finally (and quite recently) appeared seemingly making a shareholder who had taken bonus or discount shares liable for the "water" to a solvent, going corporation, the assumption was made that creditors were, even under such statutes, the beneficiaries of the legislation and often, by express statutory provisions, creditors were named as such.[31] One important case only has been found, and that one out of Delaware, which has held that a solvent corporation may collect from one receiving bonus or discount shares as fully paid the difference between what he gave and the par value of the shares.[32] Such a holding is not only justified under statutes adopting what has become known as "the statutory obligation theory," but it makes sense even without the aid of broad statutory prohibitions against accepting less than par in whatever consideration is permitted. Had the courts originally deciding the bonus and discount cases been alive to the basic reasons for the cushion called "capital stock," they would have insisted upon the payment of par, holding nugatory that part of the shareholder's contract for payment of less than par. And they would have given a solvent corporation the legal remedy upon the reformed contract. Here, again,

---

31. See West's Ann.Cal.Corp.Code §§ 1110 and 1300. Ballantine and Sterling, California Corporation Laws § 126 (1949 ed.), state that § 1300 made the duty of a shareholder to pay par value for his shares a statutory as well as a contractual one, and that "The duty is created for the benefit of creditors and other shareholders." The opportunity, thought the authors, was there for the court to put bonus and discount shares on the same basis as partially paid shares where a solvent corporation had its cause of action for the unpaid price. But when the opportunity arose in Bing Crosby Minute Maid Corp. v. Eaton, 46 Cal.2d 484, 297 P.2d 5 (1956), the court retained the "fraud" or "holding out" theory which had been set out in the leading case of Rhode v. Dock-Hop Co., 184 Cal. 367, 194 P.

11, 12 A.L.R. 449 (1920). The court indicated that the legislature must use "clear language" showing an intent "to broaden the basis of liability" in order to obtain the court's approval of the statutory obligation theory. See also 1957 Cumulative Supplement to 2B N.C.Gen.Stat. § 55–53(b) (1), which makes the watered stockholder liable to the corporation "only if there is reasonable ground to believe that creditors or shareholders may have relied on such excess or overvaluation . . . ."

32. Scully v. Automobile Finance Co., 12 Del.Ch. 174, 109 A. 49 (1920). Involved was a plan of carrying on business which had no novelty, and future services which, under the statute, were not proper consideration.

as in some other areas of corporation law, lawyers were too smart for the judges who had to decide the cases.

§ 5. The Doctrine of Equitable Contribution among Shareholders—Prevention of the Dilution of Shares

A serious problem arises when shares of the same class are issued at approximately the same time but at different prices; or similar shares are later issued to outsiders at less than the intrinsic value of shares outstanding or less than the market will bring. Shares issued at a lower price than their value necessarily dilute the value of similar existing shares. This danger exists in shares having a par value as well as in those of the no-par variety, though the greater danger lies in the latter type. Naturally, if par value shares are sold to outsiders at par when their actual value is substantially above that mark, dilution will result. While par value shares may not normally be legally issued for all purposes as fully paid for a consideration less than par, no-par value shares, theoretically, may be issued for any price.

Statutes have recently prescribed the method of fixing the price of no-par shares and, when they do not, the board of directors has that authority. It was originally assumed that the power to fix the price was discretionary and that any price could be set. Such an assumption, however, has little validity, for an unlimited exercise of this power would permit the board, in substance, to give away a part of the existing shareholders' equity in the corporate property. Because of this possibility, a protective doctrine has evolved which, in effect, prohibits an arbitrary sale of shares of the same issue to others at different prices unless the differential in price can be supported by a showing of "business and commercial facts" sufficient to convince a board, in the exercise of fair business judgment, that the difference in price is justified.[33] The fact that the shares are incapable of being sold at a higher price than set would clearly indicate that the authority to set the price has not been abused—that adequate business facts exist to warrant a difference in price. The necessity of the corporation to secure new capital on a low market may well require some sacrifice in the existing shareholders' proportionate interest in the corporation. Likewise, the sale of the same class of stock at the same time to different parties at different prices is legitimate if the compensating advantages to the corporation are sufficiently reasonable.[34]

33. Bodell v. General Gas & Electric Corp., 15 Del.Ch. 420, 140 A. 264 (1927); Atlantic Refining Co. v. Hodgman, 13 F.2d 781, 788 (3d Cir., 1926), cert. denied 273 U.S. 731, 47 S.Ct. 240, 71 L.Ed. 863 (1926).

34. See note 33, supra. Minn.Stat. Ann. § 301.16 in part provides: "Shares with or without par value shall not be allotted for a cash consideration which is unfair to the then shareholders nor for a consid-

Where preemptive rights exist in shares later issued below their value, the shareholder has the opportunity to save the dilution in his present shares by purchasing his proportion of the new issue. And, as Professor Berle has well stated: "It may well be that courts of equity would allow greater flexibility and latitude of discretion to directors where the old stockholders had this right, than would be the case where no such privilege was granted." [35]

§ 6.　Legal Consequences of Watered Stock

(a) Stock issued as a bonus or at a discount for cash. Where shares have a par value or where a selling price has been placed upon no-par shares thus putting them in a category similar to that of par value shares, if such shares are sold below par or the stated value of no-par shares, discount shares result. What legal consequences follow? Since the established rule is that as between a solvent corporation and the shareholder there can be no recovery of the difference between the contract price and par or the stated value in case of no-par shares,[36] only the rights of creditors remain to be examined.

While there is usually some constitutional or statutory provision prohibiting "fictitious issues" of stock or indebtedness and making such issues "void," or providing generally that each shareholder shall be liable for any balance due on the stock held by him, or providing more specifically that shares having a par value may not be issued for a consideration less than their par value, such provisions have not generally been found necessary to support holdings protecting creditors who cannot be paid out of the corporation's assets.[37] As far as creditors are concerned, the full cushion of par value was intended to relieve their fall.

eration other than cash upon a valuation thereof which is unfair to such shareholders; . . ." Compare 1957 (Cum.Supp. to 2B N.C. Gen.Stat. § 55–53(a) (4).

35. Berle, Studies in the Law of Corporation Finance 89 (1928).

36. "No suit could have been maintained by the company to collect the unpaid stock for such a purpose. The shares were issued as full paid, on a fair understanding, and that bound the company." Scovill v. Thayer, 105 U.S. 143, at 154, 26 L.Ed. 968 (1881).

37. Constitutional provisions making "fictitious" issues "void" may be found in a number of states including Mont.Const. Art. XV, § 10; Neb.

Const. Art. XII, § 6, which also requires an "equivalent in money paid or labor done, or property actually received and applied to the purpose for which such corporation was created . . ." New Jersey has a statutory provision that "No fictitious stock shall be issued." N.J.S.A. 14:3–9. Conn.Gen.Stat. 1949, § 5173, provides: "Each stockholder, whether an original subscriber or not, shall be liable for any balance due on the stock held by him." And Or.Rev.Stat.1953, § 57.100(1) reads: "Shares having a par value may be issued for such consideration expressed in dollars, not less than the par value thereof, as shall be fixed from time to time by the board of directors."

At first, the courts based their holdings on the trust fund theory, though there was no fund nor any contract for a fund to supply the trust *res*. Under this theory, the better cases held that prior as well as subsequent creditors were protected and even those creditors who gave credit with knowledge of the watered stock received like protection.[38] The logical fallacy that there was a trust fund led to what has become the majority view in this country that creditors' rights rest on reliance upon the false representation that when par value shares are issued full payment has been made in the quality of consideration required or will be made by virtue of a promise to pay the full amount.[39] Since there could be no reliance by creditors who gave credit prior to the watered stock issue, such creditors could not complain. And, if they had actual knowledge of the water at the time they gave credit, they had no standing in court because of the lack of reliance. Thus, only subsequent creditors and those without notice of the water were protected. Reliance was in a real sense made fictitious by a rule which made lack of reliance an affirmative defense to be pleaded and proved by the defendant-shareholder rather than to be averred and proved by the creditor.[40] And while the trust fund terminology persisted in numerous cases, many courts were either confused or intentionally using the fraud or "holding out" theory to support their holdings. Thus, where the trust fund theory is mentioned and, in the same breath, it is stated that only subsequent creditors and creditors without notice are protected, it is obvious that the true

---

38. Williams, Executor v. Chamberlain, 123 Ky. 150, 94 S.W. 29, at 32 (1906), involved an Arizona corporation. Williams subscribed for 5,-000 shares of $1 par value stock, paying the contract price of $500 or 10 cents per share. In a creditors' bill, it was held that all creditors were entitled to recover to the extent of the water if necessary to pay such debts. But see Stevens, Corporations 872 (2d ed. 1949), who states: "The trust fund doctrine is predicated upon the creditors' presumed reliance upon the full payment of the par value of outstanding shares."

39. The leading case is Hospes v. Northwestern Manufacturing & Car Co., 48 Minn. 174, 50 N.W. 1117, 15 L.R.A. 470 (1892). Next in importance is probably Rhode v. Dock Hop Co., 180 Cal. 367, 194 P. 11, 12 A.L.R. 437 (1920).

40. Woodward, Jr. v. Sonnesyn, 162 Minn. 397, 203 N.W. 221 (1925), cert.

denied sub. nom. Bruce v. Sonnesyn, 269 U.S. 567, 46 S.Ct. 25, 70 L.Ed. 415 (1925). At page 405 of 162 Minn. it is stated: "Defendants are presumed to be liable, to the extent of their bonus stock, for all subsequent claims allowed against the corporation in the absence of affirmative proof of facts exempting them from liability." And in Randall Printing Co. v. Sanitas Mineral Water Co., 120 Minn. 268, 139 N.W. 606, at 608 (1913), Bunn, J., wrote: "While the basis of the liability of the stockholders to the creditors for unpaid stock subscriptions is fraud, it is fraud in law, constructive fraud, rather than actual fraud; and it is not necessary for the creditors to prove affirmatively that they trusted the corporation in reliance upon the subscription." Minn.Stat.Ann. § 301.15, subd. 5, now requires creditors to prove their reliance thus changing the common law rule on the burden of proof.

trust fund theory is not being applied. Likewise, where the court reaches the conclusion that a receiver or trustee in bankruptcy may not sue—that the suit is in tort and personal to the creditor —it is impossible to reconcile trust fund terminology with the court's conclusion.

Even under statutes which either specifically require that the full par value or stated value of no-par shares be paid or which inferentially indicate the same, courts have had a hard time shaking off the fraud or "holding out" theory. This has been unfortunate. The most recent example has occurred under a modern statute which the draftsmen had predicted was sufficient to warrant the adoption of the more reasonable statutory obligation theory and the abandonment of the fraud theory.[41] The case involved the rights of a judgment creditor of an insolvent corporation against the holder of watered par value stock. The statute provided that "The value of the consideration to be received by a corporation for the issue of shares having par value shall be at least equal to the par value thereof," with three specific exceptions which require directorial determination of the fact that the shares cannot be sold at par, exceptions not involved in this case.[42] The evidence tended to show that the plaintiff believed that the defendant's corporation had an original capital of $25,000, which was correct, and that the only balance sheet the plaintiff had seen showed a capital of $33,000, which was not misrepresented. The defendant shareholder had answered that the plaintiff did not rely upon the par value of the shares issued. The lower court had given the plaintiff judgment with no finding on the matter of reliance. Reliance would be of no significance if the statutory obligation theory were adopted; but it would be material if the fraud theory still prevailed. The upper court, in spite of the broad statutory language and the draftsmen's comment on the breadth of the section, affirmed an order granting a new trial because of the absence of a finding on the issue of reliance or no reliance, thus keeping alive the fraud theory. Said the court: "The statute (§ 1110, Cal.Corp.Code) does not expressly impose an obligation to creditors. Most jurisdictions having similar statutes have applied the misrepresentation theory obviously on the ground that creditors are sufficiently protected against stock watering schemes under that theory." [43] In

41. Ballantine and Sterling, California Corporation Laws § 126 (1949 ed.) had so predicted.

42. West's Ann.Cal.Corp.Code § 1110, as amended by L.1957, c. 2261, § 6. See note 69, infra, for the exceptions.

43. Bing Crosby Minute Maid Corporation v. Eaton, Sr., 46 Cal.2d 484, 297 P.2d 5, at 9 (1956). But see West's Ann.Cal.Corp.Code § 1306 providing the machinery for recovery by judgment creditors with execution returned unsatisfied against shareholders for the amount due on their shares.

view of the state of the law prior to 1931 when § 1110 was enacted, the court felt that the legislature would have used "clear language expressing an intent to broaden the basis of liability of holders of watered stock had it entertained such an intention."

A basic fallacy in the fraud theory is that creditors rely upon the stated capital of a corporation in granting credit. Even if they have had access to a recent balance sheet of the company, they are much more interested in the ratio of liquid assets to current liabilities than they are in the fictitious liability item which appears as "stated capital" or "capital stock." Likewise, they are interested in the reputation which the company has acquired through paying its debts promptly. Basicly, then, both the trust fund and the fraud theories depend upon a policy which roughly prescribes that if shareholders are to obtain limited liability through the process of incorporation they must, as far as creditors are concerned, give a substitute for personal liability to the extent of the full par value of the shares for which they have subscribed, no matter what their agreement with the company was.

The statutory obligation theory recognizes this policy as one legislatively prescribed. Though the shareholder's contract calls for payment of less than par, or no payment at all, when creditors prior or subsequent, whether with or without notice of the water, or whether they have participated in the issue of watered stock, cannot obtain satisfaction from the assets of the company, they may pursue the shareholders who have not paid par for their shares on the basis that there is a statutory obligation to pay the full par value under such circumstances.[44] There is still a problem of whether the statute has made the obligation one owing to the corporation or to the creditors themselves. If the obligation is held to be one belonging to the corporation, then its receiver or trustee in bankruptcy or assignee for the benefit of creditors may pursue the shareholder to recover this corporate asset for the benefit of creditors,[45] a thing not permitted under the fraud theory without statutory aid for the cause of action is considered personal to the deceived creditor.[46] Under the trust fund doctrine, unadulterated by undue exposure to the fraud theory, the *res* was considered a corporate asset and so pursuable by those

---

44. Du Pont v. Ball, 11 Del.Ch. 430, 106 A. 39, 7 A.L.R. 955 (Sup.Ct. 1918); Easton Nat. Bank v. American Brick & Tile Co., 70 N.J.Eq. 732, 64 A. 917, 8 L.R.A.,N.S., 271, 10 Ann.Cas. 84 (1906).

45. Du Pont v. Ball, supra, note 44 (receiver); Easton Nat. Bank v. American Brick & Tile Co., supra, note 44 (receiver).

46. Courtney v. Georger, 228 F. 859 (2d Cir., 1915), cert. denied 241 U. S. 660, 36 S.Ct. 448, 60 L.Ed. 1226 (1916) (Minnesota corporation); State Bank of Commerce v. Kenney Band Instrument Co., 143 Minn. 236, 173 N.W. 560 (1919) (corporation was in bankruptcy; subsequent creditors were permitted to bring personal actions against takers of watered stock).

entitled to assemble corporate assets that creditors might be satisfied. In this respect, the trust fund theory though based upon a fiction was preferable to the fraud theory; and where the fraud theory exists, as it does in many jurisdictions today, statutes should be enacted, if not already there, to permit receivers and trustees in bankruptcy to bring suit to enforce against holders of watered stock the obligation owed to creditors to pay up to par a sufficient amount to satisfy them.

Preferable, indeed, would be the adoption of the statutory obligation theory for constitutional provisions or statutes have clearly indicated that par or stated value must, in so far as creditors are concerned, be supplied in money, property or services. Preferable, too, would be holdings, in so far as they are possible under the statutory language, to the effect that the obligation to pay par or stated value is one owed to the corporation—that is, it is a corporate asset as in the trust fund theory. It should not matter when the creditor became one or whether he had notice of the water or participated in it. The statute has stated a policy of substituted capital for unlimited liability and the fund created by the sale of stock has the double aspect of securing the payment of creditors and of giving some assurance that funds derived from the sale of shares to their full par value will be used to exploit the corporate purposes. If there was ever any legitimate use for watered stock, the moment that no-par stock was legally possible, it made such use unnecessary. With this in mind, it is not unreasonable to suggest that the statutory obligation theory deserves the expansion it obtained in *Scully v. Automobile Finance Co.*[47] where a solvent corporation was permitted to recover the water in its shares on the ground that they had been issued without consideration and illegally. Said the court: "A court of equity may declare the unlawful subscription contract to be ineffective to relieve the stockholders of the legal duty to pay the par value of the stock if the interests of the corporation so demand, or it be necessary to do so in order to pay creditors of the company, or if for any reason it be equitable and just to do so."[48] In a later case where the defendants had argued that the proper remedy was assessment to the extent of the par value rather than a cancellation of the shares, the court held that where the particular issue is voidable the court may decree the form of relief most in accord with the equities of the case.[49]

---

47. 12 Del.Ch. 174, 109 A. 49 (1920).

48. 12 Del.Ch. 174, at 182–183.

49. Diamond State Brewery, Inc. **v.** De La Rigaudiere, 25 Del.Ch. 257, 17 A.2d 313 (1941). Accord: Blair **v.** F. H. Smith Co., 18 Del.Ch. 150, 156 A. 207 (1931). The defendants were allowed the option of having their bonus shares canceled or paying for them in Maclary v. Pleasant Hills, Inc., 109 A.2d 830, at 835 (Del.Ch.1954).

While the only rational basis upon which liability for watered stock is imposed is the statutory obligation theory, it should be noted that an occasional decision placed liability solely upon the contract made with the corporation. If the contract provided for bonus or discount shares, the shareholder could not be pursued by corporation or creditor beyond what his contract called for.[50] A few similar results were reached under statutes or constitutional provisions making the fictitious issue of shares "void." If the word "void" is interpreted to mean literally what it says, then there are no rights and no liability on bonus or discount shares. The issue is void. Creditors are thus defeated.[51] And a basic reason for prohibitions against the issue of bonus or discount shares is nullified. In the better holdings on "fictitious issues" the word "void" has been interpreted as "voidable" and creditors have received the protection they deserved. Such holdings have also permitted a corporate action to enforce the surrender of the excess stock, not permitting the shareholder to elect to pay the difference and retain the stock except with the corporation's consent.[52] Furthermore, under this view, a bona fide transferee from a watered shareholder is not subject to the constitutional prohibition that "all fictitious increase of stock shall be void." [53]

(b) Stock issued for overvalued property. Problems in this area center around intentional and innocent overvaluations and in the latter category whether actual value must be given or a test of good faith in ascertaining value be used as a criterion.

50. Southworth v. Morgan, 205 N. Y. 293, 98 N.E. 490, 51 L.R.A.,N.S., 56 (1912) involved discount shares in a New Jersey corporation. As far as the common law of New York is concerned, the rule in Southworth v. Morgan has been superseded by a requirement that not less than par value be accepted for par value shares. See N.Y.Stock Corp.Law §§ 69 and 70.

51. Hirschfeld v. McKinley, 78 F.2d 124 (9th Cir., 1935) (Involving an Arizona corporation). In Stone, Trustee v. Hudgens, 129 F.Supp. 273 (D.Okl.1955), the court reluctantly followed the Oklahoma law holding—with the Oklahoma constitution and decisions—that "the attempted stock issue was an absolute *nullity* giving rise to neither rights nor liabilities." (At page 275.) Collier v. Edwards, 144 Okl. 69, 289 P. 260, 69 A.L.R. 874 (1930), had held that a creditor with notice of the water could not recover from the shareholder. But payment accepted by the corporation at a later date of full par for shares originally issued at a discount validates the "void" shares making them not subject to cancellation. Oklahoma Gas & Elect. Co. v. Hathaway, 192 Okl. 626, 138 P. 2d 832 (1943). A case prior in time had held bonus or discount shares void having a status similar to an overissue of shares even in the hands of a bona fine purchaser who had purchased them from one who had knowingly taken watered stock. Lee v. Cameron, 67 Okl. 80, 169 P. 17, at 22 (1917).

52. Taylor v. Citizens' Oil Co., 182 Ky. 350, 206 S.W. 644 (1918); Oklahoma Gas & Elect. Co. v. Hathaway, supra, note 51, thus in effect holding such shares not entirely "void".

53. Taylor v. Citizens' Oil Co., supra, note 52, 206 S.W. at 650. Compare Lee v. Cameron, supra, note 51.

Little need be said about intentional overvaluations of property or services. Where both the shareholder and the corporation know of the overvaluation, the legal effect is the same as if shares had been issued at less than par for cash. And gross overvaluation is in itself evidence of fraud indicating knowledge that the value is fictitious. Even under some of the more modern statutes which make the judgment of the directors on value conclusive in the absence of actual fraud, excessive valuation is an item to be considered with other attending circumstances as indicating fraud. Thus where there was gross overvaluation and a partial failure to supply the consideration promised, the latter constituted a point of emphasis in the court's determination.[54] But it was apparent that the gross overvaluation of property with little value was the basic reason for the finding of fraud. "Indeed," said the court, "the circumstances of this case point to the conclusion that the resolutions and dealings with respect to the formula and equipment were nothing more than a veil to hide the issuance of shares without consideration." [55]

When shares are issued for a consideration other than money there has been a conflict of authority whether the test of their validity depends upon the actual or true value of the consideration or upon the good faith determination of the value. The true value rule requires actual equality of money value with the par value of the shares. Fraud, fraudulent intent, or honest opinion of shareholders receiving such stock is immaterial.[56] The foundation of the rule is traceable largely, if not entirely, to state statutes indicating a rather complete rigidity of purpose toward wiping out exaggerated valuations of property and services given for stock. The only question involved is whether the property or services are worth the par value of the stock or its actual value where shares may be legitimately issued for less than par. The rule ignores the difficulty of setting "actual" values to many things concerning which expert appraisers may differ. Furthermore, actual value to a corporation with sufficient resources to exploit an oil field, a patent, or a business may be substantially different from actual value under less favorable economic circumstances. The only legitimate inquiry is the "actual value" to the corporation itself, a determination which would normally lie in the hands of the board of directors. If the shares had been sold for cash at their par value and the board had exercised reasonable business judgment in making a purchase of property for cash of an equal amount, no one could later hold the board or the

---

54. Diamond State Brewery, Inc. v. De La Rigaudiere, supra, note 49.

55. Ibid. 17 A.2d at 317. And see Pipelife Corp. v. Bedford, 145 A.2d 206 (Del.Ch.1958).

56. Clinton Mining & Mineral Co. v. Jamison, 256 F. 577 (3d Cir., 1919).

seller of the property because of the board's mistake in judgment concerning the value of the property. It has been suggested that value to the company should depend upon whether it would be willing to pay in cash from its bank account a sum equivalent to the par value shares issued for the property or services.[57]

Methods of valuation are also involved. If the purchase price of a going business depended solely upon a sale of assets as such for shares of a face value equal to a sound appraisal value of the assets, many a purchase would be lost. Again, it is the value to the corporation at the time of purchase that counts. And frequently that value may best be ascertained by capitalizing past earnings, especially if management is to continue as before or if adequate management can be substituted.[58] But this should be distinguished from a capitalization based upon rosy hopes for the future, that is, solely upon future anticipated profits. Anticpated profits, not based upon experience, have been held to be no legitimate basis for valuation.[59] Reasonable expectation of future profits based upon past experience, however, would seem to offer a just solution in those cases where going businesses are acquired through the issue of shares. A capitalization of such profits probably offers as good a criterion of value as any yet devised. The average of past earnings is basic, but where there is a better estimate of future earnings than this average, it has been suggested that this figure should be used as the capitalization base.[60] "To the purchaser the properties are worth a figure that represents a capitalization of the earnings that he expects to make them yield." [61] Other things being equal, the law should give way to the realism of the business man and the financier in this matter. This it seems to have done where profits have previously been achieved.[62]

57. See, Receiver v. Heppenheimer, 69 N.J.Eq. 36, 61 A. 843, at page 851 (1905). "Would the property be worth that sum in cash to the company?" While property must be of equal value, considerable weight will be given to the good faith determination of value by those empowered with the issue of shares for property. (Pages 850–851.) Honest judgment without the use of due care, will not protect them. (Page 851.)

58. Railway Review v. Groff Drill & Machine Tool Co., 84 N.J.Eq. 321, 91 A. 1021 (1914), aff'd without opinion sub. nom. Sloan, Receiver v. Paul, 84 N.J.Eq. 508, 96 A. 1103 (Ct. Err. & App. 1915).

59. See, Receiver v. Heppenheimer, supra, note 57; R. H. Herron Co.

v. Shaw, 165 Cal. 668, 133 P. 488, at 490–491 (1913).

60. Guthmann and Dougall, Corporate Financial Policy 556 (3d ed. 1955). Interesting material on valuation of corporate assets for the purpose of sale will be found on pages 555–559. The method of capitalization of earnings is explained on page 556.

61. Ibid. at 557.

62. See v. Heppenheimer, supra, note 57, condemned the capitalization of anticipated future profits. But in Railway Review v. Groff Drill & Machine Tool Co., supra, note 58, previous earnings were capitalized where the value of the plant and business with small tangible assets but with the exclusive right to manufacture and sell a patented

Because of the difficulty in valuing property and services, the "good faith" rule was widely adopted and recent statutes have tended to accept this rule as the test of validity although the property or services later turn out not to have been of the value honestly established by the board.[63] Thus, if the valuation is fairly and honestly made, too high an estimate does not make the shareholder liable to corporate creditors. But a gross and obvious overvaluation of property for shares is strong evidence of fraud in an action against a shareholder by a creditor to hold him for the water in his shares.[64]

As a matter of practical application of the two rules, it is doubtful whether the results obtained under one can differ materially from the results obtainable under the other. Either rule anticipates reasonable care in the making of a determination and while true value literally anticipates no mistakes in judgment no matter how great the care in determining the value, actually due care cannot be ignored. The test is the value to the corporation, a thing which must be ascertained from the standpoint of the incorporators, shareholders or directors within whose province the determination of value legally rests. The facts evident at the time of making the determination and the manner in which they were considered and acted upon in placing a value on property or services, including good faith and the use of due care, are pertinent to the issue in either case, or should be, though the proponents of true value would disagree. The thought processes through which the determination was made must be retraced and an analysis must be made, by men usually less capable, of those elements which went into the final determination of *value to the corporation*. If important elements of value were not considered under either rule the lack of due care may be the point of attack.

article in this country was involved.

63. The leading case is Coit v. Gold Amalgamating Co., 119 U.S. 343, 7 S.Ct. 231, 30 L.Ed. 420 (1886). For another excellently stated case, see Coffin v. Ransdell, Receiver, 110 Ind. 417, 11 N.E. 20 (1887).

64. Ibid.; Diamond State Brewery, Inc. v. De La Rigaudiere, supra, note 49. And see Pipelife Corp. v. Bedford, supra note 55. Statutes vary. Most provide that, in the absence of fraud, the judgment of the board or the shareholders, as the case may be, as to value shall be conclusive. A.L.I. Model Bus. Corp.Act § 18 (Rev.1953); West's Ann.Cal.Corp.Code § 1112; Mich. Gen.Corp.Act, § 21 (in terms of "bad faith" and "failure to exer-

cise reasonable care in determining such value"); Wis.Bus.Corp. Law § 180.15(3) (similar to A.L.I. Model Act, supra). One statute makes an attack on valuation (however gross) almost impossible by requiring proof, other than the difference between the value of property or services given for par value shares and the fair value so determined by the persons making the same, that the determination was "knowingly and intentionally made" at a greater value than fair value to the corporation. Ohio Rev.Code § 1701.19 (A) (4). For criticism of this legislation, see Emerson, The New Ohio General Corporation Law: Some Comments and Some Comparisons, 24 U. of Cin.L.Rev. 463, at 476–478 (1955).

If there is gross overvaluation, lack of due care or of good faith, one or both, may be emphasized as well as lack of actual value. However, the use of the term "good faith" connotes some elasticity of thought and action which the term "actual value" does not have. In that respect, the "good faith" terminology serves a useful purpose in this difficult process of determining the value of services and of property of various sorts.

§ 7. Legitimate Exception to Issuing Par Value Shares at Less than Par

A few common law cases recognized an exception to the general rule that par value shares may not be issued at less than par as far as creditors are concerned. In the famous case of *Handley* v. *Stutz* [65] the defendants had purchased bonds of a face value of $45,000 and had received an equal amount in par value shares as a bonus. This purchase occurred after the company had unsuccessfully tried to operate its mine and sell the coal from it and when the company was heavily in debt with further losses probable unless funds could be raised to salvage the operation. Shares at the time could be sold for no more than half their par value and the bonds could not have been floated without the bonus shares. Considering the risk taken by the subscribers, the price paid for the stock and bonds was considered reasonable. Under such circumstances the court held the defendants not liable to creditors of the then insolvent company. Facts that, while in economic straits, the company was still a "going concern" or "active corporation" with its original capital depleted and that the sale of its shares at less than par was for the purpose of "recuperating itself and providing new conditions for the successful prosecution of its business" were emphasized in the opinion. Cautious language, this, giving little leeway for expansion of the doctrine and lending no encouragement to companies whose shares were not selling at par where the motive was to finance for further expansion rather than for resuscitation.[66] However, under the rule of *Handley v. Stutz,* stock issued as fully paid must have been issued for the quality of consideration permitted and for a quantity which had some fair or reasonable equivalent to the value of the shares so issued.

As might be expected, some jurisdictions failed to recognize the necessity for an exception to the general rule and required

---

65. 139 U.S. 417, 11 S.Ct. 530, 35 L. Ed. 227 (1891). Similarly, Clark v. Bever, 139 U.S. 96, 11 S.Ct. 468, 35 L.Ed. 88 (1891); Fogg v. Blair, 139 U.S. 118, 11 S.Ct. 476, 35 L.Ed. 104 (1891).   But see Jackson v. Trevor, 64 Iowa 469, 20 N.W. 764 (1884).

66. In Harmon v. Himes, 77 F.2d 375 (D.C.Cir.1935), the attempt was made without success to use the principle of Handley v. Stutz to a corporation newly formed and not yet in operation as a business.

the payment of par when necessary to protect creditors in spite of the impossibility of issuing shares at a value equal to par.[67] The earlier statutes were conveniently vague in their statement of requirements so that it was possible for an honest difference of opinion whether the rule of *Handley v. Stutz* or one contrary to it should apply. The practical impossibility of selling new but unissued shares at par when the same shares on the market were selling at less than par was a possible point of emphasis for an argument that, for whatever corporate purpose, such shares might be legally sold at less than par. The danger of misleading creditors, however, was thought to be too great for a flat rule without limitations such as were imposed in *Handley v. Stutz*. And Machen who recognized the necessity-argument thought that the reasoning was fallacious and that the proper course to pursue in such cases was to reduce the nominal capital until it corresponded with the actual capital at which point the old shares would be worth par and the new ones might likewise be issued at par.[68]

Many modern statutes have made obsolete the rule of *Handley v. Stutz* for they require, at least for the benefit of creditors, the payment of par for shares with a par value. And the majority of jurisdictions have not had occasion to pass upon the precise point. An occasional new statute permits the issue of shares at less than par but with definitely stated restrictions concerning the circumstances under which par value shares may be issued.[69] And the common law rule that treasury shares may be

---

67. Enright v. Heckscher, 240 F. 863 (2d Cir., 1917) (while the New Jersey statute did not differ materially in substance from those involved in the cases in note 65, supra, the court interpreted it as if it did differ); New Haven Trust Co. v. Gaffney, 73 Conn. 480, 47 A. 760 (1901) (the answer to which the plaintiff's demurrer was sustained sets out facts similar to those in Handley v. Stutz, the company, however, being in the insurance business).

68. 1 Machen § 779 (1908). Ballantine, Corporations at 470 (Rev. ed. 1946), favors a broader rule than that stated in Handley v. Stutz and sees no reason why a going corporation should not be able legally to sell its par shares at their market price when it is below par.

69. West's Ann.Cal.Corp.Code § 1110, as amended by L.1957, c. 2261, § 6, provides for the issue of par value shares at less than par, (1) when the board determines such shares cannot be sold at par, (2) when par shares are issued on conversion upon a determination of the board that the convertible securities cannot be sold unless made convertible into par shares at the price fixed, less than par, and (3) when securities are issued with an option to purchase fully paid shares at less than par if the directors determine that their issuance is in the best interests of the corporation. Under § 1900(a) par shares issued at less than par under § 1110 must be capitalized at the agreed consideration. Other statutes permitting the issue of par value shares at less than par are: Burns' Ind.Ann.Stat., 1948 Replacement vol., 1957 Cum.Pocket Supp., § 25–205 (c) (if articles provide for issue at less than par); Flack's Ann.Code of Md.1951, Art. 23, § 16(e) and (f) and § 20; 3 Va. Code of 1950, 1956 Replacement vol.,

sold at less than par finds expression in a number of statutes.[70] It seems doubtful whether this exception, without some qualifications, can be sustained. That treasury shares could be legally sold at less than par was based upon the assumption that par had originally been paid for them. But, obviously, if they have been paid for at their par value and been later purchased back by the corporation at the same figure, their later sale at less than par has the same practical effect as in the case of a sale of unissued shares at less than par. If par has been paid for them and they have later been *given* to the corporation by the shareholder, par has not only been paid but retained and the amount capitalized, and any further amount procured on resale gives creditors and shareholders a further cushion. In both cases treasury shares result. In the latter case there is justification for the rule; in the former, it is impossible to see any justification. However, if the corporation has repurchased its shares at less than par, no practical damage is done if they are reissued later at that figure or a higher one less than par. But the general proposition that treasury shares may be resold at any price is too broad a principle and needs a cutting down to fit the particular situation.

§ 8. Creditors in Search of a Procedure for Recovery in Case of Unpaid Subscriptions and Watered Stock

Shares sold at par or at a stated value, in case of no-par shares, which have not been fully paid for must be distinguished from discount or bonus shares. The shareholder's contract to pay par or stated value constitutes a corporate asset and, if no provision has been made for a definite date of payment, the purchase price is due upon a call made by the corporation. Statutes of limitation start running upon the contract date of payment or upon the date of the call. And a corporate receiver, trustee in bankruptcy or assignee for the benfit of creditors may pursue shareholders who have not paid the full purchase price when the price is due.[71] Corporate inability to pay creditors is not basic, this asset being collectible by a solvent, going corporation.

Since the trust fund theory proceeds on the conviction that the corporation is the trustee for creditors when necessity re-

§ 13.1–17. Ohio formerly permitted such an issue, but the present act does not authorize it.

A number of statutes provide for the issue of par value shares at such discount from par as does not exceed reasonable compensation incurred in the sale or underwriting of such shares. N.C.Bus.Corp.Act (2B N.C.Gen.Stat., 1957 Cum.Supp.) § 55–46(c) (1); Ohio Rev.Code §

1701.18(A) (2); A.L.I.Model Bus. Corp.Act § 20 (Rev.1953).

70. N.C.Bus.Corp.Act § 55–46(c) (2); Ohio Rev.Code § 1701.18(A) (3); A.L.I.Model Bus.Corp.Act § 17 (Rev.1953).

71. Spencer v. Anderson, 193 Cal. 1, 222 P. 355, 35 A.L.R. 822 (1924); In re Remington Auto. & Motor Co., 153 F. 345, at 346 (2d Cir., 1907).

quires that shareholders of bonus or discount shares pay a portion or all of the water in their shares, remedies available stem from the basic idea that the corporation owns the fund and is the proper party to bring the action to acquire it. Representatives of the corporation, such as its receiver, trustee in bankruptcy, and assignee for the benefit of creditors are thus in a position to sue.[72] And, as the liability to absorb the water does not arise until the corporate assets prove insufficient, the statute of limitations does not start running in the shareholder's favor until the necessity for payment has been ascertained and an authorized demand of payment made.[73]

The statutory obligation theory proceeds parallel to the trust fund theory when the statute is phrased in such a manner as to indicate that the corporation is the proper person to sue on behalf of the creditors. Corporate representatives indicated in the paragraph above are proper parties to bring the suit based, as in the trust fund theory, upon an implied promise to pay the full par value when the necessity arises. But if the statute clearly runs in favor of creditors, the normal route would be by a suit brought either by a creditor in his individual right or a class action brought by one or more creditors for the benefit of all similarly situated.[74] A creditor's bill in equity brought by a judgment creditor with writ of execution returned unsatisfied is the generally approved procedure but local holdings and statutes will have to be consulted on this matter.[75]

---

72. Scovill v. Thayer, 105 U.S. 143, 26 L.Ed. 968 (1881) (trustee in bankruptcy); In re Newfoundland Syndicate, 196 F. 443 (D.N.J.1912) (trustee in bankruptcy), modified in 201 F. 443 (3d Cir., 1913); In re Remington Auto. & Motor Co., supra, note 71; Merola v. Fair Lawn Newspaper Printing Corp., 135 N.J. Eq. 152, 36 A.2d 290 (Ct.Err. & App.1944).

73. Scovill v. Thayer, supra, note 72, 105 U.S. at 158.

74. See Frink v. Carman Distributing Co., 97 Colo. 211, 48 P.2d 805 (1935), where the statutory obligation was to creditors.

75. Statutes also frequently require the obtaining of a judgment against the corporation with writ of execution returned unsatisfied in whole or in part before the creditor may proceed against shareholders holding stock not fully paid. See N.Y.Stock Corp. Law §§ 70 and 73. Under this statute, neither a trustee in bankruptcy (Granger & Co. v. Allen, 214 App.Div. 367, at 370, 212 N.Y.S. 356, at 360 (1925), aff'd sub nom. Empire Produce Co. v. Allen, 244 N.Y. 587, 155 N.E. 907 (1927)), nor an assignee for the benefit of creditors (Thompson v. Knight, 74 App. Div. 316, 77 N.Y.S. 599 (1902)), nor a receiver (Bostwick v. Young, 118 App.Div. 490, 496, 103 N.Y.S. 607 (1907), aff'd without opinion in 194 N.Y. 516, 87 N.E. 1115 (1909)) may bring the action, the holder of such stock being personally liable to the creditors of the corporation. Furthermore, all the shareholders subject to liability who are within the jurisdiction and solvent should be made parties defendant since the liability under the statute is joint and not several. 4 White on New York Corporations §§ 71 and 73 (12th ed. 1948).

On the other hand, Ohio Rev.Code § 1701.18(F) and (G) makes shareholders (of watered stock) liable to the *corporation*, with no suggestion that the liability is only when the corporation is unable to pay its creditors. Accord: Mich.Gen.Corp.

Since the fraud or holding out theory is based upon a type of deceit and reliance is a necessary element, the remedy belongs to the creditor of the corporation personally and he is the proper person to sue. Because this is no asset of the corporation, its receiver, trustee in bankruptcy and assignee for the benefit of creditors have no interest upon which to base a claim, that is, barring some statutory aid. It has been pointed out that an action based upon a shareholder's contract to pay the full subscription price differs from that founded upon the creditor's right to pursue the holder of bonus or discount shares under the fraud theory in that the first action is one sounding in contract, the second, in tort. "The two classes of actions present many points of similarity, and the failure to distinguish between them has led to unfortunate confusion, particularly in the earlier cases. Both are creditors' bills in equity, both are actions by a creditor of a corporation, seeking the aid of equity for the satisfaction of his claim out of assets not reachable by the ordinary processes of the law, and in both (but for different reasons) the plaintiff is required to allege and prove the recovery of a judgment against the corporation and the return of execution *nulla bona* (or that the corporation has become insolvent). But here the similarity ceases." [76] The creditor may have had a contract action against the corporation, but under the fraud theory his action against the shareholder is in tort based upon the false representation that the corporate capital has been paid in full. The creditor, however, cannot recover on this basis until he has been injured by the misrepresentation; thus, the necessity for obtaining a judgment against the corporation and pursuing the corporate property first. The statute of limitations against the action starts running when judgment has been recovered and a writ of execution has been returned *nulla bona* or, according to some holdings, the notorious insolvency of the corporation will start the statute running.[77] And, under this theory, the appropriate tort statute of limitations is applicable.

Where the suit is by creditor's bill rather than by a receiver or trustee in bankruptcy, it has usually been held that the bill can only be maintained on behalf of all creditors and not simply for the benefit of the creditor or creditors bringing the action.[78]

Act § 21; Minn.Stat.Ann. § 301.15, subd. 4. West's Ann.Cal.Corp.Code § 1110, though drafted to express the statutory obligation theory, was interpreted to codify the previous "fraud" or "holding out" theory. See page 405, supra.

76. Spencer v. Anderson, 193 Cal. 1, 222 P. 355, at 356–357, 35 A.L.R. 822 (1924).

77. Ibid. See Ann., When does Statute of Limitations begin to run against an action by, or in behalf of, creditors of a corporation on unpaid stock or subscriptions? 35 A.L.R. 832 (1925).

78. Handley v. Stutz, 137 U.S. 366, at 369, 11 S.Ct. 117, 118, 34 L.Ed. 706 (1890).

However, local statutes should be consulted for some have been held to give the individual creditor his cause of action against the shareholder who has not paid the full par value for his shares.[79] And, while the general rule makes the corporation a necessary and indispensable party, where the corporation has been adjudged a bankrupt, or has been dissolved, or where it is impossible to obtain service upon the corporation and the only relief sought is upon the shareholder's individual several liability, legitimate exceptions have been made.[80] But this would seem also to depend upon the theory adopted as the basis for the shareholder's liability. The trust fund and the statutory obligation theories, the latter in so far as the remedy is a corporate one, demand a rule making indispensable the corporation as a party defendant. A creditor's bill in such cases is somewhat analogous to a shareholder's derivative action.

But where the fraud theory is applicable, it would seem that, while the unsuccessful pursuit of possible legal remedies against the corporation would be a condition precedent to the bringing of a creditor's bill, the joining of the corporation as a party defendant in the bill itself would be unnecessary. As we have seen, the basis of the remedy is deceit and the remedy is available only to creditors prior in point of time to the issue of watered stock and to those only who were not cognizant of the water when they gave credit. No equitable corporate asset is involved. And while the best practical solution would be along the lines developed in case of the trust fund and statutory obligation theories, the strong accent on the notion that this is a tort action individual in nature prevents judicial acceptance of it. In fact, it is a misnomer to call the creditor's action under this theory a creditor's bill as the asset sought to be applied to the creditor's judgment is not, under the fraud theory, an equitable asset of the corporation. Minnesota, which, under its common law, adopted the fraud theory and under its corporation statute retained it, has made express provision for a corporate cause of action but only for the benefit of subsequent creditors.[81] Such legislation is wise as it guarantees equality of treatment to all creditors entitled to share in the "water" and permits representatives of the corporation such as receivers, assignees for the benefit of creditors and

---

79. Chisnell v. Ozier Co., 140 Ohio St. 355, 44 N.E.2d 464 (1942), interpreting an Ohio statutory provision existing at that time.

80. Stewart v. Ahern, 32 F.2d 864 (9th Cir., 1929), involving an Idaho corporation which, apparently, could not be served in California where the shareholder resided.

The case was decided upon a pleading defect.

81. Minn.Stat.Ann. § 301.15, subd. 4. By § 301.15, subd. 5, creditors are not presumed to have extended credit relying upon corporate compliance with the requirements of this section.

trustees in bankruptcy to bring the action for the benefit of the described creditors.

There is still a divergence of judicial opinion in the bankruptcy cases as to whether the trustee in bankruptcy may enforce only the shareholders' liability which the corporation might have enforced or whether he may also pursue the shareholders where, under the local law, only the creditors of the corporation had that right. The cases are conflicting and those which permit the trustee to enforce the liability in both types of case are, from the practical standpoint, preferable.[82] It has been pointed out that most of the case law antedates the 1938 amendment to § 70(c) of the Bankruptcy Act which expressly gave the trustee the rights of a judgment creditor with a lien.[83] Of course where the local law permits neither the corporation nor the creditor to pursue the holder of watered stock, as in Oklahoma, the trustee is in no better position.[84]

As to the liability of the shareholder upon his contract to pay for his shares or upon his bonus or discount shares, the general rule is that his liability is several and not joint. Hence, other shareholders similarly liable need not be joined as parties defendant, but may be and frequently are.[85] However, if a shareholder pays a judgment rendered against him, he is entitled to equitable contribution from fellow-shareholders similarly liable and, if he so elects before trial, he may be entitled to a receiver upon proper motion, or he may file a cross-bill for the purpose of discovering other shareholders who have not fully paid for their shares, have them brought into the suit, so that contribution may be enforced in the suit.[86] In no case will he be held for more than the par value of his shares (or the contract price above that) or the stated value in the case of no-par shares unless some further statutory liability exists.

Where a corporation has been decreed insolvent and it has been judicially determined that an assessment must be made to liquidate the corporate debts, holdings have varied as to the ne-

---

82. See 3 Remington, Bankruptcy § 1202 (Rev. ed. Henderson, 1957), for cases pro and con. 2 Glenn, Fraudulent Conveyances and Preferences § 608 (Rev. ed. 1940), suggests that "perhaps" a pragmatic rule permitting general recovery, whether creditors are prior or subsequent, or whether with knowledge, might be desirable.

83. Ibid. See note 75, supra, on the New York law.

84. Stone, Trustee v. Hudgens, 129 F.Supp. 273 (D.Okl.1955).

85. The early important case was Hatch v. Dana, 101 U.S. 205, at 214, 25 L.Ed. 885 (1879), which involved defendants who held shares upon which the corporation had called not more than 30% of their subscriptions. All the shareholders were not made defendants. But see note 75, supra, where the New York statute was interpreted to create joint and not several liability, thus requiring all solvent shareholders within the jurisdiction to be made parties defendant.

86. Ibid., 101 U.S. at 214.

cessity of bringing into the suit all shareholders who are liable and solvent so that each shareholder may pay only his proper proportion of the corporate debts, thus settling the matter of equitable contribution in the one suit.[87]   Usually statutes have been the determining factor and some inconvenience has resulted from minority holdings which confined a receiver, or trustee in bankruptcy, to collecting only the amount which, with the other assets of the company, will pay the corporate debts and costs of receivership, or bankruptcy.[88]   Determination of the amount necessary to satisfy debts and costs and the necessity for and rate of assessment are usually held to be within the power of the court without notice to the shareholders or the opportunity to be heard.[89]   But a plenary action to enforce the assessment is necessary if the shareholder refuses to pay so that he may have his day in court on defenses apart from those matters legally determinable summarily in the first proceeding.

§ 9.   Avoiding Unpaid Stock Problems by the use of No-par Shares

While no-par value shares may not be issued for a consideration different from the quality prescribed by the law, their quan-

---

87. In See, Receiver v. Heppenheimer, 69 N.J.Eq. 36, 61 A. 843 (1905), only a few of the large shareholders were defendants. They were held up to the par value of their watered shares for the claims proved in the receivership, plus costs including lawyers' fees of creditors and of the receiver, fees of the receiver and expenses that might be incurred in enforcing the decree. The court reserved in the decree the right of the defendant-shareholders who paid to use the decree to aid in obtaining contribution from shareholders not served. In John W. Cooney Co. v. Arlington Hotel Co., 11 Del.Ch. 286, 101 A. 879 (Ch.1917), mod. and aff'd sub nom. Du Pont v. Ball, 11 Del.Ch. 430, 106 A. 39, 7 A.L.R. 955 (Sup.Ct.1918), the chancellor gave a conditional decree which could make one large shareholder liable to the extent of the total debts, since his individual liability extended beyond the amount of such debts. The decree specifically reserved his right of contribution against those who did not pay.

88.   Philips v. Slocomb, 35 Del. 462, at 466, 167 A. 698 (1933); Merola v. Fair Lawn Newspaper Printing Corp., 135 N.J.Eq. 152, 36 A.2d 290 (Ct.Err. & App.1944). But see Note, 33 Mich.L.Rev. 1059 (1935), citing authority contra. Much authority supports the view that the receiver may collect the full amount due on the shareholder's contract leaving the matter of equitable contribution to be determined later. This simplifies the administration of the insolvent corporation's estate, making the accounting problems much simpler.

89.   "This is grounded in the principle that a stockholder is so far an integral part of the corporation that, in the view of the law, he is privy to the proceedings touching the body of which he is a member. He is in such privity with the corporation as to be a party to the assessment proceeding through representation by the corporation." Merola v. Fair Lawn Newspaper Printing Corp., supra, note 88, 36 A. 2d at 292. But in this case it was held that the shareholders were entitled to their day in court on the "propriety and quantum of the assessment . . ." See also In re Bell Tone Records, Inc., 91 F.Supp. 642, at 644 (D.N.J.1950).

tity, as far as creditors are concerned, can lend no hope that the actual consideration was of a given amount or that it was substantial. This does not mean, however, that no-par shares cannot be "watered." If a stated value has been set for no-par shares, whether that value was set by the incorporators and appeared in the articles of incorporation, or whether the board of directors set the price for their sale, for all practical purposes such no-par value shares are equivalent to shares having a par value of like amount. Shareholders taking them with notice of their stated value, either for cash, property or services of a value known to be less than the stated value, incur the same hazards as if they had accepted par value shares similarly watered.[90] But if no-par value shares of whatever number are accepted for property or services without placing a dollar-price upon them, creditors have no basis under any of the theories previously discussed to hold such shareholders.[91] And the same has been held true in case of bonus shares of the no-par variety.[92] For accounting pur-

90. Norton v. Lamb, 144 Kan. 665, 62 P.2d 1311 (1936). The corporate charter set the price for no-par shares at $1.

91. G. Loewus & Co., Inc. v. Highland Queen Packing Co., 125 N.J.Eq. 534, 6 A.2d 545 (1939). Here, no-par shares were issued without a price upon them but in the minutes of the board was placed the statement, "It is understood that the said shares of stock shall be issued at the price of $20 per share and representing a total value of $6,000," which was much in excess of the value given for the shares. The court found the meaning of the statement "not clear" but found no intent of the parties that $6,000 should be paid in, or that even the difference between the value of the consideration and $6,000 should be paid in. Had the price been fixed at $20 per share, the defendant having notice of this, the court assumed that payment of less would create watered stock. Israels, infra, note 92, rightly criticises this case at 1290–1291. Livingston v. Adams, 226 Mo.App. 824, 43 S.W.2d 836 (1931), cert. denied by Missouri Supreme Court (1932), involved the issue of no-par shares to promoters for a nominal consideration but with a statement in the articles that the amount of capital with which the corporation would begin business was $5,000, $2,000 being in cash and $3,000 in proper-

ty actually received. The shareholders so taking were held liable to creditors to the extent of the water. This is comparable to issuing no-par shares at a stated value, that is X-number of shares for $5,000. As to shareholders whose interests may have been diluted, see § 402, supra.

92. Johnson v. Louisville Trust Co., 293 F. 857, 36 A.L.R. 785 (6th Cir., 1923), cert. denied in 264 U.S. 585, 44 S.Ct. 334, 68 L.Ed. 862 (1924). Unless some consideration can be found for their issue, it would seem that they are void shares which could, in a suit to cancel them, be regained by the corporation. See Israels, Problems of Par and No-Par Shares: A Reappraisal, 47 Col. L.Rev. 1279, at 1283 (1947). But if any consideration was given for them, they will not be cancelled, at least in the absence of a clear abuse of discretion by the board of directors. West v. Sirian Lamp Co., 28 Del.Ch. 90, 37 A.2d 835 (1944). The grant of an exclusive license to use a patent is prima facie evidence of property within the term of the Delaware statute and ordinarily sufficient consideration to justify the issuance of corporate stock. Id. v. id., 28 Del. Ch. 398, 44 A.2d 258 (1945). Some of the no-par shares in the Louisville Trust Co. case had been issued for a nominal consideration and the court rightly held that

poses the board will have to place a value on the services or property thus acquired and capitalize the shares used to make the purchase. But this is a duty of the board and not of the recipient of the shares, and if the board sets up false values it may be liable for the misrepresentation but not the innocent recipient.[93] It has been suggested that where the board is permitted to apply part of the consideration to paid-in surplus the actual value or something under the actual value might be capitalized and the rest, representing inflated value, could be thrown into paid-in surplus.[94] The dangers seem obvious and, while the author of this suggestion based it upon the nonexistence of a case where "liability was sought to be imposed for inflation reflected in surplus rather than in stated capital" he realized that it would indeed be but a slight extension of the fraud theory to hold a shareholder accepting no-par shares under such circumstances when he was cognizant of the intended manipulation of the balance sheet. One who relies upon such a balance sheet should be protected although in this case there is no misrepresentation of the capital stock position. From the balance sheet statement of a "paid-in surplus" or "capital surplus," one is led to believe that there are X-dollars of asset value as a further present cushion when, in fact, there is nothing.

It is suggested that, either during promotion or later, when property or services of a value difficult to ascertain with reasonable accuracy are involved, the property or services be transferred under an agreement that X-number of no-par shares shall be the purchase price without reference to any stated value for the shares. In fact, if the recipient of the shares has notice that they already have a stated value, he will be in no different position from one who accepts par value shares of like description. And if he has knowledge that the board intends to carry the no-par value shares so transferred at a stated figure on the corporation's books of account and balance sheet, his position would seem to be no different. Without such knowledge he has no obligation to do more than accept X-number of no-par shares for Blackacre, a patent right, or any other thing within the quality of consideration permitted by the statute, however problematical the value may be. And, of course, if he participates in the setting of the value of the thing transferred, he should be sure that its value is not exaggerated.

these were issued for a valid consideration.

93. See G. Loewus & Co., Inc. **v.** Highland Queen Packing Co., supra, note 91, where the board may have done this. Directors were held for balance sheet inflation where balance sheet was submitted to Dun & Bradstreet in Brown-Wales Co. v. Barber, 88 N.H. 103, 184 A. 855 (1936); Crescent Mfg. Co. v. Hansen, 174 Wash. 193, 24 P.2d 604 (1933).

94. Israels, supra, note 92, at 1293, 1297–1298.

It should be apparent that shareholder-risk can be minimized by the use of a low par value share, for example a 5 or 10 cent par value, and being careful to issue no more in the aggregate than will equal the conservative value of the property or services given for the shares. In recent years certain tax advantages have encouraged the use of low par value shares instead of no-par shares.[95] And since there is no longer any public feeling against purchasing shares of a low par value at a price frequently many times the par value there is little practical difficulty in obtaining finances in this manner. The equitable contribution rule may be avoided by notice of the issue of X-number of shares for X-property of X-value prior to the subscription for or sale of similar par value shares at substantially higher than par prices. A safer method would be to incorporate these facts into the subscription agreement itself. There is the further argument, in any case, that the business importance of corporate promotion is sufficient to warrant different prices for the same class of shares sold at approximately the same time.

§ 10. Position of Transferees of Watered Stock

Transferees of shares not fully paid who took them with notice of this fact are liable in the same manner as if they had been the original owners of such shares.[96] Transferees without notice, whether the theory be trust fund, statutory obligation, or fraud, are free from liability on bonus or discount shares.[97] And where the transferee does not become liable, the transferor does not lose his liability. Some cases have indicated that, even if the transferee has become liable the transferor does not by this fact lose his liability.[98] And if, in order to avoid liability, he transfers his watered shares to one who becomes liable but is insolvent, the transferor remains liable.

---

95. Ibid. at 1292. This advantage has disappeared under a statute enacted after this volume went to press. 26 U.S.C.A. § 4321 was amended so that the stamp tax on a sale or transfer of shares is imposed on the "actual value" of the shares whether of the par or no-par value type. 27 U.S.Law Week 66 (August 26, 1958).

96. Bonbright, Shareholders' Defenses Against Liability to Creditors on Watered Stock, 25 Col.L.Rev. 408, at 418 (1925); Smith v. Donges, 73 F.2d 620 (3d Cir., 1934); Easton Nat. Bank v. American Brick & Tile Co., 69 N.J.Eq. 326, 60 A. 54, at 57–58 (1905).

97. 2 Glenn, Fraudulent Conveyances and Preferences § 609 (Rev. ed. 1940). But see Shugart v. Maytag, 188 Iowa 916, 176 N.W. 886 (1920), holding that under a South Dakota statute the transferee without notice is liable. The case is of little value after Gray Construction Co. v. Fantle, 62 S.D. 345, 253 N.W. 464 (1934), which held contrariwise on its own statute.

98. Bonbright, supra, note 96, at 418; Wolcott v. Waldstein, 86 N.J. Eq. 63, 97 A. 951 (1916).

§ 11.   Shares under the English Law

The English law has not yet authorized the issue of no-par value shares although they have been used in Canada for many years and there has been considerable agitation for them in England. An expert committee appointed by the government in 1952 made its report in January of 1954 recommending action and finding that there was a strong case for permitting the issue of such shares and a real demand for them due largely to "the ever-increasing disparity between paid-up capital and capital employed." [99]   Shares of par value only are legally permissible and these may not be sold below par except under very exceptional circumstances as provided by § 57 of the Companies Act of 1948 which, among other things, requires an order of the court sanctioning the issue of such shares at a discount "upon such terms and conditions as it thinks fit."   The most recent English work on company law states in a short footnote that "This permission is so rarely resorted to that further consideration of it is unnecessary." [1]

Whereas par value shares must be issued at not less than par, when they are sold above par the difference must appear in the balance sheet as "Share Premium Account" and is treated differently from the item "Paid-in Surplus" or "Capital Surplus" in the United States. Prior to 1948, such premiums were, however, considered part of the distributable surplus of the company and dividends could be paid from them. Since 1948 they have been treated quite differently and, for most purposes, as though they were capital. [2]

It has been pointed out that there are two loopholes through which shares have been issued at less than par: (1) for over-valued property given for shares since the company's valuation is final unless inadequacy of consideration appears on the face of the transaction or unless there is fraud; and (2) through a statutory provision permitting payment of a commission of not more than ten percent of the amount for which the shares are issued to take up shares, a provision made primarily if not solely for the benefit of underwriters. But the broad phrasing of the section seems to have encouraged a violation of its primary object by some companies making a general offering with an allowance, or discount, of ten percent. [3]

---

99. Cole, Morley and Scott, Corporate Financing in Great Britain, 12 The Business Lawyer 324, at 334 (1957).

1. Gower, Modern Company Law 104, footnote 13 (1954).

2. Cole, Morley and Scott, supra, note 99, at 333; Gower, supra, note 1, at 106, and § 56 of the English Companies Act of 1948.

3. Gower, supra, note 1, at 105; 53 of the English Companies Act of 1948.

While the rule applied in case of par value shares is a firm one, in practice issued share capital may be composed of partly paid shares and of "uncalled capital" which latter has the quality of a guaranteed fund as far as creditors are concerned. On the balance sheet only the paid-up capital is shown as a liability which, of course, is contrary to our concept in America. The continental practice is similar to our own also.[4] § 60 of the English Act provides: "A limited company may by special resolution determine that any portion of its share capital which has not been already called up shall not be capable of being called up except in the event and for the purposes of the company being wound up, and thereupon that portion of its share capital shall not be capable of being called up except in the event and for the purposes aforesaid." This provision seems to approach closely the statutory obligation theory adopted by some jurisdictions in this country. In actual practice, however, Professor Gower states that, with the exception of banks and insurance companies, paid-up capital on allotment of shares is traditionally required.[5] Only in case of liquidation may the unsecured creditors avail themselves of uncalled capital[6] which, again, is contrary to the practice in the United States. But "uncalled capital" is said to be such a rarity as to call for very little discussion in the English texts.[7]

§ 12.   Shareholders' Preemptive Right to Later Issues of Shares

While there has been much contention as to the extent of the right called "preemptive," the traditional views discussed in the cases, whether or not the discussion was necessary to the decision at hand, are along the following lines. The preemptive right was a judicial invention, equitable in character, to permit a shareholder to keep his proportionate interest in voting power, earnings and assets of the company through the right to subscribe to new shares subsequently issued for cash in the proportion then held by him in shares outstanding. Except under conditions to be shortly discussed, there was no preemptive right to shares of the original issue. If there had been, the first prospective subscriber approached would have been entitled to 100 percent of the shares initially issued. Furthermore, subscribers are said to take such shares with a clear understanding that the initial subscription shall be consummated before they have any right to the preservation of their proportional status.

The doctrine arose at a time when the small, closely held corporation was in the process of development and goes back at

4. Gower, supra, note 1, at 103.

5. Ibid.

6. Gower, supra, note 1, at 562.

7. Ibid.

least 150 years in this country.[8] Behind it was the thought that the existing shareholders were the owners and were entitled to have their ownership continued in the same proportion except as a change of fractional interest resulted from inter-shareholder transfers and those made to others. With but one class of common shares outstanding, the preemptive right to a successive issue of the same class or of another class was simple of application, whether preemption was rationalized as being a right to retain proportionate voting control or a similar interest in earnings, assets, or both.

The application of the doctrine, uncontrolled by statute or charter provisions, becomes increasingly difficult as new classes of shares are used, some of which have no voting rights, some having limited rights as to voting and as to dividends and participation in assets upon dissolution, some being convertible into common shares which may be of the nonvoting variety but with the other attributes of common shares. Many variations may be invented. As to common shares, every type of preferred share authorized and issued would compete in earnings and hence be subject to preemption. After the first issue of preferred if another preferred issue is floated carrying prior preferences as to dividends or as to assets upon dissolution, a possibility under modern statutes, the common and preferred already outstanding would both have preemptive rights under the prevailing theory so as to keep their respective proportionate interest in earnings and assets. But if the second preferred issue provides for dividends and distribution of assets after the first preferred, then only the common shareholders would have the preemptive right. If the corporation proposes a bond issue convertible into common shares, the usual case, or into preferred shares of any kind, the common shareholders will (or may) lose their proportionate interest unless the preemptive right exists in such a case. More complications result if a new preferred issue carries conversion rights to common. And the matter of how to preserve the particular proportionate interest becomes difficult,[9] and frequently impossible, where several different issues of shares are outstanding and another is contemplated with still different preferences. Such complications occur but rarely in the closely held corporation, but they are sufficiently frequent in publicly held corporations to warrant close statutory regulation.[10]

8. Gray v. Portland Bank, 3 Mass. 364, 3 Am.Dec. 156 (1807), is said to be the first case on preemptive rights. But see Drinker, The Preemptive Right of Shareholders to Subscribe to New Shares, 43 Harv. L.Rev. 586, at 590–593 (1930), where he reaches the conclusion that the case did not involve that issue.

This article contains an excellent analysis of the early leading cases.

9. N.Y.Stock Corp.Law (58 McKinney's Consol.L. of N.Y.Ann.1951) § 39, subd. 5, makes specific provision for this difficulty.

10. See Frey, Shareholders' Preemptive Rights, 38 Yale L.J. 563, at 566,

Whether a new issue of shares is subject to preemption is generally determined by asking whether the proportionate rights of the present shareholders as to voting, dividends, or corporate assets are, or may be, cut down by the new issue. If they are, the preemptive right exists unless the new issue comes within one of the exceptions courts have made in order to reach practical results thought not possible otherwise.

Confinement of preemptive rights rigidly to *new issues* of shares would do injustice to present shareholders particularly where the authorized initial issue is large and the corporation has no present intent of selling it all immediately. Similar injustice may be done unless some limitation is placed upon the time during which the initial issue is to be sold. Consequently, where the corporation has decided presently to issue only a certain number of shares less than all which have been authorized, or where conditions have materially changed due to the lapse of time so that it would be inequitable to follow the basic exception to the rule of preemption, some courts have held that a preemptive right exists in shares later issued from the initial shares authorized.[11]

Exceptions to the preemptive right have been judicially made where shares have been issued for property,[12] or in case of merger or consolidation,[13] or in payment of a debt,[14] or from treasury shares that have not been retired and later "resurrected,"[15] or from shares which have first been offered to shareholders having

footnote 11, setting out some combinations of shareholders' provisions.

11. Ross Transport, Inc. v. Crothers, 185 Md. 573, 45 A.2d 267 (1946). The court did not find it necessary to take this approach, though it indicated clearly its validity, but accepted the principle that officers and directors who were the purchasers were trustees who had violated their trust by purchasing at their own sale. In Dunlay v. Avenue M Garage & Repair Co., Inc., 253 N.Y. 274, 170 N.E. 917, at 919 (1930), the court stated: "The issued stock may be related to the unissued stock as stock for immediate issue to stock for future expansion. In such case the preemptive right might not be denied." See also Yasik v. Wachtel, 25 Del. Ch. 247, 17 A.2d 309 (1941), where shares of original issue were sold considerably later but the court viewed the corporate plan as one contemplating the issue of all of its

initial shares and found that the corporation was all the time in need of capital.

12. Thom v. Baltimore Trust Co., 158 Md. 352, 148 A. 234 (1930).

13. Musson v. New York & Queens Elect. Lt. & Pow. Co., 138 Misc. 881, 247 N.Y.S. 406 (Sup.Ct.1931).

14. Dunlay v. Avenue M Garage & Repair Co., supra, note 11. But see dictum in Hodge v. Cuba Co., 142 N.J.Eq. 340, 60 A.2d 88, at 93 (1948).

15. Hammer v. Werner, 239 App.Div. 38, 265 N.Y.S. 172, at 177 (1933). "When a corporation buys its own stock to retire it or hold it indefinitely, such stock may cease to be true treasury stock within the rule permitting reissue without affording stockholders to participate ratably." (At page 178.) In Dunn v. Acme Auto & Garage Co., 168 Wis. 128, 169 N.W. 297 (1918), the stock was purchased, retired and reissued.

preemptive rights when such shareholders have elected not to subscribe to the shares they were entitled to.[16] Most of these exceptions are based upon the supposed or actual practical necessity for their exception, although courts have rarely gone into this matter of real necessity with any thoroughness. Having become entangled in a maze of difficulties in the application of the preemptive principle, exceptions were bound to follow as a matter of course. But had the proponents of the rule that voting shares only should have a preemptive right in order to keep up their proportionate voting interest in shares having the right to vote been followed, few difficulties would have resulted.[17]

When the preemptive right exists the corporation must give the shareholders a reasonable time in which to subscribe and to arrange for the payment of the new shares, a rule which tends to frustrate the corporation in obtaining prompt and sure financing, but necessary nevertheless if the right is to be of value.[18] And since there is no requirement that shares subject to preemption be sold to the then shareholders at their par value, it is quite possible that an investment banker or other single outside financing agency would be willing to purchase the whole block at a price per share that the shareholders would not wish to subscribe for them, thus penalizing the corporation from making a single contract in the first instance. And the delay caused by first presenting the opportunity of purchase to the shareholders may be sufficient to defeat the legitimate objective of the corporation—the securing of finances at the best possible figure and with the least expenditure of time and money. As one able writer has put it, "[A]s applied to large corporations, with stock widely distributed, the rule constitutes an unnecessary refinement which in the long run works to the disadvantage of the shareholders, whose substantial rights are sufficiently protected by the enforcement of the fiduciary duty of the directors." [19]

---

16. Drinker, op. cit. supra, note 8, at 604.

17. See Frey, op. cit. supra, note 10, at 572 et seq. Professor Frey suggests this rule: "Unless otherwise provided by statute or in the articles of association, every holder of voting shares has a right that the corporation shall not create any voting shares, without first offering to him that proportion thereof which the number of votes possessed by him at a time reasonably fixed by the board of directors bears to the total number of votes then possessed by all voting shareholders." (Pages 572–573.) He denies that this is not the common law rule, and the rest of his article gives the reasons for his belief. And see Drinker, op. cit. supra, note 8, at 598–599.

18. Bennett v. Baum, 90 Neb. 320, 133 N.W. 439 (1911), in which it was held that a mere 5 days was unreasonable. On the other hand, a 60-day notice was held valid in Van Slyke v. Norris, 159 Minn. 63, 198 N.W. 409 (1924). And, in Hoyt v. Great American Ins. Co., 201 App.Div. 352, 194 N.Y.S. 449 (1922), a space of some 24 days between notice and a call for half the subscription price was held sufficient.

19. Drinker, op. cit. supra, note 8, at 601. See his illustration at 600.

It is probable that the right of preemption has, in many cases, been used by "professional privateers" [20] who take advantage of the right that they may be bought off at a high figure so that the financing may proceed without further serious objection. In a corporation whose shares are widely distributed it is rare indeed that an individual owns or controls a sufficient number of shares to give his preemptive right a large enough value to pursue it for the shares involved. The fiduciary duty of the director to secure the best price possible for the issue protects the present shareholders against a dilution of their shares; their fiduciary duty not to issue shares to themselves or to others for the purpose of changing the voting control is sufficient to protect the shareholders in their voting rights. And if shares are to be sold at less than their present value, a valid business reason will have to be produced to warrant the sale at that price or the shares must be offered to present shareholders at the price, thus giving them the chance to keep their proportionate interest in the assets and not have their shares diluted.

Assignable subscription warrants are usually used when a corporation is about to issue shares subject to the preemptive right. Whether or not the warrant states that it is assignable, as a matter of law, it probably is. This gives the shareholder who does not wish to take advantage of his right the possibility of selling it to another who desires the shares which his assignor was entitled to. And if the shares are being sold below their actual market value, it gives the warrant-holder the opportunity to prevent part or all of the dilution which would otherwise result from a sale to third persons. It seems apparent that any restrictions upon the transfer of such warrants would have to be reasonable as in other cases of restraints upon the alienation of property of this type.

In case of the actual issue to outside subscribers of shares to which present shareholders have a preemptive right, the shareholder has a remedy at law against the corporation for damages incurred by reason of such violation.[21] Prior to the issue, he may enjoin it [22] or he may obtain a mandatory order permitting him to subscribe [23] or, if the shares have been issued

---

20. A good example is General Investment Co. v. Bethlehem Steel Corp., 88 N.J.Eq. 237, 102 A. 252 (1917), where this term and "professional agitator" are used.

21. Gray v. Portland Bank, 3 Mass. 364, 3 Am.Dec. 156 (1807); Stokes v. Continental Trust Co., 186 N.Y. 285, 78 N.E. 1090 (1906). In the latter case, the shares had been issued to a banker. The action was brought to compel the corporation to issue to the plaintiff the shares his preemptive right assured him, or, if impossible to do that, to grant damages. He obtained damages.

22. Dousman v. Wisconsin & Lake Superior Mining & Smelting Co., 40 Wis. 418 (1876).

23. Hammond v. Edison Illuminating Co., 131 Mich. 79, 90 N.W. 1040 (1902).

to ones who knew of the preemptive right and knew that it had not been waived, or have been issued to the directors or officers who are charged with such notice, he may compel a cancellation of such shares.[24]

(a) Preemptive right statutes. Had the courts developed a concept which recognized the opportunity to subscribe to new issues of shares as a privilege rather than a right, statutes might well have been unnecessary. For example, the Maryland court has permitted this opportunity "when the privilege can be exercised consistently with the object which the disposition of the additional stock is legally designed to accomplish." [25] Thus, in a recent case where a Maryland corporation found it necessary to issue preferred shares convertible into common at the rate of 50 shares of common for 1 share of preferred in order to secure a large loan for rehabilitation purposes from the Reconstruction Finance Corporation, the court used the above test and held that the common shareholders were properly barred from participation.[26] Or had the proponents of the rule basing the preemptive right solely upon the retention of proportionate voting control been followed, statutes would have been unnecessary. The English common law apparently did not recognize a preemptive right, and a recent leading work has suggested that, in a small private company, a provision should be made permitting preemption, for otherwise majority directors may issue new shares to the injury of the minority.[27]

The statutes have varied from the extreme of providing for no preemptive rights unless the articles make provision for them [28] to the retention of preemptive rights unless otherwise

---

24. Ross Transport, Inc. v. Crothers, 185 Md. 573, 45 A.2d 267 (1946). This was a derivative suit by a shareholder of a Maryland corporation to have shares issued to officers and their immediate families cancelled. While the court based its opinion on breach of trust of its officers, it made clear that the treatment of cancellation would have been applied on the preemptive right argument as well. See also Schmidt v. Pritchard, 135 Iowa 240, 112 N.W. 801 (1907); Bennett v. Baum, supra, note 18.

25. Thom v. Baltimore Trust Co., 158 Md. 352, at 356, 148 A. 234, at 235 (1929). The court used both the term "privilege" and "right" in its discussion.

26. Todd v. Maryland Casualty Co., 155 F.2d 29, at 39 (7th Cir., 1946).

Said the court at page 39: "It is fantastic to think that it could have obtained this amount of money ($12,500,000) or any considerable portion thereof by a sale of Common Stock to its then existing Common stockholders." Might this also be classified as another "practical necessity" case? Flack's Ann. Code of Md.1951, Art. 23, § 26(a) (8), after setting forth seven situations where preemptive rights are not given unless otherwise provided for in the charter, provides no preemptive rights with respect to: "(8) Any other issuance of shares where the applicability of preemptive rights is impracticable."

27. Gower, Modern Company Law 346 (1954).

28. West's Ann.Cal.Corp.Code § 1106: "Unless the articles provide other-

provided in the articles,[29] or to a provision that unless otherwise provided there shall be no preemptive rights in specifically described situations.[30] Some statutes have spelled out in great detail the possibilities available, but usually with the broad exception, "unless otherwise provided by the articles." [31]

A grave danger exists today when options to purchase shares are so generously granted to high corporate officials because of the absence in some statutes of provisions to protect the shareholders from the granting of such wholesale rights. As Professor Frank Emerson has recently written of the Ohio statute: "In spite of current abuse and criticism of executive stock option and sales plans, no effective protection for shareholders has been provided. The only existing limitation, preemptive rights, may be denied by the articles of incorporation and are not applicable to treasury shares." [32]

Even in California where the preemptive right no longer exists except when specifically provided in the articles, the fiduciary principle that directors and officers may not use their positions for their own personal advantage, either to make a profit for themselves, to obtain or retain control, or to discriminate between shareholders, has its restraining influence on directorial action.[33] This, of course, is within the prophecy of an earlier writer who also wrote: "It is submitted that the law

wise, the board of directors may issue shares, option rights, or securities having conversion or option rights, without first offering them to shareholders of any class." And see § 1108 for special provisions in case of an employee stock-purchase plan. See also Burns' Ind.Ann.Stat. 1933, 1948 Repl. vol., 1957 Cum. Pocket Supp. § 25–205(i), which similarly abolishes preemptive rights.

29. Ill.Bus.Corp.Act § 24, as amended by L.1957, S.B. 266: "The preemptive right of a shareholder to acquire additional shares, whether then or thereafter authorized, of a corporation may be limited or denied to the extent provided in the articles of incorporation." Special provisions follow for employee stock-purchase plans. Somewhat similar is the A.L.I.Model Bus.Corp. Act § 24 (Rev.1953), but it specifically saves the preemptive right (unless otherwise provided in the articles) to "unissued or treasury shares" thus making certain that the right applies also to treasury shares.

30. Mich.Gen.Corp.Act § 31, as amended by L.1947, Act No. 209.

31. Ohio Rev.Code § 1701.15; 2B N.C. Gen.Stat.1957 Supp. § 55–56 ("(a) The charter may enlarge, limit or deny what would otherwise be the preemptive rights of shareholders." Then follows subpar. (b) providing specifically but with the usual "Except as otherwise provided in the charter or in this section," etc.) These two statutory sections of Ohio and North Carolina, both recently framed, offer an interesting comparison. For ample coverage and simplicity of statement, the Maryland statute warrants study. See Flack's Ann.Code of Md.1951, Art. 23, § 26.

32. Emerson, The New Ohio General Corporation Law: Some Comments and Some Comparisons, 24 U. of Cin.L.Rev. 463, at 475 (1955).

33. Schwab v. Schwab-Wilson Machine Corp., Ltd., 13 Cal.App.2d 1, 55 P.2d 1268 (1936). Likewise, as to the issue of treasury shares to change control. Elliott v. Baker, 194 Mass. 518, 80 N.E. 450 (1907).

should be changed by statute to require the incorporators to specify in the articles whether or not the preemptive right to subscribe to new shares is reserved, and if so for what classes of shares." [34] This would assure the closely held company of the important right of continued proportionate control except as outstanding shares changed hands. And the fiduciary principle would, in the main, protect shareholders where no preemptive rights existed. The publicly held corporation could then secure its financing without fear of injunction or mandatory order. Except as to those who believe in carrying corporate democracy to extreme limits of impracticality the results would seem to be good, and possible damage to shareholders remote.

Where, under a corporation's articles or under the common law without the aid of a statute preemptive rights exist, they may probably be eliminated by an amendment to the articles through the statutorily prescribed vote of the shareholders. The cases are not entirely uniform in this respect, but the general statutory authority to alter "special rights" and that which permits amendment to the extent that such provisions might have been originally placed in the articles have both been held sufficient to sustain the elimination of preemptive rights.[35] And some modern statutes permit amendment specifically to remove such rights.[36]

§ 13. The Preferred Share Contract

There is a basic rule that all shares of stock in a corporation are equal unless made otherwise by contract. Common shares, for example, are, without more, equal, each being entitled to the same dividend, voting rights, preemptive right to new issues, and to an equal distribution after creditors are paid upon dissolution. However, common shares are frequently classified as Class A and Class B, one class having no voting rights but both being equal in every other respect. Under such circumstances, there has in reality been created a preferred stock, for the voting

---

34. Drinker, The Preemptive Right of Shareholders to Subscribe to New Shares, 43 Harv.L.Rev. 586, at 615; 588 (1930).

35. Gottlieb v. Heyden Chemical Corp., 33 Del.Ch. 82, 92 et seq., 90 A.2d 660, at 666–667 (Sup.Ct.1952); Milwaukee Sanitarium v. Lynch, 238 Wis. 628, 300 N.W. 760, 138 A.L.R. 521 (1941), Ann., 138 A.L.R. 526 (1942), on "Stockholders' privilege as to acquisition of new issue of stock by corporation." But see Albrecht, Maguire & Co. v. General Plastics, Inc., 256 App.Div.

134, 9 N.Y.S.2d 415 (1939), aff'd without opinion, 280 N.Y. 840, 21 N.E.2d 887 (1939), requiring more specific statutory authority which is now supplied in N.Y.Stock Corp. Law § 35, subd. 2(H).

36. See Hodge v. Cuba Co., 142 N.J. Eq. 340, 60 A.2d 88 (1948), discussing the New Jersey statute. West's Ann.Cal.Corp.Code § 3601 (f), as amended by L.1957, c. 2261, § 17, permits amendments "to enlarge or restrict or revoke existing preemptive rights of any class or classes of shares."

right is a distinct and valuable preference. However, such voting shares, strangely enough, are not commonly labeled preferred shares.

The layman thinks of preferred stock in terms of preferences concerning dividends and perhaps of assets upon dissolution. But the preference possibilities are many, and, under modern statutes, several classes of preferred shares may be outstanding each with special preferences and each with a number of series with more limited preferences within the class. The possibilities are legion and they may be used in tailoring the preferential cloth to fit the financial occasion. In the last analysis, what preferences are given will be controlled by the necessity of the corporation and the public demand for shares sufficiently attractive to be purchased.

§ 14. Where is the Preferred Share Contract to be Found?

Unless by statutory command, the shareholder's contract may be found in the articles or certificate of incorporation, in the company's by-laws, in resolutions authorizing the issue of shares, in the share-certificate itself, or parts of the contract may be found in several of these. Modern statutes, however, have tended to require that the share-contract be placed in the articles or an amendment to them, which is the proper place for this important contract whether the statute requires it to be there or not.[37] The fact that the corporate charter constitutes a public record open to all who wish to inspect it, is reason enough, aside from its permanence. One should not have to search several documents or records to ascertain what the contract is. Thus, where the statute requires the share-contract to be in the charter, a by-law passed by the unanimous vote of the shareholders giving a preference cannot be effective in creating one.[38]

Modern statutes generally provide that the preferred share contract or a summary of its provisions be also contained in the share-certificate and, if other classes of shares are authorized, that their express terms or a summary thereof be placed there also.[39] If the statute requires more than a reference to the articles containing the contracts of perhaps several classes of preferred shares, and the naming of the place where a copy of the articles may be found, the stock certificate may be cluttered with fine print to the point where either a magnifying glass is necessary to read it or the certificate itself may be of near-newspaper

---

37. See 2B N.C.Gen.Stat.1957 Cum. Supp. § 55–7(4) and § 55–42; Ohio Rev.Code § 1701.04(A) (4) and § 1701.06; A.L.I. Model Bus.Corp. Act § 48(e) and (f) (Rev.1953).

38. Gaskill v. Gladys Belle Oil Co., 16 Del.Ch. 289, 146 A. 337 (1929).

39. Ohio Rev. Code (Gen.Corp.Law of 1955) § 1701.25; A.L.I. Model Bus.Corp.Act § 21 (Rev.1953).

size. Lawyers are hesitant to use a summary, when such is permitted, for fear of a later judicial castigation that the statement is less than the summary required.

§ 15.　Distinction between Preferred Shares and Debtor Obligations Such as Bonds

One who owns shares in a corporation is an owner, sometimes called an equitable owner, of the corporation. On the other hand, an owner of a bond, whether secured or unsecured, is a creditor entitled to compete for the corporate assets with other creditors and, if secured, to take precedence over the unsecured creditors. A shareholder, whether preferred or common, may not compete with corporate creditors, nor is he entitled to have his share purchased by the company, unless by virtue of a contract to purchase or redeem, and even then he will not be allowed to take advantage of such a contract when creditors will stand to lose thereby. When a shareholder shares in a distribution of a surplus he obtains a "dividend." The bondholder's return is by way of "interest" and this is payable out of any funds, whereas dividends are almost universally limited to payment out of excess values remaining after certain legally required deductions have been made and the stated capital item is taken into consideration.

The drafting problems are indicated by a number of rules which have come about through the interpretation of bungled drafts of the preferred contract. In recent years particularly some "bungling" seems to have been done intentionally so that, for federal income tax purposes, the share-contract would look like a debt rather than an ownership interest in the corporation.[40] Interest could then be deducted as an expense in arriving at taxable income. Thus, where "debenture stock" was issued with a promise to pay the par value at the end of the corporate existence, "interest" to be payable "out of profits only" but to be cumulative, stock to be redeemable on any "interest date" at $105 plus accrued "interest" thereon, such stock ranking after general creditors but prior to common stock upon dissolution, it was properly held that this was stock and not debtor long term paper and hence, for taxing purposes, the fund out of which interest had been paid was taxable corporate income.

Relevant points of emphasis are the manner of treatment by the parties, the maturity date of the par or principal amount and the right of the holder to enforce payment, the relative rank on dissolution—whether this security may compete with cor-

---

40. John Kelley Co. v. Comm'r, 326
U.S. 521, 66 S.Ct. 299, 90 L.Ed. 278
(1946).

porate creditors——, income payable only out of profits or out of any funds, participation in management and the right to vote. While bondholders may, under some statutes, be given voting rights, normally they have no such rights. The absence of voting rights through contractual removal is also a normal thing in preferred shares but, frequently, upon a stated condition of failure to pay dividends for a specified period, such shares are given, by the contract, a limited voting right. The factors of greatest significance in the determination that the "debenture stock" above was actually cumulative preferred stock and not a debt were the provisions limiting payment of "interest" to profits only, the placing of the holders in a secondary position to general creditors upon dissolution, thus sharing the risk which owners must share with their co-owners, and the lack of a maturity date and the right to enforce payment of the principal sum by some appropriate legal remedy.[41] The failure to fix a maturity date of the principal sum has frequently been emphasized as being of utmost significance in making the determination that the security is a share rather than a bond.[42] The fact that the instrument is called a share or a bond or the use of the term "interest" instead of "dividend," or the fact that it is redeemable either at the request or demand of the corporation or the owner, or any combination of these is significant only if the facts actually support the instrument in the basic essentials which the law has laid down.

A determination that the instrument is a bond rather than a share of stock is also important in liquidations and reorganizations under state and federal statutes for if it is a debt it will be entitled to a higher priority and thus share in the liquidation or reorganization whereas the share may, if the financial condition of the company is too bad, be wiped out. In federal bankruptcy proceedings there are also advantages in being a bondholder.[43]

41. Jordon Co. v. Allen, 85 F.Supp. 437 (D.Ga.1949). See also Com'r v. Schmoll Fils Associated, Inc., 110 F.2d 611 (2d Cir., 1940), noted in 40 Col.L.Rev. 1084 (1940); Jewel Tea Co., Inc. v. United States, 90 F.2d 451, 112 A.L.R. 182 (2d Cir., 1937).

42. Ibid.; O'Neal v. Automobile Piston & Parts Co., 188 Ga. 380, 4 S.E. 2d 40, 123 A.L.R. 850 (1939); U. S. v. South Georgia Ry. Co., 107 F.2d 3 (5th Cir., 1939) (No fixed maturity date but "interest" was payable out of capital when necessary). And see Helvering, Com'r v. Richmond, F. & P. R. Co. infra, note 44, where there was no fixed maturity date.

43. See Ballantine, Lattin and Jennings, Cases and Materials on Corporations, Introductory Note, 686–687 (2d ed. 1953).

§ 16. The Effect of "Guaranteed" Dividends or a Contract to Redeem upon a Stated Date

When the corporate issuer contracts to pay dividends in terms guaranteeing the payment of them, subscribers to such shares are likely to be misled by assuming that the guarantee assures a flow of dividends as long as the company has *any funds* available. If this were so, the shareholder would be in a position comparable to that of the bondholder. And if, added to his supposed valid contract of guarantee, his contract calls for redemption on a stated date, he may be misled into believing that, as in case of a bond, an absolute maturity date has been set for the payment of the principal amount.

Probably the most that the issuer's contract of guarantee can mean is that the shareholder has a cumulative preferred share which would have been so without the guarantee, provided his contract contained nothing contrariwise.[44] The issuer can only pay dividends out of the profits or surpluses which the jurisdiction of corporate birth permits. If the contract specifically calls for payment out of capital, the agreement would be held unlawful and void; that is, provided the contract is a share-contract and not a bond. And the redemption provision which seems to say that upon the date specified the amount stated will be paid and the share redeemed is necessarily limited to payment out of funds from which redemption may be made in the jurisdiction of corporate birth, and both the common law and statutory provisions tend to permit redemption out of capital if creditors will not be injured in the process. Hence, there is a limitation which the subscriber to such shares may not suspect.

A distinction must be made, however, between guarantees made by the issuer and those made by others, whether natural persons or corporations. Such guarantees may be valid but in the case of the guarantee made by another corporation there is still the problem of whether such guarantees are intra vires. Modern statutes have frequently given specific authority to do this, particularly when the guarantee is upon a subsidiary's or parent's shares.[45] And, of course, if the guarantee has a close enough connection with the guarantor's business so that it can be said to be reasonably necessary or conducive to that business, it may thus avoid the ultra vires objection.

---

44. See the excellent discussion of these problems by Rogers, J., in Hazel Atlas Glass Co. v. Van Dyk & Reeves, Inc., 8 F.2d 716 (2d Cir., 1925), cert. denied 269 U.S. 570, 46 S.Ct. 26, 70 L.Ed. 417 (1925). But see Helvering, Com'r v. Richmond, F. & P. R. Co., 90 F.2d 971 (4th Cir., 1937).

45. Ibid. The guarantee of payment of dividends in this case was by two natural persons. See page 180, supra, for a discussion of surety and guaranty promises by corporations.

§ 17. The Cumulative Preferred Contract

The term "cumulative preferred" has acquired a well-understood meaning in the law. It means that dividends accumulate at the rate agreed upon for all years following the issue of the shares without regard to whether a fund exists out of which payment might have been made and that such dividends must be paid before any dividend may be paid upon the common shares.[46] Thus, if for any reason the cumulative preferred dividend is not paid for one or more years in the past, and there is a fund out of which such a dividend might be paid in the present year, the directors, if they now declare a dividend, must first declare and pay the full amount of the accumulation to the preferred before they may pay one to the common or other junior shareholders. They can, of course, declare a dividend of less than the full amount to the preferred with a carry-over to the future but they cannot declare a dividend upon the common shares until eventually the full accumulated dividend is paid the preferred shareholders. Thus, the cumulative preferred dividend does not depend upon whether it was earned in any particular year just so a fund eventually exists out of which a dividend may be legally declared.

As long as corporate earnings are sufficiently great to pay dividends thus contracted for as they come due and to pay reasonable dividends to the junior shares, there is clear sailing. But where cumulative dividends have piled up because of economic distress and there is little hope of ever paying them or at least of paying anything upon the common shares for a long period, drastic reformation of the preferred shareholder's contract is sometimes sought through shareholder action directed at fundamental change. This topic is discussed at another point in this book and need not be repeated here.[47] But the possibility of protecting the preferred shareholder against such a fundamental change should be mentioned. The requirement in his contract that, for such a change, all shares of his class shall have a vote with the additional provision that, before such a change may be made, a large proportion of the shares of his class must vote affirmatively for such change will at least give some assurance that there will not be hasty judgment by the junior shareholders who see no dividends in sight for years to come if payment must first be made of the accumulated dividends to the preferred. Some statutes give voting rights to classes of shares which may be prejudiced by the fundamental change, whether or not the shares in such classes have voting rights in other situa-

---

46. Bank of America v. West End Chemical Co., 37 Cal.App.2d 685, 100 P.2d 318 (1940).

47. See Chapter 11, infra.

tions. But not all statutes give even a vote upon such an occasion, so the drafting problem becomes important in any case.

It takes no words of art to create cumulative preferred shares and a simple statement that dividends at the specified rate per annum shall be paid prior to the payment of any dividends upon the common shares, and that such dividends shall be cumulative, will suffice. A usual provision is that the dividend shall be so much per annum payable at designated quarterly periods or payable semi-annually at stated dates, or when, as and if declared by the board of directors. But no matter how positive the statement is that the company will pay such a dividend, before the board may make a declaration of it there must be a fund from which dividends may be legally declared and paid.[48] And if there is no fund, the dividend will have to be passed by the board, the cumulation being payable out of proper funds acquired at a later date.

A simple rule has become established that if the contract calls for payment of dividends prior to the payment of common dividends, the result is cumulative preferred stock without further words or terminology.[49] Or, as was succinctly put by Circuit Judge Rogers: ". . . unless a contrary intention appears, dividends on preferred stock are cumulative, and arrearages in one year are payable in subsequent years, when there are sufficient profits, before dividends can be paid on the common stock.".[50]

Unlike a bondholder's voting right (if any) which must be given specifically in his contract, the preferred shareholder has a voting right unless it has been taken away by his contract.[51] This is based upon the rule that all shares are equal unless made unequal by contract. But even this rule has its limitations. Suppose the preferred contract does not mention any participation in dividends beyond the amount stated in the contract and the preferred and common shareholders have been paid an amount equal to the annual dividend called for by the preferred contract. May the board declare a further dividend out of proper funds to the common shareholders alone or must there be equal participation in whatever additional is declared? A similar problem also arises upon liquidation of a corporation if a sufficient fund remains after the payment of creditors and the expense of liquidation and the preferred shareholder, as is usually the case, has a contract calling for payment of the par value of his shares prior to the

48. See page 467 et seq. for a discussion of the legal funds available for dividends.

49. Hazel Atlas Glass Co. v. Van Dyk & Reeves, Inc., supra note 44.

50. Ibid. at 720.

51. Ibid.

payment of anything to the common shareholders. Practically all of the case authority has held that, unless participation rights beyond the stated dividend or liquidation preferences are specifically provided for, there are no participation rights in either situation.[52]   However, in drafting a preferred contract it is wise to state that the dividend is so much per annum "and no more" and, likewise, that upon dissolution the par value and an amount equal to the undeclared but accrued dividends "and no more" shall first be paid to the preferred shareholder, the remainder to go to the common shareholders. If there are several classes of preferred, the statements will vary but if there is no participating preferred, a clause should make this clear. And if it is intended to make a class of preferred a participating preferred the amount of participation should be specifically stated.

One preference which is usually included in the cumulative preferred shareholder's contract is payment of the capital contribution and the accrued unpaid dividends prior to a distribution of assets to the common shareholders upon dissolution. Junior shareholders argued that the term "dividends" carried with it the same requirement of a legally proper fund out of which dividends might be declared and paid when the company was a going concern, and some early authority supported this argument. But most modern authority has done a better job analyzing the probable meaning of the term when used in connection with priority in payment upon a dissolution. The creditors must always be paid before assets may be distributed to preferred or common shareholders upon dissolution. After their payment, there is nothing to prevent the distribution of the balance remaining in any way the contracting parties agree. In effect, the recent cases have interpreted such provisions as if they gave a dissolution preference of the capital contribution plus "an amount equal to the accrued, undeclared dividends." [53] Wise draftsmanship would at least avoid the term "dividends" unless qualified to show that payment upon dissolution may be made out of assets of the corporation, whether or not there is a surplus or other legally prescribed fund out of which a going concern might pay

---

52. James F. Powers Foundry Co. v. Miller, 166 Md. 590, 171 A. 842 (1934).   Contra: Sternbergh v. Brock, 225 Pa. 279, 74 A. 166 (1908). Scottish Ins. Corp. v. Wilsons & Clyde, [1949] A.C. 462; Re Isle of Thanet Elect. Co., [1949] 2 All.E.R. 1060. Both English cases held that preferred shares with preferences upon dissolution were not entitled to participate beyond their liquidation preference unless participation was spelled out in the contract. Earlier English cases held a contrary view and permitted participation beyond the liquidation preference on dissolution. Gower, Modern Company Law 361 (1954); Ballantine, Corporations 508 (Rev. ed. 1946).

53. Penington v. Commonwealth Hotel Const. Corp., 17 Del.Ch. 394, 155 A. 514, 75 A.L.R. 1136 (1931); Hay v. Hay, 38 Wash.2d 513, 230 P.2d 791 (1951).

dividends. It should be said that when the preferred contract contains no statement of any preferences upon dissolution the preferred and common shares will share proportionately in the distribution of assets, each share being equal since no provision of the contract made them unequal.

What constitutes dissolution, liquidation or a winding-up should be specifically spelled out in the contract. In the absence of such a provision, it has usually been held that a merger, consolidation, or sale of all the assets of a corporation for shares in the purchasing corporation, thus making it a holding company, is not a dissolution coming within the scope of the term used in the contract creating the dissolution preference.[54] The term so used in the preferred share contract means statutory or judicial dissolution (in some jurisdictions) as inherent in a court of equity. Good draftsmanship demands that an express exception of mergers, consolidations, and sales or leases of the corporate assets be made.

§ 18.　The Non-cumulative Preferred Contract

An elementary rule applicable to dividends is that the board has the discretion to declare or not to declare them. Unless there is an abuse of this discretion, a thing which courts have not frequently found, the board's determination is final. The application of this rule to the most common type of non-cumulative preferred stock—the discretionary dividend type—has been the source of much controversy. Contrary to cumulative preferred stock, if there was no fund from which dividends could have been declared in a particular year, such shares may not later receive that year's dividend from a fund realized at a prior or later period. And if a smaller dividend has been paid than the contract provided for, the deficit cannot later be recouped from past or future earnings. But quite as important and much more dangerous is another basic majority rule, applicable to the optional dividend type of non-cumulative shares, that when the directors, in the proper exercise of their powers to declare or not to declare a dividend, pass one, it is gone forever though there was a fund out of which it might legally have been declared and paid.[55] Thus, it is accurate today to state that, on this type of

---

54. Buck v. Kleiber Motor Co., 97 F.2d 557, 98 F.2d 903 (9th Cir., 1938) (sale of assets); Windhurst v. Central Leather Co., 105 N.J.Eq. 621, 149 A. 36 (Ch.1930) (merger); Anderson v. Cleveland-Cliffs Iron Co., 87 N.E.2d 384, at 395–396 (Ohio App. 1948) (consolidation).

55. It was thought that Wabash Railway Co. v. Barclay, 280 U.S. 197, 50 S.Ct. 106, 74 L.Ed. 368 (1930), left, at least, a small hope that the directors had the power later to declare out of a fund by-passed originally by them, but still remaining at a subsequent dividend paying period, a past dividend. Mr. Justice Holmes had stated that "the claim for that year is gone and cannot be asserted at a later

non-cumulative preferred stock, dividends do not accumulate if not paid, whether earned or not.[56]   And it does not matter whether the board has determined to use the fund from which dividends might have been declared upon capital improvements or for other legitimate purposes; or because it is thought unwise this year to distribute the fund in dividends. It may be needed as working capital. The question of the necessity for so doing has no bearing on the legal rule.[57]

Apparently the abuse of directorial discretion is the only argument this type of non-cumulative preferred shareholder has to upset the board's determination. And, due to the harshness of the result of the application of the rule, courts should listen with a sympathetic ear to assertions of abuse of discretion. In fact, what might well not be considered an abuse of discretion in failing to declare a dividend on cumulative preferred shares might, quite as well, be considered an abuse of discretion in case of non-cumulative shares. With the law as it is, there should be no market for such shares. They have been used frequently in reorganizations where the security holders of the defunct corporation had no choice in the matter.

As we have seen, any language which indicates that dividends are to be cumulative, no matter what the phraseology, will create cumulative dividend shares. Where dividends are, by the contract, chargeable against net earnings and surplus generally, such dividends are cumulative.[58] But if they are payable only from the earnings of each year, being allocable only to that year, they are non-cumulative. Good draftsmanship, however, would incdlude the word "non-cumulative" in addition to other terms indicating that such dividends may be declared and paid only out of profits of the year when earned.

Less dangerous to the shareholder is non-cumulative preferred stock of the mandatory type. The contract may impose a duty upon the board to declare dividends to the extent of the funds available for the particular year, that is, to the extent of

---

date," and that "the right for that year was gone." See W. H. S. Stevens, The Discretion of Directors in the Distribution of Non-cumulative Preferred Dividends, 24 Geo.L.J. 371, at 377–379 (1936); ibid., Rights of Non-cumulative Preferred Stockholders, 34 Col.L. Rev. 1439, at 1446–1447 (1934). But Guttman v. Illinois Central R. Co., 189 F.2d 927 (2d Cir., 1951), cert. denied 342 U.S. 867, 72 S.Ct. 107, 96 L.Ed. 652 (1951), struck down the hope by holding that directors had no such discretionary power.

56. The present writer has questioned whether such stock should be termed "preferred." See Lattin, Is Non-cumulative Preferred Stock in Fact Preferred? 25 Ill.L. Rev. 148 (1930).

57. Guttman v. Illinois Central R. Co., supra, note 55.

58. In re Louisville Gas & Elect. Co., 77 F.Supp. 176 (D.Del.1948); Garrett v. Edge Moor Iron Co., 22 Del.Ch. 142, 194 A. 15 (Ch.1937), aff'd sub nom. Pennsylvania Co. for Insurances, etc. v. Cox, 23 Del. Ch. 193, 199 A. 671 (Sup.Ct.1938).

the earnings of the particular year. This prevents the passing of a dividend and its consequent loss by taking from the directors their discretion in passing such dividends when they are possible of declaration.

Besides the discretionary and mandatory types of non-cumulative preferred stock is one which has grown up in New Jersey, sometimes called the "dividend credit" or "cumulative-if-earned" type. Under the New Jersey view, the board has the discretion to pass a dividend which might have been paid to the non-cumulative preferred shareholders but, if it does, a dividend credit to the extent that the fund was capable of paying such a dividend results. From such dividend credits, dividends in arrears on non-cumulative shares must first be paid before common shareholders are entitled to any.[59] But earnings which have been retained for corporate uses and upon which there is a "dividend credit" may be partially or entirely lost in carrying on the business and, if they are, the non-cumulative preferred shareholders have no claim upon subsequent earnings to replenish what had previously been a dividend credit.[60]

The New Jersey dividend credit rule, according to some commentators, had its origin in a statute which authorized the issue of preferred shares and contained a command that "the corporation shall set apart or pay the said dividends to the holders of non-cumulative preferred stock before any dividends shall be paid on the common stock." [61] But the court, in the case just cited, thought that the statute was neither more nor less than a definition of the equitable rights of the preferred shareholders. The statute has since been amended but this has had no apparent influence on the cases, and the statutory origin of the rule, if such it is, seems to have been forgotten.[62]

There have been dicta in some recent New Jersey decisions indicating inroads upon the dividend credit theory. Thus, in *Dohme v. Pacific Coast Co.* it was said:[63] "Annual net earnings or surplus consisting of withheld annual net earnings may in

59. Sanders v. Cuba Railroad Co., 21 N.J. 78, 120 A.2d 849 (1956), is the most recent important case on the New Jersey view and contains citations to all of the important earlier cases in that state.

60. Justice Jacobs in Sanders v. Cuba Railroad Co., supra, note 59, recognized this sharing of losses by the non-cumulative shareholders.

61. See Moran v. United States Cast Iron Pipe & Foundry Co., 95 N.J. Eq. 389, at 395, 123 A. 546 (1924), quoting the statute.

62. The statutory origin is not mentioned in Justice Jacobs' opinion in Sanders v. Cuba Railroad Co., supra, note 59.

63. 5 N.J.Super. 477, 68 A.2d 490, at 497 (1949). See also Agnew v. American Ice Co., 2 N.J. 291, 66 A.2d 330, 10 A.L.R.2d 232 (1949). Compare Lich v. United States Rubber Co., 39 F.Supp. 675 (D.N. J.1941), aff'd 123 F.2d 145 (3d Cir., 1941).

the discretion of the directors be applied to legitimate corporate
purposes such as payment of debts, reduction of deficits, capital
improvements or extensions, and other ordinary business requirements, and to the extent that they are so used the inchoate
right of non-cumulative preferred stockholders in such funds
is lost or terminated." However, it is believed that such dicta
are unfounded and that Justice Jacobs has pointed the ultimate
path of the New Jersey decisions when he emphasized the equitable factors which, he felt, played a significant part in the development of the dividend credit doctrine, and stated specifically
that if a position contrary to the true dividend credit theory as
previously formulated be taken, "then the board of directors may
largely nullify the effectiveness of the dividend credit doctrine
by its manner of handling annual profits which have been earned
but have not been declared as dividends on non-cumulative preferred stock." [64]   And, at another point he asserts: "This much
is quite apparent—if the common stockholders, who generally
control the corporation and will benefit most by the passing of
the dividends on the preferred stock, may freely achieve that
result without any dividend credit consequences, then the preferred stockholders will be substantially at the mercy of others
who will be under temptation to act in their own self-interest." [65]

In drafting provisions for non-cumulative preferred contracts, care should be taken in making specific what type of
non-cumulative contract is intended. The discretionary dividend
type should make clear the power of the board to pass non-cumulative dividends and that once passed they are gone forever. The
mandatory type should be expressed in such language that when
a fund is available from which dividends may be declared, the
directors must declare a dividend to the extent of the fund. If
a dividend credit is to be set up, the contract should be specific
in setting it up and in protecting it against such invasions as
the dicta in a few New Jersey cases have indicated. There is no
good reason why a court which has a contract as general as those
frequently found in non-cumulative provisions to interpret should
not accept the view of the New Jersey courts on equitable grounds
of fairness. It has always seemed doubtful to this writer that
the term "non-cumulative" had such a fixed meaning that it could
not be so interpreted.[66] However, the manner in which the contract is stated may require the interpretation that once a dividend is legitimately passed, it is gone forever.

---

64. Sanders v. Cuba Railroad Co.,
supra, note 59, 120 A.2d at 853.
See also Note, New Jersey Dividend
Credit for Non-cumulative Preferred Stock, 55 Mich.L.Rev. 132
(1956).

65. Ibid. at 852.

66. Lattin, Is Non-cumulative Preferred Stock in Fact Preferred?
25 Ill.L.Rev. 148 (1930).

§ 19. Redemption Provisions in Preferred Shares—Callable Common Shares

Preferred shares of whatever kind usually carry a provision for redemption upon the demand of the corporation, occasionally at the request of the shareholder. If there is no provision for redemption, preferred, like common shares, are not redeemable. If such shares are to be regained by the corporation it must purchase them from shareholders who consent to sell, or receive them as a gift, and in either case they become treasury shares. It is unusual to find common shares with a call or redemption provision and under some corporation statutes it is not legally possible to make them redeemable by a provision in the contract.[67] However, a recent Massachusetts decision has sustained an amendment to the corporate charter making common shares redeemable, the corporation being one incorporated under the local statute.[68] The redemption device in common shares may be useful in case of employee stock purchase plans and in corporations where the stock is closely held and it is desired to keep it that way.

Even if the corporation statute permits it, it is poor policy to draft a redemption provision giving the shareholder the right to demand or request redemption. His demand may be made at a time when funds exist out of which redemption can be made but when the corporation sorely needs to keep its funds intact. Redemption provisions should always give the corporation the option of redeeming upon the conditions stated and thus preserve to it the right of choice of time and circumstances. Some statutes indicate that the contract must give the corporation the option.[69]

Redemption is based upon contract and its terms must be strictly followed in the calling of stock for this purpose.[70] Thus, where the right to redeem does not arise until a stated date has been reached, the corporation may not make its demand and force compliance before that time.[71] And if it does not make its elec-

---

67. Starring v. American Hair & Felt Co., 21 Del.Ch. 380, 191 A. 887 (Ch.1937), aff'd on opinion below, 21 Del.Ch. 431, 2 A.2d 249 (Sup. Ct. 1937).

68. Lewis v. H. P. Hood & Sons, Inc., 331 Mass. 670, 121 N.E.2d 850, 48 A.L.R.2d 383, Ann. at 392 (1954). See Note, Callable Common Stock, 68 Harv.L.Rev. 1240 (1955), which gives some excellent practical reasons supporting callable common stock. Policy questions are considered from page 1244.

69. West's Ann.Cal.Corp.Code § 1101, as amended by L.1957, c. 2261, § 4, states that "the right of redemption shall be exercisable at the option of the corporation only . . . ." But the same section permits compulsory redemption contracts to redeem out of sinking funds established for that purpose.

70. State ex rel. Waldeman v. Miller-Wohl Co., 3 Terry (42 Del.) 73, 28 A.2d 148 (Del.Super.Ct.1942).

71. Matter of Colby v. Imbrie & Co., Ltd., 126 Misc. 457, 214 N.Y.S. 53

tion to redeem within a reasonable time after the date set, the court may hold that the right to redeem has been lost.[72] The corporation may not delay unreasonably (nor may the shareholder when he has the option) and thus take advantage of what the future may offer. Furthermore, if the contract provides for redemption "whether by lot or pro rata or otherwise," the court is pretty likely to do what the Delaware court did with such a provision and hold that the method chosen must be "by lot, by pro rata, or in like manner," thus doing violence to what the draftsman may have intended by the use of the words "or otherwise."[73]

Provisions which state a day certain for redemption or those which give the shareholder the option of redemption upon demand are sometimes called compulsory redemption provisions for, in effect, the shares must be redeemed if there is a fund from which this may be legally done. Thus, where such a fund exists, if the board is unwilling to use it to redeem, the court will force the board to do so.[74] Creditors, of course, must be protected for the shareholder does not acquire a creditor status by virtue of the redemption provision. It has been said that "A preferred stockholder, in his relation to the creditors of a corporation, is not a creditor of such corporation, and cannot as against the creditors enforce any right he may have against the corporation. However, as between him and the corporation, or the other stockholders in it, there is no good reason why he should not be treated as a creditor where he has a demand against the corporation which can only be enforced as a debt."[75] A compulsory redemption provision was "the demand" in the case quoted from and, while the corporation was apparently in bad shape financially, no allegation had been made by the defendants of present insolvency or that the redemption would make it insolvent. Summary judgment for the plaintiff was sustained. In case of compulsory redemption, the burden of proving that there is not a fund from which the redemption may legally be made is usually placed upon the corporation or those resisting payment.

While a general majority rule pertaining to the purchase of its own shares by a corporation requires that the purchase be out of surplus and not out of capital, redemption has been held

(Sup.Ct.1926), aff'd 216 App.Div. 713, 214 N.Y.S. 819 (1926).

72. Corporation was given option to redeem "at the end of five years" but attempted to redeem some 12 years later. The court held that the phrase contemplated that redemption would be made within a reasonable time after 5 years.

Thompson v. Fairleigh, 300 Ky. 144, 187 S.W.2d 812 (1945).

73. State ex rel. Waldeman v. Miller-Wohl Co., supra, note 70.

74. Mueller v. Kraeuter & Co., 131 N.J.Eq. 475, 25 A.2d 874 (1942).

75. Schneider v. Foster-Thornburg Hdwe. Co., 33 F.Supp. 271, at 272 (D.W.Va.1940).

legally possible out of capital provided creditors are protected. Thus, in redemption, the stated capital item may generally be ignored and if the reasonable value of the corporate assets exceeds corporate liabilities with a balance sufficient to pay for the shares redeemed, and with a reasonable probability that creditors will not be injured, the redemption will be legal. Modern statutes, with some variation, have permitted a redemption from funds which could not have been used for dividend purposes or for the purchase of the corporation's own shares except in a few exceptional cases.[76]

It is important to note that either a purchase or redemption of its shares by a corporation out of any but a surplus fund has the practical effect of reducing capital without going through the prescribed procedures for doing this. However, unless such shares are formally retired and the stated capital reduced in accordance with the statutory provisions, the reacquired shares are treated as treasury shares. As such, they are not assets and, if carried as such on the corporate books and balance sheets, this would not only constitute erroneous accounting but would also give a false impression of the condition of the company. Until reissued, these shares are, like other unissued shares, pieces of paper without present value.

An even greater problem arises when a corporation redeems shares under a contract by which it has promised to pay a premium and back dividends, for example to redeem $100 par value shares at $110, if redemption is had prior to a stated date, plus arrearages of cumulative dividends. What funds may properly be used to pay the premium and dividend components? Some statutes specifically provide for the reduction of stated capital by retiring shares upon redemption and charging the stated capital account with an amount not to exceed the capital represented by the shares.[77] General statutes providing for a reduc-

---

76. West's Ann.Cal.Corp.Code §§ 1706, 1708 (redemption may be made from capital plus a few exceptional cases of purchases of its own shares). West's Ann.Cal.Corp. Code § 1708 protects liquidation preferences of shares remaining outstanding which have prior or equal claims to the assets. 2B N.C. Gen.Stat., 1957 Cum.Supp. § 55–52; Ohio Rev.Code § 1701.35(B) permits the corporation to purchase its own shares or to redeem them out of capital, but adequately protects creditors; A.L.I.Model Bus. Corp. Act § 60 (redemption) and § 5 (purchase of its own shares) (Rev.1953).

77. Del.Gen.Corp.Law § 243, as amended in L.1955, c. 467, § 2; Ohio Rev.Code § 1701.35(A) (1) and (B), the latter subsection limiting redemption to the stated capital represented by the redeemed shares, any premium on back dividends coming necessarily from surpluses from which dividend distributions could be made. Under § 1701.36(B), redeemable shares "redeemed, purchased or otherwise acquired" are deemed retired, and by § 1701.31(A) stated capital is reduced "by an amount equal to the stated capital of such" shares. Under A.L.I.Model Bus. Corp. Act

tion of stated capital would normally be sufficient for this purpose without the special authorization. But neither type of
statute covers the payment of accrued dividend and premium
components. Surpluses capable of use in the payment of dividends, whether limited to earned surplus or extending more widely to paid-in surplus or reduction surplus, could be used (and
would have to be) for the payment of accrued dividends. But
any surplus which might be legally distributed to shareholders
could be used to pay the premium component.

An interesting problem arises when the board unconditional-
ly calls for redemption all or a part of a redeemable issue in
accordance with the terms of the contract and later attempts
to rescind its action. It has been held that directors have no
power to modify or rescind their previous call since, like the
declaration of a dividend out of a proper fund, the board action
has created a debt in favor of the shareholder.[78] And, where a
solvent corporation gave its promissory note to redeem some of
its shares, but later became insolvent, the shareholder was permitted to assert his claim as a creditor since the debt had been
created at a time when legally the corporation could redeem its
shares.[79] Had the promissory note been given for shares purchased rather than redeemed, the rule sustained by the great
weight of authority is that a proper fund must exist at the time
of payment, not simply at the time of executing the note, for the
purchase to be held legal.[80] There is no good reason for the
distinction.

§ 61, shares redeemed are cancelled
but the filing of a statement of cancellation restores them to the status
of authorized but unissued shares
unless the articles provide that they
shall not be reissued. If the articles provide for no reissue of the
shares, the filing of the statement
of cancellation constitutes an
amendment to the articles and has
the effect of reducing "the number
of shares of the class so cancelled
which the corporation is authorized
to issue by the number of shares
so cancelled." This effects a reduction of stated capital. Under
§ 60, a redemption may not be made
by an insolvent corporation (see
§ 2(n) where "insolvent" is defined
as inability to pay debts as they
mature) nor when the redemption
would make it insolvent, nor upon
one other stated exception aimed
at protecting other shareholders
with claims on involuntary dissolution.

78. Taylor v. Axton-Fisher Tobacco
Co., 295 Ky. 226, 173 S.W.2d 377,
148 A.L.R. 834 (1943); Fox v. Johnson & Wimsatt, Inc., 127 F.2d 729
(D.C.Cir., 1942).

79. Campbell v. Grant Trust & Savings Co., 97 Ind.App. 169, 182 N.E.
267 (1932).

80. The general rule is well discussed in Robinson v. Wangeman,
75 F.2d 756, at 757 (5th Cir., 1935).
Contra, but standing practically
alone is Wolff v. Heidritter Lumber
Co., 112 N.J.Eq. 34, 163 A. 140 (1932).
The majority holdings permit American corporations to purchase their
own shares. American law is practically alone in permitting this
practice. In fact, in many countries, the purchase is a penal of-
fense. Nussbaum, Acquisitions by
a Corporation of its Own Stock,
35 Col.L.Rev. 971, at 976, 991–992
(1935). Levy, Purchase by Corpora-

§ 20. Sinking Funds for Redemption Purposes

Like bonds, preferred share contracts may contain provisions for the setting aside of a specified proportion of annual earnings for the purpose of redeeming preferred shares. In fact, for sinking fund redemption purposes, funds legally available, whether from surplus, annual earnings, or from stated capital, may be used.[81] Provisions will vary, but commonly dividends to date will first be required to be paid to the preferred shareholders and then a certain percentage of what remains of the funds available for redemption will be required to be set aside for redemption purposes prior to the payment of dividends upon junior issues. Or the contract may call for the setting aside of a certain proportion of the total par or redemption price of the preferred shares. In any case, a common provision prohibits the setting aside of a redemption fund as long as any dividends remain unpaid on the preferred shares.

It has been held that the mere setting aside of a fund by depositing it into a special bank account in trust for the preferred shareholders whose shares are to be redeemed, does not in itself create a debtor-creditor relationship between the corporation and its shareholders; consequently, where the depository-bank failed prior to payment, the corporation was still contractually bound to redeem and pay for its preferred shares.[82] However, this must necessarily depend upon whether the sinking or redemption fund is merely additional security offered the preferred shareholder or whether the trustee was created as the agent of the shareholders rather than of the corporation.[83] The contract should be definite on this point for, without the shareholder's consent to the appointment of an agent to receive the fund for him, the argument would appear to be in his favor that the fund is held in trust for the corporation, not for him. That is, that the fund is merely security for redemption. Thus payments into a redemption fund do not discharge the obligation unless a contrary intent is shown in the agreement.[84]

§ 21. Convertible Preferred Shares

Whereas the redemption provision permits the corporation to regain its preferred shares and thus give to the common shareholders who bear the greater risk the position of sole owners, a provision which permits the conversion of preferred shares into

tion of Its Own Stock, 15 Minn.L. Rev. 1 at 38 (1930), favors the minority American doctrine in his very thorough article on this subject.

81. Buxbaum, Preferred Stock—Law and Draftsmanship, 42 Calif.L.Rev. 243, at 269 (1954).

82. La Salle Hotel Realty Co. v. Taft, 85 F.2d 339 (7th Cir., 1936), noted in 23 Va.L.Rev. 333 (1937).

83. Note, Sinking Funds, 24 Va.L. Rev. 293, at 299 (1938).

84. Ibid. at 300.

common gives the preferred shareholder the opportunity to take advantage of a successful venture by giving up whatever rights he has under his preferred contract for the rights of a common shareholder. The contract will state the time during which and the conditions under which conversion may be had, including a statement of the number of shares of common he may acquire for his preferred shares. In the redemption provision some point must be stated at which shareholder interests cease, usually upon demand and offer of payment, or demand and deposit of an amount in trust for the shareholder for payment to him. If there is a redemption as well as a conversion clause, a point at which conversion is no longer possible—perhaps upon the call for redemption or after a stated period following a call for re-demption—should be included so that no conversion may be made after that time.

Convertible preferred shares also need protection against possible dilution of the shares which the preferred shareholder may obtain by his option to convert. If such shares are split or there are stock dividends, he should, on conversion, be able to obtain the proportionate number of shares he would have obtained had he converted prior to the split or dividend. If there is a reduction in their par value or in their stated value, an adjust-ment should be possible so that his conversion right will not suffer. Merger or consolidation may defeat his right and pro-tection is needed in such a change. The problems are many, and, in case of convertible shares, the contractual provisions are of necessity somewhat complicated.[85] An imaginative draftsman will visualize the possibilities and will leave little to the imagina-tion of the parties or of the judge who may later have to interpret his draft.

§ 22. Classes and Series of Shares—"Blank" Stock

A new class of shares not yet provided for by the articles must be authorized by the shareholders. If there are outstanding common and preferred shares, or perhaps several classes of preferred shares, their terms may be changed only upon a vote by shareholders in the prescribed statutory manner. Even if several classes have been authorized by the articles but as yet have not been issued, a shareholders' vote on an amendment to change the dividend rate, the redemption provisions, the voting rights, etc., would be necessary unless a simpler method of doing this has been authorized. And today, statutes frequently per-mit shares to be issued in series within a class giving power to the directors, if the articles so provide, to supply certain of the

85. On drafting problems generally see Buxbaum, op. cit. supra note 67a, and for convertible preferred,

contract terms such as the rate of dividend, rate of redemption, dissolution terms, etc., so that there will be that elasticity necessary to procure funds quickly and without shareholder action on terms which the then market warrants. Because of the authorization of the directors to supply many of the terms, this is sometimes called "blank stock."

The new North Carolina statute is illustrative of the trend in such statutes. It provides for classes and series within classes. It requires either express charter authorization or shareholder resolution to give the directors the power to fix preferences, limitations and relative rights of the shares of each class (if not already fixed) provided for in the charter and to establish series within classes when they have not already been established. If the directors are given the power without limitation, they may prescribe the preferences, limitations and relative rights of the authorized classes. They may create series within the classes. But "all shares of the same class shall be identical except as to the following relative rights and preferences, as to which there may be variations between different series within a class: (1) The rate of dividend. (2) The price at and the terms and conditions on which shares may be redeemed. (3) The amount payable upon shares in the event of involuntary liquidation. (4) The amount payable upon shares in event of voluntary liquidation. (5) Sinking fund provisions for the redemption or purchase of shares. (6) The terms and conditions on which shares may be converted, if the shares of any series are issued with the privilege of conversion." [86] Other provisions protect already issued preferred shares in certain respects. Authority is specifically limited to supplying terms in case of unissued shares, no power being granted to make changes in issued shares. A "Statement of Classification of Shares" is required to be executed and filed with the Secretary of State.[87] This must be done prior to the issue of such shares. The shareholders may thus give the directors broad powers in writing the share contracts or keep a good deal or all of the power in themselves. Other statutes of a similar nature exist, the Delaware statute being perhaps the broadest and the most dangerous in its possibilities.[88]

---

see page 279 et seq. An excellent analysis of the problems involved in preparing a preferred share contract will be found in Jennings' P-H Students Corporation Law Service, page 12,002 and following.

86. 2B N.C.Gen.Stat., 1957 Cum. Supp. § 55–41.

87. Ibid. § 55–42(c), (d) and (e).

88. Del.Corp.Law of 1953, § 151 as amended by L.1957, c. 121, § 4. See Berle's criticism of the undue breadth of the Delaware provision in Corporate Devices for Diluting Stock Participations, 31 Col.L.Rev. 1239, at 1264 (1931); and of the New York and Delaware provisions in Berle and Warren, Cases and Materials on the Law of Business

§ 23. Voting Rights of Preferred Shares

The contract usually provides that the exclusive voting power for the election of directors, and for all other purposes, shall be possessed by the holders of common stock unless the company shall be in default in respect to the declaration and payment of a stated number of quarterly, semi-annual or annual dividends. Then, a voting right may be given until all back dividends are declared and paid, the right varying from an exclusive voting right to elect directors (and for all other purposes) during the period of default, to a more limited right of participating in the vote with the common shareholders, a right which offers little protection unless the common shares are fewer in number than the preferred, or perhaps extending to a right to elect a certain number of board members during the period of default.[89] Such contracts should be clear as to what, if any, conditions precedent must be met by the preferred shareholders when it appears that there has been default entitling them to exercise their right, the period during which the preferred shares may vote, whether such voting power is limited to the election of directors or is given for other purposes as well, and the point at which the common shareholders revert to their former sole voting position. As a practical matter, it is important that the contract not require the passing of dividends for *successive* dividend periods, but rather for a total of eight quarterly, four semi-annual, two annual, etc., periods.[90] It is perhaps wiser to protect the preferred shareholder by providing for voting rights sufficient to control the election of a majority of the board, or one more or less than a majority, when the earnings of the corporation fall below a certain level, thus not waiting until the evil day when it is necessary to pass dividends.

Organization (Corporations) 636–637 (1948). The first two North Carolina subsections cited in note 73 supra have, I believe, remedied the defects which Berle criticizes. Ohio Rev.Code (Gen.Corp.Law of 1955) § 1701.06(A) (12) provides that the "express terms" of shares (which express terms must be in the articles) may include a statement giving the board authority to adopt amendments to the articles (see also § 1701.06(B)) concerning unissued and treasury shares of any class. The A.L.I.Model Bus. Corp.Act § 15 (Rev.1953) permits directors to function, when specifically so authorized by the shareholders, in fixing and determining the relative rights and preferences of the shares of any series but not the preferences, etc., of classes of shares.

89. Ellingwood v. Wolf's Head Oil Refining Co., 27 Del.Ch. 356, 38 A. 2d 743, 154 A.L.R. 406 (1944) (contract gave sole right upon default).

90. See Ballantine, Lattin and Jennings, Cases and Materials on Corporations, footnote 1, page 702 (2d ed. 1953); for drafting suggestions on voting provisions, see Jennings, P-H Students Corporation Law Service, pages 12,032–12,035, 12,050–12,052 (1950).

§ 24. The Transfer of Shares—Methods

The Uniform Stock Transfer Act lists all states except Pennsylvania, which state has substituted the provisions of the Uniform Commercial Code for those of the USTA which it had originally adopted in 1911, effective in 1912, as having adopted this Act.[91] It is also in force in the District of Columbia and Hawaii. The USTA provides two methods by which shares may be transferred: (1) By delivery of the stock certificate indorsed in blank or to a specified person by the one appearing by the certificate to be the owner of the shares; or (2) by delivery of a certificate and a separate written assignment or power of attorney to sell, assign or transfer the "same or the shares represented thereby," signed by the person appearing by the certificate to be the owner of such shares. Although the certificate of stock or other formal corporate documents may purport to provide for the transfer of shares only on the books of the corporation, or require registration by a registrar or transfer by a transfer agent, the statutory provisions stated above are nevertheless applicable.[92] The term "transfer" is defined in the Act as the "transfer of legal title." [93] An attempted transfer of title without a delivery of the certificate has the effect of a promise to transfer, and any obligation thereunder is determined by the law concerning the formation and performance of contracts.[94] Thus, as between the buyer and seller, the methods of disposing of or obtaining title to shares are here definitely established.

But what of gifts or pledges or of sales and purchases where the unindorsed share is delivered to the donee, pledgee or buyer with the proper intent? § 9 of the Act imposes an obligation on the owner so delivering, in the absence of an agreement to the contrary, to complete the transfer by making the proper indorsement, the transfer taking place as of the time when the indorsement is made. Specific performance is also provided for.[95]

The certificate when properly indorsed (whether the indorsement was procured by fraud, duress or mistake), or when

91. 6 U.L.A. (1922), 1957 Cum.Annual Pocket Part. There is some variation from the Act in several states. Massachusetts and Kentucky have also recently adopted the Uniform Commercial Code.

92. § 1, USTA. To the effect that stock certificates and the shares represented by them may be transferred only in the manner prescribed in the USTA, see In re Estate of Davis, 95 Ohio App. 452, 120 N.E.2d 907 (1953). And see

Nagano v. McGrath, 187 F.2d 753 (7th Cir., 1951).

93. § 22 USTA.

94. § 10 USTA.

95. A gift inter vivos by delivery of an unindorsed certificate was held valid and the corporation was required to transfer the stock on the books, the donor having died, in Reinhard v. Sidney B. Roby Co., 110 Misc. 152, 179 N.Y.S. 781 (1920); Connell's Estate, 282 Pa. 555, 128 A. 503, 38 A.L.R. 1362 (1925).

accompanied by the separate written assignment or power of attorney prescribed, is as effective in the hands of a bona fide purchaser for value from a thief, finder, or person entrusted with it, as in case of negotiable instruments generally under similar circumstances. While it has sometimes been stated that under the USTA shares are "more nearly negotiable than they formerly were," [96] § 5 of the Act actually gives full negotiability to certificates of stock.[97] Common law cases prior to the adoption of the USTA must be analyzed in the light of the negotiable provisions of the Act.[98] In order to make attachments upon or levies against shares of stock under the Act, the certificate must be actually seized, or surrendered to the issuing corporation, or its transfer enjoined.[99] And unless the certificate has been lost or destroyed, the corporation cannot be compelled to issue a new certificate until the old one is surrendered to it.[1]

For the purpose of notice of shareholders' meetings, payment of dividends and for the corporate records generally, corporations require a "transfer" on the company's books. The indorsed certificate is turned over to the company or its transfer agent and the transfer is entered on the stock transfer ledger, the old certificate being cancelled and a new certificate being issued in the transferee's name. Thus the transferee becomes a shareholder of record and the company is protected when it gives notices to him or pays dividends to him when it has no

96. Edgerly v. First Nat. Bank of Boston, 292 Mass. 181, 197 N.E. 518 (1935). Prior to the USTA, the common law protected the bona fide purchaser or pledgee from one entrusted with a stock certificate indorsed in blank or with separate assignment or power of attorney. However, where thieves or finders of such instruments sold them to bona fide purchasers, the latter were not protected. Ballantine and Lattin, Cases and Materials on Corporations, Note on page 689 (1st ed. 1939). By § 22 of the Act, "'Certificate' means a certificate of stock in a corporation organized under the laws of this state or of another state whose laws are consistent with this act." The same section defines "State" as including "state, territory, district and insular possession of the United States." Thus, a problem arises as to transfers of shares of corporations formed under the laws of foreign countries. See Sun Insurance Office, Ltd., of London v. Leshevsky, 31 F.Supp. 952 (D.Mass.

1940). With all our states in accord on the thorough negotiability of shares, should a return to the common law be made when transfers in those states are of shares in corporations organized under the laws of foreign sovereign states? Or should a court make its determination on the basis of a "new" common law as evidenced by the will of the people in this legislation?

97. See also §§ 6 and **7.**

98. See Knight v. Shutz, 141 Ohio St. 267, 47 N.E.2d 886 (1941) (stock certificates issued by Ohio corporations since July 1, 1911, the date the USTA became effective in Ohio, possess the quality of full negotiability); Peckinpaugh v. Noble, 238 Mich. 464, 213 N.W. 859, 52 A. L.R. 941 (1927) (the main purpose of the USTA was to give full negotiability to certificates of stock).

99. § 13 USTA.

1. Ibid. See § 17 USTA on lost or destroyed certificates.

other notice that he is not entitled to them. But as far as title to the shares themselves is concerned, when one of the transfer methods prescribed by the USTA has been used nothing is added title-wise by virtue of a transfer on the books of the company.[2] Furthermore, it has been held that the mere placing of shares in the name of the purchaser without a transfer of the physical possession of the certificate does not constitute a "transfer" within the meaning of the Act.[3]

§ 25. Transfer of Shares—Wrongful Refusal to Transfer—Duty of Corporation or its Transfer Agent When Shares Appear to be Held in a Representative Capacity

An unwarranted refusal by a corporation to transfer on its books to a new owner shares represented by a properly indorsed certificate constitutes a breach of an implied promise to register the transfer and also a conversion of the shares.[4] Likewise, at common law, the wrongful cancelling of the owner's certificate of stock and the unauthorized issuing of a certificate to another in place of it is a conversion.[5] Thus, where a transfer was made on tendering a certificate with a forged indorsement, it was held that a conversion resulted.[6] In such a case, the owner may elect to compel the corporation to issue a like number of shares to him in lieu of a recovery of their value.[7] A bona fide purchaser of a stolen stock certificate to which the thief had forged the owner's indorsement was held, as in the analogous case of the conversion of personalty, to be a converter of the innocently held shares.[8]

Since the enactment of the Uniform Stock Transfer Act by which certificates for shares are made thoroughly negotiable, bona fide purchasers from thieves or finders of properly indorsed certificates can require the corporation to transfer the shares to their names on the corporate books and compel the issue of new certificates to them. As in other situations, however, the corporation having notice of the theft may temporarily refuse to transfer the shares to the new owner until it has had an opportunity to investigate the circumstances which make the holder a bona fide purchaser. Bare possession of a certificate indorsed in blank, for example, does not necessarily constitute

---

2. U. S. v. Rosebush, 45 F.Supp. 664 (D.Wis.1942).

3. In re Broomhall, Killough & Co., Inc., 47 F.2d 948 (D.N.Y.1930).

4. Case v. Citizens' Bank of Louisiana, 100 U.S. 446, 25 L.Ed. 695 (1879); Herrick v. Humphrey Hardware Co., 73 Neb. 809, 103 N. W. 685, 119 Am.St.Rep. 917 (1905); 12 Fletcher, Cyc. of Corp., § 5523 (Perm. ed., 1957 Rev.Vol.).

5. Drug, Inc. v. Hunt, 35 Del. (5 W. W.Harr.) 339, 168 A. 87 (1933).

6. West v. Tintic Standard Mining Co., 71 Utah 158, 263 P. 490, 56 A. L.R. 1190 (1928).

7. Ibid.

8. Pierpoint v. Hoyt, 260 N.Y. 26, 182 N.E. 235, 83 A.L.R. 1195 (1932).

ownership for all purposes. The corporation may not ignore, except at its peril, conflicting claims of which it has notice or where it has reasonable doubt as to the title or right of the person demanding registration. However, its refusal should be qualified for the purpose of investigation, and promptness in making up its mind is essential.[9] In extreme cases where the rights of rival claimants are not clear, interpleader may be used to settle the adverse claims, or, where possible, a declaratory judgment may be sought.

Where adverse claims are presented by one not holding the duly indorsed certificate, the initial preference would seem to be with the holder of the certificate. At least one state has solved this by a statute requiring the adverse claimant to give written notice of his claim and within five days thereafter give adequate security or an indemnity bond to protect the corporation and its transfer agent in their refusal to transfer the stock. The adverse claimant must, within 60 days of his notice, start an action to determine his rights in the shares. Failure to give the notice, to post security, or to start an action exempts the corporation and its transfer agent from liability for transferring the shares and issuing a new certificate to the holder of the old one.[10]

One of the most severe obligations placed upon corporations is by virtue of a common law rule which makes a corporation liable for an unauthorized transfer of shares registered on its books in the name of a person as trustee or other fiduciary or agent. The effect of the holdings is to make the corporation or its transfer agent a supervisor of the trustee to see that he does not violate the terms of the trust with reference to the shares.[11] Where the corporation registers a transfer with actual knowledge that the trustee is breaching his trust, a clear case of corporate liability is present, whether the shares are in the name of the trustee individually or as trustee. But the weight of authority goes further and requires the corporation, where shares are registered as those of a trustee, to inquire whether the trustee, under the trust, has the power to transfer them. And the obligation exists whether the trustee is described as one under a particular will or deed of trust, or for specific beneficiaries, or where the simple description is "trustee."[12] Professor Scott

9. Leff v. N. Kaufman's Inc., 342 Pa. 342, 20 A.2d 786, 139 A.L.R. 267 (1941), noted in 27 Cornell L.Q. 101 (1941). See Ann., 139 A.L.R. 273 (1942), on the "Right or duty of a corporation to transfer stock on books to one presenting properly indorsed certificate, because of knowledge or suspicion of conflicting rights of registered holder or of third person."

10. West's Ann.Cal.Corp.Code § 2410 (formerly Cal.Civ.Code § 328a). And see § 2409 where the corporation has reasonable doubt of the right to transfer.

11. 3 Scott, Trusts § 325 (2d ed. 1956).

12. 3 Scott, op. cit. supra § 325.

and others have questioned the wisdom of putting this responsibility upon the corporation or its transfer agent, for the corporation, unlike the purchaser from a known trustee, is merely a "stakeholder" and not one who benefits from the transfer. "The effect of imposing a duty on the corporation to supervise the administration of a trust is seriously to obstruct the administration of trusts and to increase the expenses of administration." [13] The English law wisely does not require the corporation to ascertain the authority of the trustee to transfer the shares.[14] It has been pointed out that the American view has encouraged a trustee to register the shares so held in his own name individually, thus not disclosing that he is a fiduciary and so avoiding the legal problem, a practice which has been rightly condemned.[15]

Fortunately, there is considerable legislation in the various states today which changes the common law rule. § 3 of the Uniform Fiduciaries Act, which Act has been adopted in 20 states, the District of Columbia and Hawaii,[16] provides that there is no duty in the corporation or its transfer agent to inquire whether the registered fiduciary is committing a breach of trust in making the transfer, or to see that he is performing his fiduciary obligation. The corporation becomes liable, under this Act, however, if it registers a transfer with actual knowledge that the fiduciary is breaching his trust in making the transfer, "or with knowledge of such facts that the action in registering the transfer amounts to bad faith." But this Act is not applicable to shares registered in the name of the deceased owner. The executor or administrator must produce his authority to make a transfer of such shares. Local statutes must be consulted on these problems as other statutes of somewhat similar import to the Uniform Act exist. Some, too, go much further than the provisions of the Uniform Act.[17]

§ 26. Lost and Stolen Certificates

The Uniform Stock Transfer Act provides that "Except where a certificate is lost or destroyed, such corporation shall not be compelled to issue a new certificate for the stock until the old certificate is surrendered to it." [18] The negotiability of stock certificates makes such a provision not only reasonable, but necessary, for the shares are merged in the certificate itself and bona fide purchasers of properly indorsed certificates are pro-

13. Ibid., same section, at page 2348; also § 326.6, page 2372.

14. In re Perkins, 24 Q.B.D. 613 (1890); Companies Consolidation Act, 1908, 8 Edw. VII, c. 69, § 27.

15. 3 Scott, op. cit. supra, note 11, at page 2349.

16. 9B U.L.A., Miscellaneous Acts 17 (1957).

17. See Ohio Rev.Code §§ 1339.02 and 2109.29. And see Article 8, Uniform Commercial Code, §§ 8–308(1), 8–402 and 8–403 (1957 official text).

18. § 13, last sentence.

tected.   Negotiable bills of lading and warehouse receipts are
analogous in this respect to shares under the Act.   And the prohibition against attaching the shares unless the certificate is
seized by the officer or is surrendered to the corporation or its
transfer enjoined meshes in with the above provision.   However
where a certificate has been lost or destroyed (or stolen), a court
may order the issue of a new certificate upon satisfactory proof of
its loss or destruction and upon the giving of a bond sufficient to
protect the corporation or any person injured by virtue of the
certificate which remains outstanding.[19]

§ 27.   "Lost" Shareholders—Unclaimed Dividends and Other Distributions

The problem of "lost" security holders is an old one.   Notices are sent, dividend checks mailed, and other distributions
forwarded to the record holder at his address on the corporate
books.   Or the record holder may be a broker holding the shares
for the real owner who cannot be found to pay over dividends
and other benefits.   Returned with the usual notation "Not at
this address" or "Addressee unknown" other attempts at finding
him fail.   Is the dividend or other distribution to be considered
abandoned property?   Must the corporation hold as trustee for
the "lost" shareholder or is it entitled to hold for the use of the
shareholders of known addresses after the statute of limitations
has run?   Does it escheat to the state of incorporation?   To the
state of last known address of the shareholder?   Or to some
other state such as that of the principal place of business of the
corporation if it differs from the state of incorporation?   What
effect will the running of the statute of limitations have on the
problem?   Without the aid of a statute indicating who is entitled
to benefits which are unable to be conferred because their owners cannot be found, may the corporation or the record-owner-
broker do more than deposit cash and other distributions with
a depositary for safekeeping, hoping that eventually the shareholder or his successor in interest will make himself known?
There is a scarcity of legislation concerning this important
problem, a near vacuum that should be filled.

Cash dividends become a debt owing to the shareholder the
moment they are declared or upon the date the holders of record
become entitled to them.   It would be natural to assume that the
statute of limitations would start running as of that time, especially if the corporation has made a reasonable effort to locate
the shareholder.[20]   But courts have more frequently held, in the

19.   § 17 USTA.

20.   See Jacques v. White Knob Copper & Development Co., 260 App.

Div. 640, 23 N.Y.S.2d 326 (1940);
Frey, Noteworthy Decisions in the
Law of Private Corporations: 1940–

cases involving lost shareholders, that the statute does not start running until there has been a demand and/or a refusal to pay; that the corporation is a trustee or quasi-trustee of the declared dividends and must anticipate a demand, perhaps years later.[21]

It is probable that the chief reason why most courts have been reluctant to start the statute running upon the declaration of the dividend for or the accrual of other rights to the lost shareholder is the apparent injustice of cutting him off as a creditor or owner when he has had no notice of the debt owing him or of his other property rights, and in the case of property rights not describable as debts there are other inherent difficulties. The retention, too, of good public relations comes in for reasonable emphasis.[22] But, even so, the doctrine has been carried "beyond the requirements of any rationale based on notice and [the courts] have applied it without considering whether the shareholder ever received notice or whether reasonable efforts were made by the corporation to give notice to him." [23]

While as yet there is meager statutory coverage of the problem, some statutes provide that distributions upon the winding up and dissolution of the corporation be turned over to the state treasurer or a bank or trust company to be held for the person entitled to the fund.[24] The Connecticut statute steers the benefits, upon liquidation, to the state's general fund.[25] Arizona, on the other hand, gives the benefit to the school fund.[26]

Some states make provision for the distribution of unclaimed funds without reference to corporate liquidation, New Jersey's statute providing for escheat to the state.[27] And the Supreme Court in the cited case stated in a dictum that escheat

1945, 94 U. of Pa.L.Rev. 265, at 280 (1946), calls this an "unfortunate decision." English, and American minority courts, hold that the statute starts running when the right to demand dividends is perfected. Note, the Lost Shareholder, 62 Harv.L.Rev. 295, at 297 (1948).

21. Holly Sugar Corp. v. Wilson, 101 Colo. 511, 75 P.2d 149 (1937) (18 years in this case), noted in 13 Wash.L.Rev. 334 (1938); Ballantine, Lattin and Jennings, Cases and Materials on Corporations 776 (2d ed. 1953).

22. But see Mastellone v. Argo Oil Co., 46 Del. 102, 82 A.2d 379 (Sup. Ct.1951), where the court cut off rights in an analogous case.

23. Note, The Lost Shareholder, 62 Harv.L.Rev. 295, at 297 (1948).

24. West's Ann.Cal.Corp.Code §§ 5009, 5010, as amended by Cal.Stat.1957, c. 1020, p. 2257, §§ 1 and 2.

25. Conn.Gen.Corp.Law (1949) §§ 5236, 5237.

26. In re Hull Copper Co., 46 Ariz. 270, 50 P.2d 560, 101 A.L.R. 664 (1935), noted in 45 Yale L.J. 720 (1936); Ann., "Disposition of interest or rights in corporation represented by stock the owner of which cannot be found, 101 A.L.R. 670 (1936); Ariz.Const. § 8, Art. 11 (school fund gets the benefit).

27. See Standard Oil Co. v. New Jersey, 341 U.S. 428, 71 S.Ct. 822, 95 L.Ed. 1078 (1951); Ohio Rev.Code § 1701.34 (a 6-year statute of limitations). See also West's Ann.Cal. Code of Civ.Proc. § 1570, as amended by Cal.Stat.1957, c. 1020, p. 2258, § 4, and § 1578.

proceedings in New Jersey, which was the corporate birthplace, were entitled to full faith and credit in other states so as to prevent the event of a second escheat.[28] A difficult legal problem would arise where the state of the principal place of corporate business or the state of the last known domicile of the unfound shareholder should each make an escheat claim. Either or both might be considered logical points for escheat, though the state of incorporation offers the simplest and most certain point. And when a broker is record holder of the lost shareholder's shares, must he hold in trust for the eventual possible return of the true owner or of his heirs or devisees? And, if his state has an escheat statute, must he turn the ordinary and extraordinary dividends, benefits and dissolution distributions over to the state of his domicile or must he return them to the state of incorporation or the state of last known domicile of the true owner?[29]

Statutes are necessary to give direction to what happens, and when, in case shareholders cannot be found after a reasonable search. It would make good sense to require the corporation or its representative to retain the benefit for the lost shareholder and his successor in interest for a stated period and then permit distribution to the known shareholders. An alternative might well be a conditional escheat to the state to hold for the lost shareholder but with authority to use the fund during the interval between escheat and the finding of the lost shareholder or his successor when the fund, with or without interest, would be paid to him. And, in any case, the passing of a stated time period should make the escheat absolute.[30]

The problem is a practical one causing expense year after year to numerous corporations with lost shareholders. Several reasonable solutions via the statutory route are possible. And, of course, cash and property dividends in usual course, share dividends, redemption payments, and distributions upon dissolution and winding-up should all come in for treatment, as should securities issued upon merger, consolidation and reorganization.

28. See Note, Escheat of Corporate Dividends, 65 Harv.L.Rev. 1408 (1952); Note, The Lost Shareholder, 62 Harv.L.Rev. 295 (1948).

29. See thoughtful note in 65 Harv. L.Rev. 1408 (1952) on Escheat of Corporate Dividends.

30. See Note, 62 Harv.L.Rev. 295, at 298–299 (1948).

Chapter 10

DIVIDENDS

§ 1. General Rule of Discretion; Practical and Policy Considerations

Dividends are the food upon which investors feed and thrive. The profits from which they are derived and the wise use in their distribution as dividends and in the retention of some for future corporate development or emergency spell increased value to the shares and satisfaction to the shareholders. However, a too generous or a too frugal use of profits for dividends may produce insolvency in the one case and shareholder dissatisfaction and lower stock values in the other, with the additional threat of a shareholder's suit to compel the declaration of a dividend.

The general rule recognized by all courts is that it is within the sole discretion of the directors to declare or not to declare a dividend when a legal fund is available and, barring an abuse of discretion, the court will not interfere. A court, then, will not substitute its own ideas of dividend policy for those of the directors who have presumably been chosen by the owners to use their honest discretion and good business judgment in arriving at this, as well as other determinations. In view of the varied economic, "political" and taxing incidents that must be considered in making a decision of whether funds should be retained or distributed, the rule is a wise one. But as a brake upon directorial discretion, a principle recognizing the right of participation by the shareholders in all the net earnings of the company not reasonably needed for legitimate corporate purposes ought to have equal weight. Some courts have held that a mandatory provision in the share-contract requiring a declaration when funds are available is a valid one though it takes away the board's discretion to this extent.[1] The rule of directorial discretion has frequently, perhaps generally, been too sacredly respected by the courts.

§ 2. Right to Dividends—Compelling a Declaration

Bad faith of directors has no infallible distinguishing features. Intense hostility of the controlling group; high salaries,

1. New England Trust Co. v. Penobscot Chemical Fibre Co., 142 Me. 286, 50 A.2d 188 (1946); Crocker v. Waltham Watch Co., 315 Mass. 397, 53 N.E.2d 230 (1944); Note, Compelling Declaration of Dividends by Contract Construction, 39 Ill.L.Rev. 90 (1944). But see Lindgrove v. Schluter & Co., 256 N.Y. 439, at 444, 176 N.E. 832 (1931).

bonuses and corporate loans to officers in control; exclusion of
the minority from the opportunity and benefit of corporate employment; the design of those in control to retain earnings so
that they may purchase shares at a low figure produced by a nig-
gardly dividend policy; the retention of earnings to save a high-
income-bracket majority from higher income taxes if dividends
are paid—all are relevant evidence of bad faith.[2] If these are mo-
tivating causes for not declaring dividends, they amount to bad
faith as a matter of law. Other situations demand careful
scrutiny as, for example, where life beneficiaries and remainder-
men, the latter being in control, are involved.[3] And the frequent
charge by a minority in a close corporation that the majority, by
a policy of meager dividends, is attempting to freeze the minority
out is a potent bit of convincing evidence of abuse of discretion.[4]

While no particular attention, except in New Jersey, has
been given the non-cumulative shareholder of the discretionary
dividend type, it should take much less to show abuse of directorial discretion in passing dividends when they could have been declared and paid, for the excellent reason that once passed they are,
under present law, lost forever. This rule constitutes a blanket
invitation to directors to pass dividends so that the common
shareholders, in a later dividend paying period, may be the beneficiaries. It is all too easy to cover up the actual motive by setting
up apparently valid reasons for the board's action.[5]

The fact that the corporation has accumulated large profits
in excess of its needs, particularly if the profits are principally
in cash or other liquid form, is a persuasive argument to encourage a court to compel the declaration and payment of a dividend.[6]
Another is where the reasons for failing to declare a dividend are
not related to the conduct of the corporation's business, as where
the alleged reason was that the dividends would, if declared, go to
a solely owned corporation of the dominant shareholder, thus
being subject to an income tax by both corporations and later by
the dominant shareholder when his solely owned corporation distributed a dividend to him.[7] Another compelling reason today
for a court's forcing a dividend is the taxing fact that earnings or

2. Gottfried v. Gottfried, 73 N.Y.S.2d
    692 (Sup.Ct.1947).

3. See Schmitt v. Eagle Roller Mill
    Co., 199 Minn. 382, 272 N.W. 277
    (1937); City Bank Farmers' Trust
    Co. v. Hewitt Realty Co., 257 N.Y.
    62, 177 N.E. 309, 76 A.L.R. 881
    (1931).

4. Jones v. Motor Sales Co., 322 Pa.
    492, 185 A. 809 (1936).

5. See Comment, Forcing Preferred
    Dividends: The Chicago Great

Western Settlement, 19 U. of Chi.L.
Rev. 878 (1952).

6. Whittemore v. Continental Mills,
    98 F.Supp. 387 (D.Me.1951); Dodge
    v. Ford Motor Co., 204 Mich. 459,
    170 N.W. 668, 3 A.L.R. 413 (1919).
    This was an extreme case of failure
    to declare adequate dividends from
    more than adequate liquid assets
    derived from earnings.

7. Ibid.

profits permitted to accumulate beyond the "reasonably anticipated needs of the business" receive a very heavy accumulated
earnings surtax.[8] Dividends should be distributed to avoid the
surtax unless there are unusually persuasive reasons for not distributing them.

§ 3. Suit to Compel Declaration of Dividends—Type of Suit—Essential Parties

New York has recently, and badly, held that an action to
compel the corporation to declare and pay a dividend is a shareholders' derivative suit and thus subject to the conditions imposed upon the plaintiffs in such suits.[9] Fortunately, majority
opinion holds that the suit may be brought in a representative
capacity by one or more shareholders on behalf of all others similarly situated — an equitable class action making unnecessary
the joinder of numerous plaintiffs having similar interests.[10] According to this better authority, the corporation is not a nominal
defendant as it is in a derivative action. In suits to compel dividends, the corporation is a real party defendant, and a necessary
party to the action.[11] The right to dividends is an incident of
stock ownership. It is the shareholder who is injured, and not
the corporation, when dividends have been wrongfully withheld
by it. The action is thus one personal to the shareholder.

In such a suit, the corporation and (probably) the directors
who can be served should be joined as parties-defendant. Should
all or a majority of the directors be joined, since it would take a
quorum of a majority to declare a dividend if not ordered by the
court? While there is some conflict in the cases (and there are
not many cases on this point) the better and probably the more
numerous ones do not require a majority of the directors to be
made defendants since, in many cases, it would be impossible to

---

8. I.R.C. of 1954 §§ 531, 532 and 533,
26 U.S.C.A. §§ 531, 532 and 533. See
Note on High Surtax on Improperly
Accumulated Surplus: Section 102
of the Internal Revenue Code, Ballantine, Lattin and Jennings, Cases
and Materials on Corporations 765
(2d ed. 1953). Former section 102
was essentially similar to the 1954
provisions. See also Note, Personal
Liability of Shareholder-Directors
for Accumulating Earnings Which
Led to Subjection of Corporation to
§ 102 Taxes, 61 Harv.L.Rev. 1058
(1948).

9. Gordon v. Elliman, 306 N.Y. 456,
119 N.E.2d 331 (1954) (a 4–3 decision
in which Judge Fuld wrote an il-

luminating dissent). See, for comments on the case in the lower
court: DeCapriles and Prunty, Corporations, 28 N.Y.U.L.Rev. 1428
(1953); 41 Calif.L.Rev. 546 (1953);
53 Col.L.Rev. 437 (1953); 38 Cornell
L.Q. 244 (1953).

10. Dodge v. Ford Motor Co., supra,
note 6; Stevens v. U. S. Steel Corp.,
68 N.J.Eq. 373, 375–376, 59 A. 905
(1905); Whittemore v. Continental
Mills, supra note 6; Knapp v.
Bankers Securities Corp., 230 F.2d
717 (3d Cir.1956); Ballantine, Corporations 556 (Rev. ed. 1946).

11. Stevens v. U. S. Steel Corp., supra, note 10.

get service upon all or a majority.[12] An even better reason was given by Circuit Judge Goodrich in a recent case [13] in which he recognized the usual discretionary directorial rule but reasoned: "It is to be observed that when a court steps in and orders the payment of a dividend, the corporate affairs have reached the point where the judgment of the directors is no longer controlling." [14] Hence, even if all the directors are brought in as defendants "they are not called upon to exercise any business discretion. The case has passed that point." Any formal action by the board after a decree forcing a declaration of dividends "is nothing but a ministerial act" and is based upon a mandate, not by the vote of the board. Thus, it would seem to follow, as Judge Goodrich concludes: " . . . [I]f there is a corporate defendant properly subject to suit within the state and the plaintiff makes out a legal right against the corporation and the corporation has property within the state as well as being subject to suit, the chancellor can accomplish the result the plaintiff is entitled to have accomplished." [15]

§ 4. Manner of Declaring Dividends—Legal Effect

Assume that there is a proper fund from which dividends may be declared and paid, a topic yet to be considered, and that the board decides to declare a cash dividend of so much per share. The resolution may state quite simply that the board hereby declares a dividend of $2 per common share (there being but one class of shares) payable on the first day of the following month. Shareholders on the date of the declaration are said to be creditors of the corporation from the time of declaration so that if they transfer their shares after this date but before the date of payment, they and not their transferees are entitled to the dividend.[16] The effect of the declaration, of course, is not to segre-

12. Whittemore v. Continental Mills, supra, note 6 (2 of 5 directors were served. The rest were outside the jurisdiction and could not be served); Kroese v. General Steel Castings Corp., 179 F.2d 760 (3d Cir., 1950) (3 out of 12 directors were served, the plaintiff alleging that there was no one state or federal district where a majority of the board could be served), cert. denied 339 U.S. 983, 70 S.Ct. 1026, 94 L.Ed. 1386 (1950); W. Q. O'Neall Co. v. O'Neall, 108 Ind.App. 116, 25 N.E.2d 656 (1940). *Contra:* Schuckman v. Rubenstein, 164 F.2d 952 (6th Cir., 1947), cert. denied 333 U.S. 875, 68 S.Ct. 905, 92 L.Ed. 1151 (1948); see note criticising Schuckman case in 61 Harv.L.Rev. 1253

(1948). Notes on Kroese case, supra, will be found in 36 Cornell L.Q. 744 (1951); 49 Mich.L.Rev. 275 (1950); 35 Minn.L.Rev. 93 (1950); 98 U. of Pa.L.Rev. 753 (1950).

13. Kroese v. General Steel Castings Corp., supra, note 12. N. C. Bus. Corp. Act § 55–50(k), in part, contains this provision: "Any action by a shareholder to compel the payment of dividends may be brought against the directors, or against the corporation with or without joining the directors as parties."

14. Ibid. (Kroese case) at 763.

15. Ibid. at 765.

16. Ellis v. Proprietors of Essex Merrimack Bridge, 2 Pick. (19 Mass.)

gate any particular fund from the property of the corporation, though occasionally a court without accounting experience states the contrary, but to warrant posting the historical event on the books of the corporation by reducing the surplus account and crediting the dividends payable account by the amount of the dividend. However, if the dividend was declared from funds legally available for this purpose, the shareholders entitled to share in the dividend may even compete with other corporate creditors if the evil day of insolvency arrives before payment of the dividend.[17] But statutes will have to be examined on this matter since some not only prohibit the declaration of dividends out of something less than surplus but prohibit payment as well.

Customarily, the directors will not use the simple resolution in the example above but will declare a dividend on X-date payable to shareholders of record on Y-date, payment to be made on Z-date. In such a case, courts have divided on the matter of when the debtor-creditor relationship arises, one view being that the date of declaration of the dividend creates that status,[18] the other view taking the position that the directors may determine the date upon which the debt arises and have done so by indicating that the dividend is payable to shareholders of record on Y-date.[19] Whichever view is taken, the corporation will be protected if it pays to the shareholder of record when it has no notice that a transferee has superior rights. But an important problem may arise when the view taken is that no debt arises until Y-date for there is the possibility, a slight one true, that the fund legally available at X-date will not be available on Y-date. And if no fund then exists out of which a proper dividend may be declared, it seems quite obvious that the previous declaration is a nullity

243 (1824); Beers v. Bridgeport Spring Co., 42 Conn. 17 (1875).

17. Lowene v. American Fire Insurance Co., 6 Paige Ch. 482 (N.Y.1837). But would this be so under statutes prohibiting the declaration or payment of dividends at a time when the corporation is insolvent or where the dividend will impair capital? The rule which permits competition with creditors is questionable. Compare the corporation's purchase of its own shares out of a proper fund where payment for the same is attempted at a time when there is no proper fund. See Ballantine, Corporations 561 (Rev. ed. 1946).

18. First Nat. Bank & Trust Co. v. Glenn, 36 F.Supp. 552 (D.Ky.1941); Helvering, Com'r v. McGlue's Est.,

119 F.2d 167 (4th Cir., 1941) (involved a New York corporation and court applied the New York law); Com'r v. Cohen, 121 F.2d 348 (5th Cir., 1941) (Texas law was applied). Leading case of Ford v. Snook, 205 App.Div. 194, 199 N.Y.S. 630 (1923), aff'd per curiam, 240 N.Y. 624, 148 N.E. 732 (1925), was thought not to be changed by Judge Dobie in the case of McGlue's Est., supra, because of a provision contained in § 62 of the N.Y.Stock Corp.Law.

19. Richter & Co. v. Light, 97 Conn. 364, 116 A. 600 (1922), is the leading case; Nutter v. Andrews, 246 Mass. 224, 142 N.E. 67 (1923); Munro v. Mullen, Adm'r, 100 N.H. 130, 121 A. 2d 312 (1956) (involving a Massachusetts corporation); In re Estate of Wuichet, 138 Ohio St. 97, 33 N.E. 2d 15 (1941).

and that the status of debtor-creditor cannot arise on Y-date. Thus, it would seem wise if a present declaration is intended to go into the future for any unusual length of time for the board to indicate its intent of making the dividend payable to shareholders of record on the declaration date, payments to be made at intervals indicated by the board, future rights in the dividend declared to be a matter of contract between the present record holder and his transferee.

May the board rescind its resolution to declare cash dividends when it finds special reasons for so doing? It has been held that if the dividend has once been legally declared there may be no revocation by the board because a property right (the debt) has been created.[20] Shareholders could, of course, consent to a revocation if their consent was unanimous. There may be very valid reasons for rescinding a declaration of dividends, such as a corporate disaster whereby money values existing at the time of the declaration have been irretrievably lost, for example by the destruction of an important asset upon which there was no insurance, or because of the economic debacle of the "banking holidays" of 1933, the latter event justifying the retention of the funds from which the dividend was declared as additional working capital until the emergency was over, or even justifying a complete revocation. A postponement of payment would seem to be justified and, in case of such real emergencies, should not the declaration be considered as carrying with it a condition subsequent to the effect that the declaration is final and absolute unless grave circumstances arise before payment, upon which occurrences the board may rescind? There are dangers, of course, to this approach for, upon the declaration of the dividend and notice to the public, the shares take on an additional value and if there may be rescission at will the board may play fast and loose for their own benefit, a thing to be condemned. However, if the rules applicable to meetings be applied, the resolution declaring dividends could at least be reconsidered at any time during the meeting at which it was adopted which would include an adjournment of the same to a later time, especially if no public notice were given of the board's previous action.[21]

---

20. Bryan v. Welch, 74 F.2d 964 (10th Cir., 1935), cert. denied 295 U.S. 748, 55 S.Ct. 826, 79 L.Ed. 1693 (1935).

21. Dean Stevens favors a broader rule, namely, that directors have discretion to declare dividends and the same should be true of rescinding them. The courts, in both cases, would handle abuses of discretion. Stevens, Corporations 460 (2d ed.

1949). See Ford v. Easthampton Rubber Thread Co., 158 Mass. 84, 32 N.E. 1036, 20 L.R.A. 65, 35 Am.St. Rep. 462 (1893), where the court permitted a rescission of the declaration of a dividend at a meeting held a short time after the one at which the declaration was passed upon, there being no notice to shareholders or to the public of the declaration.

Where a dividend resolution is not final because its rate is subject to the president's discretion, or there is authorization to pay whenever in a named officer's judgment funds are available, or to pay at a stated rate and at stated times until such time as the board shall otherwise order, it does not create a present debt as a fully declared dividend.[22] However, the fact that no date is set for payment is not controlling. If the resolution has been without reservation, the dividend will be payable in a reasonable time.

Courts have distinguished between a cash and a stock dividend, holding that in the latter type there may be revocation by the board since no debt has been created.[23] Another and better reason sometimes assigned for the rule is that the shareholder's interest in the assets of his company is no different after the additional shares have been issued as a dividend from what it was before; consequently he has not been injured by the failure to issue.[24] However, had the share dividend been carried through there would have been frozen into permanent capital a part of the surplus which would presumably be devoted to corporate use for the further making of profits. And while the shareholder derives no greater property interest by the issue of another piece of paper, he does find it more convenient, in case he desires to sell, to have these share-dividend units to use instead of splitting his larger units. Perhaps this is just another case of *de minimis non curat lex*. The inconvenience does not add up to much.

Mention should be made of the fact that, under various statutes, share dividends may be permitted out of values resulting in special surpluses on the balance sheet which would not warrant the distribution of a cash or property dividend. For example, either the common law or a statute may make illegal a cash dividend from book surpluses derived from a revaluation of assets, particularly of the permanent asset type, but permit a stock dividend under these circumstances. Unrealized appreciation resulting in book surpluses constitutes a dangerous threat to cred-

22. Good examples are: U. S. v. Baldy, 108 F.2d 591 (9th Cir., 1939); Maloney v. Western Cooperage Co., 103 F.2d 992 (9th Cir., 1939); Alexander & Alexander v. U. S., 22 F. Supp. 921 (D.Md.1938). But compare Northwestern Marble & Tile Co. v. Carlson, 116 Minn. 438, 133 N.W. 1014, Ann.Cas.1913B, 552 (1912) (a declaration of cash or stock dividends to be paid when directors judge that business conditions warrant payment was held to be payable within a reasonable time). Semble: Billingham v. E. P. Gleason Mfg. Co., 101 App.Div. 476, 91 N.Y.S. 1046 (Sup.Ct.1905), aff'd 185 N.Y. 571, 78 N.E. 1099 (1906), where dividends were declared payable "at pleasure" of corporation and court held that this meant within a reasonable time.

23. Staats v. Biograph Co., 236 F. 454, L.R.A.1917B, 728 (2d Cir. 1916) (recognizing the rule that the declaration of a stock dividend may be rescinded at any time prior to the actual issuance of the stock).

24. Terry v. Eagle Lock Co., 47 Conn. 141 (1879).

itors and senior shareholders if allowed to be used for cash dividends. But while the distribution of a stock dividend freezes unrealized values into permanent capital, it does not have the effect of taking anything out of the corporate pocketbook to the detriment of either creditors or senior shareholders. And, of course, the stock dividend must be distinguished from "split-ups" of shares which result from an amendment to the corporate articles dividing shares of a particular class into more units, such as providing that existing shares shall be split two for one or in any other number of desired units, there being no change in the stated capital item. The result of splitting up shares into more units is simply to dilute each share without disturbing the total value of the new shares which, theoretically, should equal the value of the shares being split. Actually, as experience has shown, the value of the total split shares on the market frequently exceeds the value of the total original shares. The explanation of this phenomenon must come from incidents outside the values represented upon the balance sheet.

What has been stated above applies to dividends in shares of the dividend-declaring company and not to shares of other companies distributed as a dividend. Such alien shares are considered a property dividend and are the same as a dividend in cash.[25] And it has been held that, where a dividend had been declared payable in cash or in shares of his company's stock at the shareholder's election, this was not a stock dividend.[26] This may well be as far as a taxing statute is involved, but how can one say that there is no stock dividend to those shareholders who elect to take shares instead of cash?

While stock dividends do not require any statutory or charter provisions for their authorization, and in many states there are as yet no statutory provisions for such dividends, recently legislation, here and there, has been enacted to regulate such dividends. Statutory regulation of cash and property dividends has not been applied to stock dividends, and rightly.[27] If there are sufficient unissued shares, these may be used by the board for a share dividend. Unissued shares and a sufficient surplus to be capitalized by the share dividend are the legal requirements for a

25. In re Rogers, 22 App.Div. 428, 48 N.Y.S. 175, (1897), aff'd in 161 N.Y. 108, 55 N.E. 393 (1899).

26. Kellogg v. Kellogg, 166 Misc. 791, 4 N.Y.S.2d 219 (1938). Dividend declared at stockholder's option, either in cash or in stock of the corporation, is not a "stock dividend" since a stock dividend is declared only by the directors, the court holds. "A dividend in cash with the right to purchase new stock is not a stock dividend." But compare the actual resolution declaring this dividend which is not in terms of *purchase* from a cash dividend declared. Involved was an interpretation of trust provisions.

27. Williams v. Western Union Telegraph Co., 93 N.Y. 162 (1883).

stock dividend. If there are an insufficient number of unissued shares it will be necessary first to increase the authorized capital stock of the company, and this will normally require shareholder action. After the authorization, the directors may then declare a stock dividend to the extent of the surplus available. The shareholder's interest in his corporation is not thereby increased, but the surpus is frozen by the share dividend so that it cannot later be distributed as a cash or property dividend. And, under the present federal income taxing statute, an ordinary stock dividend, whether in common or preferred shares, is not taxable income when received because there is no distribution of assets.[28] If a gain results from its later sale, this is taxable as a capital gain.

§ 5. Restrictions on Dividend Distributions—Sources Available

A basic concept running through all dividend law is that dividends may not be declared out of capital. The term "capital" is not descriptive of any particular assets such as land, buildings, inventory, cash, etc., but is value in the large sense of value of corporate assets contributed for permanent use, unless reduced by statutorily approved shareholder action, and equal, by the better view, to the aggregate par value of shares issued and outstanding plus amounts received (or promised to be paid) through the issue of no-par value shares to the extent of the amounts

---

28. I.R.C.1954, § 305(a), 26 U.S.C.A. § 305(a). But note the exceptions in § 305(b). That this has not always been so, see Eisner v. Macomber, 252 U.S. 189, 40 S.Ct. 189, 64 L.Ed. 521, 9 A.L.R. 1570 (1919) (Here it was held that a common stock dividend paid to common shareholders where no other shares were outstanding was not income under the federal income tax provisions); Koshland v. Helvering, Com'r, 298 U.S. 441, 56 S.Ct. 767, 80 L.Ed. 1268, 105 A.L.R. 756 (1936) (Where a dividend of common shares to holders of preferred shares with liquidation preferences plus accrued dividends and no more was held taxable as income since it gave the shareholder a proportional interest essentially different from that represented by his preferred shares); Strassburger v. Com'r, 318 U.S. 604, 63 S.Ct. 791, 87 L.Ed. 1029 (1943) (Preferred stock was distributed as a dividend to the sole owner of the common shares and it was held that this did not constitute taxable income; that, "in order to render

a stock dividend taxable as income, there must be a change brought about by the issue of shares as a dividend whereby the proportional interest of the stockholder after the distribution was essentially different from his former interest"). In Chamberlain v. Comm'r, 207 F.2d 462 (6th Cir., 1953), the preferred stock received as a dividend was immediately sold to an insurance company and the Tax Court held this taxable as income. The Court of Appeals reversed, looking only to the time of share dividend distribution to ascertain the effect—that the sale was to be considered a sale of a capital asset. "Such profit is conceded to be taxable. The issue is whether it is taxable as income from a cash dividend or as income resulting from a long-term capital gain." (Page 472.) This type of bail-out was made impossible by I.R.C. 1954, § 306. See Guide to Internal Revenue Code of 1954, 26 U.S.C.A. pp. 18–22 on §§ 305 and 306 of the Code.

which are capitalized, plus other values which have been added through the capitalization of surpluses upon a declaration of share dividends, plus any other amounts capitalized from surplus.[29] The values so capitalized are for the purpose of carrying on the business and as a cushion for creditors. Hence, the rule which prohibits a declaration of a dividend out of capital is for the protection of creditors and of shareholders. As we shall see presently, there is an exception to the rule when the corporation is what is known as a "wasting asset" corporation.

The item which represents a fictitious liability on the right side (liability side) of the balance sheet, and which is variously called "Capital Stock" or "Stated Capital" or "Legal Capital", represents the dollar value of assets on the left side (asset side) of the balance sheet which must not be used for dividend purposes. This is not a fund but a "quantum" as Professor Ballantine has termed it. If inroads are made into these values by losses, such losses must ordinarily be recouped to the amount of the stated capital figure, or the stated capital be reduced by the statutorily prescribed method, before dividends are possible out of surpluses that turn up. There are, as we shall presently see, some statutes which permit the declaration and payment of dividends out of current earnings though the capital may be impaired, but these are exceptional and dangerous in the sense that creditors and senior security holders may lose the cushion, or some of it, which was supposedly for their protection.

(a) Dividend statutes. In general, three basic types of statute exist: (1) the insolvency type; (2) the impairment of capital, or balance sheet type; and (3) the earned surplus, or net profits type. There are some statutes that combine types.

The insolvency type prohibits the declaration and/or payment of a dividend when there is insolvency or where the payment would render the corporation insolvent.[30] When the term insolvent is used there is always the problem of whether the legislature meant to use the term in the bankruptcy sense of balancing assets against liabilities, or in the equity sense of the inability to meet obligations and debts as they mature. The California statute excellently provides that there may be no declaration of dividends when the corporation is insolvent in either sense.[31] Even

---

29. "All the net assets together equal capital and surplus. Legal capital is not a *res*, but a *quantum* or mathematical limit below which amount assets may not lawfully be withdrawn by the shareholders." Ballantine and Hills, Corporate Capital and Restrictions Upon Dividends Under Modern Corporation Laws, 23 Calif.L.Rev. 229, at 232 (1935).

30. See Mass.G.L.(Ter.Ed.) ch. 156, § 37; Miss.Gen.Corp.Law § 5328.

31. West's Ann.Cal.Corp.Code § 1501. Similarly, A.L.I.Model Bus.Corp. Act §§ 40 and 2(n), defining "insolvent" (Rev.1953).

if there were an earned surplus or net profits out of which dividends might be declared in states that have the net profits or surplus test, the insolvency test, if tied to the other, may well make impossible a distribution of a dividend under the equity definition of insolvency. And, of course, if net assets must be figured—as they should—by including the stated capital item as a liability, the insolvency test, as adopted in bankruptcy, would bar a dividend except where a surplus shows up by subtracting liabilities, including stated capital, from total assets, after deductions have been made for depreciation, bad debts, etc., which good accounting as well as the law requires.

The "impairment of capital" or balance sheet type of statute prohibits the declaration of dividends which will impair the corporation's capital or while it is impaired, or unless the value of assets remaining after the payment of the dividend is at least equal to its total liabilities including "capital." [32] Or the statute may be framed in some such fashion as the Delaware one which, in part, provides that dividends may be declared "out of its net assets in excess of its capital." [33]

Unless the statute defines with precision the term "capital" a problem remains as to just what is meant by this term. A recent case had to interpret a statutory provision that "Dividends of profit may be made by the directors, but the capital shall not thereby be reduced, until all debts due from the corporation are paid." The court saw three possibilities: (1) that "capital" might mean the dollar value received on the issuance of the stock as the consideration for it; (2) that it could mean the par value at issuance; or (3) that "capital" might mean the actual capital at the opening of the current, accounting period. A reduction of capital section of the statute prohibited corporations from dividing any of the corporate property so "as to reduce their stock below its par value, until all debts are paid . . . ." Thus, by examining both sections, the court concluded that "capital" in the first section meant the aggregate par value of the outstanding capital stock of the corporation.[34] The court was then posed with the further problem of what was meant by "profits." Admitting that the term, standing alone, was capable of several interpretations including that of the gain made by a business or through an investment when both receipts and expenses were taken into account, and a sum determined by the "excess of the aggregate value of all assets over the liabilities including the capital stock," the court chose the latter as being in harmony with the whole

32. N.Y.Stock Corp.Law § 58.

33. Del.Gen.Corp.Law § 170 (old § 34). The Delaware statute also permits dividends out of net profits for the fiscal year then current and/or the preceding year.

34. George E. Warren Co. v. U. S., 76 F.Supp. 587 (D.Mass.1948), interpreting the Maine statute.

tenor of the two statutory provisions and interpreted "capital stock" to mean the aggregate par value of the corporation's outstanding shares, the only kind of shares it had issued.

The terms "capital" and "capital stock" have been used to mean various things to different courts and some times to the same court so that much confusion has resulted. A new term, "stated capital," made necessary by the advent of no-par shares offers less confusion for it has had no interpretation which has been at variance with its intended meaning, legal capital. It appears as a liability—a fictitious one for the corporation is not bound to pay it—in the form of X-dollars, a figure which represents the aggregate par value of shares of that type issued and outstanding, the total amount capitalized in the case of no-par value shares, any amounts transferred from the surplus account to the capital account when stock dividends have been distributed or when there has been simply a transfer to increase capital, less any amounts that have resulted from a statutorily authorized reduction of stated capital. It is a "quantum"—a value figure— which remains the same no matter what the condition of the company may be until there has been a change made by legally recognized procedures. It would be well for courts and legislatures to abandon the old term and substitute in its stead the term "stated capital" which cannot be confused with anything else in the capital category. Unless assets reasonably valued exceed total liabilities including stated capital, there is nothing from which dividends could be declared without having the declaration out of capital. And the basic concept that dividends may not be declared out of capital would be violated. A few statutes have provided for the declaration of dividends out of surpluses *and also* out of profits derived during a stated period such as the present year and perhaps the preceding one. These we shall consider shortly.

The third type of dividend statute carries with it the "net profits" test, sometimes described in a statute in terms of "earned surplus." [35] Other descriptive phrases may be joined such as "net profits or actual surplus," [36] or "surplus . . . or net profits arising from business," [37] this latter statute also carrying a provision against the dividing, withdrawing or otherwise paying to the shareholders any part of the capital stock or of reducing it except in the manner prescribed by law. If the terms used are solely confined to a declaration out of profits, or net profits, or out of earnings, there is still the matter of what is

---

35. West's Ann.Cal.Corp.Code § 1500 uses the term "earned surplus." But cash or property dividends are also provided for out of other funds. Tex.Bus.Corp.Act, Art. 2.38, provides for cash or property dividends out of the "unreserved and unrestricted earned surplus." And see Art. 4.13C.

36. Conn.Gen.Corp.Law § 5140.

37. N.J.Gen.Corp.Law § 14:8–19.

meant. Do these terms mean an excess of assets over liabilities including stated capital? The earned surplus account from corporate birth? For the current year? Or is the meaning confined to what the profit and loss statement shows as a profit for the current year, or from the corporate birth? [38]

It has been said that in order to have "undivided profits" or "surplus" the net assets of the corporation must exceed its stated capital.[39] But, thought Circuit Judge Dobie in *United States* v. *Riely*,[40] the term "net earnings" in the Virginia statute under construction was not synonymous with these terms. Thus, it was held that the statute giving power to declare dividends "out of net earnings, or out of its net assets in excess of its capital" made it possible for the corporation to declare dividends out of current profits while capital was impaired. "Manifestly," wrote Judge Dobie, "net earnings (on the one hand) and excess of assets over capital (on the other hand) are utterly distinct and separate. Either may exist, or not exist, as to a specified period, with, or without the other."

Two things were stressed: (1) that there were no creditors involved, and (2) the position of the comma. But it has been pointed out that where courts have accepted the "profits" criterion and applied an income test rather than one which balances assets against liabilities including stated capital, they have usually included realized gains which have accumulated from the beginning of corporate existence to the present and have not picked out, as Judge Dobie did, gains accumulated in any specific period.[41] And if there have been losses during a part of the entire corporate life which have at least equalled any periodic gains, there is nothing from which dividends may be declared. In fact, these holdings have generally considered that the legislature has used terms in the alternative, not to give two chances for board action, but (perhaps) to be doubly sure that, in any event, dividends will not be declared out of capital or when capital is impaired; that dividends must come from values ascertained by deducting stated capital from net assets, the difference being usually described as "surplus." Where statutes have used the term "profits" or "net profits" and have specified an alternative based on asset valuation, the failure to specify some particular account-

38. See Ballantine, Lattin and Jennings, Cases and Materials on Corporations 789 (2d ed. 1953).

39. Willcuts v. Milton Dairy Co., 275 U.S. 215, at 218, 48 S.Ct. 71, at 72, 72 L.Ed. 247 (1927).

40. 169 F.2d 542 (4th Cir., 1948), cert. denied 335 U.S. 908, 69 S.Ct. 411, 93 L.Ed. 441 (1949). For the present Virginia statute which permits dividends in cash or property from "unreserved and unrestricted earned surplus . . . or out of capital surplus, howsoever arising. . . ." See Va.Stock Corp. Act of 1956, § 13.1–43, and § 13.1–18 defining stated capital.

41. Note, 62 Harv.L.Rev. 130 (1948). See severe criticism of the holding in 34 Va.L.Rev. 860 (1948)

ing period for ascertaining "profits" has usually been interpreted to mean that no alternative source is really meant.[42] Was more emphasis given to the placing of the comma than ought to have been? Should the strongest basic concept in dividend law, that dividends must not be declared out of capital or when capital is impaired, be overridden by what the dictionary describes as "a mark of punctuation (,) used to indicate the smallest interruptions in continuity of thought or grammatical construction?"

§ 6. Importance of the Legal Capital Concept

The various terms used to convey the "legal capital" meaning are not important if the term used, whether it be "capital stock," "capital," "stated capital," "legal capital," or some other term be understood. The confusion comes from previous judicial constructions which have not been uniform.

If corporate officials have an accurate knowledge of the reasons behind the item of legal or stated capital, they will not be likely to declare or distribute dividends from values which should be kept intact for the safety of creditors and shareholders. However, unless conservative accounting has produced a balance sheet of accurate or near-accurate asset values, a distortion may result in the "surplus" or "earned surplus" figure (if one turns up) from which a dividend is declared. Better, by far, for the protection of creditors and senior shareholders and for the corporation itself, is the listing of assets below their true value than above it, for dividends will then come out of a surplus which is smaller than otherwise, and thus capital will not be dissipated. And this, of course, is one reason why inventories under one accounting concept are carried on the balance sheet at cost or market value whichever is lower, and why diminution in value of corporate assets should be taken into consideration, at least for dividend-declaration purposes.

Stated simply, the net assets equal capital and surplus. And legal or stated capital, which is merely a mathematical (or value) figure, represents in dollars the amount in assets (capital) which may not be withdrawn by the shareholders. This is the quantum which has frequently been called a "trust fund" for the benefit of creditors, another term which, for the sake of clarity, should also be abandoned. In the descriptive language of Ballantine and Hills, "The legal capital may be compared with a certain level marked by a gauge upon the corporate reservoir of assets. If the assets stand above that level, they may be drawn off for the shareholders. If the assets fall below that level, the

---

42. Ballantine and Hills, Corporate Capital and Restrictions Upon Dividends Under Modern Corpora-   tion Laws, 23 Calif.L.Rev. 229, 242 (1935).

remaining supply must be reserved for business purposes and for creditors." [43] In general, the stated capital figure is derived from the consideration received or to be received for the corporation's issued shares, plus any surpluses frozen by stock dividends or transferred to stated capital without a further issue of shares, less any amount by which stated capital has been reduced through permissive statutory procedures.[44]

If inflated values have been assigned to assets transferred to the corporation for shares, or shares of the par value variety have been sold for less than par, a distortion, which has dangerous possibilities if not corrected prior to a dividend declaration, results. In such a case it has been held that profits are to be ascertained by reference to the "capital stock paid in," and not to the nominal share capital, that is, the stated capital, measured by the aggregate par value of the issued shares.[45] The statute under construction permitted dividends from surplus, or net profits arising from its business but prohibited the dividing, withdrawing, or in any way paying to shareholders any part of the "capital stock." The court looked only to see that the value of the present corporate assets exceeded that of the "actual assets" with which the company began business. The prohibition against dissipating capital, held the court, was "to prevent the frittering away of the actual assets with which the company is to do business, not the nominal assets which it has never received, and for which it still has a claim against the subscribers of unpaid stock." [46]

Better cases, but fewer, have held that the water must first be squeezed out before profits or a surplus exists out of which

43. Ibid. at 234 and 235.

44. § 2(j), A.L.I. Model Business Corporation Act (Rev. 1953), defines "stated capital" and the "Comment" following it states that this term was used "to avoid the ambiguity which has frequently resulted from the use of the terms 'capital' and 'capital stock.' " § 2(k), (*l*) and (m) respectively define "surplus," "earned surplus," and "capital surplus."

45. Goodnow v. American Writing Paper Co., 73 N.J.Eq. 692, 69 A. 1014 (1908), aff'g 72 N.J.Eq. 645, 66 A. 607 (1907); United Light & Power Co. v. Grand Rapids Trust Co., 85 F.2d 331 (6th Cir., 1936). But compare the manner of treatment by an administrative agency. Common stock with initial watering of $3,-000,000 was denied the right to dividends until this amount had accumulated. Northwestern Electric Co.

v. Federal Power Commission, 321 U.S. 119, 64 S.Ct. 450, 88 L.Ed. 596 (1944). In Peters v. United States Mortgage Co., 13 Del.Ch. 11, 114 A. 598 (1921), the court emphasized the then wording of the Delaware statute of "capital stock paid in" to reach the result of the Goodnow case. The statute has since been amended. See Del.Gen.Corp.Law § 154 concerning the determination of the amount of capital.

46. Goodnow v. American Writing Paper Co., supra, note 45, 69 A. at 1016. The difficulty with the last clause of this quotation seems obvious. If there is watered stock the traditional view does not put any liability upon the holders except for the benefit of creditors. If there is a promise to pay the additional amount, then the stock is not watered. See the discussion of this problem at page 414, supra.

dividends may be declared.[47]   And with the many statutes existing today which specifically prohibit the issue of par value shares
for less than par, there is no good reason why a court should hesitate to freeze sufficient earnings to take up the deficiency created
by issuing stock at less than par.[48]   This is another point at which
courts should condemn the watering of stock not only when it
has a bearing upon the payment of debts but even when the corporation itself, though perfectly solvent, withholds earnings to
take up the water in prior issues of shares.

A similar problem arises when the corporation has not taken
account of items such as depreciation, obsolescence—whether actual or through a decline of patronage, sometimes called "external
obsolescence"—, and depletions.[49]   Where reasonable deductions
for depreciation, obsolescence, or depletions (except in wasting
asset corporations), would have resulted in eliminating a surplus
derived through a failure to take account of these items, a declaration of a dividend could not be made without impairing capital.[50]

§ 7.   How Funds (Values) are Determined from Which Divi-dends may be Declared

Certain phases of this problem have already been discussed
in the sections above.   Basicly, any determination must be founded upon good accounting principles and, for the most part, courts
have been willing to follow them barring some local statute which
seemed to point otherwise.[51]   It is clear today that, for dividend
purposes, depreciation and depletion of corporate assets must be
taken into consideration in the process of establishing asset values on the balance sheet before a remainder (surplus) may be ascertained by deducting liabilities, including stated capital, from
the aggregate value of assets.   The contrary rule exists in England and was expressed early by Lindley, L. J., that "fixed capital

47.   Shaw v. Ansaldi Co., Inc., 178
      App.Div. 589, at 600, 165 N.Y.S. 872
      (1917); Nat. Newark & Essex Bank-
      ing Co. v. Durant Motor Co., 124
      N.J.Eq. 213, 1 A.2d 316 (Ch. 1938),
      aff'd 125 N.J.Eq. 435, 5 A.2d 767 (Ct.
      Err. & App.1939).

48.   On watered stock generally, see
      page 403 et seq., supra.

49.   See United Light & Power Co. v.
      Grand Rapids Trust Co., 85 F.2d
      331 (6th Cir., 1936), modifying and
      affirming 7 F.Supp. 511 (D.Mich.
      1931).   "In dete.mining true market
      value and impairment of capital,
      depreciation, in its ordinarily ac-

cepted sense, is always an element
for consideration."   This is equally
true of obsolescence, held the court.

50.   Ibid. in trial court, 7 F.Supp. at
      523: "If theoretical accounting fails
      to record obvious facts, the duty of
      the board of directors in consider-
      ing declaration of dividends is not
      performed unless such facts are
      given due weight and considera-
      tion."

51.   See N.C.Bus.Corp. Act of 1957,
      § 55–49 which specifically authorizes
      "accepted principles of sound ac-
      counting practice" except where the
      statute requires a different stand-
      ard.

may be sunk and lost, and yet the excess of current receipts over current payments may be divided, but that floating or circulating capital must be kept up, as otherwise it will enter into and form part of such excess, in which case to divide such excess without deducting the capital which forms part of it will be contrary to law." [52] Thus, the English law does not require that depreciation or depletion of fixed assets be taken account of before dividends may be declared. Even with current assets, apart from those described as "circulating capital" which probably means stock in trade in the narrowest sense,[53] the English law does not require a decrease in value to be taken into account before dividends may be declared. This practice is not to be praised, however.

Modern statutes are defining stated capital, some accepting one common law view that, as far as par value shares outstanding are concerned, the amount in cash or property accepted for them, though below the aggregate par value of such shares, constitutes the value that represents capital which must not be paid out in dividends.[54] Others, and it is believed to be the better type of statute, define the term so that the par value must be represented by assets equal to it.[55] Such statutes at least make clear what was not clear under the decisions defining "capital stock" or "capital" or, perhaps, "share capital." These definitions, however, do not cover another difficult problem of how the values are to be determined at the time of the declaration of the dividend.

After stating the requirement that depreciation must be taken into account in ascertaining funds (values) available for dividends, the further question must be asked: What accounting concept of depreciation may or must be accepted, for there are several? [56] Practically all tangible capital assets except land de-

---

52. Verner v. General and Commercial Investment Trust, [1894] 2 Ch. 239, at 266 (C.A.): "The law is much more accurately expressed by saying that dividends cannot be paid out of capital than by saying that they can only be paid out of profits."

53. Gower, Modern Company Law 113 (1954).

54. Va.Stock Corp. Act of 1956, § 13.1–18 provides: "In case of the issuance by a corporation of shares having a par value the consideration received therefor shall constitute stated capital . . ." etc. As to no-par value shares under the same section, the directors may allocate any part of the consideration to capital surplus to the extent provided by the subscription contract. If there is no contractual provision

then, within a period of 60 days after the issuance of the shares, the directors may allocate up to 25% of the consideration to capital surplus. But N.C.Bus.Corp. Act of 1957, § 55–47(b) (2) requires the entire amount of consideration received or to be received for no-par shares to be capitalized except such portion as the board prior to or at the time of issuance designates as paid-in surplus.

55. N.C.Bus.Corp. Act of 1957, § 55–47(b) (1); Ohio Rev.Code § 1701.30 (A); A.L.I.Model Bus.Corp.Act § 2 (j) (Rev.1953).

56. Is it to be straight-line, accelerated depreciation, a present value appraisal, retirement or replacement accounting? Does it matter if reputable accountants recognize it for a particular business? See,

preciate, and land were it used for farming without a replenishment of minerals consumed or of eroded topsoil would depreciate as farming land. Depreciation accounting has as its aim the distributing of the cost or other basic value of such capital assets over the period of estimated life of the particular asset in some systematic manner. Thus, if the useful life of a particular piece of machinery is estimated at ten years, provision is made in each accounting period for a proportionate deduction which, over the estimated life period, will equal the cost or value of the item less its salvage value at the end. This periodic charge to expense is generally placed in an account called "Reserve for Depreciation." Where a corporation figures depreciation on a cost less salvage basis, deducting equal amounts in each accounting period over the estimated life of the asset, this is called straight-line depreciation accounting. It is, perhaps, the most common method used by industrial corporations. Probably any sound accounting practice concerning depreciation would be sustained by the courts. Thus, dividends are not payable out of nonexistent values when proper deductions are made due to the loss in value of an asset through depreciation. Even where the preferred shareholder's contract calls for a mandatory declaration of dividends when a proper fund exists, the corporation is justified in making, and probably must make adequate provision for depreciation.[57] But depreciation charges may be excluded by specific contract or where reasonably to be implied, either in a shareholder's contract or in a profit-sharing agreement, at least where creditors will not be prejudiced,[58] and where the statute does not require, as a few now do, that depreciation be taken into consideration.

Basicly the same problem arises in the matter of notes or accounts receivable, and in the diminution in value of assets which have been purchased at a higher price than the market existing at the time of the declaration of the dividend. A certain percentage of notes and accounts receivable will not be recoverable, and a deduction of an estimated percentage must be made for bad debts or dividends may be declared illegally out of values never to be realized.[59] The traditional carrying of inventories of finish-

Hills, The Law of Accounting and Financial Statements 94 et seq. (1956). There is a good discussion in Dodd and Baker's Cases and Materials on Corporations, Note on Depreciation, 1018 et seq. (2d ed. 1951).

57. Pardee v. Harwood Elect. Co., 262 Pa. 68, 105 A. 48 (1918). And, even in a wasting asset corporation, a charge should be set up against earnings to cover depreciation of the smelting and refining plants of a mining corporation. Wittenberg v. Federal Mining & Smelting Co., 15 Del.Ch. 147, 165, 133 A. 48 (Ch. 1926), aff'd 15 Del.Ch. 409, 138 A. 347 (1927).

58. Boothe v. Summit Coal Co., 55 Wash. 167, 104 P. 207 (1909); Purdue v. Ralph, 100 F.2d 518 (5th Cir., 1938).

59. Vogtman v. Merchants' Mortgage & Credit Co., 20 Del.Ch. 364, 178 A. 99 (1935); Cannon v. Wiscassett Mills Co., 195 N.C. 119, 141 S.E. 344 (1928).

ed or raw materials at cost or market price whichever is lower is another instance of conservative accounting which works toward the same end. And where there is a diminution in value of any asset or group of assets due to whatever cause, as where the corporation had purchased stocks and bonds at a cost of some $400,000 more than the present market value, the court quite properly held that this "unrealized diminution" in value must be deducted from the assets of the company for the purpose of determining whether profits or a deficit existed.[60] No matter what the balance sheet shows, held the court, the test is whether or not the value of the assets exceeds the debts and the liability to shareholders (stated capital) and this anticipates that all assets must be taken at their actual value.

But if assets are taken at their "actual value" what happens when such fixed assets as land, buildings or long-lived machinery, or current assets such as inventory, or the stock and bonds in the case in the preceding paragraph, have actually increased in value? Should unrealized appreciation in value be permitted to function in the acceptance of values for cash dividend purposes? Good accounting, and quite as good law, have decreed that unrealized appreciation must not be used for this purpose. There is much less danger, of course, in permitting its use when current assets are involved than in case of land, buildings and equipment which are not meant to be disposed of. Current finished-product assets will presumably be sold and the profit realized within a short time; or perhaps current inventory of raw materials will shortly be manufactured and put upon the market and the anticipated values realized. But the certainty is too risky. The practice has been allowed in New York under a statute providing that "No stock corporation shall declare or pay any dividend which shall impair its capital or capital stock, nor while its capital or capital stock is impaired," which provisions were thought to be the controlling ones of the section. Justice Walter, in the trial court, held that the terms "capital" and "capital stock" used in this statute meant the amount, i. e. the value, of property equal to the number of dollars specified as the par value of paid-up issued shares (or as the stated value of no-par shares), and that when the corporate net assets exceeded that number of dollars, the excess, whether contributed by the shareholders or otherwise obtained, was surplus or surplus profits and might be distributed as dividends. Other New York cases had used the term "otherwise obtained" and "accumulated" and there were some indications to the effect that a surplus might consist of increases arising from a revaluation of fixed assets. Said Justice Walter: "It thus

60. George E. Warren Co. v. United States, 76 F.Supp. 587 (D.Mass. 1948).

appears that after using the surplus and surplus profits terminology for practically a hundred years the legislature completely abandoned it, and I think that it is quite significant as indicating a conscious intent to get away from the idea of profits earned as a result of completed transactions as the sole source of dividends." [61] Since it is legitimate for corporations to borrow to pay dividends out of a proper fund, the creditors may eventually find themselves "out on a limb" because of dividends paid from unrealized values based upon appreciation in asset values, even of land not intended for sale.

It is believed that the better and much safer rule prohibits the payment of dividends out of surpluses derived from a revaluation of assets, i.e., out of unrealized appreciations in value. Besides recognizing the possible danger to creditors and to shareholders by virtue of dissipating the margin of safety provided by the stated capital concept, Justice Stern, aided by a specific statute, wrote: "The reason why a purely conjectural increase in valuations cannot be considered for the purpose of dividends is because such reappraisals, however apparently justified and accurate for the time being, are subject to market fluctuations, are merely anticipatory of future profit, and may never be actually *realized* as an asset of the company." [62]

Some of the modern statutes specifically providing against the use of unrealized appreciation values for dividend purposes contain a clause such as "unless the amount thereof shall have been transferred to, or included in, its stated capital." [63] Other statutes specifically permit a stock dividend from such a surplus.[64] The former may be interpreted, as it was in the case cited, as a permission to use such values, when a surplus turns up, to declare and distribute a stock dividend, thus freezing the values for the time being and taking nothing from the creditors or shareholders. But a danger does exist by virtue of the possibility of later reducing stated capital through statutory procedures and producing a "reduction surplus" which could be distributed to the shareholders. If this type of maneuvering should be attempted, the statutory prohibition against using unrealized appreciation for cash dividends would still warrant a court's

61. Randall v. Bailey, 23 N.Y.S.2d 173, at 180 (Sup.Ct.1940), aff'd 288 N.Y. 280, 43 N.E.2d 43 (1942). See Note, 65 Harv.L.Rev. 1339 (1952). Also, Notes in 10 U. of Chi.L.Rev. 350 (1943); 54 Harv.L.Rev. 505 (1941); 89 U. of Pa.L.Rev. 822 (1941); 50 Yale L.J. 306 (1940).

62. Berks Broadcasting Co. v. Craumer, 356 Pa. 620, 52 A.2d 571, at 574 (1947), discussed in Note, 96 U. of Pa.L.Rev. 123 (1947).

63. Ibid. discussing the Pennsylvania statute, 52 A.2d at 574–575.

64. Ohio Rev.Code § 1701.33(A). § 1701.32(F) prohibits the use of a surplus arising from unrealized appreciation of assets to reduce or write off any deficit in earned surplus, or the creation of a reserve.

cracking down upon this indirect method which violates, at least, the spirit of the prohibition.

Unrealized appreciation has been recognized for the restricted purpose of absorbing losses but with a warning that, until there has been an actual realization of a profit on the assets so revalued, a surplus so created may not be used for dividend purposes.[65] Some of the modern statutes likewise make provision for reducing or eliminating losses by such a procedure.[66] It seems questionable whether either the common law or statutes should permit the use of surpluses arising from unrealized appreciation for even this limited purpose. Stock dividends permitted by a number of statutes are relatively harmless for they take nothing from creditors or shareholders. But the elimination of losses by applying unrealized appreciation in values is likely to be as destructive in the long run as cash or property dividends from surpluses arising from similar revaluations.

"Good will" is an intangible asset which, if carried at more than a nominal value, has similar possibilities of danger when this item is included among the assets after business experience has indicated that the enterprise is a truly going concern—that customers do return again and again with their patronage. Good will has been defined as "the advantage or benefit, which is acquired by an establishment, beyond the mere value of the capital, stock (in trade), funds, or property employed therein, in consequence of the general public patronage and encouragement, which it receives from constant and habitual customers, on account of its local position, or common celebrity, or reputation for skill or affluence, or punctuality, or from other accidental circumstances or necessities, or even from ancient partialities or prejudices."[67] It is something which, in point of time, has had a substantial existence in the market place. If an enterprise has been purchased, part of the consideration may have gone to pay for the good will which the enterprise had previously acquired, and this is an asset which may be legitimately set up as one on the purchaser's books. This would be so whether the enterprise purchased had or had not previously carried good will on its own books as an asset. However, it has been said that "With more prudence than logic, accounting practice forbids the creator of good will from valuing in its Balance Sheet the clientele which

65. Titus v. Piggly Wiggly Corp., 2 Tenn.App. 184 (1925).

66. N.C.Bus.Corp. Act of 1957, § 55–49(e) and (i). § 55–50 permits the payment of cash or property dividends from a "capital surplus" created in whole or in part by revaluing corporate assets upward provided the two legitimate sources for such dividends are unavailable and then only to shares entitled to preferential dividends. But see § 1701.32(F) of the Ohio Rev.Code, supra, note 64.

67. Eisenstadt Mfg. Co. v. J. M. Fisher Co., 241 F. 241, at 244 (1st Cir., 1917), quoting from Story on Partnership, § 99.

it has gained and which it could sell for value if it wished." [68] Yet, it has been allowed and there would seem to be about the same reasons for not setting it up as there are in revaluing assets and setting them up at their increased values.[69] The dangers are about the same, for with fixed assets of the tangible variety there is permanence of acquisition with no intent to sell unless the company goes out of business. It is, of course, the same with good will, for good will proceeds with the enterprise, not without it. And as with unrealized appreciations in value, when the time comes to sell the enterprise, good will may amount to little or nothing.

Mention has been made of the creation of a surplus through the reduction of stated capital, thus diminishing the cushion for creditors and senior shareholders. If there are no senior, but only common shareholders, such a reduction in accordance with the authorized statutory procedures followed by a pro rata distribution to shareholders would be legal. Existing creditors, however, should be protected against loss (and some of the statutes specifically protect against this); and if the distribution results in the corporation's inability to pay its debts, there would be a transfer in fraud of creditors, which would warrant recovery from the shareholders receiving the fund to the extent necessary to pay such creditors.[70] Recent statutes have tended to give the corporation the cause of action for the recovery of insolvency and capital impairment dividends which procedure makes for greater simplicity than where creditors must sue. It also has the effect of giving the trustee in bankruptcy, if bankruptcy there is, the cause of action for the benefit of the creditors.

In the case of the distribution of a reduction surplus, the court is posed with a true application of the "trust fund theory" as the capital was intended to furnish a cushion for present creditors as long as any exist.[71] If after such a reduction of stated capital the corporation is inadequately capitalized for the normal

---

68. Hills, The Law of Accounting and Financial Statements 105 (1957).

69. Randall v. Bailey, supra, note 61, where good will of $3,000,000 was entered in the corporate books three years after the Bush Terminal Company was formed, this amount in stock having been issued to Mr. Bush earlier, presumably for his promotion services. For over 20 years the item appeared on the company's balance sheets. The court permitted it to stand.

70. See the Uniform Fraudulent Conveyance Act §§ 4 and 5, and § 2(1) which defines "insolvent." 20 states have adopted this act prior to 1957. The same problem of what is meant by "insolvency" exists unless, as here, the legislation defines the term. And see the Bankruptcy Act § 67d (11 U.S.C.A. § 107(d)) and compare it with U.F.C.A. § 2(1). Section 70e of the Bankruptcy Act (11 U.S.C.A. § 110(e)) gives the trustee in bankruptcy the right to avoid fraudulent transfers.

71. Wood v. Dummer, 3 Mason 308, 30 Fed.Cas. 435, No. 17,944 (C.C.D. Me.1824).

business risks, problems of shareholder liability arise which are similar to those existing in case of the original inadequate capitalization of the corporation.[72]

It may be supposed that preferred shareholders exist when a stated capital reduction has been made of capital represented by common shares. This, of course, has the effect of reducing the cushion of protection upon which senior shareholders are entitled to rely. Particularly vicious is the effect where the preferred shares carry a preference upon dissolution. It is also disadvantageous to preferred shareholders since a distribution of the resulting reduction surplus leaves just that much less capital to work for the ultimate corporate objectives. In one important case, a substantial statutory reduction of stated capital applicable to common shares was held to be an alteration of preferred shareholder rights entitling those who dissented to an appraisal of and payment for their shares.[73] The practical effect of reducing stated capital, whether the reduction surplus is distributed or not, is to put the corporation in a position to pay more easily dividends to the common shares as this part of stated capital liability is no longer required to be figured in ascertaining an earned surplus. And where there has been common capital impairment, a statutorily prescribed reduction will make it unnecessary to replenish the deficit through future earnings and thus restore the protective cushion. Both creditors and senior shareholders must take their chance that capital may be lost in carrying on the business. They must likewise assume the risk of statutorily prescribed reductions in stated capital. However, an adequately drafted preferred share contract will protect such senior shares against the dissipation of capital assets through the reduction of stated capital.

When a corporation receives more consideration for its par value shares than par, or capitalizes less than it has received for its no-par shares, the excess is sometimes called "paid-in surplus" or "capital surplus." A similar surplus results when shares already capitalized have been donated to the company and it sells these treasury shares for what they will bring. Such surpluses should be carried on the corporate books and financial statements as a separate surplus item indicating its source. If a subsequent issue of par value shares is sold at a higher price than par, it may have been sold thus so that present shareholders would not have their interest in the the company's assets diluted; that is, that shareholders' interests be equalized.[74] Or, it may be that the

72. See p. 68 et seq., supra, this text.

73. Matter of Kinney, 279 N.Y. 423, 18 N.E.2d 645 (1939), commented upon in 39 Col.L.Rev. 1037 (1939) and 52 Harv.L.Rev. 1011 (1939).

74. See Note, Declaration of Dividends from Paid-in Surplus, 31 Col. L.Rev. 844, at 850 (1931), where it is suggested that where premiums are paid to equalize rights of unt-

market price, for whatever reason, was higher than par. The result is the same. This is not, as has sometimes been argued, an "accretion" to capital. There is no such thing, the result being a type of surplus which, under many statutes, is legally usable for dividends.[75] In other words, legal or stated capital remains at the same figure until increased or decreased by authorized statutory procedures, and the assets which constitute the protection to creditors and shareholders remain at the same value figure.[76]

Profits derived through the purchase and sale of an asset originally intended for permanent corporate use, such as real estate in the form of land or buildings, are likewise not "accretions to capital," but, like other profits, may figure in the matter of dividends.[77] Whether they do may need close interpretation where the particular statute provides for dividends from "earned surplus" or from profits, net profits or surplus profits, though it would seem that they would. If the statute is phrased in terms of "profits arising from the business," reasonable interpretation would justify a contrary result. Where distributions are made to shareholders out of extraordinary funds, they are entitled to know their source so that they may not be misled into believing that their corporation is wallowing in profits when in fact the distribution is from a source not likely to turn up again soon. Some statutes require such a notice.

There is little restriction by state legislation placed upon the creation or use of paid-in surplus. Delaware, for example, gives the directors the authority to assign substantially all of the consideration received for no-par shares to paid-in surplus, thus making this fund available for dividends.[78] By the use of this

standing shares in an accumulated surplus, the paid-in surplus should be considered earned surplus.

75. Equitable Life Assurance Society of the United States v. Union Pacific Ry. Co., 212 N.Y. 360, 106 N.E. 92, L.R.A.1915D, 1052 (1914). The defendant, a Utah corporation, retired a convertible bond issue by cancelling $175 face value of bonds for each $100 par value share of stock, thus realizing a premium of $75 as if this had been paid additionally in cash for the share of stock. A total of $15,000,000 was thus created as paid-in surplus. Under the present English law, premiums paid for shares must appear in the balance sheet as "Share Premium Account" and not be distributed as dividends. See page 423, supra, of this text.

76. See Note, Accretion of Capital as a Basis for Dividends, 14 Col.L.Rev. 524 (1914).

77. Lubbock v. British Bank of South America, [1892] 2 Ch. 198. But whatever profit or windfall gain there is must pass through the regular channels of bookkeeping before dividends may be declared. Foster v. New Trinidad Lake Asphalt Co., [1901] 1 Ch. 208; Cross v. Imperial Continental Gas Ass'n, [1923] 2 Ch. 553.

78. Del.Gen.Corp.Law of 1953, § 154. Ohio Rev.Code § 1701.30(B) (1), requires the amount received to be capitalized unless, prior to the execution and delivery of the share certificates, those legally permitted to fix the consideration specify the portion to be capitalized. In case of shares with a preference upon

technique, prohibitions against the payment of dividends out of capital may be avoided. But there is also real danger to the preferred shareholders of no-par shares since amounts they have paid which have been credited to paid-in surplus can ordinarily be used to pay dividends on junior shares and even to purchase such shares. Statutes which confine dividends to surplus profits arising from the business, or which impliedly suggest this limitation, are difficult, if not impossible, to interpret as including paid-in surplus as profits from the business except, perhaps, upon the theory that the premium paid has, as its basis, the equalizing of shareholder-interest in the earned surplus then existing.[79] But even if the particular statute can be interpreted to permit the payment of dividends and the purchase of the corporation's shares from paid-in surplus—and most of the statutes can be so interpreted—, a court would be justified in using its equity powers to protect senior shares against the use of a paid-in surplus acquired through a sale of these same shares to pay dividends to junior shareholders or to purchase junior shares. And it has been said that "Even where the paid-in surplus has been contributed by *junior shares*, it may be improper to permit use of such paid-in surplus for dividends on or purchases of the junior shares." [80] As yet the case law is scarce on these problems. This

involuntary liquidation of the corporation, limited protection is provided for. Paid-in surplus is designated as "capital surplus" and cash, property, or stock dividends may be paid from it. § 1701.33(A), but notice of the source must be given shareholders under § 1701.33(F). N.C.Bus.Corp.Act of 1957, § 55–47 (b) (2), requires the agreed consideration of no-par shares to be capitalized except such portion as the board of directors prior to or at the time of issuance of the shares designates as paid-in surplus. The A.L.I.Model Bus.Corp.Act, § 19, requires the entire consideration for no-par shares to be capitalized unless the corporation shall determine that only a part thereof shall be stated capital. "Within a period of sixty days after the issuance of shares without par value, the board of directors may allocate to capital surplus not more than twenty-five per cent of the consideration received for the issuance of such shares." Shares with preferences in corporate assets have limited protection in case of involuntary dissolution.

79. Merchant & Insurers Reporting Co. v. Schroeder, 39 Cal.App. 226, 178 P. 540 (1918), which apparently involved an initial paid-in surplus and not one acquired through equalizing shareholders' interests. The court held the entire proceeds to be part of the corporation's capital stock; hence, not profits from the business. Sed quaere, the capitalization of the full amount paid for the shares? The case might well have been decided on the ground that such premiums do not amount to "surplus profits arising from the business." West's Ann.Cal.Corp. Code § 1901 now provides that such premiums shall be credited to paid-in surplus. See Roberts v. Roberts-Wicks Co., 184 N.Y. 257, 77 N.E. 13 (1906), interpreting a preferred share contract with dividend preferences "out of the surplus profits arising from the business of the company" as not applying to a reduction surplus. Accord: Hull v. Pfister & Vogel Leather Co., 235 Wis. 653, 294 N.W. 18 (1940) (reduction surplus not "profits").

80. Dodd and Baker's Cases and Materials on Corporations 1135 (2d ed. 1951).

gives the opportunity to create an adequate and protective common law when the problems arise.

Close to the problems of paid-in surplus are those arising from a statutory reduction of stated capital, some phases of which have been considered above. This, too, is sometimes described as a paid-in surplus though the more accurate term is reduction surplus. To one unacquainted with the judicial mind, a surplus derived through a stated capital reduction would look very much like capital and, if it were distributed, would appear to be a return of capital assets. But, in one of the few cases involving the use of a reduction surplus—in this case arising from a consolidation of two corporations—as a fund from which dividends might be paid, the court stated: "If we do not look behind the organization of the new corporation, but consider only what happened at the time of organization, the surplus would fall in the class of a paid-in surplus resulting from the receipt of assets, upon issuance of the stock of the corporation, in excess of the par value of the stock. There is ample authority for the proposition that premiums realized from the sale of stock may be regarded as profits out of which dividends may be paid." [81] Even more extreme and unrealistic was the court's opinion that an earned surplus wiped out by losses was restored upon a reduction of stated capital and might then qualify (as formerly) as an "earned surplus." Since the dividend statute did not limit dividends to "current earnings," the court held that the reduction surplus could be distributed to the preferred shareholders in accordance with their contract and to common shareholders so long as the corporation was solvent and provided payment would not render it insolvent, and provided also that payment would not diminish the amount of the "capital" of the corporation. The term "capital" was interpreted to mean "capitalized assets" having the same meaning as "capital stock," that is, as stated or legal capital. The same dangers to senior shareholders exist in this situation as in the case of dividends paid from paid-in surplus, as has already been pointed out.

Some statutes have given limited protection to senior shareholders upon a stated capital reduction. A usual limitation is that the reduction must not fall below the liquidation preferences, if any, of the preferred shares, nor below the aggregate par value shares without liquidation preferences to remain outstanding after the reduction.[82] Further protection is given by

---

81. Graham v. Louisville Transit Co., 243 S.W.2d 1019, at 1022, 28 A.L.R. 2d 1171 (Ky.1951). See also Haggard v. Lexington Utilities Co., 260 Ky. 261, 84 S.W.2d 84 (1935), cited by the court in the Graham case.

82. West's Ann.Cal.Corp.Code § 1904, as amended in 1955; A.L.I. Model Bus.Corp.Act § 63, last paragraph. And see § 41(c) and (d) concerning distributions in partial liquidation.

some statutes through provisions that limit distributions from a reduction surplus to dividends to preferred shareholders and to the redemption and purchase of preferred shares.[83]   However, reduction surpluses have been authorized to be used to eliminate losses or deficits.[84]   Since this puts the corporation in a position to pay from future earnings creating a surplus dividends to junior shareholders, the practical result is to permit to this extent a dividend out of a reduction surplus.   And, by such a reduction of stated capital, there is withdrawn from further use the assets represented by the amount of stated capital reduced.

§ 8.   "Wasting Asset" Corporations

When a corporation is organized to exploit a specific asset such as a mine, an oil field, a piece of land, or a patent, with no intention of continuing in business after such exploitation, the corporation is usually described as a wasting asset corporation. The shareholders, naturally, hope to obtain a profit from the venture and to receive back their capital investment.   As in case of other corporations, the various assets used to accomplish this task, such as buildings, machinery, tools, etc., are subject to charges of depreciation, depletion and other accounting procedures already discussed, since replacement may be necessary before the mission has been consummated.   But deductions for depletion or amortization of the asset or assets of the wasting type are held not legally necessary for the purpose of determining funds available for dividends, at least where but one class of stock is outstanding.   As long as creditors are protected, the return of capital by driblets, rather than through periodic reductions of stated capital and a distribution of a resulting reduction surplus, or upon final liquidation of the company, is not legally condemned.[85]   This is an exception to the basic rule that dividends must not be paid out of capital.   But shareholders, for their own protection, should be notified of the fact that such a dividend constitutes a partial distribution of capital.

Where shares with a preference as to assets upon dissolution are in the picture, unless provision is made for the future day when dissolution occurs, the preferred shareholders will eventually find themselves with no assets from which their dissolution

83.   West's Ann.Cal.Corp.Code § 1906. West's Ann.Cal.Corp.Code § 1504(b) permits share dividends out of both paid-in surplus and reduction surplus.

84.   Ohio Rev.Code § 1701.32(F) requires shareholder action; Ill.Bus. Corp.Act § 60a.

85.   Lee v. Neuchatel Asphalt Co., 41 Ch.Div. 1 (C.A.1889).   While pre-ferred and common shares were involved, there was apparently no preference in assets upon dissolution.   Accord: Excelsior Water & Mining Co. v. Pierce, 90 Cal. 131, 27 P. 44 (1891) (mining company); Mellon v. Mississippi Wire Glass Co., 77 N.J.Eq. 498, 78 A. 710 (1910) (patents were the assets).

preferences may be satisfied. In such a case, where capital was already depleted but the directors had voted dividends to both the preferred and the common shareholders, the preferred shareholders sought an injunction against paying the declared dividend to the common shareholders and against any dividend to common shares until the impairment of capital by the depletion of the ore bodies had been restored. In the alternative they asked for an injunction against paying dividends on common shares until a reserve equal to the difference between the net value of the existing assets and the par value of the outstanding preferred shares had been set up. A demurrer by the corporation was overruled, the chancellor stating: "It seems clear to me that on fundamental principles of right and justice, the complainants as preferred stockholders possessing a prior claim on capital assets have an equity which entitles them to protection against the proposed whittling away of those assets for the benefit of the less favored common stockholders." [86] While the chancellor found neither a surplus nor net profits existing, he further stated in a dictum that he inclined to the view that the dividend on the preferred was permissible, but not that on the common. In the final hearing, the finding was made that the assets exceeded the preferred share capital, so that current profits were payable, the statute in the meantime having been amended to permit dividends from current profits.[87]

Several statutes now expressly provide for wasting asset corporations. However, there is no uniformity of expression. The California statute confines the wasting asset category to corporations "engaged solely or substantially in the exploitation" of such assets, or when "organized solely or substantially to liquidate specific assets." [88] The Ohio act provides:[89] "If the articles of a corporation engaged in whole or in part in the exploitation of mines, timber, oil wells, gas wells, quarries, or other natural resources so provide, the corporation may compute its surplus for the purpose of paying dividends without making any deduction or allowance for the depletion of said assets incidental to the exploitation and sale thereof." Does this broad statement warrant any deviation for the purpose of protecting shareholders with dissolution preferences? Or does a provision contained in a pri-

---

86. Wittenberg v. Federal Mining & Smelting Co., 15 Del.Ch. 147, 133 A. 48, at 53 (Ch. 1926), aff'd 15 Del.Ch. 409, 138 A. 347, 55 A.L.R. 1 (Sup.Ct. 1927).

87. Ibid. 15 Del.Ch. 351, 138 A. 352 (Ch. 1927). For notes on the case, see 12 Cornell L.Q. 79 (1926); 40 Harv.L.Rev. 318 (1926); 26 Mich.L. Rev. 448 (1928).

88. West's Ann.Cal.Corp.Code § 1503. The liquidation preference of senior shares has protection under this section.

89. Ohio Rev.Code § 1701.33(E). Somewhat similar is N.C.Bus.Corp. Act of 1957, § 55–50(d). There is also a provision for liquidating specific assets of other kinds. § 55–50 (e) (2).

or subsection of the same section that "No dividend shall be paid to the holders of shares of any class in violation of the rights of the holders of any other class . . . " warrant an interpretation similar to that in *Wittenberg*?

In order for the wasting asset privilege to function under the Ohio act, the articles of incorporation must provide for dividends without allowing for depletion, which is an unusual provision capable of giving some warning to shareholders. And while the California statute more broadly defines wasting assets, the Ohio statute confines such to natural resources, thus eliminating the privilege in the exploitation of patents or leases or the assets (other than natural resources) in an estate. The American Law Institute Model Business Corporation Act also requires a provision in the articles of incorporation authorizing dividends in cash "out of depletion reserves," if such dividends are to be made from this source, and also confines the privilege to corporations engaged in exploiting natural resources. Shareholders must also be informed of the source of such dividends concurrently with their distribution.[90]

There has been a good deal of criticism by legal scholars of the doctrine and of statutes which have furthered its application. Without statutory aid, it is questionable whether courts should permit a distribution of capital without using the statutorily approved method of reducing stated capital.[91] The danger to creditors and senior shareholders is obvious. And, whether with or without statutory aid, where the corporation does not use the reduction of stated capital provisions in the statute, the court should insist upon the setting up of sufficient reserves to protect creditors and senior shareholders who stand to lose if some of the statutory provisions are to be interpreted literally.[92] If the reasons for requiring a stated capital are kept clearly in mind, no court should go wrong on the measure of protection to which creditors and senior shareholders are entitled.

§ 9. Alternative Sources of Dividends

A number of statutes today provide alternative sources from which dividends may be declared and paid. The Delaware provisions of 1927 served as a model. Under this statute dividends may be declared and paid out of net assets in excess of the

90. A.L.I.Model Bus.Corp.Act § 40(b) (Rev. 1953).

91. See Ballantine, Corporations 587 (Rev. ed. 1946). He contends that the American decisions are based upon "erroneous English decisions" and that there is "no sufficient reason or need" for the doctrine.

92. But see Mellon v. Mississippi Wire Glass Co., 77 N.J.Eq. 498, 78 A. 710 (1910), where the court refused, in the absence of a provision in the share contract, to set up a sinking fund for the preferred.

corporation's capital or, if this fund (excess) does not exist, out of its net profits for the fiscal year then current and/or the preceding fiscal year.[93] While there has not been unanimous agreement in the construction of statutes authorizing in general terms payment of dividends alternatively out of net earnings, *or* out of net assets in excess of stated capital, the better and weight of authority has insisted upon a statutory provision, such as that contained in the Delaware statute, that the alternative net profits provision be specific as to the time when net profits were earned. Without such a provision, the statutory construction has usually been that the legislature intended but one fund, keeping stated capital intact, to be possible for dividends, that is, net profits over the entire corporate life to the time of the declaration of dividends.[94]

The result of alternative provisions of the Delaware type is to permit dividends out of current profits even when capital is impaired. Such dividends have sometimes been described as "nimble dividends." However, under the Delaware statute, preferred shareholders are given limited protection. It has been pointed out that no significant construction of the terms "net profits" or "net earnings" has appeared; that the meaning of "current" fiscal year is not clear.[95] It would seem as obvious here, as elsewhere in determining funds for dividends, that recognized accounting principles must be used in ascertaining what are profits or earnings; that notice must be taken of those items which good accounting procedures require in corporate profit and loss or income statements; that is, that those charges which good accounting practice would recognize as proper against current income should be made, and nothing further.[96]

In the last analysis, good accounting procedures must decide the important doubts about the nimble dividend statutes. The fact that the law has generally followed such procedures when known gives encouragement that it will continue to follow them when new problems arise. Where accountants are not in agreement, the court, as in the past, will have to make its decision on

93. Del.Gen.Corp.Law § 170; West's Ann.Cal.Corp.Code § 1500(b), as amended in 1957, is somewhat similar. Both attempt to protect the liquidation preference. See also Minn.Bus.Corp.Act § 301.22. N.C. Bus.Corp.Act § 55–50(a) (1) and (2) permits dividends out of earned surplus or (2) "Out of the amount of net profits earned during the current or preceding accounting period, each said period to be not less than six months or more than one year in duration, regardless of any impairment of stated capital." The California provision authorizes dividends from "net profits earned during the preceding accounting period, which shall not be less than six months nor more than one year in duration."

94. See discussion at pp. 471–472, supra, this text.

95. Dodd and Baker's Cases and Materials on Corporations 1158 (2d ed. 1951).

96. See Kehl, Corporate Dividends 64, 65, 151 et seq. (1941) for reasonable solutions.

what it considers the best thinking on the particular matter. Barring clear statutory provisions, dividend law is in the realm of what might be called the common law of accounting, an area upon which lawyers, unless they have an accounting background, should tread lightly. Courts might well accept as common law a provision in one of the most up-to-date corporation statutes, reading: [97] "Except where provisions of this chapter specifically require a standard or impose additional limitations, the assets of a corporation may, for the purpose of determining the lawfulness of dividends or of distributions or withdrawals of corporate assets to or for the shareholders, be carried on the books in accordance with generally accepted principles of sound accounting practice applicable to the kind of business conducted by the corporation." It is believed that, in so far as courts have touched upon dividend and other distribution problems, this section restates what common law there is.

§ 10. Consolidated Balance Sheets

Consolidated financial statements are used for the purpose of showing the financial condition of a parent and its subsidiaries as if they were one enterprise. For the purpose of ascertaining whether a fund exists from which dividends may be declared, it has been held that a consolidated balance sheet may not be used.[98] When dividends are declared by the subsidiaries, the obligations so created belong to the parent company and, like other things of value, after passing through the corporate books of account in the usual manner, may turn up as part of a proper fund out of which the parent may pay dividends. However, until the subsidiaries have declared dividends, the consolidated balance sheet represents, to the extent of earnings or surpluses capable of paying dividends, unrealized appreciations in value. And these, as we have already seen, may not, by the better view, be used as a basis for dividends. However, it is probable that the use of a consolidated balance sheet as a basis for dividends is not as dangerous as declarations out of unrealized appreciations in value of fixed assets, or even of assets which are fairly liquid, since the parent has control of the subsidaries' activities and can readily make dividends from its subsidiaries available out of funds which the law permits for such use.

Because of this control over the declaration of its subsidiaries' dividends, there is a real danger, particularly to senior shareholders in the parent, and especially to noncumulative pre-

97. N.C.Bus.Corp.Act of 1957, § 55–49(b).

98. Cintas v. American Car & Foundry Co., 131 N.J.Eq. 419, 25 A.2d 418 (Ch. 1942), aff'd 132 N.J.Eq. 460, 28 A.2d 531 (1942).

ferred shareholders, that dividends legally possible from the subsidiaries will be retarded for ulterior purposes.[99]

Another problem presented by parent-subsidiary dealings with each other is that of paper profits of either or both not yet realized in specie. May such paper profits be used to increase the surplus of the dividend-declaring unit? The general rule has been that such inter-company book profits are in the category of unrealized appreciation and thus may not be used to increase the surplus account.[1] And, of course, the same rule applies to unrealized profits in dealings between subsidiaries.

§ 11. Liability of Directors for Declaring and Paying Illegal Dividends

The liability of directors generally for their wilful and negligent acts is discussed elsewhere in this text.[2] The rules are similar in the declaration of dividends to those in other situations unless statutory provisions have set up a different standard. Thus, at common law, unless directors have wilfully or negligently declared and paid dividends from an improper source, they are neither liable to the corporation's creditors nor to the corporation or its shareholders.[3] And, barring circumstances which may reasonably lead directors to doubt the reports of company officials, they may safely rely upon balance sheets and statements of profit and loss presented to them by such representatives.

Some of the earlier statutes providing that directors must not make dividends except from surplus profits arising from the business, nor must they divide, withdraw or pay to the shareholders any part of the capital stock, were interpreted as absolute and without exception even where the dividend was declared in good faith and with due care. And where the statute made the directors who participated jointly and severally liable to the corporation, and to its creditors, it was sometimes construed to permit the corporation to recover, even where creditors were not injured, although the shareholders had received the benefit of the illegally declared dividend. It was thought not "inequitable that stockholders who have innocently participated in the distribution of the illegal dividends should have their stock restored to its normal value by contribution from the directors who have impaired the capital without being first required to pay back the

---

99. See note in 56 Harv.L.Rev. 132 (1942) which discusses the Cintas case in note 98, above.

1. Irving Trust Co. v. Gunder, 152 Misc. 83, 271 N.Y.S. 795 (Sup.Ct. 1934).

2. See page 241 et seq., this text.

3. See Note, The Statutory Responsibility of Directors for Payment of Dividends Out of Capital, 35 Yale L.J. 870, at 870–871 (1926).

dividend so paid to them." [4]   It was stated that "As a general rule, good faith on the part of the directors in declaring dividends from capital instead of from surplus profits is not a defense in a suit to recover the statutory liability." [5]

This was harsh doctrine which might reasonably have been softened by reading into the statute the necessity of bad faith or negligence if directors were to be held for what otherwise might be a mere mistake of judgment, or no mistake at all of theirs but of their appointed officials. And it has been held by a substantial majority that, without the aid of a statute, there may be no recovery from the directors by the shareholders or on their behalf, as this would require a paying over to shareholders again what they had already received in dividends.[6] However, in a two-class situation, would not the senior shares have superior equities in case illegal dividends, say, had been paid to junior shares? Would not common shareholders have a legitimate claim against directors who had paid illegal dividends to preferred shareholders?

Recent statutes have mitigated the harshness of some of the older statutes, though rigidly harsh ones still exist in some states. Some of the better statutes allow directors to rely upon corporate financial statements represented to them by the president or officer in charge of the books as being correct, or certified by independent public or certified public accountants fairly to represent the company's financial condition. Some further permit directors to take the assets at their book value in determining an amount distributable as dividends if done in good faith.[7] Under some statutes, knowledge of the director that dividends are improper must be shown.[8] Under others, he must have assented to the improper distribution.[9] Negligence in ascertaining

4. Southern California Home Builders v. Young, 45 Cal.App. 679, 188 P. 586, at 588 (1920). This case was decided under an older California statute. The California court was quoting from Appleton v. American Malting Co., 65 N.J.Eq. 375, 54 A. 454, at 456 (1903). The New Jersey statute was shortly amended. The actual damage to the corporation was held to be the amount its capital had been depleted by the unlawful dividends.

5. Southern California Home Builders v. Young, supra note 4, 188 P. at 593. Accord: Quintal v. Greenstein, 142 Misc. 854, 256 N.Y.S. 462 (Sup.Ct.1932), aff'd 236 App.Div. 719, 257 N.Y.S. 1034 (1932).

6. Spiegel v. Beacon Participations, Inc., 297 Mass. 398, 8 N.E.2d 895 (1937). The rights of creditors were not prejudiced. There was no statute governing recovery. The action was a derivative one, and the corporation was solvent. See also Turquand v. Marshall, L.R. 4 Ch.App. 376 (C.A.1869). But compare Loan Society of Philadelphia v. Eavenson, 248 Pa. 407, 94 A. 121 (1915), where a solvent corporation recovered illegal dividends from directors on the ground that otherwise a necessity might later arise to pay debts out of capital.

7. A.L.I.Model Bus.Corp.Act § 43(a) and (e); Del.Gen.Corp.Law § 172; Ill.Bus.Corp.Act § 42(h); Mo.Gen. and Bus.Corp.Law § 351.345.

8. Iowa Gen.Corp.Law § 491.41.

9. Vt.Gen.Corp.Law § 5824.

facts will not suffice under such provisions. There has been a tendency to require wilful or negligent action, as at common law, in recent statutes.[10]

As to the persons who may enforce directors' liability, the statutes vary. Some give the remedy to creditors;[11] others to the corporation;[12] still others to the creditors and to the corporation or shareholders.[13] Some restrict the remedy to present creditors while others also allow subsequent creditors the benefit of the remedy.[14] The statutes also vary as to whether the directors' liability is limited to the actual loss of creditors or shareholders or extends to the full amount of the illegal dividend irrespective of actual loss. There is much to be said for the latter type since the protection against diluting any but authorized funds through dividends is for present and future creditors, present and future shareholders and for senior against junior shareholders.[15]

§ 12. Liability of Shareholders who have Received Dividends Paid from an Improper Fund

Three situations under which such dividends may have been paid suggest themselves: (1) when the corporation is solvent at the time of the dividend distribution and remains solvent after it; (2) where solvency existed at the time of payment, but the corporation later became insolvent; and (3) where there was actual insolvency at the time of the dividend distribution. Situation (2) has been held by high authority to give no remedy when the shareholders have received no notice of the illegal source from which their dividends came.[16] The theory which supports this type of holding is that, so long as the dividend has not made the corporation insolvent, nothing has been taken from creditors of which they may complain. This ignores the idea that the stated capital cushion exists for creditors as well as for shareholders. Furthermore, it is claimed, shareholders "are in no better position than creditors to know the condition of the company, and it would be an unfair and unreasonable burden to require them to pay back, years after they have been spent, dividends received in good faith from a solvent corporation in regu-

---

10. West's Cal.Corp.Code § 825; Del. Gen.Corp.Law § 174; N.J.S.A. 14:-8–19.

11. See note 8, supra; Mass.Gen. Corp.Law § 37.

12. Mich.Gen.Corp.Act § 48.

13. N.Y.Stock Corp.Law § 58; Cal. Corp.Code § 825.

14. West's Ann.Cal.Corp.Code § 825 (existing creditors); Mo.Gen. and Bus.Corp.Law § 351.345 (subsequent creditors as well). See Whitfield v. Kern, 122 N.J.Eq. 332, 192 A. 48 (1937); id. v. id., 125 N.J.Eq. 511, 6 A.2d 471 (1939), which was the second appeal.

15. See Ballantine, Corporations 596 (Rev. ed. 1946).

16. McDonald, Receiver v. Williams, 174 U.S. 397, 19 S.Ct. 743, 43 L.Ed. 1022 (1899).

lar course of business." [17] There is substantial authority outside the federal area of operation sustaining the opposite viewpoint and holding shareholders liable to the extent of dividends so received for the benefit of creditors.[18]

When the corporation is insolvent at the time of the declaration and payment of the dividend, the innocent shareholders' position is held to be inferior to that of the creditors. As one court put it, "A sufficient and satisfactory ground is that money so paid after insolvency was taken from a fund held in trust for creditors and did not belong to the corporation; and it could give no title in the money it paid to one who did not receive it *bona fide* and for value." [19] There is also the further argument that this constitutes a transfer in fraud of creditors. But better still is the suggestion of Professor Ballantine that recovery is based upon the superior equity of creditors to be paid out of capital—liability of a quasi-contractual nature.[20] Statutes making directors liable in such situations do not relieve the shareholders from liability to repay such illegal dividends for the relief of creditors. The statutory remedy is a cumulative one.[21]

In situation (1) above, creditors will be paid, so they are in no position to complain. But senior shareholders may well object to such payments to junior shareholders thus reducing assets and, with this, some of their security. Statutes are gradually stating the shareholders' liability on dividends received from improper funds. The Michigan statute is in terms broad enough to make the shareholder disgorge to his corporation in the amount received by him where the dividend was not authorized by the statute.[22] A number of statutes create liability when the shareholders have knowledge of facts indicating the impropriety of the dividend.[23] The Washington statute, perhaps with more insight into the facts of corporate life, creates shareholder liability for improper dividends only where no director is liable or to the extent that the corporation is unable to collect from the director.[24] However, there are other statutes which work the opposite way, namely, to require shareholder

---

17. Bartlett v. Smith, 162 Md. 478, 160 A. 440, at 441, 161 A. 509 (1932), involving a Delaware corporation.

18. Considerable authority is cited for this view, which was rejected, in Bartlett v. Smith, supra, note 17.

19. Bartlett v. Smith, supra, note 17, 160 A. at 442.

20. Ballantine, Corporations 600 (Rev. ed. 1946).

21. Powers v. Heggie, 268 Mass. 233, 167 N.E. 314 (1929).

22. Mich.Gen.Corp.Act § 48.

23. West's Ann.Cal.Corp.Code § 1510.

24. See Fuld, Recovery of Illegal and Partial Liquidating Dividends from Stockholders, 28 Va.L.Rev. 50 (1941); Note, Actions Against Stockholders to Recover Illegal Dividends, 33 Col.L.Rev. 481 (1933); Comment, Obligation to Refund Dividends Paid Out of Capital, 30 Mich.L.Rev. 1070 (1932).

reimbursement when the directors have been held liable.[25] Without the aid of a statute, it is highly doubtful whether a director who has been held liable because of his participation in an illegal dividend distribution may have contribution from his co-directors or from shareholders. The same doubt exists as to the right of the paying director to be subrogated to any other right that the creditor might have against the corporation, its other directors or shareholders.[26]

25. West's Ann.Cal.Corp.Code § 827; 18 Okl.Stat.Ann. § 1.148a (1953).

26. See Note, Right of Director to Subrogation, Contribution or Reimbursement, Dodd and Baker's Cases and Materials on Corporations 1197–1199 (2d ed. 1951).

Chapter 11

FUNDAMENTAL CORPORATE CHANGES

§ 1. What are Fundamental Changes?

This chapter concerns those changes in corporate structure or shareholders' contracts which require shareholder action to make their authorization legally effective. They are concerned primarily with activity outside the normal course of the particular business and involve policy of a major sort. They include problems relative to the sale of all or a large part of the corporate assets, merger and consolidation, increase or reduction of stated capital, new issues of shares, changes of varying importance in the contracts of shares outstanding, and the dissolution of a solvent or "going" corporate business, a topic discussed in the following chapter.

§ 2. Major Changes at Common Law—The Charter as a Three-Way Contract

The starting point of controversy in this area is contained in the principle that the corporate charter constitutes a contract between the corporation and the state, between the corporation and its owners, and between the owners themselves. The landmark case of *Trustees of Dartmouth College v. Woodward,*[1] which concerned a non-profit educational institution created by Crown Charter in 1769 when New Hampshire was a colony of Britain, gave birth to the concept that a corporate charter is a contract between the state and the corporation which is protected by the impairment-of-obligations clause of the federal constitution. Thus, New Hampshire legislation *circa* 1816 in the form of three acts to amend the charter of Dartmouth College, legislation which would have made this institution state-controlled, was held unconstitutional. Chief Justice Marshall put it bluntly: "This is plainly a contract to which the donors, the trustees and the crown (to whose rights and obligations New Hampshire succeeds) were the original parties. It is a contract for the security and disposition of property."[2] Subsequent cases not only agreed but held that there was also a contract between the corporation and its owners and one between the owners themselves, a three-way contract of an unusual type.[3]

---

1. 4 Wheat. (17 U.S.) 518 (1819).
2. Ibid. at 643–644. And see Justice Story's concurring opinion at 690.
3. This is well expressed in Western Foundry Co. v. Wicker, 403 Ill. 260, 85 N.E.2d 722, 8 A.L.R.2d 878 (1949).

There was another principle drawn from partnership law which reinforced the third proposition. That principle was that to alter the contract of partnership, unanimous action of the partners was necessary.[4] Thus, the state was barred from impairing the obligation of the corporate contract and the owners were without power to change the contract without unanimous action, at least in case of major change. However, there was left to the state the area covered by the use of its "police power" which area could, by generous application, cover a good deal of ground. But generous application was not at this early date an acceptable method of interpretation. Had the *Dartmouth College* case held that the charter was a privilege rather than a contractual right, or had there been broad application of the police power doctrine, the course of corporation law concerning fundamental change might well have been quite different from what has actually occurred.

§ 3.   Reservation of the Power to Alter, Amend or Repeal Corporate Charters

The impact of the *Dartmouth College* case had one very significant and immediate influence on the course of future fundamental corporate changes. Justice Story, in his concurring opinion, had written: "When a private eleemosynary corporation is thus created by the charter of the crown, it is subject to no other control on the part of the crown, than what is expressly or implicitly reserved by the charter itself. Unless a power be reserved for this purpose, the crown cannot, in virtue of its prerogative, without the consent of the corporation, alter or amend the charter, or divest the corporation of any of its franchises, or add to them, or add to, or diminish, the number of its trustees, or remove any of the members, or change, or control the administration of the charity, or compel the corporation to receive a new charter. This is the uniform language of the authorities, and forms one of the most stubborn, and well-settled doctrines of the common law."[5] Though such reservations to amend had been contained in some charters prior to the time of this decision, they were not common.[6] But from this point on, clauses reserving the right to alter, amend or repeal appeared regularly in charters of corporations created by legislative grant and presently took their place in state constitutions or statutes.

4. Natusch v. Irving, 2 Coop.T.Cott 358, 47 Eng.Rep. 1196 (1824), Gow on Partnership, Appendix II, p. 404 (2d Eng.ed. 1825).

5. Trustees of Dartmouth College v. Woodward, supra, note 1, at 675.

6. E. Merrick Dodd, Dissenting Stockholders and Amendments to Corporate Charters, 75 U. of Pa.L. Rev. 585, at 592 (1927).

Thus, it was early held that, unless the articles or a statute authorized it, a prosperous corporation, or one that might be described as a "going business," could not sell all or a considerable part of its assets out of the ordinary course of business unless by the unanimous consent of its shareholders.[7] The reason usually assigned was that such a sale was a virtual dissolution of the corporation, and that a majority could not dissolve a going corporation as long as its term of life had not run. The implied contract of the shareholders was said to call for continued corporate life to the end of the designated period unless the venture proved unprofitable.[8] The exact limits of the proviso were never adequately defined.[9] There were, however, some who contended that *all* corporate powers were vested in the shareholders and that the majority had the power to bind the minority, "there being no exception to the general rule with respect to the power of consenting to a dissolution." [10]

When it came to the merger or consolidation of corporations, not only was the shareholders' contract involved but the state had legitimate interests to protect. Here, statutory authority was necessary.[11] Merger and consolidation, in the technical sense, usually include the taking on of franchises belonging to the previously existing individual corporations and the transfer of their property for shares in the company into which they are merged or consolidated, the merged or consolidated corporations usually being dissolved by the plan of merger or consolidation. In case of merger, the shareholders of companies A, B and C found themselves with an entirely different contract when they were required to exchange their shares for those of D company into which their companies had merged. Likewise, when

---

7. Cathedral Estates v. Taft Realty Corp., 157 F.Supp. 895, at 897 (D. Conn.1957), aff'd 251 F.2d 340 (2d Cir., 1957).

8. Geddes v. Anaconda Copper Mining Co., 254 U.S. 590, 41 S.Ct. 209, 65 L.Ed. 425 (1921); Sherrard State Bank v. Vernon, 243 Ill.App. 122 (1928); Kean v. Johnson, 9 N.J.Eq. 401 (1853); Abbot v. American Hard Rubber Co., 33 Barb. 578 (N.Y. 1861); Fain, Limitations on the Statutory Power of Majority Stockholders to Dissolve a Corporation, 25 Harv.L.Rev. 677 (1912).

9. See Geddes v. Anaconda Copper Mining Co., supra, note 8, 254 U.S. at 595–596, 41 S.Ct. 211.

10. Warren, Voluntary Transfers of Corporate Undertakings, 30 Harv.L. Rev. 335, at 346 (1917). And Professor Dodd has written: "Even at

common law it is by no means clear that the majority cannot sell all the assets of a corporation without regard to its financial condition, provided that the sale is made to strangers and for cash." E. Merrick Dodd, Dissenting Stockholders and Amendments to Corporate Charters, 75 U. of Pa.L.Rev. 585; ibid., 723, at 734 (1927).

11. Ferguson, Ex'r of Clearwater v. Meredith, 1 Wall. 25 (U.S.1864); Garrett v. Reid-Cashion Land & Cattle Co., 34 Ariz. 245, 270 P. 1044 (1928); The Chicago Title & Trust Co. v. Doyle, 259 Ill. 489, 102 N.E. 790 (1913); William B. Riker & Son Co. v. United Drug Co., 79 N.J.Eq. 580, 82 A. 930 (1912); Carolina Coach Co. v. Hartness, 198 N.C. 524, 152 S.E. 489 (1930); Topeka Paper Co. v. Oklahoma Pub. Co., 7 Okl. 220, 54 P. 455 (1898).

their companies were consolidated into a new corporation formed for that purpose, were their contractual incidents changed. Thus, prior to statutory provisions permitting a change of this kind upon a prescribed majority or other vote, unanimous action was required to make this fundamental change possible.

Where substantial changes are made in the purpose clause of the articles or certificate of incorporation or changes are made in the contractual provisions of shares outstanding, whether such provisions are required to be in the articles or may appear in by-laws, share certificate, or special resolutions, there must be consent on the part of all shareholders unless there has been a reservation of the right to change through the consent of a lesser number. And where the usual broad but general power to alter, amend or repeal is put to the test there may be, as we shall presently see, differences of opinion as to whether this power extends to contracts of the shareholders *inter se* or is limited to the contract of the corporation with the state. And there may likewise be differences of opinion as to how specific the statutory provision must be to warrant an interpretation that the particular change may be made, even if the court takes the position that the reserved power extends to the shareholders' contract.

§ 4. Progress of the Law after the Reservation of the Power to Alter, Amend or Repeal

To be kept in mind is the basic principle that the state, without any special reservation of a right, may alter, amend or repeal a corporate charter whenever the police power warrants such action. This principle will explain more readily, and certainly more accurately, decisions of a number of courts when they speak of "policy" or the "general welfare" or use some similar term and then point to the reserved power provision of constitution or statute as warranting the statutory change or authorization of change. There is no necessity of referring to the reserved power when the state's police power is sufficient to sustain an alteration, amendment or repeal of a charter. The police power was present prior to the enactment of such reserved powers and confusion results when courts fail to see this.[12]

---

12. See, for example, Wheatley v. A. I. Root Co., 147 Ohio St. 127, at 142–143, 69 N.E.2d 187, at 195 (1946), where Matthias, J., writes that "the purpose of the reservation is to enable the state to impose such restraints upon corporations as the Legislature may deem advisable for protection of the public." It is difficult to understand how this misconception has arisen.

Confusion also results from some of the early pronouncements in leading cases, such as the following: The effect of the reserved power is "at the least, to reserve to the legislature the power to make any alteration or amendment of a charter subject to it, which will not defeat or substantially impair the object of the grant, or any right vested under the grant, and which the legislature may deem necessary to carry into effect the purpose of the grant, or to protect the rights of the public or of the corporation, its stockholders or creditors, or to promote the due administration of its affairs." [13]   More useful, and definitely more accurate, is a later statement: "The authority of a state under the so-called reserved power is wide; but is not unlimited. The corporate charter may be repealed or amended, and, within limits not now necessary to define, the interrelations of state, corporation, and stockholders may be changed; but neither vested property rights nor the obligation of contracts of third persons may be destroyed or impaired." [14]   But even this needs explanation before it becomes of much practical value.   The implication that the contractual relationships between state and corporation, between state and shareholders, between corporation and shareholders and between shareholders *inter se* may be reached through the reserved power gives us a starting point from which to proceed, with a warning that there may be no destruction of "vested property rights" nor a disturbance of contracts between "third persons."   There was no uniform agreement, however, that the reserved power extended as far as the last statement indicates.

One line of authority proceeded upon the assumption that the state had reserved the power to amend, alter or repeal for the sole purpose of overcoming the difficulty brought to light in the *Dartmouth College* case, that is, to permit the state to amend or repeal corporate charters for the benefit of the public but not to give "a power to one part of the incorporators as against the other, which they did not have before." [15]   But when one thinks in terms of "benefit of the public," it is again apparent that the connotation is that of the police power or something pretty close to it; and it should be reiterated that there was no necessity for the reservation if it extended no further than the police power.   Furthermore, the *Dartmouth College* case did not actually demand a use of the state's police powers.   There was no serious thought that private educational corporations held any

13. Looker v. Maynard, 179 U.S. 46, at 52, 21 S.Ct. 21, at 23, 45 L.Ed. 79 (1900).

14. Coombes v. Getz, 285 U.S. 434, at 441, 52 S.Ct. 435, at 436, 76 L.Ed. 866 (1932).

15. Zabriskie v. Hackensack & N. Y. R. Co., 18 N.J.Eq. 178, at 186 (Ch. 1867).

threats sufficiently strong to convert them into state-controlled institutions.

When this narrow doctrine was applied to profit-making corporations—the business corporation—it became increasingly apparent that, as a practical solution to the varied problems within the body of the corporation's security holders, it was of little value. But even within the narrow limits of the doctrine, it might well be contended that many important contractual rights of shareholders with the corporation and among themselves, given a proper setting, become vested with a public interest in which the state is concerned.[16] Naturally, no objection can be made to changes large or small which were specifically authorized at the time of the formation of the corporation or prior to the issue of the shares incorporating the change, for these provisions definitely became a part of each shareholder's contract with his company. Thus, the remedy for narrow interpretation could come through specific provisions in new certificates of incorporation or through statutes specifically authorizing changes in shareholders' contracts where incorporation or issue of the shares came after the statutory enactment. Fortunately, the restricted view was adopted in but few jurisdictions, the majority accepting the view about to be discussed.

While it was no doubt true that the power to amend or repeal corporate charters was not reserved by the state with the conscious purpose of abolishing the necessity for unanimous action in case of fundamental corporate changes, a principle based on the analogy of the rule of *Natusch* v. *Irving*,[17] there was nothing to prevent an interpretation in accord with the lead given in the *Dartmouth College* case that there were other contractual rights involved besides those of the state and the corporation. Furthermore, the court had not spoken with a definiteness—particularly Justice Story's concurring opinion—indicating that but one of the contractual relationships would be remedied by the reservation of the power to amend. Besides, constitutional or statutory reservations of the power are, under liberal guidance as in other cases, subject to be moulded to fit circumstances not considered at the time of their promulgation. Fortunately, when the corporation was formed subsequently to the enactment reserving the power to amend or repeal, the great majority of courts considered the reservation of power a part of the shareholder's contract—a consent on his part that his contract was subject to change. And no distinction was made between legislation which purported to amend directly and that

---

16. This idea is convincingly expressed in Davis v. Louisville Gas & Electric Co., 16 Del.Ch. 157, at 163–164, 142 A. 654, at 657 (1928).

17. Note 4, supra.

which gave to a named proportion of the shareholders the right to do the same. The effect of such holdings was to give flexibility to a business carried on in the corporate form and to make it possible, when the capital structure was in need of overhauling, to accomplish this without the unanimous consent of the owners of the business. The shareholders had impliedly agreed to the use of the democratic process to accomplish in a practical business world what was often difficult and at times impossible.[18]

In short, the majority view meant this: corporations formed *prior* to the reservation of the power to amend or repeal came within the two rules established in the *Dartmouth College* case and *Natusch* v. *Irving;* those formed *after* the reservation of this power came under neither rule for the constitutional protection against impairment of the shareholders' contracts had been waived along with the unanimous consent principle if the statute, as was customary, provided for something less than unanimous consent.

But the story does not end here, for statutes were not always explicit on the matter of how far the designated majority might go in voting changes which were highly fundamental and which frequently did damage to some groups of shareholders without apparent damage to others; in fact others might be benefited. There was, too, in legislation permitting large corporate change in more specific language the danger that majorities might use their power to further their own interests, and this happened frequently enough to be the basis for holdings which placed equitable limitations upon the broad powers given to majorities.[19] The majority must act fairly toward all when its power is used. Similar equitable results were reached in the interpretation of statutes with broad but non-specific provisions for corporate change by a process of reasoning which denied the designated majority powers which were not clearly stated or spelled out.[20] In such cases it was not denied that the legislature

18. See the leading case of Durfee v. Old Colony & Fall River R., 5 Allen (87 Mass.) 230, at pp. 245–247 (1862). And in McNulty v. W. & J. Sloan, 184 Misc. 835, at 843, 54 N.Y.S.2d 253, at 261 (1945), it is stated: "The very essence of the reserved power of the Legislature is to enable it to change preferential rights of the different classes of stock in a corporation."

19. See Berle, Corporate Powers as Powers in Trust, 44 Harv.L.Rev. 1049 (1931); Berle and Means, The Modern Corporation and Private Property, 267 et seq. (1933); Lattin, Equitable Limitations on Powers of Majority Stockholders, 30 Mich.L.Rev. 645 (1932).

20. For example, see Breslav v. New York & Queens Electric Light & Power Co., 249 App.Div. 181, 291 N.Y.S. 932 (1936), aff'd without opinion, 273 N.Y. 593, 7 N.E.2d 708 (1937), where the power "to classify or reclassify any shares" was held not to include the power to make non-redeemable issued shares into redeemable ones. A refusal to permit the elimination of

had the power to make the changes attempted but only that there was no clear expression in the legislation that the particular change was anticipated.

Occasionally a court, forgetting or ignoring, or perhaps not being cognizant of the effect of prior decisions, defined the shareholder's contract with his company and his fellow shareholders as including only those powers to change which existed in the charter or by statute at the time the shares were first issued. This added to the confusion of an already difficult field of law which, if followed to its logical end, would require a tracing of shareholder status in each individual case in order to make a determination of what powers existed at the time of the issue of such shares.[21]

While the difficulties prior to the present point of discussion were formidable, a significant misconception cropped up which created more confusion. If specific authority existed for the change authorized by the required percentage of corporate owners, some courts, according to their views as to just when the statutory provisions became a part of the shareholders' contracts, would permit all manner of change except that which they classified as an alteration or destruction of "vested property interests." This is understandable, if confined to property interests such as debts created by the declaration of a dividend or property interests acquired in some other manner, for property interests may not be taken except by due process of law or with the consent of the owner or possessor. The confusion arises out of what seems to be an attempt on the part of some courts, when the opportunity arises, to remake parts of what every lawyer would consider the shareholder's contract into property interests by merely calling them such and, by so designating them, remove them from the reach of the reserve power. The purpose is noble, for justice is thought to be done. As Justice Shientag has put it: "Whenever the court was of the opin-

accrued but undeclared dividends through a broad authorization which could have been interpreted otherwise, is illustrated by Davison v. Parke, Austin & Lipscomb, Inc., 285 N.Y. 500, 35 N.E.2d 618 (1941). The statute was later amended so that it specifically authorized this and the court then sanctioned retroactive elimination in McNulty v. W. & J. Sloan, 184 Misc. 835, 54 N.Y.S.2d 253 (1945).

For an excellent case where the court, under broad statutory authoriza-

tion, permitted very material changes without requiring the statute to state more specifically what was intended, see Johnson v. Bradley Knitting Co., 228 Wis. 566, 280 N.W. 688 (1938). Likewise, McQuillen v. National Cash Register Co., 27 F.Supp. 639 (D.Md.1939), aff'd 112 F.2d 877 (4th Cir. 1940); Sherman v. Pepin Pickling Co., 230 Minn. 87, 41 N.W.2d 571 (1950), and Comment, 35 Minn.L.Rev. 90 (1950).

21. See, for a good example, Schaffner v. Standard Boiler & Plate Iron

ion that certain rights of stockholders could not be interfered with, they characterized those rights as "vested." [22]

Recent judicial battles have been fought over the status of accrued but undeclared dividends on preferred shares where the legislature has authorized their alteration or elimination. Delaware was the scene of early action on this problem, a broad amendment to § 26 of the Delaware General Corporation Law having been enacted in 1927 subsequently to the formation of the company and the issue of its shares.[23] Prior to the amendment of § 26, this section was not considered broad enough to cover the elimination of accrued dividends by charter amendment. Chief Justice Layton, taking his cue from an earlier case,[24] reviewed the leading cases involving major corporate change and concluded (1) that "where that right (to accrued dividends) was accorded protection when the corporation was formed and the stock was issued, a just public policy, which seeks the equal and impartial protection of the interests of all, demands that the right be regarded as a vested right of property secured against destruction by the Federal and State Constitutions;" [25] and (2) that, "quite apart from the constitutional question involved," § 26 as amended authorized only *amendments* to charters and "the cancellation of cumulative dividends already accrued through passage of time is not an amendment of a charter." [26] There was also, thought the court, nothing in this section indicating that the legislative intent was to make the act retrospective. A dictum recognized that the status of the shares could be changed prospectively by charter amendment, which dictum was justified by the Delaware (and majority) concept that succeeding statutes become a part of the shareholder's contract. The court rejected a suggested inference that the legislature, by its amendment to § 26 had intended that the amendment operate retrospectively, by a clear statement that, if the legislature intends to destroy "rights in the nature of a debt," it must express its intent in language so precise as to admit of no reasonable doubt. Obviously, if the right constitutes property, it would receive constitutional protection no matter what the language of the legislature.

Co., 150 Ohio St. 454, at 460, 83 N.E.2d 192, at 195 (1948).

22. McNulty v. W. & J. Sloane, 184 Misc. 835, 54 N.Y.S.2d 253 (Sup.Ct. 1945).

23. Keller v. Wilson & Co., Inc., 21 Del.Ch. 391, 190 A. 115 (1936), rev'g 21 Del.Ch. 13, 180 A. 584 (1935). Section 26, before and after the amendment to this section, is set forth at pp. 396 and 397, 21 Del. Ch., at pp. 117 and 118 of 190 A. The present comparable section is § 242 of the Delaware General Corporation Law.

24. Morris v. American Public Utilities Co., 14 Del.Ch. 136, 122 A. 696 (1923).

25. Keller v. Wilson & Co., Inc., supra, note 23, 21 Del.Ch. at 412, 190 A. at 124.

26. Keller v. Wilson & Co., Inc., supra, note 23, 21 Del.Ch. at 411 and 413, 190 A. at 124 and 125. But see Harr v. Pioneer Mechanical Corp., 65 F.2d 332 (2d Cir., 1933), cert. denied 290 U.S. 673, 54 S.Ct. 92, 78 L.Ed. 581 (1933) (involving a Delaware corporation).

Shortly thereafter a similar case arrived in the Delaware courts but with this difference—the corporation had been formed *after* the broad amendment to § 26. Chief Justice Layton, who also wrote this opinion, made it clear that the shareholder's right to accrued dividends under his contract was one which "ought to be regarded as a fixed, contractual right, not to be diminished or cancelled against his consent, but to be recognized and protected," and that there was nothing in the statute which indicated retrospective action. Among other things, he stated: "Many interrelations of the State, the corporation, and the shareholders, may be changed. But he, who contends that the State has conferred a power upon corporations, by charter amendment, to change such a substantial contractual right as the right to dividends on cumulative preferred stock accrued under the contract through time, should be able to point to statutory language so clear and precise as to permit of no reasonable doubt that a retrospective operation was intended." [27] But if the right is a vested property one, and not simply a contractual one, how could clear language wipe it out, there being neither a waiver by the shareholder nor a deprivation through due process procedures? If there are such substantial contractual rights as not to come within a broad legislative authority as distinguished from specific legislative consent to alter or amend the corporate charter, how is one to know what contractual provisions are of this importance? Chief Justice Layton's words are hardly an echo of earlier opinions to the effect that legislative power exercised under the reserve power may not be used to "defeat or substantially impair the object of the grant," [28] for such pronouncements seemed to prohibit substantial impairments no matter how explicit the language of the statute.

The New York Court of Appeals saw the fallacy of the concept that some contractual rights, notably the cumulative preferred shareholder's rights to dividends accrued but undeclared, become vested rights in as clean an analysis of the problem as has been made. Said the court through Judge Desmond: [29] "So

27. Consolidated Film Industries, Inc. v. Johnson, 22 Del.Ch. 407, at 416, 197 A. 489, at 493 (1937), aff'g 22 Del.Ch. 262, 194 A. 844 (1937). Contra: Harr v. Pioneer Mechanical Corp., supra, note 26, construing the same section of the Delaware statute. In Goldman v. Postal Telegraph, Inc., 52 F.Supp. 763, at 769 (D.Del.1943), Leahy, Dist. J., wrote: "If we must enter the realm of the implied, then the language of the present Chief Justice of Delaware certainly indicates that if Sec. 26 had specifically authorized the amendment in the Consolidated Film case, there could be no constitutional objections to such amendment. I do not think the Delaware courts have left in doubt what position they would take in disposing of the constitutional question in the instant case."

28. See page 499, supra.

29. Davison v. Parke, Austin & Lipscomb, 285 N.Y. 500, at 509, 35 N.E. 2d 618, at 622 (1941). That the right to accrued undeclared dividends is not a "vested" or "vested

it seems that only confusion results from saying that 'vested rights' are not within the contemplation of the statute. All preferential rights of stockholders are in a sense vested. They are all property rights founded upon contract. The right of priority in the distribution of corporate assets on dissolution is no less vested than the right to be paid dividends for past years out of contingent future profits. The inadequacy of the 'vested rights' test is further demonstrated by the fact that new stock may be issued with preferential rights to the assets of the corporation upon dissolution and to dividends superior to the preferential rights of the then outstanding shares . . . even superior to the right of preferred stockholders to dividends in arrears. . . . The judicial problem is not whether a particular preferential right is vested or not, but rather what was the legislative intent as to it." Four years later, the above analysis was used as a basis for the Supreme Court of the same state in its holding that the statutory authorization to eliminate accrued dividends, when taken advantage of by the stated majority of shareholders in a charter amendment, may be legitimately used to eliminate dividends already accrued under the preferred shareholder's contract.[30] Accrued, undeclared dividends are not debts; there must be a declaration of dividends before they become so. The contract between shareholders "is subject to a condition that it may be changed or altered in the manner prescribed or authorized by the Legislature." [31] It was as simple as that, thought the New York court.

In jurisdictions recognizing the "vested right" theory, the courts were soon pressed with attempts to avoid its application by several indirect devices which were meant to bludgeon dissenting shareholders into submission. A prior preference stock, when possible, would be authorized and dividends would be made payable first to the new issue, with perhaps a prior preference to assets upon dissolution. Inducements would be offered to dis-

property" right, see also Western Foundry Co. v. Wicker, 403 Ill. 260, 85 N.E.2d 722, 8 A.L.R.2d 878 (1949).

30. McNulty v. W. & J. Sloane, 184 Misc. 835, 54 N.Y.S.2d 253 (Sup.Ct. 1945). Accord: Sherman v. Pepin Pickling Co., 230 Minn. 87, 41 N.W. 2d 571 (1950), where the statute did not specifically authorize the elimination of accrued dividends. A charter amendment cancelled the $100 par value shares with their accrued dividends, the corporation issuing in their place $70 par value shares with a lower dividend rate. Contra: Wheatley v. A. I. Root Co., 147 Ohio St. 127, 69 N.E.2d 187

(1946). The statute expressly authorized the elimination of accrued dividends but the court held the statute not applicable to dividends accruing prior to its enactment. And see (on this case) Note, Amendment of Articles to Eliminate Dividends Accrued on Cumulative Preferred Shares, 32 Cornell L.Q. 586 (1947); Note, Accrued Dividends—No Mirage in Ohio, 18 U. of Cin. L.Rev. 172 (1949); Note, Accrued Preferred Stock Dividends—Charter Amendment, 45 Mich.L.Rev. 628 (1947).

31. McNulty v. W. & J. Sloane, supra, note 30, 54 N.Y.S.2d, at 260.

senting shareholders who might otherwise ask for an appraisal of and payment for their shares to encourage them to exchange their shares for the new prior preferred. Those who refused to exchange their stock found themselves holding shares concerning which they were unable to insist upon payment of their accrued dividends before the new prior preferred shareholders received theirs.[32] Since the statutes were usually broad enough to permit the issue of a new preferred stock having prior preferences to an issue outstanding, and since the shareholder was not forced to exchange his stock for new shares, the courts were able to say that there had been no destruction of his vested interest though, for all practical purposes, the accrued dividends might never be realized.

Another indirect method of eliminating accrued dividends was to use the merger and consolidation provisions of the statute. This was sometimes done by merger into a subsidiary already formed or by the formation of a subsidiary for the very purpose of merging with it to eliminate such dividends. The shareholder, in this procedure, had no choice but to take shares of the other corporation or demand an appraisal when the statute gave him that right.[33] The formal argument permitting this was that the shareholder's contract included his consent to merge or consolidate when the designated fraction of shareholders voted for this change. But, if accrued dividends amount to vested property interests, did his contract concerning merger and consolidation also include a waiver of his right to keep such interests until they were taken by due process? It seems doubtful whether shareholder consent was present here if it was not present in an amendment to the charter which specifically wiped

---

32. Johnson v. Fuller, 36 F.Supp. 744 (D.Pa.1940); Shanik v. White Sewing Machine Corp., 25 Del.Ch. 154, 15 A.2d 169 (1940); Johnson v. Lamprecht, 133 Ohio St. 567, 15 N.E.2d 127 (1938). But Patterson v. Durham Hosiery Mills, 214 N.C. 806, 260 S.E. 906 (1939), saw clearly the obvious result of effectively destroying the "vested right" and held contra to the above cases.

33. Federal United Corp. v. Havender, 24 Del.Ch. 318, 11 A.2d 331 (1940). Wrote Layton, C. J., 24 Del. Ch. at 335, 11 A.2d at 339: "Consequently, in a case where a merger of corporations is permitted by the law and is accomplished in accordance with the law, the holder of cumulative preference stock as to which dividends have accumulated may not insist that his right to the dividends is a fixed contractual right in the nature of a debt, in that sense vested and, therefore, secure against attack. Looking at the law which is a part of the corporate charter, and, therefore, a part of the shareholder's contract, he has not been deceived nor lulled into the belief that the right to such dividends is firm and stable." See also Langfelder v. Universal Laboratories, Inc., 68 F.Supp. 209 (D. Del.1946), aff'd 163 F.2d 804 (3d Cir., 1947); Anderson v. International Mineral & Chemical Corp., 295 N.Y. 343, 67 N.E.2d 573 (1946). In Hottenstein v. York Ice Machinery Corp., 136 F.2d 944 (3d Cir., 1943), a corporation was specially created for the purpose of merging one in trouble with accrued dividends.

out the right.[34] Of course, vested property rights, though constitutionally protected, may be waived in advance if a waiver can be shown.[35] However, it seems a bit absurd to assume that the consent to merge or consolidate carried with it a consent to the obliteration of vested property rights.

§ 5.   Extent to Which Fundamental Changes in Shareholders' Contracts have been Permitted

Theoretically, there would seem to be no bounds to contractual changes impliedly consented to by the shareholder through the state's reservation of the power to amend or repeal corporate charters. Whether the minority (New Jersey) or the majority (Delaware) view be taken, the only apparent difficulty is the *time* at which a future statutory authority to alter becomes effective, if at all, upon shareholders' contracts then existing. If the minority view be taken that the reserved power does not extend to the contract between the corporation and the shareholder, and shareholders *inter se*, this necessarily means that legislative authority to make the change must come prior to the issue of the shares whose contractual provisions are being altered by the authorized change. The statutory authorization thus becomes a part of the contract of shares subsequently issued. But if the majority view be accepted, each successive legislative authorization becomes a part of the contract because of the implied consent that this shall be so by virtue of the state's power to amend and repeal, which power existed at the time of the birth of the corporation. And, of course, if the articles or certificate of incorporation reserved the power to make, by majority or other fractional vote, material changes in shareholders' contracts, or even reserved the power to obliterate or alter property interests, the shareholder, by accepting the terms of his share-contract, cannot later object on the ground of lack of authority to carry through the change so authorized.[36] Whether

34. In Hottenstein v. York Ice Machinery Co., supra, note 33, at 950, Biggs, J., wrote: "If the right is a vested right of property, protected by constitutional guaranties the holder can be as little deprived of it by merger or consolidation under Section 59 as by reclassification under Section 26. If the terms of the contract between the preferred stockholder and his corporation cannot be changed by any charter amendment, the preferred stockholder is entitled to the protection of the Contract Clause, Section 10, Article 1 of the Federal Constitution. If the intervening complainant in the case at bar is being deprived of a vested right in property in violation of the Fourteenth Amendment to the Constitution of the United States, the court below should have granted the injunctive relief sought by the appellant."

35. Goldman v. Postal Telegraph, Inc., 52 F.Supp. 763, at 770, footnote 11 (D.Del.1943).

36. In Western Foundry Co. v. Wicker, 403 Ill. 260, 85 N.E.2d 722, 8 A.L.R.2d 878, Ann. at 893 (1949), the articles provided that "rights and preferences of the preferred shares may be changed and differ-

the minority or majority view is taken, there may still exist a controversy concerning the scope of a particular statutory or charter authority which is not specific in its statement.[37]

Because of the variation from state to state regulating charter amendments, a general statement of wide application is not possible. The basic principles stated above are important in prognosticating future developments in this important area and in suggesting problems in the drafting of corporate charters. However, there may be some value in stating how extensive have been some alterations in shareholders' contracts through the process of charter amendment. As to future dividend rights of preferred shareholders, there would seem to be little difficulty in altering them under the statutes in most states whether through a reduction in the dividend rate or changing cumulative dividend provisions to non-cumulative ones.[38] Important as are voting rights, the removal of cumulative voting rights has been permitted under a statute allowing changes in "special rights," as have changes eliminating voting rights of the preferred when dividends or sinking fund payments are in arrears, and changes transferring voting rights from common to preferred by amendment of the charter.[39]

Liquidation and redemption preferences have similar problems. Both may include components of accrued dividends and capital, and the capital component would seem to be quite as important as the accrued dividend component which has already been considered. However, even in jurisdictions which refuse to apply retroactively legislation permitting by direct charter amendment the elimination of accrued dividends, holdings have permitted by this direct method the elimination of the liquidation preference.[40]

ent classes of preferred stock may be created" by a two-thirds class vote of preferred stock. A cancellation of accrued dividends on preferred shares was sustained.

37. For examples, see note 20, supra.

38. Davis v. Louisville Gas & Elect. Co., 16 Del.Ch. 157, 142 A. 654 (1928) (charter amendment based upon 1927 amendment to § 26 of the Delaware General Corporation Law enacted subsequently to the issue of the shares in question); Yoakam v. Providence Biltmore Hotel Co., 34 F.2d 533 (D.R.I.1929) (under § 26 prior to its amendment in 1927, its justification being the authorization of alterations of "preferences").

39. Maddock v. Vorclone Corp., 17 Del.Ch. 39, 147 A. 255 (1929); Yoa-

kam v. Providence Biltmore Hotel Co., supra, note 38; Topkis v. Delaware Hdwe. Co., 23 Del.Ch. 125, 2 A.2d 114 (Ch.1938). However, in Faunce v. Boost Co., 15 N.J.Super. 534, 83 A.2d 649 (1951), where the statute authorizing "such other amendment, change or alteration as may be desired" was enacted subsequently to the issue of the shares, it was held that the previous contract was protected by the constitutional provision forbidding the impairment of contracts. This is explainable by the minority view which New Jersey had accepted. See Note, Corporate Amendments and the Impairment of Voting Rights, 54 Harv.L.Rev. 1368 (1941).

40. Goldman v. Postal Telegraph, Inc., supra, note 35; Morris v.

Charter amendments eliminating sinking fund provisions have been held valid and not valid in two jurisdictions applying the majority view. *Yoakam* v. *Providence Biltmore Hotel Co.*[41] held that a Delaware corporation could not legally eliminate a sinking fund provision by direct amendment to the charter, even as to the future. But a Wisconsin court, with a similar problem, held that sinking fund payments could be reduced by charter amendment.[42] One should again ask whether these contract rights are any different from others in the shareholder's contract and whether he has impliedly consented, as in other cases, to changes brought about through the reservation of the power to amend or repeal charters.

While it has been held by a court accepting the majority rule that statutory authority to "classify and reclassify" did not extend to the conversion of redeemable to non-redeemable shares, and while the court there intimated that had the statute been more specific the provision would have been considered unconstitutional since the right was a "vested property right," [43] it is apparent today that the same court, with its changed attitude on "vested property rights," would not make the same error in classifying the contractual right as a property interest.[44] However, where a rule exists which does not permit statutory authority in this area to have effect retroactively, shares already issued will not be affected by a later statute authorizing amendments making redeemable into non-redeemable stock.[45]

Merger and consolidation offer the same problem discussed in the preceding section where corporations with cumulative dividends due but undeclared are merged with or consolidated

American Public Utilities Co., 14 Del.Ch. 136, 122 A. 696 (1923) (the redemption premium component was eliminated by charter amendment). See also Williams v. National Pump Corp., 46 Ohio App. 427, 188 N.E. 756 (1933), petition in error dismissed in 126 Ohio St. 457, 186 N.E. 403 (1933) (statute was in effect, however, when plaintiff obtained his shares). In Transportation Bldg. Co. v. Daugherty, 74 Cal, App.2d 604, 169 P.2d 470 (1946), reduction of liquidation and redemption price from $50 to $30 by charter amendment was permitted.

41. 34 F.2d 533 (D.R.I.1929).

42. Johnson v. Bradley Knitting Co., 228 Wis. 566, 280 N.W. 688, 117 A.L.R. 1276 (1938).

43. Breslav v. New York & Queens Electric Light & Power Co., 249 App.Div. 181, 291 N.Y.S. 932 (1936), aff'd 273 N.Y. 593, 7 N.E.2d 708 (1937). See Cowan v. Salt Lake Hdwe. Co., 118 Utah 300, 221 P.2d 625 (1950), where a charter amendment making redeemable shares non-redeemable was upheld, the court being of the opinion that the statute authorized it.

44. See this text, pages 504–505, supra.

45. Yukon Mill & Grain Co. v. Vose, 201 Okl. 376, 206 P.2d 206 (1949). And in Outwater v. Public Service Corporation of New Jersey, 103 N.J. Eq. 461, 143 A. 729 (Ch.1928), aff'd 104 N.J.Eq. 490, 146 A. 916 (Ct. Err. & App.1929), an exchange of non-redeemable for redeemable preferred upon a merger was held unfair.

into corporations and shares are exchanged which carry no rights as to dividends already cumulated. It has been held that, upon consolidation, the change of non-redeemable preferred to redeemable preferred is legally proper;[46] and a merger plan by which non-redeemable preferred shareholders were offered either common or redeemable preferred shares was upheld.[47] As suggested in the preceding section, if direct amendment to the articles would not, in the particular jurisdiction, be considered valid, elimination of the right through an indirect method such as by merger or consolidation ought not to receive a judicial blessing.

Preemptive rights, under statutes permitting the alteration of "special rights" or permitting amendments of anything "which might have been originally provided in such articles," have been held to be legally destructible if the statutory requirements have been met.[48] There is not entire agreement on this matter when the statute is as general as the portions quoted above. The generality of statement, as in other cases, thus offers a court an opportunity to "do equity" when it believes that injustice will otherwise result, by declaring that, until the legislature makes its intention clear, the statute will be more narrowly construed than argued.

Courts have at times stressed the fact that shareholders who dissent and demand an appraisal and purchase of their shares, when the statute gives that right, have an adequate remedy, and thus sustain the particular fundamental change when they might not have done so otherwise. In a sense the real issue is avoided, namely, whether the power to amend or repeal extends to the legislative authority assumed. On the other hand, might it not be argued that the giving of the appraisal right is as near due process in this area as is possible of achievement? Somehow or other a democratic process must be achieved. Corporate business requires that it be practical. The modern method has been through a shareholder vote with a right of the dissenting owners at their option to be bought out, protective devices being provided to assure them a fair price for their shares. Whether the appraisal device is adequate and the extent of its use will shortly be discussed. But first must be considered the

46. Donohue v. Heuser, 239 S.W.2d 238 (Ky.App.1951).

47. Clarke v. Gold Dust Corp., 106 F.2d 598 (3d Cir., 1939), cert. denied 309 U.S. 671, 60 S.Ct. 614, 84 L.Ed. 1017 (1940).

48. Gottlieb v. Heyden Chemical Corp., 33 Del.Ch. 82, 90 A.2d 660, 91 A.2d 57 (Sup.Ct.1952); Milwaukee Sanitarium v. Lynch, 238 Wis. 628, 300 N.W. 760, 138 A.L.R. 521 (1941). In Albrecht, Maguire & Co. v. General Plastics, Inc., 256 App. Div. 134, 9 N.Y.S.2d 415 (1939), aff'd without opinion, 280 N.Y. 840, 21 N.E.2d 887 (1939), the court held that more specific statutory authority was needed. It was later supplied in N. Y. Stock Corp. Law § 35, subd. 2(H).

limitations upon majority action when fundamental change has been authorized through their action.

§ 6. Equitable Limitations on Majority Shareholder Action

Statutes giving a stated majority of shareholders the power to make fundamental changes are usually in broad terms without any indication that there may be some limitation on majority action.   Economic necessity and stubborn minorities called for reasonable flexibility in bringing about major corporate changes, but whenever majorities act there is the danger that they may use their power to further their own interests.   When they act in good faith and for what they conceive to be the best interests of their corporation, staying within the range of the power granted and proceeding in accordance with the prescribed formalities, their action will be sustained.   But, as one great judge has written: [49]   "The majority has the right to control; but when it does so, it occupies a fiduciary relation toward the minority, as much so as the corporation itself or its officers and directors.   If, through that control, a sale of the corporate property is made and the property acquired by the majority, the minority may not be excluded from a fair participation in the fruits of the sale."   When the interests of the corporation, as distinguished from the selfish interests of the majority, are faithfully guarded there is no minority shareholder problem. However, when the controlling group favors itself or some other group it thus far fails to act for the best interests of all and its action offers cause for attack.

Thus, where a majority voted to sell all of the corporate assets at an unfair price to a corporation organized by the same majority for the purpose of purchasing these assets, the court quite rightly held a sale under such circumstances may always be questioned; the majority may not benefit at the expense of the minority; equality of treatment is the criterion.[50]   And when one authorized device such as that provided for a sale of

49.   Justice Brandeis in Southern Pacific Co. v. Bogert, 250 U.S. 483, at 487–488, 39 S.Ct. 533, 535, 63 L.Ed. 1099 (1919).   See also Ervin v. Oregon Ry. & Nav. Co., 27 F. 625, at 633–634 (Cir.Ct.N.Y.1886), and Allied Chemical & Dye Corp. v. Steel & Tube Company of America, 14 Del.Ch. 1, at 12–13, 120 A. 486, 491 (1923).

50.   Ervin v. Oregon Ry. & Nav. Co., supra, note 49.   And see recent cases of Cathedral Estates v. Taft Realty Corp., 157 F.Supp. 895 (D. Conn.1957), aff'd 251 F.2d 340 (2d Cir., 1957); Gomberg v. Midvale Co., 157 F.Supp. 132, at 137 (D.Pa. 1955) (but where there is no showing that majority shareholders or directors are gaining a personal advantage from the sale, plaintiffs have the burden of showing "that the disparity between the value of the property to be sold and the money to be received is so unreasonable as to indicate that the sellers are recklessly indifferent to the interest of the whole body of stockholders").

assets or a dissolution is used to bring about a virtual consolidation or merger, minority shareholders may object on the ground that a direct method has been authorized for such a purpose. Frequently, there are essential differences in the vote required to accomplish the purpose by the direct method and often, too, the dissenting shareholder is given an appraisal remedy in one case and not in the other. If consolidation or merger is permitted through a pretended sale or dissolution, minority shareholders may be frozen out of a successful corporate venture by being paid their proportionate part of the selling price in either case; [51] that is, if the court considers only the device used to reach indirectly the real objective.[52] While the use of one authorized device to accomplish indirectly the objective attainable through the use of the second device has sometimes been called a "fraud upon the law," the basic reason for judicial disapproval seems to be the injustice of permitting a method of indirect approach when that approach denies the minority shareholder some of the protection or advantages offered by the more direct approach.

When a majority acts within the bounds permitted by the statute, there is a presumption that such action was fair. This is comparable to the presumption raised in favor of directors when they act within their powers.[53] But no vote short of a unanimous one can validate a fundamental change not authorized by statute or charter; and even where there is unanimous consent to changes in which the state has an interest, such as in merger or consolidation, it will be ineffective if the state has not

51. Theis v. Spokane Falls Gas Light Co., 34 Wash. 23, at 29, 74 P. 1004, 1006 (1904), was such a case. Another good recent example is Bloch v. Baldwin Locomotive Works, 75 Pa. D. & C. 24 (Del.Co.1950). Also, Lebold v. Inland Steel Co., 125 F.2d 369 (7th Cir., 1941), cert. denied 316 U.S. 675, 62 S.Ct. 1045, 86 L.Ed. 1749.

52. Fortunately, the court looks to the real objective. Ervin v. Oregon Ry. & Nav. Co., supra, note 49; Garrett v. Reid-Cashion Land & Cattle Co., 34 Ariz. 245, 270 P. 1044 (1928). In Finch v. Warrior Cement Corp., 16 Del.Ch. 44, 141 A. 54 (1928), the sale of assets provision was attempted to be used to bring about a reorganization of the company, stock being turned over to the shareholders and not into the company treasury. The court held that the minority could insist that it be a sale and not something else.

(See 141 A. at 59). And in William B. Riker & Son Co. v. United Drug Co., 79 N.J.Eq. 580, 82 A. 930 (1912), dissolution (sale of assets) provisions were used to effect a consolidation with a foreign corporation. The court held that this was a fraud upon the statute. Similarly, where one authorized device is used to accomplish indirectly something else, it is a "fraud upon the law." Doe Run Lead Co. v. Maynard, 283 Mo. 646, at 686, 223 S.W. 600 (1920). In Meyerhoff v. Bankers' Securities, Inc., 105 N.J.Eq. 76, 147 A. 105 (1929), provision for the sale of all the assets was attempted to be used to bring about a dissolution and the court required compliance with the dissolution provisions of the statute.

53. Cole v. National Cash Credit Ass'n, 18 Del.Ch. 47, 156 A. 183 (Ch. 1931).

authorized the action. In any case where the fundamental change is not authorized by law, a dissenting shareholder may, if not guilty of laches in bringing his action, enjoin its consummation. This is true even though an appraisal statute is broad enough to permit him an election, if he desires. And, prior to the enactment of appraisal statutes, where, through a vote of a majority, a corporation sold all its assets, merged or consolidated, where it appeared that the majority had exceeded its lawful powers, those not assenting to the change could claim the value of their shares on the theory that their interest in the corporation had been converted.[54]

Where a certain proportion of the shareholders is authorized to make specified fundamental changes, their action may range from making a change in order to benefit themselves, to a good faith change, where their business judgment was poor but their discretion was not abused, which latter change may be disadvantageous to all shareholders. The fiduciary obligation which majority power places upon its exercise calls for equality of treatment and utmost fairness and, where action is prompt, the majority may be restrained from consummating the change brought about by their abuse of discretion. If innocent third persons have acquired rights prior to an action brought to restrain the consummation of the fundamental change, they should, of course, be protected. If injunction, under these or other circumstances, is not a possible remedy, the minority shareholders are entitled to share in the benefits which the majority shareholders have taken unto themselves. Equality of treatment is the criterion.

However, where the proportion required to pass the resolution for fundamental change has in good faith voted for it, is the failure to use good business judgment a basis for minority shareholder attack? In an important holding it has been stated:[55] "The majority who are favoring the sale owe something more to the minority than to merely refrain from appropriating, either directly or indirectly, the corporate assets unto themselves. They owe the further duty of seeing to it that the assets shall be sold for a fair and adequate price." The court then analogized the position of the majority to that of a trustee who has authority to sell the assets of his beneficiary in which case the trustee's duty would be to secure a fair price. However, the majority when permitted to sell may exercise a sound business

---

54. See authorities cited in Lattin, Remedies of Dissenting Stockholders Under Appraisal Statutes, 45 Harv.L.Rev. 233, at 234, footnote 1.

55. Allied Chemical & Dye Corp. v. Steel & Tube Co. of America, 14

Del.Ch. 1, at 18–19, 120 A. 486 (1926). Accord: Allaun v. Consolidated Oil Co., 16 Del.Ch. 318, 147 A. 257 (Ch.1929).

judgment in fixing the price and if there has been no fraud and no abuse of discretion, and the shareholders' consent was free, the purchase price cannot be questioned.[56]

The same fiduciary principle requires fair terms and equality of participation in merger and consolidation. While a merger or consolidation differs from an out-and-out sale of corporate assets, yet from the standpoint of the merged or constituent companies, "a sale in substance is involved." [57] An undervaluation of the assets of the merged or constituent companies will result in a distribution of shares whose total value in the surviving company in case of merger or in the new company in case of consolidation will be less than the value of the assets acquired by this method. It has been said that the inadequacy in price must be so great as to lead a court to conclude that it was due to bad faith or to a reckless indifference to the rights of those injured rather than to an honest error of judgment in order to upset the merger or consolidation.[58] When it appears that there was an intentional undervaluation, actual fraud exists and the dissenting shareholder's remedies are clear. Where the dissenter bases his action upon constructive fraud founded upon an alleged discriminatory undervaluation of his company's assets, his case must be clear enough to show an abuse of discretion and not simply a failure to use good business judgment. "When the fraud charged is of this nature, it must be so plainly made out

---

56. Homer v. Crown Cork & Seal Co., 155 Md. 66, 141 A. 425 (1928); Jackson Co. v. Gardiner Inv. Co., 217 F. 350 (1st Cir., 1914), rehearing denied 220 F. 297 (1st Cir., 1915), appeal dismissed 239 U.S. 628, 36 S.Ct. 164, 60 L.Ed. 475 (1915); Gomberg v. Midvale Company, 157 F.Supp. 132 (D.Pa.1955). And in Wall v. Anaconda Copper Mining Co., 216 F. 242 at 243 (D.Mont.1914), Bourquin, Dist. J., wrote: "Motive, vendee, price consideration are all immaterial, provided the transaction be free from fraud." Later, at page 246, he stated: "Doubtless gross inadequacy might be a circumstance in a fraudulent sale." The dissenting shareholders' appraisal right was stressed. And, again, in Franzblau v. Capital Securities Co., Inc., 2 N.J.Super. 517, 64 A.2d 644 (1949), where the court stated that where a plan of reorganization is approved by the statutorily prescribed two-thirds, the fairness of the plan may not be looked into. *Sed quaere,* unless the statute makes the remedy of appraisal to dissenting shareholders the sole one. See, for example, Beechwood Securities Corp., Inc. v. Associated Oil Co., 104 F.2d 537 (9th Cir., 1939), interpreting the California statute, and Lattin, A Reappraisal of Appraisal Statutes, 38 Mich.L. Rev. 1165 (1940).

57. Cole v. National Cash Credit Ass'n, supra, note 56.

58. Allied Chemical & Dye Corp. v. Steel & Tube Co. of America, supra, note 55. A somewhat similar idea is expressed in Franzblau v. Capital Securities Co., Inc., supra, note 56. A similar test of unfairness in merger terms was expressed in Porges v. Vadsco Sales Corp., 27 Del.Ch. 127, 32 A.2d 148 (Ch.1943). Compare Barrett v. Denver Tramway Corp., 53 F.Supp. 198 (D.Del. 1943), aff'd 146 F.2d 701 (3d Cir., 1944), where Leahy, Dist. J., questioned the fairness of the plan and would have held it unfair but for the Delaware doctrine.

as to disclose a breach of trust or such maladministration as works a manifest wrong to the dissentients." [59]

While it is not necessary that the majority shareholders engineering the particular fundamental change shall benefit from the alleged inequality in order to contest it, the fact that they do will subject the transaction to closer scrutiny by a court of equity than where the transaction is at arm's length.[60] For example, where they own a greater interest in the buying company than in the selling company in the case of a sale of assets, or own a larger interest in one corporation in a merger or consolidation than in another one involved, these factors have an important bearing on self-serving at the expense of a group not in control. There is much to be said for close scrutiny in such circumstances. However, the motive of self-interest does not in itself warrant restraining the action if the terms are fair to the corporation. Thus, where majority shareholders who were also large creditors of their corporation voted to sell the corporate assets to pay these debts, the court held that the majority may "practically desert" the corporation by selling its assets and may thus deprive the minority of the opportunity to reap profits in the future by continuing in a business which had high prospects of success, provided the terms and conditions of the sale were fair to the corporation.[61] Motive, then, is unimportant where the terms are fair and equality of treatment is present.

§ 7. Appraisal Statutes and Their Place in Fundamental Change Legislation

In a recent case,[62] the court found no appraisal statute covering the sale of assets out of ordinary course. It recognized the general rule that, in the absence of express statutory authority, a majority could not force a minority to sell "regardless of the fairness of the price offered." Nor could a majority sell to itself the corporation's principal assets in order to get rid of a minority. But stated the court:[63] "Possibly statutory provision should be made whereby very small corporate minorities could be bought out at a fair price fixed by appraisal, arbitration or court finding, so that shakedown or strike suits could be avoided, and po-

---

59. Cole v. National Cash Credit Ass'n, supra, note 53, 156 A. at 187.

60. Crawford v. Mexican Petroleum Co., 130 F.2d 359 (2d Cir., 1942) (sale of assets); Homer v. Crown Cork & Seal Co., supra, note 56 (sale of assets); Lebold v. Inland S. S. Co., 82 F.2d 351 (7th Cir., 1936) (fictitious dissolution to oust a minority from a highly successful enterprise).

61. Allaun v. Consolidated Oil Co., supra, note 55.

62. Cathedral Estates v. Taft Realty Corp., 157 F.Supp. 895 (D.Conn. 1957), aff'd 251 F.2d 340 (2d Cir., 1957).

63. Ibid. at 897, opinion of Smith, Ch. J.

tentially troublesome small shareholders could be properly compensated for their holdings and the majority enabled thereby to remove the present handicap to free exercise of judgment in management." Appraisal statutes were designed to permit dissenting shareholders, if they wished, to be paid the value of their shares and retire from the company or to go along with the majority in the fundamental change so voted. The option, under such statutes, is given to the dissenting shareholder. There is no right to oust a troublesome shareholder if he elects to abide by the action of the majority.

The great majority of appraisal statutes were not intended to do more than permit shareholders who disagreed with the fundamental change to have their interests purchased and to retire from their company. An insignificant number of such statutes permit no attack upon the fairness of the plan, whatever it may be, and thus make appraisal and payment the only practical choice.[64] In other jurisdictions the dissenting shareholder may still insist upon such fairness in majority action that he will have a real choice between accepting the change or requesting payment for his interest. It seems far better policy to encourage fair play and common honesty than to accept, for matters of convenience, a doctrine which permits majorities to run roughshod over minorities even though there is some nuisance value in the threat of obstructing majority action.[65] Actually, the nuisance value is not very great. The courts have usually supported majority action unless it is so unreasonable as to indicate an abuse of majority powers. Add to this the cost to the plaintiff-shareholder bringing suit and his nuisance value seems even smaller.

Appraisal statutes vary materially on matters such as which shareholders may vote on the contemplated change, the percentage necessary to authorize the change, the formalities necessary to obtain the right to an appraisal and, most important of all, whether any appraisal right is given for the change under consideration.

64. 15 Mich.Stat.Ann. § 21.44 and § 21.54, as amended by P.A.1951, No. 239 (1955 Cum.Supp. to 15 Mich. Stat.Ann. § 21.54). The California Act also makes appraisal a sole remedy. West's Ann.Cal.Corp.Code § 4123. And see Porter v. C. O. Porter Machinery Co., 336 Mich. 437, at 456, 58 N.W.2d 135, 137 (1953); Beechwood Securities Corp., Inc. v. Associated Oil Co., 104 F.2d 537 (9th Cir., 1939), interpreting the California statute. Fraud was claimed. While the Michigan statute purports to make the appraisal remedy exclusive, see Wilgus and Hamilton, Michigan Corporation Law 323 (1932) and dictum in Porter case, supra, 336 Mich. at 456, 58 N.W.2d at 137. And see Pa.Bus.Corp.Law § 515 (D). See also Beloff v. Consolidated Edison Co. of New York, 300 N.Y. 11, 87 N.E.2d 561 (1949); Matteson v. Ziebarth, 40 Wash.2d 286, 242 P.2d 1025 (1952).

65. The arguments for appraisal as a sole remedy are presented in Ballantine and Sterling, Upsetting Mergers and Consolidations: Alternative Remedies of Dissenting Shareholders in California, 27 Calif.L.Rev. 644 (1939).

In the case of statutes authorizing a sale of all or a substantial part of the corporate assets, if a generalization can be made, it is that a sale in ordinary course does not need more than action by the directors; that, by and large, the mortgage, deed of trust or pledge of corporate assets to secure a debt needs only board action; that the sale or exchange of assets out of the ordinary and regular course of business requires shareholder action, and occasionally board action as well; and that the sale of assets of a going concern is frequently distinguished from that of one on the brink of insolvency, the latter requiring board action only. Apart from the exceptions not requiring a shareholder vote, 44 states and the District of Columbia specifically permit such transactions when authorized by the shareholders.[66] But, in 14 of these, there is no appraisal section which permits the dissenter to withdraw and be paid off.[67] This is somewhat surprising as many of these statutes permit an exchange or barter of assets and the payment in shares of the purchasing corporation or some other. However, the fact that 30 states offer appraisal rights under such circumstances indicates that the policy of protecting the dissenter in this way is well intrenched in these states.

While shareholder approval is required where substantial changes are made in the purpose clause of the articles or certificate of incorporation, there are very few statutes which permit the shareholder the election of withdrawing by corporate purchase of his shares.[68] This may reasonably be attributed to the not too wholesome custom of drafting the purpose clause broadly enough to include practically any business which the board determines will be profitable to the owners. Hence, shareholders are led to expect change. And there seems to be no doubt that the hunt for diversification of products, thought to be necessary to business success today, has also had its influence.

---

66. There are no specific statutory provisions in Arizona, Iowa, Mississippi and Wyoming.

67. Appraisal provisions to a full or lesser extent in case of sale, lease or exchange of assets exist in Connecticut, Idaho, Illinois, Indiana, Kentucky, Louisiana, Maine, Maryland, Massachusetts, Michigan, Missouri, Montana, New Hampshire, New Jersey, New Mexico, New York, North Carolina, North Dakota, Ohio, Oklahoma, Oregon, Pennsylvania, Rhode Island, South Carolina, Tennessee, Texas, Vermont, Virginia, Washington and Wisconsin. The A.L.I. Model Business Corporation Act § 74 (Rev.

1953) also permits appraisal for sales otherwise than in the ordinary course of business.

68. The following statutes permit appraisal in such a case: La.S.A.—Rev.Stat. § 12.52; Mass.Gen.Laws 1932, c. 156, § 46, as amended by L.1943, c. 38, § 2; Minn.Stat.Ann. § 301.40; Ohio Rev.Code (as amended 1955) § 1701.74 (the articles may take away this appraisal right when purposes are substantially changed); Okl.Stat.1951, Title 18, § 1.157, and see also § 1.-158; Tex.Bus.Corp.Act of 1955, Art. 5.11; Vt.Stat., Rev. of 1947, § 5821; Wash.Rev.Code 1951, § 23.-16.140.

Where merger or consolidation is the change contemplated, all states require shareholder approval, and the 46 states and the District of Columbia having appraisal statutes (Utah and West Virginia have none) provide for the purchase of dissenting owners' shares at the owners' option. Here, the shock is great enough to warrant the conclusion that no shareholder should be required to turn in his shares and accept new ones in a company into which his has merged or a newly organized one into which his and other companies have consolidated or, perhaps, to keep his shares in his own company when other companies have merged into his and new shares have been issued to others in the process.

In the very important area of material changes which affect, or may affect, the shareholder's contract, while he is usually given the right to vote upon the change if it affects adversely his class of shares, whether or not he may vote in other situations, there are surprisingly few statutes that give him the additional right of withdrawing, if he so elects, by requiring the corporation to purchase his shares.[69] What greater considerations of policy have been behind the appraisal provisions in case of merger and consolidation, and, if we are to judge by numbers, apparently more weighty policy considerations behind appraisal statutes in case of sale, lease or exchange of all or substantially all of the corporate assets, than in case of a material change in the shareholder's contract, are not clear. If the shareholder's dividend rate, redemption price, par value, dissolution preference, and a host of other preferences may be changed to his disadvantage, the policy of giving him an appraisal remedy would seem to be highly reasonable. This is probably the most dangerous area of all for the preferred shareholder. There is so much chance for manipulation of share priorities through directorial recommendation and majority vote, or through directorial discretion in corporate purchasing of preferred shares with dividends in arrears out of funds that might have been used for dividends on such shares that the appraisal remedy should be present with additional remedies to limit or prevent corporate purchases under such circumstances.[70] Shareholders generally follow like

69. These statutes permit appraisal in such cases: La.S.A.—Rev.Stat. § 12.52; Mo.Rev.Stat.1949, V.A.M. S. § 351.090(4) (a limited right); N.Y.Stock Corp.Law, § 38, subd. 11 as amended (58 McKinney's Consol.Laws of N.Y., Ann., § 38, subd. 11; N.C.Gen.Stat.1957 Cum.Supp. to Recompiled Volume, § 55–113, § 55–101(b); Ohio Rev.Code (as amended 1955) § 1701.74 (requires "substantial" prejudice to shares of a class "where the articles do not expressly or by implication provide for or permit such amendment"); Okl.Stat.1951, Title 18, § 1.157, and see § 1.158; Wash.Rev.Code 1951, § 23.16.140; Flack's Ann.Code of Md., Art. 23, § 69(a) (3) as amended by L.1953, c. 405, referring to § 10 of Art. 23 (appraisal for encroachment on shareholders' contract-rights when the charter does not reserve the right to make the particular amendment).

70. "Most subtle of all methods of getting rid of the preferred share-

sheep the recommendations made by their directors. And when economic conditions make it desirable to tamper with priorities, case histories show that some managements recommend as drastic changes in the preferred shareholders' contracts as these shareholders, under pressure, can be encouraged to accept. Thus, the common shareholders to whom management must normally look for continuation in office are all too frequently the actual beneficiaries of priority changes.[71] As Professor Conard has pointed out:[72] "The moral seems to be that shareholders can protect themselves in the courts if the courts are prepared to apply a strict standard of fairness." The absence of an appraisal right under the particular statute may also be a legitimate consideration by a court in passing upon the fairness or unfairness of a plan; but the plan itself should be fair whether or not there is an appraisal right.[73]

holders' priorities is the purchase of their shares in the open market. When dividends are current, we have not regarded purchase as a 'manipulation,' although something might be said on this point. But when the dividends are in arrears, the use of funds for purchase of shares automatically diminishes the possibility that dividends will ever be paid, by reducing the fund from which they would come. Conversely, the withholding of dividends helps to provide the fund for purchase at the same time that it reduces the market price of the shares." Conard, Manipulation of Share Priorities—The Record of 79 Listed Securities, 8 Vand.L.Rev. 55, at 59 (1954).

71. See Professor Conard's summary, op. cit. supra, note 70, at page 70. And see Porges v. Vadsco Sales Corp., 27 Del.Ch. 127, 32 A.2d 148 (Ch.1943), where a merger was the solution for the reorganization of a Delaware corporation in trouble with accrued dividends. The most recent balance sheet showed the net worth of the corporation to be $2,219,140.52; the sum of the par or fixed liquidation value of the preferred stock to be $2,116,000, with accumulated dividends of $1,839,156.67. While the common stock had no book value whatever, the common shareholders were given $\frac{1}{10}$ of a share in the surviving corporation for each share they owned, an obvious travesty on fairness. Yet the court found no

"fraud," stating: "When fraud of this nature is charged, the unfairness must be of such character and must be so clearly demonstrated as to impel the conclusion that it emanates from acts of bad faith, or a reckless indifference to the rights of others interested, rather than from an honest error of judgment." Could this have been an "honest error of judgment"? Other benefits, however, had been given the preferred shareholders. Compare Barrett v. Denver Tramway Corp., 53 F.Supp. 198 (D.Del.1943), aff'd 146 F.2d 701 (3d Cir., 1944), Judge Leahy's opinion in the trial court.

72. Conard, op. cit. supra note 70, at 67.

73. For a good illustration of a court's insistence upon a fair plan, see Wessel v. Guantanamo Sugar Co., 134 N.J.Eq. 271, 35 A.2d 215 (Ch.1944), aff'd 135 N.J.Eq. 506, 39 A.2d 431 (Ct.Err. & App.1944), where the court concluded that the only apparent purpose of the plan (to eliminate dividend arrearages) was to benefit the common shareholders who had not received dividends for 22 years. Compare Franzblau v. Capital Securities Co., Inc., 2 N.J.Super. 517, 64 A.2d 644 (1949), which held that the fairness of the plan could not be considered where the corporation had power to eliminate accrued dividends. State ex rel. Weede v. Bechtel, 239 Iowa 1298, 31 N.W.2d 853 (1948), cert. denied 337 U.S. 918, 69 S.Ct. 1161, 93 L.Ed. 1728 (1949), was in

By a recent Nebraska statute, an injunction may be obtained where the proponents of a proposed amendment fail to show that the amendment "is fair, just and equitable to all shareholders affected thereby." [74] This makes sense without the aid of a statute except where the statute makes the appraisal remedy the sole one in any case, and the chancellor's foot is long enough to reach it with the full vigor of his toe. And in California, the Securities Law requires a permit from the Corporation Commissioner to issue securities which change preferences of outstanding securities issued prior in point of time.[75] Thus, even with the broad appraisal statute which exists in that state, there is an effective control over the fairness of a plan coming within the reach of the blue sky provisions. Since equitable remedies, while available, require a suit with the attendant expenses, a supervisory power over the fairness of a plan which impinges upon outstanding security holders' rights might well be placed in an administrative body or official for the sake of economy; [76] and for the sake of speed which is always desirable in such matters.

Where there is authorization to dissolve a prosperous corporation and an honest dissolution for the purpose of going out of business is anticipated, there would seem to be no basis upon which to argue a further policy of appraisal for those dissenting. Dissolution means an end to the corporation and, after the payment of debts and expenses, the remaining assets are distributed in accordance with the shareholders' contracts and, if there are no special contracts giving preferences, then pro rata, each share being equal to every other one.

Thus, while owners have been given the right to participate in making decisions involving material or fundamental change, choices had to be made as to which owners (if less than all) should have this right, how it could be exercised (that is, through what formalities), and how large the vote or consent should be to authorize the particular change. Policy factors have dictated whether shareholders who dissent should possess the further

essence similar to the Porges case in note 71, supra, but the result, on grounds of unfairness, was contra to that case.

74. 1A Neb.Rev.Stat. § 21–1,162 (Reissue 1954). And see Latty, Exploration of Legislative Remedy for Prejudicial Changes in Senior Shares, 19 U. of Chi.L.Rev. 759 (1952).

75. West's Ann.Cal.Corp.Code § 25,-009 defining "sale" to include "exchange" or "any change in the rights, preferences, privileges, or restrictions on outstanding securi-

ties." See Dahlquist, Regulation and Civil Liability Under the California Corporate Securities Act, 33 Calif.L.Rev. 343 (1945); Note, Elimination of Dividend Arrearages on Cumulative Preferred Stock by Amendment of the Articles of Incorporation, 37 Calif.L. Rev. 129 (1949).

76. See Ballantine, Lattin and Jennings, Cases and Materials on Corporations, Note on Fairness: Judicial and Administrative Supervision of Recapitalization and Reorganizations, 1002–1005 (2d ed. 1953).

right of demanding payment of the value of their shares, thus giving them the right to retreat from the disadvantage or risk they feel the particular corporate alteration involves. A delicate balancing of interests of majority and minority owners has been necessary, for the majority owners should not be chained to what they believe to be unsound business judgment nor should the minority be bound to remain shareholders when they have similar feelings. And whether a dissenting shareholder should be able to contest more than the validity of the vote, through which the change purports to be authorized, is also a matter of policy which ought to be decided upon a balancing of the possible dangers of unlimited freedom to legislate fundamental changes through majority action and, on the other hand, of the power of a minority to prevent prompt action by threats of suits to enjoin what they claim to be unauthorized, or not accomplished in the prescribed manner, or unfair, or fraudulent. As indicated above, the nuisance value of threatened obstruction by a minority is of slight importance when the majority owners have proceeded honorably and fairly toward all owners, thus showing no abuse of discretion. It is a real threat, as it should be, in case of abuse of discretion by the majority.

§ 8. Necessity that Action of the Prescribed Majority be Authorized and Consummated by the Prescribed Procedures

No shareholder need comply with the conditions or accept the benefits of an appraisal right unless the particular fundamental change made has been authorized and has been carried through by the prescribed vote with whatever formalities the statute has set up. Being in derogation of the common law, strict compliance has been the rule with but only an occasional exception.[77] This is not to say that a statute which authorizes the sale of all or a substantial part of the corporation's assets upon a vote by the designated proportion of specified classes of shareholders must be complied with in cases where one of the purposes of the corporation is to dispose of its assets, as in case

---

77. Hill v. Page & Hill Co., 198 Minn. 30, 268 N.W. 705 (1936), rehearing denied 198 Minn. 30, 268 N.W. 927 (1936): "We think the exigency [one of the lowest points of the great depression which started in 1929] justified the corporate action [sale of corporate assets in a Minnesota corporation for shares in a Delaware corporation organized by some of the shareholders for this purpose since the life of the Minnesota corporation was about to expire] and took the case out of the rule applying to going concerns . . . No business man in his senses, handling his own affairs, would have taken any other course than that which defendants took." (268 N.W. at 706) The plaintiff, holding 22% of the stock, was not seeking appraisal but sought to have the transfer declared invalid and to compel the Delaware corporation to transfer the assets back to the Minnesota corporation.

of a "wasting asset" corporation,[78] for such a sale would be in the ordinary course of business and in furtherance of the corporate purposes. This is within the area of power possessed by the board of directors. However, too much confidence should not be placed in previous common law holdings unless the statute specifically excepts sales or transfers in ordinary course, an exception contained in a number of statutes today. In a recent case of a corporation in financial distress it was unsuccessfully argued that the board of directors had the power, under such circumstances, without a shareholder vote to dispose of the corporate assets. The court pointed to the statute which required a majority vote and which did not specifically authorize the directors to sell all or substantially all of the corporate assets when the corporation was not a going and prosperous one, or when it was in a failing condition.[79] There are some statutes, however, which permit the directors when their corporation is insolvent to act without shareholder action.[80]

Difficulties of interpretation arise when a statutory or common law exception permits board action to authorize and consummate a sale of corporate assets in ordinary course of business and allows of no appraisal right under such circumstances. What is within the phrase "ordinary course of business" or simi-

78. Jeppi v. Brockman Holding Co., 34 Cal.2d 11, 206 P.2d 847, 9 A.L.R. 2d 1297 (1949). This corporation was organized to manage and dispose of an estate. Justice Shenk dissented, two other justices concurring, on the ground that the statute made no exception in case of sales of entire assets in ordinary course. Likewise, a sale of all the real estate of a corporation organized to buy, sell and deal in real estate, is in ordinary course and in furtherance of the business. The directors, without shareholder consent, would have the power to sell. Thayer v. Valley Bank, 35 Ariz. 238, 276 P. 526 (1929); Tuttle v. Junior Bldg. Corp., 227 N.C. 146, 41 S.E.2d 365 (1947); Eisen v. Post, 3 N.Y.2d 518, 146 N.E.2d 779 (1957), two judges dissenting on ground that regular course of business should be determined on what corporation, actually does and not by what its certificate of incorporation gives it power to do. And see Matter of Miglietta, 287 N.Y. 246, 39 N.E.2d 224 (1942), where the right of appraisal was denied in case of a "salvage corporation" formed for the purpose of liquidating properties it had acquired.

Such transactions were within the ordinary course of the corporate business. Also, Pollack v. Adwood Corp., 321 Mich. 93, 32 N.W.2d 62 (1948), noted in 47 Mich.L.Rev. 411 (1949), involving a lease of the principal corporate asset. See Note, Sale of Entire Corporate Assets: When Are Statutes Authorizing and Regulating Sales Applicable? 38 Calif.L.Rev. 913 (1950).

79. Michigan Wolverine Student Co-Operative, Inc. v. Wm. Goodyear & Co., 314 Mich. 590, 22 N.W.2d 884 (1946): "It was for the members to decide whether to sell out, or to hold on to their real estate in the face of continuing losses on the prospect of increased enrollment and revival of corporate prosperity." A deed of the corporation's real property was cancelled because not authorized by the members. But compare Continental Bank & Trust Co. of New York v. W. A. R. Realty Corp., 270 App.Div. 577, 61 N.Y. S.2d 273 (1946), aff'd without opinion 295 N.Y. 877, 67 N.E.2d 517 (1946).

80. Daly v. Opelousas Insurance Agency, Inc., 181 La. 89, 158 So. 631 (1935).

lar terms is not always obvious. Perhaps no better test has been devised than that which asks "whether the property sold is essential to the transaction of the ordinary business of the corporation." [81]   And where an appraisal right is given when transfers are made out of ordinary course, and one is actually so made, neither the good faith of the directors nor that of the majority shareholders in authorizing what they consider a sale within the ordinary course of business can affect the rights of those who have dissented and complied with the conditions precedent to appraisal.[82]   And if the sale was actually out of ordinary course and the statutorily prescribed shareholder vote had not materialized, even though the board acted in good faith, consummation could be enjoined and, if already accomplished, could be upset, barring some argument of laches or estoppel.

While, generally, dissenting shareholders are put to an election under appraisal provisions, there are circumstances under which the duty to elect does not arise. Where the fundamental change is not authorized by law, a dissenting shareholder is under no duty to elect; he may enjoin its consummation.[83]   The appraisal provisions were not enacted to cover more than authorized changes. Where, through the abuse of discretion, the prescribed majority has not procured a fair price in the sale of all or a substantial part of the corporate assets, or has not provided for fair terms in case of merger or consolidation, or has taken advantage of the minority in a reclassification plan, or has used an indirect method to accomplish a purpose which has been authorized by a direct method as, for example, through a sale of assets provision to accomplish a dissolution or a merger or consolidation, a non-consenting shareholder is not put to an election. He may enjoin such action or, if the fundamental change has been consummated and he has not been guilty of laches, and innocent third parties will not be injured, he may upset what has been accomplished in this manner.[84]   He may, in a proper case, elect

---

81. Kunin v. Title Guarantee & Trust Co., 281 App.Div. 635, 121 N.Y.S.2d 220, at 224 (1953), aff'd 306 N.Y. 967, 120 N.E.2d 228 (1954), motion for reargument denied 307 N.Y. 686, 120 N.E.2d 856 (1954). The case leaned heavily on Matter of Timmis, 200 N.Y. 177, 93 N.E. 522 (1910), which, in turn, accepted earlier case law.   Wrote Judge Vann (93 N.E. at 523): "These cases and those which intervened established the law that a corporation cannot sell all its property, or even a part thereof so integral as to be essential for the transaction of its ordinary business, because

such a sale is wholly or partly an act of self-destruction and a practical dissolution without compliance with law."

82. Ibid.

83. Jones v. Rhea, 130 Va. 345, 107 S.E. 814 (1921); Eisenberg v. Central Zone Property Corp., 306 N.Y. 58, 115 N.E.2d 652 (1953).

84. Brown v. Ramsdell, 227 App.Div. 224, 237 N.Y.S. 573 (1929) (minority shareholders sued to recover from directors a loss to corporation incurred through sale of assets voted by majority because of bad faith or

to take advantage of his common law remedy for money damages for the conversion of his shares and, where there has been a wanton disregard of his rights, punitive damages may be allowed.[85] While a shareholder may consent to an abuse of discretion by board or majority shareholders, he is not bound to. To reiterate what has already been stated, fairness and equal opportunity to participate in the fruits of the fundamental change are essential to put the change beyond possibility of successful attack by the dissenter.

§ 9. Necessity of Dissenters who Desire Appraisal to Comply Strictly with the Statutory Conditions Precedent

When fundamental changes are proposed by the directors and presented to the shareholders for a vote, many shareholders are likely to be uninformed of their appraisal rights. Some statutes now require that the corporation's notice to the shareholders contain a statement enlightening them on this matter. The new North Carolina statute, for example, requires a statement (where appraisal rights are given) that dissenting shareholders are entitled to them upon compliance with the named section and the period during which they may make demand for payment of the fair value of their shares.[86] It is desirable that statutes require a statement of the conditions precedent to taking advantage of the appraisal right since some require that a dissenting shareholder vote against the proposal, others that he submit his written dissent prior to the meeting, others that he dissent and demand his appraisal remedy within a stated time, such as within so many days from the date of the shareholders' meeting. The

negligent recommendations of the directors); Robb v. Eastgate Hotel, Inc., 247 Ill.App. 261, 106 N.E.2d 848 (1952) (suit to enjoin performance of contract of sale alleging a conspiracy of majority to sell corporate assets to themselves at a grossly inadequate price); Schaffner v. Standard Boiler & Plate Iron Co., 150 Ohio St. 454, 83 N.E. 2d 192 (1948) (reclassification of shares cutting off accumulated dividends); Bloch v. Baldwin Locomotive Works, 75 Pa.D. & C. 24 (Del. Co.1950) (sale of assets amounting to a merger was held to give dissenters their appraisal right as if in fact merger section had been used); Theis v. Spokane Falls Gas Light Co., 34 Wash. 23, 74 P. 1004 (1904) (dissolution statute used when purpose was to sell assets to a new corporation majority-controlled); Meyerhoff v. Bankers' Se-

curities, Inc., 105 N.J.Eq. 76, 147 A. 105 (1929) (use of sales provisions to effect a dissolution); Outwater v. Public Service Corp. of New Jersey, 103 N.J.Eq. 461, 143 A. 729 (Ch.1928), aff'd 104 N.J.Eq. 490, 146 A. 916 (Ct.Err. & App.1929) (merger enjoined because of unfairness).

85. Equitable Trust Co. v. Columbia Nat. Bank, 145 S.C. 91, 142 S.E. 811 (1927).

86. Gen.Stat. of N. C., 1957 Cum. Supp. § 55–113. Shareholders in corporations subject to the Security and Exchange Commission's proxy regulations will have notice of their appraisal rights in case they dissent. 17 Code of Federal Regulations § 240.14a, Schedule 14A, Item 2 (Supp.1958), provides for a brief outline of appraisal rights and the procedure to perfect them.

conditions precedent have usually been interpreted strictly so that if the shareholder who desires not to go along with the fundamental change but wishes to surrender his shares for their fair value, he must have complied strictly with the statutory conditions set out.[87] There is good reason for strict compliance for, if dissenters are numerous, it may be impracticable for the corporation to proceed with the fundamental change because of the danger of upsetting its financial stability. Hence, the only safe advice is to "cross all t's and dot all i's" if the appraisal remedy is desired.[88]

§ 10.   Actions in the Alternative

Suppose a shareholder honestly believes that the action of the majority in approving a fundamental change is, for some reason, enjoinable. If not enjoinable, he would accept his appraisal right and retire from the company. May he bring an action in the alternative—to enjoin, and if he is mistaken in this, have an appraisal? Where, prior to the enactment of appraisal statutes, an action was brought in the alternative, such actions were permitted but his alternative request was for the value of his shares at the time of their conversion.[89] Authority, while

87. Re O'Brien, 182 Misc. 577, 45 N. Y.S.2d 208 (1943) (statute required filing of written objection and demand for payment before the meeting; filing of written objection held not enough); Roselle Park Trust Co. v. Ward Baking Corp., 177 Md. 212, 9 A.2d 228 (1939) (demand must be made within 20-day statutorily prescribed period or right is lost); In re Northeastern Water Co., 28 Del.Ch. 139, 38 A.2d 918 (1944) (demand in writing must be made within statutorily prescribed 20-day period, not simply mailed within that period—corporation must have received it within the period); In re Universal Pictures Co., Inc., 28 Del.Ch. 72, 37 A.2d 615 (Ch.1944) (burden is on dissenter to establish his right by performing the statutorily prescribed conditions); National Supply Co. v. Leland Stanford Junior University, 134 F.2d 689 (9th Cir., 1943), cert. denied 320 U.S. 773, 64 S.Ct. 77, 88 L.Ed. 462 (1943) (dissenting shareholders could not complain that they were not advised by corporation of their rights by a timely objection to claim the appraisal value of their shares). For as technical a holding as can be found, see Klein v. United Theaters Co., 148 Ohio St. 306, 74 N.E.2d 319 (1949). Contra: Zeeb v. Atlas Powder Co., 32 Del.Ch. 486, 87 A.2d 123 (Sup.Ct.1952).

88. Strict compliance by the corporation is also required. Voeller v. Neilston Warehouse Co., 311 U.S. 531, 61 S.Ct. 376, 85 L.Ed. 322 (1941), rev'g 136 Ohio St. 427, 26 N.E.2d 442 (1940), where the then Ohio provision required the corporation to submit what it considered the value of the dissenter's shares if it disagreed with the value he was required to state in his demand; otherwise his value was, by statute, made conclusively the value to be paid.

89. Garrett v. Reid-Cashion Land & Cattle Co., 34 Ariz. 245, 270 P. 1044 (1928); Finch v. Warrior Cement Corp., 16 Del.Ch. 44, 141 A. 54 (Ch. 1928). There were appraisal provisions but the court assumed that the plaintiffs were not proceeding under them. See also Jones v. Missouri-Edison Elect. Co., 135 F. 153 (D.Mo.1905), 144 F. 765 (8th Cir., 1906), 199 F. 64 (8th Cir., 1912), 203 F. 945 (8th Cir., 1913), 233 F. 49 (8th Cir., 1916).

not copious, has permitted suit in the alternative under appraisal statutes.[90] The difficulty in such cases is the impossibility of meeting the conditions precedent to appraisal and at the same time bringing suit in the alternative. However, the time schedule of notice of dissent and demand for appraisal was provided to give the corporation notice of the number of dissenters demanding to be paid the value of their shares so that, if the load of payment were too burdensome, the corporation could abandon the proposed fundamental change. The appraisal statutes usually provide for a corporate change of mind after the vote has been had and before consummation of the plan and, if no statutory provision had been made for this, since appraisal rights depend upon accomplishment of the fundamental change, the opportunity to retain the *status quo* would likewise be there. Hence, the starting of suit prior to the last day upon which notice and demand for an appraisal might be given would supply the company with the information it needs and more. Or, if he gives written notice that he plans to bring suit, this notice being within the time required to take advantage of his appraisal rights, and further states that he intends to bring suit in the alternative, should not this be sufficient to keep his appraisal right alive provided, at a later date, equity refuses to enjoin, thus leaving him with his alternative remedy?

It may be supposed that a shareholder in good faith might bring an action to enjoin the corporation from consummating the fundamental change without specifically claiming the alternative remedy. If he fails, must he go along with the majority or will the appraisal remedy be open to him at this late date? The company may feel reasonably sure that if he fails in his suit to enjoin, he will want to be relieved as an owner. Would it not be reasonable to hold that the appraisal remedy still remains in spite of the failure to comply with the formal requirements of the statute?

What has been said above may perhaps encourage "strike suits" but the expense of suit to the shareholder would seem partially to guarantee good faith attempts to enjoin where there is a reasonable belief that they will succeed. Again, this is a matter of policy about which reasonable men may well differ.

---

90. Petry v. Harwood Elect. Co., 280 Pa. 142, 124 A. 302 (1924); Lazenby v. International Cotton Mills Corp., 174 App.Div. 906, 160 N.Y.S. 1 (1916) (suit was not in alternative, but to enjoin, the court taking the position that since it denied injunction the shareholder had an option to take the value of his shares as of the time the consolidation took effect).

§ 11. Abandonment of Plan by Corporation after Shareholder Approval

Mention of this possibility and the most common reason for it have been made in the section above. Most statutes today make provision for abandonment, usually through action by the board of directors, not requiring a resubmission to the shareholders. As a method of acquiring a favorable large vote upon a plan involving fundamental change, the notice to the shareholders will frequently contain a statement to the effect that if a named percentage of shares is not voted for the change, management reserves the option not to make it; or if the owners of more than a stated number or percentage of shares demand their appraisal rights, the change if voted will not be consummated. The great bulk of such statutes requires the directors to submit their recommendation to the shareholders prior to taking a shareholder vote on the resolution. There may, of course be other reasons for not carrying out the plan after the shareholders have voted in favor of it. There is no valid reason, however, to question the authority of the board to abandon in good faith the plan when the statute has given this body the authority to do so.[91] However, it seems desirable as a practical matter that some limits as to when and for what purposes the directors may thus act should be set forth in a certificate of merger or other plan to be voted upon by the shareholders.[92] Time limits within which the board may, by its action alone, abandon the plan would seem particularly desirable.

§ 12. Determination of Value in Appraisal Proceedings

When a dissenting shareholder and his corporation cannot agree upon the price to be paid for his shares, that is, upon their value, the statutes generally provide for the appointment or selection of appraisers upon application therefor. If the particular statute provides for the payment to dissenters of the "market" or "fair market" value and the stock has a market value in a market of willing sellers and willing buyers, a market which might be termed normal because of sufficient transactions in the stock whose value is unaffected by unusual incidents, the appraisal should be a quite simple matter.[93] The statutes usually provide that the valuation shall be as of the day previous to the consummation of the vote without reference to any appreciation or depreciation resulting from the event.

---

91. Hoit v. American Bantam Car Co., 69 F.Supp. 731 (D.Pa.1947); Zobel v. American Locomotive Co., 182 Misc. 323, 44 N.Y.S.2d 33 (Sup. Ct.1943). See, generally, Fuld, Some Practical Aspects of a Merger, 60 Harv.L.Rev. 1092 (1947).

92. See Fuld, op. cit. supra, note 91, at 1096.

93. West's Ann.Cal.Corp.Code § 4300 uses the term "fair market value." See Note, 40 Calif.L.Rev. 140 (1952) on the determination of fair market value.

However, most of the appraisal statutes provide for payment of the "value" or "fair value" or "fair cash value" or are expressed in comparable terms. They, too, designate the time to which the appraisal must relate and advise that appreciation or depreciation due to the change shall not be considered by the appraisers. Such terms need interpretation for the statutes do not define them. While various contentions have been made concerning this matter, the following represents a fair consensus of opinion at the present time. Since the shareholder, by majority action, is being deprived of his investment, he is entitled to the investment value of his shares unless the statute uses descriptive terms pointing contrariwise. Investment value points toward the future with future prospects of earnings and opportunities. It also has reference to present asset value, though this is not of great weight since dissolution value is not the test. And market value, where there is a free and open market and the volume of trading in the shares is such as to constitute a fair reflection of the buying and selling public's judgment, is entitled to much weight. The New York court seems eventually to have concluded that market value is a controlling (but not the only) consideration where the market is as stated above.[94] But where there is no mar-

94. Application of Marcus, 273 App. Div. 725, 79 N.Y.S.2d 76 (1948). The appraisal and its confirmation gave the plaintiff the mean price of a share on the New York Stock Exchange on the day prior to the shareholder vote. The case is noted in 65 Harv.L.Rev. 1243 (1952).

Walter, J., in Application of Silverman, 115 N.Y.S.2d 97, at 98–99 (Sup.Ct.1952), modified in 282 App. Div. 252, 122 N.Y.S.2d 312 (1953), wrote: "Perhaps in no appraisal proceeding could it ever be said that any one criterion of value is controlling in the sense that other criteria need not be considered, but there are many appraisal proceedings in which a fair and just consideration of all possibly relevant criteria and factors may result in the emergence of one criterion which is practically, if not theoretically, controlling in that case; and where the thing being valued is the stock of a going concern and there are actual purchases and sales of such stock in substantial volume at or near to the date as of which value is to be determined, and there is no fact justifying an inference that those purchases and sales are not a fair reflection of the judgment of the buying and selling public—the opinion of informed buyers and sellers—market value is controlling at least to the extent that it would take strong and convincing evidence of some other fact, as distinguished from mere opinion, to justify a departure from it; for under those circumstances market value is not merely a composite opinion of many persons making an intensely practical appraisal in their own interest—it is actually a factual report of what willing buyers are willing to pay and willing sellers are willing to accept, and no appraiser and no court can get closer to a determination of value than that . . ." But see the Appellate Division's decision which points out the difference between shares on an exchange and those sold over the counter. A dictum in Matter of Fulton, 257 N.Y. 487, 178 N.E. 766, 79 A.L.R. 608 (1931), that where there is an active and normal market the market value is the controlling consideration is the forerunner of the later New York pronouncements. The note writer in 28 N.Y.U.L.Rev. 1021, at 1031 (1953), concludes that "The dissenting stockholder who has a market for his stock not only is deprived of an effective remedy

ket or an indifferent one for the dissident's shares, the shareholder is entitled to receive the "actual" value and in the process of ascertaining that, the appraisers should consider the "investment" value which includes the "rate of return, the security afforded that dividends will be regularly paid, the possibility that dividends will be increased or diminished, the selling price of stocks of like character, the amount of preferred stock in comparison with the common stock, the size of the accumulated surplus applicable to the payment of dividends, the record of the corporation and its prospects for the future." [95]   There is thus no definite yardstick by which shares with little or no market value can be judged.[96]

In a recent case, appraisers acting under the Delaware statute considered: (1) the net asset value of the preferred and common, (2) the fair market value of the preferred and common, (3) capitalized the earnings by taking the average earnings for the preferred and common for a 5-year period to find the earnings-dividend value of the shares, weighted the preferred and the common percentage-wise in each category upon reasonable assumptions, and came up with a valuation based upon the sum of the computations.   Vice Chancellor Seitz approved the method and gave this advice: [97]   "Conceivably, an appraiser in weighting

under the New York appraisal statute, but is penalized when he asks for one."

95. Matter of Fulton (Matter of Clark's Will), supra, note 94, 257 N.Y. at 495, 178 N.E. at 769.

96. Ohio Rev.Code § 1701, 85(C) defines "fair cash value" in willing-seller, willing-buyer terms.   Roessler v. Security Savings & Loan Ass'n, 147 Ohio St. 480, 72 N.E.2d 259 (1947), without statutory aid, had refused to adopt such a test.

97. Jacques Coe & Co. v. Minneapolis-Moline Co., 31 Del.Ch. 368, 75 A.2d 244, at 246 (1950) (the shares were not listed on any exchange but were bought and sold over the counter).   In Re General Realty & Utilities Corp., 29 Del.Ch. 480, 52 A.2d 6 (1947), the Delaware court gave asset value a 50% weight, market value and future earnings a 25% weight each.   An excellent analysis of why the market value of shares sold only over the counter does not reflect their true value, and what elements should be stressed in such a case, is contained in Application of Silverman, 282 App.Div. 252, 122 N.Y.S.2d 312

(1953), modifying 115 N.Y.S.2d 97 (Sup.Ct.1952), which had emphasized the market value above other considerations.   The appraisers' valuation of $7.50 per share was increased to $10 by the Appellate Division.

Other important cases accepting investment value as the criterion are: Sterling v. Mayflower Hotel Corp., 33 Del.Ch. 293, 93 A.2d 107, 38 A.L.R.2d 425 (Sup.Ct.1952) (merger terms were in dispute); Tri-Continental Corp. v. Battye, 31 Del. Ch. 523, 74 A.2d 71 (1950) (closed end investment company); Chicago Corp. v. Munds, 20 Del.Ch. 142, 172 A. 452 (Ch.1934) (investment company's shares were in issue); Ahlenius v. Bunn & Humphreys, 358 Ill. 155, 192 N.E. 824, 95 A.L.R. 913 (1934); Republic Finance & Investment Co. v. Fenstermaker, 211 Ind. 251, 6 N.E.2d 541 (1937); Phelps v. Watson-Stillman Co., 365 Mo. 1124, 293 S.W.2d 429 (1956); Perkins v. Public Service Co., 93 N.H. 459, 45 A.2d 210 (1945); Roessler v. Security Savings & Loan Co., 147 Ohio St. 480, 72 N.E. 2d 259 (1947); Adams v. United States Distributing Corp., 184 **Va.**

various elements of value and arriving at an appraised value might not articulate his mental processes. However, I believe an appraiser should state the monetary value which he has ascribed to the more substantial elements of value considered and the weight he has given each such element in arriving at his appraised value. I shall not pause to discuss the many infirmities involved in any evalution process. The important thing is that the appraiser must, under the statute, arrive at a dollar and cents' appraisal. Consequently, the appraiser should state the value of the elements given independent weight and the weight given to each in arriving at the appraised value. This procedure will render the valuation process a little less arbitrary and will permit a review at least on a degree basis." Actually, the appraiser in this case gave his reasons for the percentage of weight he gave to each of the items of valuation, a distinct aid to the court when asked to review the appraisal.

§ 13.   The Matter of Payment of Interest and of Costs of Appraisal

Some statutes specifically provide for the payment of interest upon the value of the dissenter's shares and the better ones make definite the time from which interest is due and the rate of interest to be applied.[98] Even if there is no provision for the payment of interest, it has been held that a dissenting sharehold-

---

134, 34 S.E.2d 244, 162 A.L.R. 1227 (1945), cert. denied 327 U.S. 788, 66 S.Ct. 807, 90 L.Ed. 1014 (1946) (Virginia corporation with statutory provision of "fair cash value"); Petition of Northwest Greyhound Lines, Inc., 41 Wash.2d 672, 251 P.2d 607 (1952) (case analyzes various items appraiser considered). However, American General Corp. v. Camp, 171 Md. 629, 190 A. 225 (1937), held "fair value" to mean "intrinsic value on liquidation." 190 A. at 229. And see Ariz.Rev.Stat. § 10–347 (pro rata share of the fair value of the net assets—as of the time of the consolidation meeting).

See also, Levy, Rights of Dissenting Shareholders to Appraisal and Payment, 15 Cornell L.Q. 420 (1930); Weiner, Payment of Dissenting Stockholders, 27 Col.L.Rev. 547 (1927); Lattin, Remedies of Dissenting Stockholders Under Appraisal Statutes, 45 Harv.L.Rev. 234 (1931).

98. Rev.Code of Wash.1951, §§ 23.-16.140 and 23.16.160 provide for in-

terest at 6% from the date of corporate authorization of the fundamental change. Ohio Rev.Code § 1701.85(B) provides that judgment be rendered for the fair cash value "with interest at such rate and from such date as the court shall fix in said judgment." N.C.Gen. Stat.1957 Cum.Supp. § 55–113(3) (e) contains a provision for the appraised value as of the date prescribed in this section "together with interest thereon to the date of such confirmation" by the court. Under West's Ann.Cal.Corp.Code § 4311, interest at 7% from the date of judgment is payable. See also, ibid. § 4304. A.L.I. Model Business Corp.Act § 71 (Rev.1953) provides (in case dissenters and corporation cannot agree on the value of the shares) for interest in an appraisal proceeding from the day prior to the vote approving merger or consolidation to the date of the judgment. Similarly, upon a sale of the entire assets out of ordinary course. § 74, ibid.

er is entitled to it as a matter of simple justice from the date of the consummation of the fundamental change.[99] Most of the case law where this question has arisen has taken the opposite view and has denied interest on the inelastic basis that the proceeding for appraisal is statutory in nature and hence the court functions only as a special tribunal with the limited powers which the statute gives it.[1] This sounds a bit antiquated at this late date and ignores the fact that legislation frequently fails to cover the whole ground and must, therefore, be filled in by reasonable construction. Where a statutory lacuna such as this exists, it should be remedied promptly by amending legislation.[2] However, even where no statute provides for interest, where a time is set for the corporation to pay the appraisal value, there is little doubt that a shareholder would be entitled to interest from that date to the date of actual payment.[3]

Appraisals can be expensive, and the threat of the imposition of their costs upon either the corporation or the dissenting shareholders may be a means of economic duress favoring settlement without using the appraisal process. Unless a shareholder has a sufficient monetary interest in the corporation to warrant the risk of being required to pay a part or all of the appraisal costs, where the court has discretion to impose them, he is likely to "sell out" at a price he would not otherwise have accepted. Where the statute makes no provision for them, it has been held that the court has no power to assess costs of appraisal, at least where the action is one at law.[4] On the other hand, it was successfully argued in a recent important case that the appraisal statute was somewhat analogous to statutes permitting controversies to be settled by arbitration and to make an agreement to that end; that in such cases, arbitrators are expected to be paid, and that all parties to the agreement are equally liable for

---

99. Skipworth v. Federal Water & Gas Corp., 185 Misc. 248, 56 N.Y.S. 2d 804 (Sup.Ct.1945) (suit against surviving corporation in a consolidation of Delaware corporations, § 61 of the Del.Corp.Law not then providing for payment of interest). But Meade v. Pacific Gamble Robinson Co., 30 Del.Ch. 509, 58 A.2d 415 (Sup.Ct.1948), set the New York court right on this by holding § 61 as then existing did not permit a charge of interest. However, Del. Corp.Law § 262(h), now applicable, makes provision for interest but with no indication of the date from which it is to be figured.

1. Pittston Co. v. O'Hara, 191 Va. 886, 63 S.E.2d 34, at 39 (1951),

states: "Where the statute does not provide for interest the court has no discretion to award interest." An appeal of the case was dismissed as involving no federal question in 342 U.S. 803, 72 S.Ct. 38, 96 L.Ed. 608 (1951). Accord: Meade v. Pacific Gamble Robinson Co., supra, note 99; In re Janssen Dairy Corp., 2 N.J.Super. 580, 64 A.2d 652 (1949).

2. See Del.Corp.Law § 262(h) which now makes provision for interest.

3. Meade v. Pacific Gamble Robinson Co., supra, note 99.

4. Schultz v. Mountain Telephone Co., 364 Pa. 266, 72 A.2d 287 (1950)

payment of the arbitrators' fees.   The court applied the principle, holding that "the statute implies a like obligation of the parties in these proceedings to share between them the payment of reasonable fees to the appraisers." [5]   It specifically required the corporation to pay one-half and the petitioners one-half, "the latter to be paid by each petitioner in the proportion that the amount of the award to her for her stock bears to the aggregate of the awards to all petitioners."   Attorneys' fees and expenses, and those of accountants and stenographers were not allowed. Such expenses are ones of litigation and as in other cases, unless there is statutory authorization, they are damnum absque injuria and without redress.

Some of the modern statutes provide that the costs of the proceeding, including the fee and costs of the appraisers, shall be assessed by the court as may appear equitable.[6]   And where the statute so provides an appellate court will not disturb the apportionment made by the trial court unless it appears that there was an abuse of discretion.[7]   In some states, statutes provide that the corporation must pay the costs when the appraisal value exceeds the offer which the corporation is required to make.[8]   This type of statute should have the effect of producing

5.   In re Janssen Dairy Corp., supra, note 1, 64 A.2d at 656.

6.   Petition of Northwest Greyhound Lines, Inc., 41 Wash.2d 672, 251 P.2d 607 (1952), without reference to any statutory provision assessed 50% to the corporation and 50% to the shareholders, the latter to share in proportion to their stockholding interest.   However, Rev. Code of Wash.1951, § 23.16.160, provides as in the text statement above.   See N.C.Gen.Stat.1957 Cum. Supp. § 55–113(3) (e).

7.   Meade v. Pacific Gamble Robinson Co., 30 Del.Ch. 509, 58 A.2d 415 (Sup.Ct.1948) (the Chancellor taxed all costs against the corporation where it appeared that the shareholder had not acted in bad faith in his demands); Tri-Continental Corp. v. Battye, 31 Del.Ch. 523, 74 A.2d 71 (Sup.Ct.1950), rev'g 31 Del.Ch. 101, 66 A.2d 910 (1949).

8.   West's Ann.Cal.Corp.Code § 4313 (by § 4304, the corporation is required to make an offer to dissenters to purchase their shares "at a price deemed by the corporation to represent their fair market value"); Ark.Gen.Corp. Act § 64–703 (including attorney's and appraiser's fees as the court shall deem

equitable);   Fla.Stat.Ann. § 608.23 (2) (including attorney's and appraiser's fees);   N.Y.Stock Corp. Law § 21 (when offer of corporation (if made) is substantially less than the appraisal value, the shareholder may be allowed appraisers' and experts' fees).   While, under § 21, subd. 5, the costs and expenses are determined by the court and "shall be assessed against the corporation," if the shareholders' failure to accept the corporation's offer (if one is made) was "arbitrary and vexatious or not in good faith" the court may assess all or a part of the costs as it deems equitable against any or all of the dissenters. See Application of Deutschmann, 113 N.Y.S.2d 823 (Sup.Ct.1952), modified on other grounds in 281 App.Div. 14, 116 N.Y.S.2d 578 (1952). And where the corporation made no offer, it was held that all costs were properly assessed against the corporation.   Application of Silverman, 282 App.Div. 252, 122 N.Y.S.2d 312 (1953).   The New York statute on costs is well worth studying.   See Note, Appraisal of Corporate Dissenters' Shares: Apportioning the Proceeding's Financial Burdens, 60 Yale L.J. 337 (1951).

legitimate good faith offers by the company because of the risk of having to pay the entire costs if its offer, even in good faith, is too low. The requirement that the corporation, under the circumstances set out, must offer what it considers the fair value of its dissenting shares is preferable to requiring the shareholder to submit what he considers the fair value. The corporation has the means of knowing what its shares are worth while the shareholder, without the aid of accountants and appraisers, can know only what the market is bringing, if the shares are listed or are reported on an over-the-counter basis. The scales should be balanced, too, by leaving a judicial discretion to assess a part or all of the costs against the petitioning shareholders and those who join them when it appears that they acted in an arbitrary and vexatious manner, or not in good faith.[9] Provisions giving the court the power to assess the costs as it deems equitable give this opportunity without special words to that effect. Local statutes and their interpretation must be pursued for an understanding of the particular local scene.

§ 14. From What Funds may Appraisal Payments be made?

In any case where the appraisal payments must be made by a purchase of a corporation's own shares, and the appraisal statute does not state from what funds its shares may be purchased, an old problem presents itself. Must such purchases be made from an existing corporate surplus or may they be paid for out of capital provided the corporation is not thereby made insolvent and creditors will not be injured. In straight purchases of its own shares, majority opinion at common law and most statutes enacted on this matter have confined such purchases to earned surplus or a surplus created in some other manner. The more liberal holdings and some modern statutes, however, provide for ordinary purchases from capital, that is, from a balance resulting from deducting debts and liabilities not including stated capital from the value of total assets, with a common proviso that creditors not be jeopardized thereby. And, as pointed out earlier in this book, redemptions of shares have usually been permitted out of balances similarly arrived at.[10]

Since appraisal rights are for the double purpose of permitting the designated majority to change fundamentally the corporate course and to give the dissenter an "out" under circumstances which to him create the necessity, it would be rea-

---

9. See N.Y.Stock Corp.Law § 21, subd. 5, mentioned in note 8 supra.

10. See Chapter 9, § 19, this book; Winchell v. Plywood Corp., 324 Mass. 171 85 N.E.2d 313 (1949) (purchase may be made out of capital where creditors will not be injured); West's Ann.Cal.Corp.Code §§ 1706(d) and 1708 (purchases may be out of capital but creditors and senior shareholders are protected).

sonable to apply the more liberal rule and permit the corporation to purchase its dissenters' shares from capital with restrictions similar to those applied in case of redemption.[11] It would be strange indeed if the majority shareholders were permitted successfully to argue that the capital must be kept intact for their benefit. The statutes themselves give the warning by granting dissenters the appraisal right. Should a court take the view that the usual rule of purchase of the corporation's own shares out of surplus applies, the corporation should be enjoined from consummating the proposed fundamental change, thus forcing it to create a surplus by reducing its stated capital, if this is legally possible, and paying off the dissenters from the reduction surplus. If this is not possible, then the corporation should be restrained until it has sufficient funds legally applicable to the purchase of its shares which are subject to purchase under the appraisal provisions. Under the statutes, the corporation will know, prior to consummation of the intended fundamental change, the number of shares it will be compelled to buy. It can predict what its ultimate liability to outgoing shareholders will be. It should know what funds are legally available for this purpose. Charged with this knowledge and capable, under modern statutes, of abandoning the fundamental change without a shareholder-vote, the directors would be taking a long chance of incurring individual liability if they proceeded to play fast and loose with appraisal rights they know or should know exist.

Where the fundamental change is a merger or consolidation, modern statutes usually require the surviving company into which others have merged, or the new corporation formed for the purpose of consolidating two or more companies to pay the dissenting shareholders who qualify under the appraisal statute, thus placing the dissenters in a position comparable to that of creditors of the absorbed companies.[12] The problem is not one of purchasing one's own shares but of paying off creditors created by the merger or consolidation as a matter of law. Wise statutes have contained a further provision, as does the Florida statute, that "If the consolidated or merged corporation shall fail to pay the amount of the (appraisal) judgment within ten (10) days after the same shall become final, it may be enforced as other judgments." [13] Under the Washington statute a shareholder is not entitled to payment of his shares on appraisal, "unless the value of the corporate assets which would remain after

11. Ohio Rev.Code (as amended 1955) § 1701.35(B).

12. Ohio Rev.Code (as amended 1955) §§ 1701.81(A) (6) and 1701.83

(B) (2); Del.Corp.Law § 262(b); A.L.I. Model Bus.Corp.Act § 71 Rev.1953).

13. Fla.Stat.Ann. § 608.23 (1956).

such payment would be at least equal to the aggregate amount of its debts and liabilities exclusive of capital stock." [14]

§ 15. When do Dissenting Shareholders Cease to be Shareholders?

The problem is important for, after the shareholders have voted favorably upon a fundamental change, dividends may be distributed either in cash or shares, meetings may be called where notice to shareholders must be given, and other shareholder-rights may be involved. Where nothing is stated in the statute indicating at what point shareholder status ends, it culminates when the corporation from which payment is due tenders the proper amount and demands the surrender of the dissenter's shares, since it is the consummation of the fundamental change which raises the duty to pay and the shareholder is under no obligation to surrender his shares and with them his status until tender has been made.

Modern statutes, however, have usually been specific on this matter. Some statutes provide that termination (or suspension) of shareholder status results at the time the dissenter makes demand for payment of his shares unless certain events later occur, such as the failure to apply for the appointment of an appraiser within the stated time, the dismissal of the appraisal proceeding as to such shareholder, the withdrawal of the shareholder's demand for appraisal with the corporation's consent, or the abandonment of the planned change by the corporation.[15] In case the shareholder has failed to act as the statute specifies in order to preserve his appraisal right, he will lose it and be compelled to go along with the majority shareholders. And where that happens, he is entitled to dividends declared since his demand for appraisal, and to any other shareholder benefits that others of his class have acquired. Also, in case the corporation abandons the voted change, as it may do under most statutes by directorial action, the shareholder returns to his status and is entitled to all except voting rights accruing during the suspension of his status. Modern statutes have usually made this clear,[16] though there is no reason to suspect holdings differing from these statutory provisions were they to be omitted.[17] Other statutes pro-

---

14. Rev.Code of Wash.1951, § 23.16.-170.

15. Del.Corp.Law § 262(i); Ohio Rev.Code (as amended 1955) § 1701.-85(E) (during the interval between demand and payment of the appraisal value, cash dividends are payable on the dissenters' shares to be credited on the fair cash value thereof).

16. See Del.Corp.Law § 262(i); Ohio Rev.Code § 1701.85(E).

17. Fla.Stat.Ann. § 608.23, added to statute by L.1953, c. 28170 (Fla. Stat.1957, § 608.23), is silent on the interval between demand and abandonment of the plan, but it seems clear in the manner of statement that the shareholder is entitled to all back benefits if there is abandonment.

vide that shareholder status ceases upon payment of the appraised value thus securing shareholder rights in the interval between demand and final reckoning.[18]   The California statute takes an intermediate position giving the holders of dissenting shares all the rights and privileges incident to their shares until the "fair market value" has been agreed upon or determined.[19] Some statutes require that dissenting shares demanding appraisal be turned in for the purpose of having a legend placed upon them to the effect that they have dissented and are demanding appraisal in order to give notice to a transferee of what he is purchasing.[20]

§ 16.   Formalities in Case of Sale of Assets, Merger and Consolidation

The purchase by a corporation of another corporation's assets is the simplest device to obtain assets, for the board of the purchasing corporation will possess the power without further shareholder action.   The selling corporation, however, will need the recommendation of its board (usually commanded by statute) and a shareholder vote to accomplish a sale out of ordinary course.   Conveyances of land, chattels and other property rights will take the usual form and the local Bulk Sales Act and holdings thereunder should be consulted to see whether it must be met as far as stock in trade and fixtures are concerned.

Statutes today generally permit the sale of corporate assets for securities of the buying corporation and these are conveyed to the selling corporation for the transfer of its assets, the selling corporation frequently going out of business by formal dissolution with either a sale of the shares received and a distribution pro rata in cash or a distribution of the shares themselves either directly or indirectly to the selling corporation's shareholders upon surrender of their own shares to complete the dissolution. The creditors, of course, must first be paid before the shareholders are entitled to share in the return of capital.   The simplicity of this transaction has encouraged its use in many cases where the actual practical result was a merger of two or more corporations.   Though indirect methods of merger or consolidation have been questioned, there would appear to be little danger of successful contest if the statutory provisions for sale give to dissenters rights similar to those available in case of formal merger

---

18.   Ill.Bus.Corp.Act of 1933, §§ 70 and 73 as amended by L.1957, S.B. 266; A.L.I. Model Bus.Corp.Act §§ 71 and 74.

19.   West's Ann.Cal.Corp.Code § 4315.

20.   See, for example, West's Ann.Cal. Corp.Code § 4302 (subsequent trans-

fers, also, must contain a like statement).   Ohio Rev.Code (as amended 1955) § 1701.85(A) (if corporation requests shares for purpose of placing legend thereon, the dissenters must present them for that purpose).

or consolidation. As stated previously, the undercurrent of judicial dissatisfaction with indirect procedures where direct ones are available stems primarily from the fact that appraisal remedies may not be present in the sale-of-assets transaction whereas they are present in merger and consolidation. There have also been abuses in the use of the sale-of-assets section such as the intentional freezing out of unwanted dissenters or the taking over of a prosperous corporation for majority benefit where, if the merger or consolidation process had been used, all would have been treated equally in the division of stock in the consolidated or surviving corporation. However, such matters can be adequately handled by the chancellor as earlier discussion has shown.

The terms "merger" and "consolidation" have been loosely used to mean the same thing. However, accurately used, the term "merger" means the absorption of one or more corporations by a corporation already in existence and continuing in existence after the merger, with the powers and liabilities of those companies merging into it. "Consolidation," on the other hand, is the absorption of one or more corporations into a corporation created for the very purpose of absorbing them. The articles of the new corporation will be sufficiently broad to cover the types of businesses carried on by the corporations thus consolidated. Both types of reorganization require statutory aid, and when there is a merger or consolidation of a local with a foreign corporation, the statutes of the states under which the corporations obtained their existence must each contain provisions authorizing such transactions with foreign corporations. Under such statutes, the boards of the corporations involved agree upon the terms of merger or consolidation and draw upon articles of merger or consolidation prior to submitting the fundamental change to the shareholders for their vote. This involves matters already discussed as to the fairness of the terms and a topic earlier discussed concerning the issue of shares for a consideration other than cash, since shares of the surviving corporation in a merger and those of the new corporation in a true consolidation will usually be issued directly to the shareholders of the corporations absorbed by the process, their shares being surrendered upon the issue and tender of the new shares. Before these fundamental changes may be consummated, the shareholders of each company involved in these transactions must authorize them by the required statutory majority of those entitled to vote on the consolidation or merger, and articles of merger or consolidation must be filed as directed by the statute.

Upon consummation of the merger or consolidation, the absorbed corporations are automatically dissolved while in the case of a sale of all of a corporation's assets for shares in the buying corporation there is no dissolution without further procedures under the dissolution statute. Both merger and consolidation involve as a legal consequence an assumption of debts and liabilities of the corporations absorbed. Statutes today particularly so state. In the case of a sale of corporate assets, the buying corporation is under no liability to pay the debts of the selling corporation unless it contracts to pay them. There may be, however, a following of assets into the possession of the buying corporation if the sale can be brought within the area of a fraudulent conveyance, a topic to be discussed shortly.

Prior to statutes providing for a sale of corporate assets for considerations other than cash, a shareholder could insist upon a sale of that description, though a proper exception was made in case of a sale for shares which had a readily ascertainable market value and which could be sold on an active market.[21] However, even in such a case, it was another matter indeed, in a subsequent dissolution, to force upon an unwilling shareholder the shares which his corporation had taken in exchange for its assets. If he refused to take the shares, he was entitled to his pro rata share of money for which the stock could be sold, either through a sale of the block taken as the purchase price of the assets or, more reasonably, through the sale of the shares to which he was entitled had he elected to accept them.[22] Under most of the present-day appraisal statutes, the dissenter in a case of sale of assets is entitled to receive the fair value of his shares which may differ materially from the money-value of the shares he might have elected to take in the purchasing corporation. Upon a dissolution following such a sale for securities, the preferred shareholder would be entitled to a dissolution preference (if his contract gave him such a preference) in cash, unless otherwise provided in his contract.

§ 17. Formalities in Case of an Increase or Decrease of Legal Capital

In case of the increase or decrease of the stated capital of a corporation, statutory authorization will provide the procedures necessary, such as the shareholder vote required to authorize new shares if there are not some remaining to be issued from a previous authorization, and, in the reduction of stated capital, the procedures required, such as a shareholder vote, the manner of reducing, such as the purchase or redemption and retirement of outstanding shares, the retirement of treasury shares, the reduction of the par value of outstanding par value stock, the reduc-

---

21. Geddes v. Anaconda Copper Min. Co., 254 U.S. 590, 41 S.Ct. 209, 65 L.Ed. 425 (1921).

22. See the discussion in Ballantine, Corporations § 284 (Rev. ed. 1946).

tion of capital assigned to no-par value stock, etc. If there are unissued shares stock dividends in proper cases may be the means of increasing the stated capital, the directors usually having complete authority to do this at their discretion. Where new shares are authorized, there will be the problem of pre-emptive rights, a topic already discussed,[23] and it may be necessary to amend the corporate charter or obtain a waiver from the shareholders having pre-emptive rights.

The reduction of stated capital has more problems of a serious nature than does its increase. As far as shareholders or creditors are concerned, the formal reduction of the stated capital without an accompanying or later distribution of a reduction surplus created thereby has no immediate practical effect. Shareholders and creditors have the same assets behind their shares and debts as before. However, if a reduction surplus is a proper fund for dividends in the particular state, the backlog or cushion which creditors and senior shareholders have been led to expect as further security may disappear. If such a distribution were made and because of it the corporation could not pay the debts of its present creditors, the transfer would be one in fraud of creditors and recoverable for their benefit.[24] And if the stated capital were reduced to a point insufficient to take care of the normal needs of the company, the argument of inadequate capitalization would be persuasive to hold the shareholders liable to creditors who later found the corporate assets inadequate to satisfy their debts.[25]

The better modern statutes contain specific provisions which protect, in varying degree, the senior shareholders and creditors, by placing limitations upon the reduction of stated capital and upon the distributing of a reduction surplus if one turns up through this procedure. The New York statute, for example, provides that the corporation may not reduce "the actual value of the assets" to an amount less than the aggregate of its debts and liabilities plus stated capital as reduced.[26] This does not give much protection to senior shareholders and creditors if the reduction and distribution of reduction surplus, if any, goes the full length allowed unless, possibly, the assets are in cash or may be readily converted into cash at their book value. The California statute carries more protection to both groups by providing that "No such reduction in the stated capital of the corporation shall be made to an amount less than the aggregate par value of all par value shares without liquidation preference to remain outstanding after such reduction and the aggregate amount of the

23. See Chapter 9, § 12, this book.

24. Refer back to Chapter 10, § 7, at page 480, this book, where the problem is discussed.

25. Ibid.

26. N.Y.Stock Corp.Law § 37, subd. 3.

liquidation preferences upon involuntary liquidation of preferred shares with or without par value to remain outstanding after such reduction." [27]   A further provision prohibits a distribution or withdrawal of reduction surplus "unless the board of directors determines that by such distribution or withdrawal the corporation will not be rendered unable to satisfy its debts and liabilities when they fall due and that the assets of the corporation after such distribution or withdrawal taken at their fair present value will at least equal one and one-quarter times its debts and liabilities." [28]   The directors are protected by a specific provision that if they make the determination in good faith and with reasonable care they shall not be liable to the corporation or to its creditors.   The preferred shareholders and creditors receive a fair measure of security under this statute.

But, actually, conditions have not changed radically since the short but critical article by Professor Callahan appeared some twenty years ago in which he reached the conclusion that "the great majority of corporation acts offer the creditor little security in the reduction situation." [29]   He pointed out that the creditor is interested in current assets and these are meat for shareholders who receive a distribution from reduction surplus; that the statutes "by setting up any ratio to be maintained between total assets and liabilities, or total assets and liabilities plus capital stock, fail in their purpose since, under them, the asset values which remain after the distribution may be entirely non-liquid, although greatly exceeding the statutory requirement as to amount." [30]   He concluded that legislation, to be sufficiently protective, must have reference to a "ratio between the liquid, or 'current,' assets of the corporation and the amount of unsecured claims against it." [31]   He proposed model provisions for the reduction and distribution which legislators might well study to make the reduction of capital process a safer one for creditors.[32]

With reference to protecting senior shareholders, the New York court worked out a neat solution under its appraisal statute.   A New York corporation reduced its no-par common shares

27.   West's Ann.Cal.Corp.Code § 1904, as amended in 1955.

28.   Ibid. § 1907.

29.   Callahan, 2 Ohio St.L.J. 220, at 224 (1936).

30.   Ibid. at 229.

31.   Ibid. at 231.

32.   Ibid., 238–239.   Part of Professor Callahan's short statute is as follows: "Assets of the corporation may be distributed to its shareholders up to the amount of such reduction surplus, provided that the assets remaining after such distribution and taken at their fair present value shall at least equal its debts and liabilities plus its capital stock as reduced, and provided further that the current assets of the corporation remaining after such distribution and taken at their fair present value shall equal at least twice the amount of the unsecured debts and liabilities of the corporation."

with a stated value of $10 per share to $1 per share, and transferred the resulting reduction surplus of $1,400,000 from capital to the surplus account.   This reduction in stated capital made it possible to use the surplus in the purchase of its own shares and for the payment of dividends on the common, although the corporation had not indicated that it intended to so use it.   The court held that such an alteration of the capital cushion gave the preferred shareholders the right to appraisal and payment for their shares, this constituting an alteration of a preferential right of outstanding shares.[33]

Prior to 1867, there was no provision in English law permitting a reduction of capital even where capital had been irretrievably lost.   Since that time, however, the Companies Acts have contained provisions permitting such reductions subject to protective safeguards and to the consent or ratification of the court. There is no possibility under English law for a corporation to make an outright purchase of its own shares, even out of surplus and even if the memorandum or articles of association specifically permitted this.[34]   In order to qualify for a reduction of capital under the 1948 Act, a company's articles (by-laws) must contain an authorization to reduce it or be amended so as to provide for this; there must be the passing of a special resolution to reduce the capital; and, finally, the court must confirm what has been done.[35]   Reductions under this Act may be made to extinguish "uncalled capital," to cancel capital "which is lost or unrepresented by available assets," and to return capital which is beyond what the company needs.   Creditors' rights, of course, will be in issue where shareholders are relieved from paying for shares subscribed but not fully paid for, and in case of a reduction and distribution of assets where the company feels it no longer needs to continue its present capitalization.   Thus an inquiry may be made by the court, unless it feels this to be unnecessary, to ascertain whether creditors may be prejudiced.   "Only if all creditors entitled to object have consented or been paid or had their debts secured may the court make an order confirming the reduction on

33. In re Kinney, 279 N.Y. 423, 18 N.E.2d 645 (1939), reargument denied 280 N.Y. 569, 20 N.E.2d 18 (1939), interpreting § 38, subd. 9 (now subd. 11) of the N.Y.Stock Corp.Law.   Section 38, subd. 11(a), uses the phrase "alters or abolishes any preferential right."   Distribution, if made, is restricted by § 38, subd. 6.

34. Trevor v. Whitworth, 12 App. Cas. 409 (1887).   But see British & American Trustee & Finance Corp. v. Couper, [1894] A.C. 399

(House of Lords), as to the purchase by the corporation of its shares in case of capital reduction. See Chapter 5, pages 181–182, this book.   See also English Companies Act of 1948, §§ 27 and 54; Buckley on The Companies Acts, 56 et seq. and 133 et seq. (12th ed. 1949).

35. Gower, Modern Company Law 520 (1954).   Provisions for the reduction of capital will be found in Companies Act of 1948, §§ 66–71. These provisions apply to limited companies having a share capital.

such terms and conditions as it thinks fit." [36]   And, while it is not customary practice, the court may require the company to place the word "reduced" after the corporate name or publish an explanation of the reasons for the reduction. After the court has passed upon the reduction, the court's order and a statement describing the new capital structure must be filed with the "registrar" who issues a certificate which is conclusive as to full compliance with the Act.

This unusual solicitude for the rights of creditors is not particularly evident in American statutes. Furthermore, the discretion of the court extends to the rights of senior shareholders though there is skepticism in some quarters as to how well the courts have handled this discretionary duty.[37] For capital irretrievably lost, neither creditors nor shareholders have a valid objection against a paper reduction showing the then condition of the company—neither loses anything. And, since dividends (under English law) may be paid out of profits over an accounting period without reference to fixed capital previously lost, thus differing from most American authority on this problem, the creditor is not misled to believe that the original cushion will remain for his protection. And this, of course, is quite as true of senior shareholders. Losses in the current accounting period of what the English describe as "circulating capital" must be recouped before dividends, for otherwise there are no profits from which dividends may be declared.[38]

§ 18. Creditors' Rights in Sale of Assets, Merger or Consolidation and Reduction of Legal Capital

Discussion heretofore has indicated that the statutory provisions which are aimed at protecting creditors and senior shareholders in the above fundamental changes, where such provisions exist at all, are for the most part inadequate. If a sale of assets violates the 13 Elizabeth, Chapter 5, type of fraudulent transfer statute, the remedies are the same as in case of other fraudulent transfers. In such cases, the creditors may hold the selling corporation as if no fraudulent transfer had been made and may follow the assets to the extent of their value into the hands of the fraudulent transferee, whether it be natural person or corporation.

When a transfer of tangible assets has been made for shares in the purchasing corporation the question has frequently arisen

36. Gower, op. cit. supra, note 35, at 520.

37. Gower, op. cit. supra, note 35, at 521, 534, 536 and 537. If there is a formal error or there is positive proof that the reduction is unfair, the court will act.

38. Gower, op. cit. supra, note 35, at 113–115.

whether the sale is free from attack or whether the type of consideration received is insufficient to qualify, as cash or tangible property of some other variety might. A number of cases after World War I arose out of transfers made by the express companies of their assets then held by them individually as joint stock companies to a corporation organized to take over these properties by a transfer of its shares for the assets. Most of the cases held that shares were not adequate consideration for the assets and that existing creditors could pursue the assets so transferred in payment of their debts because of constructive fraud. Earlier decisions, as well, sustained the theory of these cases. Some cases holding the majority view felt that the purchasing corporation was merely the selling corporation with a new name and new organization, a mere continuation of the old company, and thus held the assets received subject to the demands of creditors of the selling corporation. Other cases, however, held that shares in the consolidating corporation constituted adequate consideration and were not fraudulent for this reason.[39] And there is much to be said for this view where the shares of the purchasing corporation have a present market value to make them readily convertible into cash by the attachment and sale of the shares by a judgment creditor of the selling corporation.

It frequently happens that, where a corporation purchases the assets of another corporation and pays therefor in its own shares, as part of the consideration it assumes the debts of the selling corporation. Without such an agreement, however, the purchasing corporation is not legally liable for the payment of the seller's debts and obligations. If the transaction is considered fraudulent in the particular jurisdiction because of the payment of the consideration in shares, the assets so transferred or their value may be pursued. Beyond this, there is no liability without a contractual assumption of it.

In the case of merger and consolidation, the transfer of the constituent corporations' assets is under modern statutes effective without more than compliance with the statute, and the debts

---

39. American Railway Express Co. v. Commonwealth, 190 Ky. 636, 228 S.W. 433 (1920). American bought all the assets of Adams Express Co. for stock in American. This left Adams with no tangible or intangible assets in Kentucky. The court held that the corporation would not be allowed "to defeat its just obligations by sale or transfer of its property for no other consideration than stock or bonds in the purchasing corporation." Contra, and representing the minority rule, is McAlister v. American Railway Express Co., 179 N.C. 566, 103 S.E. 129, 15 A.L.R. 1090 (1920). See also 1 Glenn, Fraudulent Conveyances and Preferences § 287a (Rev. ed. 1940); Note, Liability for the Obligations of the Old Company— American Railway Express Company Cases, 26 Mich.L.Rev. 913 (1928); Note, Rights of Creditors Against a Successor Corporation, 44 Harv.L.Rev. 260 (1930); Annotations, Liability of corporation for debts of predecessor, 149 A.L.R. 787 (1944); 30 A.L.R. 558 (1924).

and liabilities of the absorbed corporations are assumed by the corporations into which the constituents have merged or consolidated, usually by specific provisions in the statute. Thus there is no need for the formal conveyances necessary in a sale of assets for shares in the purchasing corporation. Courts sometimes speak of the transfer as by operation of law and use similar terms with respect to the obligation of the transferee to pay the transferor's debts and liabilities. But the usual statute makes it clear that consummation of the merger or consolidation effects these results. Thus, it may be said that unless the statute continues the existence of the constituent corporations, the only remedies available to the creditors of such constituents are against the surviving or new corporation upon its implied promise to pay, or to pursue the assets into the hands of the survivor or new corporation on the basis of fraudulent transfer, if such a basis exists. If, as is usually the case, the merger or consolidation is effected by a transfer of shares to the shareholders of the constituent corporations, there is nothing for creditors of the constituents to attach. And, as we have seen, even where shares are transferred for tangible assets in a purchase-and-sale agreement, most courts consider this as fraudulent to the creditors of the selling corporation. The fact that the statutes place liability for debts and other obligations upon the survivor or new corporation, with the traditional practice of agreements of similar character in articles of merger or consolidation, usually makes the problem moot, for the debts and obligations once paid end all controversy. But, as Professor Ballantine has shown, if one of the constituents is so thoroughly insolvent that its debts and liabilities make the successor corporation insolvent so that it cannot pay the debts of the constituents absorbed by the merger or consolidation, the creditors of a solvent constituent might well have prior equitable claims against the assets of its former debtor now in the possession of a successor whose promises cannot be carried out.[40]

While a reduction of unissued but authorized shares has no effect upon creditors or shareholders,[41] one which affects the stated capital previously contributed or contracted to be contributed carries with it danger to existing shareholders and creditors alike. Unless there is a distribution of part or all of a reduction surplus which results from an authorized reduction of stated capital, or the reduction takes the form of eliminating or reducing the obligation of shareholders to pay the subscription price for their shares, present creditors are not likely to be affected. However, the reduction of stated capital may place the corpora-

---

40. Ballantine, Corporations § 294, at page 691 (Rev. ed. 1946).

41. See State ex rel. Radio Corp. of America v. Benson, 32 Del. (2 W.W. Harr.) 576, 128 A. 107 (1924), which contains an excellent discussion of this distinction.

tion in a position to pay dividends out of a surplus which otherwise would have to replenish lost capital and, in that respect, part of the cushion upon which creditors may rely is now gone. But if the corporate assets have been fairly valued, there would be little practical effect upon the position of creditors. If there is a return to shareholders of part or all of a reduction surplus, or such a surplus is used to purchase the corporation's own shares, no matter how the surplus is described it is actually a return of capital which present creditors have a right to have applied to the payment of their debts. Where creditors give credit after a reduction of stated capital with the publicity incident to the usually prescribed procedures for reduction, there is no reason for protecting them beyond the protection they would have had in case of dealing with a corporation with an original stated capital of the amount existing after the reduction. If the reduction occurs through the redemption of the corporation's preferred shares which, under the statute, may be required to be retired and the stated capital reduced accordingly, creditors at least have notice or the means of acquiring notice of the event which, as we have seen, may usually be consummated by redemption out of capital but with the usual prohibition against this if creditors will be injured.

Even though a surplus created by the reduction of stated capital and distributed to the shareholders is actually a return of capital, present-day statutes [42] have been inclined to make specific provision authorizing its distribution in similar manner and for any purpose for which other surpluses may be used, especially for dividend purposes. Thus, where dividends are distributed from reduction surplus when they would have been prohibited had they been made out of an earned surplus as, for example, when by such a dividend distribution there is reasonable ground to believe that the corporation will be rendered unable to satisfy its obligations and liabilities, the distribution is illegal and the shareholders receiving it, after judgment unsatisfied against the corporation, may be required to disgorge it under the rules applicable in case of payment of illegal dividends in other cases.[43] But where the statute does not specify the conditions of distribution of a reduction surplus, there is no good reason for considering it in any other light than that of a liquidating dividend from capital and, under the leading case of *Wood* v. *Dummer*,[44] if

---

42. Jay Ronald Co., Inc. v. Marshall Mortgage Corp., 291 N.Y. 227, 52 N.E.2d 108 (1943).

43. Chisnell v. Ozier Co., 140 Ohio St. 355, 44 N.E.2d 464 (1942). The Ohio statute then in force was held to give the creditor an individual right against the shareholder so

that the alleging of an unsatisfied judgment against the corporation was not necessary.

44. 3 Mason 308, 30 Fed.Cas. 435, No. 17944 (C.C.D.Me.1824); Beatty v. Paterson-Garfield-Lodi Bus Co., 126 N.J.Eq. 472, 9 A.2d 686 (Ch.1939). And see Note, Capital Stock Reduc-

capital is returned before the corporate creditors are paid the shareholders receiving it may be forced to disgorge. So, too, when the statute provides that distribution must not affect or prejudice creditors' rights, or requires that assets remaining after the distribution must be sufficient to pay the debts.[45]

But the statutes which contain some provision for the distribution of reduction surplus vary considerably. Some classify reduction surplus as "capital surplus," as if shares had been sold above their par or stated value, a quite different thing. And if the statute permits a dividend from such a surplus, it may also require that a shareholder receiving a dividend of this kind or any other have notice that it is from an illegal source if creditors are to recover from them.[46] One of the most recently framed statutes, that of North Carolina, contains a provision to the effect that distributions to shareholders after a reduction of stated capital, where the distribution has been made in accordance with the statutory provisions, shall give rise to no cause of action in favor of creditors, whether their claims arose prior to or after the reduction.[47] The statute classifies reduction surplus as "capital surplus" and permits cash or property dividends out of such a surplus but these are payable only if earned surplus or net profits earned during the current or preceding accounting period are not available and then only to shares entitled to preferential dividends "and no capital surplus paid in by any class of stock may be used in payment of dividends on any class junior thereto." There are provisions for "partial liquidations" where "dividends" are paid upon shares not entitled to preferential dividends upon a determination of the board of directors that the corporate assets are in excess of its needs, and upon authorization of a majority of the shareholders of each class whether entitled to vote or not. But no distribution is permitted if thereupon the present "fair value" of the assets of the corporation is less than twice the amount of its liabilities, which offers a good deal of protection. There are other protective features in this excellently drafted statute.[48] Statutes which protect to the extent that reduction surplus distributions shall not reduce the fair value of the assets to an amount less than the total of its debts and liabilities plus the stated capital as reduced are still on the dangerous side, especially when there are contingent claims with which the remaining assets may be charged. It has been demonstrated that the stat-

tion as Affecting the Rights of Creditors, 47 Harv.L.Rev. 693 (1934).

45. See the extraordinarily valuable article by Fuld, Recovery of Illegal and Partial Liquidation Dividends From Stockholders, 28 Va.L.Rev. 50, at 58 (1941).

46. As in Chisnell v. Ozier, supra, note 44, where the statute required it and the plaintiff alleged notice of the dividend's illegal source.

47. 2B N.C.Gen.Stat., 1957 Cum. Supp. § 55–48(f).

48. 2B N.C.Gen.Stat., 1957 Cum. Supp. § 44–50.

ute may be met originally and the distribution made as prescribed; but the contingent claims may prove to be greater than anticipated and the effect is that some creditors will not be paid. This result could be prevented by a statutory prohibition against distributing a reduction surplus until all known creditors or other claimants are paid or secured by some means assuring them of payment if payment is due.[49]

§ 19. Protection of Senior Shareholders Through Adequate Drafting

Because of the drastic changes in contract rights made possible by shareholder vote under modern statutes and the consequent damage that may result to the holders of senior shares, the problem of drafting the preferred share contract to obtain reasonable protection against the more damaging changes deserves careful attention.   Basic changes such as the reduction of the preferred share dividend rate, the elimination of the right to accrued, undeclared dividends, the reduction or elimination of a sinking fund if one exists under the contract, the issue of new shares with preferences prior to those of shares outstanding, the making of redeemable shares non-redeemable and vice versa, the changing of the redemption rate or of the time of redemption if one is specified, the reduction of stated capital with a distribution of a resulting reduction surplus to junior shareholders, the use of such a surplus to purchase its own shares, and other possible changes will be thought of.

The better statutes require that the share-contracts be placed in the articles or certificate of incorporation, and they should be there whether or not the statute commands this.   The provisions which authorize fundamental changes usually provide for a stated proportionate vote *unless the articles provide* for a greater, or sometimes a smaller proportion but not less than a majority. By drafting a provision requiring a sizeable proportionate vote, there is additional protection even where the sole voting power is in the junior shares, but it would be dangerous to let the drafting end there.   It is possible to give to a class of senior shares (or others for that matter) voting rights in case of fundamental changes affecting them—and many of the present-day statutes specifically give this right—and to require a high percentage of these shares to vote affirmatively for such changes, along with whatever additional proportionate vote is required by the junior shares.   Care should be taken, however, in ascertaining whether the statute does not permit amendments to the charter by a smaller vote than that provided in the specific provision inserted in

---

49.   See Fuld, op. cit. supra, note 45, at page 59.

the charter, for the court has, in one important but questionable decision held that where such is the case an amendment by the statutorily provided proportion of shareholders may delete the previously adopted provision requiring a high proportionate vote of the class whose shares may be affected.[50] It would have been an easy thing to have cured this defect by a provision requiring a like proportionate vote of the class, plus whatever proportionate vote was necessary from other classes, to alter in any way the previously adopted charter provision, but it seems doubtful whether a careful draftsman would have expected the annihilation of his protective provision by such a warped interpretation.[51] The Ohio statute gives the proper protection by stating that "If the proposed amendment would authorize any particular corporate action which, under any applicable provision of law or under the existing articles, could be authorized only by or pursuant to a specified vote of shareholders, such amendment in order to be adopted must receive the affirmative vote so specified." [52]

Through a merger or consolidation legally consummated, a shareholder in an absorbed corporation must take the shares offered him, which shares may vary materially from those he surrendered,[53] or demand an appraisal. And, even when the contract states that "no such merger shall in any way impair the rights of the preferred stock," [54] a court may find that such a provision is in conflict with the statutory authorization and that the legislature never intended that preferred stock should not be impaired by merger. Such holdings are applications of the principle that charter provisions may not be at variance with statutory ones. However, while the draftsman cannot provide for all contingencies that may arise, he can anticipate the serious ones and can usually provide for them. In most cases where troubles have

---

50. Warren v. 536 Broad St. Corp., 6 N.J.Super. 170, 70 A.2d 782 (1950). The charter provided for a 75% vote. The statute permitted amendments to the charter by a ⅔ vote of each class. Thus, by voting to amend, a ⅔ vote was able to do what the charter provision had attempted to protect against. Compare with Sellers v. Joseph Bancroft & Sons Co., 23 Del.Ch. 13, 2 A.2d 108 (Ch.1938), on final hearing 17 A.2d 831 (Del.Ch.1941), and Ripin v. Atlantic Mercantile Co., 205 N.Y. 442, 98 N.E. 855 (1912).

51. There is a good discussion of the case and of the drafting problem in Comment, Limitations on the Amending Power in the Corporate Contract, 18 U. of Chi.L.Rev. 139 (1950).

52. Ohio Rev.Code § 1701.71(A).

53. See, for a good example, Langfelder v. Universal Laboratories, Inc., 163 F.2d 804 (3d Cir., 1947), a case where there were protective provisions but they were insufficiently strong. This case is discussed in Notes, 36 Geo.L.J. 679 (1948); 61 Harv.L.Rev. 1060 (1948); 47 Mich.L.Rev. 81 (1948).

54. Jones v. St. Louis Structural Steel Co., 267 Ill.App. 576 (1932) (involving a Delaware corporation). West's Ann.Cal.Corp.Code §§ 4123, 4318 permit contracts for the payment of specific amounts to preferred shareholders on merger or consolidation.

arisen, the draftsmanship has been faulty and, had it been good, the protection would have been there.

§ 20.   Federal Taxing Incidents in Sale of Assets for Shares, Merger or Consolidation

While a general rule recognizes a gain or loss for income tax purposes in every sale, exchange or other distribution of property, as far as corporate reorganizations are concerned they may be carried out on a tax-free basis if the Internal Revenue Code is carefully followed.   However, the subject is too detailed and complicated for discussion in a small work on corporations.   §§ 351 and 368 of the Internal Revenue Code of 1954 contain the pertinent provisions on corporate organization and reorganization, while the Guide to the Internal Revenue Code of 1954 found in 26 U.S.C.A. §§ 301 to 700, pages 42–59, contains as simple a statement as can be accurately made, with examples of tax free reorganizations.[55]   Reorganizations under the IRC include statutory mergers or consolidations, sales of assets for shares if the acquiring corporation has control of the other, as defined in the section, immediately after the transaction; or if the transferor, or one or more of its shareholders or any combination of them, has control of the transferee corporation immediately after the transfer.   There are specific statutory limitations under this last clause.[56]

---

55.   See Monatt's Tax Atlas (Federal Taxation) ¶ 43.020 et seq. (1958).

56.   I.R.C.1954 (26 U.S.C.A.) § 368. Subsection (c) of § 368 defines "control."   Tax jargon of "spin-offs," "split-offs," and "split-ups" is explained in N.Y.Univ. Eighth Annual Institute on Federal Taxation at 212–213 (1950).   If Corporation A carries on a wholesale and retail business and decides to separate the two by transferring the retail business to new Corporation B for all of B's stock which is then distributed to A's shareholders, this is called a "spin-off," if A's shareholders give up none of their shares in A; a "split-off," if A's shareholders surrender a part of their shares to A.   No gain or loss for taxing purposes is recognized to the shareholders in either case.   If Corporation A transfers its wholesale business to Corporation M and its retail business to Corporation N in exchange for all of the stock in each, and this stock is distributed to A's shareholders and A is dissolved, this is, in tax gobbledegook a "split-up."   This, too, does not result in a taxable gain or loss to the shareholders of A.   See Guide to Internal Revenue Code of 1954, containing §§ 301 to 700, at pages 54–55.

Chapter 12

DISSOLUTION AND LIQUIDATION

§ 1. Meaning of Terms "Dissolution" and "Liquidation" or "Winding Up"

In the first chapter of this book the legal distinction between the dissolution and winding up of a partnership was discussed. It was stated that dissolution anticipated the termination in point of time of the partnership business activities and that winding up involved the process of settling the partnership affairs after dissolution, the partnership continuing solely for the purpose of being wound up.[1] A similar distinction exists in corporations. While lawyers and judges frequently use the term "dissolution" or "liquidation" to include both dissolution and liquidation, the distinction is important. "Dissolution," as in partnership law, means the termination of the legal existence of the corporation so that the unit may no longer carry on under its former franchises, for it has none with which to function. Liquidation or winding up involves the process of collecting the assets, paying the creditors, and distributing whatever is left, after liquidation expenses, to the shareholders in accordance with their contracts and, if there are no special contracts, then pro rata according to their shareholding interest.

Modern statutes provide, usually in detail, for the voluntary dissolution and liquidation of the business corporation, many of them naming the directors as the liquidating officials, some providing for the appointment or election of trustees for the purpose, at least one providing for the appointment of "liquidators" for this purpose.[2] Some statutes specifically state that the corporation is to be kept alive for the purpose of liquidation and the better ones keep the corporation alive for purposes of suit by and against it, and for settling its affairs, for a definitely stated

---

1. Chapter 1, at page 11.

2. West's Ann.Cal.Corp.Code § 4801 (directors, after dissolution, have full powers to wind up); ibid. §§ 4601 and 4602 (directors may both dissolve and wind up a corporation under the circumstances set out); Ark.Stat. § 64–807 (1947) (upon dissolution directors act as trustees); Flack's Md.Ann.Code, Art. 23, § 74 (directors become trustees for liquidation purposes); La. S.A.—Rev.Stat. § 12:54B (provi-sion for appointment by the shareholders of "one or more liquidators to conduct the liquidation").

The American statutes vary as to when the corporation is dissolved. Some provide for it before liquidating; others, after liquidation. Under the English law, the liquidation comes first, for "only at the end of the winding up will the company be dissolved." Gower, Modern Company Law 548 (1954).

period such as for two or three years. Variations are numerous and the local statute should be consulted for the details of dissolution and liquidation.

§ 2. Under American Common Law

In the preceding chapter it was brought out that doubt existed at common law whether, prior to the termination of the specified time of corporate existence, the shareholders could, by majority vote, dissolve a prosperous corporation; that is, without statutory aid.[3] The generally accepted view required unanimous shareholder action and, of course, the consent of the state as it was also deemed to have an interest. When the corporation was insolvent, and probably when it was solvent but skirting on the edge of insolvency, the entire assets could be legitimately sold by majority vote and, whether or not there was dissolution in the formal sense, the corporation frequently went through all but the formal motions of surrendering its charter. It paid its debts, distributed what (if anything) remained among its shareholders, and carried on no more as a corporation. This was sometimes called a dissolution and liquidation de facto.

Professor Dodd has shown that, under the early American common law, the state, by quo warranto proceedings, could take the life of a corporation for exceeding the business purposes set forth in its charter, for disposing of so much of its property as to make it impossible to resume its business, and for failure to use its franchises for an unreasonable length of time.[4] At about the same period as these early decisions, Justice Story had surmised that "A *private* corporation created by the legislature may lose its franchises by a *misuser* or a *non-user* of them; and they may be resumed by the government under a judicial judgment upon a

---

3. That a majority could do this, see Lauman v. Lebanon Valley R. R., 30 Pa. 42 (1858) (a merger was involved, but the principle is the same); Treadwell v. Salisbury Mfg. Co., 7 Gray 393 (Mass.1856). But Kean v. Johnson, 9 N.J.Eq. 401 (Ch. 1853) and Abbot v. American Hard Rubber Co., 33 Barb. 578 (N.Y. 1861) are contra. See Dodd, infra, note 4, at 184.

4. Dodd, American Corporations Until 1860, at 59–60, 64 (1954), citing People ex rel. Attorney General v. Utica Insurance Co., 15 Johns. 358 (N.Y.Sup.Ct.1818) (corporation engaged in banking operations which a statute prohibited except by authorized persons); People v. Bank of Hudson, 6 Cow. 217 (N.Y.Sup.Ct. 1826) (assignment of so much of corporation's property as to make resumption of business impossible); Bank of Vincennes v. State, 1 Blackf. 267 (Ind.1823) (acts ultra vires its charter and a further charge that the corporation had acted fraudulently and contrary to the spirit and intent of the grant); Slee v. Bloom, 19 Johns. 456 (N.Y. Ct.Err.1822) (corporation was insolvent and had ceased to do business—creditors were allowed to pursue shareholders on theory that corporation had been dissolved within the meaning of the act which permitted creditors to hold shareholders individually liable when the corporation ceased to own any property, and when it ceased doing business).

quo warranto to ascertain and enforce the forfeiture. This is the common law of the land, and is a tacit condition annexed to the creation of every such corporation."[5] However, while a de facto dissolution might result without a surrender of the charter, dissolution to be effective as one de jure required a surrender of the charter or its forfeiture through legal proceedings. In other words, something more than misuser or nonuser was necessary.

It should be said, too, that legislative repeal of charters for "some sort of misconduct by the corporation," [6] had been sustained as a legitimate exercise of the state's reserved power to amend or repeal charters. In fact, the various constitutional and statutory reservations of this power are so stated as to warrant the belief that the legislature has the power to repeal without sufficient or any cause, any limitations being of rights or interests otherwise constitutionally protected as, for example, the taking of property without due process of law, or the impairment of contracts between the corporation and third parties. It had been early decided, however, that a creditor or other contracting party had no right to prevent the dissolution of a corporation even though the statutory authority to dissolve came after the debts were created or contracts entered into.[7] The corporate property, however, could be pursued by creditors to enforce their claims except as it may have come to rest in the hands of bona fide purchasers. The property of the dissolved corporation was considered as held in trust for the payment of its creditors and others to whom there was liability.[8] This is, of course, contrary to a statement found in early treatises to the effect that upon dissolution, the corporate debts cease to exist, the grantors of its real property have it by reversion, and the state is entitled to its personal property.[9] But, as Professor Dodd has indicated, "by 1853

5. Terrett v. Taylor, 9 Cranch 43, at 51 (U.S.1815). Quo warranto was not involved, however.

6. Dodd, op. cit. supra, note 4, at 141–142. He found but one pre-1861 case of an unlimited reserved power of repeal. McLaren v. Pennington, 1 Paige 102 (N.Y.1828).

7. Dodd, op. cit. supra, note 4, at 142, citing Mumma v. Potomac Co., 8 Pet. 281 (U.S.1834).

8. Ibid. at 142. See also Curran v. Arkansas, 15 How. 304 (U.S.1853), which was a case of amendment rather than repeal, but the principle is the same.

9. Ibid. at 143, a Blackstonian doctrine [1 Blackstone 484–485 (1765)] which Professor Dodd restates in his book. See 2 Morawetz on Private Corporations § 1031, at p. 988 (2d ed. 1886). At § 1032, he writes: "It may be doubted whether it was ever the law that equitable rights to property held by a corporation were lost by a dissolution of the company. The doctrine that the property of a dissolved corporation belongs to the King or to the original donors, was first applied in the case of ecclesiastical and municipal corporations. In these cases there were no shareholders, and seldom creditors; the property was in reality without an owner, after the particular use for which it had been given had come to an end by the dissolution of the corporation. But modern business companies differ essentially from ecclesiastical and municipal corporations, both in purpose and organization. The

(the doctrine) had become so obsolete that a state legislature lacked the constitutional power to revivify it." It was a doctrine originating from the dissolution of ecclesiastical and municipal corporations where, as Morawetz has pointed out, there were no shareholders and rarely ever creditors at the point of dissolution. There were thus no equitable rights in share-owners, as in trading corporations, and reversionary rights to real property formerly held by the corporation, in such cases, were not unjustly given to the donors; furthermore, as to personalty, who had a better claim than the King?

Hence, when early American courts held that, upon dissolution, the corporation could not sue or be sued and could no longer hold title to property, they were merely stating the fact that, having no existence as a legal person, it was a physical impossibility for the corporation to do these things. The analogy of the deceased natural person and his inability to hold property, sue or be sued, is close enough. However, just as the representative of the estate of a deceased natural person could sue and be sued and hold property, the courts held that, in equity, the corporate property was held in trust by its now owners—the shareholders—for the payment of its debts and other liabilities; that these representatives or their agents could bring actions in equity to recover moneys owed their former corporation and could, likewise, be sued in equity for moneys owed by the corporation to the plaintiffs. No better statement has been made on this subject than that of Mr. Justice Curtis in the early case of *Curran* v. *State of Arkansas*: [10]

"Indeed, if it be once admitted that the property of an insolvent trading corporation, while under the management of its officers, is a trust fund in their hands for the benefit of creditors, it follows, that a court of equity, which never allows a trust to fail for want of a trustee, would see to the execution of that trust, although by the dissolution of the corporation, the legal title to its property has been changed.   .   .   .

"Whatever technical difficulties exist in maintaining an action at law by or against a corporation after its charter has been repealed, in the apprehension of a court of equity, there is no difficulty in a creditor following the property of the corporation into the hands of any one not a bona fide creditor or purchaser, and asserting his lien thereon, and obtaining satisfaction of his just debt out of that fund specifically set apart for its payment when the debt was contracted, and charged with a trust for all

shareholders or corporators in an ordinary business company are themselves the donors of its property; each member contributes his share of the capital for the common benefit of all; and the corporation itself holds the property given it merely as trustee for its shareholders."

10.   15 How. 304, at 311 (U.S.1853).

the creditors when in the hands of the corporation; which trust the repeal of the charter does not destroy."

§ 3. Incidents Determinative of Dissolution

Blackstone, writing in 1765 the substance of a course of lectures he had given at Oxford on the "Laws of England," devotes one chapter of his Commentaries, some eighteen pages in all, to the subject of corporations. As to how dissolution results, he has this to say: "A corporation may be dissolved, 1. By Act of parliament, which is boundless in its operations. 2. By the natural death of all its members, in case of an aggregate corporation. 3. By surrender of its franchises into the hands of the king, which is a kind of suicide. 4. By forfeiture of its charter, through negligence or abuse of its franchises; in which case the law judges that the body politic has broken the condition upon which it was incorporated, and thereupon the incorporation is void. And the regular course is to bring an information in nature of a writ of *quo warranto,* to inquire by what warrant the members now exercise their corporate power, having forfeited it by such and such proceedings." [11] His short treatise on this subject lumped together corporations for the advancement of religion, of learning, of commerce and of municipal government. And he covered in this short space the corporation from its birth to its death.

Of the methods by which a corporation might be dissolved in Blackstone's day, three are of present-day interest in the business corporation field. As we have seen, the state through its reservation of the power to amend or repeal charters may take the life of a corporation to which it gave birth; by virtue of statutes which authorize dissolution upon the affirmative vote of a stated proportion of its shares or of its members, a charter may be surrendered; and, if the corporation has been guilty of major violations of its charter, the state may by a proceeding in the nature of quo warranto take its life.

Some other events by virtue of which the corporate life is lost or may be taken are the expiration of the time during which the corporation was to function, the occurrence of some condition stated in its charter, the happening of some contingency set up by statute (such as the failure to pay taxes or submit required reports), the failure or loss of some essential part of the corporate property so that it can no longer function, the failure for a considerable period of exercising its corporate powers, dissension within the body of shareholders which, due to the impossibility of breaking a deadlock in the board of directors or in the sharehold-

---

11. 1 Blackstone, Commentaries on the Law of England 485 (1765).

ers, spells ultimate disaster, and perhaps in some other cases. However, unless a statute provides for dissolution without official action or without a formal surrender by the directors or shareholders in the statutorily prescribed manner, only rarely will a court hold that dissolution results from the mere happening of an event.

Perhaps the clearest case where the argument of sudden death without formalities would seem available is where the time-period for corporate operation has expired and the officers and shareholders, not realizing the fact, have continued to operate as before. Whether the corporate life has been limited by constitutional provision, by statute, or by provision in the charter, some cases hold that the corporation ceases to exist and is dissolved without further act when the time expires unless, by specific provision, other action is necessary.[12] However, nearly all corporations created under modern statutes have perpetual existence and, under these statutes, further action would be necessary for more than a de facto dissolution. And it should be said that, under liberal holdings, statutes have at times been stretched and at other times have been broad enough to require formal action after the expiration of the corporation's life-term.[13] In *Garzo* v. *Maid of the Mist Steamboat Co.*,[14] the corporate charter expired in 1942, but the corporation innocently carried on until 1947 when it became aware of this fact. A provision enacted into the New York General Corporation Law in 1944 permitted corporations whose life-terms had ended to renew them by the approval of a majority of the shares of each class of stock, and three-fourths of the shares had approved. Minority shareholders sought to compel a dissolution and liquidation on the ground that they had a "vested right," immune from legislative interference, to have the corporation dissolved and its assets distributed. The court held that there was no such "vested right" and that the reserved power to alter corporation laws and charters was ample warrant for this legislation. Said the court:[15] "The mere ending of the corporate term did not render such reserve power inoperative. Corporations whose charters may have expired continue to have a *de jure* existence for the purpose of winding up their affairs, and, to that end, meetings may be held, corporate property conveyed, suits brought and defended, directors elected and debts paid. . . . In addition, where, as here, a corporation

---

12.   16 Fletcher, Cyc. of Corporations § 7981 (Perm. ed. 1942).

13.   See, for example, Garzo v. Maid of the Mist Steamboat Co., 303 N.Y. 516, 104 N.E.2d 882 (1952), aff'g 278 App.Div. 508, 106 N.Y.S.2d 4 (1951); Glenn v. Courier-Journal Job Printing Co., 127 F.2d 820 (6th Cir., 1942) (involving a Kentucky corporation); Cohn v. Dowling, 123 F.2d 408 (6th Cir., 1941) (involving a Michigan corporation).

14.   Supra, note 13.

15.   Supra, note 13, 104 N.E.2d at 886–887, by Fuld, J.

carries on its affairs and exercises corporate powers as before, it is a *de facto* corporation as well, but ordinarily no one but the state may question its corporate existence." The section authorizing renewal of the corporate life was held by the court to authorize the continued existence of the corporation, but "was not enacted to resuscitate a lifeless corpse or to operate in a vacuum; it was put into the law, and is here invoked, to deal with a truly functioning enterprise." [16]

Since dissolution without corporate or judicial act carries with it violent results, courts should be, and have generally been, cautious in concluding that dissolution automatically results from such things as the expiration of the corporate term of life, nonuser of the corporate franchises, the lack of required officers to carry out the corporate purposes, the acquisition of all the stock by one shareholder where more than one is required to hold shares, the failure to pay taxes or make reports, and similar violations.[17] There has been a strong judicial tendency to interpret dissolution statutes as not self-executing unless the language of the particular provision cannot be otherwise construed.

§ 4. Power of Court of Equity to Dissolve Corporations

Courts of equity were formerly reluctant to entertain actions brought by minority shareholders to dissolve a corporation unless there were statutory provisions authorizing the same. More recently, however, there has been less hesitancy on their part provided the cause of dissolution is sufficiently serious. This has been particularly true when the corporation's shares have been held closely and factions have resulted with attendant discord which has reacted adversely upon the corporate interests.[18] If

---

16. Ibid. at 887.

17. Cases in note 13, supra, illustrate the expiration of charter difficulty; Coleman DuPont Road, Inc. v. Lasher, 38 Del.Ch. 258, 84 A.2d 164 (Ch.1951) (non-user of franchise does not automatically dissolve the corporation); Buhler v. Maddison, 105 Utah 39, 140 P.2d 933 (1943); 16 Fletcher, Cyc. of Corporations § 7995 (Perm. ed. 1942) (acquisition of all of shares by one person when statute requires more than one shareholder); Isbell v. Gulf Union Oil Co., 147 Tex. 6, 209 S.W.2d 762 (1948) (failure to pay taxes does not result in dissolution but Texas statute was held to take away corporation's right to sue and defend until franchise taxes were paid). And see 16 Fletcher, Cyc. of Corporations § 7988 (Perm. ed. 1942) on self-executing provisions for forfeiture to the effect that to reach that result it takes strong and unmistakable language. Strong language will be found in Leibson v. Henry, 356 Mo. 953, 204 S.W.2d 310 (1947), two judges dissenting.

18. See Nashville Packet Co. v. Neville, 144 Tenn. 698, 235 S.W. 64, at 65 (1921), where the court stated: "Under circumstances like these, where there are such dissensions within the corporation as that its business cannot be honestly or properly managed, a court of equity will intervene at the suit of a stockholder, appoint a receiver, and wind up the affairs of the concern." The court called this a de facto dissolution, holding that, for a de jure dissolution, a statute was necessary.

the dissention is such as to work "a paralysis of corporate function," it has been said that the state has an interest which will sustain its intervention for the dissolution and liquidation of a corporation.[19]   Or where there has been fraudulent mismanagement and misappropriation of the corporate funds through the influence of majority shareholders, equitable relief through dissolution and liquidation has been held appropriate.[20]   These are cases where the remedy at law is inadequate and drastic means are necessary to protect the owners.   As one basis for holding that equity will act in such cases, an early decision explains: [21] "The corporation itself holds its property as a trust fund for the stockholders, who have a joint interest in all its property and effects, and the relation between it and its several members is, for all practical purposes, that of trustee and *cestui que trust*. . . When several persons have a common interest in property, equity will not allow one to appropriate it exclusively to himself, or to impair its value to the others.   Community of interest involves mutual obligation.   Persons occupying this relation towards each other are under an obligation to make the property or fund productive of the most that can be obtained from it for all who are interested in it; and those who seek to make profit out of it, at the expense of those whose rights in it are the same as their own, are unfaithful to the relation they have assumed, and are guilty, at least, of constructive fraud."

In the absence of a statute authorizing dissolution when there is a deadlock of the board or of the shareholders, approach through equity seems particularly desirable, for it is rare in such a case to find less than serious consequences if the deadlock continues.   A deadlock means corporate paralysis, and the seriousness of the possible consequences warrants the court's decree of dissolution and liquidation.[22]   Traditional equitable principles within the broad concept that equity acts to give such relief as justice and good conscience require are quite as applicable here as elsewhere.

While it is proabale that the weight of case authority does not yet recognize the inherent power of equity to dissolve a corporation without statutory aid,[23] it has been noted that "There

---

19. Petition of Collins-Doan Co. (Morten v. Collins), 3 N.J. 382, 70 A.2d 159, 13 A.L.R.2d 1250 (1949). This action was brought under a deadlock statute but Heher, J., wrote at page 166 of 70 A.2d: "It would seem that the particular statutory provision for dissolution is but a declaration of a power existing at common law."

20. Miner v. Belle Isle Ice Co., 93 Mich. 97, 53 N.W. 218, 17 L.R.A. 412 (1892).

21. Ibid., 53 N.W. at 223–224.

22. Levant v. Kowal, 350 Mich. 232, 86 N.W.2d 336 (1957), is a fine example of this.

23. Ann., Dissolution of corporation on ground of intracorporate dead-

is a noticeable trend, in cases decided since the turn of the century, toward recognizing the inherent power of a court of equity to grant relief in proper cases," in this area.[24] The less stringent remedy (for the moment, at least) of the appointment of a receiver to take charge of and operate a corporation for a fixed period with a proviso in the decree that if the deadlocked parties cannot adjust their differences within that time the receiver will proceed to dissolve the corporation and liquidate its properties seems like an effective means of accomplishing an adjustment if one is at all possible.[25]

§ 5. Dissolution by Agreement Concerning Same in the Corporate Charter

Since dissension in closely held corporations is of frequent occurrence it would seem advisable to provide against the usual dire results by a provision in the articles or certificate of incorporation to the effect that, upon the application of one or more shareholders holding a stated percentage of the voting shares, the corporation shall sell its assets, wind up its affairs, and be legally dissolved. Unless the particular statute in the state of birth of the corporation indicates that dissolution is possible only through the use of the statutory provisions, there would seem to be no good reason for a court's failing to support this kind of provision. Since it would appear in the corporate charter, there is a contract between state and corporation, between corporation and shareholders and between the shareholders themselves. An important Massachusetts decision has sustained a *contract* entered into between two sole shareholders and their corporation whereby the corporation agreed to cause and permit its liquidation and dissolution after the end of any year upon one shareholder's giving notice to the other, unless the one to whom notice was given should purchase the shares of the other at times and prices determined as provided in the contract.[26] Said the

lock or dissension, 13 A.L.R.2d 1260 (1950).

24. Levant v. Kowal, supra, note 22, 86 N.W.2d at 340. And see Kay v. Key West Development Co., 72 So. 2d 786, 47 A.L.R.2d 361 (Fla.1954), where the court decreed that corporation's property be sold and money distributed to the two equal owners who were deadlocked, leaving the shell of a corporation to exist. This was done under the general equity powers of the court, thus avoiding the question whether the court, without statutory aid, could dissolve the corporation. See Ann., Judicial relief other than by dissolution or receivership in cases of intracorporate deadlock, 47 A.L. R.2d 365 (1956). Some statutes specifically give to equity court the power to dissolve and wind up corporations under stated conditions. For example, see Conn.Gen.Stat. § 5226 (1949) as reenacted by L.1957, Act No. 591; Del.Corp.Law § 283.

25. See Guaranty Laundry Co. v. Pulliam, 200 Okl. 185, 191 P.2d 975, at 982 (1948).

26. Leventhall v. Atlantic Finance Corp., 316 Mass. 194, 55 N.E.2d 20, 154 A.L.R. 260 (1944); Application of Hega Knitting Mills, Inc.

court: "The rights given by this contract to Leventhal and Epstein with reference to the dissolution of the corporation and the transfer of their stock are rights that it would be natural for the stockholders owning all the stock to acquire in order to protect their interests in the corporation, although the rights acquired by them may be somewhat more extensive than those that have been frequently provided for the protection of the corporation and its stockholders. . . ." [27] The court added that "The filing of a petition by a corporation or by a stockholder under § 50 (the local dissolution section) is a privilege afforded to the corporation and to the stockholder if the conditions of the statute are complied with by the petitioner. A stockholder may or may not invoke this remedy. The contract expressly prohibited either stockholder from causing a dissolution of the corporation except as therein provided. . . . [T]here is nothing in the nature of the remedy afforded a stockholder by (this) section that he cannot waive or contract away. It comes within the general rule that one may waive the benefits of a statutory remedy provided he does not thereby contravene the public policy of the Commonwealth." [28]

§ 6.   Dissolution When Directors and Shareholders are Deadlocked—Statutory Aid

Closely held corporations at times find corporate action stifled because of an equal division of board members and shareholders holding opposing views. If such a deadlock continues for long it will result in serious non-action which may in the end spell disaster. Under such circumstances, as we have seen, equity frequently takes a hand when the threat is serious and orders a dissolution and liquidation of the corporation. It seems desirable, however, to provide for such deadlocks through statutes aimed specifically at this evil, and several statutes have so provided.[29]

In essence, these statutes provide that when there is an even number of directors who are deadlocked in the management of the corporate business and the shareholders are unable to break the deadlock, a court may, upon petition of the described peti-

(In re Aschkenasy), 124 N.Y.S.2d 115 (Sup.Ct.1953); In re Block's Will, 186 Misc. 945, 60 N.Y.S.2d 639 (Surr.Ct.1946). Compare Flanagan v. Flanagan, 273 App.Div. 918, 77 N.Y.S.2d 682 (1948), aff'd without opinion 298 N.Y. 787, 83 N.E.2d 473 (1948).

27. Leventhall v. Atlantic Finance Corp., supra, note 26, 55 N.E.2d at 23.

28. Ibid. at 26.

29. Alaska Corp.Laws § 90 (1949); West's Ann.Cal.Corp.Code §§ 4650, 4651; Ky.Rev.Stat. § 271.570 (1953); La.S.A.—Rev.Stat. § 12:55; Minn. Stat.Ann. § 301.49; N.Y.Gen.Corp. Law §§ 103, 117; Ohio Rev.Code § 1701.91(A) (4).

tioners (directors or shareholders), decree dissolution. The Ohio statute also includes an excellent additional provision for dissolution when it appears that the board contains an uneven number of directors and the shareholders are deadlocked in voting power and are unable to agree upon or vote for the election of directors as successors to directors whose terms would normally expire upon the election of successors.[30]

Generally, these statutes provide for dissolution without reference to the matter of whether it will be for the best interests of the corporation, the assumption apparently being that, in the very nature of things, the continuation of the corporate business under deadlock conditions is in itself intolerable and necessarily damaging. However, the statutes are not uniform, the New York provisions, for example, stating that "if upon the application for the final order, it shall appear that . . . a dissolution will be beneficial to the stockholders or members and not injurious to the public, the court must make a final order dissolving the corporation." [31] It has been held that "in order to be entitled to a dissolution, such dissolution must be for the benefit of the stockholders," and not injurious to the public.[32]

In general, the deadlock statutes have been construed strictly. Where a statute provided for petition for dissolution by shareholders holding forty percent of the voting power in case "the votes of its board of directors and of its stockholders are equally divided on a question affecting the general management of the affairs of the corporation," it was held that dissolution was not in order though the shareholders could not agree upon the election of new directors, since there was no equal division among the old directors and they would, under the usual rule, remain in office until new directors were elected.[33] This result, of course, does violence to the statutorily required periodic elections of directors since the deadlocked shareholders, if adamant, may continue deadlocked during several election periods. Where an equal division of directors is a condition precedent to dissolution under such statutes, dissension of an equally divided body of sharehold-

---

30. Ohio Rev.Code § 1701.91(A) (4). See also N.Y.Gen.Corp.Law § 103 (either a deadlocked board or where the votes are so divided that the shareholders cannot elect a board constitutes cause for dissolution).

31. N.Y.Gen.Corp.Law § 117.

32. In re Radom & Neidorff, Inc., 307 N.Y. 1, 119 N.E.2d 563 (1954) (corporation was functioning actively and with profit); Application of Cantelmo, 275 App.Div. 231, 88 N.Y. S.2d 604 (1949) (corporation was operating successfully). See Note, Deadlock Dissolution in New York, 27 N.Y.U.L.Rev. 300 (1952); Israels, The Sacred Cow of Corporate Existence: Problems of Deadlock and Dissolution, 19 U. of Chi.L.Rev. 778 (1952).

33. Cook v. Cook, 270 Mass. 534, 170 N.E. 455 (1930). See Ann., Dissolution of corporation on ground of intracorporate deadlock or dissension, 13 A.L.R.2d 1260, 1269 et seq., on "equal division" provisions (1950).

ers has been held insufficient to grant dissolution.[34] And it has been held that the "equal division" of stock provision is a jurisdictional prerequisite for invoking a statute permitting dissolution for this reason; that the jurisdictional prerequisite is not met if the fifty percent of shares petitioning include some shares improperly purchased with corporate funds.[35]

In closely held corporations, provisions are often made for a more than majority vote of directors or of shareholders to secure better protection to minority shareholders. Under such restrictive provisions, there may be a deadlock in the sense that there is lacking the required majority though there is not an "equal division" of directors or shareholders. Until statutes cure this defect, it is suggested that the articles or certificate of incorporation contain a specific provision for deadlock dissolution under these circumstances.[36] While there is no assurance that such additional charter provisions will in all cases be held valid, the discussion in the preceding section points the way.[37]

There is also a policy question involved as to whether dissolution should be restricted to holders of half or more of the voting shares. Some statutes, under described limited conditions, permit fewer than fifty percent to petition for dissolution where deadlock is the reason.[38]

§ 7. Usual Statutory Provisions Concerning Dissolution

In the preceding chapter were discussed mergers and consolidations, the effect of which was the dissolution of one or more corporations. And, of course, the sale of all the corporate assets with the intent of going out of business results in what has sometimes been called a dissolution de facto. As we have seen, cer-

---

34. Dorf v. Hill Bus. Co., 140 N.J. Eq. 444, 54 A.2d 761 (Ct.Err. & App. 1947); Matter of Superb Diamond Cutting Corp. (Application of Landau), 183 Misc. 876, 51 N.Y.S.2d 651 (Sup.Ct.1944).

35. In re Evening Journal Ass'n (Post-Standard Co. v. Evening Journal), 1 N.J. 437, 64 A.2d 80 (1949).

36. New York amended its statute (N.Y.Gen.Corp.Law § 103) in 1951 to harmonize with N.Y.Stock Corp. Law § 9, which latter section was added to permit provisions especially adaptable to the "incorporated partnership" or closely held corporation. Generally, see Cary, How Illinois Corporations May Enjoy Partnership Advantages: Planning for the Closely Held Firm, 48 Nw.U.L.Rev. 427 (1953).

Lattin Corporations F.P.Inc.—36

37. See § 5, supra, discussing Leventhall v. Atlantic Financial Corp., 316 Mass. 194, 55 N.E.2d 20, 154 A. L.R. 260 (1944).

38. See West's Ann.Cal.Corp.Code § 4650 (shareholders of one-third of outstanding shares); Conn.Gen. Corp.Law § 5228 (for stated reasons, shareholders holding not less than one-tenth of capital stock). Under some statutes there are provisions which protect majority shareholders in such cases by permitting them to buy off the minority. See West's Ann.Cal.Corp.Code § 4658 (holders of fifty percent or more may avoid dissolution by purchasing shares of others at their fair value with a provision for ascertaining their fair value); W.Va. Gen.Corp.Law § 3093.

tain procedures guaranteeing some fairness to dissenting shareholders were worked out through judicial decision and by statute; in the latter case, the appraisal statutes aided the dissenter to retire from the business if he desired to do so.

However, by far the most numerous dissolutions come through statutes (existing in all states today) which normally give a majority or greater proportion of shareholders an absolute right to determine whether their corporation, even a highly prosperous one, shall continue its business life. Recommendation must usually come from the board of directors that the corporation proceed to dissolve under the statutory provisions; a shareholder vote is required, except under some statutes in exceptional circumstances such as where there has been an adjudication of bankruptcy, or where the corporation has not yet begun its business career, or where it has disposed of all of its assets and has not conducted any business for a stated period, say for five years.[39] In some statutes there is provision for court supervision of the dissolution and winding up of the corporation; in others, none. There may be some statement in the statute concerning the payment of debts and providing for liabilities, and frequently taxes are mentioned as being payable prior to dissolution or liquidation. There is also the usual requirement of filing a certificate of dissolution with (usually) the secretary of state before the dissolution becomes de jure. And statutes which have been carefully drawn provide for the continuation of the corporation after dissolution for the purpose of liquidating (if dissolution precedes winding up) and for suits by and against the dissolved corporation. Some of the statutes specifically designate the directors as the liquidators; others provide for the appointment or election of trustees for this purpose. If the corporation is kept alive for the purpose of liquidation, it seems fairly obvious that the directors, whether designated in the statute or not, would be the proper persons to carry out the statutory formalities, see that creditors are paid before anything is distributed to the shareholders, and when that has been done distribute what remains in accordance with the shareholders' contracts. The courts quite properly classify the corporate property at this stage of corporate life as being a trust fund for the payment of creditors and of those who have unliquidated claims against the corporation. Local statutes should be consulted for they differ materially in some respects and any gaps have to be filled by common law concepts already discussed.

The most common provision concerning the vote required by shareholders for dissolution is a two-thirds vote, but whether all shareholders are entitled to vote on this important matter or

---

39. See West's Ann.Cal.Corp.Code §§ 4600, 4601.

whether it is confined to voting shareholders only or to voting shareholders together with classes entitled to vote because of their share-contract must be ascertained from the local statute. There is no uniformity. There are a few statutes which provide that one-half or more of the shares may determine whether or not to dissolve, and it is not uncommon for statutes to make provision for dissolution upon the written consent of all the shareholders entitled to vote on the matter. This saves a shareholders' meeting and, in closely held corporations, is a useful provision. It should be said that an occasional statute specifically permits a petition for involuntary dissolution to be filed by a shareholder, under named conditions, or by a judgment creditor after writ of execution returned unsatisfied.[40] And one statute permits a shareholder owning not less than one-tenth of the capital stock of a corporation to apply for dissolution "whenever any good and sufficient reason exists for the dissolution . . ." but such a petitioner may be bought off by other shareholders applying to the court to have his shares evaluated.[41] This provision can be very useful in closely held corporations but it is thought that broad equity powers would be just as effective when "good and sufficient reason" is found for dissolving such a corporation. It is a wise provision, however, to compel a dissatisfied shareholder to sell his shares to those seeking dissolution or, in case of this statute, to those who resist dissolution, if they desire to purchase them. There should be fairness, however, to the shareholder forced to sell so that he will obtain the fair value of his shares.

§ 8. Prevention of Abuse in the use of Voluntary Dissolution Provisions

While Blackstone called the voluntary death of the corporation by the unanimous choice of its members "suicide," one able writer has stated that "Voluntary death, . . . if not for the benefit of *all* the stockholders, may perhaps be more realistically described as 'murder'; yet it is not readily recognized as such because the motivation is not always apparent." [42] The author quite rightly states that a dissolution is fraudulent when the sales price is grossly inadequate; that there are cases where dissolution has been voted for the sole purpose of ousting from a prosperous company some of the shareholders, the rest keeping the reorganized company to themselves and basking in the prosperity which should have been available to all, at least until the corporation was dissolved and liquidated with the real intent of discontinuing business. And, of course, there have been purchas-

---

40. See Minn.Stat.Ann. § 301.50.

41. Conn.Gen.Stat. § 5228 (1949).

42. Hornstein, Voluntary Dissolution —A New Development in Intracorporate Abuse, 51 Yale L.J. 64, at 64 (1941).

es and use of control for some other reason than making the company prosper for the benefit of all of its owners, such as selling out a prosperous corporation because, at the time, this offered to the control-group quick profits, perhaps not as highly taxed as would be the dividends distributed or the profits retained in the business. Whatever the reason, the best interests of the control-group rather than business as such were uppermost.

There is no doubt that some courts have worked valiantly for fairness for all the owners when majorities have used their power for their own selfish purposes.[43] Perhaps motive should play a minor part, or no part at all, in the determination made by the statutory majority honestly to dissolve and go out of business. However, if majority shareholders wind up the corporate affairs and participate in a business acquiring the assets they purported to sell, but actually transferred so that they could have the benefit without sharing it with those who were thus frozen out, even though the price was fair, there is no legitimate legal argument to support them. It is suggested that courts which have floundered with the concept that the majority shareholders must have so flagrantly violated their trust that fraud can be sensed if not actually seen need better glasses for this job.[44] There is no fairness

---

43. See § 6, Chapter 11, this book. And see Lebold v. Inland Steel Co., 125 F.2d 369 (7th Cir., 1941), cert. denied 316 U.S. 675, 62 S.Ct. 1045, 86 L.Ed. 1749 (1942), where the court rectified a grossly unfair "dissolution." Noted in 10 U. of Chi. L.Rev. 77 (1942); 28 Va.L.Rev. 1132 (1942). Accord: Theis v. Spokane Falls Gas Light Co., 34 Wash. 23, 74 P. 1004 (1904). And see Lattin, Equitable Limitations on Statutory or Charter Powers Given to Majority Stockholders, 30 Mich.L.Rev. 645 (1932).

44. The rule that the inadequacy in price in a sale of assets must be so great as to lead a court to conclude that the sale was not made in good faith or was made with a reckless indifference to the rights of those injured, loses sight of this principle of fairness. See page 514, this text and cases there cited.

No truer words have ever been uttered concerning the stewardship of directors and majority shareholders than those of Lindley, Dist. J., in Lebold v. Inland Steel Co., supra, note 43, at 372: "The directors of a corporation represent it and its stockholders; the majority stock-

holders of a corporation represent it and its minority stockholders, The vote of every director and of every majority stockholder must be directed to and controlled by the guiding question of what is best for the corporation, for which he is, to all legal intents and purposes, trustee. In his voting, in his management, he is bound to be wholeheartedly, earnestly and honestly faithful to his corporation and its best interests; his own selfish interests must be ignored. If when he votes he does so against the interest of his company, against the interest of his minority and in favor of his own interest, by such selfish action, by omission of fidelity to his own duty as a trustee, he forfeits approval in a court of equity." As vigorous, too, are the words of Collin, J., in Kavanaugh v. Kavanaugh Knitting Co., 226 N. Y. 185, at 195–196, 123 N.E. 148, at 152 (1919). However, compare the language in Rossing v. State Bank of Bode, 181 Iowa 1013, 165 N.W. 254 (1917); Kirwin v. Parkway Distillery, Inc., 285 Ky. 605, 148 S. W.2d 720 (1941); Windmuller v. Standard Distilling & Distributing Co., 114 F. 491 (D.N.J.1902). But in ousting from a prosperous corporation part of its owners no matter how obstreperous they may be. The power to control, or rather its use, should be considered in no lesser light than that of the power of a trustee to deal with the trust estate and with the beneficiary. Self-dealing in whatever form it occurs should be handled with rough hands for what it is—dishonest dealing. And, while it is often difficult to discover self-dealing in mergers, consolidations, sale of all the assets or dissolution and liquidation, the difficulty makes it even more imperative that the search be thorough and relentless.

§ 9.   Effect of Dissolution

De jure dissolution ends the business life of a corporation. Unless a statute continues its life for the purpose of liquidation and of suing and being sued, a corporation no longer exists as a legal person with the incidents of such a person. Dissolution is somewhat similar to death in case of a natural person. Hence, a dissolved corporation may not sue or be sued in the state of incorporation or in any other state. Nor may it carry on except for the purpose of liquidating its assets, paying its creditors, and distributing what remains to its shareholders.[45] And even then it does not carry on as a corporation. But, as we have seen, statutes in general preserve the corporate life for these purposes, setting up named representatives to carry out the job of liquidating. Even without statutory aid, unpaid creditors may pursue the assets in equity to enforce their claims and the owners, or their representatives, may likewise proceed to collect claims to which the corporation, during its existence, became entitled. Barring some statutory provision making the owners liable beyond their obligations for stock subscribed by them, their limited liability protects them against further assessments.

The effect of dissolution upon corporate officers and agents is to annul their former powers to act for their company. A statute may, and frequently does give them authority to act in the process of winding up the corporate business, and if they confine their activities to those legally permissible to liquidators, they will incur no personal liability to creditors or owners.[46] The situation is analogous to that of a partnership which has been dissolved, the partners then having only the authority to wind up the firm's business, pay its debts, and distribute what remains in

see Outwater v. Public Service Corp., 103 N.J.Eq. 461, 143 A. 729 (Ch.Ct.1928).

45. Leibson v. Henry, 356 Mo. 953, 204 S.W.2d 310, at 315 (1947).

46. Acting beyond their authorized powers as trustees in dissolution, the trustees (liquidators) may be held personally liable for obligations thus incurred. Leibson v. Henry, supra, note 45, two judges dissenting.

accordance with winding-up principles. In neither case may business as usual be carried on after dissolution.

There has been much confusion concerning the status of executory contracts not breached prior to dissolution. As to those entered into before, and not breached prior to involuntary dissolution, some courts have held that the subsequent inability or refusal to perform does not result in liability.[47] Contrary opinion, sometimes described as the better rule, holds that executory contracts are not extinguished by dissolution.[48] There can, of course, be suits upon contracts breached prior to dissolution under either rule.[49]

The argument is persuasive that since the liquidators have the power to save the owners from loss upon contracts entered into prior to dissolution, they have the option of performing such contracts or of refusing to do so if the latter seems the better way out. Consequently, the formal argument that the corporation no longer exists and thus cannot perform the contract, or breach it for that matter, is a weak one. Is this not comparable, indeed, to the merger or consolidation of several corporations which have executory contracts outstanding, or where similar contracts exist and there is a sale of all of the assets with or without formal dissolution? It is debatable whether any distinction should be made between voluntary and involuntary dissolution, as some courts have done, thus keeping contractual liability alive where voluntary dissolution occurs, but not where dissolution is involuntary. As in case of voluntary or involuntary bankruptcy, losses due to the inability or refusal to perform executory contracts should be chargeable against the assets of the defunct or dissolved corporation.[50]

47. Warner v. Mutual Bldg. & Inv. Co., 128 Ohio St. 37, 190 N.E. 143 (1934) (such contracts are "rescinded" thus terminating the contract between corporation and other contracting party); Arnold v. H. Piper Co., 319 Ill.App. 91, 48 N.E.2d 580 (1943) (that the other contracting party may not be held liable for refusal to perform his executory contract, which refusal occurred subsequent to the (Missouri) corporation's dissolution—such contracts are "cancelled").

48. Mumma v. The Potomac Co., 8 Pet. (33 U.S.) 281 (1834); Curran v. Arkansas, 15 How. (56 U.S.) 304, at 310 (1853); Shields v. Ohio, 95 U.S. 319, at 324, 24 L.Ed. 357 (1877); Bijur v. Standard Distilling & Distributing Co., 74 N.J.Eq. 546, 70 A. 934, at 940 (Ch.Ct.1908); Peo-

ple ex rel. Palmer v. Peoria Life Ins. Co., 376 Ill. 517, 34 N.E.2d 829 (1941); State ex rel. Everett Trust & Savings Bank v. Pacific Waxed Paper Co., 22 Wash.2d 844, 157 P.2d 707, 159 A.L.R. 297 (1945). Voluntary dissolution of a corporation or discontinuance of its business does not excuse the corporation from performance of its agreements. Martin v. Star Publishing Co., 126 A.2d 238 (Del.Sup.Ct.1956).

49. Arnold v. Streck, 108 F.2d 387 (7th Cir., 1939), involving a Missouri corporation.

50. 5 Williston, Contracts § 1327 (Rev. ed. 1937), criticises only the doctrine of the leading case on voluntary or involuntary bankruptcy as constituting in itself an anticipatory breach; MacLachlan, Bankruptcy 126 (1956).

However, the same confusion does not exist in case of leases. Rights and liabilities under a lease survive dissolution unless there is a specific clause terminating the lease upon dissolution whether voluntary or involuntary. A general non-assignability clause will not suffice, the rule being the same in case of merger or consolidation.[51]

§ 10. Distribution of Assets after Payment of Debts—Whether in Kind or in Cash

There is no difficult problem if the corporate assets upon dissolution are of no greater value than the corporate debts and liabilities. Creditors come first and must be paid before the shareholders are entitled to anything; and secured creditors rank first in order. However, the distribution among general creditors must be pro rata if the assets to which they are entitled are not sufficient to pay them in full.[52] If, after the claims against the corporation have been satisfied, there remain additional assets, these or the funds acquired by their sale must be distributed to the shareholders in accordance with the provisions of their share-contracts. If there are dissolution preferences, these come first, and unless the preferred contract gives participating rights beyond the usual dissolution preferences calling for payment of the shareholder's capital contribution, plus an amount equal to any accrued but undeclared dividends, what remains will be distributed to the common shareholders in proportion to the number of common shares they hold.[53] And, of course, the legitimate expenses of dissolution and liquidation must be paid since otherwise there would be small chance of accomplishing this objective. Such expenses are sometimes held to be preferred claims,[54] and should be as far as general creditors are concerned.

Modern statutes frequently provide for public notice of a proposed voluntary dissolution and require additional notice to the corporation's creditors.[55] Provisions stating a limited time during which claims may be presented and, if not presented during that period will be barred from participation in the general assets of the company, are contained in the better statutes.[56] But many of the statutes state rather summarily the duties of the

---

51. Chester v. Master Laboratories, 148 Neb. 378, 27 N.W.2d 541 (1947); 16 Fletcher, Cyc. of Corporations § 8124 (Perm. ed. 1942).

52. Fletcher, Cyc. of Corporations § 8219 (Perm. ed. 1942). Statutes follow the rule. Fla.Stat.Ann. § 608.29(3).

53. As to the interpretation of the preferred shareholder's contract, see page 431 et seq., this text.

54. Fletcher, Cyc. of Corporations § 8222 (Perm. ed. 1942). Statutes at times spell out this preference as in Fla.Stat.Ann. § 608.29(3).

55. Examples: West's Ann.Cal.Corp. Code § 4605 as amended by L.1957, c. 2261, § 34; N.C.Gen.Stat., 1957 Cum.Supp. § 55–119.

56. West's Ann.Cal.Corp.Code § 4608 (when there is court supervision).

liquidators, whether they be directors, trustees or receivers, to collect the debts owing the corporation, pay the creditors and other claimants, and distribute whatever remains to the shareholders.[57] Perhaps such a summary statement is sufficient as it restates the common law concerning such distributions. But it is highly desirable to have a short statute of limitations after which claimants who have not presented their claims are forever barred from pursuing the assets, the liquidators or the shareholders to whom the assets have been finally distributed.

After creditors and other claimants have been paid, and the expense of liquidation has been taken care of, what remains must be returned to the shareholders. Unless the preferred share-contract provides for dissolution preferences, there are none and these shares would share with the common shares pro rata. If dissolution preferences exist, they must be satisfied through a cash settlement unless the contract gives the corporation an option to satisfy the preference by distributing corporate assets of the value of the preference, a provision not likely to be found, or the shareholder is willing to accept, in lieu of cash, the substitute. Some few statutes carry seemingly mandatory provisions that all the property be converted into cash and be distributed pro rata among the shareholders, a manifestly unwise provision.[58] While preferred shareholders are entitled to cash upon dissolution, there is no implied contract right of the common to be so treated, but courts have at times been overzealous in the matter of being sure that the minority shareholders have the benefit of the full value of their shares as established by a sale of the assets though these be capable of ratable distribution and might better have been distributed in kind than sold.[59] Fortunately, in many states, the statutes refer specifically to possible distributions of property upon dissolution.[60]

It has been rightly held, however, that a dissolution plan which provided for a property distribution to some shareholders and a cash distribution of the fair value of their shares to others, without giving the shareholder the option of receiving either, could not be justified without an agreement or statutory aid authorizing this procedure.[61] Barring an agreement or statutory provision to the contrary, the common shareholders are to be treated alike, receiving their pro rata share of assets or of cash. While it is probable that the common shareholders can be com-

---

57. Examples: Ariz.Rev.Stat. § 10-361A; Colo.Rev.Stat. § 31-6-1 (1953); Ill.Bus.Corp.Act § 79(b).

58. Example: Colo.Rev.Stat. § 31-6-4 (1953).

59. Ballantine, Corporations 734 (Rev. ed. 1946).

60. Examples: West's Ann.Cal.Corp. Code § 5003; N.C.Gen.Stat., 1957 Cum.Supp. §§ 55-118(a) (2) and 55-119.

61. In re San Joaquin Light & Power Corp., 52 Cal.App.2d 814, 127 P. 2d 29 (1942).

pelled to accept a pro rata distribution of property capable of ratable division where fairness exists, this is not true when such a distribution would be unfair and a court may properly enjoin the execution of such a plan which, for all practical purposes, will mean a sale of the assets and a distribution pro rata in cash.[62] This may mean that considerable inconvenience or expense which may accompany a distribution of certain types of property will be an adequate basis for a suit to enjoin the consummation of the plan.

§ 11. Liability of Shareholders and/or Directors for Corporate Debts after Liquidation

If a voluntary dissolution is properly carried out, neither the shareholders nor the directors or other liquidators will incur liability to creditors. From an early date it has been a basic rule that the capital stock of a corporation constitutes a trust fund for the benefit of creditors which, if distributed to shareholders, may be recovered to satisfy corporate liabilities.[63] The directors making such a distribution would also be liable, their liability being predicated upon the proposition that, as directors or liquidators, they have the duty of not divesting the corporation of all its property without giving the creditors and other claimants a reasonable opportunity to present and enforce their claims.[64] And this is true even though the corporate assets have been transferred to a buyer, who, as part of the purchase agreement, has assumed the debts and obligations of the dissolved corporation.[65] The new debtor may not be forced upon the creditor. A creditor is said to have an equitable lien on the corporate assets of which he may not be deprived without his consent.[66] Those who carry out the liquidation of a corporation have a duty of giving reasonable notice to creditors of a proposed transfer or distribution which will take assets to which creditors are entitled out of the control of their debtor.[67]

62. Shrage (Central Hanover Bank & Trust Co., Intervener) v. Bridgeport Oil Co., 31 Del.Ch. 305, 71 A. 2d 882 (Ch.1950), which involved a plan to distribute a 1/267,200 interest in oil leases which would result in expense and difficulty in the administration of the property. The court held that an unfair plan of dissolution could not be forced upon small shareholders merely because of its happy tax consequences for large shareholders.

63. Wood v. Dummer, 3 Mason 308, 30 Fed.Cas. 435, No. 17,944 (C.C.D.

Me.1824), is the leading case setting forth this principle.

64. Pierce v. United States, 255 U.S. 398, 41 S.Ct. 365, 65 L.Ed. 197 (1921); Beatty v. Paterson-Garfield-Lodi Bus Co., Inc., 126 N.J.Eq. 472, 9 A.2d 686 (1939); Darcy v. Brooklyn & N. Y. Ferry Co., 196 N.Y. 99, 89 N.E. 461 (1909).

65. Ibid.

66. Ibid.

67. Ibid.

Corporation statutes should be consulted for the specific coverage of directorial or shareholder liability in case of the distribution and receipt of funds which should have been preserved to satisfy claims against the corporation. A common provision, general in character, makes directors who declare dividends out of improper funds or who divide, withdraw or pay to shareholders (except as authorized) any part of the capital stock, or who distribute corporate assets when the corporation is insolvent or its net assets are less than its stated capital, or when such distribution will thereby render the corporation insolvent or reduce its net assets below its stated capital, liable to the extent of the distribution.[68] However, a fair number of modern statutes cover the distribution of assets upon dissolution specifically, the Ohio statute, for example, providing for directorial liability for distributing assets without paying or making provision for the payment of "all known obligations of the corporation." [69] The recent North Carolina provision reads: "The directors of a corporation who vote for or assent to any distribution of assets of a corporation to its shareholders during the liquidation of the corporation without the payment and discharge of, or making adequate provision for, all known or reasonably ascertainable debts, obligations, and liabilities of the corporation shall be jointly and severally liable to the corporation for the value of such assets which are distributed, to the extent that such debts, obligations and liabilities of the corporation are not thereafter paid and discharged." [70] The "reasonably ascertainable" clause is a good one for it tells the directors that, as liquidators, they must use reasonable care in ascertaining obligations and liabilities which neither the corporate books nor its correspondence may show.

Problems closely allied to those considered here are those arising out of the distribution of dividends out of improper funds.[71] Some statutes now specifically provide for shareholder liability in case of wrongful distributions of assets upon dissolution and liquidation. Under the Ohio statute, if a shareholder has knowledge that the distribution is contrary to law or the corporation's articles he incurs liability to the *corporation*,[72] but a further provision in the same section provides that *creditors* are not precluded from exercising such rights as they would otherwise have to enforce their claims against the assets of the corporation paid or distributed to shareholders.[73]

---

68. Ariz.Rev.Stat. § 10–196, subd. A2; Ark.Stat. § 64–606 (1947); Ind.Gen.Corp.Act § 52.

69. Ohio Rev.Code § 1701.95(A).

70. N.C.Gen.Stat., 1957 Cum.Supp. § 55–32(e).

71. The dividend problems are discussed in Ch. X, §§ 11 and 12.

72. Ohio Rev.Code § 1701.95(C).

73. Ohio Rev.Code § 1701.95(F).

The only safe way of avoiding personal liability in the dissolution and liquidation process is to comply strictly with any statutory provisions which relate to the process and, if few or no specific provisions have yet been enacted, to comply with the basic rule that creditors must first be paid before distributing what was, prior to dissolution, a part of the corporation's stated capital.

§ 12.   Corporate Liquidation under the Internal Revenue Code of 1954

Under Internal Revenue Code § 336—Regulation 39.22(a)–20—which was a new provision in 1954 adopting the rule of the regulation, as a general rule no gain or loss is recognized to a corporation on the distribution of property in partial or complete liquidation, even though the assets may have appreciated or depreciated in value since they were acquired. By another new provision,[74] gain or loss is normally not recognized upon the sale or exchange of property of the liquidating company if, within 12 months of the date of the adoption of the liquidation plan, all the corporate assets, less those kept to meet claims, are distributed in complete liquidation and the sale takes place within the 12-month period. Prior to this 1954 change, corporations in liquidating would distribute assets in kind to the shareholders in order to avoid the tax upon the corporation for capital gains made when it sold its property and distributed the consideration received to its shareholders. The shareholders receiving the proceeds were likewise taxed for any capital gain they made. The new section was enacted to eliminate the confusion caused by decisions interpreting particular attempts to avoid double capital gains taxes, which decisions involved the sensitive question of whether, actually, the corporation or the shareholder effected the sale.

There are important distinctions as to what comes within the term "property" of properly taxable income. Thus, income from the sale of inventories or stock in trade made in the ordinary course of business is recognized and taxed. And, roughly, substantially all of inventory sold to one person in bulk in the liquidating process which results in gain or loss is considered "property" and gain or loss will not be recognized on such bulk sales made within the 12-month period.[75] However, § 337 of the Internal Revenue Code does not apply to sales or exchanges made by "collapsible corporations."[76] And there are specific provi-

74. I.R.C. § 337(a) and 26 U.S.C.A. §§ 301–700, Guide to the Internal Revenue Code of 1954, pages 37 et seq. (1954).

75. I.R.C. § 337(b), 26 U.S.C.A. § 337 (b).

76. I.R.C. § 341 and see 26 U.S.C.A. §§ 301–700, Guide to the Internal

sions concerning the complete liquidation of subsidiary corporations.[77]

The subject is too specialized and complicated to discuss further in a book primarily devoted to the law of private corporations.[78] However, as has been indicated at other points in this text, the taxing problems are important and will probably continue to be so until the Internal Revenue Code has been thoroughly overhauled and simplified. The changes are so frequent that the lawyer who would keep himself abreast of both the advances in the field of corporations and those within the area of corporate and other business association taxation has a real job on his hands. The expert in taxation is a necessary colleague to the corporate expert in the several areas of business associations where tax savings may be made.

Revenue Code of 1954, pages 38 et seq.

77. See § 332, I.R.C., and 26 U.S.C.A. §§ 301–700, Guide to the Internal Revenue Code of 1954, pages 31 et seq.

78. There is an excellent analysis in Cohen, Gelberg, Surrey, Tarleau and Warren, Corporate Liquidations Under the Internal Revenue Code of 1954, 55 Col.L.Rev. 37–55 (1955).

TABLE OF CASES

References are to pages

Y

Z

INDEX

References are to pages

References are to pages

END OF VOLUME